Workshop on Cognitive Modeling and Computational Linguistics (CMCL 2021)

Online
10 June 2021

ISBN: 978-1-7138-3020-7

Printed from e-media with permission by:

Curran Associates, Inc.
57 Morehouse Lane
Red Hook, NY 12571

Some format issues inherent in the e-media version may also appear in this print version.

Association for Computational Linguistics
209 N. Eighth Street
Stroudsburg, Pennsylvania 18360

Phone: 1-570-476-8006
Fax: 1-570-476-0860

acl@aclweb.org

Additional copies of this publication are available from:

Curran Associates, Inc.
57 Morehouse Lane
Red Hook, NY 12571 USA
Phone: 845-758-0400
Fax: 845-758-2633
Email: curran@proceedings.com
Web: www.proceedings.com

CMCL 2021

The Workshop on Cognitive Modeling and Computational Linguistics

Proceedings of the Workshop

June 10, 2021
Online Event

Introduction

Welcome to the Workshop on Cognitive Modeling and Computational Linguistics (CMCL)!!

We reached the 11th edition of CMCL, the workshop of reference for the research at the intersection between Computational Linguistics and Cognitive Science. This is the 2nd edition in a row that will be held entirely online because of the COVID-19 pandemic. Although we won't have the possibility of meeting in person in charming Mexico City, the program of CMCL 2021 is one of the richest and most interesting in the recent history of the workshop. We received 26 regular paper submissions and 17 were accepted for publication, for a total acceptance rate of 65.3%. We also received 4 non-archival submissions (extended abstracts or cross-submissions), 2 of which were accepted for presentation.

This year's accepted papers spanned a highly diverse range of questions centering on language, cognition, and computation. Several papers unified computational methods with neurobehavioral data, including EEG, MEG, and fMRI. Many of the papers leveraged state-of-the-art, transformer-based language models to distinguish between two competing theories of sentence processing. Still others probed the differences between language comprehension and language production, and whether it is feasible to treat them similarly for the purposes of explaining language use. Outside of sentence processing, accepted papers also probed the relationship between language and emotion; the graph structure of phonology; and lexical comprehension. Accepted papers spanned several grammatical formalisms, including Combinatory Categorial Grammar, Construction Grammar, and dependency grammars, in addition to statistical approaches. These diverse perspectives on cognition modeling and computational linguistics promote our scientific community's continued growth.

Additionally, as a novelty of this year's edition, we have organized a shared task on eye-tracking data prediction for English, and we accepted 10 system description papers. The ability to accurately model gaze features is vital to advance our understanding of language processing. Therefore, we posed the challenge of predicting token-level eye-tracking metrics recorded during natural reading. The participating teams submitted predictions generated mainly with two approaches: (1) Tree-based boosting algorithms with extensive feature engineering and (2) neural networks trained for regression such as fine-tuning transformer-based language models. The features for training the systems included surface features, lexical and syntactic features, token probability features, and text complexity metrics, as well as representations from state-of-the-art language models, such as BERT, RoBERTa, and XLNet. The winning team presented a linguistic feature-based approach.

Also for this year, the contribution of our PC members in thoroughly reviewing and selecting the best papers has been invaluable. Here we wish to deeply thank all of them for their time and effort.

We also thank Afra Alishahi and Zoya Bylinskii, our keynote speakers, for having accepted our invitation.

Finally, thanks again to our sponsors: the Japanese Society for the Promotion of Sciences and the Laboratoire Parole et Langage. Through their generous support, we have been able to offer fee waivers to PhD students who were first authors of accepted papers, and to offset the participation costs of the invited speakers.

The CMCL 2021 Organizing Committee

Organizing Committee

Emmanuele Chersoni, The Hong Kong Polytechnic University
Nora Hollenstein, University of Copenaghen
Cassandra Jacobs, University of Wisconsin
Yohei Oseki, University of Tokyo
Laurent Prévot, Aix-Marseille University
Enrico Santus, Bayer

Program Committee

Laura Aina, Pompeu Fabre University of Barcelona
Raquel Garrido Alhama, Tilburg University
Louise Gillian Bautista, University of the Philippines
Klinton Bicknell, Duolingo
Philippe Blache, Aix-Marseille University
Lucia Busso, Aston University
Christos Christodoulopoulos, Amazon
Aniello De Santo. University of Utah
Vesna Djokic, University of Amsterdam
Micha Elsner, Ohio State University
Raquel Fernández, University of Amsterdam
Thomas François, Catholic University of Louvain
Robert Frank, Yale University
Stefan Frank, Radboud University of Nijmegen
Stella Frank, University of Trento
Diego Frassinelli, University of Kostanz
Abdellah Fourtassi, Aix-Marseille University
John Hale, University of Georgia
Yu-Yin Hsu, The Hong Kong Polytechnic University
Tim Hunter, UCLA
Samar Husain, IIT Delhi
Jordan Kodner, Stony Brook University
Gianluca Lebani, University Ca' Foscari Venezia
Alessandro Lenci, University of Pisa
Ping Li, The Hong Kong Polytechnic University
Fred Mailhot, DialPad
Mohammad Momenian, The Hong Kong Polytechnic University
Karl Neergaard, University of Macau
Ludovica Pannitto, University of Trento
Bo Peng, Yunnan University
Sandro Pezzelle, University of Amsterdam
Stephen Politzer-Ahles, The Hong Kong Polytechnic University
Vito Pirrelli, ILC-CNR Pisa
Jakob Prange, Georgetown University
Carlos Ramisch, Aix-Marseille University
Giulia Rambelli, University of Pisa
Roi Reichart, Technion – Israel Institute of Technology

Rachel A Ryskin, University of California Merced
Lavinia Salicchi, The Hong Kong Polytechnic University
Marco Senaldi, McGill University
Friederike Seyfried, The Hong Kong Polytechnic University
William Schuler, Ohio State University
Cory Shain, Ohio State University
Lonneke Van Der Plas, University of Malta
Yao Yao, The Hong Kong Polytechnic University

Table of Contents

Conference Program

June 10, 2021, Mexico City (GMT-5)

9:00–9:15 **Introduction**

9:15–10:15 **Keynote Talk 1**

9:15–10:15 *Grounded Language Learning, from Sounds and Images to Meaning*
Afra Alishahi

10:15–10:30 **Break**

10:30–12:00 **Oral Presentations 1**

Non-Complementarity of Information in Word-Embedding and Brain Representations in Distinguishing between Concrete and Abstract Words
Kalyan Ramakrishnan and Fatma Deniz

Human Sentence Processing: Recurrence or Attention?
Danny Merkx and Stefan L. Frank

Modeling Incremental Language Comprehension in the Brain with Combinatory Categorial Grammar
Miloš Stanojević, Shohini Bhattasali, Donald Dunagan, Luca Campanelli, Mark Steedman, Jonathan Brennan and John Hale

June 10, 2021, Mexico City (GMT-5) (continued)

12:00–13:00 Lunch break

13:00–14:30 Oral Presentations 2

A Multinomial Processing Tree Model of RC Attachment
Pavel Logacev and Noyan Dokudan

That Looks Hard: Characterizing Linguistic Complexity in Humans and Language Models
Gabriele Sarti, Dominique Brunato and Felice Dell'Orletta

Accounting for Agreement Phenomena in Sentence Comprehension with Transformer Language Models: Effects of Similarity-based Interference on Surprisal and Attention
Soo Hyun Ryu and Richard Lewis

14:30–14:45 Break

14:45–15:00 Shared Task Presentation

CMCL 2021 Shared Task on Eye-Tracking Prediction
Nora Hollenstein, Emmanuele Chersoni, Cassandra L. Jacobs, Yohei Oseki, Laurent Prévot and Enrico Santus

15:00–16:30 Poster Session

LangResearchLab_NC at CMCL2021 Shared Task: Predicting Gaze Behaviour Using Linguistic Features and Tree Regressors
Raksha Agarwal and Niladri Chatterjee

TorontoCL at CMCL 2021 Shared Task: RoBERTa with Multi-Stage Fine-Tuning for Eye-Tracking Prediction
Bai Li and Frank Rudzicz

LAST at CMCL 2021 Shared Task: Predicting Gaze Data During Reading with a Gradient Boosting Decision Tree Approach
Yves Bestgen

Team Ohio State at CMCL 2021 Shared Task: Fine-Tuned RoBERTa for Eye-Tracking Data Prediction
Byung-Doh Oh

June 10, 2021, Mexico City (GMT-5) (continued)

June 10, 2021, Mexico City (GMT-5) (continued)

Evaluating the Acquisition of Semantic Knowledge from Cross-situational Learning in Artificial Neural Networks
Mitja Nikolaus and Abdellah Fourtassi

Representation and Pre-Activation of Lexical-Semantic Knowledge in Neural Language Models
Steven Derby, Barry Devereux and Paul miller

Relation Classification with Cognitive Attention Supervision
Erik McGuire and Noriko Tomuro

Graph-theoretic Properties of the Class of Phonological Neighbourhood Networks
Rory Turnbull

Contributions of Propositional Content and Syntactic Category Information in Sentence Processing
Byung-Doh Oh and William Schuler

The Effect of Efficient Messaging and Input Variability on Neural-Agent Iterated Language Learning
Yuchen Lian, Arianna Bisazza and Tessa Verhoef

Capturing Phonotactic Learning Biases with a Simple RNN
Max Nelson, Brandon Prickett and Joe Pater

16:30–17:30 Keynote Talk 2

16:30–17:30 *The Importance of Individualized Text Formats for Readability*
Zoya Bylinskii

June 10, 2021, Mexico City (GMT-5) (continued)

17:30–17:45 Closing Remarks

Non-Complementarity of Information in Word-Embedding and Brain Representations in Distinguishing between Concrete and Abstract Words

Kalyan Ramakrishnan
Indian Institute of Technology Madras
kalyan0821@yahoo.com

Fatma Deniz[†‡]
[†]University of California, Berkeley
[‡]Electrical Engineering and Computer Science
Technische Universität Berlin
fatma@berkeley.edu

Abstract

Word concreteness and imageability have proven crucial in understanding how humans process and represent language in the brain. While word-embeddings do not explicitly incorporate the concreteness of words into their computations, they have been shown to accurately predict human judgments of concreteness and imageability. Inspired by the recent interest in using neural activity patterns to analyze distributed meaning representations, we first show that brain responses acquired while human subjects passively comprehend natural stories can significantly distinguish the concreteness levels of the words encountered. We then examine for the same task whether the additional perceptual information in the brain representations can complement the contextual information in the word-embeddings. However, the results of our predictive models and residual analyses indicate the contrary. We find that the relevant information in the brain representations is a subset of the relevant information in the contextualized word-embeddings, providing new insight into the existing state of natural language processing models.

1 Introduction

Language comprises concrete and abstract words that are distinctively used in everyday conversations. Concrete words refer to entities that can be easily perceived with the senses (e.g., "house", "blink", "red"). On the other hand, abstract words refer to concepts that one cannot directly perceive with the senses (e.g., "luck", "justify", "risky"), but relies on the use of language to understand them (Brysbaert et al., 2014).

This categorization of words based on their concreteness is rooted in theoretical accounts in cognitive science. One such account is the Dual Coding Theory (Paivio, 1971, 1991), according to which two separate but interconnected cognitive systems represent word meanings, i.e., a non-verbal system that encodes *perceptual* properties of words and a verbal system that encodes *linguistic* properties of words. Concrete concepts can be easily imagined and are represented in the brain with both verbal and non-verbal codes. Abstract concepts are less imaginable and are represented with only verbal codes. For example, one can readily picture as well as describe the word *bicycle* (e.g., "has a chain", "has wheels"), but relies more on a verbal description for the word *bravery*.

The concreteness of words has since been used as a differentiating property of word meaning representations. Previous studies in natural language processing (NLP) have examined the word-embedding spaces of concrete and abstract words and showed: (i) distinct vector representations of the two categories within and across languages (Ljubešić et al., 2018), and (ii) high predictability of concreteness scores from pre-trained word-embeddings (Charbonnier and Wartena, 2019).

Neurolinguistic studies have shown an extensive, distributed network of brain regions representing the conceptual meaning of words (Mitchell et al., 2008; Wehbe et al., 2014; Huth et al., 2016). Among these, regions more closely involved in sensory processing have been shown to respond favorably to concrete words (Binder et al., 2005) over abstract words. Hill et al. (2014) argued that concrete and abstract concepts must be represented differently in the human brain by showing through a statistical analysis that concrete concepts have fewer but stronger associations in the mind with other concepts, while abstract concepts have weak associations with several other concepts.

Wang et al. (2013) showed that functional Magnetic Resonance Imaging (fMRI) signals of brain activity recorded as subjects attempted to decide which two out of a triplet of words were most similar contained sufficient information to classify the concreteness level of the word triplet, providing

Proceedings of the Workshop on Cognitive Modeling and Computational Linguistics, pages 1–11
Online Event, June 10, 2021. ©2021 Association for Computational Linguistics

further evidence of the dissimilar representations of the two categories in the brain. However, it remains an open question whether the brain responses within the semantic system can directly predict concreteness levels in the more challenging setting of *naturalistic* word stimuli (e.g., words encountered while reading a story). Moreover, given the human brain's expertise in generating and processing *perceptual* as well as *linguistic* information, one could expect the brain representations to provide information that complements the word-embeddings purely learned from linguistic contexts, improving their predictive capability. We address both these questions in this paper.

While several related works exist, the following limitations prompted a new study: (i) Anderson et al. (2017) indirectly decoded the brain representations for concrete and abstract nouns with the help of word-embeddings and convolutional neural network image representations. Instead of building a predictive model, the authors used a similarity metric to determine which signal in a pair of fMRI signals corresponds to which word in a pair of words. However, a direct, supervised decoding approach (as adopted here) would provide more substantial evidence about the strengths and weaknesses of the different information modalities. (ii) Brysbaert et al. (2014) found word concreteness scores to be highly correlated with both *visual* and *haptic* perceptual strength. However, multi-modal methods (Anderson et al., 2017; Bhaskar et al., 2017) have incorporated only visual features (as the second source of information) instead of general *perceptual* features into their predictions. By incorporating brain representations in our models, we do not miss out on such perceptual information (e.g., the adjectives "silky", "crispy", and "salty" are concrete but not as imagery-inducing as the adjective "blue"). (iii) In contrast to previous studies that have required participants to actively imagine a randomly presented word stimulus[1] (before being given a few seconds to "reset" their thoughts) during the brain data acquisition task (Anderson et al., 2012; Wang et al., 2013; Anderson et al., 2017), we adopt a task where participants would read highly engaging natural stories (without unnatural pauses), enabling them to process the word stimuli in a more realistic context.

To summarize, our objectives with this paper are twofold. First, we investigate how well human brain representations can predict the concreteness levels of words encountered in natural stories using simple, supervised learning algorithms. Second, we investigate whether brain representations encode information that may be missing from word-embeddings trained on a text corpus in making the concrete/abstract distinction. We believe that answering such questions will shed light on the current state of human and machine intelligence and on the ways to incorporate human language processing information into NLP models.

2 Related Work

A few studies have shown that the concreteness (and imageability) of words can be directly predicted with high accuracy from precomputed word-embeddings using supervised learning algorithms. Recently, Charbonnier and Wartena (2019) used a combination of word-embeddings and morphological features to predict the word concreteness and imageability values provided in seven publicly available datasets. Ljubešić et al. (2018) extended the idea to perform a cross-lingual transfer of concreteness and imageability scores by exploiting pretrained bilingual aligned word-embeddings (Conneau et al., 2017).

Multi-modal models that use both linguistic and perceptual information have been shown to outperform language models at various NLP tasks, such as learning concrete or abstract word embeddings (Hill and Korhonen, 2014; Lazaridou et al., 2015), concept categorization (Silberer and Lapata, 2014), and compositionality prediction (Roller and Schulte im Walde, 2013). However, Bhaskar et al. (2017) found that the concreteness of nouns could be predicted equally well from the textual, visual, and combined modalities. This suggests that the textual and visual modalities independently provided reliable, non-complementary information to represent both concrete and abstract nouns.

Several studies have addressed the idea of decoding neural activity patterns recorded in subjects when presented with certain textual or visual stimuli. Anderson et al. (2017) applied linguistic and visually-grounded computational models to decode the fMRI representations of a set of concrete and abstract nouns. They, too, reported no decoding advantage for multi-modal combinations over the linguistic model. Anderson et al. (2012) demonstrated that fMRI signals contained sufficient information to perform a 7-way classification of a

[1]e.g., one word would be presented every $10s$.

set of words into WordNet-based (Miller, 1995) taxonomic categories.

Lately, there has been an increasing research interest at the intersection of neuroimaging and language models (Jain and Huth, 2018; Abnar et al., 2019; Gauthier and Levy, 2019; Hollenstein et al., 2019; Toneva and Wehbe, 2019; Jain et al., 2020; Caucheteux and King, 2020; Schrimpf et al., 2020). In an interesting study, Schwartz et al. (2019) finetuned the BERT language model to predict the fMRI responses of text-reading participants to obtain representations that encode brain-activity-relevant semantic information. While the modified representations could better predict neural activity and even generalize to new participants, this inclusion of brain-relevant bias *did not* improve or degrade the model's performance on downstream NLP tasks.

3 Data Collection

3.1 Stimulus and fMRI data

We briefly describe the functional Magnetic Resonance Imaging (fMRI) data-collection procedure here and refer the reader to Deniz et al. (2019) for specific details.

Nine participants were asked to read 11 autobiographical narrative stories taken from *The Moth Radio Hour* podcast. We used six participants' data in our experiments. The stories are each 10-15 minutes long and were chosen to cover a wide range of topics. Each story was first aligned to its transcript by applying the UPenn Forced Aligner (Yuan and Liberman, 2008) and Praat (Boersma and Weenink, 2001) on the narration audio. Timestamps for word-occurrences were then obtained from Praat's TextGrid as a list of entries of the form (w_i, t_i) representing the ith word and its onset time, respectively. Using this *word-representation* list for each story, each word in the story was displayed one-by-one at the center of a screen for a duration equal to its duration in the spoken version.

Each fMRI scan consists of a sequence of voxel-responses[2] acquired at a fixed repetition-time ($TR = 2.0045s$) with a voxel-size of $2.24 \times 2.24 \times 4.1mm$. A separate scan was conducted for each subject and presented story (all analysis was done within subjects). The acquired volumetric fMRI responses for each subject were first preprocessed to correct for motion and then aligned to the first scan's temporal average, using the FMRIB Linear Image Registration Tool (FLIRT) from FSL v5.0 (Jenkinson et al., 2002; Jenkinson and Smith, 2001). A Savitzky–Golay filter (Schafer, 2011) with a $120s$ window was applied to remove low-frequency voxel-response drift from the signal. Finally, the voxel-responses for each story were z-scored separately so that they have zero mean and unit variance across all acquisitions for the story.

We note that an equivalent analysis could be carried out through a listening task since the elicited brain representations have been shown to be largely invariant to the stimulus modality (Deniz et al., 2019).

3.2 Concreteness Ratings

We used the dataset collected by Brysbaert et al. (2014), consisting of concreteness ratings for 39,954 English words. Each word was rated by around 25 participants (recruited through Amazon Mechanical Turk) on a 1-5 scale so that the most concrete words are assigned the highest score of 5, and the most abstract words are assigned the lowest score of 1. For each word, the average rating (and standard deviation) across all raters was recorded.

3.3 Word-Embeddings

We extracted the 768-dimensional activations from the final hidden layer of the Generative Pre-trained Transformer (GPT-2) (Radford et al., 2019) to obtain contextualized representations for the words in the stories. The reasons for selecting GPT-2 in this work are due to the findings of Schrimpf et al. (2020). First, GPT-2 was constrained to use unidirectional attention in the same way humans process text in a left-to-right fashion. Second, the authors find that models best matching human language processing are precisely those trained for a *next* word prediction objective (such as the GPT family).

4 Data Preparation

Rating and Vectorizing Using the word-representation for each story and a list of the fMRI acquisition-times (identical for all subjects), we partitioned the words into disjoint *chunks* so that all words in a chunk correspond to the same acquisition. Therefore, all words read by the subjects within a duration of 1 TR from the start of the acquisition pulse were included in the same chunk.

[2] voxel = volumetric pixel.

We used GPT-2 to vectorize each word in a story by supplying all words in the story leading up to it[3] as context and extracting the network's hidden layer representation corresponding to the last input position. To rate the words in the story, we first lowercased and lemmatized them and then used the Brysbaert et al. (2014) concreteness dataset to assign a rating to each word in a chunk. Only around 7% of all words in the stories were not covered by the dataset and were dropped before subsequent analysis.

We stored the ith preprocessed functional image of each subject as an N_b-dimensional *voxel-response vector* $\vec{b}_i$, where N_b denotes the number of voxels for that subject's brain. Typical values for N_b were found to lie in the 70k-90k range (with a mean of 80976 and a standard deviation of 6173, across subjects).

Downsampling Since the rate at which the text stimulus was presented to the subjects (the narration rate) is higher than the rate of fMRI data acquisition (2.0045s per acquisition), several words may occur within the TR corresponding to a single acquisition and will all fall under the same chunk. Therefore, we downsampled the stimulus to match the acquisition rate before further analysis by averaging out the concreteness ratings (r_w) and word-embeddings ($\vec{e}_w$) within each TR. Thus, the *chunk-rating* and *chunk-embedding* for chunk C_i are given by:

$$r_i = \frac{1}{|C_i|} \sum_{w \in C_i} r_w$$

$$\vec{e}_i = \frac{1}{|C_i|} \sum_{w \in C_i} \vec{e}_w$$

Stacking We temporally stacked the voxel-response vectors, chunk-embeddings and chunk-ratings, first within each story and then across all 11 stories to obtain (i) a per-subject *voxel-response matrix* $B \in \mathbb{R}^{T \times N_b}$, (ii) an *embedding matrix* $E \in \mathbb{R}^{T \times D}$, and (iii) a *rating vector* $\vec{r} \in \mathbb{R}^T$, where T denotes the total number of fMRI acquisitions across all stories per subject, and D denotes the dimensionality of the word-embedding space. $D = 768$ for GPT-2, and 11 stories with an average duration close to 12.5 min per story gives $T = 4028$.

[3]or as many as allowed by the model's capacity.

5 Predictive Models

5.1 Word-Embedding based model

We consider the task of classifying words as *concrete* or *abstract* (based on their concreteness ratings) using the word-embeddings (chunk-embeddings, $\vec{e}_i$) as explanatory variables. For this, we first defined a *concreteness threshold* τ as follows: any word is labeled *concrete* if its assigned rating is strictly greater than τ, and is labeled *abstract* otherwise. We take $\tau = 3$.

We then segregated the data into *well-defined* classes by discarding any chunks that were found to consist of a mixture of concrete and abstract words (as defined above). This retains roughly 42% of all chunks ($T^s < T$), resulting in the following *strict* counterparts to the embedding matrix and rating vector obtained in Section 4: (i) $E^s \in \mathbb{R}^{T^s \times D}$, and (ii) $\vec{r}^s \in \mathbb{R}^{T^s}$, with the superscript ^{s} denoting that only chunks satisfying the strictly concrete/abstract property are being considered. We binary-encoded $\vec{r}^s$ into the boolean vector $\vec{y}^s \in \{0, 1\}^{T^s}$, so that $y_i^s = 1$ if the corresponding chunk is strictly concrete and $y_i^s = 0$ otherwise. Our specific choice for the concreteness threshold ($\tau = 3$) produces a dataset that is approximately balanced between the two classes and is a natural choice for a 1-5 scale.[4]

We learned the $E^s \to \vec{y}^s$ mapping for each subject through $L2$-regularized logistic regression. We trained on 75% of the available data and picked the best value for the regularization parameter C through 5-fold cross-validation. We report the accuracy, recall, and F1 score of the classifier in our results.

An important variable in cognitive processing is the frequency with which words are encountered in language. High-frequency words are often perceived and processed faster than low-frequency words (van Heuven et al., 2014). Thus, word frequency could be a confounding variable to our objective if its distribution over the concrete words significantly differs from its distribution over the abstract words encountered in the stories. To check if this is the case, we computed the distribution of SUBTLEX-US (Brysbaert and New, 2009) word frequencies separately over all concrete vs. abstract words encountered by the subjects. However, a Kolmogorov-Smirnov test showed that the computed distribution over the concrete words was *not*

[4]Out of all strictly concrete/abstract chunks, 52% were labeled concrete, and 48% were labeled abstract.

significantly different from the distribution over the abstract words ($ks = 0.056, p = 0.063$).

5.2 Voxel-Response based model

Voxel Selection With up to 90,000 voxel-responses recorded per fMRI acquisition, not all voxels may be relevant to our objective of predicting the concreteness of word stimuli (Binder et al., 2005).

A standard voxel selection method is to manually determine regions of interest (ROIs) in the brain by analyzing the fMRI responses recorded in an auxiliary functional localizer task (Fedorenko et al., 2010) and select voxels from only these regions. However, this comes at the risk of being too restrictive. For example, one might inadvertently exclude regions in the brain encoding relevant sensory processing information in favor of regions encoding linguistic information. Given our objective to investigate whether brain representations contain any such additional information over word-embeddings, we avoided ROI-based methods for voxel selection.

We instead selected voxels based on their fractions of potentially-explainable response variance across time steps. This may be estimated separately for each voxel by recording different versions of its (time-varying) response corresponding to repeated presentations (Hsu et al., 2004) of the same stimulus-sequence. Assume that one story is repeatedly presented N times to a given subject and b represents a voxel being analyzed. If $b_t^{(n)}$ represents its response at time step t corresponding to the nth repetition, then its mean response across repetitions is $b_t = \frac{1}{N}\sum_{m=1}^{N} b_t^{(m)}$. The following equations estimate the fraction of potentially-explainable variance for b assuming the voxel-responses are z-scored across all time steps for the story:

$$ev(b) = \frac{1}{N}\sum_{n=1}^{N} [1 - \underset{t}{Var}(b_t^{(n)} - b_t)]$$

$$\overline{ev}(b) = ev(b) - \frac{1}{N-1}(1 - ev(b))$$

Thus, $\overline{ev}(b)$ is analogous to the adjusted R^2 of a (perfect) model that always predicts the mean response (b_t) across repetitions. A larger value indicates that the voxel responds consistently to repetitions of the same stimulus. Each subject was presented the last story $N = 2$ times, and the top-V voxels with the highest $\overline{ev}$ values were retained. From this, we obtain the desired reduced form $\hat{B} \in \mathbb{R}^{T \times V}$. The optimal number of semantic voxels V was chosen separately for each subject to maximize performance on the validation set (described next).

Prediction Task Blood-oxygen-level-dependent (BOLD) signals in the brain typically persist for 8-10s after stimulus onset (Ashby, 2019). Since each chunk covers nearly 2s of stimulus presentation, we expect the response to each chunk to be jointly encoded by the first, second, third, and fourth (reduced) voxel-response vectors that *follow* the current acquisition. However, including the first or fourth acquisition significantly degraded predictive performance. We posit that this degradation occurs because the voxel-response vectors recorded one or four TRs after the current acquisition are more prone to be directly affected by words falling in chunks preceding or succeeding the chunk of interest.

With this observation, we modeled the brain's representation of the stimulus in chunk C_i to be of the form $f(\vec{\hat{b}}_{i+2}, \vec{\hat{b}}_{i+3})$, where $\vec{\hat{b}}_{i'}$ represents the reduced voxel-response vector from the i'th acquisition. We therefore constructed the *reduced+delayed* voxel-response matrix $\hat{B}^{+} \in \mathbb{R}^{T \times 2V}$ by replacing each row of $\hat{B}$ with the concatenation of the *second* and *third* rows that succeed it.[5]

For classification, we first discarded chunks that are not strictly concrete/abstract and obtained $\hat{B}^{+s} \in \mathbb{R}^{T^s \times 2V}$. We then used regularized logistic regression to learn the per-subject $\hat{B}^{+s} \rightarrow \vec{y}^s$ mapping. The training procedure is identical to the one followed in Section 5.1.

Statistical Significance We determined the statistical significance of our classification results using a label-permutation method (Ojala and Garriga, 2009) with cross-validated accuracy as the chosen test statistic. Here, the distribution of a test statistic under the null hypothesis (that data and labels are independent) is estimated by training and evaluating the classifier on several randomized versions of the original data (by permuting classification labels). The p-value is then calculated as the proportion of randomized samples where the classifier performs better than it does on the original sample. We ran 100 iterations per subject.

[5] For rows that are ≤ 3 positions from the end, we used zero-padding for consistent dimensions.

6 Comparing the Representations

6.1 Combined model

First, we combined the word-embedding and voxel-response stimulus representations (obtained in Section 4 and Section 5.2) for each subject, by stacking the word-embedding matrix (E) and the reduced+delayed voxel-response matrix ($\hat{B}^{+}$) along the feature dimension to obtain the combined stimulus matrix $C \in \mathbb{R}^{T\times(D+2V)}$. Limiting the data to *strict* chunks yields the matrix $C^s \in \mathbb{R}^{T^s\times(D+2V)}$, which was then used for the classification task.

The rationale behind combining representations is the following. If the information encoded by the word-embedding and voxel-response representations were indeed complementary, the combined model should fare better at the prediction task than the two individual models because it now has access to information that was missing in either representation.

The classification task (predicting $\vec{y}^s$) and its training procedure are identical to those described in Section 5.1.

6.2 Residual Classification

Next, we attempted to *remove* the information present in each representation from the other and then train the classification model using the resulting representation. This procedure is described below.

1. *Removing voxel-response information from word-embeddings:* For each subject, we learned a linear mapping $L \in \mathbb{R}^{2V\times D}$ from $\hat{B}^{+s}$ to E^s through multivariate ridge regression (Haitovsky, 1987). We then computed the residuals $E_r^s \in \mathbb{R}^{T^s\times D}$ in a cross-validated manner as follows, and used the residuals for the classification task:

$$E_r^s = E^s - \hat{B}^{+s} \cdot L$$

2. *Removing word-embedding information from voxel-responses:* For each subject, we learned the linear mapping $L' \in \mathbb{R}^{D\times 2V}$ from E^s to $\hat{B}^{+s}$ through multivariate ridge regression. We then computed the residuals $\hat{B}_r^{+s} \in \mathbb{R}^{T^s\times 2V}$ in a cross-validated manner as follows, and used the residuals for the classification task:

$$\hat{B}_r^{+s} = \hat{B}^{+s} - E^s \cdot L'$$

Statistical Significance To statistically validate that any observed decrease in a residual model's performance compared to the corresponding non-residual model is really due to shared information between the representations (and not due to overfitting/chance), we adopted a "residual-permutation" procedure similar to that in Section 5.2.

Here, an empirical null distribution is created by training and evaluating each residual model above with several randomized versions of whichever representation is to be *regressed out*. The randomization is performed by permuting this representation over all time steps. The p-value is then calculated as the fraction of such residual models with cross-validated accuracies *lower* than that of the true (non-randomized) residual model. We ran 100 iterations per subject.

7 Results

We use the abbreviations **E** for the word-embedding based model, **B** for the voxel-response based (brain) model, **E+B** for the combined-representation model, **E-B** for the word-embedding model with voxel-response information removed, and **B-E** for the voxel-response model with word-embedding information removed. Figure 1 shows the classification accuracies of all models across the six subjects.

7.1 Individual models

Table 1 shows the average accuracy, recall, and F1 score of E and B.

B achieved an average classification accuracy of 69% and F1 score of 71%, and performed significantly higher than chance under the label-permutation test ($p \leq 9 \times 10^{-3}$) for each subject. This indicates that the fMRI signals triggered due to words encountered by subjects in natural stories encode enough information to significantly distinguish their concreteness levels under the current predictive framework. Evidently, this information must be useful above and beyond the noise present in the fMRI data unique to the data acquisition process. To our knowledge, the ability to classify the concreteness of *naturalistic* word stimuli from their induced brain representations in a direct, supervised fashion has not been shown in the existing literature.

E achieved a comparatively higher classification accuracy of 87%, which is in agreement with existing research (in non-naturalistic settings) on the pre-

Model	Performance (Mean ± S.D.)		
	Accuracy	Recall	F1 score
E	$\mathbf{0.87}$	0.88	0.87
B	$\mathbf{0.69 \pm 2.5\%}$	$0.77 \pm 2.6\%$	$0.71 \pm 2.4\%$
E+B	$\mathbf{0.86 \pm 1.9\%}$	$0.86 \pm 2.6\%$	$0.85 \pm 2.0\%$

Table 1: Classification metrics across the six participants for the word-embedding based (*E*), voxel-response based (*B*) and combined (*E+B*) models.

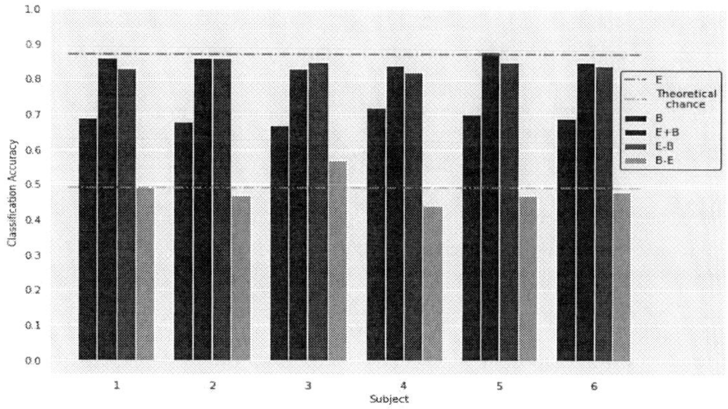

Figure 1: Variation in classification accuracies of all models over the six subjects' data.

dictability of word concreteness and imageability using word-embeddings as explanatory variables (Charbonnier and Wartena, 2019; Ljubešić et al., 2018).

7.2 Comparative models

Table 1 shows the average accuracy, recall, and F1 score of *E*, *B*, and *E+B*.

As argued in Section 1, we expect the additional sensory processing information encoded in the voxel-responses to complement the linguistic/contextual information encoded in the word-embeddings. Consequently, the combined model should fare better at distinguishing the concreteness of words in the stories.

However, our results indicate otherwise. The performance of *E+B* ($86 \pm 1.9\%$) was not significantly different from *E* (87%) under a 1-sample t-test ($t = -2.33, p = 0.07, df = 5$, 2-tail), meaning the combined model is only as good as the word-embedding based model at the task considered. Therefore, the information present in the voxel-responses relevant to differentiating between concrete and abstract words is already well-encoded by the word-embeddings, and the former does not complement the latter. On the other hand, the performance of *E+B* ($86 \pm 1.9\%$) was significantly higher than *B* ($69 \pm 2.5\%$) under a paired t-test ($t = 17.77, p = 5 \times 10^{-6}, df = 5$, 1-tail). This indicates that the word-embeddings may even contain useful extra information above that in the fMRI signals (note that we already demonstrated the effectiveness of our predictive framework in significantly distinguishing word-concreteness purely from fMRI signals). We explore this idea further next.

Table 2 shows the average accuracy, recall, and F1 score of the residual models *E-B* and *B-E*.

The results of the residual analyses are surprising. First, *E-B* achieved an average accuracy of 84%, which was significant under the residual-permutation test ($p \leq 9 \times 10^{-3}$) for each subject. The performance of *E-B* ($84 \pm 1.7\%$) was also significantly lower than *E* (87%) across subjects under a 1-sample t-test ($t = -4.71, p = 2.6 \times 10^{-3}, df = 5$, 1-tail). This shows that removing the voxel-response information from the word-embeddings marginally affects its ability to classify word concreteness. More strikingly, *B-E* achieved an average accuracy of 48%, which is lower than the theoretical chance accuracy of 50% (see Figure 1). This result was significant under the residual-permutation test ($p \leq 9 \times 10^{-3}$) for each subject, ruling out the possibility that the

Residual Model	Performance (Mean $\pm$ S.D.)		
	Accuracy	Recall	F1 score
E-B	$\mathbf{0.84 \pm 1.7\%}$	$0.85 \pm 2.4\%$	$0.84 \pm 1.4\%$
B-E	$\mathbf{0.48 \pm 9.1\%}$	$0.60 \pm 5.8\%$	$0.55 \pm 5.6\%$

Table 2: Classification metrics across the six participants for the two residual models.

Misclassified example	Ground-truth label
... And so at the earliest opportunity ...	abstract
... with this kind of curious compassion. And ...	abstract
... to suggest I might find myself on such a wayward path ...	abstract
... . Kind of blissfully unaware of what was ...	abstract
... start to get a little tricky. My husband ...	abstract
... couple amens and some applause and then everybody ...	concrete
... you know, for hundred dollars a night maybe ...	concrete

Table 3: Examples of chunks frequently misclassified by the voxel-response model. The exact phrase falling within the chunk is in dark color. We find that a majority of such misclassifications come from the abstract category.

huge performance decrease was merely caused by overfitting/chance. Across subjects too, the performance of *B-E* ($48 \pm 9.1\%$) was significantly lower than *B* ($69 \pm 2.5\%$) under a paired t-test ($t = -8.52, p = 1.8 \times 10^{-4}, df = 5$, 1-tail).

Therefore, while removing the word-embedding information from the voxel-responses fully *eliminates* the latter's predictive capability (a 30% decrease), going the other way around only has a marginal effect on predictive performance (a 3% decrease). These results show not only that the fMRI signals do not provide complementary information to the word-embeddings in making the concrete/abstract distinction, but that the relevant information in the voxel-responses is really a *subset* of the relevant information in the word-embeddings. This is a surprising result, considering the task was to distinguish a property of words theorized to fundamentally affect how the human brain represents language. We summarize our findings and provide some additional observations about this work next.

8 Conclusion

This paper has three key findings. First, we showed that words encountered in natural stories could be classified based on concreteness purely from the neural activity elicited as subjects passively comprehended the stories, using a direct, supervised approach.

Second, we showed that in making the concrete/abstract distinction, contextualized word-embeddings (i.e., GPT-2) **do not** benefit from the inclusion of information from the accompanying fMRI signals, despite evidence from several neurolinguistic studies of the human brain exhibiting fundamentally different representations over the two categories.

Finally, we found that while the residual information remaining in fMRI signals after regressing out word-embedding information can no longer distinguish concrete from abstract words, the residual information in word-embeddings beyond the fMRI signals performs significantly at this task. This shows that the information in the voxel-responses important to our prediction task is a **subset** of the corresponding information in the contextualized word-embeddings.

Our results should be interpreted in light of the following observations:

A limitation of our work is that while the voxel-responses and word-embeddings (from GPT-2) considered provide contextualized stimulus representations, the Brysbaert et al. (2014) dataset provides non-contextualized ratings for each word. We partially addressed this discrepancy by formulating the prediction task as a *classification* problem since the available labels are now much more likely to match ground-truth. I.e., it is reasonable to assume that the broad binary concreteness class of a word will rarely be modified by context as much as the continuous scores would. Future work could overcome this limitation by developing the ideas from the recently introduced CONcreTEXT task[6]

[6]`https://github.com/lablita/CONcreTEXT`

Metric	Model				
	E	*B*	*E+B*	*E-B*	*B-E*
Spearman's ρ (Mean $\pm$ S.D.)	0.85	$\mathbf{0.42 \pm 0.03}$	0.84 ± 0.02	0.80 ± 0.03	$\mathbf{0.09 \pm 0.05}$

Table 4: Spearman's rank-correlation coefficients ($\rho \in [-1, 1]$) between predicted and true ratings across the six participants.

of computing contextualized rating scores. We still report regression results in Table 4 for completeness and observe that they are consistent with our findings (e.g., *B-E* can no longer predict word concreteness as suggested by its near-zero rank-correlation). Finally, we find that repeating our analyses with non-contextualized word2vec embeddings (Mikolov et al., 2013) also yielded *qualitatively* identical results as in Section 7.2, indicating that our three conclusions above hold for word-embeddings more generally.

Another observation is that while *B* ($69 \pm 2.5\%$) significantly distinguishes concrete from abstract words, it still does not perform as well as *E* (87%) at this task. There could be two reasons for this difference. First, *B* does not handle abstract stimuli as well as *E* does. Quantitatively, while *B* achieves a recall of $77 \pm 2.6\%$ on concrete chunks, its recall on abstract chunks is significantly lower at $63 \pm 3.6\%$. On the other hand, *E* shows nearly identical performances over the categories. Table 3 shows some of *B*'s misclassified examples common to as many as four out of six subjects. Out of the 29 such common misclassifications, 19 (65.5%) were found to be abstract. This could indicate that neural activity patterns are not as informative for abstract stimuli as concrete stimuli, which is in agreement with psycholinguistic studies demonstrating verbal processing advantages for concrete concepts over abstract concepts (Holmes and Langford, 1976; Kroll and Merves, 1986; Romani et al., 2008). Second, the temporal resolution of functional Magnetic Resonance Imaging may be too coarse (Gauthier and Levy, 2019; Schwartz et al., 2019) for optimal performance on our task (we had to downsample the stimulus in Section 4). Nevertheless, our findings are important. Applying the current predictive framework on the fMRI signals produced highly significant results, and it is under such a framework that the above conclusions were made. Future work could explore the differences in decoding neural activity from naturalistic stimuli with imaging methods of different temporal resolutions (e.g., EEG, MEG) to determine which method should be used for which kind of task.

To conclude, we believe that this paper will inspire future work to take up the following exciting directions: Which natural language processing tasks may benefit from incorporating human language processing information into the existing frameworks? Are there ways of including such information to expose avenues for improvement in these models?

References

Samira Abnar, Lisa Beinborn, Rochelle Choenni, and Willem H. Zuidema. 2019. Blackbox meets blackbox: Representational Similarity and Stability Analysis of Neural Language Models and Brains. *CoRR*, abs/1906.01539.

Andrew Anderson, Tao Yuan, Brian Murphy, and Massimo Poesio. 2012. On discriminating fMRI representations of abstract WordNet taxonomic categories. In *Proceedings of the 3rd Workshop on Cognitive Aspects of the Lexicon*, pages 21–32, Mumbai, India. The COLING 2012 Organizing Committee.

Andrew J. Anderson, Douwe Kiela, Stephen Clark, and Massimo Poesio. 2017. Visually Grounded and Textual Semantic Models Differentially Decode Brain Activity Associated with Concrete and Abstract Nouns. *Transactions of the Association for Computational Linguistics*, 5:17–30.

F Gregory Ashby. 2019. *Statistical analysis of fMRI data*. MIT press.

Sai Abishek Bhaskar, Maximilian Köper, Sabine Schulte Im Walde, and Diego Frassinelli. 2017. Exploring Multi-Modal Text+Image Models to Distinguish between Abstract and Concrete Nouns. In *Proceedings of the IWCS workshop on Foundations of Situated and Multimodal Communication*.

J. R. Binder, C. F. Westbury, K. A. McKiernan, E. T. Possing, and D. A. Medler. 2005. Distinct Brain Systems for Processing Concrete and Abstract Concepts. *Journal of Cognitive Neuroscience*, 17(6):905–917.

Paul Boersma and David Weenink. 2001. PRAAT, a system for doing phonetics by computer. *Glot International*, 5(9/10):341–345.

M. Brysbaert and Boris New. 2009. Moving beyond Kučera and Francis: A critical evaluation of current word frequency norms and the introduction of a new and improved word frequency measure for American English. *Behavior Research Methods*, 41:977–990.

Marc Brysbaert, Amy Beth Warriner, and Victor Kuperman. 2014. Concreteness ratings for 40 thousand generally known English word lemmas. *Behavior Research Methods*, 46(3):904–911.

Charlotte Caucheteux and Jean-Rémi King. 2020. Language processing in brains and deep neural networks: computational convergence and its limits. *bioRxiv*.

Jean Charbonnier and Christian Wartena. 2019. Predicting Word Concreteness and Imagery. In *Proceedings of the 13th International Conference on Computational Semantics - Long Papers*, pages 176–187, Gothenburg, Sweden. Association for Computational Linguistics.

Alexis Conneau, Guillaume Lample, Marc'Aurelio Ranzato, Ludovic Denoyer, and Hervé Jégou. 2017. Word Translation Without Parallel Data. *CoRR*, abs/1710.04087.

Fatma Deniz, Anwar O. Nunez-Elizalde, Alexander G. Huth, and Jack L. Gallant. 2019. The Representation of Semantic Information Across Human Cerebral Cortex During Listening Versus Reading Is Invariant to Stimulus Modality. *Journal of Neuroscience*, 39(39):7722–7736.

Evelina Fedorenko, Po-Jang Hsieh, Alfonso Nieto-Castañón, Susan Whitfield-Gabrieli, and Nancy Kanwisher. 2010. New Method for fMRI Investigations of Language: Defining ROIs Functionally in Individual Subjects. *Journal of Neurophysiology*, 104(2):1177–1194. PMID: 20410363.

Jon Gauthier and Roger Levy. 2019. Linking artificial and human neural representations of language. In *Proceedings of the 2019 Conference on Empirical Methods in Natural Language Processing and the 9th International Joint Conference on Natural Language Processing (EMNLP-IJCNLP)*, pages 529–539, Hong Kong, China. Association for Computational Linguistics.

Yoel Haitovsky. 1987. On Multivariate Ridge Regression. *Biometrika*, 74(3):563–570.

Felix Hill and Anna Korhonen. 2014. Learning Abstract Concept Embeddings from Multi-Modal Data: Since You Probably Can't See What I Mean. In *Proceedings of the 2014 Conference on Empirical Methods in Natural Language Processing (EMNLP)*, pages 255–265, Doha, Qatar. Association for Computational Linguistics.

Felix Hill, Anna Korhonen, and Christian Bentz. 2014. A Quantitative Empirical Analysis of the Abstract/Concrete Distinction. *Cognitive Science*, 38(1):162–177.

Nora Hollenstein, Antonio de la Torre, Nicolas Langer, and Ce Zhang. 2019. CogniVal: A Framework for Cognitive Word Embedding Evaluation. In *Proceedings of the 23rd Conference on Computational Natural Language Learning (CoNLL)*, pages 538–549, Hong Kong, China. Association for Computational Linguistics.

V.M. Holmes and J. Langford. 1976. Comprehension and recall of abstract and concrete sentences. *Journal of Verbal Learning and Verbal Behavior*, 15(5):559 – 566.

Anne Hsu, Alexander Borst, and Frédéric E Theunissen. 2004. Quantifying variability in neural responses and its application for the validation of model predictions. *Network: Computation in Neural Systems*, 15(2):91–109. PMID: 15214701.

Alexander Huth, Wendy Heer, Thomas Griffiths, Frédéric Theunissen, and Jack Gallant. 2016. Natural speech reveals the semantic maps that tile human cerebral cortex. *Nature*, 532:453–458.

Shailee Jain and Alexander Huth. 2018. Incorporating Context into Language Encoding Models for fMRI. In *Advances in Neural Information Processing Systems*, volume 31. Curran Associates, Inc.

Shailee Jain, Vy Vo, Shivangi Mahto, Amanda LeBel, Javier S Turek, and Alexander Huth. 2020. Interpretable multi-timescale models for predicting fMRI responses to continuous natural speech. In *Advances in Neural Information Processing Systems*, volume 33, pages 13738–13749. Curran Associates, Inc.

Mark Jenkinson, Peter Bannister, Michael Brady, and Stephen Smith. 2002. Improved Optimization for the Robust and Accurate Linear Registration and Motion Correction of Brain Images. *NeuroImage*, 17(2):825 – 841.

Mark Jenkinson and Stephen Smith. 2001. A global optimisation method for robust affine registration of brain images. *Medical Image Analysis*, 5(2):143 – 156.

Judith F Kroll and Jill S Merves. 1986. Lexical access for concrete and abstract words. *Journal of Experimental Psychology: Learning, Memory, and Cognition*, 12(1):92.

Angeliki Lazaridou, Nghia The Pham, and Marco Baroni. 2015. Combining Language and Vision with a Multimodal Skip-gram Model. In *Proceedings of the 2015 Conference of the North American Chapter of the Association for Computational Linguistics: Human Language Technologies*, pages 153–163, Denver, Colorado. Association for Computational Linguistics.

Nikola Ljubešić, Darja Fišer, and Anita Peti-Stantić. 2018. Predicting Concreteness and Imageability of Words Within and Across Languages via Word Embeddings. In *Proceedings of The Third Workshop on Representation Learning for NLP*, pages 217–222, Melbourne, Australia. Association for Computational Linguistics.

Tomas Mikolov, Ilya Sutskever, Kai Chen, Greg S Corrado, and Jeff Dean. 2013. Distributed Representations of Words and Phrases and their Compositionality. In C. J. C. Burges, L. Bottou, M. Welling, Z. Ghahramani, and K. Q. Weinberger, editors, *Advances in Neural Information Processing Systems 26*, pages 3111–3119. Curran Associates, Inc.

George A. Miller. 1995. WordNet: A Lexical Database for English. *Commun. ACM*, 38(11):39–41.

Tom M. Mitchell, Svetlana V. Shinkareva, Andrew Carlson, Kai-Min Chang, Vicente L. Malave, Robert A. Mason, and Marcel Adam Just. 2008. Predicting Human Brain Activity Associated with the Meanings of Nouns. *Science*, 320(5880):1191–1195.

M. Ojala and G. C. Garriga. 2009. Permutation Tests for Studying Classifier Performance. In *2009 Ninth IEEE International Conference on Data Mining*, pages 908–913.

Allan Paivio. 1971. *Imagery and Verbal Processes*. Holt, Rinehart and Winston.

Allan Paivio. 1991. Dual Coding Theory: Retrospect and Current Status. *Canadian Journal of Psychology/Revue Canadienne de Psychologie*, 45(3):255–287.

Alec Radford, Jeff Wu, Rewon Child, David Luan, Dario Amodei, and Ilya Sutskever. 2019. Language Models are Unsupervised Multitask Learners.

Stephen Roller and Sabine Schulte im Walde. 2013. A Multimodal LDA Model integrating Textual, Cognitive and Visual Modalities. In *Proceedings of the 2013 Conference on Empirical Methods in Natural Language Processing*, pages 1146–1157, Seattle, Washington, USA. Association for Computational Linguistics.

Cristina Romani, Sheila Mcalpine, and Randi C. Martin. 2008. Concreteness Effects in Different Tasks: Implications for Models of Short-Term Memory. *Quarterly Journal of Experimental Psychology*, 61(2):292–323. PMID: 17853203.

R. W. Schafer. 2011. What Is a Savitzky-Golay Filter? [Lecture Notes]. *IEEE Signal Processing Magazine*, 28(4):111–117.

Martin Schrimpf, Idan Blank, Greta Tuckute, Carina Kauf, Eghbal A. Hosseini, Nancy Kanwisher, Joshua Tenenbaum, and Evelina Fedorenko. 2020. The neural architecture of language: Integrative reverse-engineering converges on a model for predictive processing. *bioRxiv*.

Dan Schwartz, Mariya Toneva, and Leila Wehbe. 2019. Inducing brain-relevant bias in natural language processing models. In H. Wallach, H. Larochelle, A. Beygelzimer, F. d'Alché-Buc, E. Fox, and R. Garnett, editors, *Advances in Neural Information Processing Systems 32*, pages 14123–14133. Curran Associates, Inc.

Carina Silberer and Mirella Lapata. 2014. Learning Grounded Meaning Representations with Autoencoders. In *Proceedings of the 52nd Annual Meeting of the Association for Computational Linguistics (Volume 1: Long Papers)*, pages 721–732, Baltimore, Maryland. Association for Computational Linguistics.

Mariya Toneva and Leila Wehbe. 2019. Interpreting and improving natural-language processing (in machines) with natural language-processing (in the brain). In H. Wallach, H. Larochelle, A. Beygelzimer, F. d'Alché-Buc, E. Fox, and R. Garnett, editors, *Advances in Neural Information Processing Systems 32*, pages 14954–14964. Curran Associates, Inc.

Walter J. B. van Heuven, Pawel Mandera, Emmanuel Keuleers, and Marc Brysbaert. 2014. Subtlex-UK: A New and Improved Word Frequency Database for British English. *Quarterly Journal of Experimental Psychology*, 67(6):1176–1190. PMID: 24417251.

Jing Wang, Laura B. Baucom, and Svetlana V. Shinkareva. 2013. Decoding abstract and concrete concept representations based on single-trial fMRI data. *Human Brain Mapping*, 34(5):1133–1147.

Leila Wehbe, Brian Murphy, Partha Talukdar, Alona Fyshe, Aaditya Ramdas, and Tom Mitchell. 2014. Simultaneously Uncovering the Patterns of Brain Regions Involved in Different Story Reading Subprocesses. *PLOS ONE*, 9(11):1–19.

Jiahong Yuan and Mark Liberman. 2008. Speaker identification on the SCOTUS corpus. *Acoustical Society of America Journal*, 123(5):3878.

Human Sentence Processing: Recurrence or Attention?

Danny Merkx
Radboud University
Nijmegen, The Netherlands
d.merkx@let.ru.nl

Stefan L. Frank
Radboud University
Nijmegen, The Netherlands
s.frank@let.ru.nl

Abstract

Recurrent neural networks (RNNs) have long been an architecture of interest for computational models of human sentence processing. The recently introduced Transformer architecture outperforms RNNs on many natural language processing tasks but little is known about its ability to model human language processing. We compare Transformer- and RNN-based language models' ability to account for measures of human reading effort. Our analysis shows Transformers to outperform RNNs in explaining self-paced reading times and neural activity during reading English sentences, challenging the widely held idea that human sentence processing involves recurrent and immediate processing and provides evidence for cue-based retrieval.

1 Introduction

Recurrent Neural Networks (RNNs) are widely used in psycholinguistics and Natural Language Processing (NLP). Psycholinguists have looked to RNNs as an architecture for modelling human sentence processing (for a recent review, see Frank et al., 2019). RNNs have been used to account for the time it takes humans to read the words of a text (Monsalve et al., 2012; Goodkind and Bicknell, 2018) and the size of the N400 event-related brain potential as measured by electroencephalography (EEG) during reading (Frank et al., 2015; Rabovsky et al., 2018; Brouwer et al., 2017; Schwartz and Mitchell, 2019).

Simple Recurrent Networks (SRNs; Elman, 1990) have difficulties capturing long-term patterns. Alternative RNN architectures have been proposed that address this issue by adding gating mechanisms that control the flow of information over time; allowing the networks to weigh old and new inputs and memorise or forget information when appropriate. The best known of these are the Long Short-Term Memory (LSTM; Hochreiter and Schmidhuber, 1997) and Gated Recurrent Unit (GRU; Cho et al., 2014) models.

In essence, all RNN types process sequential information by recurrence: Each new input is processed and combined with the current hidden state. While gated RNNs achieved state-of-the-art results on NLP tasks such as translation, caption generation and speech recognition (Bahdanau et al., 2015; Xu et al., 2015; Zeyer et al., 2017; Michel and Neubig, 2018), a recent study comparing SRN, GRU and LSTM models' ability to predict human reading times and N400 amplitudes found no significant differences (Aurnhammer and Frank, 2019).

Unlike the LSTM and GRU, the recently introduced Transformer architecture is not simply an improved type of RNN because it does not use recurrence at all. A Transformer cell as originally proposed (Vaswani et al., 2017) consists of self-attention layers (Luong et al., 2015) followed by a linear feed forward layer. In contrast to recurrent processing, self-attention layers are allowed to 'attend' to parts of previous input directly.

Although the Transformer has achieved state-of-the art results on several NLP tasks (Devlin et al., 2019; Hayashi et al., 2019; Karita et al., 2019), not much is known about how it fares as a model of human sentence processing. The success of RNNs in explaining behavioural and neurophysiological data suggests that something akin to recurrent processing is involved in human sentence processing. In contrast, the attention operations' direct access to past input, regardless of temporal distance, seems cognitively implausible.

We compare how accurately the word surprisal estimates by Transformer- and GRU-based language models (LMs) predict human processing effort as measured by self-paced reading, eye tracking and EEG. The same human reading data was used by Aurnhammer and Frank (2019) to compare RNN types. We believe the introduction of the Transformer merits a simi-

Proceedings of the Workshop on Cognitive Modeling and Computational Linguistics, pages 12–22
Online Event, June 10, 2021.

lar comparison because the differences between Transformers and RNNs are more fundamental than among RNN types. All code used for the training of the neural networks and the analysis is available at `https://github.com/DannyMerkx/next_word_prediction`

2 Background

2.1 Human Sentence Processing

Why are some words more difficult to process than others? It has long been known that more predictable words are generally read faster and are more likely to be skipped than less predictable words (Ehrlich and Rayner, 1981). Predictability has been formalised as surprisal, which can be derived from LMs. Neural network LMs are trained to predict the next word given all previous words in the sequence. After training, the LM can assign a probability to a word: it has an expectation of a word w at position t given the preceding words $w_1, ..., w_{t-1}$. The word's surprisal then equals $-\log P(w_t|w_1, ..., w_{t-1})$.

Hale (2001) and Levy (2008) related surprisal to human word processing effort in sentence comprehension. In psycholinguistics, reading times are commonly taken as a measure of word processing difficulty, and the positive correlation between reading time and surprisal has been firmly established (Mitchell et al., 2010; Monsalve et al., 2012; Smith and Levy, 2013). The N400, a brain potential peaking around 400 ms after stimulus onset and associated with semantic incongruity (Kutas and Hillyard, 1980), has been shown to correlate with word surprisal in both EEG and MEG studies (Frank et al., 2015; Wehbe et al., 2014).

In this paper, we compare RNN and Transformer-based LMs on their ability to predict reading time and N400 amplitude. Likewise, Aurnhammer and Frank (2019) compared SRNs, LSTMs and GRUs on human reading data from three psycholinguistic experiments. Despite the GRU and LSTM generally outperforming the SRN on NLP tasks, they found no difference in how well the models' surprisal predicted self-paced reading, eye-tracking and EEG data.

2.2 Comparing RNN and Transformer

According to (Levy, 2008), surprisal acts as a 'causal bottleneck' in the comprehension process, which implies that predictions of human processing difficulty only depend on the model architecture

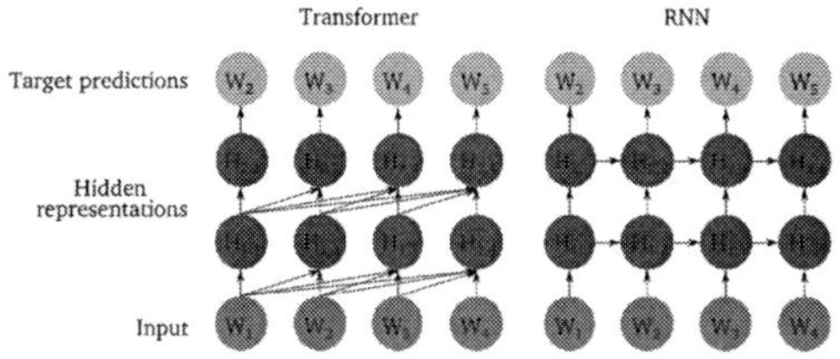

Figure 1: Comparison of sequential information flow through the Transformer and RNN, trained on next-word prediction.

through the estimated word probabilities. Here we briefly highlight the difference in how RNNs and Transformers process sequential information. The activation flow through the networks is represented in Figure 1.[1]

In an RNN, incoming information is immediately processed and represented as a hidden state. The next token in the sequence is again immediately processed and combined with the previous hidden state to form a new hidden state. Across layers, each time-step only sees the corresponding hidden state from the previous layer in addition to the hidden state of the previous time-step, so processing is immediate and incremental. Information from previous time-steps is encoded in the hidden state, which is limited in how much it can encode so decay of previous time-steps is implicit and difficult to avoid. In contrast, the Transformer's attention layer allows each input to directly receive information from all previous time-steps.[2] This basically unlimited memory is a major conceptual difference with RNNs. Processing is not incremental over time: Processing of word w_t is not dependent on hidden states H_1 through H_{t-1} but on the unprocessed inputs w_1 through w_{t-1}. Consequently, the Transformer cannot use implicit order information, rather, explicit order information is added to the input.

However, a uni-directional Transformer can also use implicit order information as long as it has multiple layers. Consider $H_{1,3}$ in the first layer which is based on w_1, w_2 and w_3. Hidden state

[1] Note that the figure only shows how activation is propagated through time and across layers, not how specific architectures compute the hidden states (see Elman (1990); Hochreiter and Schmidhuber (1997); Cho et al. (2014); Vaswani et al. (2017) for specifics on the SRN, LSTM, GRU and Transformer, respectively).

[2] Language modelling is trivial if the model also receives information from future time-steps, as is commonly allowed in Transformers. Our Transformer is thus uni-directional, which is achieved by applying a simple mask to the input.

$H_{1,3}$ does not depend on the order of the previous inputs (any order will result in the same hidden state). However, $H_{2,3}$ depends on $H_{1,1}, H_{1,2}$ and $H_{1,3}$. If the order of the inputs w_1, w_2, w_3 is different, $H_{1,3}$ will be the same hidden state but $H_{1,1}$ and $H_{1,2}$ will not, resulting in a different hidden state at $H_{2,3}$.

Unlike Transformers, RNNs are inherently sequential, making them seemingly more plausible as a cognitive model. Christiansen and Chater (2016) argue for a 'now-or-never' bottleneck in language processing; incoming inputs need to be rapidly recoded and passed on for further processing to prevent interference from the rapidly incoming stream of new material. In line with this theory, Futrell et al. (2020) proposed a model of lossy-context surprisal based on a lossy representation of memory. Recurrent processing, where input is forgotten as soon as it is processed and only available for subsequent processing through a bounded-size hidden state, is more compatible with these theories than the Transformer's attention operation.

3 Methods

We train LMs with Transformer and GRU architectures and compare how well their surprisal explains human behavioural and neural data. Although a state-of-the-art pre-trained model can achieve higher LM quality, we opt to train our own models for several reasons. Firstly, the predictive power of surprisal increases with language model quality (Goodkind and Bicknell, 2018), so to separate the effects of LM quality from those of the architectural differences, the architectures must be compared at equal LM capability. We also need to make sure both models have seen the same sentences. Training our own models gives us control over training material, hyper-parameters and LM quality to make a fair comparison.

Perhaps most importantly, we test our models on previously collected human sentence processing data. Most popular large-scale pre-trained models use efficient byte pair encodings as input rather than raw word tokens. This is a useful technique for creating the best possible LM, but also a crucial mismatch with how our test material was presented to the human subjects. It is not possible to directly compare the surprisal generated on BPEs to whole-word measures such as gaze durations and reading times.

3.1 Language Model Architectures

We first trained a GRU model using the same architecture as Aurnhammer and Frank (2019): an embedding layer with 400 dimensions per word, a 500-unit GRU layer, followed by a 400-unit linear layer with a tanh activation function, and finally an output layer with log-softmax activation function. All LMs used in this experiment use randomly initialised (i.e., not pre-trained) embedding layers.

We implement the Transformer in PyTorch following Vaswani et al. (2017). To minimise the differences between the LMs, we picked parameters for the Transformer such that the total number of weights is as close as possible to the GRU model. We also make sure the embedding layers for the models share the same initial weights. The Transformer model has an embedding layer with 400 dimensions per word, followed by a single Transformer layer with 8 attention heads and a fully connected layer with 1024 units, and finally an output layer with log-softmax activation function. The total number of parameters for our single-layer GRU and Transformer models are 9,673,137 and 9,581,961 respectively.

We also train two-layer GRU and Transformer models. Neural networks tend to increase in expressiveness with depth (Abnar et al., 2019; Giulianelli et al., 2018) and a second layer allows the Transformer to use implicit order information, as explained above. While results (see Section 4.2) showed that the two-layer Transformer outperformed the single-layer Transformer in explaining the human reading data, the Transformer did not further benefit from an increase to four layers so we include only the single and two layer models. We did not see a performance increase in the two-layer GRU over the the single-layer GRU and therefore did not try to further increase its layer depth.

3.2 Language Model Training

We train our LMs on Section 1 of the English Corpora from the Web (ENCOW 2014; Schäfer, 2015), consisting of sentences randomly selected from the web. We first exclude word tokens containing numerical values or punctuation other than hyphens and apostrophes, and treat common contractions such as 'don't' as a single token. Following Aurnhammer and Frank (2019) we then select the 10,000 most frequent word types from ENCOW. 134 word types from the test data (see Section 3.3) that were not covered by these most frequent words are added for a final vocabulary of 10,134 words. We select the sentences from ENCOW that consist only of words in the vocabulary and limit the sentence length to 39 tokens (the longest sentence in the test data). Our training data contains 5.9M sentences with a total of 85M tokens.

The LMs are trained on a standard next-word prediction task with cross-entropy loss. In the Transformer, we apply a mask to the upper diagonal of the attention matrix such that each position can only attend to itself and previous positions. To account for random effects of weight initialisation and data presentation order we train eight LMs of each type and share the random seeds between LM types so each random presentation order and embedding layer initialisation is present in both LM types. The LMs were trained for two epochs using stochastic gradient descent with a momentum of 0.9. Initial learning rates (0.02 for the GRU and 0.005 for the Transformer) were chosen such that the language modelling performance of the GRU and Transformer models are as similar as possible. The learning rate was halved after $\frac{1}{3}$, $\frac{2}{3}$, and all sentences during the first epoch and then kept constant over the second epoch. LMs were trained on minibatches of ten sentences.

3.3 Human Reading Data

We use the self paced reading (SPR, 54 participants) and eye-tracking (ET, 35 participants) data from Frank et al. (2013) and the EEG data (24 participants) from Frank et al. (2015). In these experiments, participants read English sentences from unpublished novels. In the SPR and EEG experiments, the participants were presented sentences one word at a time. In the SPR experiment the reading was self paced while in the EEG experiment words had a fixed presentation time. In the ET experiment, participants were shown full sentences while an eye tracking device monitored which word was fixated. The SPR stimuli consist of 361 sentences, with the EEG and ET stimuli being a subset of the 205 shortest SPR stimuli. The experimental measures representing processing effort of a word are reading time for the SPR data (time between key presses), gaze duration for the ET data (time a word is fixated before the first fixation on a different word) and N400 amplitude for the EEG data (average amplitude at the centroparietal electrodes between 300 and 500 ms after word onset; Frank et al., 2015).

We exclude from analysis sentence-initial and -final words, and words directly followed by a comma. From the SPR and ET data we also exclude the word following a comma, and words with a reading time under 50 ms or over 3500 ms. From the EEG data we exclude datapoints that were marked by Frank et al. (2015) as containing artifacts. The numbers of data points for SPR, ET, and EEG were 136,727, 33,001, and 32,417, respectively.

3.4 Analysis Procedure

At 10 different points during training (1K, 3K, 10K, 30K, 100K, 300K, 1M, 3M sentences and after the first and second epoch) we save each LM's parameters and estimate a surprisal value on each word of the 361 test sentences.

3.4.1 Linear Mixed Effects Regression

Following Aurnhammer and Frank (2019), we analyse how well each set of surprisal values predicts the human sentence processing data using linear mixed effects regression (LMER) models with the *MixedModels* package in Julia (Bates et al., 2019). For each datasets (SPR, ET, and EEG) we fit a baseline LMER model which takes into account several factors known to influence processing effort. The dependent variables for the SPR and ET models are log-transformed reading time and gaze duration, respectively; for the EEG model it is the size of the N400 response. All LMER models include log-transformed word frequency (taken from SUBTLEXus; Brysbaert and New, 2009), word length (in characters) and the word's position in the sentence as fixed effects.

Spill-over occurs when processing a word is not yet completed when the next word is read (Rayner, 1998).To account for spill-over in the SPR and ET data we include the previous word's frequency and length. For the SPR data, we include the previous word's reading time to account for the high correlation between consecutive words' reading times. For the EEG data, we include the baseline activity (average amplitude in the 100 ms before word onset). All fixed effects were standardised, and all LMER models include two-way interaction effects between all fixed effects, by-subject and by-item (word token) random intercepts, and by-subject random slopes for all fixed effects.

After fitting the baseline models, we include the surprisal values (for SPR and ET also the previous word's surprisal) as fixed effects, but no new interactions. For each LMER model with surprisal, we calculate the log-likelihood ratio with its corresponding baseline model, indicating the decrease in model deviance due to adding the surprisal measures. The more the surprisal values decrease the model deviance, the better they predict the human reading data. We call this log-likelihood ratio the goodness-of-fit between the surprisal and the data. Surprisal from the early stages of training often received a negative coefficient, contrary to the expected longer reading times and higher N400 amplitude for higher surprisal. This could be caused by collinearity, most likely between surprisal and the log-frequency, which was confirmed by their very high correlation ($> .9$) and Variance Inflation Factors (> 15) (Tomaschek et al., 2018). Apparently, the neural networks are very sensitive to word frequency before they learn to pick up on more complex relations in the data. We indicate affected goodness-of-fit scores by adding a negative sign and excluded these scores from the next stage of analysis.

3.4.2 Generalised Additive Modelling

As said before, it is well known that surprisal values derived from better LMs are a better fit to human reading data (Monsalve et al., 2012; Frank et al., 2015; Goodkind and Bicknell, 2018). We use generalised additive modelling (GAM) to assess whether the LMs differ in their ability to explain the human reading data at equal language modelling capability, that is, because of their architectural differences and not due to being a better LM. The log-likelihood ratios obtained in the LMER analyses are a measure of how well each LM explains the human reading data. We use each LM's average log probability over the datapoints used in the LMER analyses as a measure of the LM's language modelling capability. Separate GAMs are fit for each of the three datasets, using the R package *mgcv* by (Wood, 2004). LM type (single-layer GRU, two-layer GRU, etc.) is used as an unordered factor so that separate smooths are fit for each LM type. Furthermore, we add training repetition (i.e., the random training order and embedding initialisation) as a random smooth effect.

4 Results

4.1 LM Quality and Goodness-of-Fit

Figure 2 shows the goodness-of-fit values from the LMER models and the smooths fit by the GAMs. Overall we see the expected relationship where higher LM quality results in higher goodness of fit. The LM quality increases monotonically during training, meaning the clusters seen in the scatterplots correspond to the points during training where the network parameters were stored. The models do seem to reach similar levels of LM quality at the end of training: The average log probability of the best LM (two-layer Transformer) is only 0.17 higher than the worst LM (two-layer GRU).

4.2 GAM Comparisons

The bottom row of Figure 2 shows the estimated differences between the GAM curves in the middle row. The two-layer GRU does not seem to improve over the single-layer GRU. It outperforms the single-layer GRU only in the early stages of training on the EEG data, with the single-layer GRU outperforming it in the later stages and on the SPR data. The two-layer GRU also reaches lower LM quality on all datasets. For the Transformers we see the opposite, with the two-layer Transformer outperforming the single-layer Transformer on the N400 data at the end of training and never being outperformed by its shallower counterpart. The two-layer Transformer reaches a higher maximum LM quality on all datasets.

For the comparison between architectures, we only compare the best model of each type, i.e., the single-layer GRU and two-layer Transformer. The GRU outperforms the Transformer in the early stages of training (3K-300K sentences) on the N400 data, but the Transformer outperforms the GRU at the end of training on both the SPR and N400 data. On the gaze duration data, there are some performance differences with the Transformers and GRUs outperforming each other at different points during training but there are no differences in the later stages of training.

4.3 Shorter and Longer Sentences in SPR

The SPR data contains a subset of sentences longer (in number of characters) than those in the EEG/ET data. As the Transformer has unlimited memory of past inputs, the presence of longer sentences could explain why it outperformed the GRU on the SPR data. We repeated the analysis of the single- and two-layer GRUs and Transformers but only on those sentences from the SPR data that also occurred in the EEG/ET data. On these shorter sentences, there are no notable performance differences between any of the LM architectures (Figure

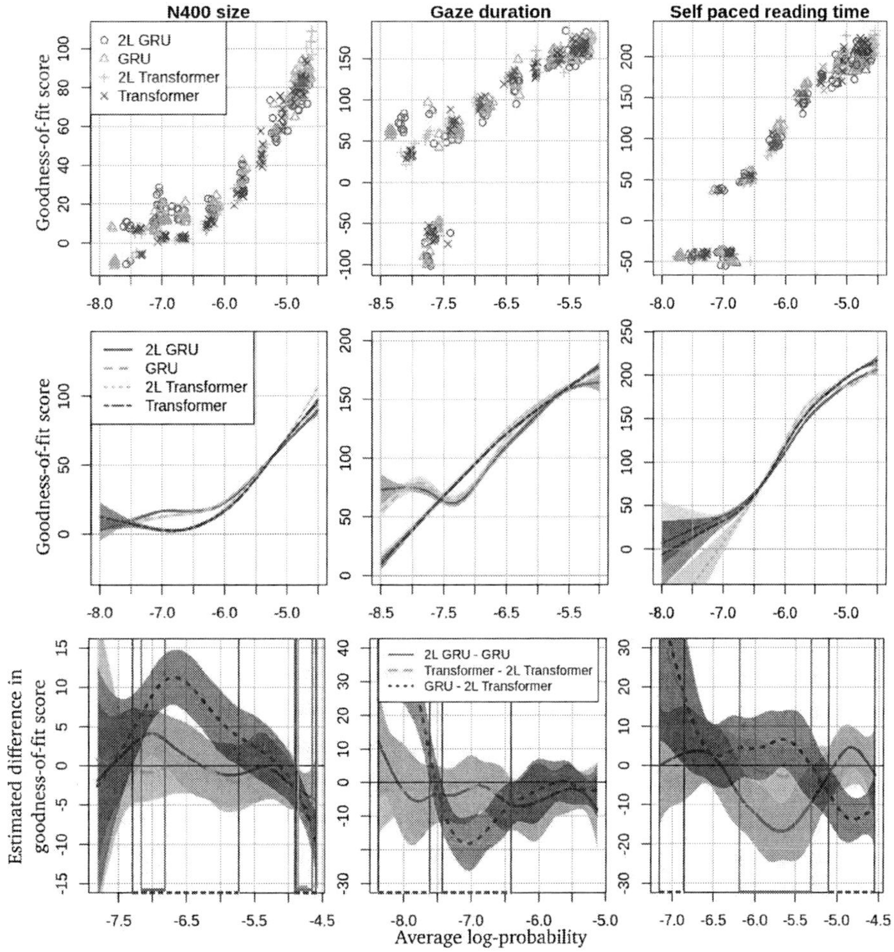

Figure 2: Top row: results of the linear mixed effects regression analysis grouped by LM type. These scatter plots show the resulting goodness-of-fit values plotted against the average log-probability over the included test data. Negative goodness-of-fit indicates effects in the unexpected direction. Middle row: smooths resulting from the GAMs fitted on the goodness-of-fit data (excluding negative values), with their 95% confidence intervals. Bottom row: estimated differences in goodness-of-fit score. The markings on the x-axis and the vertical lines indicate intervals where zero is not within the 95% confidence interval. Each curve represents a comparison between two models, with an estimated difference above zero meaning the first model performed better and vice versa for differences below zero.

3). When we test on only those sentences that were not included in the EEG/ET experiments (i.e., the longer sentences), the Transformers outperform the GRUs as they did on the complete SPR dataset.

5 Discussion

We trained several language models based on Transformer and GRU architectures to investigate how well these neural networks account for human reading data. At equal LM quality, the Transformers generally outperform the GRUs. It seems that their attention-based computation allows them to better fit the self-paced reading and EEG data. This is an unexpected result, as we considered the Transformer's unlimited memory and access to past inputs implausible given current theories on human language processing.

Notably, the Transformer outperformed the GRU on the two datasets where sentences were presented to participants word by word (SPR and EEG). Neurophysiological evidence suggests that natural (whole sentence) reading places different demands on the reader than word-by-word reading, leading to different encoding and reading strategies (Metzner et al., 2015). Metzner et al. speculate that word-by-word reading places greater demand on working memory, leading to faster retrieval of previously processed material. This seems to be supported by our results; the Transformer has direct access to previous inputs and hidden states and is better at explaining the RT and N400 data from the word-by-word reading experiments. However, when we split the SPR data by sentence length, the results suggest that the Transformers' advantage is mainly due to performing better on the longer SPR sentences. On the other hand, the Transformer did outperform the GRU on the EEG dataset which contains only the shorter subset of sentences. The question remains whether the Transformer's unlimited memory is an advantage on longer sentences only, or if it could also explain why it performs better on data presented word-by-word. This question could be resolved with new data gathered in experiments where the same set of stimuli is used in SPR and EEG. Furthermore, future research could do a more specific error analysis to identify on which sentences the Transformer performs better, and perhaps even on which sentences the GRU performs better. Such an analysis may reveal the models are sensitive to certain linguistic properties allowing us to form testable hypotheses.

Surprisingly, adding a GRU layer did not improve performance, and even hurt it on reading time data, despite previous research showing that increasing layer depth in RNNs allows them to capture more complex patterns in linguistic data (Abnar et al., 2019; Giulianelli et al., 2018). The Transformers did show improvement when adding a second layer but did not improve much with four layers. As explained in Section 2, a single-layer Transformer cannot make use of implicit order information in the sequence. When adding a single layer to our Transformer, the second layer operates no longer on raw input embeddings but on contextualised hidden states allowing the model to utilise implicit input order information. Further layers increase the complexity of the model but do not make such a fundamental difference in how input is processed. In future work we could investigate how powerful this implicit order information is, and whether multi-layer Transformer LMs no longer require the additional explicit order information.

Our results raise the question how good recurrent models are as models of human sentence processing if they are outperformed by a cognitively implausible model. However, one could also interpret the results in favour of Transformers (and the attention mechanism) being plausible as a cognitive model. While unlimited working memory is certainly implausible, some argue that the capacity of working memory is even smaller than often thought (only 2 or 3 items) and that language processing depends on rapid direct-access retrieval of items from storage (McElree, 1998; Lewis et al., 2006). Cue based retrieval theory posits that items are rapidly retrieved based on how well they match the cue (Parker et al., 2017). This is compatible with the attention mechanism used in Transformers which, simply put, weighs previous inputs based on their similarity to the current input. Cue-based retrieval models due have a recency bias due to decaying activation of memory representations but it is possible to implement a similar mechanism in Transformers (Peng et al., 2021).

Interestingly, Lewis et al. (2006) claims that serial order information is retrieved too slowly to support sentence comprehension. However, our two-layer Transformer outperforms the single layer Transformer, presumably due to order information implicitly arising as a natural result from the attention operation being performed. The use of serial order information could be compatible with cue-

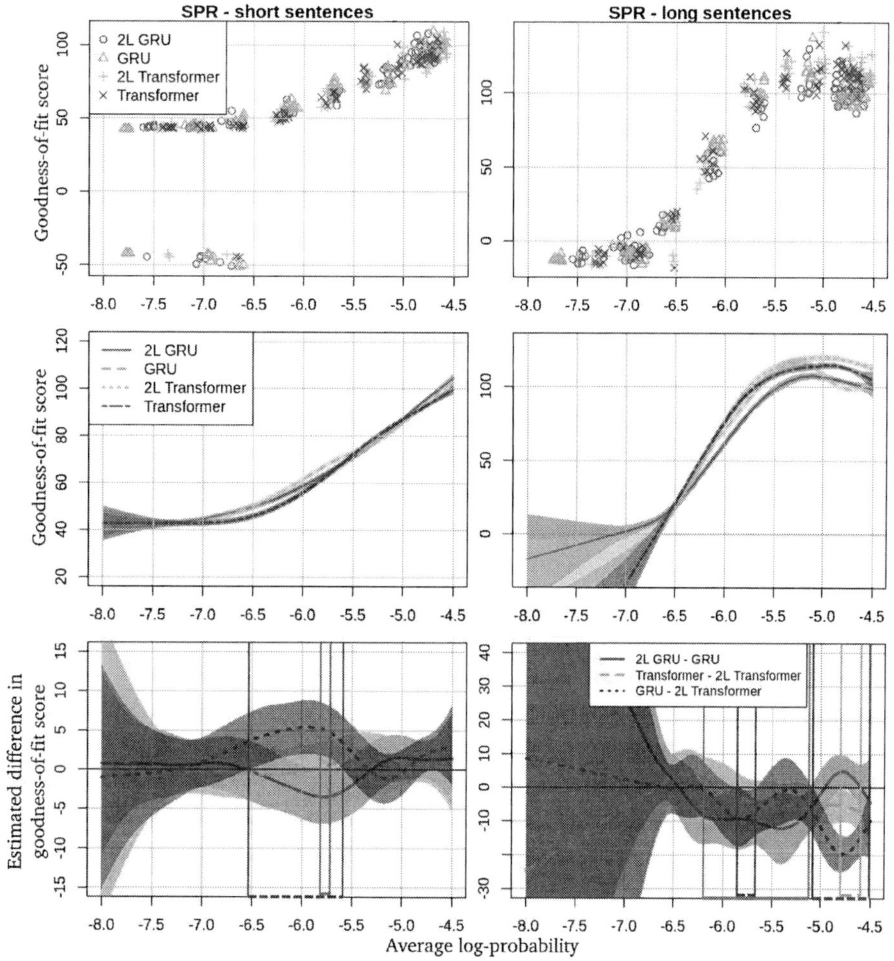

Figure 3: Top row: the results of the linear mixed effects regression analysis on the SPR data, where the data is split by whether the sentences were present in the ET/EEG experiment or not. These scatter-plots show the resulting goodness-of-fit values plotted against the average surprisal over the included test data. Middle row: the smooths resulting from the GAMs fitted on the goodness-of-fit data, with their 95% confidence intervals. Bottom row: the estimated differences in goodness-of-fit score with intervals where 0 is not withing the 95% confidence interval marked by vertical lines and markers on the x-axis. Each curve represents a comparison between two models, with an estimated difference above zero meaning the first model performed better and vice versa for differences below zero.

based retrieval models if the order information can naturally arise from the retrieval operations.

In conclusion, we investigated how the Transformer architecture holds up as a model of human sentence processing compared to the GRU. Our Transformer LMs are better at explaining the EEG and SPR data which contradicts the widely held idea that human sentence processing involves recurrent and immediate processing with lossy retrieval of previous input and provides evidence for cue-based retrieval in sentence processing.

Acknowledgements

The research presented here was funded by the Netherlands Organisation for Scientific Research (NWO) Gravitation Grant 024.001.006 to the Language in Interaction Consortium.

References

Samira Abnar, Lisa Beinborn, Rochelle Choenni, and Willem Zuidema. 2019. Blackbox meets blackbox: Representational similarity and stability analysis of neural language models and brains. In *Proceedings of the 2019 ACL Workshop BlackboxNLP: Analyzing and Interpreting Neural Networks for NLP*, pages 191–203, Florence, Italy. Association for Computational Linguistics.

Christoph Aurnhammer and Stefan L Frank. 2019. Comparing gated and simple recurrent neural network architectures as models of human sentence processing. In *Proceedings of the 41st Annual Conference of the Cognitive Science Society*, pages 112–118.

Dzmitry Bahdanau, Kyunghyun Cho, and Yoshua Bengio. 2015. Neural machine translation by jointly learning to align and translate. In *Proceedings of the 3rd International Conference on Learning Representations, ICLR 2015*.

Douglas Bates, Phillip Alday, Dave Kleinschmidt, José Bayoán Santiago Calderón, Andreas Noack, Tony Kelman, Milan Bouchet-Valat, Yakir Luc Gagnon, Simon Babayan, Patrick Kofod Mogensen, Morten Piibeleht, Michael Hatherly, Elliot Saba, and Antoine Baldassari. 2019. Juliastats/mixedmodels.jl: v2.2.0.

Harm Brouwer, Matthew W. Crocker, Noortje J. Venhuizen, and John C. J. Hoeks. 2017. A neurocomputational model of the N400 and the P600 in language processing. *Cognitive Science*, 41:1318–1352.

Marc Brysbaert and Boris New. 2009. Moving beyond Kučera and Francis: A critical evaluation of current word frequency norms and the introduction of a new and improved word frequency measure for American English. *Behavior Research Methods*, 41(4):977–990.

Kyunghyun Cho, Bart Van Merriënboer, Caglar Gulcehre, Dzmitry Bahdanau, Fethi Bougares, Holger Schwenk, and Yoshua Bengio. 2014. Learning phrase representations using RNN encoder-decoder for statistical machine translation. In *Proceedings of the 2014 Conference on Empirical Methods in Natural Language Processing (EMNLP)*, pages 1724–1734.

Morten H. Christiansen and Nick Chater. 2016. The Now-or-Never bottleneck: A fundamental constraint on language. *Behavioral and Brain Sciences*, 39:E62.

Jacob Devlin, Ming-Wei Chang, Kenton Lee, and Kristina Toutanova. 2019. Bert: Pre-training of deep bidirectional transformers for language understanding. In *Proceedings of the 17th Annual Conference of the North American Chapter of the Association for Computational Linguistics*, pages 4171–4186.

Susan F. Ehrlich and Keith Rayner. 1981. Contextual effects on word perception and eye movements during reading. *Journal of Verbal Learning and Verbal Behavior*, 20:641–655.

Jeffrey L. Elman. 1990. Finding structure in time. *Cognitive Science*, 14(2):179–211.

Stefan L. Frank, Padraic Monaghan, and Chara Tsoukala. 2019. Neural network models of language acquisition and processing. In Peter Hagoort, editor, *Human Language: from Genes and Brains to Behavior*, pages 277–291. Cambridge, MA: The MIT Press.

Stefan L. Frank, Irene F. Monsalve, Robin L. Thompson, and Gabriella Vigliocco. 2013. Reading time data for evaluating broad-coverage models of English sentence processing. *Behavior Research Methods*, 45(4):1182–1190.

Stefan L. Frank, Leun J. Otten, Giulia Galli, and Gabriella Vigliocco. 2015. The ERP response to the amount of information conveyed by words in sentences. *Brain and Language*, 140:1–11.

Richard Futrell, Edward Gibson, and Roger P Levy. 2020. Lossy-Context Surprisal: An Information-Theoretic Model of Memory Effects in Sentence Processing. *Cognitive Science*, 44(3):e12814.

Mario Giulianelli, Jack Harding, Florian Mohnert, Dieuwke Hupkes, and Willem Zuidema. 2018. Under the hood: Using diagnostic classifiers to investigate and improve how language models track agreement information. In *Proceedings of the 2018 EMNLP Workshop BlackboxNLP: Analyzing and Interpreting Neural Networks for NLP*, pages 240–248, Brussels, Belgium. Association for Computational Linguistics.

Adam Goodkind and Klinton Bicknell. 2018. Predictive power of word surprisal for reading times is a linear function of language model quality. In *Proceedings of the 8th Workshop on Cognitive Modeling and Computational Linguistics (CMCL 2018)*, pages 10–18.

John Hale. 2001. A probabilistic Earley parser as a psycholinguistic model. In *Proceedings of the Second Meeting of the North American Chapter of the Association for Computational Linguistics*, pages 1–8.

Hiroaki Hayashi, Yusuke Oda, Alexandra Birch, Ioannis Konstas, Andrew Finch, Minh-Thang Luong, Graham Neubig, and Katsuhito Sudoh. 2019. Findings of the third workshop on neural generation and translation. In *Proceedings of the 3rd Workshop on Neural Generation and Translation*, pages 1–14.

Sepp Hochreiter and Jürgen Schmidhuber. 1997. Long short-term memory. *Neural Computation*, 9(8).

Shigeki Karita, Nanxin Chen, Tomoki Hayashi, Takaaki Hori, Hirofumi Inaguma, Ziyan Jiang, Masao Someki, Nelson E. Y. Soplin, Ryuichi Yamamoto, Xiaofei Wang, Shinji Watanabe, Takenori Yoshimura, and Wangyou Zhang. 2019. A comparative study on transformer vs rnn in speech applications. In *2019 IEEE Automatic Speech Recognition and Understanding Workshop (ASRU)*, pages 449–456.

Marta Kutas and Steven A. Hillyard. 1980. Reading senseless sentences: brain potentials reflect semantic incongruity. *Science*, 207(11):203–206.

Roger Levy. 2008. Expectation-based syntactic comprehension. *Cognition*, 106(3):1126–1177.

R.L. Lewis, S. Vasishth, and J. A. Van Dyke. 2006. Computational principles of working memory in sentence comprehension. *Trends in Cognitive Science*, 10:447–454.

Minh-Thang Luong, Hieu Pham, and Christopher D. Manning. 2015. Effective approaches to attention-based neural machine translation. In *Proceedings of the 2015 Conference on Empirical Methods in Natural Language Processing*, pages 1412–1421.

Brian McElree. 1998. Attended and non-attended states in working memory: Accessing categorized structures. *Journal of Memory and Language*, 38(2):225–252.

Paul Metzner, Titus von der Malsburg, Shravan Vasishth, and Frank Rösler. 2015. Brain responses to world knowledge violations: A comparison of stimulus- and fixation-triggered event-related potentials and neural oscillations. *Journal of Cognitive Neuroscience*, 27(5):1–10.

Paul Michel and Graham Neubig. 2018. MTNT: A testbed for machine translation of noisy text. In *Proceedings of the 2018 Conference on Empirical Methods in Natural Language Processing*, pages 543–553. Association for Computational Linguistics.

J. Mitchell, M. Lapata, V. Demberg, and F. Keller. 2010. Syntactic and semantic factors in processing difficulty: An integrated measure. In *Proceedings of the 48th Annual Meeting of the Association for Computational Linguistics*, page 196–206.

Irene F. Monsalve, Stefan L. Frank, and Gabriella Vigliocco. 2012. Lexical surprisal as a general predictor of reading time. In *Proceedings of the 13th Conference of the European Chapter of the Association for Computational Linguistics, Proceedings*, pages 398–408.

D. Parker, M. Shvartsman, and J. A. Van Dyke. 2017. *Language processing and disorders*, chapter The cue-based retrieval theory of sentence comprehension: New findings and new challenges. Cambridge Scholars Publishing.

Hao Peng, Nikolaos Pappas, Dani Yogatama, Roy Schwartz, Noah Smith, and Lingpeng Kong. 2021. Random feature attention. In *The Ninth International Conference on Learning Representations*.

Milena Rabovsky, Steven S. Hansen, and James L. McClelland. 2018. Modelling the n400 brain potential as change in a probabilistic representation of meaning. *Nature Human Behaviour*, 2:693–705.

Keith Rayner. 1998. Eye movements in reading and information processing: 20 years of research. *Psychological Bulletin*, 124(3):372–422.

Roland Schäfer. 2015. Processing and querying large web corpora with the COW14 architecture. In *Proceedings of the 3rd Workshop on the Challenges in the Management of Large Corpora*, pages 28–34.

Dan Schwartz and Tom Mitchell. 2019. Understanding language-elicited EEG data by predicting it from a fine-tuned language model. In *Proceedings of the 2019 Conference of the North American Chapter of the Association for Computational Linguistics: Human Language Technologies, Volume 1 (Long and Short Papers)*, pages 43–57, Minneapolis, Minnesota. Association for Computational Linguistics.

Nathaniel J. Smith and Roger Levy. 2013. The effect of word predictability on reading time is logarithmic. *Cognition*, 128:302–319.

Fabian Tomaschek, Peter Hendrix, and R. Harald Baayen. 2018. Strategies for addressing collinearity in multivariate linguistic data. *Journal of Phonetics*, 71:249–267.

Ashish Vaswani, Noam Shazeer, Niki Parmar, Jakob Uszkoreit, Llion Jones, Aiden N. Gomes, Lukasz Kaiser, and Illia Polosukhin. 2017. Attention is all you need. In *Proceedings of the 31st Conference on Neural Information Processing Systems*, pages 6000–6010.

L. Wehbe, A. Vaswani, K. Knight, and T. Mitchell. 2014. Aligning context-based statistical models of language with brain activity during reading. In *Proceedings of the 2014 Conference on Empirical Methods in Natural Language Processing*, pages 233–243.

S. N. Wood. 2004. Stable and efficient multiple smoothing parameter estimation for generalized additive models. *Journal of the American Statistical Association*, 99(467):673–686.

Kelvin Xu, Jimmy Lei Ba, Ryan Kiros, Kyunghyun Cho, Aaron Courville, Ruslan Salakhutdinov, Richard S. Zemel, and Yoshua Bengio. 2015. Show, attend and tell: Neural image caption generation with visual attention. In *Proceedings of the 32nd International Conference on Machine Learning*, volume 37, pages 169–176.

Albert Zeyer, Patrick Doetsch, Paul Voigtlaender, Ralf Schluter, and Hermann Ney. 2017. A comprehensive study of deep bidirectional lstm rnns for acoustic modeling in speech recognition. In *Proceedings of the 2017 IEEE International Conference on Acoustics, Speech and Signal Processing*, pages 2462–2466.

Modeling Incremental Language Comprehension in the Brain with Combinatory Categorial Grammar

Miloš Stanojević[1*] **Shohini Bhattasali**[3] **Donald Dunagan**[2]
Luca Campanelli[2,5] **Mark Steedman**[1] **Jonathan R. Brennan**[4] **John Hale**[2]
[1]University of Edinburgh, UK [2]University of Georgia, USA
[3]University of Maryland, USA [4]University of Michigan, USA [5]Haskins Laboratories, USA

Abstract

Hierarchical sentence structure plays a role in word-by-word human sentence comprehension, but it remains unclear how best to characterize this structure and unknown how exactly it would be recognized in a step-by-step process model. With a view towards sharpening this picture, we model the time course of hemodynamic activity within the brain during an extended episode of naturalistic language comprehension using Combinatory Categorial Grammar (CCG). CCG has well-defined incremental parsing algorithms, surface compositional semantics, and can explain long-range dependencies as well as complicated cases of coordination. We find that CCG-derived predictors improve a regression model of fMRI time course in six language-relevant brain regions, over and above predictors derived from context-free phrase structure. Adding a special Revealing operator to CCG parsing, one designed to handle right-adjunction, improves the fit in three of these regions. This evidence for CCG from neuroimaging bolsters the more general case for mildly context-sensitive grammars in the cognitive science of language.

1 Introduction

The mechanism of human sentence comprehension remains elusive; the scientific community has not come to an agreement about the sorts of abstract steps or cognitive operations that would best-explain people's evident ability to understand sentences as they are spoken word-by-word. One way of approaching this question begins with a competence grammar that is well-supported on linguistic grounds, then adds other theoretical claims about how that grammar is deployed in real-time processing. The combined theory is then evaluated against observations from actual human language processing. This approach has been successful in accounting for eye-tracking data, for instance starting from Tree-Adjoining Grammar and adding a special Verification operation (Demberg et al., 2013).

In this spirit, the current paper models the hemodynamics of language comprehension in the brain using complexity metrics from psychologically-plausible parsing algorithms. We start from a mildly context-sensitive grammar that supports incremental interpretation,[1] Combinatory Categorial Grammar (CCG; for a review see Steedman and Baldridge, 2011). We find that CCG offers an improved account of fMRI blood-oxygen level dependent time courses in "language network" brain regions, and that a special Revealing parser operation, which allows CCG to handle optional postmodifiers in a more human-like way, improves fit yet further (Stanojević and Steedman, 2019; Stanojević et al., 2020). These results underline the consensus that an expressive grammar, one that goes a little beyond context-free power, will indeed be required in an adequate model of human comprehension (Joshi, 1985; Stabler, 2013).

2 A Focus on the Algorithmic Level

A step-by-step process model for human sentence parsing would be a proposal at Marr's (1982) middle level, the algorithmic level (for a textbook introduction to these levels, see Bermúdez, 2020, §2.3). While this is a widely shared research goal, a large proportion of prior work linking behavioral and neural data with parsing models has relied upon

*Correspondence to m.stanojevic@ed.ac.uk

[1]This work presupposes that sentence interpretation for the most part reflects compositional semantics, and that comprehension proceeds by and large incrementally. This perspective does not exclude the possibility that highly frequent or idiosyncratic patterns might map directly to interpretations in a noncompositional way (see Ferreira and Patson, 2007; Blache, 2018 as well as Slattery et al., 2013; Paolazzi et al., 2019 and discussion of Bever's classic 1970 proposal by Phillips 2013). de Lhoneux et al. (2019) shows how to accommodate these cases as multi-word expressions in a CCG parser. Bhattasali et al. (2019) maps brain regions implicated in these two theorized routes of human sentence processing.

Proceedings of the Workshop on Cognitive Modeling and Computational Linguistics, pages 23–38
Online Event, June 10, 2021.

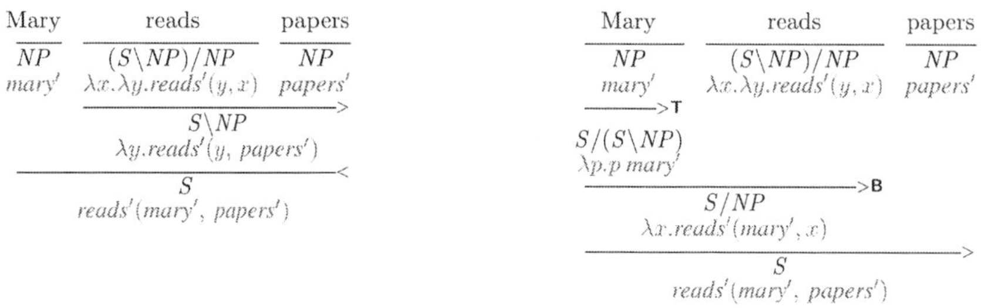

(a) Right-branching derivation. (b) Left-branching derivation.

Figure 1: Semantically equivalent CCG derivations.

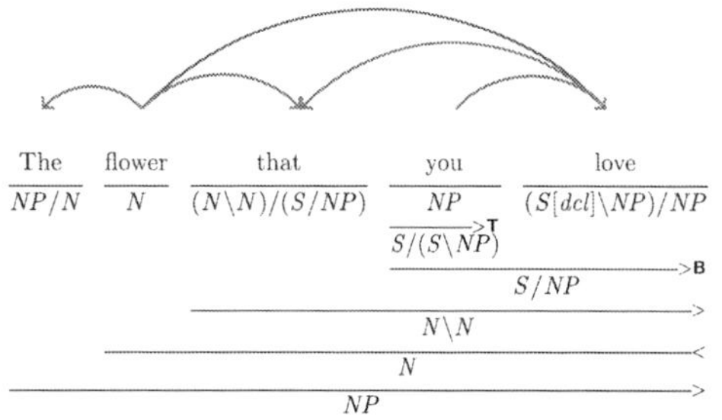

Figure 2: CCG derivation and extracted semantic dependencies for a relative clause from the Little Prince. Red highlighting indicates filler-gap relationship.

the surprisal linking hypothesis, which is not an algorithm. In fact surprisal wraps an abstraction barrier around an algorithmic model, deriving predictions solely from the probability distribution on that model's outputs (for a review see Hale, 2016). This abstraction is useful because it allows for the evenhanded comparison of sequence-oriented models such as ngrams or recurrent neural networks against hierarchical, syntax-aware models. And indeed in eye-tracking, this approach confirms that some sort of hierarchical structure is needed (see e.g. Fossum and Levy, 2012; van Schijndel and Schuler, 2015). This same conclusion seems to be borne out by fMRI data (Henderson et al., 2016; Brennan et al., 2016; Willems et al., 2016; Shain et al., 2020).

But precisely because of the abstraction barrier that it sets up, surprisal is ill-suited to the task of distinguishing ordered steps in a processing mechanism. We therefore put surprisal aside in this paper, focusing instead on complexity metrics that are nearer to algorithms; the ones introduced below in §5.3 all map directly on to tree traversals. By counting derivation tree nodes, these metrics track work that the parser does, rather than the rarity of particular words or ambiguity of particular constructions.[2]

Previous research at the algorithmic level has been limited in various ways. Brennan et al. (2016) used an expressive grammar, but it was not broad coverage and the step counts were based on derived X-bar trees rather than the derivation trees that would need to be handled by a provably correct parsing algorithm (Stanojević and Stabler, 2018). Brennan et al. (2020) used a full-throated parser but employed the Penn Treebank phrase structure without explicit regard for long-distance dependency. Figure 2 shows an example of one of these dependencies.

3 Why CCG?

CCG presents an opportunity to remedy the limitations identified above in section 2. As already mentioned, CCG is appropriately expressive (Vijay-Shanker and Weir, 1994). And it has special characteristics that are particularly attractive for incremental parsing. CCG can extract filler-gap dependencies such as those in the object relative clause in Figure 2, synchronously and incrementally building surface compositional semantics (cf. Demberg 2012).[3] CCG also affords many different ways of

[2]Counting derivation-tree nodes dissociates from surprisal. Brennan et al. (2020) addresses the choice of linking hypothesis empirically by deriving both step-counting and surprisal predictors from the same parser. The former but not the latter predictor significantly improves a regression model of fMRI timecourse in posterior temporal lobe, even in the presence of a co-predictor derived from a sequence-oriented language model.

[3]The derivations in Figure 1 and 2 use type-raising as a parser operation. In the definition of CCG from Steedman (2000) type-raising is not a syntactic, but a lexical operation. The reason why we use it as a parsing operation is because that is the way it was defined in the CCGbank (Hockenmaier and Steedman, 2007) and because it is implemented as such in all broad coverage parsers. Type-raising contributes to the complexity metric described in Section 5.3

deriving the same sentence (see Figure 1). These alternative derivations all have the same semantics, so from the point of view of comprehension they are all equally useful. Steedman (2000, §9.2) argues that this flexible constituency is the key to achieving human-like incremental interpretation without unduly complicating the relationship between grammar and processor. Incremental interpretation here amounts to delivering updated meaning-representations at each new word of the sentence. Such early delivery would seem to be necessary to explain the high degree of incrementality that has been demonstrated in laboratory experiments (Marslen-Wilson, 1973; Altmann and Steedman, 1988; Tanenhaus et al., 1995).

Other types of grammar rely upon special parsing strategies to achieve incrementality. Eager left-corner parsing (LC) is often chosen because it uses a finite amount of memory for processing left- and right-branching structures (Abney and Johnson, 1991). Resnik (1992) was the first to notice a similarity between eager left-corner CFG parsing and shift-reduce parsing of CCG left-branching derivations. In short, forward type-raising $>\mathbf{T}$ is like LC prediction while forward function-composition $>\mathbf{B}$ is like LC completion (both of these combinators are used in Figure 2). However, CCG has other combinators that make it even more incremental. For instance, in a level one center embedding such as "Mary gave John a book" a left-corner parser cannot establish connection between *Mary* and *gave* before it sees *John*. CCG includes a generalized forward function composition $>\mathbf{B}^2$ that can combine type-raised *Mary* $S/(S\backslash NP)$ and *gave* $((S\backslash NP)/NP)/NP$ into $(S/NP)/NP$.

To our knowledge, the present study is the first to validate the human-like processing characteristics of CCG by quantifying their fit to human neural signals.

4 The Challenge of Right Adjunction for Incremental Parsing

A particular grammatical analysis may be viewed as imposing ordering requirements on left-to-right incremental parser operations; it obligates certain operations to wait until others have finished. A case in point is right adjunction in sentences such as "Mary reads papers daily." (see Figure 3a). Here the parser has built "Mary reads papers" eagerly, as it should be expected from any parser with human-like behavior, but then it encountered the adjunct

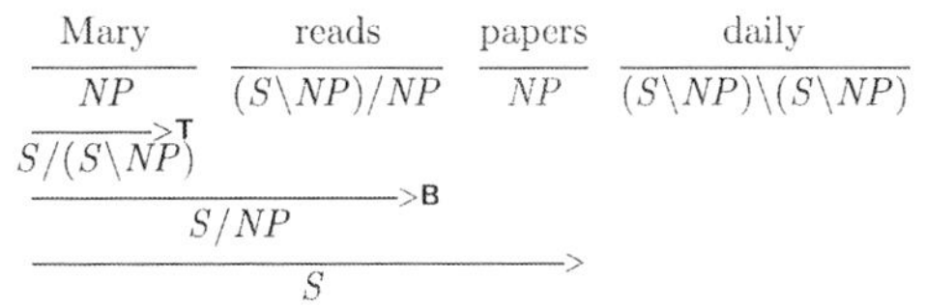

(a) Problem — $S\backslash NP$ that needs to be modified was never built.

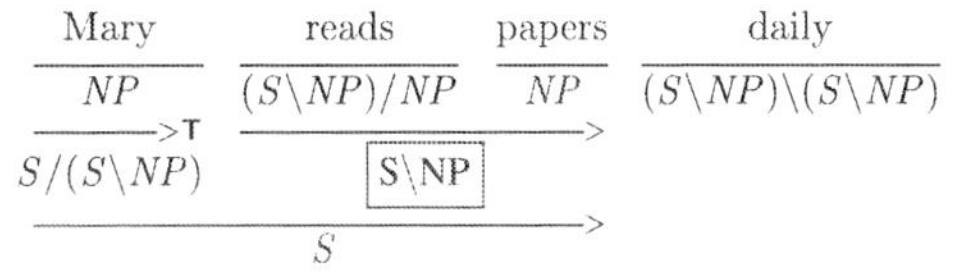

(b) Incremental tree rotation *reveals* the needed node of type $S\backslash NP$.

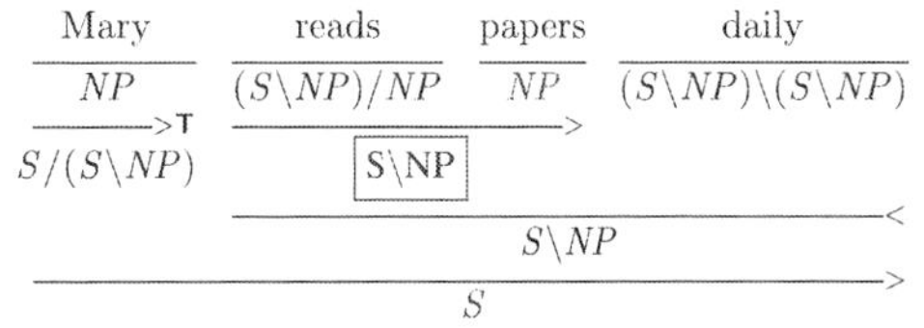

(c) Right adjunct is attached to the revealed node.

Figure 3: Right adjunction. The right spine of each derivation is highlighted in blue. The boxed node S\NP is revealed after tree rotation. Psycholinguistic implications are detailed in Stanojević et al. (2020).

"daily". This adjunct is an optional postmodifier of the verb phrase "reads papers." It could be analyzed using the rule *VP* → *VP AdvP* where "daily" is a one-word adverbial phrase adjunct of VP. With this rule, a context-free phrase structure parser will be forced either (i) to backtrack upon seeing "daily" or (ii) to leave the VP open for postmodification (Hale, 2014, pages 31–33 opts for the latter). Neither of these alternatives is particularly appealing from the perspective of cognitive modeling, and indeed Sturt and Lombardo (2005) report a pattern of eye-tracking data that appears to be inconsistent with CCG. They suggest that CCG's account of conjunction, itself analyzable as adjunction, imposes an ordering requirement that cannot be satisfied in psycholinguistically-realistic way.

Sturt and Lombardo's 2005 finding is an important challenge for theories of incremental interpretation, including neurolinguistic models based on LC parsing (Brennan and Pylkkänen, 2017; Nelson et al., 2017). Stanojević and Steedman (2019) offer a crucial part of a solution to this problem.

First, they relax the notion of attaching of a right-adjunct: an adjunct does not have to attach to the top category of the tree but it can attach to any node on the *right spine* of the derivation, as long as the attachment respects the node's syntactic type. In Figure 3a the *right spine* is highlighted in blue. However, none of the constituents on the right spine can be modified by "daily" because the constituent that needs to be modified, "reads papers" was never built; it is not part of the left-branching derivation. To address this, the Stanojević and Steedman parser includes a second innovation: it applies a special *tree-rotation* operation that transforms left-branching derivations into semantically equivalent right-branching ones. In Figure 3b this operation produces a new right spine, *revealing* a node of type $\boxed{S\backslash NP}$, which is the type assigned to English verb phrases in CCG. In Figure 3c the adjunct "daily" is properly attached to this boxed node via Application, a CCG rule that is used quite generally across many different constructions.

The idea of attaching right-adjuncts to a node of an already-built tree has appeared several times before (Pareschi and Steedman, 1987; Niv, 1994; Ambati et al., 2015; Stanojević and Steedman, 2019) and in all cases it crucially leverages CCG's flexible constituency as shown in Figure 1. See Stanojević et al. (2020) for more detailed treatment of Sturt and Lombardo's construction using predictive completion. The present study examines whether or not the addition of the Revealing operation increases the fidelity of CCG-derived parsing predictions to human fMRI time course data.

5 Methods

We follow Brennan et al. (2012) and Willems et al. (2016) in using a spoken narrative as a stimulus in the fMRI study. Participants hear the story over headphones while they are in the scanner. The neuroimages collected during their session serve as data for regression modeling with word-by-word predictors derived from the text of the story.

5.1 The Little Prince fMRI Dataset

The English audio stimulus was Antoine de Saint-Exupéry's *The Little Prince*, translated by David Wilkinson and read by Karen Savage. It constitutes a fairly lengthy exposure to naturalistic language, comprising 19,171 tokens, 15,388 words and 1,388 sentences, and lasting over an hour and a half. This is the fMRI version of the EEG corpus described in Stehwien et al. (2020). It has been used before to investigate a variety of brain-language questions unrelated to CCG parsing (Bhattasali et al., 2019; Bhattasali and Hale, 2019; Li et al., 2018). Prior to parsing, number expressions were spelled out i.e. 42 as "forty two" and all punctuation was removed.

5.1.1 Participants

Participants comprised fifty-one volunteers (32 women and 19 men, 18-37 years old) with no history of psychiatric, neurological, or other medical illness or history of drug or alcohol abuse that might compromise cognitive functions. All strictly qualified as right-handed on the Edinburgh handedness inventory (Oldfield, 1971). All self-identified as native English speakers and gave their written informed consent prior to participation, in accordance with the university's IRB guidelines. Participants were compensated for their time, consistent with typical practice for studies of this kind. They were paid $65 at the end of the session. Data from three out of the 51 participants was excluded because they did not complete the entire session or moved their head excessively.

5.1.2 Presentation

After giving their informed consent, participants were familiarized with the MRI facility and assumed a supine position on the scanner gurney. The presentation script was written in PsychoPy (Peirce, 2007). Auditory stimuli were delivered through MRI-safe, high-fidelity headphones (Confon HP-VS01, MR Confon, Magdeburg, Germany) inside the head coil. Using a spoken recitation of the US Constitution, an experimenter increased the volume until participants reported that they could hear clearly. Participants then listened passively to the audio storybook for 1 hour 38 minutes. The story had nine chapters and at the end of each chapter the participants were presented with a multiple-choice questionnaire with four questions (36 questions in total), concerning events and situations described in the story. These questions served to assess participants' comprehension. The entire session lasted around 2.5 hours.

5.1.3 Data Collection

Imaging was performed using a 3T MRI scanner (Discovery MR750, GE Healthcare, Milwaukee, WI) with a 32-channel head coil at the Cornell MRI Facility. Blood Oxygen Level Dependent (BOLD) signals were collected using a T2 -weighted echo planar imaging sequence (repetition time: 2000 ms, echo time: 27 ms, flip angle: 77deg, image acceleration: 2X, field of view: 216×216 mm, matrix size 72×72, and 44 oblique slices, yielding 3 mm

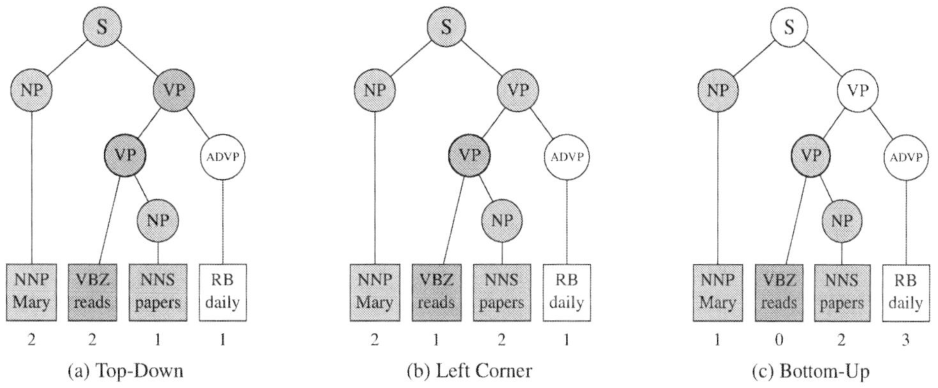

Figure 4: Different parsing strategies for constituency trees. Below each word is a complexity measure associated with that word. It is equivalent to the number of round nodes visited by the parser when the word is being integrated.

isotropic voxels). Anatomical images were collected with a high resolution T1-weighted ($1\times1\times1$ mm^3 voxel) with a Magnetization-Prepared RApid Gradient-Echo (MP-RAGE) pulse sequence.

5.1.4 Preprocessing

Preprocessing allows us to make adjustments to improve the signal to noise ratio. Primary preprocessing steps were carried out in AFNI version 16 (Cox, 1996) and include motion correction, coregistration, and normalization to standard MNI space. After the previous steps were completed, ME-ICA (Kundu et al., 2012) was used to further preprocess the data. ME-ICA is a denoising method which uses Independent Components Analysis to split the T2*-signal into BOLD and non-BOLD components. Removing the non-BOLD components mitigates noise due to motion, physiology, and scanner artifacts (Kundu et al., 2017).

5.2 Grammatical Annotations

We annotated each sentence in *The Little Prince* with phrase structure parses from the *benepar* constituency parser (Kitaev and Klein, 2018). Previous studies have used the Stanford CoreNLP parser, but *benepar* is much closer to the current state-of-the-art in constituency parsing. To find CCG derivations we used *RotatingCCG* by Stanojević and Steedman (2019; 2020).

5.3 Complexity Metric

The complexity metric used in this study is the number of nodes visited in between leaf nodes, on a given traversal of a derivation tree. This corresponds to the number of parsing actions that would be taken, per word, in a mechanistic model of human comprehension (see e.g. Kaplan, 1972; Frazier, 1985). These numbers (i.e. written below the leaves of the trees in Figure 4) are intended as predictions about sentence processing effort, which may be reflected in the fMRI BOLD signal (see discussion of convolution with hemodynamic response function in §6.2).

For constituency parses we examine bottom-up (aka shift-reduce parsing), top-down, and left-corner parsing. Figure 4 shows all these parsing strategies on an example constituency tree. This Figure highlights three points: (a) that the complexity metrics correspond to visited nodes of the tree (b) that they are incremental metrics, computed word by word and (c) that alternative parsing strategies lead to different predictions.

In CCG all natural parsing strategies are bottom-up. The main difference among them is what kind of derivation they deliver. We evaluate right-branching derivations, left-branching derivations and revealing derivations; the latter are simply left-branching derivations with the addition of the Revealing operation. To compute this we get the best derivation from a CCG parser and then convert it to the three different kinds of semantically equivalent derivations using the *tree-rotation* operation (Niv, 1994; Stanojević and Steedman, 2019).

In the case of revealing derivations we count only the nodes that are constructed with reduce and right-adjunction operations, but we do not count the nodes constructed with tree-rotation. This is because tree-rotation is not an operation that introduces anything new in the interpretation — tree-rotation only helps the right-adjunction operation reveal the constituent that needs to be modified.

All parsing strategies have the same total number of nodes, but only differ in the abstract timing of those nodes' construction. In general, left-branching derivations construct nodes earlier than do the corresponding right-branching derivations. However, in the case of right-adjunction both left- and right-branching derivations delay construction of many nodes until the right-adjunct is consumed. This is not the case with the revealing derivations that are specifically designed to allow flexibility with right-adjuncts.

5.4 Hypotheses

Using the formalism-specific and parsing strategy-specific complexity metrics defined above in §5.3, we evaluate three hypotheses.

Hypothesis 1 (H1): *CCG improves a model of fMRI BOLD time courses above and beyond context-free phrase structure grammar.*

Mildly context-sensitive grammars like CCG capture properties of sentence structure that are only very inelegantly covered by context-free phrase structure grammars. For instance, the recovery of filler-gap dependency in Figure 2 follows directly from the definition of the combinators. This hypothesis supposes that the brain indeed does work to recover these dependencies, and that that work shows up in the BOLD signal.

Hypothesis 2 (H2): *The Revealing parser operation explains unique variability in the BOLD signal, variability not accounted for by other CCG derivational steps.*

As described above in §4, Revealing allows a CCG parser to handle right-adjunction gracefully. This hypothesis in effect proposes that this enhanced psychological realism should extend to fMRI.

Hypothesis 3 (H3): *Left-branching CCG derivations improve BOLD activity prediction over right-branching.*

Left-branching derivations provide maximally incremental CCG analyses. If human processing is maximally incremental, and if this incrementality is manifested in fMRI time courses, then complexity metrics based on left-branching CCG derivations should improve model fit over and above right-branching.

6 Data Analysis

6.1 Regions of Interest

We consider six regions of interest in the left hemisphere: the pars opercularis (IFG_oper), the pars triangularis (IFG_tri), the pars orbitalis (IFG_orb), the superior temporal gyrus (STG), the superior temporal pole (sATL) and the middle temporal pole (mATL). These regions are implicated in current neurocognitive models of language (Hagoort, 2016; Friederici, 2017; Matchin and Hickok, 2020). However evidence suggests that particular sentence-processing operations could be localized to different specific regions within this set (Lopopolo et al., 2021; Li and Hale, 2019; Brennan et al., 2020). We use the parcellation provided by the automated anatomical labeling (AAL) atlas (Tzourio-Mazoyer et al., 2002) for SPM12. For each subject, extracting the average blood-oxygenation level-dependent (BOLD) signal from each region yields 2,816 data points for each region of interest (ROI). These data served as dependent measures in the statistical analyses described below in §6.3.

6.2 Predictors

The predictors of theoretical interest are the parser-derived complexity metrics described above in section 5.3. To these we add additional covariates that are known to influence human sentence processing. The first of these is Word Rate, which has the value 1 at the offset of each word and zero elsewhere. The second is (unigram) word Frequency. This is a log-transformed attestation count of the given word type in a corpus of movie subtitles (Brysbaert and New, 2009). The third is the root-mean-squared (RMS) intensity of the audio. Finally we include the fundamental frequency f0 of the narrator's voice as recovered by the RAPT pitch tracker (Talkin, 1995). These control predictors serve to rule out effects that could be explained by general properties of speech perception (cf. Goodkind and Bicknell 2021; Bullmore et al. 1999; Lund et al. 2006). The word-by-word complexity metrics are given timestamps according to the offsets of the words with which they correspond.

In order to use these predictors to model the BOLD signal, we convolve the time-aligned vectors with the SPM canonical hemodynamic response function which consists of a linear combination of two gamma functions and links neural activity and the estimated BOLD signal (see e.g.

Henson and Friston, 2007). After convolution, each of the word-by-word metrics of interest is orthogonalized against convolved word rate to remove correlations attributable to their common timing. Figure 7 in the Appendix reports correlations between these predictors.

6.3 Statistical Analyses

Data were analyzed using linear mixed-effects regression.[4] All models included random intercepts for subjects. Random slopes for the predictors were not retained either because of convergence failures or because they did not alter the pattern of results.

A theory-guided, model comparison framework was used to contrast alternative hypotheses (articulated in §5.4). The Likelihood Ratio test was used to compare the fit of competing regression models (for an introduction, see Bliese and Ployhart, 2002). Effects were considered statistically significant with $\alpha = 0.008$ ($0.05/6$ regions, following the Bonferroni procedure).[5]

As a quantitative comparison between ROIs was not directly relevant for the research questions at issue, statistical analyses were carried out by region. This approach, as compared to examining the effects of, and the interactions between, all ROIs and predictors in the same analysis, reduced the complexity of the models and facilitated parameter estimation.

Hypothesis H1 was tested by examining the overall predictive power of the CCG-derived predictors over and above a baseline model that included word rate, word frequency, sound power, fundamental frequency, and word-by-word node counts derived from all three phrase structure parsing strategies:

(I) *BOLD* ∼ *word_rate* + *word_freq* + *RMS* + *f0* + *bottom-up* + *top-down* + *left-corner* ***{CCG-left* + *CCG-right* + *CCG-revealing}***

To test H2, we examined whether node counts incorporating the Reveal operation explained BOLD signal variability over and above a baseline model that included, in addition to the variables in (I), node counts from left branching and right branching CCG derivations:

(II) *BOLD* ∼ *word_rate* + *word_freq* + *RMS* + *f0* + *bottom-up* + *top-down* + *left-corner* + *CCG-left* + *CCG-right* ***{CCG-revealing}***

Last, for H3 in section 5.4, we tested whether word-by-word traversals of left branching CCG derivations accounted for any significant amount of BOLD signal variability over and above right branching. This amounts to asking whether CCG processing is maximally eager or maximally delayed.

(III) *BOLD* ∼ *word_rate* + *word_freq* + *RMS* + *f0* + *bottom-up* + *top-down* + *left-corner* + *CCG-right* ***{CCG-left}***

7 Results

Behavioral results on the comprehension task showed attentive listening to the spoken narrative with average response accuracy of 90% (SD = 3.7%).

7.1 H1: CCG-specific effects

The first question that we investigated was whether CCG derivations would account for any significant amount of BOLD activity over and above bottom-up, top-down, and left-corner phrase structure parsing strategies in addition to baseline covariates (i.e. as introduced above in §5.3 and depicted in Figure 4). The overall predictive power of the three CCG derivations emerged to significantly improve the models fit in all six regions examined, thus providing strong support for H1. For all analyses, the complete tables of results are provided in the Appendix (Tables 1 to 6).

To better understand the source of those effects, we followed-up with an additional set of analyses in which we contrasted one CCG parsing strategy at a time against the same baseline model. These CCG parsing strategies exhibit a region-specific pattern of fits which is summarized in Figure 5.[6]

7.2 H2: The Revealing parser operation

The second hypothesis, H2 in section 5.4, is about hemodynamic effects of the Revealing operation. The results summarized in Figure 6 supported this hypothesis: the CCG-revealing predictor significantly improved model fit to the BOLD signal in three of six ROIs examined (IFG_tri, IFG_oper,

[4]Regression analyses used the lme4 R package (version 1.1-26; Bates et al., 2015).

[5]A Bonferroni correction of $0.05/6$ reflects the fact each of the three hypotheses was tested with a single Likelihood Ratio test per ROI, irrespective of the number of variables in the models compared.

[6]The direction of the effects for the analyses in both Figure 5 and 6 was not affected by the correlation among variables (Figure 7 in the Appendix).

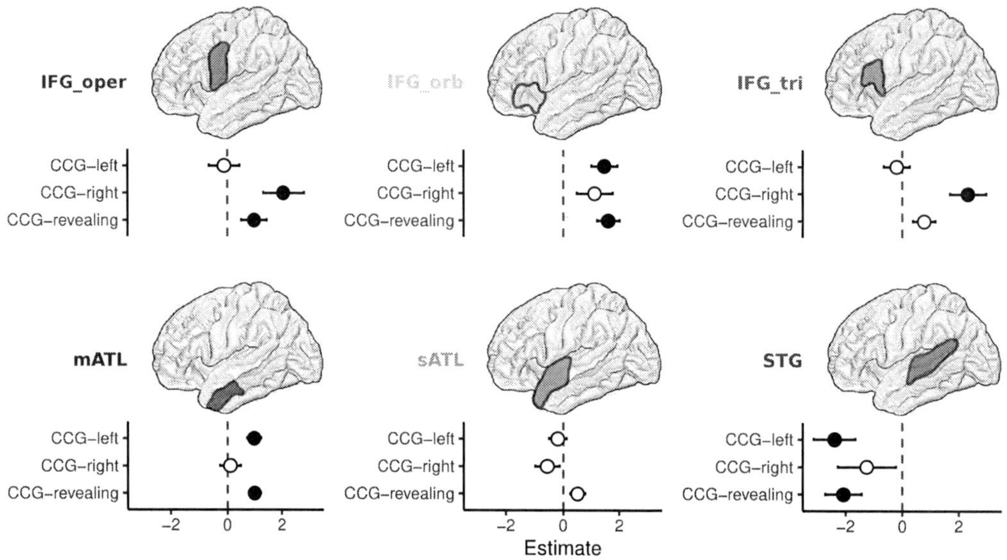

Figure 5: CCG derivation effects by ROI. Coefficient point estimates ± SE. Filled points indicate that the predictor significantly improved model fit. Note that for IFG_oper the CCG-revealing predictor is only marginally significant after Bonferroni correction across ROIs.

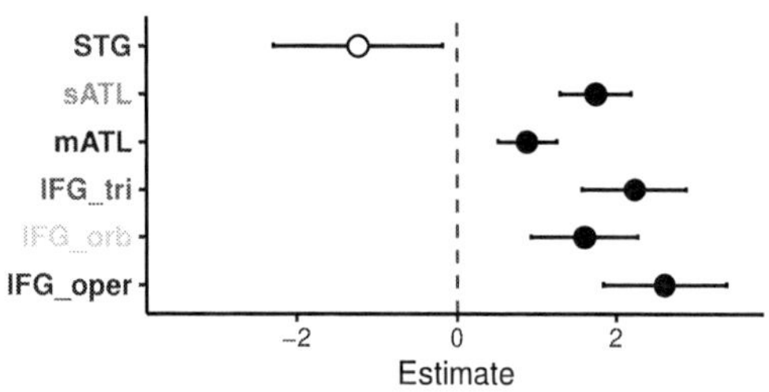

Figure 6: Effects of the CCG-revealing predictor by ROI. Coefficient point estimates ± SE. Filled points indicate that the predictor significantly improved model fit. Note that for IFG_orb and mATL, the effects became only marginally significant after Bonferroni correction.

sATL) and marginally significant in two others after Bonferroni correction (IFG_orb and mATL). The positive sign of the statistically significant coefficients in Figure 6 indicates that, as expected, increased processing cost, as derived from the CCG-revealing parser, was associated with increased BOLD activity.

7.3 H3: Left- versus Right-branching

In the last set of analyses, we investigated whether left-branching CCG derivations improve BOLD activity predictions over right-branching derivations (H3 in section 5.4).

It emerged that the CCG-left predictor significantly improved model fit in IFG_tri, IFG_orb, STG, mATL, and, but only marginally significant after Bonferroni correction, IFG_oper. These findings, overall, indicate the ability of left branching CCG derivations to account for a unique amount of BOLD activity during language processing.

8 Discussion

The improvement that CCG brings to modeling fMRI time courses — over and above predictors derived from well-known context-free parsing strategies — confirms that mildly context-sensitive grammars capture real aspects of human sentence processing, as suggested earlier by Brennan et al. (2016). We interpret the additional improvement due to the Revealing operation as neurolinguistic evidence in support of that particular way of achieving heightened incrementality in a parser. While it is possible that other incremental parsing techniques might adequately address the challenge of right adjunction (see §4 above) we are at present unaware of any that are supported by evidence from human neural signals. The patterning of fits across regions aligns with the suggestion that different kinds of processing, some more eager and others less so, may be happening across the brain (cf. Just and Varma 2007). For instance the explanatory success of predictors derived from left-branching and Revealing derivations in the middle temporal pole (mATL) supports the idea that this region tracks tightly time-locked, incremental language combinatorics[7] while other regions such as the inferior frontal gyrus (IFG) hang back, waiting to process linguistic relationships until the word at which they would be integrated into a right-branching CCG derivation (roughly consistent with Friederici, 2017; Pylkkänen, 2019).

In the superior temporal gyrus (STG) the sign of the effect changes for CCG-derived predictors. This is the unique region where Lopopolo et al. (2021) observe an effect of phrase structure processing, as opposed to dependency grammar processing. This could be because our CCG is lexicalized. Of course, the CCGbank grammar captures many other aspects of sentence structure besides lexical dependencies (see Hockenmaier and Steedman 2007).

Shain et al. (2020) use a different, non-combinatory categorial grammar to model fMRI time courses. Whereas this earlier publication employs the surprisal linking hypothesis to study predictive processing, the present study considers instead the parsing steps that would be needed to recover grammatical descriptions assigned by CCG. This distinction can be cast as the difference between Marr's computational and algorithmic levels of analysis, as suggested above in §2. But besides the choice of vantage point, there are conceptual differences that lead to different modeling at both levels. For instance, the generalized categorial grammar of Shain et al. (2020) is quite expressive and may go far beyond context-free power. But in that study it was first flattened into a probabilistic context-free grammar (PCFG) to derive surprisal predictions. The present study avoids this step by deriving processing complexity predictions directly from CCG derivations using node count. This directness is important when reasoning from human data, such as neural signals, to mathematical properties of formal systems, such as grammars (see discussion of Competence hypotheses in Steedman, 1989).

[7]This predictive relationship between left-branching derivations in middle temporal pole timecourses is observed in (the brains of) native speakers of English, a head-initial language. An exciting direction for future work concerns the possibility that the brain bases of language processing might covary with typological distinctions like head direction (cf. Bornkessel-Schlesewsky and Schlesewsky, 2016).

This prior work by Shain et al. (2020) includes a telling observation: that surprisal from a 5-gram language model improves fit to brain data, over and above a PCFG. Shain et al. hypothesize that this additional contribution is possible expressly because of PCFGs' context-freeness, and that a (mildly) context-sensitive grammar would do better. The results reported here are consistent with this suggestion.

9 Conclusion and Future Work

CCG, a mildly context-sensitive grammar, helps explain the time course of word-by-word language comprehension in the brain over and above Penn Treebank-style context-free phrase structure grammars regardless of whether they are parsed left-corner, top-down or bottom-up. This special contribution from CCG is likely attributable to its more realistic analysis of "movement" constructions (e.g. Figure 2) which would not be assigned by naive context-free grammars. CCG's flexible approach to constituency may offer a way to understand both immediate and delayed subprocesses of language comprehension from the perspective of a single grammar. The Revealing operation, designed to facilitate more human-like CCG parsing, indeed leads to increased neurolinguistic fidelity in a subset of brain regions that have been previously implicated in language comprehension.

We look ahead in future work to quantifying the effect of individual complexity metrics across brain regions using alternative metrics related to surprise and memory (e.g. Graf et al., 2017). This future work also includes investigation of syntactic ambiguity, for instance via beam search along the lines of Crabbé et al. (2019) using the incremental neural CCG model of Stanojević and Steedman (2020).

Acknowledgements

This material is based upon work supported by the National Science Foundation under grant numbers 1903783 and 1607251. The work was supported by an ERC H2020 Advanced Fellowship GA 742137 SEMANTAX grant.

Ethical Considerations

The fMRI study described in section 5.1 was approved by Cornell University's Institutional Review Board under protocol ID #1310004157

References

Steven P. Abney and Mark Johnson. 1991. Memory requirements and local ambiguities of parsing strategies. *Journal of Psycholinguistic Research*, 20:233–249.

Gerry Altmann and Mark Steedman. 1988. Interaction with context during human sentence processing. *Cognition*, 30:191–238.

Bharat Ram Ambati, Tejaswini Deoskar, Mark Johnson, and Mark Steedman. 2015. An Incremental Algorithm for Transition-based CCG Parsing. In *Proceedings of the 2015 Conference of the North American Chapter of the Association for Computational Linguistics: Human Language Technologies*, pages 53–63. Association for Computational Linguistics.

Douglas Bates, Martin Mächler, Benjamin M. Bolker, and Steven C. Walker. 2015. Fitting linear mixed-effects models using lme4. *Journal of Statistical Software*, 67(1):1–48.

José Luis Bermúdez. 2020. *Cognitive science: an introduction to the science of the mind.* Cambridge University Press.

Shohini Bhattasali, Murielle Fabre, Wen-Ming Luh, Hazem Al Saied, Mathieu Constant, Christophe Pallier, Jonathan R. Brennan, R. Nathan Spreng, and John T. Hale. 2019. Localising memory retrieval and syntactic composition: An fMRI study of naturalistic language comprehension. *Language, Cognition and Neuroscience*, 34(4):491–510.

Shohini Bhattasali and John Hale. 2019. Diathesis alternations and selectional restrictions: A fMRI study. *Papers from the Annual Meeting of the Chicago Linguistic Society*, 55:33–43.

Philippe Blache. 2018. Light-and-deep parsing: A cognitive model of sentence processing. In Thierry Poibeau and Aline Villavicencio, editors, *Language, Cognition and Computational Models*, pages 27–52. Cambridge University Press, Cambridge, U.K.

Paul D. Bliese and Robert E. Ployhart. 2002. Growth modeling using random coefficient models: Model building, testing, and illustrations. *Organizational Research Methods*, 5(4):362–387.

Ina Bornkessel-Schlesewsky and Matthias Schlesewsky. 2016. The importance of linguistic typology for the neurobiology of language. *Linguistic Typology*, 20(3):303.

Jonathan Brennan, Yuval Nir, Uri Hasson, Rafael Malach, David J. Heeger, and Liina Pylkkänen. 2012. Syntactic structure building in the anterior temporal lobe during natural story listening. *Brain and Language*, 120(2):163–173.

Jonathan R. Brennan, Chris Dyer, Adhiguna Kuncoro, and John T. Hale. 2020. Localizing syntactic predictions using recurrent neural network grammars. *Neuropsychologia*, 146:107479.

Jonathan R. Brennan and Liina Pylkkänen. 2017. MEG evidence for incremental sentence composition in the anterior temporal lobe. *Cognitive Science*, 41(S6):1515–1531.

Jonathan R. Brennan, Edward P. Stabler, Sarah E. Van Wagenen, Wen-Ming Luh, and John T. Hale. 2016. Abstract linguistic structure correlates with temporal activity during naturalistic comprehension. *Brain and Language*, 157-158:81–94.

Marc Brysbaert and Boris New. 2009. Moving beyond Kučera and Francis: A critical evaluation of current word frequency norms and the introduction of a new and improved word frequency measure for American English. *Behavior research methods*, 41(4):977–990.

Edward T. Bullmore, Michael J. Brammer, Sophia Rabe-Hesketh, Vivienne A. Curtis, Robin G. Morris, Steve C.R. Williams, Tonmoy Sharma, and Philip K. McGuire. 1999. Methods for diagnosis and treatment of stimulus-correlated motion in generic brain activation studies using fMRI. *Human brain mapping*, 7(1):38–48.

Robert W. Cox. 1996. AFNI: software for analysis and visualization of functional magnetic resonance neuroimages. *Computers and Biomedical research*, 29(3):162–173.

Benoit Crabbé, Murielle Fabre, and Christophe Pallier. 2019. Variable beam search for generative neural parsing and its relevance for the analysis of neuro-imaging signal. In *Proceedings of the 2019 Conference on Empirical Methods in Natural Language Processing and the 9th International Joint Conference on Natural Language Processing (EMNLP-IJCNLP)*, pages 1150–1160, Hong Kong, China. Association for Computational Linguistics.

Miryam de Lhoneux, Omri Abend, and Mark Steedman. 2019. Investigating the effect of automatic MWE recognition on CCG parsing. In Yannick Parmentier and Jakub Waszczuk, editors, *Representation and parsing of multiword expressions: current trends*, pages 183–215. Language Science Press.

Vera Demberg. 2012. Incremental derivations in CCG. In *Proceedings of the 11th International Workshop on Tree Adjoining Grammars and Related Formalisms (TAG+11)*, pages 198–206, Paris, France.

Vera Demberg, Frank Keller, and Alexander Koller. 2013. Incremental, predictive parsing with psycholinguistically motivated Tree-Adjoining Grammar. *Computational Linguistics*, 39(4):1025–1066.

Fernanda Ferreira and Nikole D. Patson. 2007. The 'good enough' approach to language comprehension. *Language and Linguistics Compass*, 1(1-2):71–83.

Victoria Fossum and Roger Levy. 2012. Sequential vs. hierarchical syntactic models of human incremental sentence processing. In *Proceedings of the*

3rd Workshop on Cognitive Modeling and Computational Linguistics (CMCL 2012), pages 61–69, Montréal, Canada. Association for Computational Linguistics.

Lyn Frazier. 1985. Syntactic complexity. In David R. Dowty, Lauri Karttunen, and Arnold M. Zwicky, editors, *Natural language parsing: Psychological, computational, and theoretical perspectives*, chapter 4, pages 129–189. Cambridge University Press.

Angela D. Friederici. 2017. *Language in Our Brain: The Origins of a Uniquely Human Capacity*. MIT Press.

Adam Goodkind and Klinton Bicknell. 2021. Local word statistics affect reading times independently of surprisal. *arXiv preprint arXiv:2103.04469*.

Thomas Graf, James Monette, and Chong Zhang. 2017. Relative clauses as a benchmark for Minimalist parsing. *Journal of Language Modelling*, 5:57–106.

Peter Hagoort. 2016. MUC (Memory, Unification, Control): a model on the neurobiology of language beyond single word processing. In Gregory Hickok and Steven L. Small, editors, *Neurobiology of language*, chapter 28. Elsevier.

John Hale. 2016. Information-theoretical complexity metrics. *Language and Linguistics Compass*, 10(9):397–412.

John T. Hale. 2014. *Automaton Theories of Human Sentence Comprehension*. CSLI, Stanford.

John M Henderson, Wonil Choi, Matthew W Lowder, and Fernanda Ferreira. 2016. Language structure in the brain: A fixation-related fMRI study of syntactic surprisal in reading. *Neuroimage*, 132:293–300.

Rik Henson and Karl Friston. 2007. Convolution models for fMRI. In Karl J. Friston, John T. Ashburner, Stefan J. Kiebel, Thomas E. Nichols, and William D. Penny, editors, *Statistical parametric mapping: the analysis of functional brain images*, chapter 14. Academic Press.

Julia Hockenmaier and Mark Steedman. 2007. CCGbank: A corpus of CCG derivations and dependency structures extracted from the Penn Treebank. *Computational Linguistics*, 33(3):355–396.

Aravind K. Joshi. 1985. Tree adjoining grammars: How much context-sensitivity is required to provide reasonable structural descriptions? In David R. Dowty, Lauri Karttunen, and Arnold M.Editors Zwicky, editors, *Natural Language Parsing: Psychological, Computational, and Theoretical Perspectives*, page 206–250. Cambridge University Press.

Marcel Just and Sashank Varma. 2007. The organization of thinking: What functional brain imaging reveals about the neuroarchitecture of complex cognition. *Cognitive, Affective, & Behavioral Neuroscience*, 7:153–191.

Ronald M. Kaplan. 1972. Augmented transition networks as psychological models of sentence comprehension. *Artificial Intelligence*, 3:77–100.

Nikita Kitaev and Dan Klein. 2018. Constituency parsing with a self-attentive encoder. In *Proceedings of the 56th Annual Meeting of the Association for Computational Linguistics (Volume 1: Long Papers)*, pages 2676–2686, Melbourne, Australia. Association for Computational Linguistics.

Prantik Kundu, Souheil J Inati, Jennifer W Evans, Wen-Ming Luh, and Peter A. Bandettini. 2012. Differentiating BOLD and non-BOLD signals in fMRI time series using multi-echo epi. *Neuroimage*, 60(3):1759–1770.

Prantik Kundu, Valerie Voon, Priti Balchandani, Michael V. Lombardo, Benedikt A. Poser, and Peter A. Bandettini. 2017. Multi-echo fMRI: A review of applications in fMRI denoising and analysis of BOLD signals. *NeuroImage*, 154:59 – 80.

Jixing Li, Murielle Fabre, Wen-Ming Luh, and John Hale. 2018. Modeling brain activity associated with pronoun resolution in English and Chinese. In *Proceedings of the First Workshop on Computational Models of Reference, Anaphora and Coreference*.

Jixing Li and John Hale. 2019. Grammatical predictors for fMRI time-courses. In Robert C. Berwick and Edward P. Stabler, editors, *Minimalist parsing*, pages 159–173. Oxford University Press.

Alessandro Lopopolo, Antal van den Bosch, Karl-Magnus Petersson, and Roel M. Willems. 2021. Distinguishing syntactic operations in the brain: Dependency and phrase-structure parsing. *Neurobiology of Language*, 2(1):152–175.

Torben E. Lund, Kristoffer H. Madsen, Karam Sidaros, Wen-Lin Luo, and Thomas E. Nichols. 2006. Non-white noise in fMRI: does modelling have an impact? *Neuroimage*, 29(1):54–66.

David Marr. 1982. *Vision: A computational investigation into the human representation and processing of visual information*. Freeman.

William Marslen-Wilson. 1973. Linguistic structure and speech shadowing at very short latencies. *Nature*, 244:522–523.

William Matchin and Gregory Hickok. 2020. The cortical organization of syntax. *Cerebral Cortex*, 30(3):1481–1498.

Matthew J. Nelson, Imen El Karoui, Kristof Giber, Xiaofang Yang, Laurent Cohen, Hilda Koopman, Sydney S. Cash, Lionel Naccache, John T. Hale, Christophe Pallier, and Stanislas Dehaene. 2017. Neurophysiological dynamics of phrase-structure building during sentence processing. *Proceedings of the National Academic of Sciences*, 114(18):E3669–E3678.

Michael Niv. 1994. A psycholinguistically motivated parser for CCG. In *Proceedings of the 32nd annual meeting on Association for Computational Linguistics*, pages 125–132. Association for Computational Linguistics.

Richard C. Oldfield. 1971. The assessment and analysis of handedness: the Edinburgh inventory. *Neuropsychologia*, 9(1):97–113.

Caterina Laura Paolazzi, Nino Grillo, Artemis Alexiadou, and Andrea Santi. 2019. Passives are not hard to interpret but hard to remember: evidence from online and offline studies. *Language, Cognition and Neuroscience*, 34(8):991–1015.

Remo Pareschi and Mark Steedman. 1987. A Lazy Way to Chart-parse with Categorial Grammars. In *Proceedings of the 25th Annual Meeting on Association for Computational Linguistics*, ACL '87, pages 81–88, Stroudsburg, PA, USA. Association for Computational Linguistics.

Jonathan W. Peirce. 2007. Psychopy—Psychophysics software in Python. *Journal of Neuroscience Methods*, 162(1):8–13.

Colin Phillips. 2013. Parser-grammar relations: We don't understand everything twice. In Montserrat Sanz, Itziar Laka, and Michael K. Tanenhaus, editors, *Language Down the Garden Path: The Cognitive and Biological Basis of Linguistic Structures*, pages 294–315. Oxford University Press.

Liina Pylkkänen. 2019. The neural basis of combinatory syntax and semantics. *Science*, 366(6461):62–66.

Philip Resnik. 1992. Left-corner parsing and psychological plausibility. In *Proceedings of the 14th International Conference on Computational Linguistics, COLING 92*, pages 191–197.

Cory Shain, Idan Asher Blank, Marten van Schijndel, William Schuler, and Evelina Fedorenko. 2020. fMRI reveals language-specific predictive coding during naturalistic sentence comprehension. *Neuropsychologia*, 138:107307.

Timothy J. Slattery, Patrick Sturt, Kiel Christianson, Masaya Yoshida, and Fernanda Ferreira. 2013. Lingering misinterpretations of garden path sentences arise from competing syntactic representations. *Journal of Memory and Language*, 69(2):104–120.

Edward P. Stabler. 2013. The epicenter of linguistic behavior. In Montserrat Sanz, Itziar Laka, and Michael K. Tanenhaus, editors, *Language Down the Garden Path: The Cognitive and Biological Basis for Linguistic Structures*, chapter 17, pages 316–323. Oxford University Press.

Miloš Stanojević and Edward Stabler. 2018. A Sound and Complete Left-Corner Parsing for Minimalist Grammars. In *Proceedings of the Eighth Workshop on Cognitive Aspects of Computational Language Learning and Processing*, pages 65–74. Association for Computational Linguistics.

Miloš Stanojević and Mark Steedman. 2019. CCG Parsing Algorithm with Incremental Tree Rotation. In *Proceedings of the 2019 Conference of the North American Chapter of the Association for Computational Linguistics: Human Language Technologies, Volume 1 (Long and Short Papers)*, pages 228–239, Minneapolis, Minnesota. Association for Computational Linguistics.

Miloš Stanojević and Mark Steedman. 2020. Max-Margin Incremental CCG Parsing. In *Proceedings of the 58th Annual Meeting of the Association for Computational Linguistics*, pages 4111–4122, Online. Association for Computational Linguistics.

Miloš Stanojević, John Hale, and Mark Steedman. 2020. Predictive Processing of Coordination in CCG. In *Proceedings of the 33rd Annual CUNY Conference on Human Sentence Processing*, Amherst, Massachusetts. University of Massachusetts.

Mark Steedman. 1989. Grammar, Interpretation, and Processing from the Lexicon. In *Lexical Representation and Process*. MIT Press.

Mark Steedman. 2000. *The Syntactic Process*. MIT Press, Cambridge, MA.

Mark Steedman and Jason Baldridge. 2011. Combinatory categorial grammar. In Robert D. Borsley and Kersti Börjars, editors, *Non-transformational syntax: formal and experimental models of grammar*, chapter 5. Wiley-Blackwell.

Sabrina Stehwien, Lena Henke, John Hale, Jonathan Brennan, and Lars Meyer. 2020. The Little Prince in 26 languages: Towards a multilingual neurocognitive corpus. In *Proceedings of the Second Workshop on Linguistic and Neurocognitive Resources*, pages 43–49.

Patrick Sturt and Vincenzo Lombardo. 2005. Processing coordinated structures: Incrementality and connectedness. *Cognitive Science*, 29(2):291–305.

David Talkin. 1995. A robust algorithm for pitch tracking (RAPT). In W. B. Kleijn and K. K. Paliwal, editors, *Speech coding and synthesis*, pages 495–518. Elsevier.

Michael Tanenhaus, Michael Spivey-Knowlton, Kathleen Eberhard, and Julie Sedivy. 1995. Integration of visual and linguistic information in spoken language comprehension. *Science*, 268:1632–1634.

Nathalie Tzourio-Mazoyer, Brigitte Landeau, Dimitri Papathanassiou, Fabrice Crivello, Olivier Etard, Nicolas Delcroix, Bernard Mazoyer, and Marc Joliot. 2002. Automated anatomical labeling of activations in spm using a macroscopic anatomical parcellation of the MNI MRI single-subject brain. *Neuroimage*, 15(1):273–289.

Marten van Schijndel and William Schuler. 2015. Hierarchic syntax improves reading time prediction. In *Proceedings of the 2015 Conference of the North American Chapter of the Association for Computational Linguistics: Human Language Technologies*, pages 1597–1605, Denver, Colorado. Association for Computational Linguistics.

K. Vijay-Shanker and David J. Weir. 1994. The equivalence of four extensions of context-free grammars. *Mathematical Systems Theory*, 27:27–511.

Roel M Willems, Stefan L. Frank, Annabel D Nijhof, Peter Hagoort, and Antal van den Bosch. 2016. Prediction during natural language comprehension. *Cerebral Cortex*, 26(6):2506–2516.

Appendix

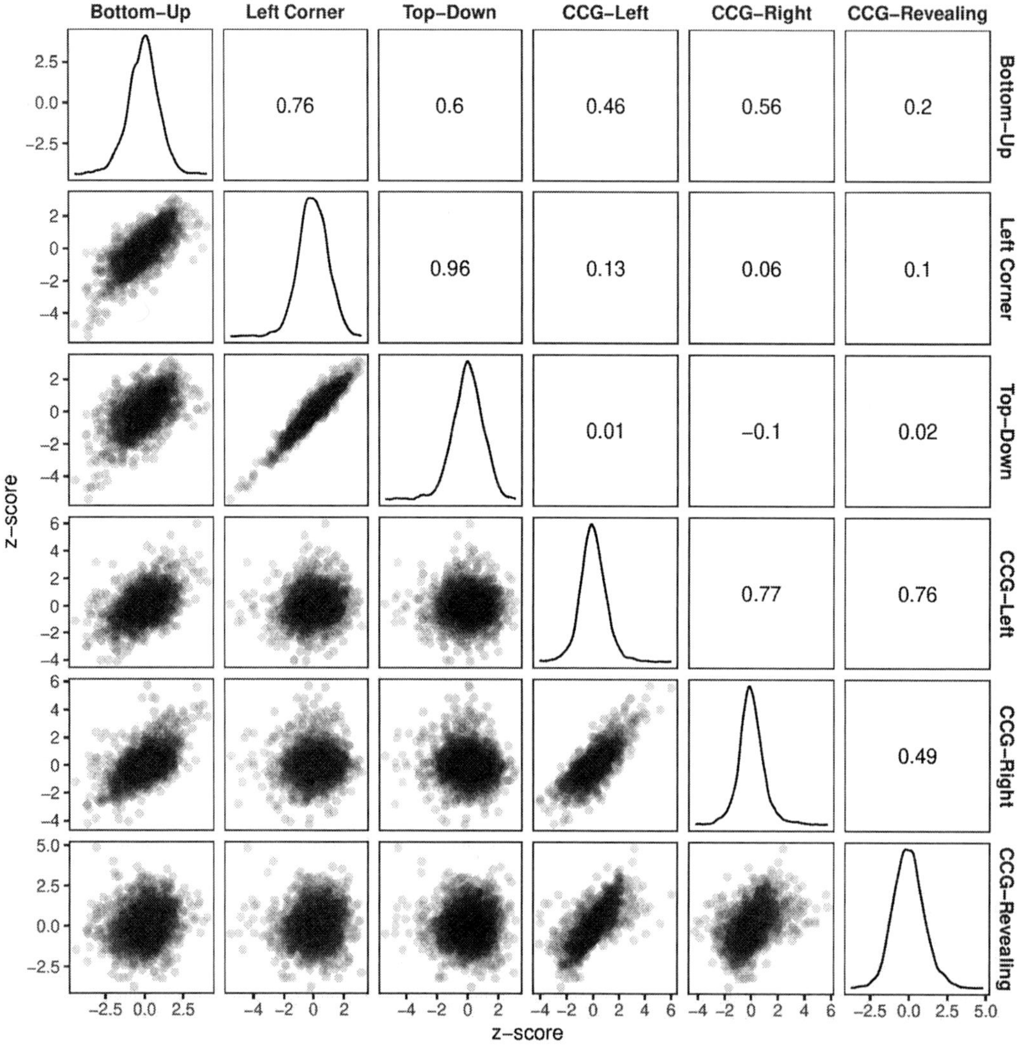

Figure 7: Scatterplot matrix with density plots and Pearson correlation coefficients for phrase structure and CCG derivations.

Hypothesis 1

Model 1: $BOLD \sim word\_freq + word\_rate + RMS + f0 + bottomup + leftcorner + topdown$
Model 2: $BOLD \sim word\_freq + word\_rate + RMS + f0 + bottomup + leftcorner + topdown + CCG\_left + CCG\_right + CCG\_revealing$

Region	AIC_1^a	AIC_2^b	ΔAIC^c	$\chi^2(3)$	p
IFG_oper	1762175	1762156	-19.26	25.26	<0.001
IFG_orb	1717590	1717579	-10.31	16.31	0.001
IFG_tri	1715945	1715913	-32.10	38.1	<0.001
mATL	1562113	1562092	-20.92	26.92	<0.001
sATL	1604738	1604726	-12.09	18.09	<0.001
STG	1843201	1843194	-7.20	13.2	0.004

Table 1: Hypothesis 1, CCG-specific effects: CCG_left + CCG_right + CCG_revealing. [a]Akaike Information Criterion for the baseline model (model 1). [b]Akaike Information Criterion for model 2. [c]$AIC\_2 - AIC\_1$. Bonferroni adjusted significance threshold: $0.05/6 = 0.008$.

Hypothesis 1: Follow-up analyses

Model 1: $BOLD \sim word\_freq + word\_rate + RMS + f0 + bottomup + leftcorner + topdown$
Model 2: $BOLD \sim word\_freq + word\_rate + RMS + f0 + bottomup + leftcorner + topdown + CCG\_right$

Region	AIC_1^a	AIC_2^b	ΔAIC^c	$\chi^2(1)$	p
IFG_oper	1762175	1762170	-5.42	7.42	0.007
IFG_orb	1717590	1717589	-1.03	3.03	0.082
IFG_tri	1715945	1715934	-11.25	13.25	<0.001
mATL	1562113	1562115	1.91	0.09	0.770
sATL	1604738	1604739	0.31	1.69	0.193
STG	1843201	1843201	0.51	1.49	0.223

Table 2: Hypothesis 1, CCG-specific effects: CCG_right. [a]Akaike Information Criterion for the baseline model (model 1). [b]Akaike Information Criterion for model 2. [c]$AIC\_2 - AIC\_1$. Bonferroni adjusted significance threshold: $0.05/6 = 0.008$.

Model 1: $BOLD \sim word\_freq + word\_rate + RMS + f0 + bottomup + leftcorner + topdown$
Model 2: $BOLD \sim word\_freq + word\_rate + RMS + f0 + bottomup + leftcorner + topdown + CCG\_left$

Region	AIC_1^a	AIC_2^b	ΔAIC^c	$\chi^2(1)$	p
IFG_oper	1762175	1762177	1.96	0.04	0.846
IFG_orb	1717590	1717582	-8.12	10.12	0.002
IFG_tri	1715945	1715947	1.81	0.19	0.666
mATL	1562113	1562101	-11.53	13.53	<0.001
sATL	1604738	1604740	1.60	0.4	0.527
STG	1843201	1843192	-8.52	10.52	0.001

Table 3: Hypothesis 1, CCG-specific effects: CCG_left. [a]Akaike Information Criterion for the baseline model (model 1). [b]Akaike Information Criterion for model 2. [c]$AIC\_2 - AIC\_1$. Bonferroni adjusted significance threshold: $0.05/6 = 0.008$.

Model 1: $BOLD \sim word\_freq + word\_rate + RMS + f0 + bottomup + leftcorner + topdown$
Model 2: $BOLD \sim word\_freq + word\_rate + RMS + f0 + bottomup + leftcorner + topdown + CCG\_revealing$

Region	AIC_1^a	AIC_2^b	ΔAIC^c	$\chi^2(1)$	p
IFG_oper	1762175	1762173	-2.18	4.18	0.041
IFG_orb	1717590	1717576	-14.00	16	<0.001
IFG_tri	1715945	1715943	-1.77	3.77	0.052
mATL	1562113	1562096	-16.49	18.49	<0.001
sATL	1604738	1604737	-1.67	3.67	0.055
STG	1843201	1843192	-8.51	10.51	0.001

Table 4: Hypothesis 1, CCG-specific effects: CCG_revealing. [a]Akaike Information Criterion for the baseline model (model 1). [b]Akaike Information Criterion for model 2. [c]$AIC\_2 - AIC\_1$. Bonferroni adjusted significance threshold: $0.05/6 = 0.008$.

Hypothesis 2

Model 1: $BOLD \sim word\_freq + word\_rate + RMS + f0 + bottomup + leftcorner + topdown + CCG\_left + CCG\_right$
Model 2: $BOLD \sim word\_freq + word\_rate + RMS + f0 + bottomup + leftcorner + topdown + CCG\_left + CCG\_right + CCG\_revealing$

Region	AIC_1^a	AIC_2^b	ΔAIC^c	$\chi^2(1)$	p
IFG_oper	1762165	1762156	-9.34	11.34	0.001
IFG_orb	1717583	1717579	-4.03	6.03	0.014
IFG_tri	1715922	1715913	-9.68	11.68	0.001
mATL	1562096	1562092	-4.01	6.01	0.014
sATL	1604741	1604726	-14.32	16.32	<0.001
STG	1843193	1843194	0.61	1.39	0.239

Table 5: Hypothesis 2, CCG Revealing operation. [a]Akaike Information Criterion for the baseline model (model 1). [b]Akaike Information Criterion for model 2. [c]$AIC\_2 - AIC\_1$. Bonferroni adjusted significance threshold: $0.05/6 = 0.008$.

Hypothesis 3

Model 1: $BOLD \sim word\_freq + word\_rate + RMS + f0 + bottomup + leftcorner + topdown + CCG\_right$
Model 2: $BOLD \sim word\_freq + word\_rate + RMS + f0 + bottomup + leftcorner + topdown + CCG\_right + CCG\_left$

Region	AIC_1^a	AIC_2^b	ΔAIC^c	$\chi^2(1)$	p
IFG_oper	1762170	1762165	-4.49	6.49	0.011
IFG_orb	1717589	1717583	-5.25	7.25	0.007
IFG_tri	1715934	1715922	-11.18	13.18	<0.001
mATL	1562115	1562096	-18.82	20.82	<0.001
sATL	1604739	1604741	1.93	0.07	0.788
STG	1843201	1843193	-8.32	10.32	0.001

Table 6: Hypothesis 3, Left- versus Right-CCG parsing. [a]Akaike Information Criterion for the baseline model (model 1). [b]Akaike Information Criterion for model 2. [c]$AIC\_2 - AIC\_1$. Bonferroni adjusted significance threshold: $0.05/6 = 0.008$.

A Multinomial Processing Tree Model of RC Attachment

Pavel Logačev
Boğaziçi University
Department of Linguistics
34342 Istanbul, Turkey
pavel.logacev@gmail.com

Noyan Dokudan
Boğaziçi University
Department of Linguistics
34342 Istanbul, Turkey
noyan.dokudan@gmail.com

Abstract

In the field of sentence processing, speakers' preferred interpretation of ambiguous sentences is often determined using a variant of a discrete choice task, in which participants are asked to indicate their preferred meaning of an ambiguous sentence. We discuss participants' degree of attentiveness as a potential source of bias and variability in such tasks. We show that it may distort the estimates of the preference of a particular interpretation obtained in such experiments and may thus complicate the interpretation of the results as well as the comparison of the results of several experiments. We propose an analysis method based on multinomial processing tree models (Batchelder and Riefer, 1999) which can correct for this bias and allows for a separation of parameters of theoretical importance from nuisance parameters. We test two variants of the MPT-based model on experimental data from English and Turkish and demonstrate that our method can provide deeper insight into the processes underlying participants' answering behavior and their interpretation preferences than an analysis based on raw percentages.

1 Introduction

One of the key questions in the field of sentence processing has been: *What does the human sentence processing mechanism do when confronted with an ambiguity?* A variety of different proposals regarding online disambiguation strategies have been made over the years, such as the Garden-path Theory (Frazier, 1987), the Tuning Hypothesis (Cuetos et al., 1996), the Competition-Integration Model (McRae et al., 1998) and many others. Their diverging predictions have led to a significant body of empirical research documenting, among other things, substantial cross-linguistic variation in the interpretation of ambiguous sentences: For instance, Cuetos and Mitchell (1988) compared the RC attachment preferences of English and Spanish speakers in ambiguous sentences like (1) and (2), in which the relative clause *'who had an accident'* can attach either to the NP headed by the first noun (N1, *'daughter'*) or to the NP headed by the second noun (N2, *'colonel'*).[1]

Cuetos and Mitchell presented Spanish-speaking and English-speaking participants with ambiguous sentences like (1) and (2) and asked them to answer comprehension questions like *'Who had an accident?'*. Participants' responses indicated that English sentences like (1) were assigned an N2 interpretation in 61% of the cases, while their Spanish counterparts like (2) were assigned an N1 interpretation in 72% of the cases. The authors interpret this finding as an argument against a cross-linguistically universal parsing strategy in the resolution of RC attachment ambiguities.

(1) The journalist interviewed the daughter$_{N1}$ of the colonel$_{N2}$ [who had an accident].

(2) El periodista entrevisto a la hija$_{N1}$
The journalist interviewed to the daughter
del coronel$_{N2}$ [que tuvo el accidente].
of the colonel [who had an accident].

Although disambiguation strategies seem to be at least partially determined by the linguistic properties of a given language, various other factors appear to influence the resolution of RC attachment ambiguities. For example, in a questionnaire study, Gilboy et al. (1995, inter alia) demonstrated a substantial influence of construction type. They asked participants to indicate which of the two available noun phrases was modified by the RC in several constructions. They found that the percentage of N2 attachment responses ranged between approximately 20% to 70% for their English sentences and

[1] To any ambiguity in the context of typologically diverse languages, we will refer to the two interpretation options as *N1 attachment* and *N2 attachment*, with N1 and N2 referring to the order of occurrence of the noun phrases head nouns instead of the more common terms *high attachment* and *low attachment*.

Proceedings of the Workshop on Cognitive Modeling and Computational Linguistics, pages 39–47
Online Event, June 10, 2021.

between 10% to 80% for their Spanish sentences. Grillo et al. (2015) also conducted a two-alternative forced-choice (2AFC) task in which English speakers choose between N1 and N2 as the attachment sites for the RC to indicate their interpretation of the sentence. They showed that English speakers, who had previously been claimed to prefer N2 attachment, preferred N1 attachment in more than 50% of the cases when a small clause reading was possible.

RC attachment preferences have also been studied in Turkish, where the order of the RC and the complex noun phrase is reversed, compared to English and Spanish. In a questionnaire study with sentences like (3), Kırkıcı (2004) found that animacy may affect attachment preferences such that when both NPs were [+human], there was no significant difference between the proportions of the N1 and N2 attachment, while an N1 attachment manifested when both NPs were [-human]. Contrary to this finding, Dinçtopal-Deniz (2010) found an across-the-board preference for N1 attachment in Turkish. In her questionnaire study, monolingual Turkish speakers read Turkish sentences with ambiguous RC-attachment and answered questions about them by indicating one of two options on each trial. The results of this study showed that participants preferred N1 attachment over N2 attachment: 66% percent of the responses indicated an N1 interpretation of the sentence.

(3) Şoför [şehir merkezin-de oturan]$_{RC}$
driver city center-in living
profesörün$_{N1}$ sekreterini$_{N2}$ gördü.
professor's secretary saw
'The driver saw the secretary of the professor who was living in the city center.'

2 The Role of Guessing

What most of the above studies of RC attachment preferences have in common is that they use some variant of a discrete choice task, in which participants select one of two response options to indicate their interpretation of the ambiguity. The relative proportion of responses indicating N1 and N2 attachment, respectively are interpreted as estimates of the magnitude of N1 or N2 attachment. A potential complication in interpreting the percentage of responses favoring an alternative in this way is that participants' responses may not always reflect their interpretation. At least on some trials, participants may process the sentence only partially or fail to pay attention to it altogether. In such cases, participants' question responses must be based on an incomplete or nonexistent representation, and are more likely to resemble guesses than informed responses.

Evidence for such incomplete processing comes from the widely known fact that participants' accuracy in experimental tasks is often far from perfect, even for relatively simple tasks such as acceptability judgments: For example, Dillon and Wagers (2019) found in an *offline* acceptability judgment study that ungrammatical sentences like (4) are judged acceptable on 18% of the trials. Since it appears unlikely that sentences like (4) are considered grammatical and interpretable when fully processed, the explanation for such responses must lie in their incomplete processing followed by guessing.

(4) *Who do you think that the new professor is going to persuade anyone?

One way of conceptualizing a simple generative model of erroneous responses in relatively simple discrete choice tasks is to assume that at least some participants on some occasions fail to pay attention to the stimulus, and as a result, select a random response. If so, the relation between the probability of response *X* being actually preferred to alternative responses (p_X) and the probability of observing response *X* (p'_X) can be formalized as in equation 1: p'_X is the weighted average of (i) the probability of *X* being preferred to the alternative when the stimulus is fully attended to (p_X) and (ii) the probability of selecting *X* when the stimulus is *not* attended to (g_X), where a is the probability of attending to the stimulus.

$$p'_X = a \cdot p_X + (1 - a) \cdot g_X \qquad (1)$$

Equation 1 illustrates that under the above assumptions, the proportion of responses indicating a preference for *X* conflates multiple factors. As a result, many preference estimates for *X* (p'_X) are compatible with a wide range of underlying preferences (p_X) under different assumptions regarding participants' degree of attentiveness and guessing behavior (a and g_X).

Table 1 illustrates this problem. It shows several parameter combinations which can account for a preference of 65% for *X* in a binary choice task. Such a finding may reflect (i) the absence of an

	p_X	a	g_X	p'_X
2	0.5	0.7	1	0.65
1	0.9	0.7	0.06	0.65
3	0.1	0.35	0.945	0.65

Table 1: Example combinations of parameters that may lead to an observed preference of approximately 65% according to equation 1.

underlying preference (table 1, row 1), (ii) the presence of a much stronger preference (table 1, row 2), and (iii) even a strong preference towards the alternative to X (table 1, row 3).

Given that participants in most if not all psycholinguistic tasks produce a sizeable amount of erroneous responses, it appears *a priori* quite plausible that such mechanisms are also at play in attachment preference studies. This means that empirical estimates of attachment preferences (p'_X) are likely to be (i) *biased towards the guessing parameter* g_X to a degree determined by a, and (ii) are likely to *vary between studies* as a function of the between-study differences in a and g_X. In the following, we propose a method for disentangling the contributions of attachment preferences and guessing using multinomial processing tree models (MPT; Erdfelder et al., 2009; Batchelder and Riefer, 1999) based on response patterns in unambiguous baseline sentences. We will first assess the empirical adequacy of two alternative MPT models on two experiments in English and Turkish, in which participants answered polar comprehension questions about sentences with ambiguous and unambiguous RC attachment. We will then compare the two experiments with regard to the parameter estimates obtained from the MPT models.

3 Experiments

To evaluate our method, which will be presented in the next section, we used question-answering data from two experiments in which participants read sentences with ambiguous and unambiguous RC attachments and answered polar comprehension questions about them.

3.1 Experiment 1

We used the RC question-answering data from Swets et al.'s (2008) self-paced reading experiment in English (N=48). In this experiment, participants read sentences like (5) in three attachment conditions and answered comprehension questions about RC attachment similar to (6) on every trial. All comprehension questions required a *'yes'/'no'* answer. One-half of the questions asked whether the RC modified the noun phrase headed by N1, and the other half asked about N2.

RC attachment was disambiguated by means of gender (mis)match between the reflexive in the RC and the RC head noun. Each participant read 36 experimental sentences. Unambiguous sentences had correct answers, while the responses to ambiguous sentences indicated how readers disambiguated the sentence, thus reflecting their RC attachment preference.

(5) a. AMBIGUOUS ATTACHMENT
The maid$_{N1}$ of the princess$_{N2}$ [who scratched *herself* in public] ...

b. N1 ATTACHMENT
The son$_{N1}$ of the princess$_{N2}$ [who scratched *himself* in public] ...

c. N2 ATTACHMENT
The son$_{N1}$ of the princess$_{N2}$ [who scratched *herself* in public] ...

... was terribly humiliated.

(6) COMPREHENSION QUESTION
Did the maid/princess/son scratch in public?

Figure 1 (left panel) shows the average percentages of *'yes'* responses to comprehension questions by attachment condition and question type (questions about N1 or N2).

3.2 Experiment 2

The second set of question-answering data came from an unpublished self-paced reading experiment on RC attachment in Turkish (N=99). In an experimental design similar to Swets et al., participants read sentences like (7). Because Turkish relative clauses are pre-nominal, the RC *who hit each other* preceded the complex noun phrase *the fans of the football players*. All RCs contained a reciprocal anaphor (*each other*), which allowed us to disambiguate the RC attachment by means of number marking on the head nouns as RCs with the reciprocals can only modify plural noun phrases. When only one of the nouns was plural, the sentence was unambiguous, and ambiguous when both nouns were plural since they were both licit attachment sites for the RC.

Participants were asked *'yes'/'no'* comprehension questions, like (8), which were always about

RC attachment. The comprehension question asked about the event mentioned in the RC and whether one of the nouns was involved in that event. Each participant read 42 experimental sentences. One-half of the questions asked whether the RC modified the noun phrase headed by N1, and the other half asked about N2. The experiment was conducted online on *ibexfarm* (Drummond, 2013). All participants were undergraduate students at Boğaziçi University and native speakers of Turkish. Figure 1 (right panel) shows the average percentages of *'yes'* responses to comprehension questions by attachment condition and question type (question about N1 or N2).

(7) Dün akşam, [birbirini döven]$_{RC}$ ...
Yesterday evening, each other hit

a. AMBIGUOUS ATTACHMENT

futbolcu-lar-ın$_{N1}$ hayran-lar-ı$_{N2}$ ...
footballer-PL-GEN fan-PL-POSS

b. N1 ATTACHMENT

futbolcu-lar-ın hayran-ı ...
footballer-PL-GEN fan.SG-POSS

c. N2 ATTACHMENT

futbolcu-nun hayran-lar-ı ...
footballer.SG-GEN fan-PL-POSS

... stadyumu hemen terk etti.
stadium immediately leave did.

'The fan(s) of the football player(s) who hit each other left the stadium immediately, yesterday evening.'

(8) COMPREHENSION QUESTION
Futbolcu(lar)/hayran(lar) dövüşte yer almış mı?
'Was/were the football player(s)/fan(s) involved in the fight?'

3.3 Results

The average percentages of *'yes'* responses in figure 1 indicate a substantial number of errors in unambiguous experimental conditions in both experiments, such as *'no'*-responses to N1 questions and *'yes'*-responses to N2 questions about N1 attachment sentences.

The average accuracy in answering questions about unambiguous sentences was 79% (SE = 1.3) in Swets et al.'s English experiment, and 66.5% (SE = 2.5) in our Turkish experiment.

The responses in the ambiguous attachment conditions indicate an N2 attachment preference in the English as 58% (SE = 2.1) of the response were

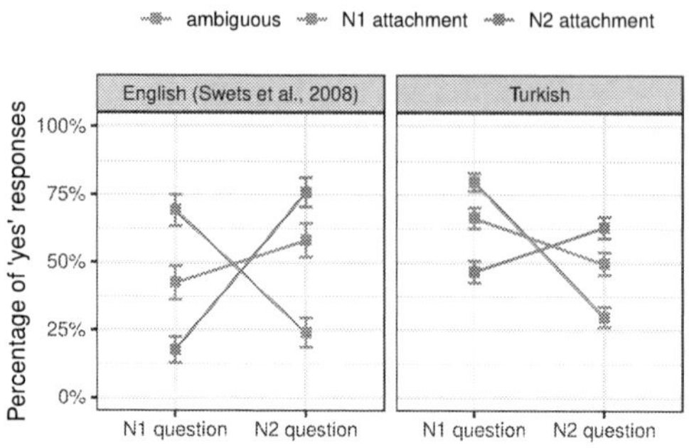

Figure 1: Average percentages of *'yes'* responses by attachment condition (color) and question type (x-axis). Error bars indicate 95% within-subject CIs.

compatible with N2 attachment (*'yes'* responses to N2 questions and *'no'* responses to N1 questions). Meanwhile, the Turkish data indicated an N1 preference as 58% (SE = 1.9) of the question responses were compatible with an N1 interpretation of the sentence. In both cases, the preferred attachment option is *local*, i.e., adjacent to the RC and is consistent with prior research.

Even though the estimates of the magnitude of the attachment preference are coincidentally equal, the magnitude of the preference for local attachment may not be. This is due to the presence of a substantial number of erroneous responses in unambiguous conditions in both experiments. Their presence indicates a substantial number of *guessing trials*, and thus suggests that not all N1- or N2-compatible responses in ambiguous indicate that the participant has successfully formed an N1- or N2 attachment interpretation of the sentence as they may have been generated by the same extraneous cognitive process that generates erroneous responses in the unambiguous attachment conditions.

The problem is exacerbated by the fact the response accuracy is particularly low in the N2 attachment condition in Experiment 2 (58.2%). A possible reason for this is that even on trials resulting in an N2 interpretation, the parser always attempts to construct an N1 attachment structure first because, in Turkish, unlike in English, potential attachment sites are processed sequentially after the relative clause has already been processed. As a result, the presence of a discarded alternative N1 attachment structure (e.g., Staub, 2007) could interfere with the retrieval of the correct structure during question answering in N2 attachment conditions. If, as a result of retrieval failure, participants resort to guessing, we would expect to observe a substantial number of erroneous responses following N2 attachment sentences or ambiguous sentences which were ultimately disambiguated towards N2 attachment.

In the next section, we present two models of erroneous responses and then use them to estimate the magnitude of the actual strength of the attachment preference.

4 MPT Models of Question-Answering and Attachment

In accounting for the influence of extraneous cognitive processes, we considered two mechanisms that may generate erroneous question responses, and implemented both as multinomial processing tree (MPT) models (Batchelder and Riefer, 1999). In the following sections, we will use the model with the better empirical fit to obtain less biased estimates of the attachment preferences in the ambiguous conditions.

MPT models offer a way to formalize hypotheses about how a mixture of several latent processes generates a categorical response (cf. Erdfelder et al., 2009, for an overview). That is, under the assumption that different sequences of events may occur on different trials, the latent processes hypothesized to be involved in processing are represented as a probability tree, with each path through the processing tree corresponding to unique combinations of cognitive processes which give rise to a particular response, along with the probabilities of each path. Importantly, this formalization provides a framework in which the probabilities of relevant latent processes can be estimated. We will use them to estimate the magnitude of the RC attachment preference in Turkish and English.

4.1 Model 1

The first mechanism we considered as a potential explanation for erroneous responses is that participants sometimes fail to attend to or successfully process the stimulus or the comprehension question and simply press a random button. We hypothesize that this may happen due to inattentiveness, careless responding, distractions in the environment, mind-wandering (e.g., Smallwood, 2011), (temporary) fatigue, or failure to allocate sufficient processing resources towards the experimental task. We will subsume all of these factor under the umbrella term *inattentiveness*.

The failure to process the stimulus is assumed to affect all three attachment conditions to the same degree. When participants do successfully comply with the task, they always respond to comprehension questions correctly in unambiguous conditions, while in ambiguous conditions, they sometimes adopt an N1 attachment interpretation of the sentence, and sometimes an N2 attachment, and answer comprehension questions in accordance with the adopted disambiguation of the ambiguous structure.

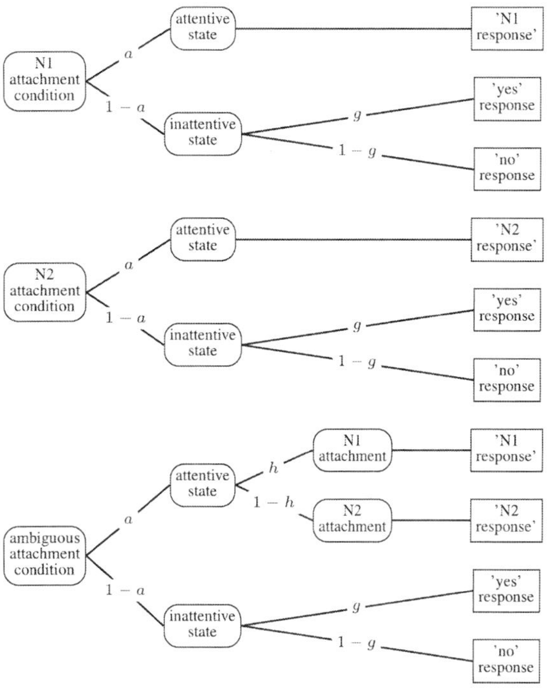

Figure 2: An MPT model of question answering with equal error rates for (i) N1 attachment, (ii) N2 attachment, and (iii) ambiguous sentences.

The assumptions of this account are illustrated in figure 2. The processing tree at the top illustrates how events during the processing of an N1 attachment sentence can unfold: On any given N1 attachment trial, a participant may be in an attentive state (with probability a) or an inattentive state (with probability $1 - a$). If the participant is in an attentive state throughout the trial (i.e., during reading and question answering), they will form a memory trace of the sentence they read, and later use it to correctly answer a comprehension question. This is illustrated in the top branch of the N1 attachment condition schematic in figure 2, where *'N1 response'* stands for *'yes'* responses to N1 questions and *'no'* responses to N2 questions.

If the participant is in an inattentive state at any point during the trial (i.e., during reading or question answering), they will either fail to form a memory trace of the sentence they read or will fail to use it to answer the comprehension question. On those occasions, they will respond *'yes'* with probability g, and *'no'* with probability $1 - g$. This is illustrated in the bottom branch of the N1 attachment condition MPT schematic in figure 2.

As a result of these assumptions, the probability of a *'yes'* response in the N1 attachment condition is as given in equation 3, where I_{N1} (as in eq. 2) is an indicator variable which is 1 for N1 comprehension questions (such as *'Did N1 do RC?'*) and 0 for N2 comprehension questions such (as *'Did N2 do RC?'*).

$$I_{N1} = \begin{cases} 1, & \text{for trials with N1 questions} \\ 0, & \text{for trials with N2 questions} \end{cases} \quad (2)$$

$$p_{Y|N1} = a \cdot I_{N1} + (1 - a) \cdot g \quad (3)$$

The processing assumptions for the N2 attachment (middle, figure 2) condition and the ambiguous condition (bottom, figure 2) follow a similar logic, with the probability of a *'yes'* response given by equations 4 and 5.

$$p_{Y|N2} = a \cdot (1 - I_{N1}) + (1 - a) \cdot g \quad (4)$$

An important assumption about the hypothesized processes in ambiguous attachment conditions is that when readers are in an attentive state, they disambiguate ambiguous sentences either towards an N1 interpretation (with probability h) or an N2 interpretation (with probability $1 - h$). We make no assumptions about whether that happens during reading or at the question answering stage.

$$p_{Y|A} = a \cdot [h \cdot I_{N1} + (1 - h) \cdot (1 - I_{N1})] + (1 - a) \cdot g \quad (5)$$

Importantly, we make no assumptions as to what may bring on inattentiveness and whether it occurs predominantly during reading or question answering. The key assumption of this account, however, is that this process affects all attachment conditions to the same degree.

4.2 Model 2

The second model included an additional possible source of erroneous responses that may not affect all attachment conditions equally. We hypothesized that, as observed in the unambiguous conditions of Experiment 2, one of the two interpretations (N1 or N2 attachment) could be more prone to failure, in that it may be less likely to be successfully created during reading, or less likely to be successfully recalled during question answering.

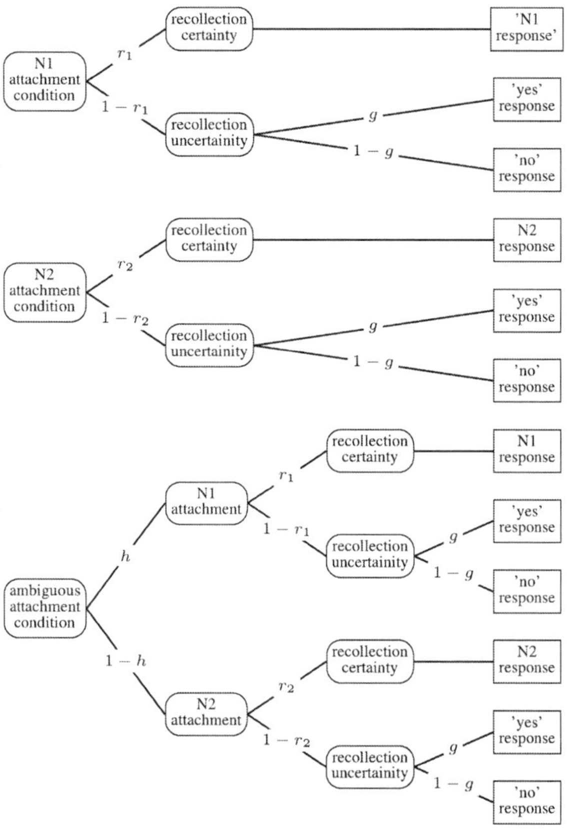

Figure 3: An MPT model of question answering with different error rates for N1 attachment and N2 attachment processes.

We formalized the assumption of different error rates associated with N1 and N2 attachment in the model in figure 3. The hypothesized structure of unambiguous N1 and N2 attachment trials is similar to Model 1 in figure 2. Each attachment process (N1 and N2 attachment) is associated with a probability of complete recollection certainty (r_1 and r_2, respectively) which reflects the probability that the correct sentence structure is (i) constructed during reading and (ii) later correctly recalled during the question answering phase. If the correct sentence structure is constructed and recalled, participants respond in accordance with the structure they constructed. Otherwise, they select a random response, i.e., *'yes'* with a probability of g and *'no'* with a probability of $1-g$. The probability of a *'yes'* response for all attachment conditions is given in equations 6, 7, 8.

In the ambiguous condition (figure 3, bottom), the recollection certainty and recollection uncertainty nodes are nested under the RC attachment nodes because the probabilities of the recollection certainty and uncertainty states depend on which RC attachment was chosen.

$$p_{Y|N1} = r_1 \cdot I_{N1} + (1 - r_1) \cdot g \quad (6)$$

$$p_{Y|N2} = r_2 \cdot (1 - I_{N1}) + (1 - r_2) \cdot g \quad (7)$$

$$p_{Y|A} = h \cdot p_{Y|N1} + (1 - h) \cdot p_{Y|N2} \quad (8)$$

Importantly, Model 2 (fig. 3) subsumes Model 1 (fig. 2) and therefore does not exclude the influence of an additional attention-related processes that affect all attachment conditions equally. This is because it can be re-parameterized as $(1 - r_1) = (1 - a) + (1 - r'_1)$ and $(1 - r_2) = (1 - a) + (1 - r'_2)$, such that the guessing rates in N1 and N2 attachment conditions, $(1 - r_1)$ and $(1 - r_2)$, can be interpreted as the sums of the attention-related guessing rate $(1 - a)$ and the condition-specific guessing rates $(1 - r'_1)$ and $(1 - r'_2)$.

5 Method

We implemented both MPT models[2] in *brms* and *rstan* (Bürkner, 2018; Stan Development Team, 2020) in R (R Core Team, 2018) according to equations 3-8. We fitted the models to each experiment separately, using 4 MCMC chains with $1,000$ warm-up and $3,000$ post-warm-up iterations. For the sake of computational convenience, we estimated all model parameters on the logit scale, and in the following, we will use θ' to refer to the logit-transform of any parameter θ.

We used mildly informative Gaussian priors for all logit-transformed population parameters in both models: $h', g' \sim N(0,1)$, and $a, r_1, r_2 \sim N(0,1)$.

[2]All code has been made available at `https://git.io/JODKF`

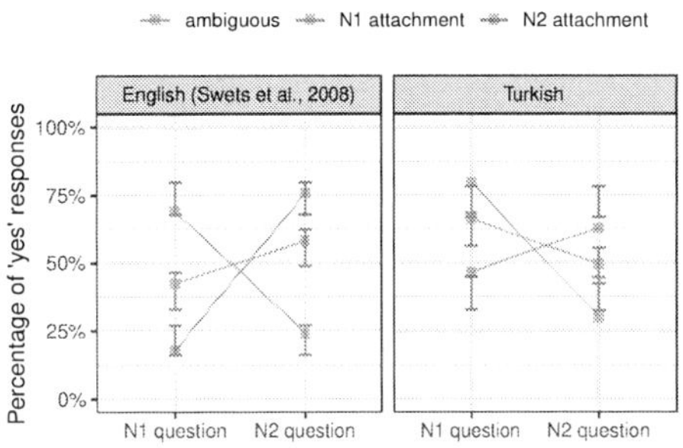

Figure 4: Average percentages of *'yes'* responses in the experiments, and 95% posterior prediction intervals based on Model 1 by attachment condition and question type.

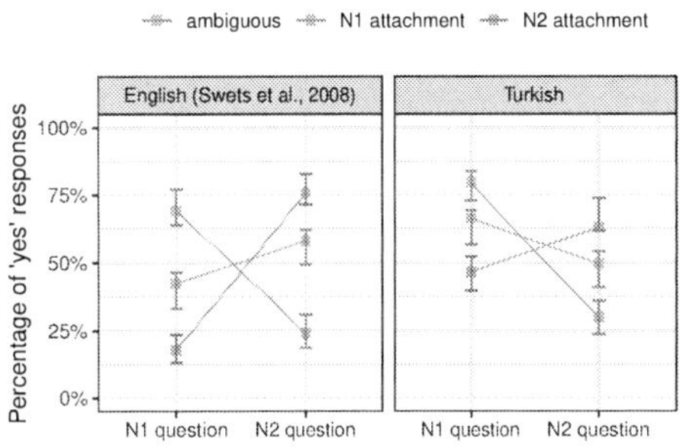

Figure 5: Average percentages of *'yes'* responses in the experiments, and 95% posterior prediction intervals based on Model 2 by attachment condition and question type.

To account for individual differences in all parameters, we used hierarchical models with by-subject intercepts for all parameters, where each participant k's responses were modeled as a function of population-level parameters θ with subject subject-level adjustments $\delta_{\theta,k}$, with $\theta'_k = \theta' + \delta_{\theta',k}$, where the by-subject adjustments are distributed as $\delta_{\theta',k} \sim N(0, \sigma_{\theta'})$.

6 Model Comparison

Figures 4 and 5 show the average percentages of *'yes'* responses by experiment (circles and connecting lines) alongside 95% posterior predictive intervals generated by, Model 1 and 2, respectively (error bars).

Figure 4 shows that although Model 1 could approximate the experimental findings it systematically overestimated the proportion of responses compatible with the preferred RC attachment (N2 in English, N1 in Turkish) in both unambiguous conditions: For example, in the N1 attachment con-

	English	Turkish
	$\widehat{elpd}$	$\widehat{elpd}$
model 1	-511.3 (18.1)	-796.4 (15.0)
model 2	-469.4 (14.8)	-750.5 (13.5)
	$\Delta\widehat{elpd}$	$\Delta\widehat{elpd}$
model 2-1	41.9 (11.6)	45.9 (9.3)

Table 2: Estimates of expected log pointwise predictive density ($\widehat{elpd}$) by model for each experiment and differences between model $\widehat{elpd}$s. Standard errors in brackets.

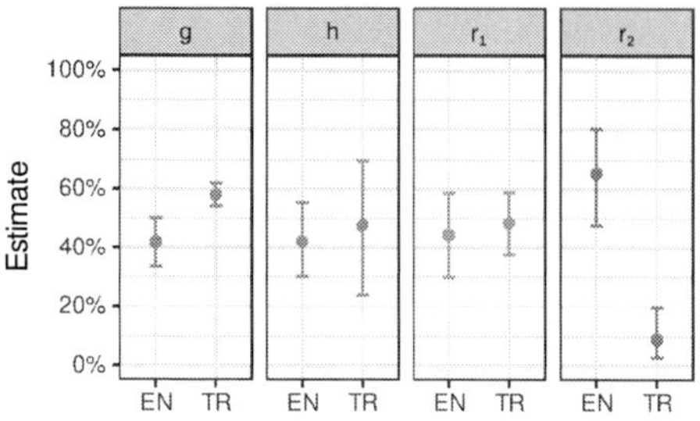

Figure 6: Population parameter estimates and 95% credible intervals for all four parameters of Model 2 (g, h, r_1, r_2) for both experiments, English (EN) and Turkish (TR).

dition in English, the number of *'yes'* responses to N1 questions and *'no'* responses to N2 questions were slightly overestimated. Similarly, in the N2 attachment condition in Turkish, the model underestimated the percentages of *'yes'* responses to N1 questions and *'no'* responses to N2 questions. Figure 5 shows that Model 2 appeared to have fewer systematic deviations, and appeared to fit the data quite well.

In order to compare the models more formally, we using PSIS-LOO-CV (Vehtari et al., 2017) to compute each model's expected log pointwise predictive density (ELPD). ELPD provides an estimate of the model's out-of-sample performance and thus penalizes additional model flexibility, which puts Models 1 and 2 on an equal footing although Model 2 has more parameters. Table 2 shows the ELPD estimates ($\Delta\widehat{elpd}$), as well as the differences between models in $\Delta\widehat{elpd}$ along with their respective standard errors. Larger values indicate better performance.

Both $\Delta\widehat{elpd}$ estimates are relatively large relative to their standard errors, and thus point towards Model 2 having better out-of-sample performance. This finding suggests that the two attachment processes are affected by the error-generating process to different degrees.

7 Results

Having established Model 2 as an adequate model of RC attachment in the context of question-answering, we used its parameter estimates to understand the pattern of responses in the experimental data: Figure 6 shows the Model 2 population parameter estimates for both experiments as well as 95% credible intervals for all four parameters. In addition to the difference in the guessing bias g between experiments, it also shows a lot of uncertainty in the estimates of the attachment parameter h, which represents the probability with which the parser adopts an N1 attachment interpretation over an N2 attachment structure in ambiguous attachment conditions. Both estimates of the N1 attachment probability have rather wide credible intervals, with 42% ($CrI = [30; 55]$) for the English experiment and 48% ($CrI = [24; 70]$) for the Turkish experiment. While the estimate for English is consistent with weak evidence for an N2 attachment preference, the estimate for Turkish indicates no clear preference.

The explanation for the surprising absence of evidence for an N1 attachment preference in the parameter h in Turkish lies in the the substantial difference between the successful recall probabilities r_1 (49%, $CrI = [38; 59]$) and r_2 (9%, $CrI = [3; 20]$), which indicate that N1 interpretations were successfully processed and recalled with a higher probability than their N2 counterparts. According to the assumptions of Model 2, this leads to a question response pattern which appears to suggest an N1 preference even when there isn't one ($h = 0.5$): When participants decide to adopt an N1 interpretation, their question responses indicate N1 attachment on most trials – sometimes due to successful recall of the N1 interpretation, and at other times as a result of guessing. When participants decide to adopt an N2 interpretation, however, they fail to recall the correct interpretation most of the time, and thus engage in guessing. Importantly, guesses result in N1 responses 50% of the time, since questions about N1 and N2 interpretations are balanced. As a result, a substantial difference between r_1 and r_2, such that $r_1 < r_2$ will lead to more N1 responses than N2 responses to questions about ambiguous sentences because

N1 interpretations are more successfully recalled, even if ambiguous sentences are assigned N1 interpretations only 50% of the time.

Whatever the source of higher error rates in the N2 attachment conditions in the Turkish experiment is, our MPT analysis suggests that what appears as a weak N1 attachment preference in our Turkish experiment is actually a consequence of a large number of guessing trials associated with N2 attachment. In sum, our analysis shows that (i) the N2 attachment preference in the English experiment appears to hold up even when guessing trials are taken into account, and (ii) that what appears to be an N1 attachment preference in Turkish is readily explained by the processing difficulty associated with processing and recalling N2 attachment structures in Turkish.

8 Summary

Based on the assumption that readers sometimes do not allocate the required amount of attention to the task they are performing, we have discussed a previously neglected source of bias and variability that may affect studies of attachment preferences and of interpretation preferences more generally. We attempted to account for the role of guessing as a strategy used in answering comprehension questions when the answer is not known. We argue that understanding the role of guessing in discrete choice tasks is crucial because data consisting of responses to comprehension questions where participants sometimes fail to arrive at a full interpretation of the structure may be confounded. To this end, we proposed an MPT-based analysis method that allows to de-confound parameters of theoretical importance from nuisance parameters such as the guessing rate. We tested two variants of the MPT-based model on experimental data from English and Turkish, and demonstrated that this method can provide further insight into the processes underlying participants' answering behavior as well as their attachment preferences.

References

William H. Batchelder and David M. Riefer. 1999. Theoretical and empirical review of multinomial process tree modeling. *Psychonomic Bulletin & Review*, 6(1):57–86.

Paul-Christian Bürkner. 2018. Advanced Bayesian multilevel modeling with the R package brms. *The R Journal*, 10(1):395–411.

Fernando Cuetos and Don C. Mitchell. 1988. Cross-linguistic differences in parsing. *Cognition*, 30(1):73–105.

Fernando Cuetos, Don C. Mitchell, and Martin Corley. 1996. Parsing in different languages. In *Language Processing in Spanish*. Erlbaum, Hillsdale, NJ.

Brian Dillon and Matthew Wagers. 2019. Approaching gradience in acceptability with the tools of signal detection theory. Preprint, Open Science Framework.

Nazik Dinçtopal-Deniz. 2010. Relative clause attachment preferences of Turkish L2 speakers of English. In Bill VanPatten and Jill Jegerski, editors, *Language Acquisition and Language Disorders*. John Benjamins Publishing Company, Amsterdam.

A. Drummond. 2013. Ibex farm.

E. Erdfelder, T. Auer, B. Hilbig, A. Aßfalg, M. Moshagen, and L. Nadarevic. 2009. Multinomial Processing Tree Models: A Review of the Literature. *Journal of Psychology*, 217(3):108–124.

Lyn Frazier. 1987. Sentence Processing: A Tutorial Review. In Max Coltheart, editor, *Attention and Performance XII*. Erlbaum, Hillsdale, NJ.

E. Gilboy, J.-M. Sopena, C. Clifton, and L. Frazier. 1995. Argument structure and association preferences in Spanish and English complex NPs. *Cognition*, 54(2):131–167.

Nino Grillo, João Costa, Bruno Fernandes, and Andrea Santi. 2015. Highs and Lows in English Attachment. *Cognition*, 144:116–122.

Bilal Kırkıcı. 2004. The processing of relative clause attachment ambiguities in Turkish. *Turkic Languages*, 8:111–121.

K. McRae, M.J. Spivey-Knowlton, and M.K. Tanenhaus. 1998. Modeling the Influence of Thematic Fit in On-line Sentence Comprehension. *Journal of Memory and Language*, 38(3).

R Core Team. 2018. *R: A Language and Environment for Statistical Computing*. R Foundation for Statistical Computing, Vienna, Austria.

J. Smallwood. 2011. Mind-wanderingwhile reading. *Language and Linguistics Compass*, 5(2):63–77.

Stan Development Team. 2020. RStan: the R interface to Stan. R package version 2.19.3.

A. Staub. 2007. The return of the repressed. *Journal of Memory and Language*, 57(2):299–323.

B. Swets, T. Desmet, C. Clifton, and F. Ferreira. 2008. Underspecification of syntactic ambiguities: Evidence from self-paced reading. *Memory & Cognition*, 36(1):201–216.

A. Vehtari, Gelman A., and Gabry J. 2017. Practical bayesian model evaluation using leave-one-out cross-validation and waic. *Statistics and Computing*, 27.

That Looks Hard: Characterizing Linguistic Complexity in Humans and Language Models

Gabriele Sarti [1,2] **Dominique Brunato** [2] **Felice Dell'Orletta** [2]

[1] University of Trieste, International School for Advanced Studies (SISSA), Trieste
[2] Istituto di Linguistica Computazionale "Antonio Zampolli" (ILC-CNR), Pisa
ItaliaNLP Lab – *italianlp.it*
gabriele.sarti996@gmail.com
{dominique.brunato, felice.dellorletta}@ilc.cnr.it

Abstract

This paper investigates the relationship between two complementary perspectives in the human assessment of sentence complexity and how they are modeled in a neural language model (NLM). The first perspective takes into account multiple online behavioral metrics obtained from eye-tracking recordings. The second one concerns the offline perception of complexity measured by explicit human judgments. Using a broad spectrum of linguistic features modeling lexical, morpho-syntactic, and syntactic properties of sentences, we perform a comprehensive analysis of linguistic phenomena associated with the two complexity viewpoints and report similarities and differences. We then show the effectiveness of linguistic features when explicitly leveraged by a regression model for predicting sentence complexity and compare its results with the ones obtained by a fine-tuned neural language model. We finally probe the NLM's linguistic competence before and after fine-tuning, highlighting how linguistic information encoded in representations changes when the model learns to predict complexity.

1 Introduction

From a human perspective, linguistic complexity concerns difficulties encountered by a language user during sentence comprehension. The source of such difficulties is commonly investigated using either *offline measures* or *online behavioral metrics*. In the offline framework, complexity ratings can be elicited either by assessing errors in comprehension tests or collecting explicit complexity judgments from readers. Instead, in the online paradigm, cognitive signals are collected mainly through specialized machinery (e.g., MRI scanners, eye-tracking systems) during natural or task-oriented reading. Among the wide range of online complexity metrics, gaze data are widely regarded as reliable proxies of processing difficulties, reflecting both low and high-level complexity features of the input (Rayner, 1998; Hahn and Keller, 2016). Eye-tracking measures have recently contributed to significant improvements across many popular NLP applications (Hollenstein et al., 2019a, 2020) and in particular on tasks related to linguistic complexity such as *automatic readability assessment* (ARA) (Ambati et al., 2016; Singh et al., 2016; González-Garduño and Søgaard, 2018), obtaining meaningful results for sentence-level classification in easy and hard-to-read categories (Vajjala and Lučić, 2018; Evaldo Leal et al., 2020; Martinc et al., 2021). However, readability levels are conceptually very different from cognitive processing metrics since ARA corpora are usually built in an automated fashion from parallel documents at different readability levels, without explicit evaluations of complexity by target readers (Vajjala and Lučić, 2019). A different approach to complexity assessment that directly accounts for the perspective of readers is presented in the corpus by Brunato et al. (2018), where sentences are individually labeled with the *perception of complexity* of annotators, which may better reflect the underlying cognitive processing required by readers to parse the sentence. This consideration is supported by recent results highlighting the unpredictability of outliers in perceived complexity annotations, especially for sentences having complex syntactic structures (Sarti, 2020).

Given the relation between complexity judgments elicited from annotators and online cognitive processing metrics, we investigate whether the connection between the two perspectives can be highlighted empirically in human annotations and language model representations. We begin by leveraging linguistic features associated with a variety of sentence-level structural phenomena and analyzing their correlation with offline and online complexity metrics. We then evaluate the performance of models using either complexity-related explicit

Proceedings of the Workshop on Cognitive Modeling and Computational Linguistics, pages 48–60
Online Event, June 10, 2021.

features or contextualized word embeddings, focusing mainly on the neural language model ALBERT (Lan et al., 2020). In this context, we show how both explicit features and learned representations obtain comparable results when predicting complexity scores. Finally, we focus on studying how complexity-related properties are encoded in the representations of ALBERT. This perspective goes in the direction of exploiting human processing data to address the interpretability issues of unsupervised language representations (Hollenstein et al., 2019b; Gauthier and Levy, 2019; Abnar et al., 2019). To this end, we rely on the *probing task* approach, a recently introduced technique within the area of NLMs interpretability consisting of training diagnostic classifiers to probe the presence of encoded linguistic properties inside contextual representations (Conneau et al., 2018; Zhang and Bowman, 2018). We observe that fine-tuning on online and offline complexity produces a consequent increase in probing performances for complexity-related features during our probing experiments. This investigation has the specific purpose of studying whether and how learning a new task affects the linguistic properties encoded in pretrained representations. In fact, while pre-trained models have been widely studied using probing methods, the effect of fine-tuning on encoded information was seldom investigated. For example, Merchant et al. (2020) found that fine-tuning does not impact heavily the linguistic information implicitly learned by the model, especially when considering a supervised probe closely related to a downstream task. Miaschi et al. (2020) further demonstrated a positive correlation between the model's ability to solve a downstream task on a specific input sentence and the related linguistic knowledge encoded in a language model. Nonetheless, to our knowledge, no previous work has taken into account sentence complexity assessment as a fine-tuning task for NLMs. Our results suggest that the model's competencies during training are interpretable from a linguistic perspective and are possibly related to its predictive capabilities for complexity assessment.

Contributions To our best knowledge, this is the first work displaying the connection between online and offline complexity metrics and studying how they are represented by a neural language model. We a) provide a comprehensive analysis of linguistic phenomena correlated with eye-tracking data and human perception of complexity, addressing similarities and differences from a linguistically-motivated perspective across metrics and at different levels of granularity; b) compare the performance of models using both explicit features and unsupervised contextual representations when predicting online and offline sentence complexity; and c) show the natural emergence of complexity-related linguistic phenomena in the representations of language models trained on complexity metrics.[1]

Metric Level	Description	Label
Offline (Perceptual)	Perceived complexity annotation on a 1-to-7 Likert scale.	PC
Online (Early)	Duration of the first reading pass in milliseconds.	FPD
Online (Late)	Total fixation count	FXC
	Total duration of all fixations in milliseconds	TFD
Online (Contextual)	Duration of outbound regressive saccades in milliseconds	TRD

Table 1: Sentence-level complexity metrics. We refer to the entire set of gaze metrics as ET (eye-tracking).

	Perc. Complexity	Eye-tracking
domain	news articles	literature
aggregation	avg. annotators	words sum + avg. participants
filtering	IAA + duplicates	min length
# sentences	1115	4041
# words	21723	52131
avg. sent. length	19.48	12.90
avg. word length	4.95	4.60

Table 2: Descriptive statistics of the two sentence-level corpora after the preprocessing procedure.

2 Data and Preprocessing

Our study leverages two corpora, each capturing different aspects of linguistic complexity:

Eye-tracking For online complexity metrics, we used the monolingual English portion of GECO (Cop et al., 2017), an eye-tracking corpus based on the novel "The Mysterious Case at Styles" by Agatha Christie. The corpus consists of 5,386 sentences annotated at word-level with eye-movement records of 14 English native speakers. We select four online metrics spanning multiple

[1] Code and data available at `https://github.com/gsarti/interpreting-complexity`

Annotation Level	Linguistic Feature Description	Label
Raw Text	Sentence length (tokens), word length (characters)	n_tokens, char_per_tok
	Words and lemmas type/token ratio	ttr_form, ttr_lemma
POS Tagging	Distribution of UD and language-specific POS tags	upos_dist_*, xpos_dist_*
	Lexical density	lexical_density
	Inflectional morphology of auxiliaries (mood, tense)	aux_mood_*, aux_tense_*
Dependency Parsing	Syntactic tree depth	parse_depth
	Average and maximum length of dependency links	avg_links_len, max_links_len
	Number and average length of prepositional chains	n_prep_chains, prep_chain_len
	Relative ordering of main elements	subj_pre, subj_post, obj_pre, obj_post
	Distribution of dependency relations	dep_dist_*
	Distribution of verbal heads	vb_head_per_sent
	Distribution of principal and subordinate clauses	princ_prop_dist, sub_prop_dist
	Average length of subordination chains	sub_chain_len
	Relative ordering of subordinate clauses	sub_post, sub_pre

Table 3: Description of sentence-level linguistic features employed in our study.

phases of cognitive processing, which are widely considered relevant proxies for linguistic processing in the brain (Demberg and Keller, 2008; Vasishth et al., 2013). We sum-aggregate those at sentence-level and average their values across participants to obtain the four online metrics presented in Table 1. As a final step to make the corpus more suitable for linguistic complexity analysis, we remove all utterances with fewer than 5 words. This design choice is adopted to ensure consistency with the perceived complexity corpus by Brunato et al. (2018).

Perceived Complexity For the offline evaluation of sentence complexity, we used the English portion of the corpus by Brunato et al. (2018). The corpus contains 1,200 sentences taken from the Wall Street Journal section of the Penn Treebank (McDonald et al., 2013) with uniformly-distributed lengths ranging between 10 and 35 tokens. Each sentence is associated with 20 ratings of perceived-complexity on a 1-to-7 point scale. Ratings were assigned by English native speakers on the CrowdFlower platform. To reduce the noise produced by the annotation procedure, we removed duplicates and sentences for which less than half of the annotators agreed on a score in the range $\mu_n \pm \sigma_n$, where μ_n and σ_n are respectively the average and standard deviation of all annotators' judgments for sentence n. Again, we average scores across annotators to obtain a single metric for each sentence.

Table 2 presents an overview of the two corpora after preprocessing. The resulting eye-tracking (ET) corpus contains roughly four times more sentences than the perceived complexity (PC) one, with shorter words and sentences on average.

3 Analysis of Linguistic Phenomena

As a first step to investigate the connection between the two complexity paradigms, we evaluate the correlation of online and offline complexity labels with linguistic phenomena modeling a number of properties of sentence structure. To this end, we rely on the Profiling-UD tool (Brunato et al., 2020) to annotate each sentence in our corpora and extract from it $\sim$100 features representing their linguistic structure according to the Universal Dependencies formalism (Nivre et al., 2016). These features capture a comprehensive set of phenomena, from basic information (e.g. sentence and word length) to more complex aspects of sentence structure (e.g. parse tree depth, verb arity), including properties related to sentence complexity at different levels of description. A summary of most relevant features in our analysis is presented in Table 3.

Figure 1 reports correlation scores for features showing a strong connection ($|\rho| > 0.3$) with at least one of the evaluated metrics. Features are ranked using their Spearman's correlation with complexity metrics, and scores are leveraged to highlight the relation between linguistic phenomena and complexity paradigms. We observe that features showing a significant correlation with eye-tracking metrics are twice as many as those correlating with PC scores and generally tend to have higher coefficients, except for total regression duration (TRD). Nevertheless, the most correlated features are the same across all metrics. As expected, sentence length (*n_tokens*) and other related fea-

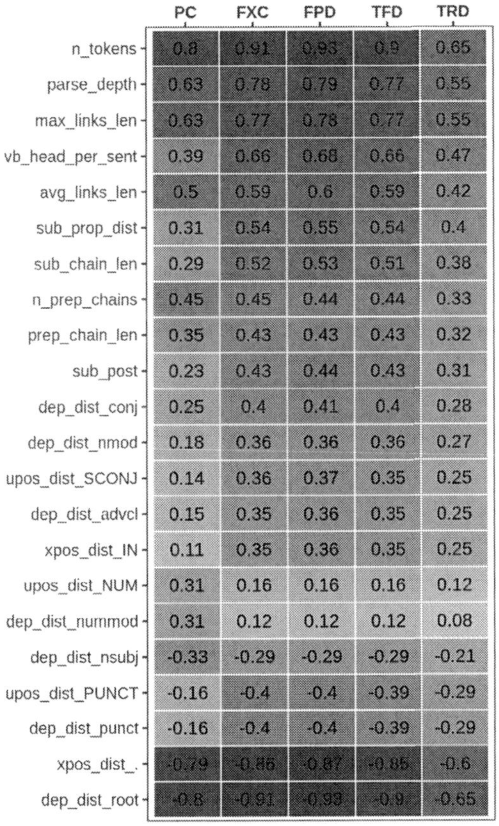

Figure 1: Ranking of the most correlated linguistic features for selected metrics. All Spearman's correlation coefficients have $p < 0.001$.

tures capturing aspects of structural complexity occupy the top positions in the ranking. Among those, we also find the length of dependency links (*max_links_len, avg_links_len*) and the depth of the whole parse tree or selected sub-trees, i.e. nominal chains headed by a preposition (*parse_depth, n_prep_chains*). Similarly, the distribution of subordinate clauses (*sub_prop_dist, sub_post*) is positively correlated with all metrics but with stronger effect for eye-tracking ones, especially in presence of longer embedded chains (*sub_chain_len*). Interestingly, the presence of numbers (*upos_NUM, dep_nummod*) affects only the explicit perception of complexity while it is never strongly correlated with all eye-tracking metrics. This finding is expected since numbers are very short tokens and, like other functional POS, were never found to be strongly correlated with online reading in our results. Conversely, numerical information has been identified as a factor hampering sentence readability and understanding (Rello et al., 2013).

Unsurprisingly, sentence length is the most correlated predictor for all complexity metrics. Since many linguistic features highlighted in our analysis are strongly related to sentence length, we tested whether they maintain a relevant influence when this parameter is controlled. To this end, Spearman's correlation was computed between features and complexity tasks, but this time considering bins of sentences having approximately the same length. Specifically, we split each corpus into 6 bins of sentences with 10, 15, 20, 25, 30 and 35 tokens respectively, with a range of ± 1 tokens per bin to select a reasonable number of sentences for our analysis.

Figure 2 reports the new rankings of the most correlated linguistic features within each bin across complexity metrics ($|\rho| > 0.2$). Again, we observe that features showing a significant correlation with complexity scores are fewer for PC bins than for eye-tracking ones. This fact depends on controlling for sentence length but also on the small size of bins for the whole dataset. As in the coarse-grained analysis, TRD is the eye-tracking metric less correlated to linguistic features, while the other three (FXC, FPD, TFD) show a homogeneous behavior across bins. For the latters, vocabulary-related features (token-type ratio, average word length, lexical density) are always ranked on top (and with a positive correlation) in all bins, especially when considering shorter sentences (i.e. from 10 to 20 tokens). For PC, this is true only for some of them (i.e. word length and lexical density). At the same time, features encoding numerical information are still highly correlated with the explicit perception of complexity in almost all bins. Interestingly, features modeling subordination phenomena extracted from fixed-length sentences exhibit a reverse trend than when extracted from the whole corpus, i.e. they are negatively correlated with judgments. If, on the one hand, we expect an increase in the presence of subordination for longer sentences (possibly making sentences more convoluted), on the other hand, when length is controlled, our findings suggest that subordinate structures are not necessarily perceived as a symptom of sentence complexity. Our analysis also highlights that PC's relevant features are significantly different from those correlated to online eye-tracking metrics when controlling for sentence length. This aspect wasn't evident from the previous coarse-grained analysis. We note that, despite controlling sentence length,

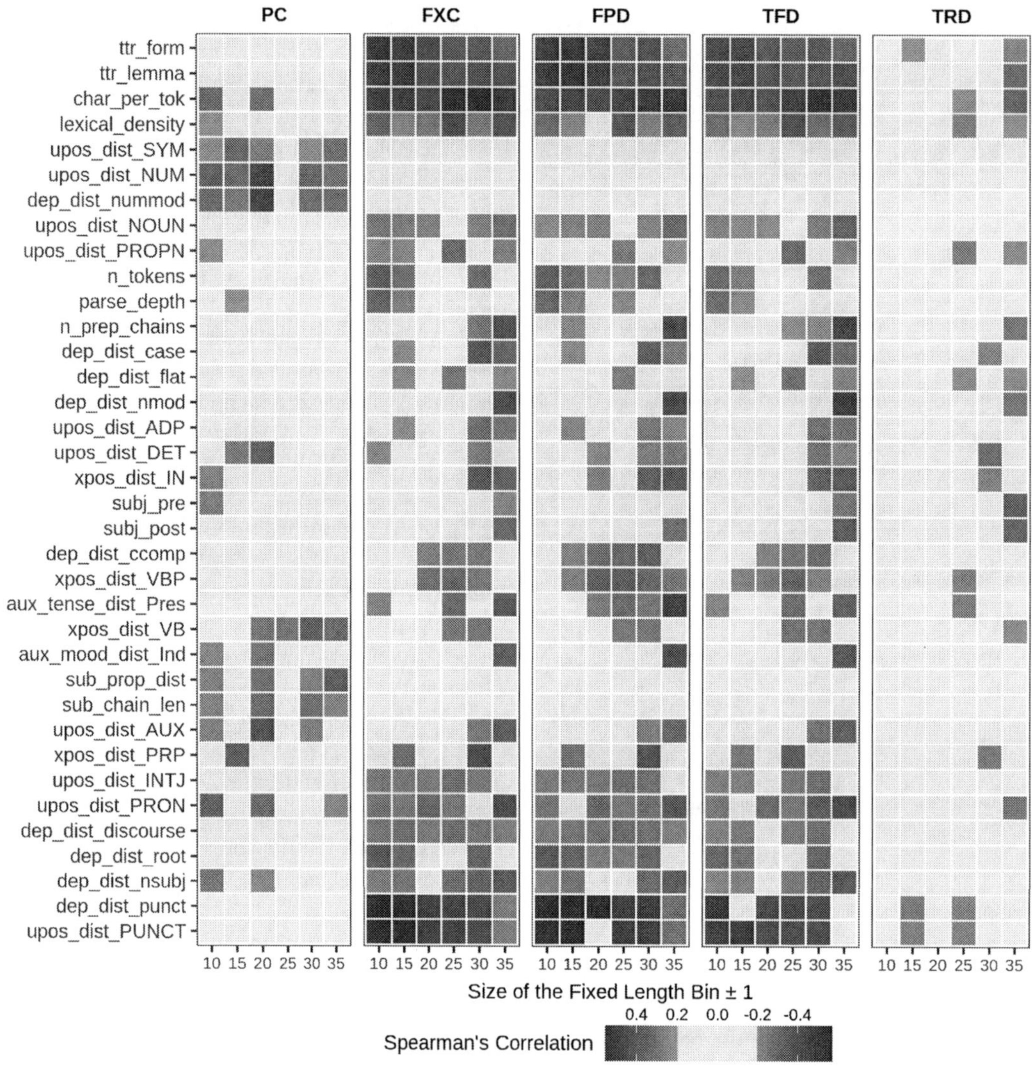

Figure 2: Rankings of the most correlated linguistic features for metrics within length-binned subsets of the two corpora. Coefficients ≥ 0.2 or ≤ -0.2 are highlighted, and have $p < 0.001$. (Bins from 10 to 35 have sizes of 173, 163, 164, 151, 165, and 147 sentences for PC and 899, 568, 341, 215, 131, and 63 sentences for gaze metrics.)

gaze measures are still significantly connected to length-related phenomena. This can be possibly due to the ± 1 margin applied for sentence selection and the high sensitivity of behavioral metrics to small changes in the input.

4 Predicting Online and Offline Linguistic Complexity

Given the high correlations reported above, we proceed to quantify the importance of explicit linguistic features from a modeling standpoint. Table 4 presents the RMSE and R^2 scores of predictions made by baselines and models for the selected complexity metrics. Performances are tested with a 5-fold cross-validation regression with fixed random seed on each metric. Our baselines use average metric scores of all training sentences (Average) and average scores of sentences binned by their length in # of tokens (Length-binned average) as predictions. The two linear SVM models leverage explicit linguistic features, using respectively only n_tokens (SVM length) and the whole set of $\sim$100 features (SVM feats). Besides those, we also test the performances of a state-of-the-art Transformer neural language model relying entirely on contextual word embeddings. We selected ALBERT as a

	PC		FXC		FPD		TFD		TRD	
	RMSE	R^2	RMSE	R^2	RMSE	R^2	RMSE	R^2	RMSE	R^2
Average	.87	.00	6.17	.06	1078	.06	1297	.06	540	.03
Length-binned average	.53	.62	2.36	.86	374	.89	532	.85	403	.45
SVM length	.54	.62	2.19	.88	343	.90	494	.86	405	.45
SVM feats	**.44**	.74	**1.77**	**.92**	**287**	**.93**	**435**	.89	400	.46
ALBERT	**.44**	**.75**	1.98	.91	302	**.93**	**435**	**.90**	**382**	**.49**

Table 4: Average Root-Mean-Square Error and R^2 for complexity predictions of two average baselines, two SVMs relying on explicit features and a pretrained language model with contextualized word embeddings using 5-fold cross-validation. ALBERT learns eye-tracking metrics in a multitask setting over parallel annotations.

lightweight yet effective alternative to BERT (Devlin et al., 2019) for obtaining contextual word representations, using its last-layer [CLS] sentence embedding as input for a linear regressor during fine-tuning and testing. We selected the last layer representations, despite having strong evidence on the importance of intermediate representation in encoding language properties, because we aim to investigate how final layers encode complexity-related competences. Given the availability of parallel eye-tracking annotations, we train ALBERT using multitask learning with hard parameter sharing (Caruana, 1997) on gaze metrics.[2]

From results in Table 4 we note that: i) the length-binned average baseline is very effective in predicting complexity scores and gaze metrics, which is unsurprising given the extreme correlation between length and complexity metrics presented in Figure 1; ii) the SVM feats model shows considerable improvements if compared to the length-only SVM model for all complexity metrics, highlighting how length alone accounts for much but not for the entirety of variance in complexity scores; and iii) ALBERT performs on-par with the SVM feats model on all complexity metrics despite the small dimension of the fine-tuning corpora and the absence of explicit linguistic information. A possible interpretation of ALBERT's strong performances is that the model implicitly develops competencies related to phenomena encoded by linguistic features while training on online and offline complexity prediction. We explore this perspective in Section 5.

As a final step in the study of feature-based models, we inspect the importance accorded by the SVM feats model to features highlighted in previous sections. Table 5 presents coefficient ranks produced by SVM feats for all sentences and for the 10 ± 1 length bin, which was selected as the broadest subset. Despite evident similarities with the previous correlation analysis, we encounter some differences that are possibly attributable to the model's inability in modeling non-linear relations. In particular, the SVM model still finds sentence length and related structural features highly relevant for all complexity metrics. However, especially for PC, lexical features also appear in the top positions (e.g. *lexical density*, *ttr_lemma*, *char_per_tok*), as well as specific features related to verbal predicate information (e.g. *xpos_dist_VBZ,_VBN*). This holds both for all sentences, and when considering single length-binned subsets. While in the correlation analysis eye-tracking metrics were almost indistinguishable, those behave quite differently when considering how linguistic features are used for inference by the linear SVM model. In particular, the fixation count metric (FXC) consistently behaves in a different way if compared to other gaze measures, even when controlling for length.

5 Probing Linguistic Phenomena in ALBERT Representations

As shown in Table 4, ALBERT performances on the PC and eye-tracking corpora are comparable to those obtained using a linear SVM with explicit linguistic features. To investigate if ALBERT encodes the linguistic knowledge that we identified as strongly correlated with online and perceived sentence complexity during training and prediction, we adopt the *probing task* testing paradigm. The aim of this analysis is two-fold: i) probing the presence of complexity-related information encoded by ALBERT representations during the pre-training

[2]Additional information on parameters and chosen training approach is presented in Appendix A.

	All Sentences					Bin 10±1				
	PC	FXC	FPD	TFD	TRD	PC	FXC	FPD	TFD	TRD
n_tokens	1	1	1	1	1	-36	5	1	1	2
char_per_tok	2	2	12	10	16	3	1	3	3	19
xpos_dist_VBN	5	-37	76	77	75	28	9	26	21	42
avg_links_len	6	-6	7	7	7	11	-8	-23	-30	-46
n_prep_chains	7	3	10	9	8	-44	16	50	41	48
dep_dist_compound	9	7	58	61	49	13	12	60	51	47
vb_head_per_sent	10	4	4	6	3	2	-9	31	36	-33
max_links_len	56	5	2	2	2	-32	-30	36	30	-39
parse_depth	34	-36	3	3	4	-17	-1	22	24	12
sub_post	28	-33	8	8	9	-28	-40	33	34	48
dep_dist_conj	17	31	11	13	10	37	-37	46	56	-48
upos_dist_NUM	15	39	70	72	72	4	/	/	/	/
ttr_form	-42	28	77	74	-26	17	2	3	2	1
prep_chain_len	53	12	16	16	14	-48	-23	43	39	42
sub_chain_len	24	-14	19	19	32	-30	-43	56	55	35
dep_dist_nsubj	11	-16	-8	-8	-9	-2	31	-18	-19	-29
upos_dist_PRON	-16	-13	-7	-6	-8	-44	-21	-5	-8	-38
dep_dist_punct	-21	-3	-4	-4	-4	-20	-3	-2	-2	-2
dep_dist_nmod	-20	-2	55	50	50	-9	3	28	17	15
xpos_dist_.	-11	15	-1	-1	-1	-6	43	-24	-30	32
xpos_dist_VBZ	-9	20	82	-33	-30	24	14	20	40	-47
dep_dist_aux	-8	17	-30	-29	77	32	27	39	31	45
dep_dist_case	-7	-34	25	22	34	8	-6	62	44	-21
ttr_lemma	-4	21	-22	-28	-11	-4	-45	4	4	9
dep_dist_det	-3	52	42	40	21	-27	-36	17	14	5
sub_prop_dist	-2	29	6	5	5	26	28	63	59	21
lexical_density	-1	-1	26	25	20	-37	-5	5	6	10

Table 5: Rankings based on the coefficients assigned by SVM feats for all metrics. Top ten positive and negative features are marked with orange and cyan respectively. "/" marks features present in less than 5% of sentences.

process, especially in relation to analyzed features; and ii) verifying whether, and in which respect, this competence is affected by a fine-tuning on complexity assessment tasks.

To conduct the probing experiments, we aggregate three UD English treebanks representative of different genres, namely: EWT, GUM and ParTUT by Silveira et al. (2014); Zeldes (2017); Sanguinetti and Bosco (2015), respectively. We thus obtain a corpus of 18,079 sentences and use the Profiling-UD tool to extract n sentence-level linguistic features $\mathcal{Z} = z_1, \ldots, z_n$ from gold linguistic annotations. We then generate representations $A(x)$ of all sentences in the corpus using the last-layer [CLS] embedding of a pretrained ALBERT base model without additional fine-tuning, and train n single-layer perceptron regressors $g_i : A(x) \rightarrow z_i$ that learn to map representations $A(x)$ to each linguistic feature z_i. We finally evaluate the error and R^2 scores of each g_i as a proxy to the quality of representations $A(x)$ for encoding their respective linguistic feature z_i. We repeat the same evaluation for ALBERTs fine-tuned respectively on perceived complexity (PC) and on all eye-tracking labels with multitask learning (ET), averaging scores with 5-fold cross-validation. Results are shown on the left side of Table 6.

As we can see, ALBERT's last-layer sentence representations have relatively low knowledge of complexity-related probes, but the performance on them highly increases after fine-tuning. Specifically, a noticeable improvement is obtained on features that were already better encoded in base pretrained representation, i.e. sentence length and related features, suggesting that fine-tuning possibly accentuates only properties already well-known by the model, regardless of the target task. To verify that this isn't the case, we repeat the same experiments on ALBERT models fine-tuned on the smallest length-binned subset (i.e. 10±1 tokens) presented in previous sections. The right side of Table 6 presents these results. We know from our length-binned analysis of Figure 2 that PC scores are mostly uncorrelated with length phenomena,

	Base		PC		ET		PC Bin 10±1		ET Bin 10±1	
	RMSE	R^2	RMSE	R^2	RMSE	R^2	RMSE	R^2	RMSE	R^2
n_tokens	8.19	.26	4.66	**.76**	2.87	**.91**	8.66	.18	6.71	**.51**
parse_depth	1.47	.18	1.18	**.48**	1.04	**.60**	1.50	.16	1.22	**.43**
vb_head_per_sent	1.38	.15	1.26	**.30**	1.14	**.42**	1.44	.09	1.30	**.25**
xpos_dist_.	.05	.13	.04	**.41**	.04	**.42**	.04	.18	.04	**.38**
avg_links_len	.58	.12	.53	**.29**	.52	**.31**	.59	.10	.56	**.20**
max_links_len	5.20	.12	4.08	**.46**	3.75	**.54**	5.24	.11	4.73	**.28**
n_prep_chains	.74	.11	.67	**.26**	.66	**.29**	.72	.14	.69	**.21**
sub_prop_dist	.35	.09	.33	.13	.31	**.22**	.34	.05	.32	.15
upos_dist_PRON	.08	.09	.08	.14	.08	.07	.07	**.23**	.08	.15
upos_dist_NUM	.05	.08	.05	.06	.05	.02	.05	**.16**	.05	.06
dep_dist_nsubj	.06	.08	.06	.10	.06	.05	.05	**.17**	.06	.11
char_per_tok	.89	.07	.87	**.12**	.90	.05	.82	**.22**	.86	.14
prep_chain_len	.60	.07	.57	**.17**	.56	**.19**	.59	.12	.56	**.18**
sub_chain_len	.70	.07	.67	**.15**	.62	**.26**	.71	.04	.66	**.16**
dep_dist_punct	.07	.06	.07	.06	.07	**.14**	.07	.06	.07	**.14**
dep_dist_nmod	.05	.06	.05	.07	.05	.06	.05	.09	.05	.09
sub_post	.44	.05	.46	**.12**	.44	**.18**	.47	.05	.45	**.14**
dep_dist_case	.07	.05	.06	.06	.07	.08	.07	.07	.07	.10
lexical_density	.14	.05	.13	.03	.13	.03	.13	**.13**	.13	**.13**
dep_dist_compound	.06	.04	.06	.05	.06	.03	.06	.10	.06	.07
dep_dist_conj	.04	.03	.04	.04	.04	.04	.05	.02	.04	.03
ttr_form	.08	.03	.08	.05	.08	.05	.08	.05	.08	.05
dep_dist_det	.06	.03	.06	.02	.06	.04	.06	.03	.06	.03
dep_dist_aux	.04	.02	.04	.01	.04	.01	.04	.06	.04	.04
xpos_dist_VBN	.03	.01	.03	.00	.03	.00	.03	.01	.03	.00
xpos_dist_VBZ	.04	.01	.04	.01	.04	.02	.04	.02	.04	.02
ttr_lemma	.09	.01	.09	.06	.09	.06	.09	.04	.09	.03

Table 6: RMSE and R^2 scores for diagnostic regressors trained on ALBERT representations, respectively, without fine-tuning (Base), with PC and eye-tracking (ET) fine-tuning on all data (left) and on the 10 ± 1 length-binned subset (right). **Bold** values highlight relevant increases in R^2 from Base.

while ET scores remain significantly affected despite our controlling of sequence size. This also holds for length-binned probing task results, where the PC model seems to neglect length-related properties in favor of other ones, which were the same highlighted in our fine-grained correlation analysis (e.g. word length, numbers, explicit subjects). The ET-trained model confirms the same behavior, retaining strong but lower performances for length-related features. We note that, for all metrics, features that were highly relevant only for the SVM predictions, such as those encoding verbal inflectional morphology or vocabulary-related ones (Table 5), are not affected by the fine-tuning process. Despite obtaining the same accuracy of a SVM, the neural language model seem to address the task more similarly to humans when accounting for correlation scores (Figure 2). A more extensive analysis of the relation between human behavior and predictions by different models is deemed interesting for future work.

To conclude, although higher probing tasks performances after fine-tuning on complexity metrics should not be interpreted as direct proof that the neural language model is exploiting newly-acquired morpho-syntactic and syntactic information, they suggest an importance shift in NLM representation, triggered by fine-tuning, that produces an encoding of linguistic properties able to better model the human assessment of complexity.

6 Conclusion

This paper investigated the connection between eye-tracking metrics and the explicit perception of sentence complexity from an experimental standpoint. We performed an in-depth correlation analysis between complexity scores and sentence-level properties at different granularity levels, highlighting how all metrics are strongly connected to sentence length and related properties, but also revealing different behaviors when controlling for length. We then evaluated models using explicit linguistic features and unsupervised word embeddings to predict complexity, showing comparable performances across metrics. We finally tested the encoding of linguistic properties in the contextual representations of a neural language model, noting the natural emergence of task-related linguistic properties within the model's representations after the training process. We thus conjecture that a relation subsists between the linguistic knowledge acquired by the model during the training procedure and its downstream performances on tasks for which the morphosyntactic and syntactic structures play a relevant role. For the future, we would like to test comprehensively the effectiveness of tasks inspired by the human language learning as intermediate steps to train more robust and parsimonious neural language models.

7 Broader Impact and Ethical Perspectives

The findings described in this work are mostly intended to evaluate recent efforts in the computational modeling of linguistic complexity. This said, some of the models and procedures described can be clearly beneficial to society. For example, using models trained to predict reading patterns may be used in educational settings to identify difficult passages that can be simplified, improving reading comprehension for students in a fully-personalizable way. However, it is essential to recognize the potentially malicious usage of such systems. The integration of eye-tracking systems in mobile devices, paired with predictive models presented in this work, could be used to build harmful surveillance systems and advertisement platforms using gaze predictions for extreme behavioral manipulation. In terms of research impact, the experiments presented in this work may provide useful insights into the behavior of neural language models for researchers working in the fields of interpretability in NLP and computational psycholinguistics.

References

Samira Abnar, Lisa Beinborn, Rochelle Choenni, and Willem Zuidema. 2019. Blackbox meets blackbox: Representational similarity & stability analysis of neural language models and brains. In *Proceedings of the 2019 ACL Workshop BlackboxNLP: Analyzing and Interpreting Neural Networks for NLP*, pages 191–203, Florence, Italy. Association for Computational Linguistics.

Bharat Ram Ambati, Siva Reddy, and Mark Steedman. 2016. Assessing relative sentence complexity using an incremental CCG parser. In *Proceedings of the 2016 Conference of the North American Chapter of the Association for Computational Linguistics: Human Language Technologies*, pages 1051–1057, San Diego, California. Association for Computational Linguistics.

Dominique Brunato, Andrea Cimino, Felice Dell'Orletta, Giulia Venturi, and Simonetta Montemagni. 2020. Profiling-UD: a tool for linguistic profiling of texts. In *Proceedings of the 12th Language Resources and Evaluation Conference*, pages 7145–7151, Marseille, France. European Language Resources Association.

Dominique Brunato, Lorenzo De Mattei, Felice Dell'Orletta, Benedetta Iavarone, and Giulia Venturi. 2018. Is this sentence difficult? do you agree? In *Proceedings of the 2018 Conference on Empirical Methods in Natural Language Processing*, pages 2690–2699, Brussels, Belgium. Association for Computational Linguistics.

Rich Caruana. 1997. Multitask learning. *Machine Learning*, 28:41–75.

Alexis Conneau, German Kruszewski, Guillaume Lample, Loïc Barrault, and Marco Baroni. 2018. What you can cram into a single $&!#* vector: Probing sentence embeddings for linguistic properties. In *Proceedings of the 56th Annual Meeting of the Association for Computational Linguistics (Volume 1: Long Papers)*, pages 2126–2136, Melbourne, Australia. Association for Computational Linguistics.

Uschi Cop, Nicolas Dirix, Denis Drieghe, and Wouter Duyck. 2017. Presenting GECO: An eyetracking corpus of monolingual and bilingual sentence reading. *Behavior Research Methods*, 49(2):602–615.

Deepset. 2019. FARM: Framework for adapting representation models. GitHub repository: `https://github.com/deepset-ai/FARM`.

Vera Demberg and Frank Keller. 2008. Data from eyetracking corpora as evidence for theories of syntactic processing complexity. *Cognition*, 109(2):193 – 210.

Jacob Devlin, Ming-Wei Chang, Kenton Lee, and Kristina Toutanova. 2019. BERT: Pre-training of deep bidirectional transformers for language understanding. In *Proceedings of the 2019 Conference of the North American Chapter of the Association for Computational Linguistics: Human Language Technologies, Volume 1 (Long and Short Papers)*, pages 4171–4186, Minneapolis, Minnesota. Association for Computational Linguistics.

Sidney Evaldo Leal, João Marcos Munguba Vieira, Erica dos Santos Rodrigues, Elisângela Nogueira Teixeira, and Sandra Aluísio. 2020. Using eye-tracking data to predict the readability of Brazilian Portuguese sentences in single-task, multi-task and sequential transfer learning approaches. In *Proceedings of the 28th International Conference on Computational Linguistics*, pages 5821–5831, Barcelona, Spain (Online). International Committee on Computational Linguistics.

Jon Gauthier and Roger Levy. 2019. Linking artificial and human neural representations of language. In *Proceedings of the 2019 Conference on Empirical Methods in Natural Language Processing and the 9th International Joint Conference on Natural Language Processing (EMNLP-IJCNLP)*, pages 529–539, Hong Kong, China. Association for Computational Linguistics.

Ana Valeria González-Garduño and Anders Søgaard. 2018. Learning to predict readability using eye-movement data from natives and learners. In *AAAI Conference on Artificial Intelligence 2018*. AAAI Conference on Artificial Intelligence.

Michael Hahn and Frank Keller. 2016. Modeling human reading with neural attention. In *Proceedings of the 2016 Conference on Empirical Methods in Natural Language Processing*, pages 85–95, Austin, Texas. Association for Computational Linguistics.

Nora Hollenstein, Maria Barrett, and Lisa Beinborn. 2020. Towards best practices for leveraging human language processing signals for natural language processing. In *Proceedings of the Second Workshop on Linguistic and Neurocognitive Resources*, pages 15–27, Marseille, France. European Language Resources Association.

Nora Hollenstein, Maria Barrett, Marius Troendle, Francesco Bigiolli, Nicolas Langer, and Ce Zhang. 2019a. Advancing nlp with cognitive language processing signals. *arXiv preprint arXiv:1904.02682*.

Nora Hollenstein, Antonio de la Torre, Nicolas Langer, and Ce Zhang. 2019b. CogniVal: A framework for cognitive word embedding evaluation. In *Proceedings of the 23rd Conference on Computational Natural Language Learning (CoNLL)*, pages 538–549, Hong Kong, China. Association for Computational Linguistics.

Zhenzhong Lan, Mingda Chen, Sebastian Goodman, Kevin Gimpel, Piyush Sharma, and Radu Soricut. 2020. ALBERT: A Lite BERT for self-supervised learning of language representations. In *International Conference on Learning Representations*.

Matej Martinc, Senja Pollak, and Marko Robnik-Šikonja. 2021. Supervised and Unsupervised Neural Approaches to Text Readability. *Computational Linguistics*, 47(1):141–179.

Ryan McDonald, Joakim Nivre, Yvonne Quirmbach-Brundage, Yoav Goldberg, Dipanjan Das, Kuzman Ganchev, Keith Hall, Slav Petrov, Hao Zhang, Oscar Täckström, Claudia Bedini, Núria Bertomeu Castelló, and Jungmee Lee. 2013. Universal Dependency annotation for multilingual parsing. In *Proceedings of the 51st Annual Meeting of the Association for Computational Linguistics (Volume 2: Short Papers)*, pages 92–97, Sofia, Bulgaria. Association for Computational Linguistics.

Amil Merchant, Elahe Rahimtoroghi, Ellie Pavlick, and Ian Tenney. 2020. What happens to BERT embeddings during fine-tuning? In *Proceedings of the Third BlackboxNLP Workshop on Analyzing and Interpreting Neural Networks for NLP*, pages 33–44, Online. Association for Computational Linguistics.

Alessio Miaschi, Dominique Brunato, Felice Dell'Orletta, and Giulia Venturi. 2020. Linguistic profiling of a neural language model. In *Proceedings of the 28th International Conference on Computational Linguistics*, pages 745–756, Barcelona, Spain (Online). International Committee on Computational Linguistics.

Joakim Nivre, Marie-Catherine de Marneffe, Filip Ginter, Yoav Goldberg, Jan Hajič, Christopher D. Manning, Ryan McDonald, Slav Petrov, Sampo Pyysalo, Natalia Silveira, Reut Tsarfaty, and Daniel Zeman. 2016. Universal Dependencies v1: A multilingual treebank collection. In *Proceedings of the Tenth International Conference on Language Resources and Evaluation (LREC'16)*, pages 1659–1666, Portorož, Slovenia. European Language Resources Association (ELRA).

Keith Rayner. 1998. Eye movements in reading and information processing: 20 years of research. *Psychological bulletin*, 124 3:372–422.

Luz Rello, Susana Bautista, Ricardo Baeza-Yates, Pablo Gervás, Raquel Hervás, and Horacio Saggion. 2013. One half or 50%? an eye-tracking study of number representation readability. In *Human-Computer Interaction – INTERACT 2013*, pages 229–245, Berlin, Heidelberg. Springer Berlin Heidelberg.

Manuela Sanguinetti and Cristina Bosco. 2015. *Part-TUT: The Turin University Parallel Treebank*, pages 51–69. Springer International Publishing, Cham.

Gabriele Sarti. 2020. UmBERTo-MTSA @ AcCompl-It: Improving complexity and acceptability prediction with multi-task learning on self-supervised annotations. In *Proceedings of Seventh Evaluation Campaign of Natural Language Processing and Speech Tools for Italian. Final Workshop (EVALITA 2020)*, Online. CEUR.org.

Natalia Silveira, Timothy Dozat, Marie-Catherine de Marneffe, Samuel Bowman, Miriam Connor, John Bauer, and Chris Manning. 2014. A gold standard dependency corpus for English. In *Proceedings of the Ninth International Conference on Language Resources and Evaluation (LREC'14)*, pages 2897–2904, Reykjavik, Iceland. European Language Resources Association (ELRA).

Abhinav Deep Singh, Poojan Mehta, Samar Husain, and Rajkumar Rajakrishnan. 2016. Quantifying sentence complexity based on eye-tracking measures. In *Proceedings of the Workshop on Computational Linguistics for Linguistic Complexity (CL4LC)*, pages 202–212, Osaka, Japan. The COLING 2016 Organizing Committee.

Sowmya Vajjala and Ivana Lučić. 2018. OneStopEnglish corpus: A new corpus for automatic readability assessment and text simplification. In *Proceedings of the Thirteenth Workshop on Innovative Use of NLP for Building Educational Applications*, pages 297–304, New Orleans, Louisiana. Association for Computational Linguistics.

Sowmya Vajjala and Ivana Lučić. 2019. On understanding the relation between expert annotations of text readability and target reader comprehension. In *Proceedings of the Fourteenth Workshop on Innovative Use of NLP for Building Educational Applications*, pages 349–359, Florence, Italy. Association for Computational Linguistics.

Shravan Vasishth, Titus von der Malsburg, and Felix Engelmann. 2013. What eye movements can tell us about sentence comprehension. *Wiley interdisciplinary reviews. Cognitive science*, 4 2:125–134.

Thomas Wolf, Lysandre Debut, Victor Sanh, Julien Chaumond, Clement Delangue, Anthony Moi, Pierric Cistac, Tim Rault, Remi Louf, Morgan Funtowicz, Joe Davison, Sam Shleifer, Patrick von Platen, Clara Ma, Yacine Jernite, Julien Plu, Canwen Xu, Teven Le Scao, Sylvain Gugger, Mariama Drame, Quentin Lhoest, and Alexander Rush. 2020. Transformers: State-of-the-art natural language processing. In *Proceedings of the 2020 Conference on Empirical Methods in Natural Language Processing: System Demonstrations*, pages 38–45, Online. Association for Computational Linguistics.

Amir Zeldes. 2017. The GUM corpus: creating multilayer resources in the classroom. *Language Resources and Evaluation*, 51:581–612.

Kelly Zhang and Samuel Bowman. 2018. Language modeling teaches you more than translation does: Lessons learned through auxiliary syntactic task analysis. In *Proceedings of the 2018 EMNLP Workshop BlackboxNLP: Analyzing and Interpreting Neural Networks for NLP*, pages 359–361, Brussels, Belgium. Association for Computational Linguistics.

	Model & Tokenizer Parameters		
heads dimension	1-Layer Dense		
max seq. length	128		
embed. dropout	0.1		
seed	42		
lowercasing	✗		
tokenization	SentencePiece		
vocab. size	30000		
	Training Parameters		
	PC	ET	Probes
fine-tuning	standard	multitask	multitask
freeze LM w	✗	✗	✓
weighted loss	-	✓	✗
CV folds	5	5	5
early stopping	✓	✓	✗
training epochs	15	15	5
patience	5	5	-
evaluation steps	20	40	-
batch size	32	32	32
learning rate	1e-5	1e-5	1e-5

Table 7: Model, tokenizer and training parameters used for fine-tuning ALBERT on complexity metrics.

A Parametrization and Fine-tuning Details for ALBERT

We leverage the pretrained albert-base-v2 checkpoint available in the HuggingFace's Transformer framework (Wolf et al., 2020) and use adapted scripts and classes from the FARM framework (Deepset, 2019) to perform multitask learning on eye-tracking metrics. Table 7 presents the parameters used to define models and training procedures for experiments in Sections 4 and 5.

During training we compute MSE loss scores for task-specific heads for the four eye-tracking metrics (ℓ_{FXC}, ℓ_{FPD}, ℓ_{TFD}, ℓ_{TRD}) and perform a weighted sum to obtain the overall loss score ℓ_{ET} to be optimized by the model:

$$\ell_{ET} = \ell_{FXC} + \ell_{FPD} + \ell_{TFD} + (\ell_{TRD} \times 0.2)$$

The use of ℓ_{TRD} was shown to have a positive impact on the overall predictive capabilities of the model only when weighted to prevent it from dominating the ℓ_{ET} sum.

Probing tasks on linguistic features are performed by freezing the language model weights and training 1-layer heads as probing regressors over the last-layer [CLS] token for each feature. In this setting no loss weighting is applied, and the regressors are trained for 5 epochs without early stopping on the aggregated UD dataset.

B Examples of Sentences from Complexity Corpora

Table 8 presents examples of sentences randomly selected from the two corpora leveraged in this study. We highlight how eye-tracking scores show a very consistent relation with sentence length, while PC scores are much more variable. This fact suggests that the offline nature of PC judgments makes them less related to surface properties and more connected to syntax and semantics.

C Models' Performances on Length-binned Sentences

Similarly to the approach adopted in Section 3, we test the performances of models on length-binned data to verify if performances on length-controlled sequences are consistent with those achieved on the whole corpora. RMSE scores averaged with 5-fold cross validation over the length-binned sentences subsets are presented in Figure 3. We note that ALBERT outperforms the SVM with linguistic features on nearly all lengths and metrics, showing the largest gains on intermediate bins for PC and gaze durations (FPD, TFD, TRD). Interestingly, overall performances of models follow a length-dependent increasing trend for eye-tracking metrics, but not for PC. We believe this behavior can be explained in terms of the high sensibility to length previously highlighted for online metrics, as well as the variability in bin dimensions (especially for the last bin containing only 63 sentences). We finally observe that the SVM model based on explicit linguistic features (SVM feats) performs poorly on larger bins for all tasks, sometimes being even worse than the bin-average baseline. While we found this behavior surprising given the positive influence of features highlighted in Table 4, we believe this is mostly due to the small dimension of longer bins, which negatively impacts the generalization capabilities of the regressor. The relatively better scores achieved by ALBERT in those, instead, support the effectiveness of information stored in pretrained language representations when a limited number of examples is available.

Length bin	Sentence	PC Score
Bin 10±1	It hasn't made merger overtures to the board.	2.15
Bin 15±1	For most of the past 30 years, the marriage was one of convenience.	1.45
Bin 20±1	Shanghai Investment & Trust Co., known as Sitco, is the city's main financier for trading business.	3.35
Bin 25±1	For fiscal 1988, Ashland had net of $224 million, or $4.01 a share, on revenue of $7.8 billion.	4.55
Bin 30±1	C. Olivetti & Co., claiming it has won the race in Europe to introduce computers based on a powerful new microprocessor chip, unveiled its CP486 computer yesterday.	4.25
Bin 35±1	The White House said he plans to hold a series of private White House meetings, mostly with Senate Democrats, to try to persuade lawmakers to fall in line behind the tax cut.	2.9

Length bin	Sentence	FPD	FXC	TFD	TRD
Bin 10±1	Evidently there was a likelihood of John Cavendish being acquitted.	1429	7.69	1527	330
Bin 15±1	I come now to the events of the 16th and 17th of that month.	1704	9.71	1979	467
Bin 20±1	Who on earth but Poirot would have thought of a trial for murder as a restorer of conjugal happiness!	2745	15.38	3178	1003
Bin 25±1	He knew only too well how useless her gallant defiance was, since it was not the object of the defence to deny this point.	3489	19.77	4181	1012
Bin 30±1	I could have told him from the beginning that this obsession of his over the coffee was bound to end in a blind alley, but I restrained my tongue.	3638	21.36	4190	1010
Bin 35±1	There was a breathless hush, and every eye was fixed on the famous London specialist, who was known to be one of the greatest authorities of the day on the subject of toxicology.	4126	23.14	4814	1631

Table 8: Example of sentences selected from all the length-binned subset for the Perceived Complexity Corpus (top) and the GECO corpus (bottom). Scores are aggregated following the procedure described in Section 2. Reading times (FPD, TFD, TRD) are expressed in milliseconds.

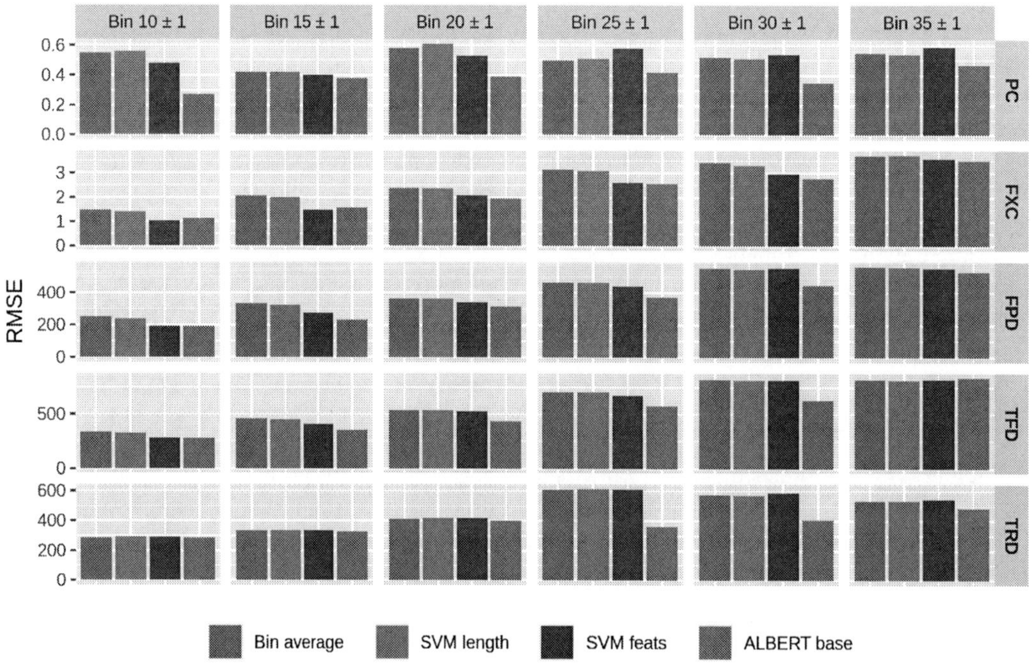

Figure 3: Average Root Mean Square Error (RMSE) scores for models in Table 4, performing 5-fold cross-validation on the same length-binned subsets used for the analysis of Figure 2. Lower scores are better.

Accounting for Agreement Phenomena in Sentence Comprehension with Transformer Language Models: Effects of Similarity-based Interference on Surprisal and Attention

Soo Hyun Ryu
Department of Psychology
University of Michigan
soohyunr@umich.edu

Richard L. Lewis
Department of Psychology
University of Michigan
rickl@umich.edu

Abstract

We advance a novel explanation of similarity-based interference effects in subject-verb and reflexive pronoun agreement processing, grounded in surprisal values computed from a pretrained large-scale Transformer model, GPT-2. Specifically, we show that surprisal of the verb or reflexive pronoun predicts *facilitatory interference effects* in ungrammatical sentences, where a distractor noun that matches in number with the verb or pronoun leads to faster reading times, despite the distractor not participating in the agreement relation. We review the human empirical evidence for such effects, including recent meta-analyses and large-scale studies. We also show that *attention patterns* (indexed by entropy and other measures) in the Transformer show patterns of diffuse attention in the presence of similar distractors, consistent with cue-based retrieval models of parsing. But in contrast to these models, the attentional cues and memory representations are learned entirely from the simple self-supervised task of predicting the next word.

1 Introduction

Deep Neural Network (DNN) language models (LeCun et al., 2015; Sundermeyer et al., 2012; Vaswani et al., 2017) have recently attracted the attention of researchers interested in assessing their linguistic competence (Chaves, 2020; Da Costa and Chaves, 2020; Ettinger, 2020; Wilcox et al., 2018, 2019) and potential to provide accounts of psycholinguistic phenomena in sentence processing (Futrell et al., 2018; Linzen and Baroni, 2021; Van Schijndel and Linzen, 2018; Wilcox et al., 2020). In this paper we show how attention-based transformer models (we use a pre-trained version of GPT-2) provide the basis for a new theoretical account of facilitatory interference effects in subject-verb and reflexive agreement processing. These effects, which we review in detail below, have played an important role in psycholinguistic theory because they show that properties of noun phrases that are not the grammatical targets of agreement relations may nonetheless exert an influence on processing time at points where those agreement relations are computed.

The explanation we propose here is a novel one grounded in surprisal (Hale, 2001; Levy, 2008), but with origins in graded attention and similarity-based interference (Van Dyke and Lewis, 2003; Lewis et al., 2006; Jäger et al., 2017). We use surprisal as the key predictor of reading time (Levy, 2013), and through targeted analyses of patterns of attention in the transformer, show that the model behaves in ways consistent with cue-based retrieval theories of sentence processing. The account thus provides a new integration of surprisal and similarity-based interference theories of sentence processing, adding to a growing literature of work integrating noisy memory and surprisal (Futrell et al., 2020). In this case, the noisy representations arise from training the transformer, and interference must exert its influence on reading times through a *surprisal bottleneck* (Levy, 2008).

The remainder of this paper is organized as follows. We first provide an overview of some of key empirical work in human sentence processing concerning subject-verb and reflexive pronoun agreement. We then provide a brief overview of the GPT-2 architecture, its interesting psycholinguistic properties, and the method and metrics that we will use to examine the agreement effects. We then apply GPT-2 to the materials used in several different human reading time studies. We conclude with some theoretical reflections, identification of weaknesses, and suggestions for future work.

2 Agreement Interference Effects in Human Sentence Processing

One long-standing focus of work in sentence comprehension is understanding how the structure of human short-term memory might support and con-

Proceedings of the Workshop on Cognitive Modeling and Computational Linguistics, pages 61–71
Online Event, June 10, 2021.

strain the incremental formation of linguistic dependencies among phrases and words (Gibson, 1998; Lewis, 1996; Lewis et al., 2006; Miller and Chomsky, 1963; Nicenboim et al., 2015). A key property of human memory thought to shape sentence processing is *similarity-based interference* (Miller and Chomsky, 1963; Lewis, 1993, 1996). Figure 1 shows a simple example of how such interference arises in cue-based retrieval models of sentence processing, as a function of the compatibility of *retrieval targets* and *distractors* with retrieval *cues* (Lewis and Vasishth, 2005; Lewis et al., 2006; Van Dyke and Lewis, 2003) (Corresponding sentences are from Wagers et al. (2009)'s Exp 4–6 shown in Table 1). *Inhibitory interference effects* occur when features of the target perfectly match the retrieval cue and features of a distractor partially matches, while *facilitatory interference effects* occur when the features of both target and distractor partially match the features of retrieval cue.

In this study, we focus on interference effects in subject-verb number agreement and reflexive pronoun-antecedent agreement, specifically in languages where the agreement features include *syntactic number* which is morphologically marked on the verb or pronoun. In such cases, number is plausibly a useful retrieval cue, and it is easy to manipulate the number of distractor noun phrases to allow for carefully controlled empirical contrasts.

Interference in subject-verb agreement. Previous studies (Pearlmutter et al., 1999; Wagers et al., 2009; Dillon et al., 2013; Lago et al., 2015; Jäger et al., 2020) attest to both *inhibitory* interference (slower processing in the presence of an interfering distractor) and *facilitatory* interference (faster processing in the presence of an interfering distractor), but the existing empirical support for inhibitory interference is weak, and many studies fail to find any evidence for it (Dillon et al., 2013; Lago et al., 2015; Wagers et al., 2009). There is stronger evidence for facilitatory effects, which arise in ungrammatical structures where the verb or pronoun fails to agree in number with the structurally correct target noun phrase, but where either an intervening or preceding distractor noun phrase does match in number. Example A. below illustrates, taken from Wagers et al. (2009), where the subject and verb are boldfaced and the distractor noun is underlined:

A. The **slogan** on the <u>posters</u> **were** designed to get attention.

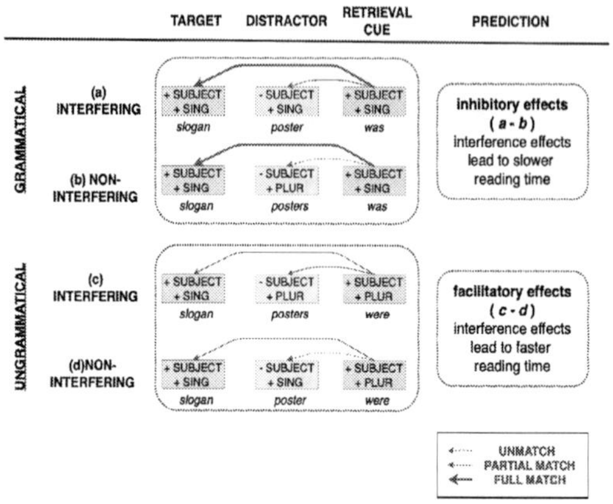

Figure 1: How facilitatory and inhibitory interference effects arise in subject-verb dependency creation in cue-based retrieval parsing. The critical manipulation concerns the overlap of number feature between the distractor, target, and retrieval cue.

A Bayesian meta-analysis of agreement phenomena was recently conducted with an extensive set of studies (Jäger et al., 2017; Vasishth and Engelmann, 2021). Their analysis of first-pass reading times from eye-tracking experiments on subject-verb number agreement is shown in Figure 1. The evidence from the meta-analysis is consistent with a very small or nonexistent inhibitory interference effect in in the grammatical conditions, with a small but robust facilitatory interference effects in the ungrammatical conditions. Concerned that the existing experiments did not have sufficient power to detect the inhibitory effects, Nicenboim et al. (2018) ran a large scale eye-tracking study (185 participants) with materials designed to increase the inhibition effect, and did detect a 9ms effect (95% credible posterior interval 0–18ms). This represents the strongest evidence to date for inhibitory effects in grammatical agreement structures, but even this evidence indicates the effect may be near zero.

Interference in reflexive pronoun agreement. Example B. below shows a pair of sentences from Dillon et al. (2013) used to probe facilitatory effects in reflexive pronoun agreement (again, the target antecedent and pronoun are boldfaced and the distractor is underlined):

B. (1) *interfering* The basketball **coach** who trained the star <u>players</u> usually blamed **themselves** for the ...

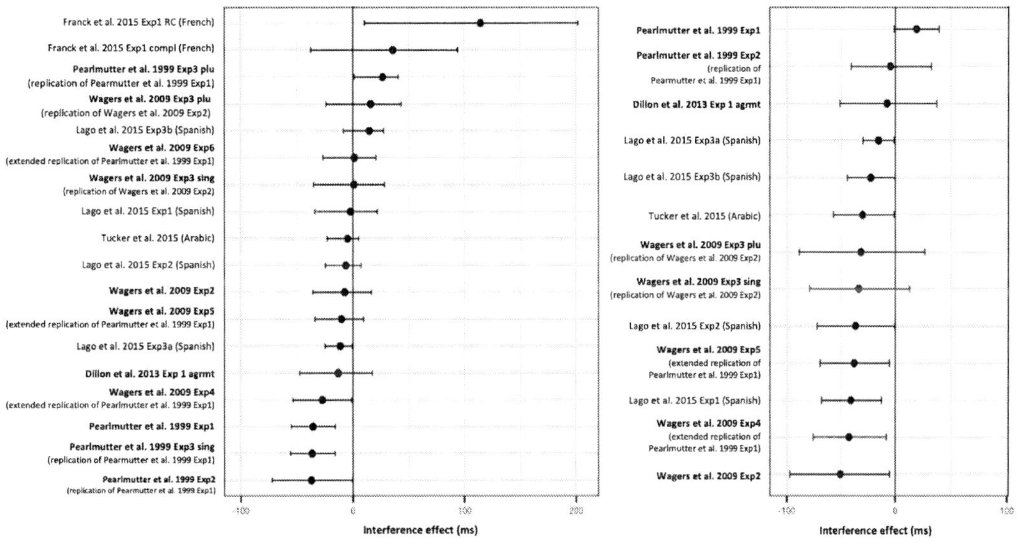

(a) Interference effects in grammatical sentences

(b) Interference effects in ungrammatical sentences

Figure 2: Results of the meta-analysis on subject-verb number agreement from Vasishth and Engelmann (2021). The materials from boldfaced studies are those that we used in our GPT-2 experiments.

(2) *non-interfering* The basketball **coach** who trained the star player usually blamed **themselves** for the ...

The empirical record concerning facilitatory effects in reflexive agreement is mixed. Some have claimed that such effects do not arise (Sturt, 2003; Xiang et al., 2009; Dillon et al., 2013), and that this is expected under a model in which the structural constraints from binding theory (Chomsky et al., 1982) serve to effectively filter candidates for retrieval—in short, the parser does not consider or make contact with the ungrammatical distractor noun phrases (Sturt, 2003; Dillon et al., 2013).

However, a recent Bayesian meta analysis of key experiments by Dillon et al. (2013) indicates substantially overlapping posterior estimates of facilitatory effects for subject-verb agreement and reflexive agreement (Vasishth and Engelmann, 2021). Concerned again about under-powered studies, Jäger et al. (2020) undertook a large scale (181 participants) eye-tracking replication and did find evidence for nearly equivalent facilitatory speedups for reflexive and subject-verb agreement (Figure 3). This result is not inconsistent with the meta-analysis, but provides stronger evidence that the facilitation effects in reflexives are real.

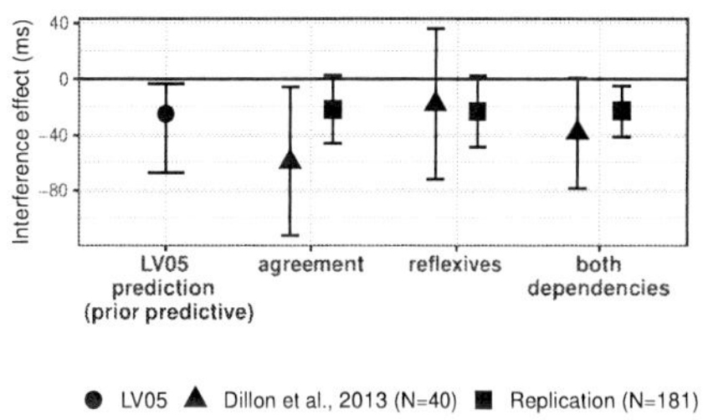

Figure 3: From Jäger et al. (2020). Posterior estimates of facilitatory interference effects in subject-verb and reflexive agreement processing in a large scale replication of Dillon et al. (2013), the original effects, and predictions from the Lewis and Vasishth (2005) model.

We take advantage of the very broad coverage of GPT-2 by having GPT-2 process the same set of sentence materials as human subjects in four different agreement experiments. To anticipate our key results, we find GPT-2 yields lower surprisal, i.e. facilitatory effects, in both subject-verb and reflexive pronoun conditions. Furthermore, we show that attention at the verb or pronoun is distributed to both target and distractor in just those conditions where the distractor matches the hypothesized number retrieval cue (Lin et al., 2019). Finally, we show that the surprisal contrasts between matching and non-matching distractors in the grammatical (inhibitory) interference conditions are essentially zero.

3 GPT-2 for Psycholinguistic Analysis

The psycholinguistic relevance of GPT-2 and its training method. GPT-2 (Generative Pre-trained Transformer-2), introduced by OpenAI in Radford et al. (2019), is a language model with a decoder-only Transformer architecture (Vaswani et al., 2017), and has achieved state-of-the-art performance in diverse downstream tasks. GPT-2 and other large-scaled language models based on transformer architectures were trained on billions of words of text, and engineered with performance in mind, not with concern for psycholinguistic plausibility. Why then should we then take them seriously as the basis of psycholinguistic models?

We believe that the new transformer-based models have three important properties that make them of psycholinguistic interest. (a) The models are among the first to serve as the basis of systems that achieve human-level performance on a range of linguistic tasks, and they directly generate a key quantity, *surprisal of the next word*, that we know is an important predictor of reading times in humans (Hale, 2001; Levy, 2008). (b) Although the data requirements are currently much greater than that for human language acquisition, the models are trained on a simple task—predict the next word—that may plausibly serve as the basis of a self-supervised learning signal in human language acquisition. The representations that arise from such learning are thus psycholinguistically interesting. (c) The learned soft-attention and parallel content-based retrieval of representations of prior input are architectural properties of the GPT models that align very closely with retrieval-based models of sentence comprehension (Lewis et al., 2006). And the structure of these psycholinguistic models was proposed as a response to the challenges of computing long-distance dependencies—the same challenge that motivated the transformer as a departure from standard recurrent architectures (Vaswani et al., 2017; Galassi et al., 2020).

Identifying specialized heads in GPT-2. Here we use the medium-sized GPT-2 which is constructed with 12 layers, each of which includes 12 attention heads. Previous studies have revealed that individual attention heads in Transformer models serve are at least partially specialized in function (Clark et al., 2019; Vig, 2019; Vig and Belinkov, 2019; Voita et al., 2019). Specifically, Voita et al. (2019) found that certain attention heads are specialized for different dependency relations.

Following Voita et al. (2019)'s method, we identified heads that are specialized for subject-verb relations and reflexive anaphora resolution. Voita et al. (2019)'s method works as follows. First, sentences are parsed using CoreNLP dependency parser (Manning et al., 2014). Then, relative string positions (e.g., one token back, two tokens back) of all instances in each syntactic dependency were counted. Considering the proportion of the most frequent relative position as the baseline, attention heads are selected as specialized for a particular dependency relation if attention is paid for the corresponding dependent at least 10% more often than the baseline. In other words, there must be some evidence that the attention head is sensitive to the dependency and not merely string position.

To find attention heads responsible for the relation between subjects and verbs, we used the CoreNLP parser on 148,376 sentences from the Brown corpus and Gutenberg corpus provided via Natural Language Toolkit (NLTK) (Bird et al., 2009), extracting 49,145 *nsubj* relations, which associate nominal subjects and their governors which are mostly verbs. The most frequent relative position for *nsubj* dependency relation is -1, which means that the nominal subjects usually come right before their governor, taking up 42% of the cases.

After analyzing the attention distribution pattern using GPT-2, we obtained four syntactic heads that were found to be partly specialized for *nsubj* dependency relations: *head4_3* (59%); *head3_6* (51%); *head6_0* (49%); *head2_9* (49%)[1]. Although we expect that the four syntactic heads responsible for *nsubj* dependency relation may play distinct roles, in our analyses here we simply use the best performing head (*head4_3*).

The same method was implemented to find attention heads responsible for reflexive anaphora resolution. The only difference was that we used NeuralCoref (Wolf et al., 2018) to count relative position of antecedents to reflexive anaphora since the dependency parser does not associate antecedents and anaphora. Out of 2,660 sentences that includes reflexive anaphora, we extracted 510 sentences where NeuralCoref identified a single unique antecedent for the reflexive pronoun. The most fre-

[1]head*n*_*m* refers to the *m*-th attention head in the *n*-th layer. Numbers in parentheses indicate accuracies of heads in paying the highest attention to the subject/antecedent by the verb/pronoun.

Table 1: A set of data included for the experiment on subject-verb agreement. (Wagers et al. (2009)'s Exp3 also included sets with plural subjects in the ungrammatical conditions.)

	Interference	Grammaticality	Example sentences
Wagers 2009 Exp 2-3	int	gram	The commentator who the **viewer trusts** ...
	non-int	gram	The commentators who the **viewer trusts** ...
	int	ungram	*The commentators who the **viewer trust** ...
	non-int	ungram	*The commentator who the **viewer trust** ...
Wagers (2009) Exp 4-6	int	gram	The **slogan** on the poster **was** designed ...
	non-int	gram	The **slogan** on the posters **was** designed ...
	int	ungram	*The **slogan** on the posters **were** designed ...
	non-int	ungram	*The **slogan** on the poster **were** designed ...
Dillon 2013 Exp 1 agrmt	int	gram	The **executive** who oversaw the middle manager apparently **was** dishonest ...
	non-int	gram	The **executive** who oversaw the middle managers apparently **was** dishonest ...
	int	ungram	*The **executive** who oversaw the middle managers apparently **were** dishonest ...
	non-int	ungram	*The **executive** who oversaw the middle manager apparently **were** dishonest ...

quent relative position for reflexive anaphora and their antecedents was -2, meaning that antecedents appear before reflexive anaphora having one word in between. The proportion of the highest relative position was 22%, requiring 24.2 % of accuracy for attention heads to be considered responsible for reflexive anaphora resolution. We found four heads whose accuracies are higher than the threshold: *head1_5* (44%); *head3_5* (39%); *head4_3* (27%); *head6_0* (25%), and we again take the best performing head (*head1_5*) for further analysis.

Metrics. We define here three metrics for our analyses: *surprisal, attention entropy from syntactic heads*, and *attention to target*. We use surprisal for making reading time predictions, but use the attention metrics to provide insight into the processing at the critical region and therefore the representations computed in the prefix before the critical region. Surprisal is thus based on the final prediction of the entire model, but the attention metrics are associated with the attention heads most specialized for our dependencies of interest.

Surprisal (Hale, 2001; Levy, 2008) is defined as the negative log probability of the word given left context.

$$\text{Surprisal}(w) = -\log_2 P(w|context) \quad (1)$$

Any use of surprisal requires adoption of some kind of language model; e.g. some past work has used probabilistic CFGs (Levy, 2008). Here we use GPT-2, which computes after each word a probability distribution over its large lexicon that is conditioned on its internal representation of the left context.

Attention to target is simply the value of the soft attention vector element that corresponds to the target word position, which we denote $\text{Attn}(w_{cue}, w_{target})$, and indicates how much attention is allocated to the target by one of the specialized attention heads (*head4_3* for subject-verb and *head1_5* for reflexives.)

Attention entropy is a variant of Shannon (1948)'s information entropy that we use as a measure of how sharply focused (low entropy) or diffuse (high entropy) the attention pattern is. (It may be thought of as a measure of the uncertainty about the attentional target, but because the attention values are not probabilities from which targets are sampled, this interpretation is not strictly warranted).

$$\text{Entropy}(w_i) = \sum_{j=1}^{i-1} \text{Attn}(w_i, w_j) \times \log_2 \text{Attn}(w_i, w_j) \quad (2)$$

where *i* refers to the location of the critical word, *j* are locations of prior words, and $\text{Attn}(w_i, w_j)$ is attention allocated to w_j from w_i.

4 Subject-verb Agreement Experiments

To investigate whether GPT-2 may predict facilitatory interference effects in subject-verb agreement, we ran GPT-2 on materials from three studies (Dillon et al., 2013; Wagers et al., 2009): 48 sets of sentences from Experiments 2-3 in Wagers et al. (2009)[2]; 24 sets of sentences from Experiments 4-7 in Wagers et al. (2009); 48 sets of sentences from Dillon et al. (2013) (See Table 1).

These three sets of sentences have in common a 2×2 structure with the factors *grammaticality* (grammatical/ungrammatical) and *interference* (interfering/non-interfering), as described above. Additionally, Wagers et al. (2009)'s Exp 3 also includes an additional condition, *subject* (singular/plural) for investigating a possible singular-plural asymmetry, i.e., asking whether interference effects are equivalent for plural (for plural verbs) and singular (for singular verbs) distractors.

Note that sentences from Experiments 2–3 in Wagers et al. (2009) involve structures in which the distractor appears *before* the target, and so test effects of *proactive interference*. Thus the distractors are also more distant from verbs than in the other experimental materials.

Results of surprisal analyses. Figure 4 shows the surprisal computed at the critical verbs in each of the experiments and in each of the four conditions separately (red dots and intervals represent means and conventional 95% confidence intervals). Surprisal matches the important qualitative pattern found in the meta-analysis of first-pass reading times: lower surprisal—facilitatory effects—are found in the ungrammatical conditions when the distractor matches the verb's number, and no inhibitory effects are found in the grammatical conditions. Furthermore, the effects are largest for the case of *retroactive* interference, where the distractor follows the target and immediately precedes the verb (Figure 4a), compared to *proactive* inteference, where the distractor precedes the target (Figure 4c). The exception is that no facilitatory effects were found when the verb is singular and the target subject is plural (see Figure 4d). But the facilitatory effect in this condition was not reliably different from zero in the meta-analysis, and it mirrors a plural-singular asymmetry (or *markedness* effect) found in agreement attraction in production.

[2]Wagers et al. (2009)'s materials are an extended and slightly modified version of Pearlmutter et al. (1999)

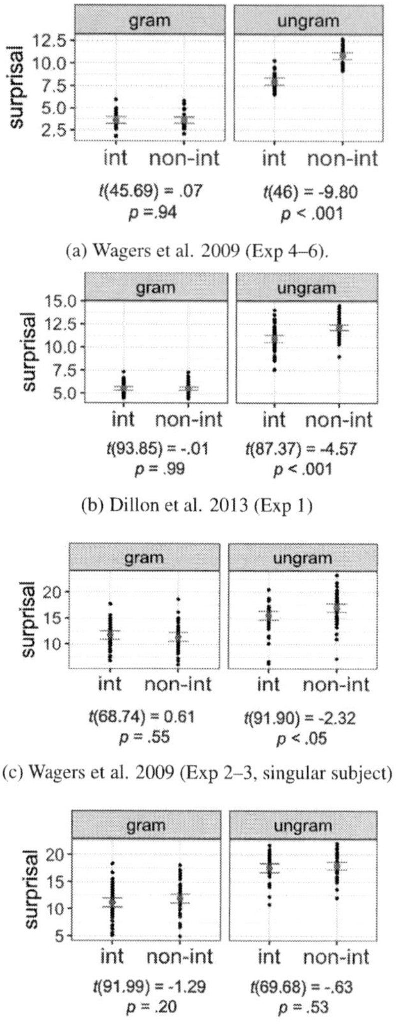

(a) Wagers et al. 2009 (Exp 4–6).

(b) Dillon et al. 2013 (Exp 1)

(c) Wagers et al. 2009 (Exp 2–3, singular subject)

(d) Wagers et al. 2009 (Exp 3, plural subject)

Figure 4: The surprisal of critical verbs computed by GPT-2 on the materials in four subject-verb number agreement experiments. Each small dot is a data point from one sentence; the red dots and intervals represent means and 95% confidence intervals.

Results of attention analyses. Our conjecture is that in the *interfering* conditions where the distractor matches the verb in number that the attention of the *nsubj*-specialized attention head *head4_3* will be distributed to both the target *and* the distractor. It is possible to visualize exactly this pattern using a tool developed by Vig (2019). Figure 5 shows an example visualization.

Analyses of the *attention entropy* and *attention to target* metrics provide quantitative evidence for

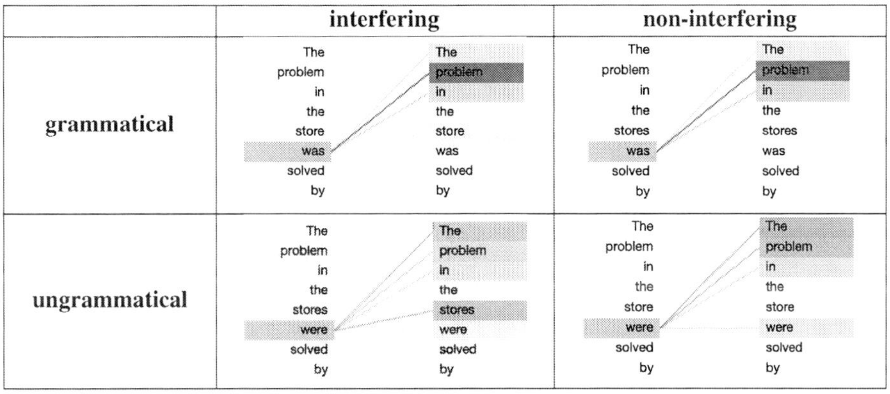

Figure 5: An example of the attention distribution of an attention head specialized for subject-verb dependencies in the four conditions of the subject-verb agreement experiments.

this conjecture: Figure 6 shows two metrics across the four datasets. The interfering conditions always show the highest value of *attention entropy* and the lowest value of *attention to target*, which means that the head most specialized for subject-verb relations distributes attention more diffusely and away from the target subject. There is evidence for the expected attention effects even in the grammatical conditions, but in these conditions there is no effect of surprisal. Thus, under a theory in which similarity-based interference exerts its effects on reading time through a *surprisal bottleneck* (Levy, 2008), no reading time differences are expected here—even though the underlying representations and attention patterns may reflect the interference.

Preliminary corpus analysis of ungrammatical subject-verb agreement sentences. One possible explanation for the observed facilitatory interference effects is that GPT-2 was exposed to ungrammatical sentences in the training data that have precisely the interference patterns of the ungrammatical sentences in our experiments. To examine such possibility, we analyzed 241 sentences randomly extracted from a Reddit corpus (Chang et al., 2020) whose subjects and verbs do not agree in number, and have either interfering or non-interfering distractors in between. The results shown in Table 2 suggest that interfering distractors occur about twice as often as non-interfering distractors in the case of singular subjects with an ungrammatical plural verb, consistent with our expectations that agreement-attraction errors in production may be evident in un-edited corpora.

But it seems unlikely that this 2:1 ratio, which

	singular subj	plural subj
interfering	80	71
non-interfering	39	51

Table 2: Results from a preliminary corpus analysis of patterns of ungrammatical subject-verb agreement. In the key case of a singular subject and a plural verb, the number of an intervening distractor is about twice as likely to be plural (interfering) rather than singular (non-interfering). See text for a discussion.

corresponds to about a 1 bit difference in surprisal, is sufficient alone to explain the observed surprisal differences. For example, in the Wagers et al Experiment 4–6, we observed about a 3 bit difference in surprisal, a 2 bit or 4x difference in probability relative to what would be expected on the basis of the corpus counts. More extensive corpus analysis is necessary to confidently rule out this explanation.

5 Reflexive Agreement Experiments

To examine whether the prediction of GPT-2 are consistent with the null interference effects argued for by Dillon et al. (2013), or show facilitatory interference effects as in the large scale Jäger et al. (2020) replication, we conducted an experiment using the same methodology as described above for the subject-verb experiments, but using the reflexive materials in Dillon et al. (2013), and focusing the attention analyses on the head most specialized for reflexive anaphor resolution. Examples of the materials are shown in Table 3.

Results of the surprisal analyses. Summaries of the surprisal (and attention metrics) measured at

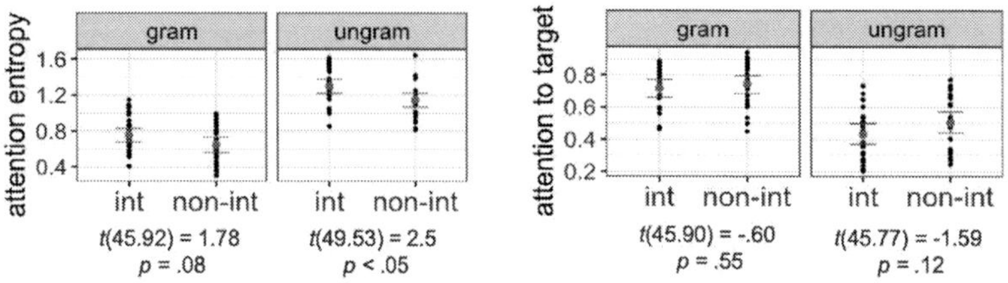

(a) Wagers et al. 2009 (Exp 4–6)

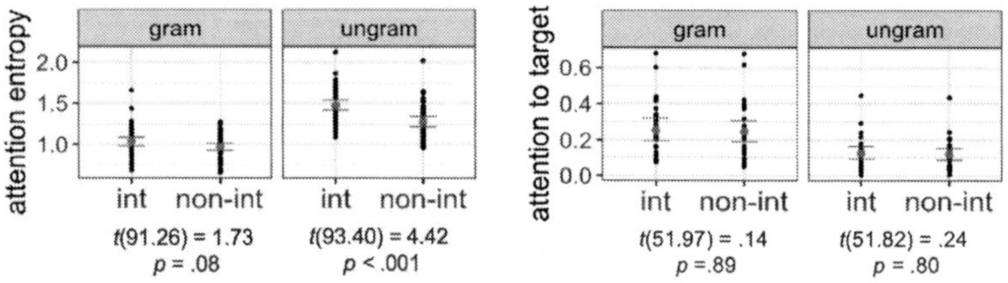

(b) Dillon et al. 2013 (Exp 1)

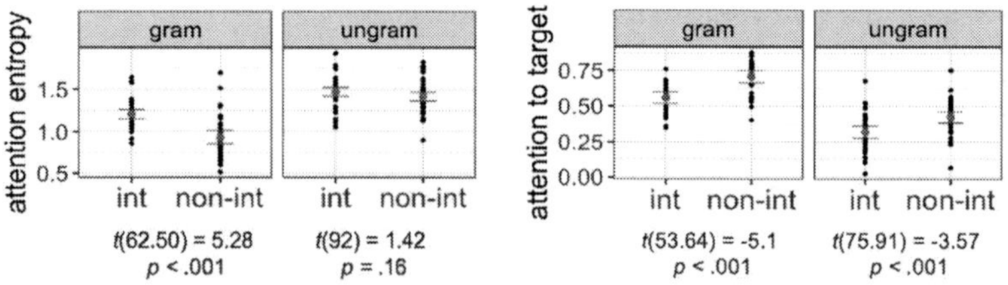

(c) Wagers et al. 2009 (Exp 3, singular subject)

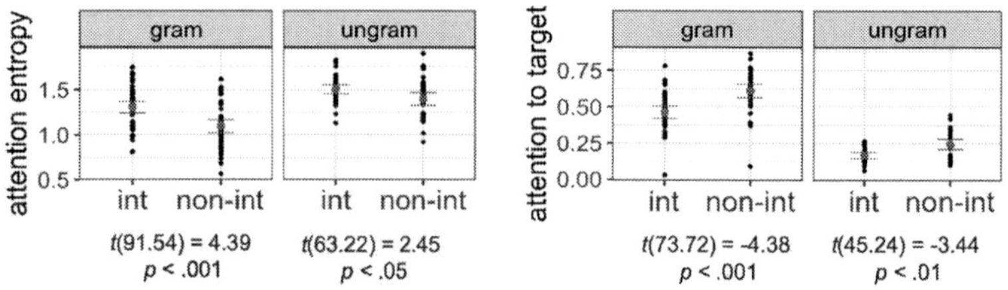

(d) Wagers et al. 2009 (Exp 3, plural subject)

Figure 6: Metrics quantifying attention patterns of the attention head most specialized for subject-verb relations, computed at the verb in the subject-verb agreement experiments.

reflexive anaphora are provided in Figure 7. Consistent with the large scale replication of Dillon et al. (2013) conducted by Jäger et al. (2020) (but inconsistent with the null results reported by Dillon et al), we found lower *surprisal* values in the ungrammatical interfering conditions, consistent with a facilitatory interference effect.

Results of the attention analyses. We found little or no differences between interfering and non-interfering cases in the two attention metrics *attention entropy* and *attention to target*. It is possible that this is because the attention head *head1_5* that we found to be partly specialized for reflexive anaphora resolution is actually not as specialized in reflexive anaphora resolution as *head4_3* specialized in *nsubj* dependency resolution. We cannot conclude yet whether there exist heads that serve this function better (that are not detected by the method of Voita et al. (2019)), whether GPT-2 is not reliably resolving the reflexive anaphora, or whether GPT-2 is doing so in a way that is dis-

	Interference	Grammaticality	Example sentences
Dillon 2013 Exp 1 reflexive	int	gram	The basketball **coach** who trained the star player usually blamed **himself** for the ...
	non-int	gram	The basketball **coach** who trained the star players usually blamed **himself** for the ...
	int	ungram	*The basketball **coach** who trained the star players usually blamed **themselves** for the ...
	non-int	ungram	*The basketball **coach** who trained the star player usually blamed **themselves** for the ...

Table 3: Examples from Dillon et al. (2013), used in the GPT-2 experiment on reflexive pronoun agreement.

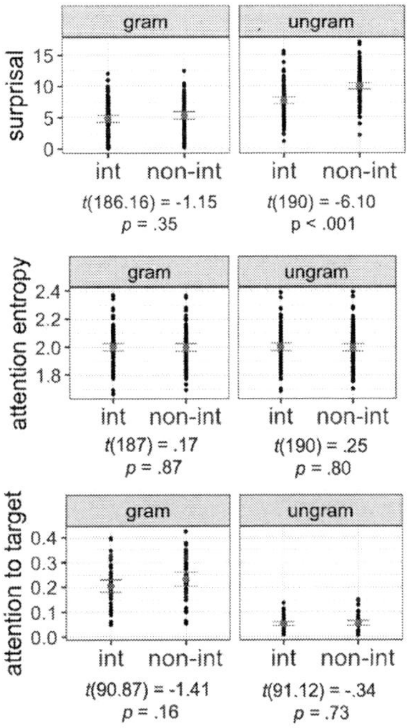

Figure 7: Results of the GPT-2 reflexive agreement experiment using materials from Dillon et al. (2013).

tributed across many attention heads.

6 Discussion and Future Directions

Effects of similarity-based interference have been the province of models of noisy memory rather than models of probabilistic expectations, because in standard probabilistic grammars the expectation for the agreement features of a licensor such as a verb or pronoun should not be conditioned upon the agreement features of constituents other than the target licensee. But we show here that a large-scale Transformer language model, GPT-2, trained only to predict the next word, nevertheless yields surprisal values that are consistent with facilitatory interference effects due to distractor noun phrases that do not participate in the agreement relations. We also confirmed that two metrics that are easily computed from the Transformers' attention mechanism, *attention entropy* and *attention to target*, show patterns in the subject-verb experiments that are consistent with cue-based retrieval models.

Our results are suggestive of a possible interesting link between surprisal and noisy memory representations. The attention patterns that we have discovered must reflect similarity between the representations of the target and distractor noun phrases. This representational similarity is the source of great generalization power, but this generalization can lead to linguistic expectations that are not derived by conventional grammatical analyses.

One limitation of our analyses of attention is that they depend on methods for identifying specialized heads for specific dependency types. It is not clear that we understand enough about Transformer models to do this reliably. But our results suggest that for at least some dependencies, these simple attention metrics and head selection methods can yield interesting insights.

The approach outlined may provide an important way to combine surprisal and noisy memory accounts, maintaining a surprisal bottleneck. Using trained Transformers has the significant theoretical advantage that the memory representations, the attention/retrieval cues, and thus the predicted similarity effects are *learned* via a self-supervised prediction task. And so such models naturally yield experience-driven sources of noisy representations that are independent of the process noise assumed in existing memory-based models. Combining the process- and experience-based noise in a single model is an important goal for psycholinguistic theory.

References

Steven Bird, Ewan Klein, and Edward Loper. 2009. *Natural language processing with Python: analyzing text with the natural language toolkit*. " O'Reilly Media, Inc.".

Jonathan P Chang, Caleb Chiam, Liye Fu, Andrew Wang, Justine Zhang, and Cristian Danescu-Niculescu-Mizil. 2020. Convokit: A toolkit for the analysis of conversations. In *Proceedings of the 21th Annual Meeting of the Special Interest Group on Discourse and Dialogue*, pages 57–60.

Rui P Chaves. 2020. What don't rnn language models learn about filler-gap dependencies? *Proceedings of the Society for Computation in Linguistics*, 3(1):20–30.

Noam Chomsky et al. 1982. *Some concepts and consequences of the theory of government and binding*. MIT press.

Kevin Clark, Urvashi Khandelwal, Omer Levy, and Christopher D Manning. 2019. What does bert look at? an analysis of bert's attention. *arXiv preprint arXiv:1906.04341*.

Jillian K Da Costa and Rui P Chaves. 2020. Assessing the ability of transformer-based neural models to represent structurally unbounded dependencies. *Proceedings of the Society for Computation in Linguistics*, 3(1):189–198.

Brian Dillon, Alan Mishler, Shayne Sloggett, and Colin Phillips. 2013. Contrasting intrusion profiles for agreement and anaphora: Experimental and modeling evidence. *Journal of Memory and Language*, 69(2):85–103.

Allyson Ettinger. 2020. What bert is not: Lessons from a new suite of psycholinguistic diagnostics for language models. *Transactions of the Association for Computational Linguistics*, 8:34–48.

Richard Futrell, Edward Gibson, and Roger P Levy. 2020. Lossy-context surprisal: An information-theoretic model of memory effects in sentence processing. *Cognitive science*, 44(3):e12814.

Richard Futrell, Ethan Wilcox, Takashi Morita, and Roger Levy. 2018. Rnns as psycholinguistic subjects: Syntactic state and grammatical dependency. *arXiv preprint arXiv:1809.01329*.

Andrea Galassi, Marco Lippi, and Paolo Torroni. 2020. Attention in natural language processing. *IEEE Transactions on Neural Networks and Learning Systems*.

Edward Gibson. 1998. Linguistic complexity: Locality of syntactic dependencies. *Cognition*, 68(1):1–76.

John Hale. 2001. A probabilistic earley parser as a psycholinguistic model. In *Second Meeting of the North American Chapter of the Association for Computational Linguistics*.

Lena A Jäger, Felix Engelmann, and Shravan Vasishth. 2017. Similarity-based interference in sentence comprehension: Literature review and bayesian meta-analysis. *Journal of Memory and Language*, 94:316–339.

Lena A Jäger, Daniela Mertzen, Julie A Van Dyke, and Shravan Vasishth. 2020. Interference patterns in subject-verb agreement and reflexives revisited: A large-sample study. *Journal of Memory and Language*, 111:104063.

Sol Lago, Diego E Shalom, Mariano Sigman, Ellen F Lau, and Colin Phillips. 2015. Agreement attraction in spanish comprehension. *Journal of Memory and Language*, 82:133–149.

Yann LeCun, Yoshua Bengio, and Geoffrey Hinton. 2015. Deep learning. *nature*, 521(7553):436–444.

Roger Levy. 2008. Expectation-based syntactic comprehension. *Cognition*, 106(3):1126–1177.

Roger Levy. 2013. Memory and surprisal in human sentence comprehension.

Richard L Lewis. 1993. An architecturally-based theory of human sentence comprehension. Technical report, CARNEGIE-MELLON UNIV PITTSBURGH PA DEPT OF COMPUTER SCIENCE.

Richard L Lewis. 1996. Interference in short-term memory: The magical number two (or three) in sentence processing. *Journal of psycholinguistic research*, 25(1):93–115.

Richard L Lewis and Shravan Vasishth. 2005. An activation-based model of sentence processing as skilled memory retrieval. *Cognitive science*, 29(3):375–419.

Richard L Lewis, Shravan Vasishth, and Julie A Van Dyke. 2006. Computational principles of working memory in sentence comprehension. *Trends in cognitive sciences*, 10(10):447–454.

Yongjie Lin, Yi Chern Tan, and Robert Frank. 2019. Open sesame: Getting inside bert's linguistic knowledge. In *Proceedings of the 2019 ACL Workshop BlackboxNLP: Analyzing and Interpreting Neural Networks for NLP*, pages 241–253.

Tal Linzen and Marco Baroni. 2021. Syntactic structure from deep learning. *Annual Review of Linguistics*.

Christopher D Manning, Mihai Surdeanu, John Bauer, Jenny Rose Finkel, Steven Bethard, and David McClosky. 2014. The stanford corenlp natural language processing toolkit. In *Proceedings of 52nd annual meeting of the association for computational linguistics: system demonstrations*, pages 55–60.

George A Miller and Noam Chomsky. 1963. Finitary models of language users.

Bruno Nicenboim, Shravan Vasishth, Felix Engelmann, and Katja Suckow. 2018. Exploratory and confirmatory analyses in sentence processing: A case study of number interference in german. *Cognitive science*, 42:1075–1100.

Bruno Nicenboim, Shravan Vasishth, Carolina Gattei, Mariano Sigman, and Reinhold Kliegl. 2015. Working memory differences in long-distance dependency resolution. *Frontiers in Psychology*, 6:312.

Neal J Pearlmutter, Susan M Garnsey, and Kathryn Bock. 1999. Agreement processes in sentence comprehension. *Journal of Memory and language*, 41(3):427–456.

Alec Radford, Jeffrey Wu, Rewon Child, David Luan, Dario Amodei, and Ilya Sutskever. 2019. Language models are unsupervised multitask learners. *OpenAI blog*, 1(8):9.

Claude E Shannon. 1948. A mathematical theory of communication. *The Bell system technical journal*, 27(3):379–423.

Patrick Sturt. 2003. The time-course of the application of binding constraints in reference resolution. *Journal of Memory and Language*, 48(3):542–562.

Martin Sundermeyer, Ralf Schlüter, and Hermann Ney. 2012. Lstm neural networks for language modeling. In *Thirteenth annual conference of the international speech communication association*.

Julie A Van Dyke and Richard L Lewis. 2003. Distinguishing effects of structure and decay on attachment and repair: A cue-based parsing account of recovery from misanalyzed ambiguities. *Journal of Memory and Language*, 49(3):285–316.

Marten Van Schijndel and Tal Linzen. 2018. Modeling garden path effects without explicit hierarchical syntax. In *CogSci*.

Shravan Vasishth and Felix Engelmann. 2021. *Sentence Comprehension as a Cognitive Process: A computational approach*. Cambridge University Press.

Ashish Vaswani, Noam Shazeer, Niki Parmar, Jakob Uszkoreit, Llion Jones, Aidan N Gomez, Łukasz Kaiser, and Illia Polosukhin. 2017. Attention is all you need. In *Advances in neural information processing systems*, pages 5998–6008.

Jesse Vig. 2019. A multiscale visualization of attention in the transformer model. In *Proceedings of the 57th Annual Meeting of the Association for Computational Linguistics: System Demonstrations*, pages 37–42.

Jesse Vig and Yonatan Belinkov. 2019. Analyzing the structure of attention in a transformer language model. In *Proceedings of the 2019 ACL Workshop BlackboxNLP: Analyzing and Interpreting Neural Networks for NLP*, pages 63–76.

Elena Voita, David Talbot, Fedor Moiseev, Rico Sennrich, and Ivan Titov. 2019. Analyzing multi-head self-attention: Specialized heads do the heavy lifting, the rest can be pruned. In *Proceedings of the 57th Annual Meeting of the Association for Computational Linguistics*, pages 5797–5808.

Matthew W Wagers, Ellen F Lau, and Colin Phillips. 2009. Agreement attraction in comprehension: Representations and processes. *Journal of Memory and Language*, 61(2):206–237.

Ethan Wilcox, Jon Gauthier, Jennifer Hu, Peng Qian, and Roger Levy. 2020. On the predictive power of neural language models for human real-time comprehension behavior. *arXiv preprint arXiv:2006.01912*.

Ethan Wilcox, Roger Levy, and Richard Futrell. 2019. What syntactic structures block dependencies in rnn language models? *arXiv preprint arXiv:1905.10431*.

Ethan Wilcox, Roger Levy, Takashi Morita, and Richard Futrell. 2018. What do rnn language models learn about filler-gap dependencies? *arXiv preprint arXiv:1809.00042*.

Thomas Wolf, James Ravenscroft, Julien Chaumond, and Maxwell Rebo. 2018. Neuralcoref: Coreference resolution in spacy with neural networks.

Ming Xiang, Brian Dillon, and Colin Phillips. 2009. Illusory licensing effects across dependency types: Erp evidence. *Brain and Language*, 108(1):40–55.

CMCL 2021 Shared Task on Eye-Tracking Prediction

Nora Hollenstein
University of Copenhagen
nora.hollenstein@gmail.com

Emmanuele Chersoni
The Hong Kong Polytechnic University
emmanuelechersoni@gmail.com

Cassandra Jacobs
University of Wisconsin
jacobs.cassandra.l@gmail.com

Yohei Oseki
University of Tokyo
oseki@g.ecc.u-tokyo.ac.jp

Laurent Prévot
Aix-Marseille University
laurent.prevot@univ-amu.fr

Enrico Santus
Bayer Pharmaceuticals
esantus@gmail.com

Abstract

Eye-tracking data from reading represent an important resource for both linguistics and natural language processing. The ability to accurately model gaze features is crucial to advance our understanding of language processing. This paper describes the Shared Task on Eye-Tracking Data Prediction, jointly organized with the eleventh edition of the Workshop on Cognitive Modeling and Computational Linguistics (CMCL 2021). The goal of the task is to predict 5 different token-level eye-tracking metrics from the Zurich Cognitive Language Processing Corpus (ZuCo). Eye-tracking data were recorded during natural reading of English sentences. In total, we received submissions from 13 registered teams, whose systems include boosting algorithms with handcrafted features, neural models leveraging transformer language models, or hybrid approaches. The winning system used a range of linguistic and psychometric features in a gradient boosting framework.

1 Introduction/Overview

The ability of accurately modeling eye-tracking features is crucial to advance the understanding of language processing. Eye-tracking provides millisecond-accurate records on where humans look, shedding lights on where they pay attention during their reading and comprehension phase (see the example in Figure 1). The benefits of utilizing eye movement data have been noticed in various domains, including natural language processing and computer vision. Not only can it reveal the workings of the underlying cognitive processes of language understanding, but the performance of computational models can also be improved if their inductive bias is adjusted using human cognitive signals such as eye-tracking, fMRI, or EEG data (Barrett et al., 2016; Hollenstein et al., 2019; Toneva and Wehbe, 2019). Thanks to the recent introduction of a standardized dataset (Hollenstein et al., 2018, 2020), it is now possible to compare the capabilities of machine learning approaches to model and analyze human patterns of reading.

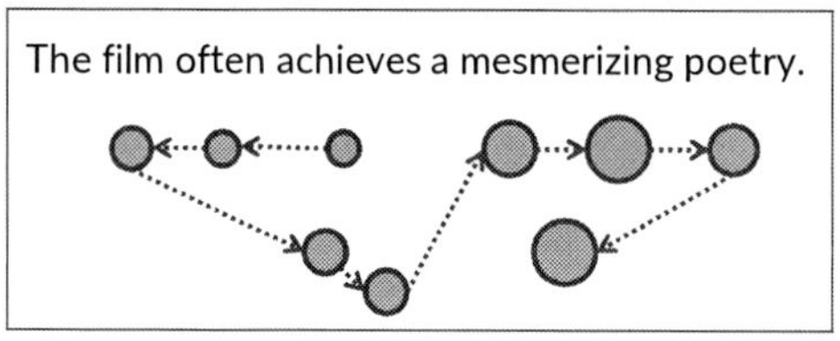

Figure 1: Example sentence from the ZuCo corpus read by a single reader. The blue dots mark fixations on the corresponding words above, a wider diameter represent a longer fixation duration.

In this shared task, we present the challenge of predicting eye word-level tracking-based metrics recorded during English sentence processing. We encouraged submissions concerning both cognitive modeling and linguistically motivated approaches (e.g., language models). All data files are available on the competition website.[1]

2 Related Work

Research on naturalistic reading has shown that fixation patterns are influenced by the predictability of words in their sentence context (Ehrlich and Rayner, 1981). In natural language processing and psycholinguistics, the most influential account of the phenomenon is surprisal theory (Hale, 2001; Levy, 2008), which claims that the processing difficulty of a word is proportional to its *surprisal*, i.e., the negative logarithm of the probabil-

[1] https://competitions.codalab.org/competitions/28176

Proceedings of the Workshop on Cognitive Modeling and Computational Linguistics, pages 72–78
Online Event, June 10, 2021. ©2021 Association for Computational Linguistics

ity of the word given the context. Surprisal theory was the reference framework for several studies on language models and eye-tracking data prediction (Demberg and Keller, 2008; Frank and Bod, 2011; Fossum and Levy, 2012). These studies use the data from the Dundee Corpus (Kennedy et al., 2003), which consists of sentences from British newspapers with eye-tracking measurements from 10 participants, as one of the earliest and most popular benchmarks.

Later work on the topic found that the perplexity of a language model is the primary factor determining the fit to human reading times (Goodkind and Bicknell, 2018), a result that was confirmed also by the recent investigations involving neural language models such as GRU networks (Aurnhammer and Frank, 2019) and Transformers (Merkx and Frank, 2020; Wilcox et al., 2020; Hao et al., 2020). Using an alternative approach, Bautista and Naval (2020) obtained good results for the prediction of eye movements with autoencoders.

In addition to the ZuCo corpus used for this shared task (see Section 4), there are several other resources of eye-tracking data for English. The Ghent Eye-Tracking Corpus (GECO; Cop et al., 2017) is composed of the entire Agatha Christie's novel *The Mysterious Affair at Styles*, for a total of $54,364$ tokens, it contains eye-tracking data from 33 subjects, both English native speakers (14) and bilingual speakers of Dutch and English (19), and comes with the Dutch counterpart. The Provo corpus (Luke and Christianson, 2017) contains 55 short English texts about various topics, with 2.5 sentences and 50 words on average, for a total of $2,689$ tokens, and eye-tracking measures collected from 85 subjects. Annotated eye-tracking corpora are also available for other languages, including German (Kliegl et al., 2006), Hindi (Husain et al., 2015), Japanese (Asahara et al., 2016) and Russian (Laurinavichyute et al., 2019), among others.

3 Task Description

In this shared task, we present the challenge of predicting eye-tracking-based metrics recorded during English sentence processing. The task is formulated as a regression task to predict the following 5 eye-tracking features for each token in the context of a full sentence:

1. NFIX (number of fixations): total number of fixations on the current word.

Feature	min	max	mean (std)
NFIX	0.0	7.25	1.1 (0.7)
FFD	0.0	296.8	77.3 (34.4)
GPT	0.0	2424.9	154.1 (143.6)
TRT	0.0	996.2	128.8 (88.6)
FIXPROP	0.0	1.0	0.67 (0.26)

Table 1: Minimum, maximum, mean and standard deviation of the feature values *before scaling* in both training and test data, after averaging across readers.

Feature	min	max	mean (std)
NFIX	0.0	100.0	15.1 (9.5)
FFD	0.0	12.2	3.2 (1.4)
GPT	0.0	100.0	6.4 (5.9)
TRT	0.0	41.1	5.3 (3.7)
FIXPROP	0.0	100.0	67.1 (26.0)

Table 2: Minimum, maximum, mean and standard deviation of the *scaled* feature values in both training and test data, after averaging across readers.

2. FFD (first fixation duration): the duration of the first fixation on the prevailing word.
3. TRT (total reading time): the sum of all fixation durations on the current word, including regressions.
4. GPT (go-past time): the sum of all fixations prior to progressing to the right of the current word, including regressions to previous words that originated from the current word.
5. FIXPROP (fixation proportion): the proportion of participants that fixated the current word (as a proxy for how likely a word is to be fixated).

The goal of the task is to train a model which predicts these five eye-tracking features for each token in a given sentence.

4 Data

We use the eye-tracking data recorded during normal reading from the freely available Zurich Cognitive Language Processing Corpus (ZuCo; Hollenstein et al., 2018, 2020). ZuCo is a combined eye-tracking and EEG brain activity dataset, which provides anonymized records in compliance with an ethical board approval and as such it does not

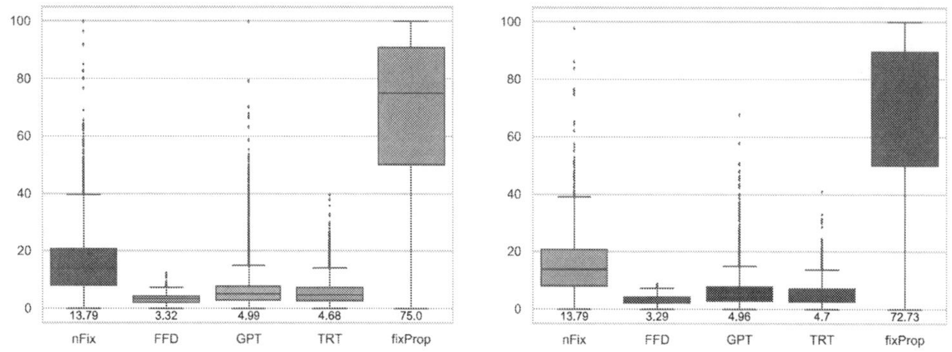

(a) Training data.

(b) Test data.

Figure 2: Boxplot showing the feature value distributions of both training and test sets. Below each box is the median value of each feature.

contain any information that can be linked to the participants.

The eye-tracking data was recorded with an Eye-Link 1000 system in a series of naturalistic reading experiments. Full sentences were presented at the same position on the screen one at a time. The participants read each sentence at their own reading speed. The reading material included sentences from movie reviews from the Stanford Sentiment Treebank (Socher et al., 2013) and a Wikipedia dataset (Culotta et al., 2006). For a detailed description of the data acquisition, please refer to the original publications. An example sentence is presented in Figure 1.

We use the normal reading paradigms from ZuCo, i.e, Task 1 and Task 2 from ZuCo 1.0, and all tasks from ZuCo 2.0. We extracted the eye-tracking data from all 12 subjects from ZuCo 1.0 and all 18 subjects from ZuCo 2.0. The dataset contains 990 sentences. All sentences were shuffled randomly before splitting into training and test sets. The training data contains 800 sentences, and the test data 190 sentences.

4.1 Preprocessing

Tokenization The tokens in the sentences are split in the same manner as they were presented to the participants during the reading experiments. Hence, this does not necessarily follow a linguistically correct tokenization. For example, the sequences "(except," and "don't" were presented as such to the reader and not split into "(", "except", "," and "do", "n't" as a tokenizer would do. Sentence endings are marked with an <*EOS*> symbol added to the last token.

Feature Extraction The eye-tracking feature values are scaled between 0 and 100 to facilitate evaluation via the mean absolute error. The features NFIX and FIXPROP are scaled separately, while FFD, GPT and TRT are scaled together since these are all dependent and measured in milliseconds. The features are averaged across all readers. The data was scaled and randomly shuffled before splitting into training and test data. Tables 1 and 2 show the ranges of the eye-tracking features before and after scaling. Figure 2 depicts the feature value distributions in both training and test sets, showing that the distributions are very similar in both splits.

5 Evaluation

In this section, we describe the evaluation procedure used to assess the submitted predictions of the participating teams.

Any additional data source was allowed to train the models, as long as it is freely available to the research community. For example, additional eye-tracking corpora, additional features such as brain activity signals, pre-trained language models, etc.

5.1 Scoring Metric

The submitted predictions are evaluated against the real eye-tracking feature values using the mean absolute error (MAE) metric, a measure of errors between paired observations including comparisons of predicted (y) versus observed (x) values for each

Rank	Team Name	MAE	NFIX	FFD	GPT	TRT	FIXPROP	Reference
1	LAST	3.813	3.879	0.655	2.197	1.524	10.812	Bestgen (2021)
2	TALEP	3.833	3.761	0.662	2.180	1.486	11.076	Dary et al. (2021)
3	TorontoCL	3.929	3.944	0.671	2.227	1.516	11.286	Li and Rudzicz (2021)
4	LangResearchLab_NC	3.949	4.039	0.674	2.248	1.568	11.216	Agarwal and Chatterjee (2021)
5	CogNLP-Sheffield	3.957	3.956	0.689	2.260	1.529	11.349	Vickers et al. (2021)
6	OSU	3.977	3.987	0.682	2.364	1.540	11.311	Oh (2021)
7	MTL782_IITD	4.064	4.115	0.719	2.264	1.622	11.599	Choudhary et al. (2021)
8	KonTra	4.216	4.263	0.698	2.756	1.682	11.683	Yu et al. (2021)
9	Sabhay_Jain	4.257	4.264	0.848	2.476	1.721	11.974	-
10	ReadMe	4.383	4.363	0.741	2.502	1.761	12.549	Balkoca et al. (2021)
11	PIHKers	4.388	4.335	0.715	3.059	1.713	12.118	Salicchi and Lenci (2021)
12	ChiSquareX	4.676	4.557	1.281	2.810	2.289	12.445	-
-	MEAN BASELINE	7.357	7.303	1.149	3.782	2.778	21.775	-
13	IIIT_DWD	9.762	8.845	1.589	4.633	3.296	30.446	-

Table 3: Overall results showing the best submission per team and the mean baseline. The teams are ranked by the MAE averaged across all five eye-tracking features (third column).

word in the test set:

$$MAE = \frac{\sum_{i=1}^{n} |y_i - x_i|}{n} \quad (1)$$

The winning system is defined as the one with the lowest average MAE across all 5 eye-tracking features.

5.2 Mean Baseline

We use the mean central tendency as a baseline for this regression problem, i.e., we calculate the mean value for each feature from the training data and use it as a prediction for all words in the test data. Table 3 shows the MAE scores achieved by this mean baseline for each eye-tracking feature.

6 Participating Teams & Systems

13 teams and a total of 42 participants registered on the competition website. All 13 teams, including 26 registered participants, submitted their predictions during the evaluation phase. Each team was allowed three submissions during the evaluation phase. Finally, 10 teams published system description papers outlining their approach (see Table 3 for all references).

Methods The participating teams submitted predictions generated from various approaches. Mainly two methods were used: (1) Boosting methods using tree-based algorithms with extensive feature extraction (e.g., CatBoost[2] or LightGBM[3]), and (2) neural network based approaches for regression such as fine-tuning transformer-based language models (Vaswani et al., 2017). Most teams achieved their best performance using an ensemble of predictors. Moreover, some teams also trained hybrid systems including both feature-based approaches and state-of-the-art language models.

Features The features included for training the systems include surface features (e.g., word length, sentence length, word positions in the sentence), lexical features (e.g., lemmas, named entities) token probability features (word frequency and n-gram metrics), syntactic features (e.g., part-of-speech tags and dependency parsing), text complexity metrics, behavioral measures, (e.g., concreteness, familiarity, age of acquisition), context features (i.e., information about the preceding and following tokens) as well as representations from state-of-the-art language models, such as BERT (Devlin et al., 2019), RoBERTa (Liu et al., 2019), and XLNet (Yang et al., 2019).

Additional data Only one team (Li and Rudzicz, 2021) used external eye-tracking data, leveraging the Provo corpus (Luke and Christianson, 2017) for additional word-level eye movement samples.

7 Results

In this section, we describe the prediction performance achieved by the participating teams. The official results of this shared task are presented in Table 3. The best results were achieved by a linguistic feature-based approach (Bestgen, 2021). As described above, other teams opted for neural

[2] `https://catboost.ai/`

[3] `https://lightgbm.readthedocs.io/en/latest/`

approaches (e.g., Li and Rudzicz, 2021 and Oh, 2021) or hybrid approaches (e.g., Yu et al., 2021 and Choudhary et al., 2021), combining linguistic features and state-of-the-art language representations.

The difficulty of predicting the individual eye-tracking features is analogous in all submitted systems. FFD is the most accurately predicted feature. This seems to suggest that the models are more capable to capture early processing stages of lexical access compared to late-stage semantic integration, indexed by TRT and NFIX.

Generally, the error for the three features representing reading times in milliseconds (FFD, GPT, and TRT), is much lower than for NFIX and FIXPROP. The latter are the features with the most variance. The mean baseline results also reveal the same patterns. The features with lower variance achieve lower MAEs. The FIXPROP feature, representing how likely a word is to be fixated, might be more challenging to predict since it is more dependent on subject-specific characteristics. Nevertheless, when comparing the MAEs of each eye-tracking feature to the mean baseline, the systems achieve the largest improvement on this feature.

8 Outlook & Conclusion

We presented the results of the first shared task on predicting token-level eye-tracking features recorded during natural sentences reading. We hope the CMCL Shared Task makes a lasting contribution to the field of linguistic cognitive modelling by providing researchers with a standard evaluation framework and a high quality dataset. Despite the limited size of the test set, many previously reached conclusions can now be tested more thoroughly and future models can be compared on a shared benchmark.

For future editions of this shared task, we see the following improvement opportunities: (1) providing an official development set during the training phase; (2) using additional metrics for assessment, such as R^2 to achieve a better understanding of the submitted models; (3) extending the dataset to include additional eye-tracking data from other English corpora, as well as including data from other languages such as Dutch or Russian (e.g., Cop et al., 2017 or Laurinavichyute et al., 2019).

References

Raksha Agarwal and Niladri Chatterjee. 2021. LangResearchLab_NC at CMCL2021 Shared Task: Predicting Gaze Behaviour using Linguistic Features and Tree Regressors. In *Proceedings of the NAACL Workshop on Cognitive Modeling and Computational Linguistics*.

Masayuki Asahara, Hajime Ono, and Edson T Miyamoto. 2016. Reading-Time Annotations for "Balanced Corpus of Contemporary Written Japanese". In *Proceedings of COLING: Technical Papers*.

Christoph Aurnhammer and Stefan L Frank. 2019. Evaluating Information-theoretic Measures of Word Prediction in Naturalistic Sentence Reading. *Neuropsychologia*, 134:107198.

Alişan Balkoca, Abdullah Algan, Cengiz Acarturk, and Cagri Çöltekin. 2021. Team ReadMe at CMCL 2021 Shared Task: Predicting Human Reading Patterns by Traditional Oculomotor Control Models and Machine Learning. In *Proceedings of the NAACL Workshop on Cognitive Modeling and Computational Linguistics*.

Maria Barrett, Joachim Bingel, Frank Keller, and Anders Søgaard. 2016. Weakly Supervised Part-of-speech Tagging Using Eye-tracking Data. In *Proceedings of ACL*.

Louise Gillian Bautista and Prospero Naval. 2020. Towards Learning to Read Like Humans. In *International Conference on Computational Collective Intelligence*, pages 779–791. Springer.

Yves Bestgen. 2021. LAST at CMCL 2021 Shared Task: Predicting Gaze Data During Reading with a Gradient Boosting Decision Tree Approach. In *Proceedings of the NAACL Workshop on Cognitive Modeling and Computational Linguistics*.

Shivani Choudhary, Kushagri Tandon, Raksha Agarwal, and Niladri Chatterjee. 2021. MTL782_IITD at CMCL 2021 Shared Task: Prediction of Eye-Tracking Features using BERT Embeddings and Linguistic Features. In *Proceedings of the NAACL Workshop on Cognitive Modeling and Computational Linguistics*.

Uschi Cop, Nicolas Dirix, Denis Drieghe, and Wouter Duyck. 2017. Presenting GECO: An Eyetracking Corpus of Monolingual and Bilingual Sentence Reading. *Behavior Research Methods*, 49(2):602–615.

Aron Culotta, Andrew McCallum, and Jonathan Betz. 2006. Integrating Probabilistic Extraction Models and Data Mining to Discover Relations and Patterns in Text. In *Proceedings of NAACL*.

Franck Dary, Alexis Nasr, and Abdellah Fourtassi. 2021. TALEP at CMCL 2021 Shared Task: Non Linear Combination of Low and High-level Features for Predicting Eye-Tracking Data. In *Proceedings of the NAACL Workshop on Cognitive Modeling and Computational Linguistics*.

Vera Demberg and Frank Keller. 2008. Data from Eye-tracking Corpora as Evidence for Theories of Syntactic Processing Complexity. *Cognition*, 109(2):193–210.

Jacob Devlin, Ming-Wei Chang, Kenton Lee, and Kristina Toutanova. 2019. BERT: Pre-training of Deep Bidirectional Transformers for Language Understanding. In *Proceedings of NAACL*.

Susan E. Ehrlich and Keith Rayner. 1981. Contextual Effects on Word Perception and Eye Movements During Reading. *Journal of Verbal Learning and Verbal Behavior*, 20:641–65.

Victoria Fossum and Roger Levy. 2012. Sequential vs. Hierarchical Syntactic Models of Human Incremental Sentence Processing. In *Proceedings of the NAACL Workshop on Cognitive Modeling and Computational Linguistics*.

Stefan L Frank and Rens Bod. 2011. Insensitivity of the Human Sentence-processing System to Hierarchical Structure. *Psychological Science*, 22(6):829–834.

Adam Goodkind and Klinton Bicknell. 2018. Predictive Power of Word Surprisal for Reading Times Is a Linear Function of Language Model Quality. In *Proceedings of the LSA Workshop on Cognitive Modeling and Computational Linguistics*.

John Hale. 2001. A Probabilistic Earley Parser as a Psycholinguistic Model. In *Proceedings of NAACL*.

Yiding Hao, Simon Mendelsohn, Rachel Sterneck, Randi Martinez, and Robert Frank. 2020. Probabilistic Predictions of People Perusing: Evaluating Metrics of Language Model Performance for Psycholinguistic Modeling. In *Proceedings of the EMNLP Workshop on Cognitive Modeling and Computational Linguistics*.

Nora Hollenstein, Maria Barrett, Marius Troendle, Francesco Bigiolli, Nicolas Langer, and Ce Zhang. 2019. Advancing NLP with Cognitive Language Processing Signals. *arXiv preprint arXiv:1904.02682*.

Nora Hollenstein, Jonathan Rotsztejn, Marius Troendle, Andreas Pedroni, Ce Zhang, and Nicolas Langer. 2018. ZuCo, a Simultaneous EEG and Eye-tracking Resource for Natural Sentence Reading. *Scientific Data*.

Nora Hollenstein, Marius Troendle, Ce Zhang, and Nicolas Langer. 2020. ZuCo 2.0: A Dataset of Physiological Recordings During Natural Reading and Annotation. In *Proceedings of LREC*.

Samar Husain, Shravan Vasishth, and Narayanan Srinivasan. 2015. Integration and Prediction Difficulty in Hindi Sentence Comprehension: Evidence from an Eye-Tracking Corpus. *Journal of Eye Movement Research*, 8(2).

Alan Kennedy, Robin Hill, and Joël Pynte. 2003. The Dundee Corpus. In *Proceedings of the 12th European Conference on Eye Movement*.

Reinhold Kliegl, Antje Nuthmann, and Ralf Engbert. 2006. Tracking the Mind During Reading: The Influence of Past, Present, and Future Words on Fixation Durations. *Journal of Experimental Psychology*, 135(1):12.

AK Laurinavichyute, Irina A Sekerina, SV Alexeeva, and KA Bagdasaryan. 2019. Russian Sentence Corpus: Benchmark Measures of Eye Movements in Reading in Cyrillic. *Behavior Research Methods*, 51(3):1161–1178.

Roger Levy. 2008. Expectation-based Syntactic Comprehension. *Cognition*, 106(3):1126–1177.

Bai Li and Frank Rudzicz. 2021. TorontoCL at CMCL 2021 Shared Task: RoBERTa with Multi-Stage Fine-Tuning for Eye-Tracking Prediction. In *Proceedings of the NAACL Workshop on Cognitive Modeling and Computational Linguistics*.

Yinhan Liu, Myle Ott, Naman Goyal, Jingfei Du, Mandar Joshi, Danqi Chen, Omer Levy, Mike Lewis, Luke Zettlemoyer, and Veselin Stoyanov. 2019. RoBERTa: A Robustly Optimized BERT Pretraining Approach. *arXiv preprint arXiv:1907.11692*.

Steven G Luke and Kiel Christianson. 2017. The Provo Corpus: A Large Eye-tracking Corpus with Predictability Norms. *Behavior Research Methods*, pages 1–8.

Danny Merkx and Stefan L Frank. 2020. Comparing Transformers and RNNs on Predicting Human Sentence Processing Data. *arXiv preprint arXiv:2005.09471*.

Byung-Doh Oh. 2021. Team Ohio State at CMCL 2021 Shared Task: Fine-Tuned RoBERTa for Eye-Tracking Data Prediction. In *Proceedings of the NAACL Workshop on Cognitive Modeling and Computational Linguistics*.

Lavinia Salicchi and Alessandro Lenci. 2021. PIHKers at CMCL 2021 Shared Task: Cosine Similarity and Surprisal to Predict Human Reading Patterns. In *Proceedings of the NAACL Workshop on Cognitive Modeling and Computational Linguistics*.

Richard Socher, Alex Perelygin, Jean Wu, Jason Chuang, Christopher D Manning, Andrew Ng, and Christopher Potts. 2013. Recursive Deep Models for Semantic Compositionality over a Sentiment Treebank. In *Proceedings of EMNLP*.

Mariya Toneva and Leila Wehbe. 2019. Interpreting and Improving Natural Language Processing (in Machines) with Natural Language Processing (in the Brain). In *Advances in Neural Information Processing Systems*, pages 14928–14938.

Ashish Vaswani, Noam Shazeer, Niki Parmar, Jakob Uszkoreit, Llion Jones, Aidan N Gomez, Łukasz Kaiser, and Illia Polosukhin. 2017. Attention Is All You Need. In *Advances in Neural Information Processing Systems*, pages 5998–6008.

Peter Vickers, Rosa Wainwright, Harish Tayyar Madabushi, and Aline Villavicencio. 2021. CogNLP-Sheffield at CMCL 2021 Shared Task: Blending Cognitively Inspired Features with Transformer-based Language Models for Predicting Eye Tracking Patterns. In *Proceedings of the NAACL Workshop on Cognitive Modeling and Computational Linguistics*.

Ethan Gotlieb Wilcox, Jon Gauthier, Jennifer Hu, Peng Qian, and Roger Levy. 2020. On the Predictive Power of Neural Language Models for Human Real-Time Comprehension Behavior. *arXiv preprint arXiv:2006.01912*.

Zhilin Yang, Zihang Dai, Yiming Yang, Jaime Carbonell, Russ R Salakhutdinov, and Quoc V Le. 2019. XLNet: Generalized Autoregressive Pretraining for Language Understanding. *Advances in Neural Information Processing Systems*, 32:5753–5763.

Qi Yu, Aikaterini-Lida Kalouli, and Diego Frassinelli. 2021. KonTra at CMCL 2021 Shared Task: Predicting Eye Movements by combining BERT with Surface, Linguistic and Behavioral Information. In *Proceedings of the NAACL Workshop on Cognitive Modeling and Computational Linguistics*.

LangResearchLab_NC at CMCL2021 Shared Task: Predicting Gaze Behaviour Using Linguistic Features and Tree Regressors

Raksha Agarwal, Niladri Chatterjee
Indian Institute of Technology Delhi
Hauz Khas, Delhi-110016, India
raksha.agarwal@maths.iitd.ac.in
niladri@maths.iitd.ac.in

Abstract

Analysis of gaze data behaviour has gained momentum in recent years for different NLP applications. The present paper aims at modelling gaze data behaviour of tokens in the context of a sentence. We have experimented with various Machine Learning Regression Algorithms on a feature space comprising the linguistic features of the target tokens for prediction of five Eye-Tracking features. CatBoost Regressor performed the best and achieved fourth position in terms of MAE based accuracy measurement for the ZuCo Dataset.

1 Introduction

Eye-Tracking data or Gaze data compiles millisecond-accurate records about where humans look while reading. This yields valuable insights into the psycho-linguistic and cognitive aspects of various tasks requiring human intelligence. Eye-Tracking data has been successfully employed for various downstream NLP tasks, such as part of speech tagging (Barrett et al., 2016), named entity recognition (Hollenstein et al., 2018), sentiment analysis (Mishra et al., 2018), text simplification (Klerke et al., 2016), and sequence classification (Barrett and Hollenstein, 2020) among others. Development of systems for automatic prediction of gaze behaviour has become an important topic of research in recent years. For example, Klerke et al. (2016) and Mishra et al. (2017) used bi-LSTM and CNN, respectively for learning different gaze features. In the present work, Eye-Tracking features for words/tokens of given sentences are learned using Tree Regressors trained on a feature space comprising the linguistic properties of the target tokens. The proposed feature engineering scheme aims at encoding shallow lexical features, possible familiarity with the readers, interactions of a target token with other words in its context, and statistical language model features.

2 Task Setup

The shared task is designed to predict five Eye-Tracking features namely, number of fixations (nF), first fixation duration (FFD), total reading time (TR), go-past time (GP) and, fixation proportion (fxP). ZuCo Eye-Tracking dataset is used for the present task (Hollenstein et al., 2021, 2020, 2018). The dataset contains three subsets corresponding to Train, Trial and Test which contains 700, 100, and 191 sentences, respectively. Their respective token counts are 13765, 1971, and 3554. Each input token is uniquely represented by a tuple $< sid, wid >$, where sid is the sentence_id and wid is the word_id. Mean Absolute Error (MAE) is used for evaluation.

3 Feature Engineering

For the above-mentioned task, linguistic features for a given input token are extracted in order to encode the lexical, syntactic, and contextual properties of the input token. Additionally, familiarity of the input token and its collocation with surrounding words is also modelled as explained below.

3.1 Shallow Lexical Features

It is intuitive that the lexical properties of a given input token have an effect on the amount of time spent on reading the word. Features, such as Number of letters (Nlets), vowels (Nvow), syllables (Nsyl), phonemes (Nphon), morphemes (Nmorph), and percentage of upper case characters (PerUp) in the input token are used to model shallow lexical characterstics of the target token. A feature (IsNamed) is used to indicate whether the input token is a Named Entity. The language of etymological[1] origin, e.g., Latin, French of the target token is also considered as a feature, named EtyOrig.

In addition, several Boolean features have been used for characterization of the input token. The

[1] https://pypi.org/project/ety/

Proceedings of the Workshop on Cognitive Modeling and Computational Linguistics, pages 79–84
Online Event, June 10, 2021. ©2021 Association for Computational Linguistics

input tokens, which are the last words of the respective sentences, are suffixed by the string <EOS>. These are identified by a Boolean feature (IsLast). The <EOS> string is removed for further feature extraction. Two Boolean features (IsNumber, Hyphen) are used to indicate whether the input token is numeric, and whether the target token contains multiple words connected using hyphens, respectively. To indicate that the input token is a possesive word, a Boolean feature is used (IsPossessive). The identification has been done with the help of POS tag of SpaCy library and presence of apostrophe. A Boolean feature (StartPunct) is used to identify inputs starting with a puntuation character, these punctuations are removed for further feature extraction. Furthermore, we have considered two sentence level features namely, the total number of tokens in the sentence (LenSent), and the relative position (Relpos) of the input token in the sentence.

3.2 Modelling Familiarity

In the present work, the familiarity of a token is modelled using various frequency based features as described below.

A Boolean feature (IsStopword) is used to indicate whether the token is a stopword or not. It has been observed that the gaze time for stopwords, such as *a*, *an*, *of*, is much less in comparison with uncommon words, such as *grandiloquent* $< 457, 20 >$, and *contrivance* $< 715, 4 >$. This feature has been extracted using NLTK's list of English stopwords.

Corpus based features are used to indicate the common usage of input tokens. A Boolean feature (InGoogle) indicates whether the input token belongs to the list of the 10,000 most common English words, as determined by n-gram frequency analysis of the Google's Trillion Word Corpus[2]. Similarly, to indicate the presence of input tokens in the list of 1000 words included in Ogden's Basic English[3], a Boolean feature (InOgden) is used.

Frequency based features are also used to model the familiarity of input tokens. The following features are used: Frequency of input token in Ogden's Basic English (OgdenFreq), Exquisite Corpus (ECFreq) and, SUBTLEX (SUBTFreq). Exquisite Corpus[4] compiles texts from seven different domains. SUBTLEX contains frequency of 51 million words calculated on a corpus of Movie Subtitles. Contextual Diversity (ConDiversity) reported in SUBTLEX is also used as a feature. Contextual Diversity is computed as the percentage of movies in which the word appears. Furthermore, frequency of the input tokens given in the L count of (Thorndike and Lorge, 1944), and London-Lund Corpus of English Conversation by (Brown, 1984) are also used as features (TLFreq, BrownFreq).

The probability of the input token calculated using a bigram and trigram character language models are also considered as feature (CharProb2, CharProb3). The probability is lower for words where letters have unusual ordering. For example, consider the tokens *crazy* $< 350, 3 >$ and *czar* $< 525, 28 >$, $CharProb2(crazy) > CharProb2(czar)$ because the letter bigram *cr* (cry, crazy, create, cream, secret) is more common than bigram *cz* (czar, eczema) amongst English words. The letter bigram and trigram probabilities are calculated using letter counts from Google's Trillion Word Corpus[5]. Suppose a word W consist of N letters $W = l_1 \ldots l_N$ then, the corresponding feature value is calculated as:

$$CharProb2(W) = \frac{1}{N-1} \sum_{i=1}^{N-1} log_{10} P(l_i l_{i+1})$$

$$CharProb3(W) = \frac{1}{N-2} \sum_{i=1}^{N-2} log_{10} P(l_i l_{i+1} l_{i+2})$$

3.3 Modelling Context

There is a significant variation in the amount of time spent on comprehending the semantics of a word in different sentences. Variation in fixation time for the token *early* in different sentences is presented in Table 1. To model this variation, it is important to include features with respect to the context of the input word. Both simple Universal POS tag (UniTag) and detailed Penn POS tag (PennTag) of the input token extracted using SpaCy are considered as features. The POS of a target word depends on the context in which it appears as shown in Table 2.

Number of synsets (Nsyn), hyponyms (Nhypo) and hypernyms (Nhyper) extracted from NLTK WordNet are also used as features. These features are calculated considering the synsets having the same POS tag as the input token. The Dependency tree of a sentence helps to understand the relationship between different words of a given sentence.

[2] https://github.com/first20hours/google-10000-english

[3] http://ogden.basic-english.org

[4] https://pypi.org/project/wordfreq/

[5] http://norvig.com/ngrams/count_2l.txt, http://norvig.com/ngrams/count_3l.txt

id	nF	FF	GP	TR	fxP
$< 252, 3 >$	21.91	4.44	7.55	7.08	100
$< 618, 5 >$	15.33	4.18	4.18	5.28	83.3
$< 533, 15 >$	9.19	3.03	3.22	3.22	61.1

Table 1: Variation in fixation time for the token ***early***

sid	Sentence	Uni/Penn
366	After the show was cancelled, he played a handyman on the series The Facts of Life.	NOUN/ NN
460	A classy item by a legend who may have nothing left to prove but still has the chops and drive to show how its done.	VERB/ VB

Table 2: POS feature for the token ***show***

In this respect, the dependency tag of the input token with its syntactical head (DepTag) and, POS tag of the head (HeadPOS) are considered as features. Additionally, two features are extracted from the dependency tree, namely, depth of the input token in the tree (TokDepth), and the number of children of the input token (NChild).

3.4 Language Model Features

Statistical n-gram language models help to model collocation of words in sentences, and to determine the probability of a sequence of words. In the present work, we use a trigram language model trained on the Gigaword corpus[6] to extract two features (FragScore3, FragScore5) which measure the language model score of a word sequence containing the input token and the context words in the sentence in a window of 3 and 5, respectively.

Suppose the input sentence is denoted by $S = w_1 w_2 \ldots w_N$ and w_n is the target token where $n \in 1, 2, \ldots N$. Let P_3 denote the trigram language model probability then,

$$FragScore3(w_n) = log_{10} P_3(w_j \ldots w_n \ldots w_k)$$

$$FragScore5(w_n) = log_{10} P_3(w_r \ldots w_n \ldots w_t)$$

where $j = max(1, n-3)$, $k = min(N, n+3)$, $r = max(1, n-5)$ and $t = min(N, n+5)$.

We use an n-gram language model to calculate the conditional probability of a word given the preceding n-1 words. In particular, two features corresponding to the average conditional probabilities (AvgCondP3,AvgCondP2) have been extracted using the aforementioned trigram language model and a bigram model trained on Google's Trillion Word Corpus[7]. For words near the sentence boundary, the average is adjusted accordingly. If P_2 denotes the bigram language model probability then,

$$AvgCondP3(w_n) = \frac{1}{3} \sum_{k=n}^{n+2} P_3(w_k \mid w_{k-1}, w_{k-2})$$

$$AvgCondP2(w_n) = \frac{1}{2} \sum_{k=n}^{n+1} P_2(w_k \mid w_{k-1})$$

Sentences with higher perplexity have uncommon word sequences which may require more time to comprehend. Perplexity of the sentence calculated using tri-gram language model is also considered as a feature (Perplexity).

$$Perplexity(S) = \sqrt[N]{1/P_3(w_1 w_2 \ldots w_N)}$$

4 Description of Algorithms

Experiments were conducted using the following machine learning regression algorithms:

- Partial Least Square Regression (PLS): This method aims at fitting a linear regression model by projecting the dependent and independent variables into a new space.
- Neural Network (NN): NN based regression method aims at predicting the value of the dependent variable as a function of input variables via a collection of interconnected nodes.
- Decision Tree (DT): The regression model is built in the form of a tree structure by breaking the dataset into smaller subsets.
- Random Forest (RF): RF regressor fits a multitude of decision trees on various sub-samples of the dataset, and uses averaging to improve accuracy and control over-fitting.
- XGBoost (XG) : Here, weakly learned decision trees are turned into strong learners by training upon residuals instead of aggregation (Chen and Guestrin, 2016).
- Light Gradient Boosting Machine (LG) : This method uses a histogram-based boosting algorthim which uses a specialised Gradient-based one-sided sampling of data points of large gradients (Ke et al., 2017).

[6] lm_giga_64k_nvp_3gram.zip

[7] http://norvig.com/ngrams/

- CatBoost (CB): This method takes advantage of the categorical features which are otherwise converted to numerical features in traditional gradient boosting algorithms. CB uses oblivious trees as base predictors which uses same splitting criterior accross the entire level of the tree, and hence are less prone to overfitting (Prokhorenkova et al., 2018).

Since five target Eye-Tracking metrics had to be predicted, Multioutput (MO) and Regressor Chain (RC) algorithms were deployed using sklearn.

5 Experimental Details

The input tokens containing only punctuations were removed. The Eye-Tracking feature for token '&' is assigned a fixed value [8]. For all other punctuation tokens, the assigned Eye-Tracking feature value is 0. SpaCy[9] is used for POS tagging, lemmatization, dependency parsing and NER. Stopword feature, Corpus features and Frequency features as described in Section 3.2 were extracted after lower casing and lemmatizing the input token. For RC the order is tuned between the 120 possibilities and the *max_depth* denoted as d, is tuned between 1 to 15. For NN the number of intermediate dense layers is tuned between 1 to 4, the layer dimension is tuned between {10, 25, 50, 100, 150, 200, 250, 300, 500} and dropouts is tuned randomly between 0 to 1. ReLU activation function is used in the intermediate dense layers, batch size is set to 32, learning rate is set to 0.005, and MAE is minimized using Adam optimizer (Kingma and Ba, 2015).

6 Results

The individual MAE for the five predicted features along with overall MAE for various regression techniques are reported in Table 3. For NN, two dense layers with dimension 100 and 200, respectively and corresponding dropouts 0.13 and 0.02, respectively were used. In the present work, CB outperforms other regression algorithms. This can be attributed to the permutation-driven ordered boosting technique of CB and effective use of categorical features. It can be observed that CB+MO performed the best on the Test Dataset. CB+RC with order (0,4,1,2,3) improved the performance for the Trial Dataset however, it did not have the same effect for the Test Data. The MAE of the proposed system is within 0.14 of the top performer.

[8] mean of Eye-Tracking values of '&' in the training set

[9] https://spacy.io/

7 Analysis

System predictions are presented in Table 4. The model had the highest MAE for the token $< 824, 16 >$ which contained alphanumeric characters because the features failed to capture its properties. For the token $< 900, 9 >$, the gold labels are 0, but the system predicts positive values. The true gaze features nF, GP, and TR for multi-hyphenated and repeated token, viz. $< 874, 20 >$ is found to be higher than the predicted values. However, the prediction of the system for the tokens $< 951, 5 >$ and $< 976, 26 >$ are close to the true values. The MAE for the token '*with*' in sentence 828 is very low while in sentence 933, it is very high. This is because there is large variation in the true Eye-Tracking values while the variation is low in the predicted values.

To analyze the importance of each feature, the corresponding feature is eliminated and the CB+MO model is trained on the reduced feature space. It was observed that elimination of each individual feature increased the error and thus, each feature plays an important role in the overall performance of the system. The MAE on the Trial Set corresponding to individual features are reported in Table 5. The feature *Relpos*, which indicates the relative position of token in the sentence, emerged as the most important feature.

8 Conclusion and Future Work

Automatic prediction of Gaze features without human intervention is important for scalability of these features for tasks involving large datasets. The Shared Task aims at prediction of five Eye-Tracking features for each token of a given sentence. In the present work, a set of linguistic features focused on representing the shallow lexical characteristics of the token, rarity of the token, and interaction and collocation of the target token with its context are extracted. CB+MO regressor trained on the above feature space secured fourth rank on the Shared Task. Error analysis indicates that there is high variation of Eye-Tracking features for the same words in different contexts. However, the proposed system does not capture this variation. In future we would like to incorporate more features in order to represent the context of the target token more effectively.

		Trial						Test					
Technique	d	nF	FF	GP	TR	fxP	MAE	nF	FF	GP	TR	fxP	MAE
CB+RC (0,4,1,2,3)	6	3.92	0.64	2.25	1.49	10.7	**3.79**	4.04	0.68	2.27	1.56	11.3	3.98
CB+MO	6	3.92	0.63	2.27	1.51	10.7	3.81	4.04	0.67	2.25	1.57	11.2	**3.95**
RF+MO	11	4.03	0.64	2.41	1.56	10.9	3.90	4.21	0.69	2.37	1.64	11.4	4.06
LG+MO		4.04	0.64	2.43	1.56	10.8	3.90	4.10	0.67	2.35	1.59	11.2	3.99
XG+ MO		4.05	0.65	2.40	1.57	10.9	3.92	4.21	0.69	2.40	1.63	11.5	4.09
DT+MO	7	4.32	0.68	2.58	1.70	11.6	4.18	4.51	0.73	2.53	1.78	12.3	4.37
NN		4.65	0.75	2.55	1.77	12.9	4.52	4.90	0.78	2.65	1.89	13.9	4.82
PLS+MO		4.79	0.73	3.10	1.85	13.2	4.74	4.95	0.78	3.21	1.93	13.8	4.93

Table 3: Mean Absolute Error values

		Predicted					Gold					
id	word	nF	FF	GP	TR	fxP	nF	FF	GP	TR	fxP	MAE
$< 824, 16 >$	111Senator	24.9	4.1	8.7	8.2	88.3	97.7	5.8	33.4	41.1	100	28.8
$< 900, 9 >$	counts.<EOS>	13.6	3.7	16.5	5.3	71.3	0.0	0.0	0.0	0.0	0.0	22.1
$< 874, 20 >$	great-great-great-great-great	37.8	4.7	17.2	14.8	96.1	86.1	3.8	30.8	31.1	89.7	17.1
$< 951, 5 >$	side-splittingly	42.5	4.9	12.1	15.3	99.8	42.5	4.3	14.3	14.8	100	0.69
$< 976, 26 >$	Rice's	17.8	4.0	6.4	6.5	83.4	17.2	4.4	6.4	6.4	83.3	0.23
$< 828, 9 >$	with	10.6	2.4	3.2	3.2	56.7	10.3	2.1	3.2	2.7	58.3	0.55
$< 933, 5 >$	with	11.0	2.5	3.4	3.5	58.3	14.9	3.2	7.0	5.1	75.0	5.31

Table 4: System predictions

Feature Group	Feature Space	MAE	Feature Group	Feature Space	MAE
	w/o Nlets	3.8474		w/o IsStopword	3.8158
	w/o Nvow	3.8169		w/o InGoogle	3.8190
	w/o Nsyl	3.8264		w/o InOgden	3.8177
	w/o Nphon	3.8231		w/o OgdenFreq	3.8256
	w/o Nmorph	3.8255		w/o ECFreq	3.8173
	w/o PerUp	3.8206	Familiarity	w/o SUBTFreq	3.8161
	w/o IsNamed	3.8180		w/o ConDiversity	3.8154
Shallow Lexical	w/o EtyOrig	3.8214		w/o TLFreq	3.8118
	w/o IsLast	3.8243		w/o BrownFreq	3.8160
	w/o IsNumber	3.8209		w/o CharProb2	3.8203
	w/o Hyphen	3.8261		w/o CharProb3	3.8236
	w/o IsPossesive	3.8176		w/o UniTag	3.8112
	w/o StartPunct	3.8183		w/o PennTag	3.8186
	w/o LenSent	3.8388		w/o NSyn	3.8194
	w/o RelPos	**3.8725**		w/o Nhypo	3.8201
	w/o FragScore3	3.8166	Context	w/o Nhyper	3.8233
	w/o FragScore5	3.8313		w/o DepTag	3.8206
Language Model	w/o AvgCondP2	3.8263		w/o HeadPOS	3.8192
	w/o AvgCondP3	3.8190		w/o TokDepth	3.8247
	w/o Perplexity	3.8169		w/o NChild	3.8178

Table 5: MAE scores for individual feature elimination

Acknowledgements

Raksha Agarwal acknowledges Council of Scientific and Industrial Research (CSIR), India for supporting the research under Grant no: SPM-06/086(0267)/2018-EMR-I. The authors thank Kushagri Tandon and Shivani Choudhary for helpful discussions.

References

Maria Barrett, Joachim Bingel, Frank Keller, and Anders Søgaard. 2016. Weakly supervised part-of-speech tagging using eye-tracking data. In *Proceedings of the 54th Annual Meeting of the Association for Computational Linguistics (Volume 2: Short Papers)*, pages 579–584, Berlin, Germany. Association for Computational Linguistics.

Maria Barrett and Nora Hollenstein. 2020. Sequence labelling and sequence classification with gaze: Novel uses of eye-tracking data for natural language processing. *Language and Linguistics Compass*, 14(11):1–16.

Gordon DA Brown. 1984. A frequency count of 190,000 words in the london-lund corpus of english conversation. *Behavior Research Methods, Instruments, & Computers*, 16(6):502–532.

Tianqi Chen and Carlos Guestrin. 2016. Xgboost: A scalable tree boosting system. In *Proceedings of the 22nd ACM SIGKDD International Conference on Knowledge Discovery and Data Mining*, KDD '16, page 785–794, New York, NY, USA. Association for Computing Machinery.

Nora Hollenstein, Emmanuele Chersoni, Cassandra Jacobs, Yohei Oseki, Laurent Prévot, and Enrico Santus. 2021. CMCL 2021 shared task on eye-tracking prediction. In *Proceedings of the Workshop on Cognitive Modeling and Computational Linguistics*.

Nora Hollenstein, Jonathan Rotsztejn, Marius Troendle, Andreas Pedroni, Ce Zhang, and Nicolas Langer. 2018. Zuco, a simultaneous eeg and eye-tracking resource for natural sentence reading. *Scientific data*, 5(1):1–13.

Nora Hollenstein, Marius Troendle, Ce Zhang, and Nicolas Langer. 2020. ZuCo 2.0: A dataset of physiological recordings during natural reading and annotation. In *Proceedings of the 12th Language Resources and Evaluation Conference*, pages 138–146, Marseille, France. European Language Resources Association.

Guolin Ke, Qi Meng, Thomas Finley, Taifeng Wang, Wei Chen, Weidong Ma, Qiwei Ye, and Tie-Yan Liu. 2017. Lightgbm: A highly efficient gradient boosting decision tree. In *Advances in Neural Information Processing Systems*, volume 30. Curran Associates, Inc.

Diederik P. Kingma and Jimmy Ba. 2015. Adam: A method for stochastic optimization. In *3rd International Conference on Learning Representations, ICLR 2015, San Diego, CA, USA, May 7-9, 2015, Conference Track Proceedings*.

Sigrid Klerke, Yoav Goldberg, and Anders Søgaard. 2016. Improving sentence compression by learning to predict gaze. In *Proceedings of the 2016 Conference of the North American Chapter of the Association for Computational Linguistics: Human Language Technologies*, pages 1528–1533, San Diego, California. Association for Computational Linguistics.

Abhijit Mishra, Kuntal Dey, and Pushpak Bhattacharyya. 2017. Learning cognitive features from gaze data for sentiment and sarcasm classification using convolutional neural network. In *Proceedings of the 55th Annual Meeting of the Association for Computational Linguistics (Volume 1: Long Papers)*, pages 377–387, Vancouver, Canada. Association for Computational Linguistics.

Abhijit Mishra, Srikanth Tamilselvam, Riddhiman Dasgupta, Seema Nagar, and Kuntal Dey. 2018. Cognition-cognizant sentiment analysis with multitask subjectivity summarization based on annotators' gaze behavior. *Proceedings of the AAAI Conference on Artificial Intelligence*, 32(1).

Liudmila Prokhorenkova, Gleb Gusev, Aleksandr Vorobev, Anna Veronika Dorogush, and Andrey Gulin. 2018. Catboost: unbiased boosting with categorical features. In *Advances in Neural Information Processing Systems*, volume 31. Curran Associates, Inc.

Edward Lee Thorndike and Irving Lorge. 1944. The teacher's word book of 30,000 words.

TorontoCL at CMCL 2021 Shared Task: RoBERTa with Multi-Stage Fine-Tuning for Eye-Tracking Prediction

Bai Li[1,2], **Frank Rudzicz**[1,2,3]
[1] University of Toronto, Department of Computer Science
[2] Vector Institute for Artificial Intelligence
[3] Unity Health Toronto
{bai, frank}@cs.toronto.edu

Abstract

Eye movement data during reading is a useful source of information for understanding language comprehension processes. In this paper, we describe our submission to the CMCL 2021 shared task on predicting human reading patterns. Our model uses RoBERTa with a regression layer to predict 5 eye-tracking features. We train the model in two stages: we first fine-tune on the Provo corpus (another eye-tracking dataset), then fine-tune on the task data. We compare different Transformer models and apply ensembling methods to improve the performance. Our final submission achieves a MAE score of 3.929, ranking 3rd place out of 13 teams that participated in this shared task.

1 Introduction

Eye-tracking data provides precise records of where humans look during reading, with millisecond-level accuracy. This type of data has recently been leveraged for uses in natural language processing: it can improve performance on a variety of downstream tasks, such as part-of-speech tagging (Barrett et al., 2016), dependency parsing (Strzyz et al., 2019), and for cognitively-inspired evaluation methods for word embeddings (Søgaard, 2016). Meanwhile, Transformer-based language models such as BERT (Devlin et al., 2019) and RoBERTa (Liu et al., 2019) have been applied to achieve state-of-the-art performance on many natural language tasks. The CMCL 2021 shared task aims to add to our understanding of how language models can relate to eye movement features.

In this paper, we present our submission to this shared task, which achieves third place on the leaderboard. We first explore some simple baselines using token-level features, and find that these are already somewhat competitive with the final model's performance. Next, we describe our model architecture, which is based on RoBERTa (Figure 1). We find that model ensembling offers a substantial performance gain over a single model. Finally, we augment the provided training data with the publicly available Provo eye-tracking corpus and combine them using a two-stage fine-tuning procedure; this results in a moderate performance gain. Our source code is available at https://github.com/SPOClab-ca/cmcl-shared-task.

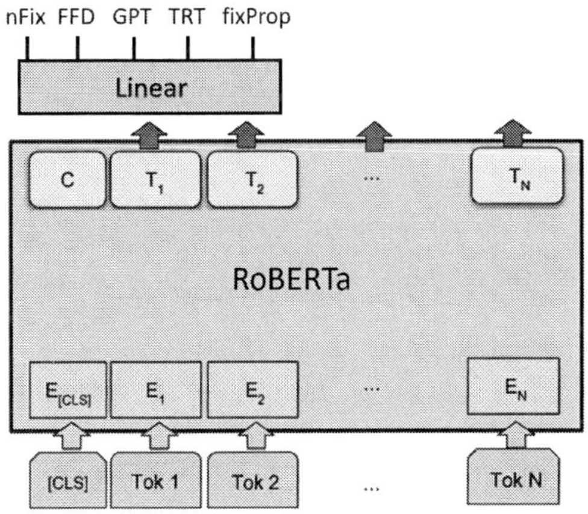

Figure 1: Our model consists of RoBERTa with a regression head on each token, which is a linear layer that predicts the 5 output features from the last layer's embeddings. The model is initialized from pretrained weights and fine-tuned on the task data.

2 Task Description

The shared task format is described in Hollenstein et al. (2021), which we will briefly summarize here. The task data consists of sentences derived from the ZuCo 1.0 and ZuCo 2.0 datasets; 800 sentences (15.7 tokens) were provided as training data and 191 sentences (3.5k tokens) were held out for evaluation. The objective is to predict five eye-tracking features for each token:

- Number of fixations on the current word (*nFix*).

Proceedings of the Workshop on Cognitive Modeling and Computational Linguistics, pages 85–89
Online Event, June 10, 2021.

Model	nFix	FFD	GPT	TRT	fixProp	All (Dev)
Median	7.208	1.162	3.547	2.732	21.179	7.165
Linear regression	4.590	0.795	2.995	1.812	13.552	4.749
SVR (RBF kernel)	4.440	0.723	2.728	1.728	12.077	4.339

Table 1: Baseline results: 'Median' is a model that always predicts the median of the training data; the linear regression and SVR models use 4 token-level surface features described in Section 3.1.

Model	nFix	FFD	GPT	TRT	fixProp	All (Dev)
BERT-base	4.289	0.704	2.645	1.678	11.155	4.094
BERT-large	4.150	0.682	2.493	1.616	11.013	3.991
RoBERTa-base	**4.066**	**0.681**	**2.443**	**1.570**	**10.981**	**3.930**
RoBERTa-large	4.156	0.681	2.468	1.623	11.047	3.995

Table 2: MAE using BERT and RoBERTa models with fine-tuning.

- First fixation duration of the word (*FFD*).
- Go-past time: the time from the first fixation of a word until the first fixation beyond it (*GPT*).
- Total reading time of all fixations of the word, including regressions (*TRT*).
- Proportion of participants that fixated on the word (*fixProp*).

The features are averages across multiple participants, and each feature is scaled to be in the range [0, 100]. The evaluation metric is the mean absolute error (MAE) between the predicted and ground truth values, with all features weighted equally.

Since each team is allowed only a small number of submissions, we define our own train and test split to compare our models' performance during development. We use the first 600 sentences as training data and the last 200 sentences for evaluation during development. Except for the submission results (Table 4), all experimental results reported in this paper are on this development train/test split.

3 Our Approach

3.1 Baselines

We start by implementing some simple baselines using token-level surface features. Previous research in eye tracking found that longer words and low-frequency words have higher probabilities of being fixated upon (Rayner, 1998). We extract the following features for each token:

- Length of token in characters.
- Log of the frequency of token in English text, retrieved using the `wordfreq`[1] library.
- Boolean of whether token contains any uppercase characters.
- Boolean of whether token contains any punctuation.

Using these features, we train linear regression and support vector regression models separately for each of the 5 output features (Table 1). Despite the simplicity of these features, which do not use any contextual information, they already perform much better than the median baseline. This indicates that much of the variance in all 5 eye-tracking features are explained by surface-level cues.

3.2 Fine-tuning Transformers

Our main model uses RoBERTa (Liu et al., 2019) with a linear feedforward layer to predict the 5 output features simultaneously from the last hidden layers of each token. In cases where the original token is split into multiple RoBERTa tokens, we use the first RoBERTa token to make the prediction. The model is initialized with pretrained weights and fine-tuned on the task data to minimize the sum of mean squared errors across all 5 features.

As the task data is relatively small, we found that the model needs to be fine-tuned for 100-150 epochs to reach optimal performance, far greater than the recommended 2-4 epochs (Devlin et al., 2019). We trained the model using the AdamW optimizer (Loshchilov and Hutter, 2018) with learning rates of {1e-5, 2e-5, 5e-5, 1e-4} and batch sizes of {8, 16, 32}; all other hyperparameters were left

[1] `https://github.com/LuminosoInsight/wordfreq/`

Model	nFix	FFD	GPT	TRT	fixProp	All (Dev)
Single Model	4.066	0.681	2.443	1.570	10.891	3.930
Ensemble of 2	3.978	0.671	2.350	1.534	10.714	3.849
Ensemble of 5	3.944	0.669	2.321	**1.521**	10.665	3.824
Ensemble of 10	**3.943**	**0.666**	**2.316**	1.522	**10.660**	**3.821**

Table 3: Ensembles of RoBERTa-base model, obtained by taking a simple mean of the predictions of individual models. This improves our overall performance by about 0.09 MAE compared to a single model, but with diminishing returns past 5 models.

Training Data	nFix	FFD	GPT	TRT	fixProp	All (Dev)	Submission
Task Only (Single)	4.066	0.681	2.443	1.570	10.891	3.930	n/a
Provo + Task (Single)	3.984	0.713	2.424	1.556	10.781	3.892	n/a
Task Only (Ensemble)	3.943	0.666	2.316	1.522	10.660	3.821	3.974
Provo + Task (ensemble)	**3.888**	**0.664**	**2.306**	**1.499**	**10.586**	**3.789**	**3.929**

Table 4: Comparison of model trained using the provided versus two-stage fine-tuning using Provo data. The additional pretraining improved overall performance by about 0.04 MAE. Our best submission is an ensemble of 10 RoBERTa-base models with two-stage fine-tuning.

at their default settings using the HuggingFace library (Wolf et al., 2020).

In addition to RoBERTa, we experiment with BERT (Devlin et al., 2019); we try both the base and large versions of BERT and RoBERTa, using a similar range of hyperparameters for each (Table 2). RoBERTa-base performed the best in our validation experiments; surprisingly, RoBERTa-large had worse performance.

3.3 Model Ensembling

We use a simple approach to ensembling: we train multiple versions of an identical model using different random seeds and make predictions on the test data. These predictions are the averaged to obtain the final submission. In our experiments (Table 3), ensembling greatly improves our performance, but with diminishing returns: the MAE of the 10-model ensemble is only marginally better than the 5-model ensemble. We use ensembles of 10 models in our final submission.

3.4 Domain Adaptation from Provo

In addition to the task data provided, we also use data from the Provo corpus (Luke and Christianson, 2018). This corpus contains eye-tracking data from 84 participants reading 2.6k words from a variety of text sources. The corpus also provides predictability norms and extracted syntactic and semantic features for each word, which we do not use.

We process the Provo data to be similar to the task data so that they can be combined. First, we identify the Provo features that are most similar to each of the output features: we map *IA_FIXATION_COUNT* to *nFix*, *IA_FIRST_FIXATION_DURATION* to *FFD*, *IA_REGRESSION_PATH_DURATION* to *GPT*, and *IA_DWELL_TIME* to *TRT*, taking the mean across all participants for each feature. For the *fixProp* feature, we calculate the proportion of participants where $IA\_DWELL\_TIME > 0$ for each word. Finally, we scale all five features to have the same mean and standard deviation as the task data, and verify that their distributions and pairwise scatterplots are similar (Figure 2).

We use two-stage fine-tuning to combine the Provo data with the task data. In two-stage fine-tuning, the entire model is fine-tuned on an auxiliary task before fine-tuning on the target task – this often yields a performance improvement, especially when the target task has a small amount of data (Pruksachatkun et al., 2020). In our case, we fine-tune the RoBERTa-base model for 100 epochs on the Provo data, then fine-tune for another 150 epochs on the task data. This gave a considerable improvement on both the development and submission scores (Table 4). Our best final submission is an ensemble of 10 identical models trained this way with different random seeds.

4 Conclusion and Future Work

We propose a simple approach to predict eye-tracking features using the RoBERTa model cus-

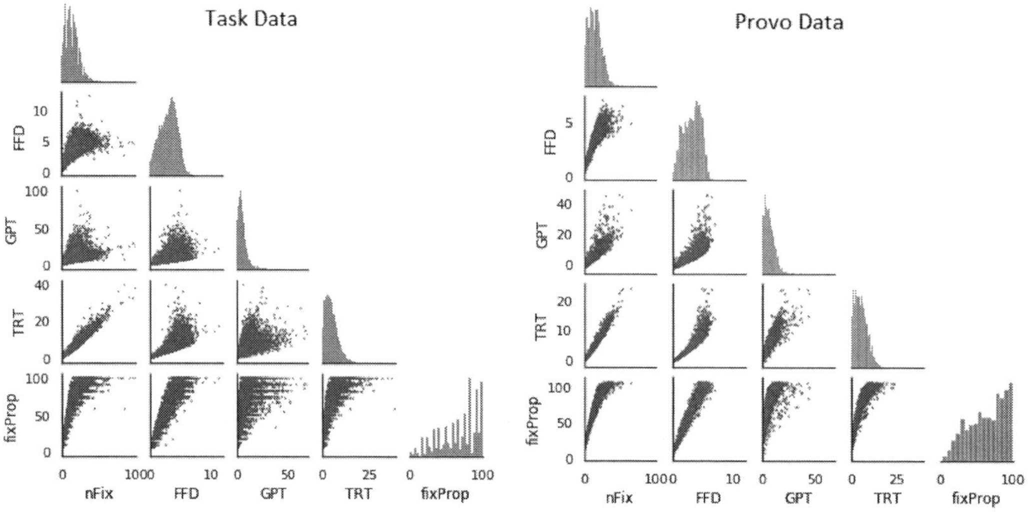

Figure 2: Distributions and pairwise scatterplots of the task data (left) and Provo data processed to match the mean and standard deviation of the task data (right).

tomized with a per-token regression head. Our initial model uses the standard fine-tuning procedure; experiments show that the performance is further improved by model ensembling and domain adaptation by two-stage fine-tuning on an intermediate eye-tracking task. Our best model achieves third place on the leaderboard.

In future work, several avenues may be explored to further improve performance. First, we did not combine our feature engineering baseline with the RoBERTa model – engineered features (such as frequency statistics or neurolinguistic norms) would provide the model with information not contained in RoBERTa. Second, we only experimented with a small subset of features from the Provo corpus for domain adaptation, whereas it is not actually necessary for the auxiliary fine-tuning task to match the target task. Thus, it may be possible to achieve better performance by fine-tuning on a different set of Provo features, or a different dataset entirely.

Acknowledgements

We thank Dr Jeanne Sinclair for her helpful discussions during this project. FR is supported by a CIFAR Chair in Artificial Intelligence.

References

Maria Barrett, Joachim Bingel, Frank Keller, and Anders Søgaard. 2016. Weakly supervised part-of-speech tagging using eye-tracking data. In *Proceedings of the 54th Annual Meeting of the Association for Computational Linguistics (Volume 2: Short Papers)*, pages 579–584.

Jacob Devlin, Ming-Wei Chang, Kenton Lee, and Kristina Toutanova. 2019. BERT: Pre-training of deep bidirectional transformers for language understanding. In *Proceedings of the 2019 Conference of the North American Chapter of the Association for Computational Linguistics: Human Language Technologies, Volume 1 (Long and Short Papers)*, pages 4171–4186.

Nora Hollenstein, Emmanuele Chersoni, Cassandra Jacobs, Yohei Oseki, Laurent Prévot, and Enrico Santus. 2021. CMCL 2021 shared task on eye-tracking prediction. In *Proceedings of the Workshop on Cognitive Modeling and Computational Linguistics*.

Yinhan Liu, Myle Ott, Naman Goyal, Jingfei Du, Mandar Joshi, Danqi Chen, Omer Levy, Mike Lewis, Luke Zettlemoyer, and Veselin Stoyanov. 2019. RoBERTa: A robustly optimized BERT pretraining approach. *arXiv preprint arXiv:1907.11692*.

Ilya Loshchilov and Frank Hutter. 2018. Decoupled weight decay regularization. In *International Conference on Learning Representations*.

Steven G Luke and Kiel Christianson. 2018. The Provo corpus: A large eye-tracking corpus with predictability norms. *Behavior research methods*, 50(2):826–833.

Yada Pruksachatkun, Jason Phang, Haokun Liu, Phu Mon Htut, Xiaoyi Zhang, Richard Yuanzhe Pang, Clara Vania, Katharina Kann, and Samuel Bowman. 2020. Intermediate-task transfer learning with pretrained language models: When and why does it work? In *Proceedings of the 58th Annual*

Meeting of the Association for Computational Linguistics, pages 5231–5247.

Keith Rayner. 1998. Eye movements in reading and information processing: 20 years of research. *Psychological bulletin*, 124(3):372.

Anders Søgaard. 2016. Evaluating word embeddings with fMRI and eye-tracking. In *Proceedings of the 1st Workshop on Evaluating Vector-Space Representations for NLP*, pages 116–121.

Michalina Strzyz, David Vilares, and Carlos Gómez-Rodríguez. 2019. Towards making a dependency parser see. In *Proceedings of the 2019 Conference on Empirical Methods in Natural Language Processing and the 9th International Joint Conference on Natural Language Processing (EMNLP-IJCNLP)*, pages 1500–1506.

Thomas Wolf, Lysandre Debut, Victor Sanh, Julien Chaumond, Clement Delangue, Anthony Moi, Pierric Cistac, Tim Rault, Rémi Louf, Morgan Funtowicz, et al. 2020. Transformers: State-of-the-art natural language processing. In *Proceedings of the 2020 Conference on Empirical Methods in Natural Language Processing: System Demonstrations*, pages 38–45, Online. Association for Computational Linguistics.

LAST at CMCL 2021 Shared Task: Predicting Gaze Data During Reading with a Gradient Boosting Decision Tree Approach

Yves Bestgen
Laboratoire d'analyse statistique des textes - LAST
Institut de recherche en sciences psychologiques
Université catholique de Louvain
Place Cardinal Mercier, 10 1348 Louvain-la-Neuve, Belgium
yves.bestgen@uclouvain.be

Abstract

A LightGBM model fed with target word lexical characteristics and features obtained from word frequency lists, psychometric data and bigram association measures has been optimized for the 2021 CMCL Shared Task on Eye-Tracking Data Prediction. It obtained the best performance of all teams on two of the five eye-tracking measures to predict, allowing it to rank first on the official challenge criterion and to outperform all deep-learning based systems participating in the challenge.

1 Introduction

This paper describes the system proposed by the Laboratoire d'analyse statistique des textes (LAST) for the Cognitive Modeling and Computational Linguistics (CMCL) Shared Task on Eye-Tracking Data Prediction. This task is receiving more and more attention due to its importance in modeling human language understanding and improving NLP technology (Hollenstein et al., 2019; Mishra and Bhattacharyya, 2018).

As one of the objectives of the organizers is to "compare the capabilities of machine learning approaches to model and analyze human patterns of reading" (https://cmclorg.github.io/shared_task), I have chosen to adopt a generic point of view with the main objective of determining what level of performance can achieve a system derived from the one I developed to predict the lexical complexity of words and polylexical expressions (Shardlow et al., 2021). That system was made up of a gradient boosting decision tree prediction model fed with features obtained from word frequency lists, psychometric data, lexical norms and bigram association measures. If there is no doubt that predicting lexical complexity is a different problem, one can think that the features useful for it also play a role in predicting eye movement during reading.

The next section summarizes the main characteristics of the challenge. Then the developed system is described in detail. Finally, the results in the challenge are reported along with an analysis performed to get a better idea of the factors that affect the system performance.

2 Data and Task

The eye-tracking data for this shared task were extracted from the Zurich Cognitive Language Processing Corpus (ZuCo 1.0 and ZuCo 2.0, Hollenstein et al., 2018, 2020). It contains gaze data for 991 sentences read by 18 participants during a normal reading session. The learning set consisted in 800 sentences and the test set in 191 sentences.

The task was to predict five eye-tracking features, averaged across all participants and scaled in the range between 0 and 100, for each word of a series of sentences: (1) the total number of fixations (nFix), (2) the duration of the first fixation (FFD), (3) the sum of all fixation durations, including regressions (TRT), (4) the sum of the duration of all fixations prior to progressing to the right, including regressions to previous words (GPT), and (5) the proportion of participants that fixated the word (fixProp). These dependent variables (DVs) are described in detail in Hollenstein et al. (2021). The submissions were evaluated using the mean absolute error (MAE) metric and the systems were ranked according to the average MAE across all five DVs, the lowest being the best.

As the DVs are of different natures (number, proportion and duration), their mean and variance are very different. The mean of fixProp is 21 times greater than that of FFD and its variance 335 times. Furthermore, while nFix and fixProp were scaled independently, FFD, GPT and TRT were scaled together. For that reason, the mean and dispersion of these three measures are quite different: FFD must necessarily be less than or equal to TRT and GPT[1].

[1]The relation between TRT and GPT is not obvious to me

Proceedings of the Workshop on Cognitive Modeling and Computational Linguistics, pages 90–96
Online Event, June 10, 2021. ©2021 Association for Computational Linguistics

These two factors strongly affect the importance of the different DVs in the final ranking.

3 System

3.1 Procedure to Build the Models

The regression models were built by the 2.2.1 version of the LightGBM software (Ke et al., 2017), a well-known implementation of the gradient boosting decision tree approach. This type of model has the advantage of not requiring feature preprocessing, such as a logarithmic transformation, since it is insensitive to monotonic transformations, and of including many parameters allowing a very efficient overfit control. It also has the advantage of being able to directly optimize the MAE.

Sentence preprocessing and feature extraction as well as the post-processing of the LightGBM predictions were performed using custom SAS programs running in SAS University (still freely available for research at `https://www.sas.com/en_us/software/university-edition.html`). Sentences were first lemmatized by the TreeTagger (Schmid, 1994) to get the lemma and POS-tag of each word. Special care was necessary to match the TreeTagger tokenization with the Zuco original one. Punctuation marks and other similar symbols (e.g., "(" or "$") were simply disregarded as they were always bound to a word in the tokens to predict. The attribution to the words of the values on the different lists was carried out in two stages: on the basis of the spelling form when it is found in the list or of the lemma if this is not the case.

The features used in the final models as well as the LightGBM parameters were optimized by a 5-fold cross validation procedure, using the sentence and not the token as the sampling unit. The number of boosting iterations was set by using the LightGBM early stopping procedure which stops training when the MAE on the validation fold does not improve in the last 200 rounds. The predicted values which were outside the [0, 100] interval were brought back in this one, which makes it possible to improve the MAE very slightly.

3.2 Features

To predict the five DVs, five different models were trained. The only differences between them were in the LightGBM parameters. There were thus all based on exactly the same features, which are described below.

since one can be larger or smaller than the other in a significant number of cases.

Target Word Length. The length in characters of the preceding word, the target word and the following one.

Target Word Position. The position of the word in the sentence encoded in two ways: the rank of the word going from 1 to the sentence total number of words and the ratio between the rank of the word and the total number of words.

Target Word POS-tag and Lemma. The POS-tag and lemma for the target word and the preceding one.

Corpus Frequency Features. Frequencies in corpora of words were either calculated from a corpus or extracted from lists provided by other researchers. The following seven features have been used:

- The (unlemmatized) word frequencies in the British National Corpus (BNC, `http://www.natcorp.ox.ac.uk/`).
- The Facebook frequency norms for American English and British English in Herdagdelen and Marelli (2017).
- The Rovereto Twitter Corpus frequency norms (Herdagdelen and Marelli, 2017).
- The USENET Orthographic Frequencies from Shaoul and Chris (2006).
- The Hyperspace Analogue to Language (HAL) frequency norms provided by (Balota et al., 2007) for more that 40,000 words.
- The frequency word list derived from Google's ngram corpora available at `https://github.com/hackerb9/gwordlist`.

Features from Lexical Norms. The lexical norms of Age of Acquisition and Familiarity were taken from the Glasgow Norms which contain judges' assessment of 5,553 English words (Scott et al., 2019).

Lexical Characteristics and Behavioral Measures from ELP. Twenty-three indices were extracted from the English Lexicon Project (ELP, Balota et al., 2007; Yarkoni et al., 2008), a database that contains, for more than 40,000 words, reaction time and accuracy during lexical decision and naming tasks, made by many participants, as well as lexical characteristics (`https://elexicon.wustl.edu/`). Eight indices come from the behavioral measures, four for each task: average response latencies (raw and standardized), standard deviations, and accuracies. Fourteen indices come from the "Orthographic, Phonological, Phonographic, and Levenshtein Neighborhood Metrics" section of the dataset. These are all the metrics provided except Freq_Greater, Freq_G_Mean, Freq_Less, Freq_L_Mean, and Freq_Rel. These are variables whose initial analyzes showed that they were redundant with those selected. The last feature is the average bigram count of a word.

Bigram Association Measures. These features indicate the degree of association between the target word and the one that precedes it according to a series of indices calculated on the basis of the frequency in a reference corpus (i.e., the BNC) of the bigram and that of the two words that compose it, using the following association measures (AMs): pointwise mutual information and t-score (Church and Hanks, 1990), z-score (Berry-Rogghe, 1973), log-likelihood Chi-square test (Dunning, 1993), simple-ll (Evert, 2009), Dice coefficient (Kilgarriff et al., 2014) and the two delta-p (Kyle et al., 2018). Most of the formulas to compute these AMs are also provided in Evert (2009) and in Pecina (2010). As these features mix together the assets of both collocations (by using association scores) and ngrams (by using contiguous pairs of words), Bestgen and Granger (2014) refer to them as *collgrams*. They make it possible not to rely exclusively on the frequency of the bigram in the corpus, which can be misleading because a bigram may be observed frequently, not because of its phraseological nature, but because it is made up of very frequent words (Bestgen, 2018). Conversely, a relatively rare bigram, composed of rare words, may be typical of the language. Since word frequency is already accounted for by the corpus frequency features, it was desirable to employ indices that reduce the impact of this factor. Originating in works in lexicography and foreign language learning (Church and Hanks, 1990; Durrant and Schmitt, 2009; Bestgen, 2017, 2019), they have recently shown their usefulness in predicting the lexical complexity of multi-word expressions (Bestgen, 2021). In the present case, it is assumed that these indices can serve as a proxy of the next word predictability (Kliegl et al., 2004).

Parameters	Run 1	Run 2
bagging_fraction	0.66	0.70
bagging_freq	5	5
feature_fraction	0.09	0.85
learning_rate	0.0095	0.0050
max_depth	11	no limit
max_bin	64	64
min_data_in_bin	2	5
max_leaves	11	30
min_data_in_leaf	7	5
n_iter	4800	(see text)

Table 1: LightGBM parameters for the first two runs.

Feature coverage. Some words to predict are not present in these lists and the corresponding score is thus missing. Based on the complete dataset provided by the organizers, it happens in:

- 1% (Google ngram) to 17% (Facebook and Twitter) of the tokens for the corpus frequency features,
- 9% for the ELP Lexical Characteristics, but a few features have as much as 41% missing values,
- 11% for the ELP Behavioral Measures,
- 18% for the Bigram AMs.

In total, sixteen tokens have missing values for all these features (Corpus Frequency, Lexical Characteristics and Behavioral Measures from ELP, and Bigram Association Measures). These tokens have however received values for the length and position features. All the missing values were handled by LightGBM default procedure.

4 Analyses and Results

4.1 Models Submitted to the Challenge

During the test phase, teams were allowed to submit three runs. My three submissions were all based on the features described above, the only differences between them resulting from changes in the LigthGBM parameters. They were set at their default values except those shown in Table 1. The official performances of the top five challenge submissions are given in Table 2.

Team	Run	Mean	nFix	FFD	GPT	TRT	fixProp
LAST	3	**3.8134**	3.879	**0.655**	2.197	1.524	**10.812**
LAST	2	3.8159	3.886	0.655	2.199	1.523	10.817
TALEP	1	3.8328	**3.761**	0.662	**2.180**	**1.486**	11.076
LAST	1	3.8664	3.943	0.662	2.237	1.545	10.944
TorontoCL	2	3.9287	3.944	0.671	2.227	1.516	11.286

Table 2: Performance (MAE) for the five best runs submitted to the challenge. Best scores are bolded.

The first submission was based on the parameters selected during the development phase. They were identical for the five DVs. For the other two submissions, a random grid search coded in python was used to try optimizing the parameters independently for each DV. The parameter space for this first random search is provided in Appendix A. As the measure of the challenge is the MAE averaged across the five DVs and as the system MAE for fixProp was up to 15 times higher than that of the other DVs, the optimized parameters for this variable were selected. Additional analyzes showed that they also made it possible to improve performance on the four other DVs. Their values are given in Table 1. Certain initial choices were only slightly modified. The value of other parameters such as the maximum number of leaves and the feature fraction were markedly increased, suggesting that the risk of overfit was relatively low (see `https://lightgbm.readthedocs.io/en/latest/Parameters-Tuning.html`). In this system, the number of iterations was optimized (thanks to the early stopping procedure) for each DV and sets at the fourth highest value: 3,740 for nFix, 3,829 for TRT, 2,861 for GPT, 3,497 for FFD, and 3,305 for fixProp.

For the third submission, a new round of random optimization was conducted by evaluating parameter values close to those selected for Run 2, independently for each DV. As it only got slightly better performance than Run 2, these parameter values are not shown to save space.

As shown in Table 2, Runs 2 and 3 ranked at the first 2 places of the challenge. This result was largely due to their better performance for fixProp since the TALEP system, second in the challenge, achieved significantly better performance for three of the five DVs, but these have less impact on the official measurement. An analysis, carried out after the end of the challenge, showed that the system would not have been more effective (average MAE of 3.8138) if, during the first optimization step, a specific model for each DV had been selected.

Using Pearson's linear correlation coefficient as a measure of effectiveness, which is unaffected by the differences in means and variability between the five DVs, Run 3 obtains an average r of 0.812 on the test set (min = 0.792 for GPT; max = 0.838 for fixProp). This value is relatively high, but it can only really be interpreted by taking into account the reliability of the average real eye-tracking feature values.

4.2 Feature Usefulness

The first part of Table 3 presents the main results of an ablation procedure aimed at examining the impact of the different types of features on the system performance. It gives the average MAE as well as the difference in percentage between each system and the best run for the average MAE and for the five DVs. It must be first stressed that all features based on lemmas and POS-tag, the two Glasgow norms and the length of the token that follows the target are useless for predicting the test set since without them the system achieves a MAE of 3.8134. They are thus discarded in all the ablation analyses. The target's positions in the sentence and the length features are clearly essential. Among the features resulting from corpora and behavioral data, it is the bigram association measures and the frequencies in the corpora that are the most useful.

Generally speaking, the feature sets have comparable utility for all DVs. However, we observe that the position in the sentences is particularly important for predicting GPT while the length of the target is more useful for nFix.

The second part of Table 3 presents an analysis of the utility of optimizing the LightGBM parameters, based on the best system. Optimizing RMSE instead of MAE is especially penalizing for GPT. Using the default values of the LightGBM param-

Models	MAE	%MAE	%nFix	%FFD	%GPT	%TRT	%fixProp
W/o behavioral data	3.849	-0.93	**-0.69**	**-1.30**	-0.75	-0.78	-1.05
W/o ELP charact.	3.859	-1.19	**-0.54**	-1.36	-0.95	-0.59	**-1.55**
W/o frequencies	3.880	-1.74	**-1.38**	-1.68	**-1.88**	-1.55	-1.87
W/o bigram AM	3.881	-1.78	-2.05	**-2.32**	**-1.39**	-1.94	-1.70
W/o length feat.	3.979	-4.35	**-5.95**	**-2.92**	-3.17	-4.43	-4.08
W/o position feat.	4.095	-7.39	-7.68	-4.44	**-22.88**	-7.48	**-4.30**
RMSE optimization	3.847	-0.87	-0.43	**0.46**	**-4.73**	-0.09	-0.43
Default Param + MAE	3.902	-2.32	-2.34	**-1.54**	**-3.52**	-2.12	-2.15
Default Param + RMSE	4.141	-8.59	-7.67	-7.65	**-12.62**	**-7.43**	-8.31
Linear Regression	4.268	-10.64	-9.04	**-7.88**	**-24.09**	-9.47	-8.26
LGBM on Length + Position	4.219	-10.63	-10.7	-11.4	**-8.18**	**-12.1**	-10.85

Table 3: Performance (MAE) of different system versions and deviation (%) from the best run ($MAE = 3.813$). Minimum and maximum values across DVs for each row are bolded.

eters is particularly penalizing when RMSE is the criterion.

A final question concerns the benefits of employing LightGBM instead of another regression algorithm when the proposed features are used. To try to provide at least a partial answer, I trained a multiple linear regression model on the basis of the features used, while adding for each feature, for which the calculation was possible, a second feature containing the logarithm of the initial value. I replaced the missing data with 0, which is probably not optimal. A stepwise regression procedure with a threshold to enter sets at $p = 0.01$ and a threshold to exit sets at $p = 0.05$ was employed to construct for each DV a model on the learning set and apply it to the test set. The results obtained are given in the second to last row of Table 3. The performances are clearly less good. It is even worse than the performance level of a LightGBM model based only on the length and position features (see the last row of Table 3). This regression system would have been ranked 10th in the challenge.

5 Conclusion

The system proposed for the 2021 CMCL Shared Task on Eye-Tracking Data Prediction was particularly effective, obtaining the first place in the challenge, but it must be kept in mind that the system that came second is superior to it for three of the five DVs. The analyzes carried out to understand its pros and cons indicate that optimizing the LightGBM parameters is quite beneficial to it as well as the different sets of features derived from corpora and behavioral data, including bigram AMs which, to my knowledge, have never been employed for this type of task.

It would have been interesting to relate these observations to the psycholinguistic literature on the factors that influence eye fixations, but this is unfortunately not possible here, for lack of space. In addition, this would first require deepening the ablation analyzes by simultaneously considering several feature sets. For instance, the lack of usefulness of the POS-tags could simply result from the links (at least partial) between them and the frequency and length of the tokens. Likewise, some of the bigram AMs are relatively sensitive to the frequency of the words that compose them (e.g., the t-score favors frequent bigrams which are usually composed of frequent words). It is thus highly probable that some of the features in the different sets (frequencies, behavioral data...) are redundant and can be removed without impairing the performance of the system. This is a potential development path.

Acknowledgements

The author wishes to thank the organizers of this shared task for putting together this valuable event and the reviewers for their very constructive comments. He is a Research Associate of the Fonds de la Recherche Scientifique - FNRS (Fédération Wallonie Bruxelles de Belgique). Computational resources were provided by the supercomputing facilities of the UCLouvain (CISM/UCL) and the Consortium des Equipements de Calcul Intensif en Fédération Wallonie Bruxelles (CECI).

References

David A. Balota, Melvin J. Yap, Keith A. Hutchison, Michael J. Cortese, Brett Kessler, Bjorn Loftis, James H. Neely, Douglas L. Nelson, Greg B. Simpson, and Rebecca Treiman. 2007. The English lexicon project. *Behavior Research Methods*, 39:445–459.

Godelieve L. M. Berry-Rogghe. 1973. The computation of collocations and their relevance in lexical studies. In Adam J Aitken, Richard W. Bailey, and Neil Hamilton-Smith, editors, *The Computer and Literary Studies*. Edinburgh University Press.

Yves Bestgen. 2017. Beyond single-word measures: L2 writing assessment, lexical richness and formulaic competence. *System*, 69:65–78.

Yves Bestgen. 2018. Evaluating the frequency threshold for selecting lexical bundles by means of an extension of the Fisher's exact test. *Corpora*, 13:205–228.

Yves Bestgen. 2019. Evaluation de textes en anglais langue ètrangère et séries phraséologiques : comparaison de deux procédures automatiques librement accessibles. *Revue française de linguistique appliquée*, 24:81–94.

Yves Bestgen. 2021. LAST at SemEval-2021 Task 1: improving multi-word complexity prediction using bigram association measures. In *Proceedings of SemEval-2021*.

Yves Bestgen and Sylviane Granger. 2014. Quantifying the development of phraseological competence in L2 English writing: An automated approach. *Journal of Second Language Writing*, 26:28–41.

Kenneth Ward Church and Patrick Hanks. 1990. Word association norms, mutual information, and lexicography. *Computational Linguistics*, 16(1):22–29.

Ted Dunning. 1993. Accurate methods for the statistics of surprise and coincidence. *Computational Linguistics*, 19(1):61–74.

Philip Durrant and Norbert Schmitt. 2009. To what extent do native and non-native writers make use of collocations? *International Review of Applied Linguistics in Language Teaching*, 47:157–177.

Stefan Evert. 2009. Corpora and collocations. In Anke Lüdeling and Merja Kytö, editors, *Corpus Linguistics. An International Handbook*, pages 1211–1248. Mouton de Gruyter.

Amac Herdagdelen and Marco Marelli. 2017. Social media and language processing: How Facebook and Twitter provide the best frequency estimates for studying word recognition. *Cognitive Science*, 41:976–995.

Nora Hollenstein, Emmanuele Chersoni, Cassandra Jacobs, Yohei Oseki, Laurent Prévot, and Enrico Santus. 2021. CMCL 2021 shared task on eye-tracking prediction. In *Proceedings of the Workshop on Cognitive Modeling and Computational Linguistics*.

Nora Hollenstein, Antonio de la Torre, Nicolas Langer, and Ce Zhang. 2019. CogniVal: A framework for cognitive word embedding evaluation. In *Proceedings of the 23rd Conference on Computational Natural Language Learning (CoNLL)*, pages 538–549, Hong Kong, China. Association for Computational Linguistics.

Nora Hollenstein, Jonathan Rotsztejn, Marius Troendle, Andreas Pedroni, Ce Zhang, and Nicolas Langer. 2018. ZuCo, a simultaneous EEG and eye-tracking resource for natural sentence reading. *Scientific Data. 5:180291*, 5(180291):1–13.

Nora Hollenstein, Marius Troendle, Ce Zhang, and Nicolas Langer. 2020. ZuCo 2.0: A dataset of physiological recordings during natural reading and annotation. In *Proceedings of The 12th Language Resources and Evaluation Conference, LREC 2020, Marseille, France, May 11-16, 2020*, pages 138–146. European Language Resources Association.

Guolin Ke, Qi Meng, Thomas Finley, Taifeng Wang, Wei Chen, Weidong Ma, Qiwei Ye, and Tie-Yan Liu. 2017. LightGBM: A highly efficient gradient boosting decision tree. In I. Guyon, U. V. Luxburg, S. Bengio, H. Wallach, R. Fergus, S. Vishwanathan, and R. Garnett, editors, *Advances in Neural Information Processing Systems 30*, pages 3146–3154. Curran Associates, Inc.

Adam Kilgarriff, Vít Baisa, Jan Bušta, Miloš Jakubíček, Vojtěch Kovář, Jan Michelfeit, Pavel Rychlý, and Vít Suchomel. 2014. The Sketch Engine: ten years on. *Lexicography*, 1(1):7–36.

Reinhold Kliegl, Ellen Grabner, Martin Rolfs, and Ralf Engbert. 2004. Length, frequency, and predictability effects of words on eye movements in reading. *European Journal of Cognitive Psychology*, 16:262–284.

Kristopher Kyle, Scott Crossley, and Cynthia Berger. 2018. The tool for the automatic analysis of lexical sophistication (TAALES): version 2.0. *Behavior Research Methods*, 50:1030–1046.

Abhijit Mishra and Pushpak Bhattacharyya. 2018. *Applications of Eye Tracking in Language Processing and Other Areas*, pages 23–46. Springer Singapore, Singapore.

Pavel Pecina. 2010. Lexical association measures and collocation extraction. *Language Resources & Evaluation*, 44:137–158.

Helmutt Schmid. 1994. Probabilistic part-of-speech tagging using decision trees. In *International Conference on New Methods in Language Processing*, pages 44–49.

Graham G. Scott, Anne Keitel, Marc Becirspahic, Bo Yao, and Sara C. Sereno. 2019. The Glasgow norms: Ratings of 5,500 words on nine scales. *Behavior Research Methods*, 51:1258–1270.

Cyrus Shaoul and Westbury Chris. 2006. USENET orthographic frequencies for 111,627 English words.

Matthew Shardlow, Richard Evans, Gustavo Paetzold, and Marcos Zampieri. 2021. SemEval-2021 task 1: Lexical complexity prediction. In *Proceedings of the 14th International Workshop on Semantic Evaluation (SemEval-2021)*.

Tal Yarkoni, David A. Balota, and Melvin Yap. 2008. Moving beyond Coltheart's N: A new measure of orthographic similarity. *Psychonomic Bulletin & Review*, 16:971–979.

A Appendix

At the request of a reviewer, the parameter space for the first random search is provided below. Those for the second random search are not provided as they did not allow to really improve the performances.

```
param_grid = {
 'max_bin': [16,32,48,64,80,96,112,128,
    160,192,224,256],
  'min_data_in_bin':[2,3,4,5,6,8,10,12,
    15,20],
  'num_leaves': [4,5,6,7,8,9,10,11,12,13,
    15,18,21,25,30],
  'learning_rate': [0.005,0.007,0.009,
    0.011,0.014,0.018,0.022,0.026,0.03,
    0.035,0.05],
  'min_data_in_leaf': [2,3,4,5,6,7,8,9,10,
    11,12,13,15,18,21,25,30],
  'max_depth': [3,4,5,6,7,8,9,10,11,12,13,
    -1],
  'feature_fraction': list(np.linspace(
    0.01, 0.90, 91)),
  'bagging_freq': list(range(3, 7, 1)),
  'bagging_fraction': list(np.linspace(
    0.50, 0.90, 9))
}
```

Team Ohio State at CMCL 2021 Shared Task: Fine-Tuned RoBERTa for Eye-Tracking Data Prediction

Byung-Doh Oh
Department of Linguistics
The Ohio State University
oh.531@osu.edu

Abstract

This paper describes Team Ohio State's approach to the CMCL 2021 Shared Task, the goal of which is to predict five eye-tracking features from naturalistic self-paced reading corpora. For this task, we fine-tune a pre-trained neural language model (RoBERTa; Liu et al., 2019) to predict each feature based on the contextualized representations. Moreover, motivated by previous eye-tracking studies, we include word length in characters and proportion of sentence processed as two additional input features. Our best model strongly outperforms the baseline and is also competitive with other systems submitted to the shared task. An ablation study shows that the word length feature contributes to making more accurate predictions, indicating the usefulness of features that are specific to the eye-tracking paradigm.

1 Introduction

Behavioral responses such as eye-tracking data provide valuable insight into the latent mechanism behind real-time language processing. Based on the well-established observation that behavioral responses reflect processing difficulty, cognitive modeling research has sought to accurately predict these responses using theoretically motivated variables (e.g. *surprisal*; Hale, 2001; Levy, 2008). Earlier work in this line of research has introduced incremental parsers for deriving psycholinguistically-motivated variables (e.g. Roark et al., 2009; van Schijndel et al., 2013), while more recent work has focused on evaluating the capability of neural language models to predict behavioral responses (Hao et al., 2020; Wilcox et al., 2020).

The CMCL 2021 Shared Task on eye-tracking data prediction (Hollenstein et al., 2021) provides an appropriate setting to compare the predictive power of different approaches using a standardized dataset. According to the task definition, the goal of the shared task is to predict five eye-tracking features from naturalistic self-paced reading corpora, namely the Zurich Cognitive Language Processing Corpus 1.0 and 2.0 (ZuCo 1.0 and 2.0; Hollenstein et al., 2018, 2020). These corpora contain eye-tracking data from native speakers of English that read select sentences from the Stanford Sentiment Treebank (Socher et al., 2013) and the Wikipedia relation extraction corpus (Culotta et al., 2006). The five eye-tracking features to be predicted for each word, which have been normalized to a range between 0 and 100 and then averaged over participants, are as follows:

- Number of fixations (nFix): Total number of fixations on the current word
- First fixation duration (FFD): The duration of the first fixation on the prevailing word
- Total reading time (TRT): The sum of all fixation durations on the current word
- Go-past time (GPT): The sum of all fixations before progressing to the right of the current word
- Fixation proportion (fixProp): The proportion of participants that fixated on the current word

In this paper, we present Team Ohio State's approach to the task of eye-tracking data prediction. As the main input feature available from the dataset is the words in each sentence, we adopt a transfer learning approach by fine-tuning a pre-trained neural language model to this task. Furthermore, we introduce two additional input features motivated by previous eye-tracking studies, which measure word length in characters and the proportion of sentence processed. Our best-performing model outperforms the mean baseline by a large margin in terms of mean absolute error (MAE) and is also competitive with other systems submitted to the shared task.

Proceedings of the Workshop on Cognitive Modeling and Computational Linguistics, pages 97–101
Online Event, June 10, 2021. ©2021 Association for Computational Linguistics

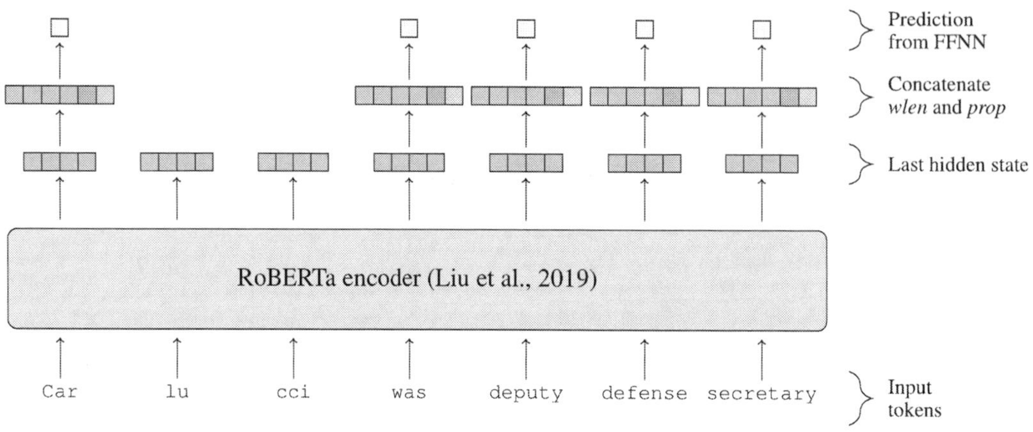

Figure 1: Model architecture for eye-tracking feature prediction.

2 Model Description

Our model relies primarily on the Transformer-based pre-trained language model RoBERTa (Liu et al., 2019) for contextualized representations of each word in the input sentence.[1] However, since RoBERTa uses byte-pair encoding (Sennrich et al., 2016) to tokenize each sentence, there is a mismatch between the number of output representations from RoBERTa and the number of words in each sentence. In order to address this issue, the model uses the representation for the first token associated with each word to make predictions. For example, if byte-pair encoding tokenizes the word `Carlucci` into `Car`, `lu`, and `cci`, the representation for `Car` is used to make predictions for the entire word `Carlucci`.[2]

Additionally, two input features based on previous eye-tracking studies are included in the model. The first is word length measured in characters (*wlen*), which captures the tendency of readers to fixate longer on orthographically longer words. The second feature is proportion of sentence processed (*prop*), which is calculated by dividing the current index of the word by the number of total words in each sentence. This feature is intended to take into account any "edge effects" that may be observed at the beginning and the end of each sentence, as well as any systematic change in eye movement as a function of the word's location within each sentence. These two features, which are typically treated as nuisance variables that are experimentally or statistically controlled for in eye-tracking studies (e.g. Hao et al., 2020; Rayner et al., 2011; Shain, 2019), are included in the current model to maximize prediction accuracy.[3]

A feedforward neural network (FFNN) with one hidden layer subsequently takes these three features (i.e. RoBERTa representation, *wlen*, and *prop*) as input and predicts a scalar value. To predict the five eye-tracking features defined by the shared task, this identical model was trained separately for each eye-tracking feature. An overview of the model architecture is presented in Figure 1.[4]

3 Training Procedures

3.1 Data Partitioning

Following the shared task guidelines, 800 sentences and their associated eye-tracking features from the ZuCo 1.0 and 2.0 corpora (Hollenstein et al., 2018, 2020) provided the data for training the model. However, a concern with using all 800 sentences to fine-tune the RoBERTa language model as described above is the tendency of high-capacity lan-

[1]Although other word representations could be used within our model architecture, the use of RoBERTa was motivated by its state-of-the-art performance on many NLP tasks. The $\text{RoBERTa}_{\text{base}}$ and $\text{RoBERTa}_{\text{large}}$ variants were explored in this work, which resulted in two different models. We used the implementation made available by HuggingFace (`https://github.com/huggingface/transformers`).

[2]Future work could investigate the use of more sophisticated approaches, such as using the average of all token representations associated with the word.

[3]Other variables typically examined in eye-tracking studies include frequency-based measures (e.g. token frequency) and prediction-based measures (e.g. various instantiations of surprisal). However, those variables were not included in our models as input features, as it was thought that the high-capacity RoBERTa model trained on a masked language modeling objective would implicitly encode such information.

[4]Code for model training and evaluation is available at `https://github.com/byungdoh/cmcl21_st`.

Model	Dev (MSE)					Test (MAE)				
	nFix	FFD	GPT	TRT	fixProp	nFix	FFD	GPT	TRT	fixProp
RoBERTa$_{\text{base}}$	28.307	**0.757**	14.780	**4.234**	**198.917**	**3.987**	0.682	**2.364**	**1.540**	11.311
RoBERTa$_{\text{large}}$	**28.023**	0.762	**14.669**	4.502	200.352	4.079	**0.668**	2.407	1.544	**11.210**
Mean baseline	91.783	2.062	35.509	13.838	662.309	7.303	1.149	3.782	2.778	21.775

Table 1: MSE on the held-out dev set and MAE on the test set for the two models.

Model	Test (MAE)				
	nFix	FFD	GPT	TRT	fixProp
Full model	3.987	0.682	2.364	1.540	11.311
-prop	3.987	0.681	2.364	1.540	11.315
-wlen	3.997	0.681	2.376	1.543	11.424
-prop,wlen	3.998	0.681	2.377	1.543	11.431

Table 2: MAE on the test set for full RoBERTa$_{\text{base}}$ model and its ablated variants.

guage models to agressively overfit to the training data (Howard and Ruder, 2018; Jiang et al., 2020; Peters et al., 2019). To prevent such overfitting, the last 80 sentences (10%; 1,546 words) were excluded from training as the dev set and were used to conduct held-out evaluation. This partitioning resulted in the final training set, which consists of 720 sentences (90%; 14,190 words).

3.2 Implementation Details

For each eye-tracking feature, the two models were trained to minimize mean squared error (MSE, Equation 1),

$$\mathcal{L}(\theta) = \frac{1}{N}\sum_{i=1}^{N}(y_i - f(\mathbf{x}_i;\theta))^2 \quad (1)$$

where $f(\cdot;\theta)$ is the model described in Section 2, $\mathbf{x}_i$ is the concatenation of three input features, y_i is the target value associated with the eye-tracking feature, and N is the number of training examples in each batch. The AdamW algorithm (Loshchilov and Hutter, 2019) with a weight decay hyperparameter of 0.01 was used to optimize the model parameters. The learning rate was warmed-up over the first 10% of training steps and was subsequently decayed linearly. The number of nodes in the hidden layer of the FFNN was fixed to half of that of the input layer. Additionally, dropout with a rate of 0.1 was applied before both the input layer and the hidden layer of the FFNN. Finally, to avoid exploding gradients, gradients with a norm greater than 1 were clipped to norm 1.

The optimal hyperparameters were found using grid search based on MSE on the held-out dev set. More specifically, the learning rate was explored within the set of $\{1 \times 10^{-5}, 2 \times 10^{-5}, 3 \times 10^{-5}, 5 \times 10^{-5}\}$, batch size was explored within the set of $\{4, 8, 16, 32, 64\}$ sentences, and the maximum number of training epochs was explored within the set of $\{8, 16, 32, 64, 128, 192\}$. During training, the model was evaluated on the dev set after every training epoch.

4 Results and Discussion

Table 1 shows the MSE on the dev set and MAE[5] on the test set for the two models. Both models strongly outperformed the baseline approach that predicts the mean value of the training set, resulting in a $\sim$40% decrease in MAE for all five features. Additionally, although the difference is small, the RoBERTa$_{\text{base}}$ model tended to perform better than the RoBERTa$_{\text{large}}$ model on the test set.[6] This suggests that models with higher capacity may not necessarily be preferable for this task, especially in light of the small amount of training data available.

To evaluate the contribution of the *wlen* and *prop* features, an ablation study was conducted using the RoBERTa$_{\text{base}}$ model. In addition to showing how useful *wlen* and *prop* information is for predicting eye-tracking features, the analysis was also thought to reveal whether or not such information is already contained within the RoBERTa representations. The two input features were ablated by simply replacing them with zeros during inference, which allowed a clean manipulation of their contribution to the final predictions.

The results in Table 2 show that the ablation of the *prop* feature made virtually no difference in the model predictions. This is most likely due to the fact that the Transformer (Vaswani et al., 2017), which the RoBERTa models are based on, includes positional encodings that allow the model to be sen-

[5]The official evaluation metric, $\frac{1}{N}\sum_{i=1}^{N}|y_i - f(\mathbf{x}_i;\theta)|$.

[6]The RoBERTa$_{\text{base}}$ model ranked 11th out of 29 submissions on the shared task (6th out of 13 participating teams).

sitive to the position of each token in the sequence. Therefore, in order to fully examine the contribution of positional information on this task, a variant of the current model using RoBERTa representations trained without positional encodings would have to be evaluated.

The ablation of the *wlen* feature resulted in a more notable difference in four out of five eye-tracking features. This indicates that information about orthographic length is both useful for eye-tracking data prediction and also orthogonal to the information captured by the RoBERTa representations. This may partially be explained by RoBERTa's use of byte-pair encoding, which can result in many short tokens for a given word (e.g. tokens `Car`, `lu`, `cci` for the word `Carlucci`). Since only the first token was used by the current models to represent each word, explicitly including information about word length seems to have contributed to making more accurate predictions. More generally, this highlights the utility of incorporating features that are specific to eye-tracking, which may not be inherent in high-capacity language models trained for a different objective.

5 Conclusion

In this paper, we present our approach to the CMCL 2021 Shared Task on eye-tracking data prediction. Our models primarily adopt a transfer learning approach by employing a feedforward neural network to predict eye-tracking features based on contextualized representations from a pre-trained language model. Additionally, we include two input features that have been known to influence eye movement, which are word length in characters (*wlen*) and proportion of sentence processed (*prop*). Our best model based on $\text{RoBERTa}_{\text{base}}$ strongly outperforms the mean baseline and is also competitive with other systems submitted to the shared task. A follow-up ablation study shows that the *wlen* feature contributed to making more accurate predictions, which indicates that explicitly incorporating features specific to the eye-tracking paradigm can complement high-capacity language models on this task.

Acknowledgments

We would like to thank the anonymous reviewers for their helpful comments.

References

Aron Culotta, Andrew McCallum, and Jonathan Betz. 2006. Integrating probabilistic extraction models and data mining to discover relations and patterns in text. In *Proceedings of the Human Language Technology Conference of the NAACL, Main Conference*, pages 296–303.

John Hale. 2001. A probabilistic Earley parser as a psycholinguistic model. In *Proceedings of the Second Meeting of the North American Chapter of the Association for Computational Linguistics on Language Technologies*, pages 1–8.

Yiding Hao, Simon Mendelsohn, Rachel Sterneck, Randi Martinez, and Robert Frank. 2020. Probabilistic predictions of people perusing: Evaluating metrics of language model performance for psycholinguistic modeling. In *Proceedings of the Workshop on Cognitive Modeling and Computational Linguistics*, pages 75–86.

Nora Hollenstein, Emmanuele Chersoni, Cassandra Jacobs, Yohei Oseki, Laurent Prévot, and Enrico Santus. 2021. CMCL 2021 Shared Task on Eye-Tracking Prediction. In *Proceedings of the Workshop on Cognitive Modeling and Computational Linguistics*.

Nora Hollenstein, Jonathan Rotsztejn, Marius Troendle, Andreas Pedroni, Ce Zhang, and Nicolas Langer. 2018. ZuCo, a simultaneous EEG and eye-tracking resource for natural sentence reading. *Scientific Data*, 5.

Nora Hollenstein, Marius Troendle, Ce Zhang, and Nicolas Langer. 2020. ZuCo 2.0: A dataset of physiological recordings during natural reading and annotation. In *Proceedings of the 12th Language Resources and Evaluation Conference*, pages 138–146.

Jeremy Howard and Sebastian Ruder. 2018. Universal language model fine-tuning for text classification. In *Proceedings of the 56th Annual Meeting of the Association for Computational Linguistics*, pages 328–339.

Haoming Jiang, Pengcheng He, Weizhu Chen, Xiaodong Liu, Jianfeng Gao, and Tuo Zhao. 2020. SMART: Robust and efficient fine-tuning for pre-trained natural language models through principled regularized optimization. In *Proceedings of the 58th Annual Meeting of the Association for Computational Linguistics*, pages 2177–2190.

Roger Levy. 2008. Expectation-based syntactic comprehension. *Cognition*, 106(3):1126–1177.

Yinhan Liu, Myle Ott, Naman Goyal, Jingfei Du, Mandar Joshi, Danqi Chen, Omer Levy, Mike Lewis, Luke Zettlemoyer, and Veselin Stoyanov. 2019. RoBERTa: A robustly optimized BERT pretraining approach.

Ilya Loshchilov and Frank Hutter. 2019. Decoupled weight decay regularization.

Matthew E. Peters, Sebastian Ruder, and Noah A. Smith. 2019. To tune or not to tune? Adapting pretrained representations to diverse tasks. In *Proceedings of the 4th Workshop on Representation Learning for NLP (RepL4NLP-2019)*, pages 7–14.

Keith Rayner, Timothy J. Slattery, Denis Drieghe, and Simon P. Liversedge. 2011. Eye movements and word skipping during reading: Effects of word length and predictability. *Journal of Experimental Psychology: Human Perception and Performance*, 37(2):514–528.

Brian Roark, Asaf Bachrach, Carlos Cardenas, and Christophe Pallier. 2009. Deriving lexical and syntactic expectation-based measures for psycholinguistic modeling via incremental top-down parsing. In *Proceedings of the 2009 Conference on Empirical Methods in Natural Language Processing*, pages 324–333.

Rico Sennrich, Barry Haddow, and Alexandra Birch. 2016. Neural machine translation of rare words with subword units. In *Proceedings of the 54th Annual Meeting of the Association for Computational Linguistics*, pages 1715–1725.

Cory Shain. 2019. A large-scale study of the effects of word frequency and predictability in naturalistic reading. In *Proceedings of the 2019 Conference of the North American Chapter of the Association for Computational Linguistics: Human Language Technologies, Volume 1 (Long and Short Papers)*, pages 4086–4094.

Richard Socher, Alex Perelygin, Jean Wu, Jason Chuang, Christopher D. Manning, Andrew Ng, and Christopher Potts. 2013. Recursive deep models for semantic compositionality over a sentiment treebank. In *Proceedings of the 2013 Conference on Empirical Methods in Natural Language Processing*, pages 1631–1642.

Marten van Schijndel, Andy Exley, and William Schuler. 2013. A model of language processing as hierarchic sequential prediction. *Topics in Cognitive Science*, 5(3):522–540.

Ashish Vaswani, Noam Shazeer, Niki Parmar, Jakob Uszkoreit, Llion Jones, Aidan N Gomez, Łukasz Kaiser, and Illia Polosukhin. 2017. Attention is all you need. In *Advances in Neural Information Processing Systems*, volume 30.

Ethan Gotlieb Wilcox, Jon Gauthier, Jennifer Hu, Peng Qian, and Roger P. Levy. 2020. On the predictive power of neural language models for human real-time comprehension behavior. In *Proceedings of the 42nd Annual Meeting of the Cognitive Science Society*, pages 1707–1713.

PIHKers at CMCL 2021 Shared Task: Cosine Similarity and Surprisal to Predict Human Reading Patterns.

Lavinia Salicchi
The Hong Kong Polytechnic University
lavinia.salicchi@connect.polyu.hk

Alessandro Lenci
Università di Pisa
alessandro.lenci@unipi.it

Abstract

Eye-tracking psycholinguistic studies have revealed that context-word semantic coherence and predictability influence language processing. In this paper we show our approach to predict eye-tracking features from the ZuCo dataset for the shared task of the Cognitive Modeling and Computational Linguistics (CMCL2021) workshop. Using both cosine similarity and surprisal within a regression model, we significantly improved the baseline Mean Absolute Error computed among five eye-tracking features.

1 Introduction

The shared task proposed by the organizers of the Cognitive Modeling and Computational Linguistics workshop (Hollenstein et al., 2021) requires participant to create systems capable of predicting eye-tracking data from the ZuCo dataset (Hollenstein et al., 2018). Creating systems to efficiently predict biometrical data may be useful to make prediction about linguistic materials for which we have few or none experimental data, and to make new hypothesis about the internal dynamics of cognitive processes.

The approach we propose relies mainly on two factors that have been proved to influence language comprehension: i.) the **semantic coherence** of a word with the previous ones (Ehrlich and Rayner, 1981) and ii.) its **predictability** from previous context (Kliegl et al., 2004). We model the first factor with the *cosine similarity* (Mitchell et al., 2010; Pynte et al., 2008) between the distributional vectors, representing the context and the target word, produced by different Distributional Semantic Models (DSM) (Lenci, 2018). We compared 10 state-of-the-art word embedding models, and two different approaches to compute the context vector. We model the predictability of a word within the context with the word-by-word *surprisal* computed with 3 of the above mentioned models (Hale, 2001; Levy, 2008). Finally, cosine similarity and surprisal are combined in different regression models to predict eye tracking data.

2 Related Works

Different word embedding models (GloVe, Word2Vec, WordNet2Vec, FastText, ELMo, BERT) have been evaluated in the framework proposed by Hollenstein et al. (2019). The evaluation is based on the model capability to reflect semantic representations in the human mind, using cognitive data in different datasets for eye-tracking, EEG, and fMRI. Word embedding models are used to train neural networks on a regression task. The results of their analyses show that BERT, ELMo, and FastText have the best prediction performances.

Regression models with different combinations of cosine similarity and surprisal, to predict (and further study the cognitive dynamics beneath) eye movements have been created by Frank (2017), who claims that, since word embeddings are based on co-occurrences, semantic distance may actually represent word predictability, rather than semantic relatedness, and that previous findings showing correlations between reading times and semantic distance were actually due to a confound between these two concepts. In his work, he uses linear regression models testing different surprisal measures, and excluding it. The results show that when surprisal is factored out, the effects of semantic similarity on reading times disappear, proving thus the existence of an interplay between the two elements.

3 Experimental Setting

3.1 Datasets

The shared task materials come from ZuCo (Hollenstein et al., 2018), that includes EEG and eye-tracking data, collected on 12 English speakers reading natural texts. The data collection has been

Proceedings of the Workshop on Cognitive Modeling and Computational Linguistics, pages 102–107
Online Event, June 10, 2021.

done in three different settings: two normal reading tasks and one task-specific reading session. The original dataset comprises $1,107$ sentences, and for the shared task 800 sentences ($15,736$ words) have been used for the training data, while the test set included about 200 sentences ($3,554$ words). Since the shared task focuses on eye-tracking features, only this latter data were available. The training dataset structure includes sentence number, word-within-sentence number, word, number of fixations (nFix), first fixation duration (FFD), total reading time (TRT), go-past time (GPT), fixation proportion (fixProp). The first three elements were part of the test set too.

Our approach includes a preliminary step of feature selection. For this purpose we also used GECO (Cop et al., 2017) and Provo (Luke and Christianson, 2018), two eye-tracking corpora containing long, complete, and coherent texts. **GECO** is a monolingual and bilingual (English and Dutch) corpus composed of the entire Agatha Christie's novel *The Mysterious Affair at Styles*. GECO contains eye-tracking data of 33 subjects (19 of them bilingual, 14 English monolingual) reading the full novel text, presented paragraph-by-paragraph on a screen. GECO is composed of $54,364$ tokens. **Provo** contains 55 short English texts about various topics, for a total of $2,689$ tokens, and a vocabulary of $1,197$ words. These texts were read by 85 subjects and their eye-tracking measures were collected in an available on-line dataset. Similarly to ZuCo, GECO and Provo data are recorded during naturalistic reading on everyday life materials. For every word in GECO and Provo, we extracted its mean total reading time, mean first fixation duration, and mean number of fixations, by averaging over the subjects.

3.2 Word Embeddings

Table 1 shows the embeddings types used in our experiments, consisting of 6 non-contextualized DSMs and 4 contextualized DSMs. The former include predict models (**SGNS** and **FastText**) (Mikolov et al., 2013; Levy and Goldberg, 2014; Bojanowski et al., 2017) and count models (**SVD** and **GloVe**) (Bullinaria and Levy, 2012; Pennington et al., 2014). Four DSMs are window-based and two are syntax-based (**synt**). Embeddings have 300 dimensions and were trained on the same corpus of about 3.9 billion tokens, which is a concatenation of ukWaC and a 2018 dump of Wikipedia.

Pre-trained contextualized embeddings include the 512-dimensional vectors produced by the three layers of the **ELMo** bidirectional LSTM architecture (Peters et al., 2018), the $1,024$-dimensional vectors in the 24 layers of **BERT-Large** Transformers (BERT-Large, Cased) (Devlin et al., 2019), the $1,600$-dimensional vectors of **GPT2-xl** (Radford et al.), and the 200-dimensional vectors produced by the **Neural Complexity** model (van Schijndel and Linzen, 2018).

3.3 Method

To predict eye tracking data we tested different regression models and several features combinations.

Feature Selection. To select the features to be used, for each word embedding model and language model we carried out a preliminary investigation computing Spearman's correlation between eye tracking features, and respectively surprisal and cosine similarity: The features with the highest correlation with biometrical data have been selected for being used in the regression model.

For each target word w in GECO, Provo and ZuCo, we measure the **cosine similarity** between the embedding of w and the embedding of the context c composed of the previous words in the same sentence. We then compute the Spearman correlation between the cosine and the eye-tracking data for w. We test two different ways of computing the context embedding:

Additive model (for every embedding type): The context vector is the sum of all its word embeddings. Because of the bidirectional nature of BERT, the input to this model needed a special pre-processing. In order to prevent that the vectors representing words within the context were computed using the target word itself, we passed to BERT a list of sub-sentences, each of which were composed of context words only. So given the sentence *The dog chases the cat*:

S[0] = ["The"]
S[1] = ["The dog"]
S[2] = ["The dog chases"]
S[3] = ["The dog chases the"]
S[4] = ["The dog chases the cat"]

Starting from the second sub-sentence, the cosine similarity is computed between the last word vector and the sum of words vectors belonging to the previous sub-sentence (list element). Therefore, to compute the cosine similarity between *cat* and the previous context, we select *cat* from S[4] and

Model	Hyperparameters
Non-contextualized DSMs	
SVD.w2	count DSM with 345K window-selected context words, window of width 2, reduced with SVD
SVD.synt	count DSM with 345K syntactically typed context words reduced with SVD
GloVe	count DSM with context window of width 2, reduced with log-bilinear regression
SGNS.w2	Skip-gram with negative sampling, context window of width 2, 15 negative examples
SGNS.synt	Skip-gram with negative sampling, syntactically-typed context words, 15 negative examples
FastText	Skip-gram with subword information, context window of width 2, 15 negative examples
Contextualized DSMs	
ELMo	Pretrained ELMo embeddings on the 1 Billion Word Benchmark
BERT	Pretrained BERT-Large embeddings on the concatenation of the Books corpus and Wikipedia
GPT2-xl	Pretrained GPT2-xl embeddings on WebText
Neural Complexity	Pretrained Neural Complexity embeddings on Wikipedia

Table 1: List of the embedding models used for the study, together with their hyperparameter settings.

$The + dog + chases + the$ from S[3].
CLS: The context vector is the embedding produced by BERT for the special token [CLS]. As for the additive model, BERT was fed with sub-sentences, and for each target word the CLS-context-vector was the one computed at the previous list element. So, looking at the previous example, for *cat* as target word, we will use the CLS vector representing all the S[3] elements.

Given the positive effect of semantic coherence on language processing, we expect that the eye-tracking data for w have a negative correlation with its cosine similarity with c: *The higher the cosine, the lower the reading time of w measured by eye-tracking*.

We then used BERT, GPT2-xl and Neural Complexity to compute word-by-word surprisal. As for the cosine similarity, for BERT the input sentences were organized in sub-sentences, and the last token, the target word, was replaced with the special tag [MASK]. Finally, we compute the Spearman correlation between the **surprisal** of w, and the eye-tracking data for the target word. Differently from the cosine, we expect the surprisal to be positively correlated with the word reading time: *The less predictable a word, the slower its processing*.

The comparison has been done between 60 possible features: 6 values of cosine similarity between non-contextualized vectors, 51 values of cosine similarity between contextualized vectors (48 from 24 layers of BERT in two different ways to compute the context vector, and 3 from ELMo, GPT2-xl and Neural Complexity), 3 values of surprisal from BERT, GPT2-xl, Neural Complexity. Based on the correlation values, we selected one cosine similarity feature and one surprisal feature, that have been combined with two variables that are well-known in the cognitive neuroscience literature for influencing eye movements: word length and word frequency, the last one computed on Wikipedia[1].

Regression Model Selection. Taking into account the Spearman's correlations, we selected one word embedding model for cosine similarity and one Language Model for surprisal. Then, different kind of regression models from Scikit-learn have been compared. More precisely, *PLS Regression, Multi-layer Perceptron Regressor, Random Forest Regressor, Linear Regression, Ridge Regression, Bayesian ridge regression, Epsilon-Support Vector Regression, Linear regression with combined L1 and L2 priors as Regularizer, Gradient Boosting Regressor*. The **metric** used to evaluate different models is the Mean Absolute Error on ZuCo's eye tracking features prediction. Once the model and the features have been selected, the **comparison** between 3 different regression settings has been done: i) surprisal only; ii) cosine similarity only; iii) surprisal + cosine similarity.
For the regression model selection, we used 2/3 of the ZuCo training set to train the model, and 1/3 for validation purposes. Once we found the best (i.e. lower MAE among eye tracking data) combination of features and regression model, the prediction on test data has been done.

4 Results and Discussion

Spearman's correlations between eye tracking features and cosine similarity showed that best performances are reached by vectors produced by BERT layer 22 CLS context (mean correlation over eye tracking features on the three datasets: -0.62), while best correlations between eye tracking data and surprisal are reached by GPT2-xl (mean correlation over eye tracking features on the three datasets: 0.40). These results led us to select as

[1] Using https://github.com/IlyaSemenov/wikipedia-word-frequency

Feature	Model	Regression model	MAE
FFD	BERTcos_GPTsurpr	GBR	0.69
FFD	GPTcos_GPTsurpr	GBR	0.69
FFD	BERTcos_GPTsurpr	RF	0.74
FFD	BASELINE	RF	0.77
fixprop	BERTcos_GPTsurpr	GBR	11.64
fixprop	GPTcos_GPTsurpr	GBR	11.78
fixprop	GPTcos_GPTsurpr	RF	12.33
fixprop	BASELINE	RF	12.75
GPT	BERTcos_GPTsurpr	GBR	2.96
GPT	GPTcos_GPTsurpr	GBR	2.978
GPT	BERTcos_GPTsurpr	LR	3.08
GPT	BASELINE	BRR	3.09
nFix	BERTcos_GPTsurpr	GBR	4.21
nFix	GPTcos_GPTsurpr	GBR	4.37
nFix	BERTcos_GPTsurpr	LR	4.49
nFix	BASELINE	LR	4.67
TRT	BERTcos_GPTsurpr	GBR	1.64
TRT	GPTcos_GPTsurpr	GBR	1.67
TRT	BERTcos_GPTsurpr	RF	1.76
TRT	BASELINE	RF	1.84

Table 2: Best three MAEs for each eye-tracking feature + baseline.

features for regression model: cosine similarity between vectors computed by BERT 22 CLS and surprisal computed by GPT2-xl. We also tested the cosine similarity between vectors computed by GPT2-xl, to have a comparison with a regression model with features produced by the same model. While performing regression model selection comparing 9 models from Scikit-learn, we also tried different combinations of features.

Table 2 shows the best 3 combinations of features and models, compared with the baseline created taking into account word frequency and word lenght only. The lowest MAEs for each eye-tracking feature were reached by a Gradient Boosting Regressor (GBR) using both the cosine similarity between vectors produced by BERT and the surprisal computed by GPT2-xl. The average MAE using the GBR model with BERT cosine and GPT2-xl surprisal was 4.22 (mean improvement compared with the baseline = 0.54), with one feature, *fixProp*, producing a MAE value significantly higher than the other eye tracking features. Since fixProp is "*the proportion of participants that fixated the current word*" (i.e., the probability of the word of being fixed), we hypothesized that the combination of phenomena influencing the likelihood of fixating a word could be captured by the other 4 eye tracking features, making them in turn good predictors of fixProp.

Therefore, we tested again the 9 regression models with Scikit-learn, this time using nFix, FFD, TRT, GPT, word lenght and word frequency as features, in every possible permutation (one per time, pairs of features, etc.). A lower MAE on fixProp on training data has been obtained using a *Random Forest* method with nFix, TRT, and GPT, reaching a MAE of 3.15.

The improvements of the final model over the baseline suggest that the information conveyed by the cosine similarity and the surprisal contributes in modeling the cognitive processing beneath reading. Our results are consistent with Pynte et al. (2008) and Mitchell et al. (2010) findings about the relation between cosine similarity and eye movements data, as well as with Hale (2001) and Levy (2008), who found surprisal to be useful in predicting reading times.
Anyway, our model performance shows that taking into account *both* the computational measures benefits the modeling. Even if Frank (2017) rises an interesting issue about the interplay between the information included in word embeddings and the one provided by the suprisal computed by language models, our results keep us from fully agree with his observations: since the joined model performed better that the ones taking into account only cosine similarity or only surprisal, it is obvious that the two measures convey exclusive and useful information, even if it is more than plausible that they share some kind of information to some extent.

In summary, we used a two-step approach: i.) the final model to predict nFix, FFD, GPT, and TRT in test data was a Gradient Boosting Regressor having as features the cosine similarity between the CLS vector (BERT) and the target word embedding, GPT2-xl surprisal, word length and word frequency; ii.) the predicted values of nFix, GPT, and TRT were used in a Random Forest to predict fixProp.

The shared task final results over the test data, revealed that our model had an average MAE of 4.3877 over all eye tracking features (the baseline was 7.3699, while the best model reached a MAE of 3.8134).

5 Conclusions

In this paper we described the system we proposed in the CMCL2021 "Shared Task: Predicting human reading patterns". We were required to create a model capable of predicting number of fixations, first fixation duration, total reading time, go-past time, and fixation proportion of each word in the ZuCo dataset. We proposed a regression model using word length and word frequency, combined with two elements that are proved to influence reading processing: the semantic coherence and the predictability of a word within the context. To compute these last two regression features we used the cosine similarity between the vector representing the context and the word embedding of the target word, and the surprisal computed by Language Models, respectively. We selected the models to produce the vectors and to compute the surprisal calculating the Spearman correlation between the cosine similarity and the eye tracking data, and between the surprisal and the same data. We then used the best cosine similarity and surprisal within a regression model, selected among 9 possible models. Our results outperformed the baseline, with a average MAE among eye tracking features just 0.5743 higher than the best model in the competition.

Our model may be improved exploring new types of regressors and word embeddings, and including new textual features such as sentence length and information regarding words immediately preceding the target ones.

References

Piotr Bojanowski, Edouard Grave, Armand Joulin, and Tomas Mikolov. 2017. Enriching Word Vectors with Subword Information. *Transactions of the Association for Computational Linguistics*, 5:135–146.

John A Bullinaria and Joseph P Levy. 2012. Extracting Semantic Representations from Word Co-Occurrence Statistics: Stop-Lists, Stemming, and SVD. *Behavior Research Methods*, 44(3):890–907.

Uschi Cop, Nicolas Dirix, Denis Drieghe, and Wouter Duyck. 2017. Presenting GECO: An Eye-Tracking Corpus of Monolingual and Bilingual Sentence Reading. *Behavior Reseach Methods*, 49(2):602–615.

Jacob Devlin, Ming-Wei Chang, Kenton Lee, and Kristina Toutanova. 2019. BERT: Pre-training of Deep Bidirectional Transformers for Language Understanding. In *Proceedings of NAACL*.

Susan E. Ehrlich and Keith Rayner. 1981. Contextual Effects on Word Perception and Eye Movements During Reading. *Journal of Verbal Learning and Verbal Behavior*, 20:641–65.

Stefan L Frank. 2017. Word Embedding Distance Does not Predict Word Reading Time. In *Proceedings of CogSci*, pages 385–390.

John Hale. 2001. A Probabilistic Earley Parser as a Psycholinguistic Model. In *Proceedings of NAACL*.

Nora Hollenstein, Emmanuele Chersoni, Cassandra Jacobs, Yohei Oseki, Laurent Prévot, and Enrico Santus. 2021. Cmcl 2021 shared task on eye-tracking prediction. In *Proceedings of the Workshop on Cognitive Modeling and Computational Linguistics*.

Nora Hollenstein, Antonio de la Torre, Nicolas Langer, and Ce Zhang. 2019. CogniVal: A Framework for Cognitive Word Embedding Evaluation. In *Proceedings of CONLL*.

Nora Hollenstein, Jonathan Rotsztejn, Marius Troendle, Andreas Pedroni, Ce Zhang, and Nicolas Langer. 2018. Zuco, a simultaneous eeg and eye-tracking resource for natural sentence reading. *Scientific Data*, 5.

Reinhold Kliegl, Ellen Grabner, Martin Rolfs, and Ralf Engbert. 2004. Length, frequency, and predictability effects of words on eye movements in reading. *European Journal of Cognitive Psychology - EUR J COGN PSYCHOL*, 16:262–284.

Alessandro Lenci. 2018. Distributional Models of Word Meaning. *Annual Review of Linguistics*, 4:151–171.

Omer Levy and Yoav Goldberg. 2014. Dependency-Based Word Embeddings. In *Proceedings of ACL*.

Roger Levy. 2008. Expectation-based Syntactic Comprehension. *Cognition*, 106(3):1126–1177.

Steven G Luke and Kiel Christianson. 2018. The Provo Corpus: A Large Eye-tracking Corpus with Predictability Norms. *Behavior Research Methods*, 50(2):826–833.

Tomas Mikolov, Kai Chen, Greg Corrado, and Jeffrey Dean. 2013. Efficient Estimation of Word Representations in Vector Space. *arXiv preprint arXiv:1301.3781*.

Jeff Mitchell, Mirella Lapata, Vera Demberg, and Frank Keller. 2010. Syntactic and Semantic Factors in Processing Difficulty: An Integrated Measure. In *Proceedings of ACL*.

Jeffrey Pennington, Richard Socher, and Christopher Manning. 2014. Glove: Global Vectors for Word Representation. In *Proceedings of EMNLP*.

Matthew E. Peters, Mark Neumann, Mohit Iyyer, Matt Gardner, Christopher Clark, Kenton Lee, and Luke Zettlemoyer. 2018. Deep Contextualized Word Representations. In *Proceedings of NAACL*.

Joel Pynte, Boris New, and Alan Kennedy. 2008. On-line Contextual Influences During Reading Normal Text: A Multiple-Regression Analysis. *Vision research*, 48(21):2172–2183.

A. Radford, Jeffrey Wu, R. Child, David Luan, Dario Amodei, and Ilya Sutskever. Language Models are Unsupervised Multitask Learners. In *Open-AI Blog*.

Marten van Schijndel and Tal Linzen. 2018. A Neural Model of Adaptation in Reading. In *Proceedings of EMNLP*.

TALEP at CMCL 2021 Shared Task: Non Linear Combination of Low and High-Level Features for Predicting Eye-Tracking Data

Franck Dary, Alexis Nasr, Abdellah Fourtassi
Aix Marseille Univ, Université de Toulon, CNRS, LIS, Marseille, France
{franck.dary,alexis.nasr,abdellah.fourtassi}@lis-lab.fr

Abstract

In this paper we describe our contribution to the CMCL 2021 Shared Task, which consists in predicting 5 different eye tracking variables from English tokenized text. Our approach is based on a neural network that combines both raw textual features we extracted from the text and parser-based features that include linguistic predictions (e.g. part of speech) and complexity metrics (e.g., entropy of parsing). We found that both the features we considered as well as the architecture of the neural model that combined these features played a role in the overall performance. Our system achieved relatively high accuracy on the test data of the challenge and was ranked 2nd out of 13 competing teams and a total of 30 submissions.

1 Introduction

The CMCL 2021 Shared Task (Hollenstein et al., 2021) aims at comparing different approaches to the task of predicting eye tracking variables. Given English text as a sequence of tokens, the goal is to predict 5 behavioural metrics (averaged over 12 human subjects).

Our approach was based on two major steps. First, we generated several features that either proved successful in previous work or that reflected our intuition about their potential in predicting eye tracking data. Second, we proposed a way for an optimal combination of these features using a simple neural network. Both steps proved to be useful in our final predictions.

The paper is organized as follows. First, in section 2, we list and describe the features we used to predict the eye-tracking data. Then, in section 3, we briefly describe the neural architecture of the model we used to combine the features. Next, in section 4, we report details about the model's training and evaluation. Finally, in section 5, we analyze and discuss the impact of each feature (as well as the impact of each group of features) on the overall performance of the model.

2 Features Generation

Before introducing the model (schematically described in Figure 1), we thought useful to first list and describe how we obtained the candidate predictive features from the original textual material of the challenge as well as from secondary sources. Our features are listed in Table 1, and can be organized into four categories: 1) Raw textual features we extracted form the proposed text, 2) Frequency values, 3) Linguistic features we obtained by annotating the proposed text in an automatic fashion, and 4) Complexity measures produced by a parser across several linguistic levels. Below are more details on each of these categories of features.

2.1 Raw Textual Features

The eight features of this group were directly extracted from the textual material of the challenge. These features are listed in Table 1 and they are self-explanatory. They include, e.g., word length, prefixes, and suffixes.

2.2 Frequencies

Every word in the text has been associated with three frequency values: the frequency of the word out of context (unigram), the frequencies of bigrams made of the current word and either the preceding or the next one. The values were computed using the Google's *One billion words benchmark for language modeling* corpus (Chelba et al., 2013).

2.3 Linguistic Features

We enriched the original textual material with three types of linguistic annotations (obtained automatically): part of speech tags, morphological tags and syntactic dependencies. Theses three types of annotations were realized using an augmented (neural network based) version our software MACAON (Nasr et al., 2011), where words in a sentence are discovered then annotated one at a time (from left to right). Annotation is based on classifiers that

Proceedings of the Workshop on Cognitive Modeling and Computational Linguistics, pages 108–113
Online Event, June 10, 2021. ©2021 Association for Computational Linguistics

take as input features about current word and its context and produce as output a probability distribution over a set of actions. Such actions posit word boundaries on the raw text, associate part of speech and morphological tags to words or link words of a sentence with syntactic dependencies. The actions that perform the prediction of syntactic dependencies are based on the transition based parsing framework (Nivre, 2003), which makes use of a stack that stores words that should be connected to words not yet discovered. The stack allows to connect words that are not adjacent in the sentence.

The classifiers are organized in an incremental architecture, i.e., once the tokenizer detected a word boundary, control jumps to the part of speech tagger, then to the morphological tagger and eventually to the syntactic parser, before going back to the tokenizer. The behaviour of the whole system is greedy, at every step, a single action is selected and performed. The action selected is the one that maximizes the probability distribution computed by the classifier.

2.4 Complexity Metrics

Besides producing linguistic labels, MACAON also produces numbers that reflect the difficulty associated with a given linguistic decision. We used these numbers to instantiate several "complexity metrics" that we used as a proxy to human difficulty to process a word (Hale, 2001). We generated two types of such complexity measures.

The first one is a measure of the "confidence" with which the system selects a given action. This confidence is based on the shape of the probability distribution produced by the system at each step. The measure used is simply the entropy of the probability distribution. A low entropy distribution corresponds to a high confidence and a high entropy to a low one. Four different measures of entropy were computed, one for every linguistic level (see Table 1).

The second kind of complexity metrics is related to the stack of the syntactic parser. One measure we used was the height of the stack. The stack has a tendency to grow when processing complex sentences, e.g., when it involves several subordinated clauses. A large value of the stack's height can therefore be interpreted as an indicator of a syntactically complex linguistic configuration. The second measure was the distance that separates in the sentence the two words on the top of the stack.

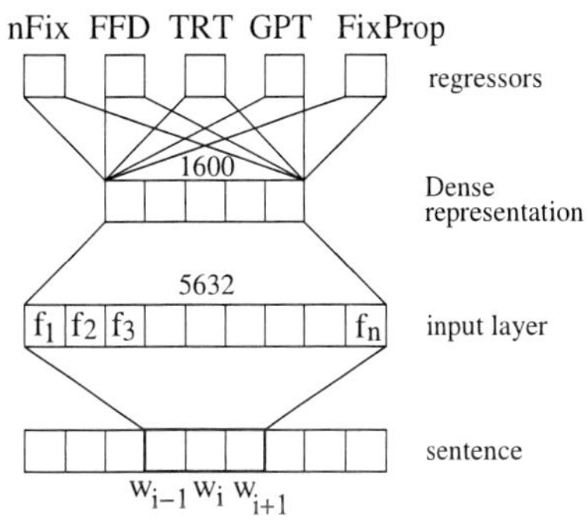

Figure 1: Model Architecture: a sliding window reads the sentence and encodes the features of the words (see Table 1) in the input layer. An MLP compresses the input layer using non linear functions. Five linear regressors predict the values of the variables.

2.5 Implementation Details

The MACAON model was trained on the concatenation of the English corpora GUM, EWT, LinES and ParTUT from Universal Dependencies (Zeman et al., 2019), for a total of 29,916 sentences and 515,228 words. It was used to process the raw[1] (untokenized) text in the ZuCo corpus. This processing yielded a tokenization of the text similar to the way UD corpora are tokenized (punctuation marks are tokens), where for each word we produced both linguisitc labels and complexity metrics. These measures were then aligned with the shared task corpus using Levenshtein distances between words. This alignment was necessary because the tokenization is different between the linguistic model output and the shared task material.

3 Features Combination

We used a simple neural network to perform a series of five regression tasks, one for each measure to predict. The regressions were realized using the architecture described in Figure 1. As is clear from the figure, all regression tasks take as input a single representation of the words being processed. This representation is optimized for the five regression tasks simultaneously. Perhaps the most complex part of the model is the encoding of the input layer because different kind of features require different encoding methods.[2]

[1]Available in the task_materials directory of the ZuCo distribution https://osf.io/q3zws/.

[2]The neural network was implemented in C++ using the PyTorch library (Paszke et al., 2019). The same software is used both to provide linguistic labels as in section 2 and to

The model is composed of three parts, each part taking as input the output of the preceding one (Figure 1).

3.1 The Input Layer

The input of the Multilayer Perceptron is a large vector that encodes all the features listed in Table 1. It is made of the concatenation of all these feature encodings for a span of three words centered on the current word. The features were encoded differently depending on their nature. For numeric values, such as word lengths or frequencies, we directly input them into our neural network. As for discrete values, such as part of speech tags, we used a dictionnary mapping each label to an embedding. Such embeddings (of size 64),[3] are learnable parameters of the model. They are randomly initialized, except for the FORM feature (see Table 1) where the embeddings were initialized on the train section of the shared task material using GloVe[4] (Pennington et al., 2014). We associated each feature with a bi-LSTM taking as input the sequence of values indicated in the *Span* column of Table 1, which define a window of width 1,2 or three, centered on the current word. The outputs of all such bi-LSTMs were concatenated, yielding a single embedding of size 5632. A dropout layer is then applied to the whole input vector, where during training 30% of the neurons are set to 0, making the network less prone to over-fitting.

3.2 The Multilayer Perceptron

It is composed of 2 linear layers (with bias), each one of size 1600. The ReLU function was applied to each layer output, and no dropout was used. The goal of the Multilayer Perceptron is to build a compact representation of the input layer that is optimized for the regression tasks.

3.3 The Decision Layer

The decision layer is simply a linear layer (with bias) of input size 1600 and output size 1. There are 5 different decision layers (one for each value to predict). Parameter of this linear layer are the only one that were not shared between the 5 predictions tasks.

predict the challenge's five oculometric measures, but with different models. The software used to train our model is available online: https://gitlab.lis-lab.fr/franck.dary/macaon/

[3]See section 4 about hyperparameters selection.

[4]Implementation: https://github.com/stanfordnlp/GloVe. Words with less than 2 occurrences were treated as unknown words, thus producing an unknown words embedding.

4 Training and Evaluation

In this section, we will describe how we trained the neural network presented in section 3 to predict all five shared task oculometric measures (nFix, FFD, TRT, GPT, fixProp), and how we proceeded for the choice of its hyperparameters such as number of layers, size of layers, size of embeddings.

During the training phase of the shared task, we decided to split the training material into train/dev/test parts of the following respective sizes 70%/15%/15%. This allowed us to use the dev part for early stopping and the test part to compare competing models on the basis of their generalization capability. We used absolute error as our loss function, and used Adagrad as our optimizer.

To decide on the values of the hyperparameters, we trained different models (changing one hyper parameter at a time) for 40 epochs on the train part of our split. As a form of early stopping, we only saved a model when its performance was the best on the dev set. Finally, we used performance on the test part of our split to compare models and decide which hyperparameter values were the best.

To train our final model, we ditched our custom split and used the entire shared task training material for a total of 7 epochs to avoid overfitting, achieving an MAE of 3.83 (the best team obtained 3.81). In Table 1 we reported that our best model had an MAE of 3.73, indicating that ditching the train/dev split was not a good idea.

5 Results and Discussion

Table 1 lists all the predictive features used in the current work and their impact on the Mean Absolute Error (MAE) — averaged over the five target measures of the challenge — both at the individual level and at the group level.

The individual MAE values were computed by training the model only on the feature at hand in addition to FREQUENCY and LENGTH, thus reflecting its performance beyond these simple baseline features[5]. As for the group-level MAE, we obtained them by training a model that takes as input all the features of the group at hand as well as the preceding groups in the table. For example, the MAE for "Raw Textual Features" was obtained by training the model on all the feature in this group only (as

[5]That's why the individual MAE values for FREQUENCY and LENGTH are identical: It is the errors of a model trained only on the baseline features made of FREQUENCY and LENGTH.

Name	Description	Span	MAE (individual)	MAE (group)
Raw Textual Features				
LENGTH	Number of letters in the word.	111	$4.20_{\pm 0.00}$	
PREFIX	First 3 letters of the word.	010	$4.15_{\pm 0.02}$	
SUFFIX	Last 3 letters of the word.	010	$4.16_{\pm 0.01}$	
FORM	Contextualized word embedding.	110	$4.05_{\pm 0.01}$	
EOS	Whether or not the word is the last of the sentence.	110	$4.15_{\pm 0.00}$	$3.87_{\pm 0.01}$
WORD_ID	Index of the word in the sentence. (Kuperman et al., 2010)	110	$4.09_{\pm 0.01}$	
SENT_ID	Index of the sentence in the text. (Genzel and Charniak, 2002)	110	$4.16_{\pm 0.01}$	
TEXT_ID	Index of the file containing the raw text.	010	$4.18_{\pm 0.00}$	
Frequencies				
FREQUENCY	Logarithm of the frequency of the word.	111	$4.20_{\pm 0.00}$	
COOC_P	Log frequency of the bigram with previous word.	111	$4.15_{\pm 0.00}$	$3.78_{\pm 0.02}$
COOC_N	Log frequency of the bigram with next word.	111	$4.17_{\pm 0.00}$	
Linguistic Features				
POS	Part of speech.	110	$4.15_{\pm 0.00}$	
MORPHO	Morphology.	110	$4.17_{\pm 0.00}$	$3.74_{\pm 0.01}$
DEPREL	Syntactic function.	110	$4.14_{\pm 0.00}$	
DEP_LEN	Distance to the syntactic governor.	110	$4.17_{\pm 0.01}$	
Complexity Metrics				
STACK_SIZE	Size of the stack when processing the word. (Gibson, 2000)	111	$4.12_{\pm 0.00}$	
STACK_DIST	Distance between the two top elements of the stack.	111	$4.14_{\pm 0.01}$	
ENT_TOK	Entropy of the tokenizer.	110	$4.22_{\pm 0.00}$	
ENT_TAG	Entropy of the part of speech tagger.	110	$4.22_{\pm 0.01}$	
ENT_MORPHO	Entropy of the morphological tagger.	110	$4.22_{\pm 0.00}$	$3.73_{\pm 0.00}$
ENT_PARSER	Entropy of the dependency parser. (Boston et al., 2008)	110	$4.23_{\pm 0.01}$	
ENT_MEAN	Mean of the entropies.	110	$4.22_{\pm 0.00}$	
ENT_MAX	Highest entropy.	110	$4.23_{\pm 0.01}$	

Table 1: Features of our model. Span defines the words taken into account in a window of length 3 centered on the current word. The first MAE column of row FEATNAME is the MAE achieved by a model using only features {FEATNAME,FREQUENCY,LENGTH}. Last MAE column is the score achieved by a model when adding this feature group (last value is for the model with all features). Results include standard deviation across 2 replications.

there is no preceding group). The MAE for "Frequencies" was obtained by training the model on all the feature in this group in addition to the features in the "Raw Textual Features" group, and so forth. Finally, the score associated with "Complexity Metrics" is the most comprehensive, including all features in the table. The goal of such nested calculation is to appreciate the role of each higher-level group above and beyond the information provided by the lower-level group of features. The four groups were ordered by the amount of effort it requires to obtain them. We did not test every combination of features.

Several conclusion can be drawn from these results. First, we found that low-level features performed very well. Indeed when combining only raw textual features and frequencies, we already had an impressive performance of MAE $= 3.78$. The linguistic features allow us to only slightly improve performance with a small gain of ΔMAE $=$ 0.04. Surprisingly enough, the complexity metrics barely added any useful information. When looking at each complexity measure individually, we found that only the measures related to the stack size of the parser added information, whereas entropy-based measures, if anything, degraded performance in the test set compared to frequency and length. This was unexpected because the literature (Demberg and Keller, 2009; Wu et al., 2010) suggest that these metrics should play a little but noticeable role in modeling oculometric features. We suspect that even if these metrics are significant in mixed effect models, they are not powerful enough to increase the predictive performance of a neural network model.

In addition to testing the contribution of the predictive features, we were curious if our way of combining these features also played a role. Thus, we compared our non-linear neural network to five linear regressions (one for each variable in the challenge) both using Table 1 features[6]. The average gain was quite large ΔMAE $= 1.23$, showing that both the features we used as well as the way we combined them played a role in the scores we obtained in this challenge.

[6]Minus FORM, PREFIX and SUFFIX because the linear model would struggle to deal with the many values that appear in the test set but not in the train set.

References

Marisa Ferrara Boston, John Hale, Reinhold Kliegl, Umesh Patil, and Shravan Vasishth. 2008. Parsing costs as predictors of reading difficulty: An evaluation using the potsdam sentence corpus. *Journal of Eye Movement Research.-ISSN*, 2(1):1–12.

Ciprian Chelba, Tomas Mikolov, Mike Schuster, Qi Ge, Thorsten Brants, Phillipp Koehn, and Tony Robinson. 2013. One billion word benchmark for measuring progress in statistical language modeling. *arXiv preprint arXiv:1312.3005*.

Vera Demberg and Frank Keller. 2009. A computational model of prediction in human parsing: Unifying locality and surprisal effects. In *Proceedings of the Annual Meeting of the Cognitive Science Society*, volume 31.

Dmitriy Genzel and Eugene Charniak. 2002. Entropy rate constancy in text. *Proceedings of the 40th Annual Meeting of the Association for Computational Linguistics (ACL'02)*.

Edward Gibson. 2000. The dependency locality theory: A distance-based theory of linguistic complexity. *Image, language, brain*, 2000:95–126.

John Hale. 2001. A probabilistic earley parser as a psycholinguistic model. In *Proceedings of the second meeting of the North American Chapter of the Association for Computational Linguistics on Language technologies*, pages 1–8. Association for Computational Linguistics.

Nora Hollenstein, Emmanuele Chersoni, Cassandra Jacobs, Yohei Oseki, Laurent Prévot, and Enrico Santus. 2021. CMCL 2021 shared task on eye-tracking prediction. In *Proceedings of the Workshop on Cognitive Modeling and Computational Linguistics*.

Victor Kuperman, Michael Dambacher, Antje Nuthmann, and Reinhold Kliegl. 2010. The effect of word position on eye-movements in sentence and paragraph reading. *Quarterly Journal of Experimental Psychology*, 63(9):1838–1857.

Alexis Nasr, Frederic Bechet, Jean-Francois Rey, Benoit Favre, and Joseph Le Roux. 2011. Macaon: An nlp tool suite for processing word lattices. In *The 49th Annual Meeting of the Association for Computational Linguistics: demonstration session*.

Joakim Nivre. 2003. An efficient algorithm for projective dependency parsing. In *Proceedings of the Eighth International Conference on Parsing Technologies*, pages 149–160.

Adam Paszke, Sam Gross, Francisco Massa, Adam Lerer, James Bradbury, Gregory Chanan, Trevor Killeen, Zeming Lin, Natalia Gimelshein, Luca Antiga, Alban Desmaison, Andreas Kopf, Edward Yang, Zachary DeVito, Martin Raison, Alykhan Tejani, Sasank Chilamkurthy, Benoit Steiner, Lu Fang, Junjie Bai, and Soumith Chintala. 2019. Pytorch: An imperative style, high-performance deep learning library. In H. Wallach, H. Larochelle, A. Beygelzimer, F. d, Alché-Buc, E. Fox, and R. Garnett, editors, *Advances in Neural Information Processing Systems 32*, pages 8024–8035. Curran Associates, Inc.

Jeffrey Pennington, Richard Socher, and Christopher D. Manning. 2014. Glove: Global vectors for word representation. In *Empirical Methods in Natural Language Processing (EMNLP)*, pages 1532–1543.

Stephen Wu, Asaf Bachrach, Carlos Cardenas, and William Schuler. 2010. Complexity metrics in an incremental right-corner parser. In *Proceedings of the 48th annual meeting of the association for computational linguistics*, pages 1189–1198.

Daniel Zeman et al. 2019. Universal dependencies 2.5. LINDAT/CLARIAH-CZ digital library at the Institute of Formal and Applied Linguistics (ÚFAL), Faculty of Mathematics and Physics, Charles University.

Appendix

Name	nFix		FFD		GPT		TRT		fixProp	
Raw Textual Features										
LENGTH	$4.30_{\pm0.00}$		$0.71_{\pm0.00}$		$2.55_{\pm0.00}$		$1.69_{\pm0.00}$		$11.75_{\pm0.00}$	
EOS	$4.28_{\pm0.00}$		$0.71_{\pm0.00}$		$2.38_{\pm0.00}$		$1.69_{\pm0.00}$		$11.71_{\pm0.00}$	
SUFFIX	$4.25_{\pm0.00}$		$0.70_{\pm0.00}$		$2.60_{\pm0.00}$		$1.66_{\pm0.00}$		$11.59_{\pm0.00}$	
TEXT_ID	$4.25_{\pm0.00}$		$0.71_{\pm0.00}$		$2.52_{\pm0.00}$		$1.67_{\pm0.00}$		$11.75_{\pm0.00}$	
PREFIX	$4.24_{\pm0.00}$	3.88	$0.70_{\pm0.00}$	0.67	$2.59_{\pm0.00}$	2.21	$1.66_{\pm0.00}$	1.54	$11.57_{\pm0.00}$	11.06
SENT_ID	$4.16_{\pm0.00}$		$0.70_{\pm0.00}$		$2.55_{\pm0.00}$		$1.64_{\pm0.00}$		$11.75_{\pm0.00}$	
WORD_ID	$4.11_{\pm0.00}$		$0.70_{\pm0.00}$		$2.52_{\pm0.00}$		$1.61_{\pm0.00}$		$11.52_{\pm0.00}$	
FORM	$4.11_{\pm0.00}$		$0.69_{\pm0.00}$		$2.29_{\pm0.00}$		$1.60_{\pm0.00}$		$11.54_{\pm0.00}$	
Frequencies										
FREQUENCY	$4.30_{\pm0.00}$		$0.71_{\pm0.00}$		$2.55_{\pm0.00}$		$1.69_{\pm0.00}$		$11.75_{\pm0.00}$	
COOC_N	$4.28_{\pm0.00}$	3.76	$0.71_{\pm0.00}$	0.66	$2.44_{\pm0.00}$	2.13	$1.68_{\pm0.00}$	1.44	$11.73_{\pm0.00}$	10.91
COOC_P	$4.28_{\pm0.00}$		$0.70_{\pm0.00}$		$2.46_{\pm0.00}$		$1.67_{\pm0.00}$		$11.66_{\pm0.00}$	
Linguistic Features										
DEP_LEN	$4.28_{\pm0.00}$		$0.71_{\pm0.00}$		$2.48_{\pm0.00}$		$1.68_{\pm0.00}$		$11.73_{\pm0.00}$	
MORPHO	$4.26_{\pm0.00}$		$0.70_{\pm0.00}$		$2.56_{\pm0.00}$		$1.67_{\pm0.00}$		$11.68_{\pm0.00}$	
POS	$4.23_{\pm0.00}$	3.69	$0.70_{\pm0.00}$	0.65	$2.56_{\pm0.00}$	2.12	$1.65_{\pm0.00}$	1.43	$11.59_{\pm0.00}$	10.79
DEPREL	$4.21_{\pm0.00}$		$0.70_{\pm0.00}$		$2.56_{\pm0.00}$		$1.66_{\pm0.00}$		$11.57_{\pm0.00}$	
Complexity Metrics										
ENT_TOK	$4.32_{\pm0.00}$		$0.71_{\pm0.00}$		$2.62_{\pm0.00}$		$1.69_{\pm0.00}$		$11.73_{\pm0.00}$	
ENT_PARSER	$4.31_{\pm0.00}$		$0.71_{\pm0.00}$		$2.66_{\pm0.00}$		$1.69_{\pm0.00}$		$11.78_{\pm0.00}$	
ENT_MORPHO	$4.31_{\pm0.00}$		$0.71_{\pm0.00}$		$2.62_{\pm0.00}$		$1.69_{\pm0.00}$		$11.77_{\pm0.00}$	
ENT_MAX	$4.30_{\pm0.00}$		$0.71_{\pm0.00}$		$2.66_{\pm0.00}$		$1.69_{\pm0.00}$		$11.78_{\pm0.00}$	
ENT_MEAN	$4.30_{\pm0.00}$	3.67	$0.71_{\pm0.00}$	0.65	$2.62_{\pm0.00}$	2.12	$1.69_{\pm0.00}$	1.43	$11.75_{\pm0.00}$	10.80
ENT_TAG	$4.30_{\pm0.00}$		$0.71_{\pm0.00}$		$2.60_{\pm0.00}$		$1.69_{\pm0.00}$		$11.78_{\pm0.00}$	
STACK_DIST	$4.23_{\pm0.00}$		$0.70_{\pm0.00}$		$2.50_{\pm0.00}$		$1.67_{\pm0.00}$		$11.63_{\pm0.00}$	
STACK_SIZE	$4.20_{\pm0.00}$		$0.70_{\pm0.00}$		$2.48_{\pm0.00}$		$1.65_{\pm0.00}$		$11.59_{\pm0.00}$	

Table 2: Detailed results for individual features and features groups, across 5 metrics.

MTL782_IITD at CMCL 2021 Shared Task: Prediction of Eye-Tracking Features Using BERT Embeddings and Linguistic Features

Shivani Choudhary*, **Kushagri Tandon***, **Raksha Agarwal**, **Niladri Chatterjee**
Indian Institute of Technology Delhi
Hauz Khas, Delhi-110016, India
shivani@sire.iitd.ac.in,
{mas197083,raksha.agarwal,niladri}@maths.iitd.ac.in

Abstract

Reading and comprehension are quintessentially cognitive tasks. Eye movement acts as a surrogate to understand which part of a sentence is critical to the process of comprehension. The aim of the shared task is to predict five eye-tracking features for a given word of the input sentence. We experimented with several models based on LGBM (Light Gradient Boosting Machine) Regression, ANN (Artificial Neural Network) and CNN (Convolutional Neural Network), using BERT embeddings and some combination of linguistic features. Our submission using CNN achieved an average MAE of 4.0639 and ranked 7th in the shared task. The average MAE was further lowered to 3.994 in post task evaluation.

1 Introduction

Eye tracking data gauged during the process of natural and comprehensive reading can be an outset to understand which part of the sentence demands more attention. The main objective of the present experiment is to understand the factors responsible for determining how we perceive and process languages.

The CMCL-2021 shared task (Hollenstein et al., 2021) focuses on predicting the eye-tracking metrics for a word. The goal of the task is to train a predictive model for five eye-tracking feature values namely, nFix (Number of fixations), FFD (First fixation duration), TRT (Total reading time), GPT (Go past time), and fixProp (fixation proportion) for a given word of a sentence (Hollenstein et al., 2018; Inhoff et al., 2005). Here, nFix is the total number of fixations on the current word, FFD is the duration of the first fixation on the prevailing word, TRT is the sum of all fixation durations on the current word including regressions, GPT is the sum of all fixations prior to progressing to the right of the current word, including regressions to previous words that originated from the current word and fixProp is the proportion of the participants who fixated on the current word. With respect to eye-tracking data, regression refers to the backward movement of the eye required to reprocess the information in the text (Eskenazi and Folk, 2017).

In this work we have experimented with two broad categories of models: regessor based and neural networks based. Among the regressor based models, we tried with Catboost, XGboost, Light Gradient Boosting Machine (LGBM) among others. Among the Neural Network based models we have used both ANN and CNN. LGBM gave the best results among the regressor based models. CNN produced lowest MAE between CNN and ANN. In this paper we discuss the best models of each type and their corresponding parameters in detail.

The paper is divided into the following sections: Section 2 describes some details of the dataset used for the experiments. In Section 3 we discuss the data preparation approaches for feature extraction. Model details are presented in Section 4, and Section 5 presents analysis of the results. Section 6 concludes the paper. The code for the proposed system is available at https://github.com/shivaniiitd/Eye_tracking

2 Dataset Description

The present task uses the eye-tracking data of the Zurich Cognitive Language Processing Corpus (ZuCo 1.0 and ZuCo 2.0) (Hollenstein et al., 2018, 2020). The dataset is divided into two subsets Train, and Test. The data statistics are presented in Table 1. The data was arranged according to the *sentence_id* and *word_id*. The Train data set contained the values of nFix, GPT, FFD, TRT and fixProp for each word of the input sentences. We used the first 100 sentences from the Train data for validation purposes.

* Joint First Author

Proceedings of the Workshop on Cognitive Modeling and Computational Linguistics, pages 114–119
Online Event, June 10, 2021.

Dataset	No of Sentence	No of Words
Train	800	15736
Test	191	3554

Table 1: Data statistics

3 Data Pre-processing and Feature Selection

It is important to identify the features that provide essential visual and cognitive cues about each word which in turn govern the corresponding various eye-tracking metrics for the word. In the present work we have used BERT embeddings along with linguistic features (Agarwal et al., 2020) to train the predictive models.

Mean Absolute Error (MAE) was used for measuring the performance of the proposed systems for the shared task.

Before feature extraction, the following pre-processing steps were performed:

- The <EOS> tag and extra white spaces were stripped from the end of the words.
- Sentences were created by sequentially joining the words having the same *sentence_id*.
- Additionally, for CNN and ANN models punctuations were removed from the input word.

3.1 Feature Selection

Initially the essential token-level attributes were extracted as follows:

1. Syllables: The number of syllables in a token determines its pronunciation. The sentences were tokenized using the spaCy (Honnibal et al., 2020), and the syllables[1] package was used to calculate the number of syllables in each token.

2. BERT Embeddings: The Bidirectional Encoder Representations from Transformers (BERT) (Devlin et al., 2019) embeddings are contextualized word representations. We have considered the average of the embeddings from the last four hidden layers. The pytorch_pretrained _bert[2] uncased embeddings have been used to extract this feature for each token.

[1]https://github.com/prosegrinder/python-syllables

[2]https://github.com/huggingface/transformers

The above-mentioned features are extracted token-wise but in the training set some input words (which includes both singleton tokens and hyphenated phrases) contained more than one token, e.g. 'seventh-grade'

The final attributes that were used for the LGBM models according to each input word are as follows:

- BERT Embeddings: BERT embeddings for the input word is calculated by averaging the embeddings over all the tokens that make up the word, extracted using the BertTokenizer.
- Syllables: For extracting the syllables for each input word , we sum the number of syllables over all the tokens in that word.
- Word_id: This feature was supplied in the dataset. It indicates the position of each word or phrase in the sentence.
- Word_length: The total number of characters present in each input word or phrase.

Some additional features, such as POS tag, detailed tag, NER tag, dependency label and a Boolean value to indicate whether a token is present in the list of standard English stopwords or not, were also considered. However, these features have not been incorporated in the final models as these features failed to improve the models' performances. To get the values of these features for the input words, the properties of the last token in the input word are used, unless it is a punctuation. In that case the properties of the token before the punctuation are used. To account for the above, two additional features were considered:

(a) a binary feature (HasHyphen) to indicate whether the phrase contains a hyphen or not;

(b) the number of punctuation (NumPunct) in the phrase;

For illustration, for the input phrase 'Brandenburg-Kulmbach,' the feature HasHyphen is 1 and NumPunct is 2, and for the other features mentioned above, the token 'Kulmbach' was used.

4 Proposed Models

In this section we present the details of the three predictive machine learning regression models namely, LGBM, ANN and CNN.

Features	Avg_MAE		nFix	FFD	GPT	TRT	fixProp
Syllables+	**4.01**	MAE	4.02	0.69	2.52	1.58	11.24
Word_id+		λ_1	6.6	2.6	4.6	9.6	3.6
Word_length+		λ_2	12.6	12.6	9.2	0.6	3.6
BERT		NL	75	62	62	80	31
Word_id +	**4.01**	MAE	4.01	0.68	2.52	1.58	11.25
Word_length+		λ_1	4.6	1.0	4.6	9.6	10.6
BERT		λ_2	8.6	11.6	9.2	0.6	18.6
		NL	75	62	62	75	31
Syllables+	4.12	MAE	4.15	0.70	2.55	1.63	11.58
Word_length+		λ_1	4.6	5.6	3.6	3.6	9.6
BERT		λ_2	8.6	15.6	6.6	0.6	9.6
		NL	80	93	31	62	62
Syllables+	4.27	MAE	4.31	0.71	2.59	1.68	12.06
Word_id+		λ_1	4.6	2.6	1.6	4.6	7.6
BERT		λ_2	8.6	12.6	3.6	2.6	7.6
		NL	93	62	31	62	31

Table 2: LGBM Regressor Models

4.1 LGBM Model

LGBM is a Gradient Boosting Decision Tree (GBDT) algorithm which uses two novel techniques: Gradient-based One-Side Sampling (GOSS) and Exclusive Feature Bundling (EFB) to deal with a large number of data instances and large number of features respectively (Ke et al., 2017).

GOSS keeps all the data instances in the GBDT with large gradients and performs random sampling on the instances with small gradients. The sparsity of feature space in high dimensional data provides a possibility to design a nearly lossless approach to reduce the number of features. Many features in a sparse feature are mutually exclusive. These exclusive features are bundled into a single feature (called an exclusive feature bundle).

Five LGBM Regressor models from the LightGBM python package[3] were trained and tuned on varied feature spaces. These models were trained with BERT Embeddings which is present in all models as a feature, along with different combinations of linguistic features, namely, Word_id, Word_length, and Syllables.

In the context of the given problem, the following hyperparameters were tuned,

- **lambda_l1** (λ_1): It is the L1 regularization parameter.
- **lambda_l2** (λ_2): It is the L2 regularization parameter.
- **num_leaves** (NL): This is the main parameter to control the complexity of the tree model, and governs the leaf-wise growth of the tree.

The hyperparameters, namely λ_1, λ_2, and NL, the overall model MAE (Avg_MAE) calculated as average of the MAEs corresponding to each eye-tracking metric, and the individual MAE corresponding to each eye tracking metric evaluated on the test sets are described in Table 2.

4.2 Artificial Neural Network

We have applied a seven layer deep ANN for the shared task. First hidden layer has 1024 neurons, followed by 4 hidden layers of sizes 512, 256, 64 and 16 respectively. The output layer is of size 1. For each of the five eye-tracking features, we have trained separate Neural Networks. The ANN is implemented using Keras with tensorflow backend (Chollet et al., 2015). Adam optimizer (Kingma and Ba, 2017) is used to minimize the loss function (MAE). Rectified linear unit (ReLU) activation is applied on the dense layers. Hyperparameter tuning detail is presented in Section 5. The learning rate is set to decay at a rate of $e^{-0.1}$ after 15 epochs. Dropout layers with dropout rate of 0.2 was placed after the first three hidden layers.

4.3 Convolutional Neural Network

The proposed CNN model has been implemented with the following configuration. In order to capture the contextual information from the sentence, we have used a context window of size K. We split the whole sentence around that word with a sliding window of length K. We named two matrices as left and right context matrix, formed with preceding and succeeding K-1 words, respectively. If the number of words available for the sliding window is less than K then K-r rows are padded with zero, at the start for the left context matrix, and at the end

[3]https://github.com/microsoft/LightGBM

Model	Features	Avg_MAE		nFix	FFD	TRT	GPT	fixProp
CNN	Word_id+	**3.99**	MAE	4.02	0.70	**2.24**	**1.58**	11.43
	Word_length+		BS	32	32	32	32	32
	BERT		DR	0.44	0.3	0.3	0.3	0.3
			LR	1e-4	1e-4	1e-4	1e-4	1e-4
CNN	Word_id+	**4.00**	MAE	4.03	0.70	2.26	1.59	11.41
	Word_length+		BS	16	16	32	16	32
	BERT		DR	0.4	0.1	0.4	0.3	0.0
			LR	1e-4	1e-4	1e-4	1e-4	1e-4
ANN	Word_id+	**4.08**	MAE	4.06	0.71	2.37	1.58	11.68
	Word_length+		BS	64	64	32	16	64
	BERT		DR	0.2	0.0	0.2	0.0	0.0
			LR	1e-5	1e-5	1e-3	1e-4	1e-5
ANN	Word_id+	**4.08**	MAE	4.06	0.72	2.40	1.59	11.65
	Word_length+		BS	64	32	32	64	64
	BERT		DR	0.0	0.3	0.3	0.2	0.0
			LR	1e-5	1e-3	1e-3	1e-5	1e-5

Table 3: CNN model's performance

for the right context matrix. We have conducted experiments for values of K in the set {1, 2, 5, 10, 11, 12}. The best results were obtained for K=10.

The left and right context matrices are fed into two different branches of convolutional layers. The left branch has two convolutions with filter sizes 3×3 with ReLU, and 5×5 without ReLU in two separate branches. For further processing outputs from both the branches are concatenated. In the right branch, two convolution layer with 3×3 filter with ReLU are stacked.

Batch Normalization and ReLU activation are applied on the output of convolutional layers, followed by a pooling layer. The outputs of both the branches are fed into two separate convolutional layers with filter size 64 and kernel size 3×3, followed by two max pooling / average pooling layers with kernel size 2×2. Average pooling has generated the best results. The outputs of the two branches are flattened to obtain two tensors. The resulting tensors are averaged, and this acts as the input to seven fully connected layers with sizes 2048, 1024, 512, 64, 32, 16 and 1, respectively.

The padding used in the convolutional layer is 'same' which keeps the input and output dimension equal. For each of the five eye-tracking features, we have trained separate Neural Networks. The model was trained with loss function MAE, batch size of 32 and Adam optimizer. ReLU activation function is used for the fully connected layers except the output layer. The learning rate is set to decay at a rate of $e^{-0.1}$ after 15 epochs. The network has a dropout rate of 0.2 on the CNN layers and between the fully connected layers of sizes 2048, 1024, 512, and 64. Hyperparameter tuning details are described below.

Parameters	Range
NF	[32, 64]
BS	[16, 32]
LR	[1e-3, 1e-4]
DR	[0, 0.1, 0.2, 0.3, 0.4, 0.5]

Table 4: CNN Hyperparameter details

Parameters	Range
BS	[16, 32, 64]
LR	[1e-3, 1e-4, 1e-5]
DR	[0, 0.1, 0.2, 0.3, 0.4]

Table 5: ANN Hyperparameter details

4.4 Hyperparameter Tuning

Hyperparameter tuning for CNN was performed on Learning Rate (LR), Batch Size (BS), Dropout Rate (DR) and Number of Filters (NF) while ANN hyperparamter tunning was performed on learning rate, batch size, dropout rate. Hyperopt[4] library was used for grid search. For CNN and ANN the range of values for grid search parameters are presented in Table 4 and Table 5, respectively. DR in ANN was limited to 0.4 since higher value will leave very few connections. The maximum number of trials was set to 20. Pooling method variation was controlled manually. CNN models with Average pooling and NF 64 produced the lowest MAE. Additional experiments were conducted on CNN with feature set word_id, word_length and BERT was analysed for fine dropout rate of 0.42, 0.44 and 0.46 and higher batch size of 256. Learning rate was reduced by 0.2 using Keras callback API ReduceLROnPlateau. EarlyStopping was used to stop the training process if the validation loss stops decreasing.

[4]http://hyperopt.github.io/hyperopt/

Model	Features	Avg_MAE	nFix	FFD	GPT	TRT	fixProp
CNN	word_id + Length+ BERT	**3.99**	4.02	0.7	**2.24**	**1.58**	11.43
CNN	Syllables + Word_id+Length+BERT	4.00	4.03	0.70	2.26	1.59	11.41
LGBM	Word_id + Length+ BERT	4.01	**4.01**	**0.68**	2.52	**1.58**	11.25
LGBM	Syllables + Word_id + Length+ BERT	4.01	4.02	0.69	2.52	**1.58**	**11.24**

Table 6: Analysis of the best performing models

5 Results and Analysis

The comparison among top four performing models, ranked according to MAE, is presented in Table 6. CNN models with the feature space Word_id + Length + BERT , as described in Section 3.1 performed the best with MAE 3.99.

It has been observed that Word_id, Length and the BERT embeddings are all present in the feature space of the best performing models, hence these features play an important role in the determination of the eye-tracking metrics. Although, addition of Syllables to the feature space of the LGBM Model did not decrease the MAE corresponding to nFix and FFD. In case of CNN, inclusion of Syllables decreased the MAE corresponding to fixProp. The best result with feature set POS+word_len+word_id+BERT was generated by CNN with an MAE of 4.07. Removal of POS tags as a feature lead to improvement in FFD and TRT however, the overall performance decreased.

The LGBM Models give the best results corresponding to nFix, FFD and fixProp among the top 4 best performing models, While CNN based model performed the best on Avg_MAE and GPT. As we observe in Table 2, in most of the cases, the removal of Word_id and Length led to a decline in the systems' performance. It is also observed that the complex structure of Neural Networks fail to model some of the features in comparison with LGBM model. These experiments also indicate that the feature space for individual eye-tracking features may be curated separately to achieve a better accuracy.

6 Conclusion

The aim of the present work is to develop a predictive model for five eye-tracking features. Experiments were conducted using LGBM, ANN and CNN models trained on a feature space consisting of pre-trained BERT embeddings and linguistic features namely, number of syllables, POS tag, Word length and Word_id. The discussed CNN Models achieved the best performance with respect to the test data. Experiments for studying the importance of individual features indicate that POS tag has the lowest impact on the overall MAE, with respect to the CNN Models and that the addition of Syllables to the feature space in LGBM models does not improve the overall performance of the system. It is further observed that individual linguistic features lead to a varied effect on different eye-tracking metrics. Separate tuning of hyperparameters and feature space corresponding to the LGBM and Neural Network based model, for each eye-tracking metric, can improve the overall system performance.

Even though CNN architecture is more complex, but with the same set of features the LGBM regressor gave almost same results. Currently, we did not perform a rigorous hyperparameter tuning which may be taken up in future.

Acknowledgements

Shivani Choudhary acknowledges the support of DST INSPIRE, Department of Science and Technology, Government of India.

Raksha Agarwal acknowledges Council of Scientific and Industrial Research (CSIR), India for supporting the research under Grant no: SPM-06/086(0267)/2018-EMR-I. The authors thank Google Colab for the free GPU based instance.

References

Raksha Agarwal, Ishaan Verma, and Niladri Chatterjee. 2020. LangResearchLab_NC at FinCausal 2020, task 1: A knowledge induced neural net for causality detection. In *Proceedings of the 1st Joint Workshop on Financial Narrative Processing and MultiLing Financial Summarisation*, pages 33–39, Barcelona, Spain (Online). COLING.

François Chollet et al. 2015. Keras. https://keras.io.

Jacob Devlin, Ming-Wei Chang, Kenton Lee, and Kristina Toutanova. 2019. BERT: Pre-training of deep bidirectional transformers for language understanding. In *Proceedings of the 2019 Conference of the North American Chapter of the Association for Computational Linguistics: Human Language Technologies, Volume 1 (Long and Short Papers)*, pages 4171–4186, Minneapolis, Minnesota. Association for Computational Linguistics.

Michael A Eskenazi and Jocelyn R Folk. 2017. Regressions during reading: The cost depends on the cause. *Psychonomic bulletin & review*, 24(4):1211–1216.

Nora Hollenstein, Emmanuele Chersoni, Cassandra Jacobs, Yohei Oseki, and Enrico Prévot, Laurent Santus. 2021. Cmcl 2021 shared task on eye-tracking prediction. In *Proceedings of the Workshop on Cognitive Modeling and Computational Linguistics*.

Nora Hollenstein, Jonathan Rotsztejn, Marius Troendle, Andreas Pedroni, Ce Zhang, and Nicolas Langer. 2018. Data descriptor: ZuCo, a simultaneous EEG and eye-tracking resource for natural sentence reading. *Sci. Data*, 5(1):1–13.

Nora Hollenstein, Marius Troendle, Ce Zhang, and Nicolas Langer. 2020. ZuCo 2.0: A dataset of physiological recordings during natural reading and annotation. In *Proceedings of the 12th Language Resources and Evaluation Conference*, pages 138–146, Marseille, France. European Language Resources Association.

Matthew Honnibal, Ines Montani, Sofie Van Landeghem, and Adriane Boyd. 2020. spaCy: Industrial-strength Natural Language Processing in Python.

Albrecht W. Inhoff, Brianna M. Eiter, and Ralph Radach. 2005. Time course of linguistic information extraction from consecutive words during eye fixations in reading. *J. Exp. Psychol. Hum. Percept. Perform.*, 31(5):979–995.

Guolin Ke, Qi Meng, Thomas Finley, Taifeng Wang, Wei Chen, Weidong Ma, Qiwei Ye, and Tie-Yan Liu. 2017. Lightgbm: A highly efficient gradient boosting decision tree. In *Proceedings of the 31st International Conference on Neural Information Processing Systems*, NIPS'17, page 3149–3157, Red Hook, NY, USA. Curran Associates Inc.

Diederik P. Kingma and Jimmy Ba. 2017. Adam: A method for stochastic optimization.

KonTra at CMCL 2021 Shared Task: Predicting Eye Movements by Combining BERT with Surface, Linguistic and Behavioral Information

Qi Yu, Aikaterini-Lida Kalouli, Diego Frassinelli
Department of Linguistics, University of Konstanz
firstname.lastname@uni-konstanz.de

Abstract

This paper describes the submission of the team KonTra to the CMCL 2021 Shared Task on eye-tracking prediction. Our system combines the embeddings extracted from a fine-tuned BERT model with surface, linguistic and behavioral features, resulting in an average mean absolute error of 4.22 across all 5 eye-tracking measures. We show that word length and features representing the expectedness of a word are consistently the strongest predictors across all 5 eye-tracking measures.

1 Introduction

The corpora ZuCo 1.0 and ZuCo 2.0 by Hollenstein et al. (2018, 2019) contain eye-tracking data collected in a series of reading tasks on English materials. For each word of the sentences, five eye-tracking measures are recorded: 1) the number of fixations (*nFix*), 2) the first fixation duration (*FFD*), 3) the go-past time (*GPT*), 4) the total reading time (*TRT*), and 5) the fixation proportion (*fixProp*). Providing a subset of the two corpora, the CMCL 2021 Shared Task (Hollenstein et al., 2021) requires the prediction of these eye-tracking measures based on any relevant feature.

To tackle the task, we conduct a series of experiments using various combinations of BERT embeddings (Devlin et al., 2018) and a rich set of surface, linguistic and behavioral features (SLB features). Our experimental setting enables a comparison of the potential of BERT and the SLB features, and allows for the explainability of the system. The best performance is achieved by the models combining word embeddings extracted from a fine-tuned BERT model with a subset of the SLB features that are the most predictive for each eye-tracking measure. Overall, our model was ranked 8th out of 13 models submitted to the shared task.

Our main contributions are the following: 1) We show that training solely on SLB features provides better results than training solely on word embeddings (both pre-trained and fine-tuned ones). 2) Among the SLB features, we show that word length and linguistic features representing word expectedness consistently show the highest weight in predicting all of the 5 measures.

2 Describing Eye-Tracking Measures

To explore the impact of linguistic and cognitive information on eye-movements in reading tasks, we extract a set of surface, linguistic, behavioral and BERT features, as listed in Table 1.

Surface Features Given the common finding that surface characteristics, particularly the length of a word, influence fixation duration (Juhasz and Rayner, 2003; New et al., 2006), we compute various surface features at word and sentence level (e.g., word and sentence length).

Linguistic Features The linguistic characteristics of the words co-occurring in a sentence have an effect on eye movements (Clifton et al., 2007). Thus, we experiment with features of syntactic and semantic nature. The syntactic features are extracted using the Stanza NLP kit (Qi et al., 2020). For each word, we extract its part-of-speech (POS), its word type (content vs. function word), its dependency relation and its named entity type. According to Godfroid et al. (2018) and Williams and Morris (2004), word familiarity (both local and global) has an effect on the reader's attention, i.e., readers may pay less attention on words that already occurred in previous context. In this study, we treat familiarity as word expectedness and model it using three types of semantic similarity: a) similarity of the current word w_m to the whole sentence (*similarity*$_{w_m,s}$), b) similarity of the current word to its previous word (*similarity*$_{w_m,w_{m-1}}$), and c) similarity of the current word to all of its previous words within the current sentence (*similarity*$_{w_m,w_{1\ldots m-1}}$). To compute these similarity measures, we use the BERT (base) (De-

Proceedings of the Workshop on Cognitive Modeling and Computational Linguistics, pages 120–124
Online Event, June 10, 2021.

Feature Category	Feature Name
Surface Features	word length, sentence length in tokens, sentence length in characters, word length-sentence length ratio
Linguistic Features	POS, word type, named entity type, dependency relation, surprisal score, frequency score, similarity$_{w_m,s}$, similarity$_{w_m,w_{m-1}}$, similarity$_{w_m,w_{1...m-1}}$
Behavioral Features	age of acquisition, prevalence score, valence score, arousal score, dominance score, concreteness$_{human}$, concreteness$_{auto}$
BERT Features	pre-trained BERT embedding, fine-tuned BERT embedding

Table 1: The complete set of surface, linguistic and behavioral (SLB) features and the BERT features.

vlin et al., 2018) pre-trained model[1] and map each word to its pre-trained embedding of layer 11. We chose this layer because it mostly captures semantic properties, while the last layer has been found to be very close to the actual classification task and thus less suitable for our purpose (Jawahar et al., 2019; Lin et al., 2019). Based on these extracted embeddings, we calculate the cosine similarities. To measure the similarity of the current word to the whole sentence (*similarity*$_{w_m,s}$), we take the CLS token to represent the whole sentence; we also experiment with the average token embeddings as the sentence embedding, but we find that the CLS token performs better. For measuring the similarity of the current word to all of its previous words (*similarity*$_{w_m,w_{1...m-1}}$), we average the embeddings of the previous words and find the cosine similarity between this average embedding and the embedding of the current word.

Furthermore, semantic surprisal, i.e., the negative log-transformed conditional probability of a word given its preceding context, provides a good measure of predictability of words in context and efficiently predicts reading times (Smith and Levy, 2013), N400 amplitude (Zhang et al., 2020) and pupil dilation (Frank and Thompson, 2012). We compute surprisal using a bigram language model trained on the lemmatized version of the first slice (roughly 31-million tokens) of the ENCOW14-AX corpus (Schäfer and Bildhauer, 2012). As an additional measure of word expectedness, we also include frequency scores based on the US subtitle corpus (SUBTLEX-US, Brysbaert and New, 2009).

Behavioral Features As discussed in Juhasz and Rayner (2003) and Clifton et al. (2007), behavioral measures highly affect eye-movements in reading tasks. For each word in the sentence, we extract behavioral features from large collections of human generated values available online: age of acquisition (Kuperman et al., 2012), prevalence (Brysbaert et al., 2019), valence, arousal, dominance (Warriner et al., 2013) and concreteness. For concreteness, we experiment both with human generated scores (*concreteness*$_{human}$, Brysbaert et al., 2014) and automatically generated ones (*concreteness*$_{auto}$, Köper and Schulte im Walde, 2017). All behavioral measures have been centered (mean equal to zero) and the missing values have been set to the corresponding mean value.

BERT Features Given the success of current language models for various NLP tasks, we investigate their expressivity for human-centered tasks such as eye-tracking: each word is mapped to two types of contextualized embeddings. First, each word is mapped to its BERT (Devlin et al., 2018) embedding extracted from the pre-trained base model. To extract the second type of contextualized embedding, we fine-tune BERT on each of the five eye-tracking measures. Specifically, the BERT base model[2] is fine-tuned separately 5 times, one for each of the eye-tracking measures to be predicted. Based on these fine-tuned models, we extract the embedding of each word as a fixed feature vector to be used for further experimentation. This means that in this step each word is in fact mapped to five distinct embeddings, one for each fine-tuned model. In the later experimentation, we use the respective embedding based on which measure is currently predicted (e.g., the embedding extracted from the model fine-tuned for nFix is used to predict nFix).

[1] https://github.com/google-research/bert

[2] We use the regression implementation from: https://github.com/fancyerii/bert

Measure	Feature Name
nFix	**word length** (0.81), **frequency score** (0.05), word length-sentence length ratio (0.01), **similarity**$_{w_m,w_{m-1}}$ (0.01), surprisal score (0.01), similarity$_{w_m,w_{1...m-1}}$ (0.01)
FFD	**word length** (0.80), **frequency score** (0.06), **similarity**$_{w_m,w_{m-1}}$ (0.02), word length-sentence length ratio (0.02), similarity$_{w_m,w_{1...m-1}}$ (0.02), surprisal score (0.01)
GPT	**word length** (0.40), surprisal score (0.27), word length-sentence length ratio (0.06), similarity$_{w_m,s}$ (0.04), **similarity**$_{w_m,w_{m-1}}$ (0.02), **frequency score** (0.02), stop word (0.02), similarity$_{w_m,w_{1...m-1}}$ (0.02), numeral token (0.02), age of acquisition (0.01), dominance (0.01)
TRT	**word length** (0.70), **frequency score** (0.11), word length-sentence length ratio (0.03), numeral token (0.01), **similarity**$_{w_m,w_{m-1}}$ (0.01), similarity$_{w_m,s}$ (0.01), sentence length in characters (0.01)
fixProp	**word length** (0.84), **similarity**$_{w_m,w_{m-1}}$ (0.04), **frequency score** (0.03), similarity$_{w_m,w_{1...m-1}}$ (0.02)

Table 2: SLB features with importance ≥ 0.01. Features in each row are sorted by their importance in descending order. Features that are strong predictors in all 5 measures are marked in **bold**.

3 Predicting Eye-Tracking Measures

We conduct three experiments using different feature combinations, and experiment with three model architectures. The models' parameters are experimentally defined. First, we train a Linear Regression model (LR). Second, we train a Decision Tree Regressor (DT) with the *mse* (*Mean Squared Error*) criterion and a maximum depth of 7. Last, we train a Random Forest Regressor (RF) with the *mse* criterion, 15 estimators and a maximum depth of 7. Before training the models, all categorical feature values are one-hot-encoded and all numeric values are normalized within the range $[0, 1]$.

3.1 Experiment 1: Using Only SLB Features

In Experiment 1, we train the aforementioned model architectures on the full set of SLB features. Among the three models, the Random Forest Regressor achieves the best overall performance, with an average MAE across all 5 eye-tracking measures of $\overline{\text{MAE}}_{\text{RF}} = 4.059$, $\overline{\text{MAE}}_{\text{DT}} = 4.187$, $\overline{\text{MAE}}_{\text{LR}} = 4.322$. To shed light on the most predictive features for each of the eye-tracking measures, we perform feature selection based on the features' weight, i.e., the impurity-based feature importance (Gini importance) computed as the normalized total reduction of the criterion brought by that feature – the higher, the more important the feature. We select features with importance higher than 0.01, resulting in a reduced SLB feature set as shown in Table 2. This selected set is further used for Experiment 3 (see Section 3.3).

3.2 Experiment 2: Using Only BERT

Our second experiment aims at investigating the expressivity of the contextualized BERT embeddings. We experiment with the two variants of BERT embeddings (see Section 2). In the first variant, the three models use the pre-trained BERT embeddings, while in the second variant, the models use the fine-tuned BERT embeddings. The latter means that for each of the 5 eye-tracking measures, the extracted embeddings of the corresponding fine-tuned model are used and 3 models are trained for each measure, with a total of 15 models. We also experiment with the predictions directly resulting from the fine-tuning tasks, but we observe that these predictions show similar performance. This finding is in line with what is reported in Devlin et al. (2018).

3.3 Experiment 3: Enhancing BERT with SLB Features

Extracting BERT embeddings as fixed-length features instead of using the predictions directly out of the fine-tuned model allows us to extend the BERT vectors with further features. Thus, in the last experiment, we train the 3 regression models on an *extended* vector, comprising the extracted 768-dimensional BERT embedding and additional dimensions for the reduced SLB feature set of Experiment 1 (see Section 3.1). Again, two variants are tested: one using the pre-trained embeddings and the other one using the fine-tuned embeddings of the corresponding model.

4 Results and Discussion

Table 3 reports the results from all experimental settings on the development set and test set (80/20 split). Due to space limits, we only report the results of the best model in each configuration. Overall, combining the embeddings from the fine-tuned version of BERT with the surface, linguistic and behavioral features gives the best performance on

	nFix	FFD	GPT	TRT	fixProp
			DEVELOPMENT SET		
SLB	4.126 (RF)	0.675 (RF)	2.682 (RF)	1.615 (RF)	11.198 (RF)
Pre-trained BERT	4.925 (LR)	0.769 (LR)	2.967 (LR)	1.888 (LR)	13.530 (LR)
Fine-tuned BERT	4.694 (LR)	0.753 (LR)	2.811 (LR)	1.805 (LR)	13.140 (LR)
Pre-trained BERT + SLB	4.086 (LR)	0.676 (RF)	2.625 (RF)	1.597 (RF)	11.150 (RF)
Fine-tuned BERT + SLB	**3.982 (LR)**	**0.676 (RF)**	**2.572 (RF)**	**1.555 (LR)**	**11.147 (RF)**
			TEST SET (PRE-EVALUATION)		
Fine-tuned BERT + SLB	4.263 (LR)	0.698 (RF)	2.756 (RF)	1.682 (LR)	11.683 (RF)
			TEST SET (POST-EVALUATION)		
Fine-tuned BERT + SLB	4.233 (LR)	0.700 (RF)	2.751 (LR)	1.673 (LR)	11.760(RF)

Table 3: Mean absolute errors on the development and the test set. The pre-evaluation test set results are the ones submitted to the competition. We obtained the post-evaluation results after further fine-tuning.

all 5 eye-tracking measures. When we compare the predictive power of the models including only SLB features against the models trained only on BERT, we see that the embeddings are less informative than the carefully selected set of SLB features.

A closer investigation of the selected SLB features in Table 2 provides interesting insights about the nature of the features and the task.

Surface Features Among all SLB features, *word length* is consistently the predictor with the highest weight across all 5 measures. Furthermore, *word length-sentence length ratio* is among the most important contributors in 4 of the 5 measures. This confirms the observation in Hollenstein et al. (2018, p. 10) that the probability of a word being skipped reduces as word length increases.

Linguistic Features Two features for word expectedness, i.e., *frequency score* and *similarity*$_{w_m,w_{m-1}}$, also show a high predictive power for all 5 measures. This confirms previous findings by Godfroid et al. (2018) and Williams and Morris (2004). Likewise, *similarity*$_{w_m,w_{1...m-1}}$ ranks among the most important features for 4 of the 5 measures, and *surprisal score* for 3 of the 5 measures. Most importantly, surprisal score shows a much higher importance in predicting GPT, which indicates that encountering an unexpected word may cause a regressive reading to re-inspect previous words and thus increases the go-past time. On the other hand, the syntactic properties of a word (e.g., POS, dependency relation and named entity type) do not show any strong effect in our results. The only exception is that *numeral tokens* are among the most important features in predicting GPT and TRT. After a closer look into the data, we found that a majority of the numeral tokens are information about date (e.g. *November 28*; *1826-1905*). The effect of such numeral tokens could probably be explained by the nature of the data, where a majority of the sentences are biographical sentences from Wikipedia (Hollenstein et al., 2018, 2019). In such data, this numeral information is highly relevant for the context.

Behavioral Features *Dominance* and *age of acquisition* also play a significant role in predicting GPT: as indicated in the literature (Juhasz and Rayner, 2003), such behavioral measures have a strong impact on the processing time of words in context.

5 Conclusion

We presented a system of eye-tracking feature prediction which combines BERT with a rich set of surface, linguistic and behavioral (SLB) features. Overall, our three studies indicate that including not only semantic properties that can be directly extracted from text, such as embeddings and surprisal score, but also measures reflecting behavioral (e.g., dominance and age of acquisition) and surface properties (word and sentence length) has a positive impact on the performance of our models in predicting eye-tracking data.

References

Marc Brysbaert, Paweł Mandera, Samantha F McCormick, and Emmanuel Keuleers. 2019. Word prevalence norms for 62,000 English lemmas. *Behavior Research Methods*, 51(2):467–479.

Marc Brysbaert and Boris New. 2009. Moving beyond Kučera and Francis: A critical evaluation of current word frequency norms and the introduction of a new and improved word frequency measure for American English. *Behavior Research Methods*, 41(4):977–990.

Marc Brysbaert, Amy Beth Warriner, and Victor Kuperman. 2014. Concreteness ratings for 40 thousand generally known English word lemmas. *Behavior Research Methods*, 46(3):904–911.

Charles Clifton, Adrian Staub, and Keith Rayner. 2007. Eye movements in reading words and sentences. In Roger P.G. Van Gompel, Martin H. Fischer, Wayne S. Murray, and Robin L. Hill, editors, *Eye Movements*, pages 341–371. Elsevier, Oxford.

Jacob Devlin, Ming-Wei Chang, Kenton Lee, and Kristina Toutanova. 2018. BERT: Pre-training of deep bidirectional transformers for language understanding. *preprint arXiv:1810.04805*.

Stefan Frank and Robin Thompson. 2012. Early effects of word surprisal on pupil size during reading. In *Proceedings of the Annual Meeting of the Cognitive Science Society*, volume 34.

Aline Godfroid, Jieun Ahn, Ina Choi, Laura Ballard, Yaqiong Cui, Suzanne Johnston, Shinhye Lee, Abdhi Sarkar, and Hyung-Jo Yoon. 2018. Incidental vocabulary learning in a natural reading context: An eye-tracking study. *Bilingualism*, 21(3):563.

Nora Hollenstein, Emmanuele Chersoni, Cassandra Jacobs, Yohei Oseki, Laurent Prévot, and Enrico Santus. 2021. CMCL 2021 shared task on eye-tracking prediction. In *Proceedings of the Workshop on Cognitive Modeling and Computational Linguistics*.

Nora Hollenstein, Jonathan Rotsztejn, Marius Troendle, Andreas Pedroni, Ce Zhang, and Nicolas Langer. 2018. ZuCo, a simultaneous EEG and eye-tracking resource for natural sentence reading. *Scientific Data*, 5(1):1–13.

Nora Hollenstein, Marius Troendle, Ce Zhang, and Nicolas Langer. 2019. ZuCo 2.0: A dataset of physiological recordings during natural reading and annotation. *preprint arXiv:1912.00903*.

Ganesh Jawahar, Benoît Sagot, and Djamé Seddah. 2019. What does BERT learn about the structure of language? In *Proceedings of the 57th Annual Meeting of the Association for Computational Linguistics*, pages 3651–3657.

Barbara J Juhasz and Keith Rayner. 2003. Investigating the effects of a set of intercorrelated variables on eye fixation durations in reading. *Journal of Experimental Psychology: Learning, Memory, and Cognition*, 29(6):1312.

Maximilian Köper and Sabine Schulte im Walde. 2017. Improving verb metaphor detection by propagating abstractness to words, phrases and individual senses. In *Proceedings of the 1st Workshop on Sense, Concept and Entity Representations and their Applications*, pages 24–30.

Victor Kuperman, Hans Stadthagen-Gonzalez, and Marc Brysbaert. 2012. Age-of-acquisition ratings for 30,000 English words. *Behavior Research Methods*, 44(4):978–990.

Yongjie Lin, Yi Chern Tan, and Robert Frank. 2019. Open sesame: Getting inside BERT's linguistic knowledge. In *Proceedings of the 2019 ACL Workshop BlackboxNLP: Analyzing and Interpreting Neural Networks for NLP*, pages 241–253.

Boris New, Ferrand Ludovic, Pallier Christophe, and Brysbaert Marc. 2006. Reexamining the word length effect in visual word recognition: New evidence from the English Lexicon Project. *Psychonomic Bulletin & Review*, 13(1):45–52.

Peng Qi, Yuhao Zhang, Yuhui Zhang, Jason Bolton, and Christopher D. Manning. 2020. Stanza: A Python natural language processing toolkit for many human languages. In *Proceedings of the 58th Annual Meeting of the Association for Computational Linguistics: System Demonstrations*.

Roland Schäfer and Felix Bildhauer. 2012. Building large corpora from the web using a new efficient tool chain. In *Eighth International Conference on Language Resources and Evaluation (LREC)*, pages 486–493.

Nathaniel J Smith and Roger Levy. 2013. The effect of word predictability on reading time is logarithmic. *Cognition*, 128(3):302–319.

Amy Beth Warriner, Victor Kuperman, and Marc Brysbaert. 2013. Norms of valence, arousal, and dominance for 13,915 English lemmas. *Behavior Research Methods*, 45(4):1191–1207.

Rihana Williams and Robin Morris. 2004. Eye movements, word familiarity, and vocabulary acquisition. *European Journal of Cognitive Psychology*, 16(1-2):312–339.

Ye Zhang, Diego Frassinelli, Jyrki Tuomainen, Jeremy I Skipper, and Gabriella Vigliocco. 2020. More than words: Word predictability, prosody, gesture and mouth movements in natural language comprehension. *preprint BioRxiv*.

CogNLP-Sheffield at CMCL 2021 Shared Task: Blending Cognitively Inspired Features with Transformer-based Language Models for Predicting Eye Tracking Patterns

Peter Vickers*, **Rosa Wainwright***,
Harish Tayyar Madabushi and **Aline Villavicencio**

Department of Computer Science
University of Sheffield
United Kingdom

{pgjvickers1, rhwainwright1, h.tayyarmadabushi, a.villavicencio}
@sheffield.ac.uk

Abstract

The CogNLP-Sheffield submissions to the CMCL 2021 Shared Task examine the value of a variety of cognitively and linguistically inspired features for predicting eye tracking patterns, as both standalone model inputs and as supplements to contextual word embeddings (XLNet). Surprisingly, the smaller pre-trained model (XLNet-base) outperforms the larger (XLNet-large), and despite evidence that multi-word expressions (MWEs) provide cognitive processing advantages, MWE features provide little benefit to either model.

1 Introduction and Motivation

Many researchers now agree that eye movements during reading are not random (Rayner, 1998); as a result, eye-tracking has been used to study a variety of linguistic phenomena, such as language acquisition (Blom and Unsworth, 2010) and language comprehension (Tanenhaus, 2007). Readers do not study every word in a sentence exactly once, so following patterns of fixations (pauses with the eyes focused on a word for processing) and regressions (returning to a previous word) provides a relatively non-intrusive method for capturing subconscious elements of subjects' cognitive processes.

Recently, cognitive signals like eye-tracking data have been put to use in a variety of NLP tasks, such as POS-tagging (Barrett et al., 2016), detecting multi-word expressions (Rohanian et al., 2017) and regularising attention mechanisms (Barrett et al., 2018): the majority of research utilising eye-tracking data has focused on its revealing linguistic qualities of the reading material and/or the cognitive processes involved in reading. The CMCL 2021 Shared Task of Predicting Human Reading Behaviour (Hollenstein et al., 2021) asks a slightly different question: given the reading material, is it possible to predict eye-tracking behaviour?

Our ability to quantitatively describe linguistic phenomena has greatly increased since the first feature-based models of reading behaviour (i.e. Carpenter and Just (1983)). Informed by these traditional models, our first model tests 'simple' features that are informed by up-to-date expert linguistic knowledge. In particular, we investigate information about multi-word expressions (MWEs) as eye-tracking information has been used to detect MWEs in context (Rohanian et al., 2017; Yaneva et al., 2017), and empirically MWEs appear have processing advantages over non-formulaic language (Siyanova-Chanturia et al., 2017).

Our second model is motivated by evidence that Pre-trained Language Models (PLMs) outperform feature based models in ways that do not correlate with identifiable cognitive processes (Sood et al., 2020). Since many PLMs evolved from the study of human cognitive processes (Vaswani et al., 2017) but now perform in ways that do not correlate with human cognition, we wished to investigate how merging cognitively inspired features with PLMs may impact predictive behaviour. We felt this was a particularly pertinent question given that PLMs have been shown to contain information about crucial features for predicting eye tracking patterns such as parts of speech (Chrupała and Alishahi, 2019; Tenney et al., 2019) and sentence length (Jawahar et al., 2019).

We therefore had the goals of providing a competitive Shared Task entry, and investigating the following hypotheses: A) Does linguistic/cognitive information that can be *predicted* by eye-tracking features prove useful for *predicting* eye-tracking features? B) Can adding cognitively inspired features to a model based on PLMs improve performance in predicting eye tracking features?

* *Equal Contribution*

Proceedings of the Workshop on Cognitive Modeling and Computational Linguistics, pages 125–133
Online Event, June 10, 2021. ©2021 Association for Computational Linguistics

2 Task Description

The CMCL 2021 Shared Task of Predicting Reading Behaviour formulates predicting gaze features from the linguistic information in their associated sentences as a regression task. The data for the task consists of 991 sentences (800 training, 191 test) and their associated token-level gaze features from the Zurich Cognitive Language Processing Corpora (Hollenstein et al., 2018, 2020). For each word, the following measures were averaged over the reading behaviour of the participants: FFD (*first fixation duration*, the length of the first fixation on the given word); TRT (*total reading time*, the sum of the lengths of all fixations on the given word); GPT (*go past time*, the time taken from the first fixation on the given word for the eyes to move to its right in the sentence); nFix (*number of fixations*, the total quantity of fixations on a word, regardless of fixation lengths) and fixProp (*fixation proportion*, the proportion of participants that fixated the word at least once). Solutions were evaluated using Mean Absolute Error (MAE). For more details about the Shared Task, see Hollenstein et al. (2021).

3 Related Work

Transformer architectures Bidirectional Encoder Representations from Transformers (BERT) (Devlin et al., 2019) is a Language Representation model constructed from stacked Neural Network attention layers and 'massively' pre-trained on large Natural Language Corpora. In contrast with traditional language models, BERT is pre-trained in two settings: a 'cloze' task where a randomly masked word is to be predicted, and next sentence prediction. BERT or derivative models have been used to achieve state-of-the-art baselines on many NLP tasks (Devlin et al., 2019; Yang et al., 2019). Analysis studies have shown that BERT learns complex, task-appropriate, multi-stage pipelines for reasoning over natural language, although there is evidence of model bias. XLNet (Yang et al., 2019) is an autoregressive formulation of BERT which trains on all possible permutations of contextual words, and removes the assumption that predicted tokens are independent of each other.

Similar studies To our knowledge, studies that attempt to *predict* cognitive signals using language models are fairly few and far between. Djokic et al. (2020) successfully used non-Transformer word embeddings to decode brain activity recorded during literal and metaphorical sentence disambiguation. Since RNNs may be considered more 'cognitively plausible' than Transformer based models, Merkx and Frank (2020) compared how well these two types of language models predict different measures of human reading behaviour, finding that the Transformer models more accurately predicted self-paced reading times and EEG signals, but the RNNs were superior for predicting eye-tracking measures.

In a slightly different task, Sood et al. (2020) compared LSTM, CNN, and XLNet attention weightings with human eye-tracking data on the MovieQA task (Tapaswi et al., 2016), finding significant evidence that LSTMs display similar patterns to humans when performing well. XLNet used a more accurate strategy for the task but was less similar to human reading.

Though these studies may indicate that Transformer models are not the most suited to eye-tracking prediction, they are still considered State of the Art in creating broad semantic representations and general linguistic competence (Devlin et al., 2019). As such, we hoped they would allow us to investigate Carpenter and Just's speculation that the dominance of word length and frequency for predicting eye-tracking behaviour may reduce "as the metrics improve for describing higher-level factors" like semantic meaning (1983, p. 290).

4 Experimental Design[1]

We pursued both feature engineering and deep learning approaches to the task; though both methods performed well independently, there was little improvement in predictive capability when combining their features (see Table 1). As such, we developed and submitted two models: Model 1 (Feature Rich) and Model 2 (XLNet). Additional details about the feature combinations used in our final models can be found in Appendices A and C.

4.1 Linguistic Features

Each word in the training vocabulary was encoded as a one-hot vector. Since function words are more likely to be fixated than open class words (Carpenter and Just, 1983), we included POS information generated by `Spacy` (Honnibal et al., 2020) (honouring the tokenisation in the training data). We included a a binary indicator for whether a word

[1]For reproducibility purposes, our program code (including details of hyperparameters) is available here: CogNLP-Sheffield-CMCL-2021

was the first or last in its sentence to incorporate the knowledge that first and last fixations on a *line* are 5-7 letter spaces from the two respective ends (Rayner, 1998). We generated raw frequencies (proportion per million words) and Zipf frequencies (Van Heuven et al., 2014).

Finally, concreteness norms (a measure of how 'abstract' a given word is) were included as features (mean, standard deviation, and the % of participants familiar enough with the word to accurately judge its concreteness; Brysbaert et al. (2014)). We specifically tested concreteness due to the unusually large coverage of the norms.

4.2 Reading Specific Features

Word length has been empirically demonstrated as a very good predictor of gaze features in many studies (i.e. Rayner and McConkie (1976); Carpenter and Just (1983). Duration of fixation is observed to increase for words that exceed the mean saccade length (7-9 letters), and probability of fixation is reduced for words shorter than half the mean saccade length (Rayner and McConkie, 1976). Therefore, as features we included both the raw word lengths, and categorical variables representing word length as a proportion of a mean saccade length.

Since readers may store information about adjacent words (Rayner, 1975, 1998; Barrett, 2018), we also experimented with supplying features from previous and future words to each target word.

4.3 Type Summary Statistics from GECO

Following Barrett et al. (2016), we used the monolingual data from the GECO corpus (Cop et al., 2017) to generate type-level summary statistics for each word. Specifically, we averaged the gaze features across the 12 participants who completed the reading task, and normalised these features to reflect the normalisation of the Shared Task training data. We then averaged these values again at the type (word) level. For words present in the task training data but not the GECO data, we estimated the values using means for words in the GECO data of a similar frequency (according to the `wordfreq`).

4.4 Multi-word Expression Features

We generated an MWE lexicon and summary metrics using the Wikitext-103 corpus (Merity et al., 2016) and `mwetoolkit` (Ramisch, 2012). We chose Wikitext-103 since it provided a large variety of possible MWEs in a similar context to the ZuCo reading material (Hollenstein et al., 2020). We produced two indicator features for the presence of MWEs: a binary indicator, and a categorical variable summarising the syntactic pattern of the MWE, motivated by Yaneva et al.'s evidence that MWEs of different syntactic patterns display different eye-tracking characteristics (2017).

Following the method of Cordeiro et al. (2019), we joined component words of MWEs in Wikitext-103 using underscores (i.e. *climate change* became *climate_change*) and then generated Skip-gram word embeddings (Mikolov et al., 2013) for all single words and MWEs identified in Wikitext-103. Using the `feat_comp` function in `mwetoolkit` (Ramisch, 2012), these MWE embeddings were used to compute compositionality scores and weights (Cordeiro et al., 2019). [2]

MWEs identified in the training data were assigned MWE embeddings and compositionality information as features, and non-MWEs were assigned single word embeddings and zero values for compositionality.

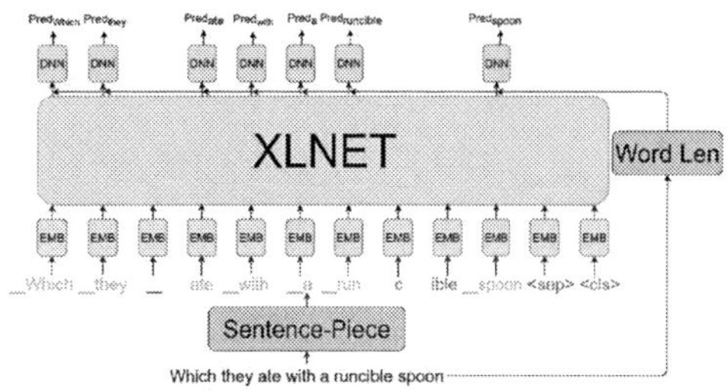

Figure 1: XLNET Feature Prediction Model

4.5 XLNet

In order to obtain Massively Pre-trained Language Model features we used XLNet. We finetuned a model that was pre-trained on BooksCorpus (Zhu et al., 2015), English Wikipedia, Giga5 (Courtney Napoles, Matthew R. Gormley, 2012), ClueWeb 2012-B (Callan et al., 2009), and Common Crawl text (Crawl, 2019). For predictions, we took the final hidden representation of the first sub-word token encoding of each word. We concatenated this feature with an integer representing the total word length in characters to encourage the model to explicitly attend to word length. We tested the effectiveness of sub-word aggregation but found this

[2]The score represents the degree to which the meaning of the MWE can be worked out from the meanings of its constituent words (i.e. 'climate change' has high compositionality, 'cloud nine' has low compositionality), and the weights estimate the semantic contribution of each word in the expression.

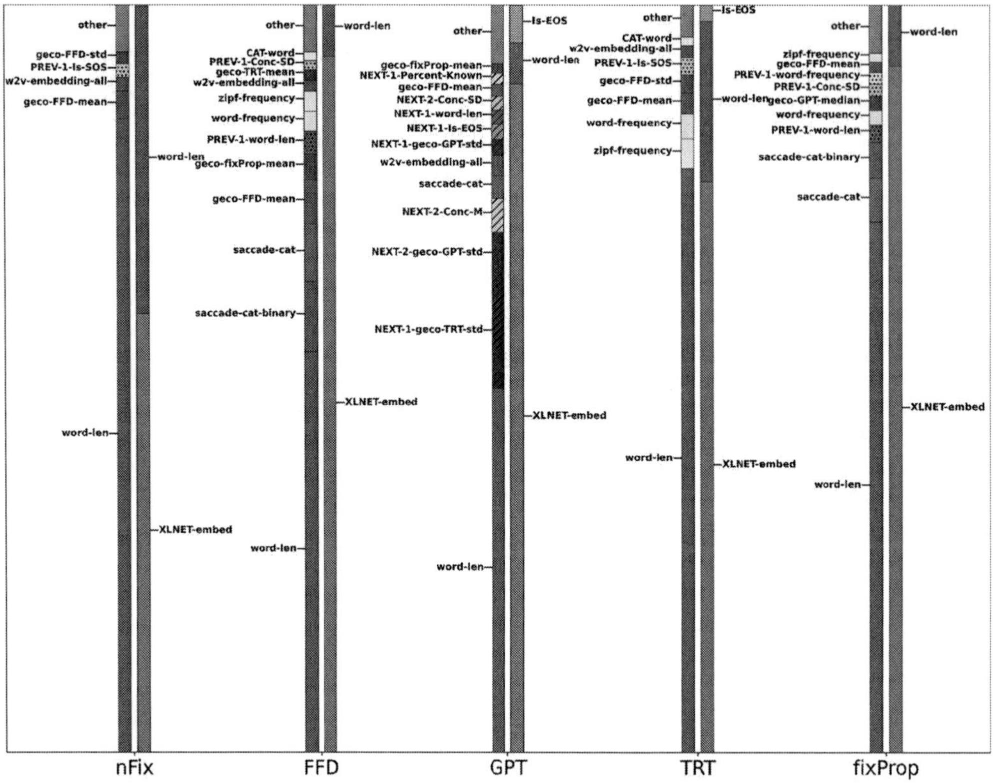

Figure 2: Feature Importance by Target for Model 1 (Left) and Model 2 (Right).

reduced the model's accuracy by an average of 0.04 MAE, which we speculate is due loss of information in the pooling operation whilst head sub-word units already contain contextual information. We then passed the concatenated sub-word and word-length features to a 3-layer dense Neural Network which was used to predict the Shared Task's five target features. This 3-layer multi-feature Network was found to be optimal through experimentation. For stability, we used the Huber loss objective, which approximates L2 loss for small values and L1 loss for large values. We trained using the AdamW optimiser and with learning rates and training duration chosen through grid search across 3-fold cross-validation, obtaining an optimal learning rate of 0.00001 and 800 epochs.

4.6 Regressors

To form predictions for the Feature Rich model we used a Random Forest Regressor implemented by `scikit-learn` (Pedregosa et al., 2011) with parameters `[max_depth = 7, n_estimators = 100, max_features = None]`. For the XLNet model, we collected the XLNet final state embeddings (identical to those fed into the DNN in Figure 1) along with the features `[word-len, CAT-pos, zipf-frequency, Is-EOS, Is-SOS]`. We then trained `scikit-learn's ElasticNetCV` for 5-fold validation with parameters `[max_iter = 10000, l1_ratio=[0.1,0.3,0.5,0.7,1], cv=5]`.

5 Results

In Table 1 we present the MAE on validation splits of the training data. This information informed our choice of model submissions alongside a preference for models using more cognitive features.

Model/Split	1	2	3	Mean
ElasticNet(XLNet + ALL Features)	3.918	3.927	3.891	3.912
Feature Rich/Model 1	**4.017**	**4.023**	**3.981**	**4.007**
BERT-base-cased	4.030	4.045	3.977	4.012
ElasticNet(BERT-base-cased)	3.986	4.024	3.969	3.993
XLNet-base-cased	3.988	3.956	3.935	3.959
XLNet-base-cased (random init)	4.608	4.722	4.695	4.675
XLNet-large-cased	3.929	4.039	3.960	3.976
ElasticNet(XLNet-base-cased)/Model 2	**3.921**	**3.924**	**3.896**	**3.914**

Table 1: Model MAE on Development Splits

We submitted two sets of predictions from Model 2 (ElasticNet(XLNet-base-cased)) and one set of predictions from Model 1 (Feature Rich). Table 2 shows the ranking of Models 1 and 2 in

Rank	Team (model)	MAE
1	LAST	3.8134
2	TALEP	3.8328
	...	
5	CogNLP@Sheffield (XLNet/Model 2)	3.9565
	...	
7	MTL782_IITD	4.0639
-	CogNLP@Sheffield (Feature Rich/Model 1)	4.0689
	...	
-	MEAN BASELINE	7.3699
13	IIIT_DWD	9.7615

Table 2: Ranking on the CMCL Shared Task Test Data.

the overall task. Our overall standing is shown to be 5th, with an MAE delta of 0.143 behind the best model. Whilst a prediction which combined Models 1 and 2 was slightly more accurate (see Table 1), we regard this improvement as within margin of error. We therefore focussed on Models 1 and 2 separately since this allowed for clearer comparisons between the two approaches.

6 Analysis and Discussion

Our results (Table 1) support both our hypotheses introduced in Section 1.

We did not anticipate that XLNet-base would outperform XLNet-large, which had more pre-training data and layers. This is possibly due to the limited amount of training data specific to the task for fine-tuning, resulting in the larger model under-fitting. We are able to confirm that the knowledge XLNet learns through massive pre-training crucial to its performance in this arena - removal of this knowledge through weight randomisation increases MAE from 3.959 to 4.675. Hence we believe that both structure and pre-training of XLNet-base contribute to its success in this task.

We use normalised permutation feature importance (see Appendix B) to better understand the value of different features and present it on a per-target basis for each model in Figure 2.

The most interesting outcome of our experiments was the fact that XLNet embeddings subsume information contained across most features except word length (especially in predicting nFix). It may be that the use of word-pieces obfuscate word length information thus requiring the explicit addition of that information. While the usefulness of features such as word length is consistent with the literature, we were surprised by the relative unimportance of MWE information given that many neurocognitive studies have demonstrated differences in how they are processed (Siyanova-Chanturia et al., 2011, 2017; Cacciari and Tabossi, 1988). An additional surprise is that even though the Skip-gram embeddings provide semantic information about single words as well as MWEs, the Feature Rich models make little use of them. Many of the Feature Rich models utilize the GECO features, which may be because they provide approximate guidance about the distributions of the various gaze features that would be difficult to learn directly given the sparsity of the training data.

7 Conclusion and Future Work

This work describes our submissions to the 2021 CMCL Shared Task: we contributed a Feature Rich model inspired by cognitive and linguistic information, and model predominantly based on contextual XLNet-base embeddings. We find that only a limited subset of the cognitive features (such as word length) are helpful in the XLNet model. To our surprise, neither XLNet-large embeddings nor MWE features provide performance improvements. However, we believe this indicates a need for further research into MWE representations as opposed to suggesting that MWEs are unimportant for creating effective cognitive models.

Acknowledgements

We are grateful to Cheng Cao, Elham Khodaei, Srivishnu Ethirajulu Krishnaraj and Ronan Ramdas Revadker for their help generating and testing the feature sets. PV and RW are supported by the Centre for Doctoral Training in Speech and Language Technologies (SLT) and their Applications funded by the UK Research and Innovation grant EP/S023062/1. RW is also supported by ZOO Digital. This work is also partially supported by the EPSRC grant EP/T02450X/1.

References

Maria Barrett. 2018. *Improving natural language processing with human data: Eye tracking and other data sources reflecting cognitive text processing.* Ph.D. thesis.

Maria Barrett, Joachim Bingel, Nora Hollenstein, Marek Rei, and Anders Søgaard. 2018. Sequence classification with human attention. In *Proceedings of CoNLL 2018*, pages 302–312.

Maria Barrett, Joachim Bingel, Frank Keller, and Anders Søgaard. 2016. Weakly Supervised Part-of-speech Tagging Using Eye-tracking Data. In *Pro-*

ceedings of ACL 2016: Short Papers, pages 579–584, Stroudsburg, PA, USA. Association for Computational Linguistics.

E. Blom and S. Unsworth. 2010. *Experimental Methods in Language Acquisition Research*. Language learning and language teaching. John Benjamins Pub. Company.

Leo Breiman. 2001. Random forests. *Machine Learning*, 45(1):5–32.

Marc Brysbaert, Amy Beth Warriner, and Victor Kuperman. 2014. Concreteness ratings for 40 thousand generally known English word lemmas. *Behavior Research Methods*, 46(3):904–911.

Cristina Cacciari and Patrizia Tabossi. 1988. The comprehension of idioms. *Journal of Memory and Language*, 27:668–683.

Jamie Callan, Mark Hoy, Changkuk Yoo, and Le Zhao. 2009. Clueweb09 data set.

P. A. Carpenter and M. A. Just. 1983. What your eyes do while your mind is reading. In Keith Rayner, editor, *Eye movements in reading: Perceptual and language processes*, pages 275–307. Academic Press., New York.

Grzegorz Chrupała and Afra Alishahi. 2019. Correlating neural and symbolic representations of language. In *Proceedings of the 57th Annual Meeting of the Association for Computational Linguistics*, pages 2952–2962, Florence, Italy. Association for Computational Linguistics.

Uschi Cop, Nicolas Dirix, Denis Drieghe, and Wouter Duyck. 2017. Presenting GECO: An eyetracking corpus of monolingual and bilingual sentence reading. *Behavior Research Methods*, 49(2):602–615.

Silvio Cordeiro, Aline Villavicencio, Marco Idiart, and Carlos Ramisch. 2019. Unsupervised compositionality prediction of nominal compounds. *Computational Linguistics*, 45(1):1–57.

Benjamin Van Durme Courtney Napoles, Matthew R. Gormley. 2012. Annotated English Gigaword. *Linguistic Data Consortium*.

Common Crawl. 2019. Common Crawl.

Jacob Devlin, Ming-Wei Chang, Kenton Lee, and Kristina Toutanova. 2019. BERT: Pre-training of deep bidirectional transformers for language understanding. In *Proceedings of the 2019 Conference of the North American Chapter of the Association for Computational Linguistics: Human Language Technologies, Volume 1 (Long and Short Papers)*, pages 4171–4186, Minneapolis, Minnesota. Association for Computational Linguistics.

Vesna G Djokic, Jean Maillard, Luana Bulat, and Ekaterina Shutova. 2020. Decoding Brain Activity Associated with Literal and Metaphoric Sentence Comprehension Using Distributional Semantic Models. *Transactions of the Association for Computational Linguistics*.

Nora Hollenstein, Emmanuele Chersoni, Cassandra Jacobs, Yohei Oseki, Laurent Prévot, and Enrico Santus. 2021. CMCL 2021 Shared Task on Eye-Tracking Prediction. In *Proceedings of the Workshop on Cognitive Modelling and Computational Linguistics*.

Nora Hollenstein, Jonathan Rotsztejn, Marius Troendle, Andreas Pedroni, Ce Zhang, and Nicolas Langer. 2018. Zuco, a simultaneous eeg and eye-tracking resource for natural sentence reading. *Scientific Data*, 5.

Nora Hollenstein, Marius Troendle, Ce Zhang, and Nicolas Langer. 2020. ZuCo 2.0: A Dataset of Physiological Recordings During Natural Reading and Annotation. Technical report.

Matthew Honnibal, Ines Montani, Sofie Van Landeghem, and Adriane Boyd. 2020. spaCy: Industrial-strength Natural Language Processing in Python.

Ganesh Jawahar, Benoît Sagot, and Djamé Seddah. 2019. What does BERT learn about the structure of language? In *Proceedings of the 57th Annual Meeting of the Association for Computational Linguistics*, pages 3651–3657, Florence, Italy. Association for Computational Linguistics.

Jing Lei, Max G'Sell, Alessandro Rinaldo, Ryan J. Tibshirani, and Larry Wasserman. 2016. Distribution-Free Predictive Inference For Regression. *Journal of the American Statistical Association*, 113(523):1094–1111.

Edward Loper and Steven Bird. 2002. Nltk: The natural language toolkit. *CoRR*.

Lucas Mentch and Giles Hooker. 2016. Quantifying Uncertainty in Random Forests via Confidence Intervals and Hypothesis Tests. *Journal of Machine Learning Research*, 17(26):1–41.

Stephen Merity, Caiming Xiong, James Bradbury, and Richard Socher. 2016. Pointer Sentinel Mixture Models. *Proceedings of ICLR 2017*.

Danny Merkx and Stefan L. Frank. 2020. Comparing transformers and rnns on predicting human sentence processing data.

Tomas Mikolov, Kai Chen, Greg Corrado, and Jeffrey Dean. 2013. Efficient estimation of word representations in vector space. In *1st International Conference on Learning Representations, ICLR 2013 - Workshop Track Proceedings*. International Conference on Learning Representations, ICLR.

Kristin K. Nicodemus, James D. Malley, Carolin Strobl, and Andreas Ziegler. 2010. The behaviour of random forest permutation-based variable importance measures under predictor correlation. *BMC Bioinformatics*, 11(1):110.

F. Pedregosa, G. Varoquaux, A. Gramfort, V. Michel, B. Thirion, O. Grisel, M. Blondel, P. Prettenhofer, R. Weiss, V. Dubourg, J. Vanderplas, A. Passos, D. Cournapeau, M. Brucher, M. Perrot, and E. Duchesnay. 2011. Scikit-learn: Machine learning in Python. *Journal of Machine Learning Research*, 12:2825–2830.

Carlos Ramisch. 2012. A generic and open framework for multiword expressions treatment: from acquisition to applications. In *Proceedings of the ACL 2012 Student Research Workshop*, September, pages 61–66. Association for Computational Linguistics.

Keith Rayner. 1975. The perceptual span and peripheral cues in reading. *Cognitive Psychology*, 7(1):65–81.

Keith Rayner. 1998. Eye Movements in Reading and Information Processing: 20 Years of Research. *Psychological Bulletin*, 124(3):372–422.

Keith Rayner and George W. McConkie. 1976. What guides a reader's eye movements? *Vision Research*, 16(8):829–837.

Radim Rehurek and Petr Sojka. 2011. Gensim–python framework for vector space modelling. *NLP Centre, Faculty of Informatics, Masaryk University, Brno, Czech Republic*, 3(2).

Omid Rohanian, Shiva Taslimipoor, Victoria Yaneva, and Le An Ha. 2017. Using Gaze Data to Predict Multiword Expressions. In *Proceedings of RANLP 2017*, pages 601–609.

Anna Siyanova-Chanturia, Kathy Conklin, Sendy Caffarra, Edith Kaan, and Walter J.B. van Heuven. 2017. Representation and processing of multi-word expressions in the brain. *Brain and Language*, 175:111–122.

Anna Siyanova-Chanturia, Kathy Conklin, and Norbert Schmitt. 2011. Adding more fuel to the fire: an eye-tracking study of idiom processing by native and non-native speakers. *Second Language Research*, 27(2):251–272.

Ekta Sood, Simon Tannert, Diego Frassinelli, Andreas Bulling, and Ngoc Thang Vu. 2020. Interpreting Attention Models with Human Visual Attention in Machine Reading Comprehension. In *Proceedings of CoNLL 2020*, pages 12–25, Stroudsburg, PA, USA. Association for Computational Linguistics.

Robyn Speer, Joshua Chin, Andrew Lin, Sara Jewett, and Lance Nathan. 2018. Luminosoinsight/wordfreq: v2.2.

Michael K Tanenhaus. 2007. Spoken language comprehension: Insights from eye movements. *The oxford handbook of psycholinguistics*.

Makarand Tapaswi, Yukun Zhu, Rainer Stiefelhagen, Antonio Torralba, Raquel Urtasun, and Sanja Fidler. 2016. MovieQA: Understanding Stories in Movies through Question-Answering. In *IEEE Conference on Computer Vision and Pattern Recognition (CVPR)*.

Ian Tenney, Patrick Xia, Berlin Chen, Alex Wang, Adam Poliak, R Thomas McCoy, Najoung Kim, Benjamin Van Durme, Sam Bowman, Dipanjan Das, and Ellie Pavlick. 2019. What do you learn from context? probing for sentence structure in contextualized word representations. In *International Conference on Learning Representations*.

Walter J B Van Heuven, Pawel Mandera, Emmanuel Keuleers, and Marc Brysbaert. 2014. SUBTLEX-UK: A new and improved word frequency database for British English. *The Quarterly Journal of Experimental Psychology*, 67(6):1176–1190.

Ashish Vaswani, Noam Shazeer, Niki Parmar, Jakob Uszkoreit, Llion Jones, Aidan N Gomez, Ł ukasz Kaiser, and Illia Polosukhin. 2017. Attention is all you need. In *Advances in Neural Information Processing Systems*, volume 30. Curran Associates, Inc.

Victoria Yaneva, Shiva Taslimipoor, Omid Rohanian, and Le An Ha. 2017. Cognitive Processing of Multiword Expressions in Native and Non-native Speakers of English: Evidence from Gaze Data. Technical report.

Zhilin Yang, Zihang Dai, Yiming Yang, Jaime Carbonell, Russ R Salakhutdinov, and Quoc V Le. 2019. Xlnet: Generalized autoregressive pretraining for language understanding. In *Advances in Neural Information Processing Systems*, volume 32. Curran Associates, Inc.

Y Zhu, R Kiros, R Zemel, R Salakhutdinov, R Urtasun, A Torralba, and S Fidler. 2015. Aligning Books and Movies: Towards Story-Like Visual Explanations by Watching Movies and Reading Books. In *2015 IEEE International Conference on Computer Vision (ICCV)*, pages 19–27.

A Features Used

We use the following features for each model. +N and +P indicate that associated data for the two next and two preceding words were included, respectively.

A.1 Model One Features

```
[CAT-pos+N+P, CAT-word+N+P,
Conc-M+N+P, Conc-SD+N+P,
Is-EOS+N+P, Is-SOS+N+P,
Percent-Known+N+P,
comp-score+N+P, comp-weights+N+P,
geco-FFD-mean+N+P,
geco-FFD-std+N+P,
geco-GPT-median+N+P,
geco-GPT-std+N+P,
geco-TRT-mean+N+P,
geco-fixProp-mean+N+P,
geco-fixProp-std+N+P,
geco-nFix-median+N+P,
geco-nFix-std+N+P,
is-mwe+N+P, is-strange+N+P,
mwe-cat+N+P, saccade-cat+N+P,
saccade-cat-binary+N+P,
w2v-embedding+N+P,
word-frequency+N+P, word-len+N+P,
zipf-frequency+N+P]
```

A.2 Model Two Features

```
[XLNET-embed, CAT-pos, Is-EOS,
Is-SOS, word-len, zipf-frequency]
```

B Permutation Feature Importance

We use permutation feature importance (Breiman, 2001) to better understand the impact of different features on each of the different models. This method measures the base error of the model against the error when one feature is randomly permuted, allowing for quantification of importance. That is for feature i:

$$FI_i = E_{base} - E_{perm_i}$$

We note that permutation methods have a tendency of attributing higher importance to correlated features (Nicodemus et al., 2010), whilst still being informative. Alternatives include per-feature retraining (Lei et al., 2016; Mentch and Hooker, 2016) which was computationally intractable within the timeframe of the CMCL task duration.

C Description of features

Feature (generated at the word-level unless specified)	Description	Data and tools used
CAT_word	One hot word encoding	
CAT_pos	Categorical encoding of Part-of-Speech tag	Honnibal et al. (2020)
Is_EOS	Binary variable indicating if word is the last in its sentence	
Is_SOS	Binary variable indicating if word is the first in its sentence	
Conc_M	Mean concreteness norm assigned to the lemmatized form of the word. Words not covered by the dataset of norms were given a'neutral' score of 3 (concreteness rated on a Likert scale from 1-5)	Brysbaert et al. (2014)
Conc_SD	Standard deviation of concreteness values assigned to lemmatized form of word. Words not covered by the dataset of norms were assigned the mean of Conc_SD for all other words	Brysbaert et al. (2014)
Percent_Known	Proportion of participants asked to estimate concreteness norms that were familiar enough with the word to judge its concreteness. Words not covered by the dataset of norms were assigned a value of 1	Brysbaert et al. (2014)
word_len	Number of characters in the word	
saccade_cat	Categorical representation of number of characters in relation to average saccade length (categories were 1-3, 4-7, 8-10 and 11+ letters)	
saccade _cat_binary	Binary categorical representation of number of characters in relation to average saccade length (categories were 1-3 letters and 4+ letters)	
word_frequency	Frequency of word per million words	Speer et al. (2018)
zipf_frequency	Frequency of word per million words on the zipf scale	Speer et al. (2018)
NEXT_n_FEAT	Attaches FEAT for the next n words to the current word (i.e. NEXT_1_Is_EOS attaches Is_EOS for the next word to the current word)	
PREV_n_FEAT	Attaches FEAT for the previous n words to the current word	
geco_FEAT_mean	Mean average of all measurements of FEAT for this word in GECO. If the word was not present in GECO, the mean of means for words with comparable frequency in natural language was used	Cop et al. (2017)
geco_FEAT_median	Median average of all measurements of FEAT for this word GECO. If the word was not present in GECO, the mean of medians for words with comparable frequency was used	Cop et al. (2017)
geco_FEAT_std	Standard deviation of all measurements of FEAT for this word in GECO. If the word was not present in GECO, mean of standard deviations for words with comparable frequency was used	Cop et al. (2017)
is_mwe	Binary indicator showing if word is part of an MWE in this context	Ramisch (2012)
mwe_cat	Categorical representation of whether the word is part of an MWE in this context, where categories are based on syntactic patterns (i.e. adjective noun compound, verb + preposition phrase)	Ramisch (2012) Loper and Bird (2002)
w2v_embedding	300 dimensional Skip-gram embedding for the word or MWE. If the word is part of an MWE in this context, the Skip-gram embedding trained for the MWE is used instead. Embeddings are trained using the Wikitext-103 corpus, where multiword expressions are reformatted to be concatenated using underscores (i.e. *multiword_expression*)	Ramisch (2012) Mikolov et al. (2013) Rehurek and Sojka (2011) Merity et al. (2016)
comp_score	Compositionality score for the MWE calculated using mwetoolkit. Words not part of MWEs are assigned a value of 0	Ramisch (2012) Cordeiro et al. (2019)
comp_weights	Weights used for each word to calculate the comp_score for the MWE (certain words may contribute more semantic meaning to an MWE than others). Words not part of MWEs are assigned a value of 0	Ramisch (2012) Cordeiro et al. (2019)
is_strange	Binary indicator of non-standard formatting or non-alphanumeric characters in the current word (generated using regular expressions)	

Team ReadMe at CMCL 2021 Shared Task: Predicting Human Reading Patterns by Traditional Oculomotor Control Models and Machine Learning

Alişan Balkoca, A. Can Algan, Cengiz Acartürk
Cognitive Science Department, Middle East Technical University
Çağrı Çöltekin
Department of Linguistics, University of Tübingen

Abstract

This system description paper describes our participation in CMCL 2021 shared task on predicting human reading patterns. Our focus in this study is making use of well-known, traditional oculomotor control models and machine learning systems. We present experiments with a traditional oculomotor control model (the EZ Reader) and two machine learning models (a linear regression model and a recurrent network model), as well as combining the two different models. In all experiments we test effects of features well-known in the literature for predicting reading patterns, such as frequency, word length and word predictability. Our experiments support the earlier findings that such features are useful when combined. Furthermore, we show that although machine learning models perform better in comparison to traditional models, combination of both gives a consistent improvement for predicting multiple eye tracking variables during reading.

1 Introduction

Oculomotor control in reading has been a well-established domain in eye tracking research. From the perspective of perceptual and cognitive mechanisms that drive eye movement control, the characteristics of the visual stimuli is better controlled in reading research than visual scene stimuli. Several computational models have been developed for the past two decades, which aimed at modeling the relationship between a set of independent variables, such as word characteristics and dependent variables, such as fixation duration and location (Kliegl et al., 2006).

Based on the theoretical and experimental research in reading, the leading independent variables include the frequency of a word in daily use, the length of the word and its sentential predictability. The term *sentential predictability* (or word predictability) is used to define predictability score which is the probability of guessing a word from the sequence of previous words of the sentence (Kliegl et al., 2004). The dependent variables include numerous metrics, including fixation duration metrics such as first fixation duration (FFD) and total gaze time on a word, as well as location and numerosity metrics such as the location of a fixation on a word and gaze-regressions.

A major caveat of the computational models that have been developed since the past two decades is that they weakly address linguistic concepts beyond the level of the fixated word, with a few exceptions, such as the spillover effects related to the preview of a next word *n+1* during the current fixation on word *n* (Engbert et al., 2005). These models are also limited in their recognition of syntactic, semantic and discourse characteristics of the text due to their complexity, despite they are indispensable aspects of reading for understanding. Machine Learning (ML) models of oculomotor control address some of those limitations by presenting high predictive power. However, the holistic approach of the learning models has drawbacks in terms of the explainability of the model underpinnings. In this study, we present experiments with a traditional model of oculomotor control in reading, namely the EZ Reader (Reichle et al., 2003), two ML models (a regression model and a recurrent network model), and their combination. We present an evaluation of the results by focusing on the model inputs that reveal relatively higher accuracy.

Accordingly, the aim of the present paper is to investigate the effectiveness of both types of models and their combinations on predicting human reading behavior as set up by the CMCL 2021 shared task (Hollenstein et al., 2021). The task is defined as predicting five eye-tracking features, namely *number of fixations* (nFix), *first fixation duration* (FFD), *total reading time* (TRT), *go-past time* (GPT), and *fixation proportion* (fixProp). The eye-tracking data of the Zurich Congitive Language

Proceedings of the Workshop on Cognitive Modeling and Computational Linguistics, pages 134–140
Online Event, June 10, 2021.

Processing Corpus (ZuCo 1.0 and ZuCo 2.0) were used (Hollenstein et al., 2018), (Hollenstein et al., 2019). Details of these variables and further information on the data set can be found in the task description paper (Hollenstein et al., 2021).

2 Methodology

We created our models and identified the input features following the findings in research on oculomotor control in reading. The previous studies have shown that word length, frequency and sentential predictability are well known parameters that influence eye movement patterns in reading (Rayner, 1998). There exist further parameters that influence eye movement characteristics. For instance, the location of a word in the sentence has been proposed as a predictor on First Fixation Duration (Kliegl et al., 2006). Therefore, we used those additional parameters to improve the accuracy of the learning models, as well as running a traditions oculomotor control model (viz., the EZ Reader) with its required parameter set. Below we present a description of the models that have been employed in the present study.

2.1 System Description

2.1.1 The EZ Reader Model

EZ Reader has been developed as a rule-based model of oculomotor control in reading. It predicts eye movement parameters, such as single fixation duration, first fixation duration and total reading time. The model efficiently addresses some of experimental research findings in the reading literature. For example, a saccade completion takes about 20-50 msec to complete, and saccade length is about 7-9 characters (Rayner, 2009). The model consists of three main processing modules. The oculomotor system is responsible for generating and executing saccades by calculating the saccade length. The visual system controls the attention of the reader. Finally, the word identification system calculates the time for identifying a word, mainly based on the word length and the frequency of word in daily use. EZ Reader accepts four arguments as its input; frequency (count in million), word length (number of characters), sentential predictability of the word, and the word itself. The output features of the model are given in Table 1.

Among those features, FFD and TT outputs of EZ Reader directly map to FFD and TRT (Total Reading Time) in the training data of the CMCL

Feature	Description
EZ-SFD	Single Fixation Duration
EZ-FFD	First Fixation Duration
EZ-GD	Gaze Duration
EZ-TT	Total Reading Time
EZ-PrF	Fixation Probability
EZ-Pr1	Probability of making exactly one fixation
EZ-Pr2	Probability of making two or more fixations
EZ-PrS	Probability of skipping

Table 1: EZ Reader output features.

EZ Reader	Training Data	MAE
TT	Total Reading Time	3.25
FFD	First Fixation Duration	9.14

Table 2: Mean Absolute Error (MAE) scores obtained by the EZ Reader model

2021 shared task. The EZ reader output features are not sufficient enough to generate mean absolute error values for each feature in the training data. Therefore we were only able to calculate mean absolute error values for FFD and TRT. Table 2 presents the Mean Absolute Error (MAE) values of the test set, when predicted by the EZ Reader model. In the design of the EZ Reader model, we assumed the simulation count as 2000 participants, which means that the model runs 2000 distinct simulations and the result scores consist of the average of the simulation results. 2000 participants is the optimum number for our case in terms of simulation time and the MAE it produces. Above 2000 participants MEA did not decrease significantly.

A major challenge in designing the EZ Reader model is that the model is not able to produce the output values for some of the words, labeling them *Infinity*. Those are usually long words with relatively low frequency. In order to find an optimal value to fill in the *Infinity* slots, we calculated the mean absolute error between TRT of the training data and the TT values of EZ Reader model results, as an operational assumption. The calculation returned 284 ms. Figure 1 shows the MAE scores over given values between 0 to 500. This value is close to the average fixation duration for skilled readers which is about 200ms - 250ms (Rayner, 1998). Therefore, we preserved the assumption in model development pipeline.

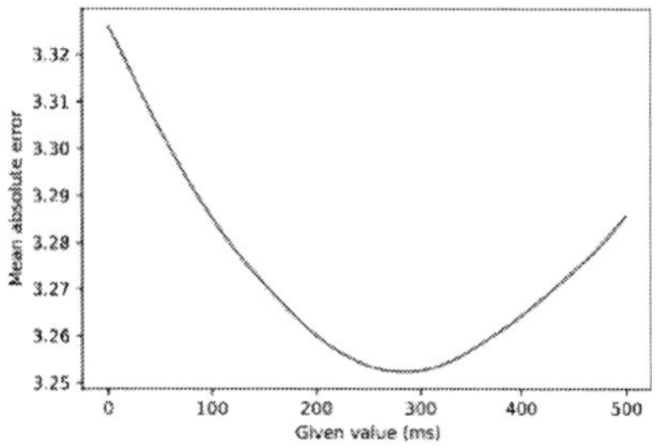

Figure 1: Mean Absolute Error scores over given values for Infinity slot

In the present study, besides calculating the mean absolute error values for the EZ Reader model, we employed the outputs of the EZ Reader model as inputs to the LSTM model. Below, we present the model for the Linear Baseline and the LSTM model.

2.1.2 Linear Baseline

Our linear model is a least-squares regression model with L2 regularization (ridge regression). The input features to the regression model include the main word-level features, frequency, word length and predictability discussed above. Word frequencies are computed using a large news corpus of approximately 2.7 million articles.[1] The predictability features are obtained using the recurrent network described in Section 2.2. Besides these features, we also include some linguistic features including the POS tag, dependency relation, and signed distance from the head, as well as named entity tag. The POS and dependency information is obtained using version 1.2 of UDPipe using the pretrained models released by the authors (Straka and Straková, 2017; Straka and Straková, 2019). We used Apache OpenNLP (Apache Software Foundation, 2014) for named entity recognition. The model input also included indicator features for beginning and end of sentence, and whether the word is combined with a punctuation mark or not (see Table 3). We also included the features from EZ-reader described in Section 2.1.1 as additional inputs to the regression model.

The predictions were based on a symmetric window around the target word, where all the above features for the target word and $\pm k$ words were concatenated. We selected the optimal window size as well as the regularization constant (alpha) for the ridge regression model via grid search. The grid search is used to determine a single same alpha and single window size for all target variables. We use the ridge regression implementation of the Python scikit-learn library (Pedregosa et al., 2011).

[1]'All the news' data set, available from `https://components.one/datasets/all-the-news-2-news-articles-dataset/`.

Feature	Description	Used in model
Word Frequency (Fr)	Word occurrence per million	LB-LSTM
Word Location	Zero based index of the word in sentence.	LB-LSTM
Word Length (WL)	Character count of the word	LB-LSTM
Word Predictability (Pr)	Probability of knowing a word before reading it	LB-LSTM
StartPunct	The presence of a punctuation before the word	LB-LSTM
EndPunct	The presence of the punctuation at the end	LB-LSTM
EndSent	Is the last word of the sentence or not	LB-LSTM
POS	Core part-of-speech category	LB
Dep	Universal syntactic relations	LB
HeadDist	Signed distance from the head	LB
Ner	Named entity category (person and company names, etc.)	LB
EZ Reader simulation outputs	see Table 1	LB-LSTM

Table 3: Input features used in Linear Baseline and LSTM model.

2.1.3 LSTM Model

The LSTM model consists of an LSTM layer with 128 units followed by two dense layers and 5-dimensional output layer. The input features of the model include word length in total number of characters, word predictability, frequency per million, the location of the word in the sentence, the presence of a punctuation before the word, the presence of the punctuation at the end, and the end of sentence, being the last word of the sentence or not. Finally, the input features included the outputs of the typical EZ Reader model (given in Table 1). The output features of the LSTM model the variables identified by the CMCL 2021 share task, namely nFix, FFD, GPT, TT, and fixProp.

2.2 Predictability Scores

Sentential predictability of a word in a context is a well-established predictor of eye movement patterns in reading (Fernández et al., 2014; Kliegl et al., 2004; Clifton et al., 2016). We used two methods to generate the predictability values. First, we used the average human predictability scores from the Provo Corpus (Luke and Christianson, 2018), which is a public eye-tracking dataset collected from real participants. The Provo Corpus includes the cloze task results in which participants are given the starting word of the sentence and expected to guess the next word. The actual word is shown after the participant's guess and prediction for the next word is expected. This process continues for all of the words. Prediction value is generated for each word in corpus by simply calculating the ratio of the correct guesses to all guesses for the word. We selected 1.0 as the default prediction value for words which does not exist in the

Model	nFix	FFD	GPT	TRT	fixProp
LAST	3.88	0.66	2.20	1.52	10.81
Linear	4.36	0.74	2.50	1.76	12.55
LSTM	4.62	0.76	3.61	1.84	13.06
Baseline	7.30	1.15	3.78	2.78	21.78

Table 4: Official scores (MAE) of our models in comparison to mean baseline and the first team (LAST) in the competition.

Features	nFix	FFD	GPT	TRT	fixProp
Fr	4.80	2.20	2.75	1.85	13.61
WL	6.73	0.77	2.78	1.84	12.94
Pr	5.64	0.85	3.11	2.15	15.17
EZ-SFD	6.26	1.00	3.11	2.34	18.21
WL x Pr x Fr	4.35	0.71	2.68	1.73	11.99
WL x Pr	4.28	0.71	2.70	1.68	12.07
EZ-SFDxFrxWLxPr	4.21	0.73	2.57	1.64	12.11

Table 5: MAE for with different feature combinations.

Provo Corpus. The mean absolute error for TRT between EZ Reader output and CMCL train data was at minimum when default prediction value is 1.0.

Second, we developed a separate LSTM model that produced sentential predictability values. For this, we trained the model by Wikipedia.[2] Since the primary goal of the model was to predict eye movement patterns per word, we built a word-level language model. The model consisted of two LSTM layers with 1200 hidden units. It was trained with a learning rate of 0.0001, and a dropout value was set to 0.2, with the Adam optimizer. After the training, we obtained the predictability scores for each word based on their sentential context. These scores were then used as an additional feature in our final model besides the other features, such as word length and frequency.

Provo Corpus predictability values are independent from the context of text used in the shared task. However using predictability values from the first method gave better results than the calculated predictability. Therefore we used Provo Corpus predictability values for the results in the following sections.

3 Results

We participated in the CMCL 2021 shared task with two submissions, one with the linear model described in Section 2.1.2, and the other with the LSTM model (Section 2.1.3). Table 4 presents the scores of our system in the competition, in comparison to mean baseline and the best system. Our systems perform substantially better than the baseline, and the difference between the scores of the participating teams are comparatively small. Among our models, the linear model performed slightly better, obtaining 10th place in the competition. However, experimenting with the LSTM model gave us more information about the basic features of eye movements in reading and their effects on fixation durations. For the remainder of this section, we will present further experiments with the LSTM model, demonstrating the effects of various features discussed above.

3.1 Further Experiments

To demonstrate the effectiveness of the features described above, we trained a number of models that employed a set of input variables in isolation, as well as the models trained by their combination. In particular, we trained a model on frequency, then predictability, and then word length. Then we trained models by their combinations as input features. Each model produced a MAE (mean absolute error) value. We then calculated the average of the MAE values for each model output (nFix, FFD, GPT, TRT, and FixProp) and their Standard Deviation (SD). Finally, we calculated how far each model was away from the average MAE in terms of the SDs. Table 5 presents MAE scores for each setting.

The figures in the Appendix A show the distance of the models from the center of the circle, where the center represents the best MAE score and the circle represents the distance covered by one SD (Standard Deviation) from the best accuracy (i.e. the center). The models that received the combination of frequency, predictability, word length and E-Z SFD (i.e., E-Z Reader's single fixation duration prediction) as the input returned the best MAE values for four of five dependent variables. As an example, consider the MAE values for the models developed for predicting the *nFix* (the number of fixations on a word). Figure 2 shows that the majority of the models that are based on features in isolation have relatively lower predictability compared to the models that take a combination of the features as the inputs. In particular, the predictability model (i.e., the model that is solely based on

[2] We use the sentence segmented corpus from `https://www.kaggle.com/mikeortman/wikipedia-sentences`.

the predictability values as the input feature) has a mean MAE value 1.75 times the SD (Standard Deviation). Similarly, the word-length model has approximately 3 times the SD from the best score, and the EZ-SFD model (i.e., the model that is solely based on the single fixation duration predictions of the EZ Reader model) has a mean MAE value far away from the mean by 2.5 times the SD value.

4 Conclusion

In this paper, we analyzed a linear baseline model and an LSTM model that employed the outputs of a traditional model as its inputs. We built models with input features in isolation, and their combination. The evaluation of the mean absolute errors (MAE) supported a major finding in reading research: The oculomotor processes in reading are influenced by multiple factors. Temporal and spatial aspects of eye movement control are determined by linguistic factors as well as low-level nonlinguistic factors (Rayner, 1998; Kliegl and Engbert, 2013). The models that employ their combinations return higher accuracy. Our findings also indicate that besides the frequently used features in the literature, the EZ-SFD (single frequency duration outputs of the EZ Reader model) may contribute to the accuracy of the learning based models. Nevertheless, given the high variability of the machine learning model outputs a systematic investigation is necessary that address several operational assumptions in the present study. In particular, future research should improve statistical analysis for comparing the model outputs. It should also address the influence of the location of a word in a sentence, besides its interaction with the duration measures. Last but not the least, future research on developing ML models of oculomotor control in reading should focus on the relationship between the aspects of the ML model design and basic findings in reading research. The GCMW (Gaze Contingent Moving Window) paradigm and the boundary paradigm (Rayner, 2014) are some examples of those findings that could be used for oculomotor control modeling.

References

Apache Software Foundation. 2014. openNLP Natural Language Processing Library. http://opennlp.apache.org/.

Charles Clifton, Fernanda Ferreira, John M. Henderson, Albrecht W. Inhoff, Simon P. Liversedge, Erik D. Reichle, and Elizabeth R. Schotter. 2016. Eye movements in reading and information processing: Keith Rayner's 40 year legacy. *Journal of Memory and Language*, 86:1–19.

Ralf Engbert, Antje Nuthmann, Eike M Richter, and Reinhold Kliegl. 2005. SWIFT: a dynamical model of saccade generation during reading. *Psychological review*, 112(4):777.

Gerardo Fernández, Diego E. Shalom, Reinhold Kliegl, and Mariano Sigman. 2014. Eye movements during reading proverbs and regular sentences: The incoming word predictability effect. *Language, Cognition and Neuroscience*, 29(3):260–273.

Nora Hollenstein, Emmanuele Chersoni, Cassandra Jacobs, Yohei Oseki, Laurent Prévot, and Enrico Santus. 2021. Cmcl 2021 shared task on eye-tracking prediction. In *Proceedings of the Workshop on Cognitive Modeling and Computational Linguistics*.

Nora Hollenstein, Jonathan Rotsztejn, Marius Troendle, Andreas Pedroni, Ce Zhang, and Nicolas Langer. 2018. ZuCo, a simultaneous EEG and eye-tracking resource for natural sentence reading. *Scientific data*, 5(1):1–13.

Nora Hollenstein, Marius Troendle, Ce Zhang, and Nicolas Langer. 2019. Zuco 2.0: A dataset of physiological recordings during natural reading and annotation. *arXiv preprint arXiv:1912.00903*.

Reinhold Kliegl and Ralf Engbert. 2013. Evaluating a computational model of eye-movement control in reading. In *Models, simulations, and the reduction of complexity*, pages 153–178. De Gruyter.

Reinhold Kliegl, Ellen Grabner, Martin Rolfs, and Ralf Engbert. 2004. Length, frequency, and predictability effects of words on eye movements in reading. *European journal of cognitive psychology*, 16(1-2):262–284.

Reinhold Kliegl, Antje Nuthmann, and Ralf Engbert. 2006. Tracking the mind during reading: The influence of past, present, and future words on fixation durations. *Journal of experimental psychology: General*, 135(1):12.

Steven G Luke and Kiel Christianson. 2018. The provo corpus: A large eye-tracking corpus with predictability norms. *Behavior research methods*, 50(2):826–833.

F. Pedregosa, G. Varoquaux, A. Gramfort, V. Michel, B. Thirion, O. Grisel, M. Blondel, P. Prettenhofer, R. Weiss, V. Dubourg, J. Vanderplas, A. Passos, D. Cournapeau, M. Brucher, M. Perrot, and E. Duchesnay. 2011. Scikit-learn: Machine learning in Python. *Journal of Machine Learning Research*, 12:2825–2830.

Keith Rayner. 1998. Eye movements in reading and information processing: 20 years of research. *Psychological bulletin*, 124(3):372.

Keith Rayner. 2009. Eye Movements in Reading: Models and Data. *Journal of Eye Movement Research*, 2(5):1–10.

Keith Rayner. 2014. The gaze-contingent moving window in reading: Development and review. *Visual Cognition*, 22(3-4):242–258.

Erik D Reichle, Keith Rayner, and Alexander Pollatsek. 2003. The EZ reader model of eye-movement control in reading: Comparisons to other models. *Behavioral and brain sciences*, 26(4):445.

Milan Straka and Jana Straková. 2017. Tokenizing, pos tagging, lemmatizing and parsing UD 2.0 with UDPipe. In *Proceedings of the CoNLL 2017 Shared Task: Multilingual Parsing from Raw Text to Universal Dependencies*, pages 88–99, Vancouver, Canada. Association for Computational Linguistics.

Milan Straka and Jana Straková. 2019. Universal dependencies 2.5 models for UDPipe (2019-12-06). LINDAT/CLARIAH-CZ digital library at the Institute of Formal and Applied Linguistics (ÚFAL), Faculty of Mathematics and Physics, Charles University.

A Appendix

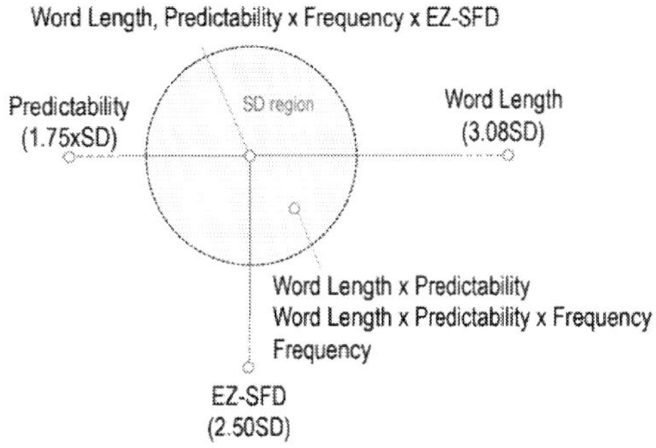

Figure 2: MAE scores for nFix

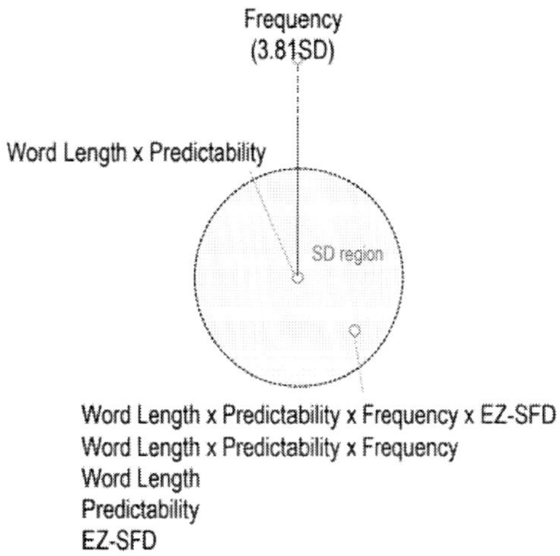

Figure 3: MAE scores for FFD

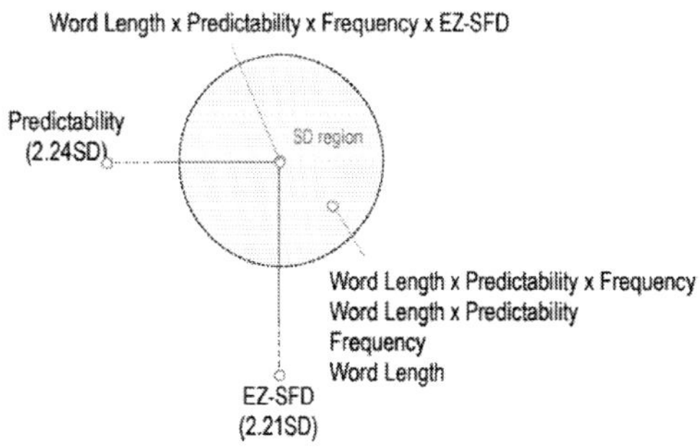

Figure 4: MAE scores for GPT

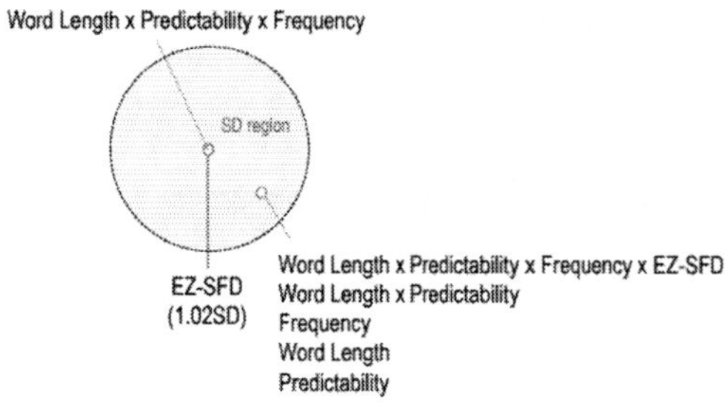

Figure 5: MAE scores for fixProp

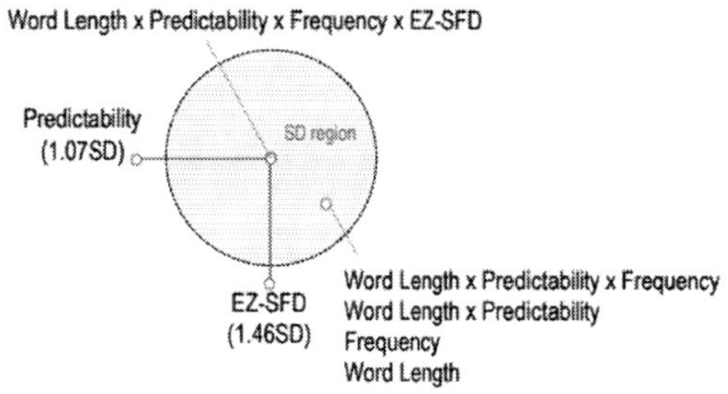

Figure 6: MAE scores for TRT

Enhancing Cognitive Models of Emotions with Representation Learning

Yuting Guo
Computer Science
Emory University
Atlanta GA 30322, USA
yuting.guo@emory.edu

Jinho D. Choi
Computer Science
Emory University
Atlanta GA 30322, USA
jinho.choi@emory.edu

Abstract

We present a novel deep learning-based framework to generate embedding representations of fine-grained emotions that can be used to computationally describe psychological models of emotions. Our framework integrates a contextualized embedding encoder with a multi-head probing model that enables to interpret dynamically learned representations optimized for an emotion classification task. Our model is evaluated on the Empathetic Dialogue dataset and shows the state-of-the-art result for classifying 32 emotions. Our layer analysis can derive an emotion graph to depict hierarchical relations among the emotions. Our emotion representations can be used to generate an emotion wheel directly comparable to the one from Plutchik's model, and also augment the values of missing emotions in the PAD emotional state model.

1 Introduction

Emotion classification has been extensively studied by many disciplines for decades (Spencer, 1895; Lazarus and Lazarus, 1994; Ekman, 1999). Two main streams have been developed for this research: one is the discrete theory that tries to explain emotions with basic and complex categories (Plutchik, 1980; Ekman, 1992; Colombetti, 2009), and the other is the dimensional theory that aims to conceptualize emotions into a continuous vector space (Russell and Mehrabian, 1977; Watson and Tellegen, 1985; Bradley et al., 1992). Illustration of human emotion however is often subjective and obscure in nature, leading to a long debate among researchers about the "correct" way of representing emotions (Gendron and Feldman Barrett, 2009).

Representation learning has made remarkable progress recently by building neural language models on large corpora, which have substantially improved the performance on many downstream tasks (Peters et al., 2018; Devlin et al., 2019; Yang et al., 2019; Liu et al., 2019; Joshi et al., 2020). Encouraged by this rapid progress along with an increasing interest of interpretability in deep learning models, several studies have attempted to capture various knowledge encoded in language (Adi et al., 2017; Peters et al., 2018; Hewitt and Manning, 2019), and shown that it is possible to learn computational representations through distributional semantics for abstract concepts. Inspired by these prior studies, we build a deep learning-based framework to generate emotion embeddings from text and assess its ability of enhancing cognitive models of emotions. Our contributions are summarized as follows:[1]

- To develop a deep probing model that allows us to interpret the process of representation learning on emotion classification (Section 3).
- To achieve the state-of-the-art result on the Empathetic Dialogue dataset for the classification of 32 emotions (Section 4).
- To generate emotion representations that can derive an emotion graph, an emotion wheel, as well as fill the gap for unexplored emotions from existing emotion theories (Section 5).

2 Related Work

Probing models are designed to construct a probe to detect knowledge in embedding representations. Peters et al. (2018) used linear probes to examine phrasal information in representations learned by deep neural models on multiple NLP tasks. Tenney et al. (2019) proposed an edge probing model using a span pooling to analyze syntactic and semantic relations among words through word embeddings. Hewitt and Manning (2019) constructed a structural probe to detect the correlations among word pairs to predict their latent distances in dependency trees. As far as we can tell, our work is the first to generate embeddings of fine-grained emotions from text and apply them to well-established emotion theories.

[1] All our resources including source codes and models are available at https://github.com/emorynlp/CMCL-2021.

Proceedings of the Workshop on Cognitive Modeling and Computational Linguistics, pages 141–148
Online Event, June 10, 2021. ©2021 Association for Computational Linguistics

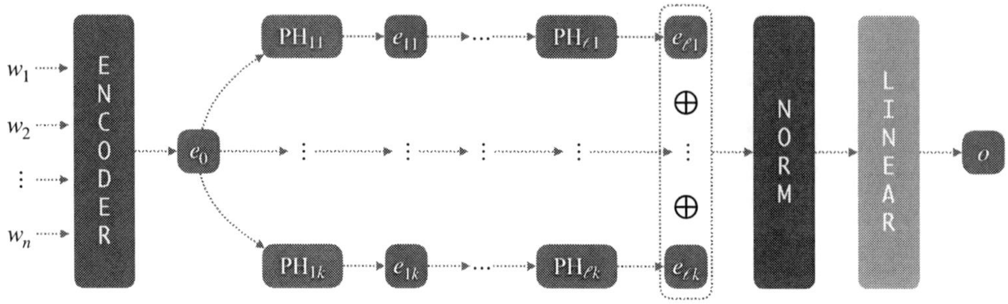

Figure 1: The overview of our deep learning-based multi-head probing model.

NLP researchers have produced several corpora for emotion detection including FriendsED (Zahiri and Choi, 2018), EmoInt (Mohammad et al., 2017), EmoBank (Buechel and Hahn, 2017), and DailyDialogs (Li et al., 2017), all of which are based on coarse-grained emotions with at most 7 categories. For a more comprehensive analysis, we adapt the Empathetic Dialogue dataset based on fine-grained emotions with 32 categories (Rashkin et al., 2019).

3 Multi-head Probing Model

We present a multi-head probing model allowing us to interpret how emotion embeddings are learned in deep learning models. Figure 1 shows an overview of our probing model. Let $W = \{w_1, \ldots, w_n\}$ be an input document where w_i is the i'th token in the document. W is first fed into a contextualized embedding encoder that generates the embedding $e_0 \in \mathbb{R}^{d_0}$ representing the entire document. The document embedding e_0 is then fed into multiple probing heads, $\mathrm{PH}_{11}, \ldots, \mathrm{PH}_{1k}$, that generate the vectors $e_{1j} \in \mathbb{R}^{d_1}$ comprising features useful for emotion classification ($j \in [1, k]$). The probing heads in this layer are expected to capture abstract concepts (e.g., positive/negative, intense/mild).

Each vector e_{1j} is fed into a sequence of probing heads where the probing head PH_{ij} is defined $\mathrm{PH}_{ij}(e_{hj}) \rightarrow e_{ij}$ ($i \in [2, \ell], j \in [1, k], h = i - 1$). The feature vectors $e_{\ell}*$ from the final probing layer are expected to learn more fine-grained concepts (e.g., ashamed/embarrassed, hopeful/anticipating). $e_{\ell}*$ are concatenated and normalized to $g_{\ell} \in \mathbb{R}^{d_{\ell} \cdot k}$ and fed into a linear layer that generates the output vector $o \in \mathbb{R}^m$ where m is the total number of emotions in the training data. It is worth mentioning that every probing sequence finds its own feature combinations. Thus, each of $e_{\ell}*$ potentially represents different concepts in emotions, which allow us to analyze concept compositions of these emotions empirically derived by this model.

4 Experiments

4.1 Contextualized Embedding Encoder

For all experiments, BERT (Devlin et al., 2019) is used as the contextualized embedding encoder for our multi-head probing model in Section 3. BERT prepends the special token `CLS` to the input document W such that $W' = \{\mathtt{CLS}\} \oplus W$ is fed into the ENCODER in Figure 1 instead, which generates the document embedding e_0 by applying several layers of multi-head attentions to `CLS` along with the other tokens in W (Vaswani et al., 2017).[2]

4.2 Dataset

Although several datasets are available for various types of emotion detection tasks (Section 2), most of them are annotated with coarse-grained labels that are not suitable to make a comprehensive analysis of emotions learned by deep learning models.

	TRN	DEV	TST	ALL
C	19,533	2,770	2,547	24,850
L	18.2 (±10.4)	19.6 (±11.4)	23.0 (±12.5)	18.9 (±10.8)

Table 1: Statistics of the Empathetic Dialogue dataset. TRN/DEV/TST: training/development/test set. C: # of documents, L: average # of tokens and its standard deviation in each document.

To demonstrate the impact of our probing model, the Empathetic Dialogue dataset is selected, that is labeled with 32 emotions on ≈25K conversations related to daily life, each of which comes with an emotion label, a situation described in text that can reflect the emotion (e.g., `Proud` → "*I finally got that promotion at work!*"), and a short two-party dialogue generated through MTurk that simulates a conversation about the situation (Rashkin et al., 2019). For our experiments, only the situation parts are used as input documents.

[2]Details about the experimental settings are provided in Section A.1.

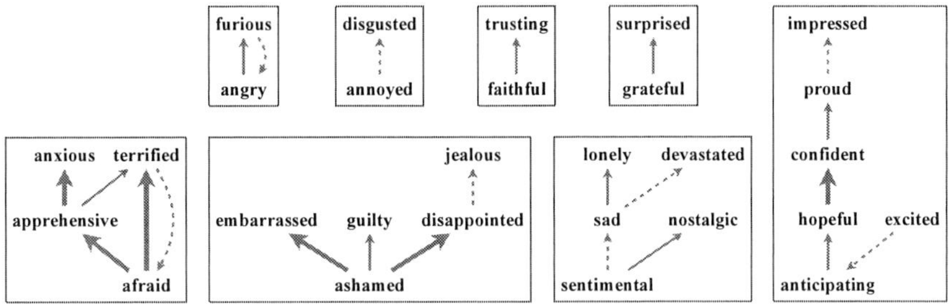

Figure 2: The overview of our deep learning-based multi-head probing model.

4.3 Results

Several multi-head probing models are developed by varying the number of probing layers and the dimension of feature vectors to find the most effective model for interpretation. For all models, a linear layer is used for every probing head such that $\text{PH}_{i*}(e_{h*}) \rightarrow w \cdot e_{h*} = e_{i*}$, where $e_{h*} \in \mathbb{R}^{1 \times d_h}$, $w \in \mathbb{R}^{d_h \times d_i}$, $e_{i*} \in \mathbb{R}^{1 \times d_i}$. The dimension of the document embedding d_0 is set to 768 for all models as configured by the pretrained BERT model.

k	128:64:32	64:32	32
2	56.9 (±0.4)	57.1 (±0.5)	56.9 (±0.5)
4	57.5 (±0.4)	58.1 (±0.5)	**57.8** (±0.5)
8	**57.8** (±0.8)	**58.2** (±0.5)	57.6 (±0.1)
16	57.2 (±0.3)	57.6 (±0.4)	57.7 (±0.6)
32	57.2 (±0.9)	57.3 (±0.4)	57.5 (±0.7)
64	56.8 (±0.6)	57.2 (±0.3)	57.4 (±0.4)

Table 2: Average accuracies and standard deviations on the test set. k: total # of feature vectors in each layer, i'th # in each column delimited by colons is the dimension of the feature vectors in the i'th probing layer.

Table 2 shows the results achieved by all models; every model is trained 3 times and the average accuracy and its standard deviation is reported. The baseline BERT model using no probing, that is to feed e_0 directly into the linear layer, is also built for comparison, showing a significantly higher accuracy of 57.6% (±0.02) than the previously reported state-of-the-art of 48% by Rashkin et al. (2019). The best result is achieved by the 2-layer probing model with 8 feature vectors, showing the accuracy of 58.2% ($d_1 = 64, d_2 = 32, k = 8$).

5 Analysis

5.1 Layer-wise Analysis

To analyze which emotional concepts are embedded in each probing layer (Section 3), we train a logistic regression model on the concatenated vector of $(e_{i1} \oplus \cdots \oplus e_{ik})$ for each layer ℓ_i with the same configuration used for the 3-layer model, 128:64:32 (Table 2), and tested on the development set. For each pair of adjacent layers (ℓ_i, ℓ_j) where $j = i+1$ and $1 \leq i \leq 2$, we measure the likelihood $H_{ij}(s,t)$ of those layers classifying each emotion s as every other emotion t as follows:

$$H_{ij}(s,t) = L(s,t) - L(t,s)$$
$$L(e_g, e_p) = \ell_j(e_g, e_p) - \ell_i(e_g, e_p)$$

where $\ell_*(e_g, e_p)$ is the proportion of the documents whose gold labels are e_g but predicted as e_p by the model trained on the layer ℓ_*. If $L(s,t) > 0$, it means that the higher layer ℓ_j tends to predict s as t more than the lower layer ℓ_i. $L(t,s) > 0$ implies the opposite, and is used as a penalty term to get a more reliable measurement of how much the higher layer is confused s for t than the lower layer.

The results are illustrated in Figure 2, where arrows pointing from one emotion s to another emotion t indicate $H_{ij}(s,j) \geq 2$. The dashed arrows and thin solid arrows correspond to the confusion likelihoods of $H_{12}(s,j)$ and $H_{23}(s,j)$ respectively, and the thick solid arrows reflect the likelihoods in those two metrics. Most emotion pairs point from coarse-grained emotions to fine-grained emotions (e.g., *angry* → *furious*, *sentimental* → *nostalgic*) except for a few pairs (*excited* → *anticipating*), implying that higher probing layers tend to learn more finer-grained emotions that lower layers.

5.2 Generation of Emotion Wheel

Plutchik (1980) introduced the emotion wheel by selecting a reference emotion and arranging others on a circle where the angles are determined by manually assessed similarities between emotion pairs. Inspired by this work, we derive an emotion wheel by creating emotion embeddings and representing each complex emotion as a weighted sum of two basic emotions. Given an emotion e and a set of documents $\mathcal{D}_e$ whose gold labels are e in the DEV set, the embedding of e can be derived as follows, where g_ℓ^d is the normalized vector in Section 3 for d.

$$r_e = \frac{1}{|\mathcal{D}_e|} \sum_{\forall d \in \mathcal{D}_e} g_\ell^d \tag{1}$$

For each complex emotion c, its combinatory basic emotion pair (b_i, b_j) and the weight $w \in [0.1, 0.9]$ are founded as follows (r_* is the embedding of b_*):

$$\begin{aligned} r_{i,j,w} &= w \cdot r_i + (1 - w) \cdot r_j \\ (b_i, b_j, w) &= \underset{\forall i, \forall j, \forall w}{\arg\max}[\text{cosine\_sim}(r_{i,j,w}, c)] \end{aligned} \tag{2}$$

Figure 3 depicts the emotion wheel auto-generated by our framework; 8 basic emotions are displayed on the outer circle and complex emotions are displayed on the edges between those basic emotions where the dot scales are proportional to the cosine_sims in Eq (2).[3] Although the only manual part in this wheel is the selection of those basic emotions from Plutchik (1980), it is compatible to the original emotion wheel in Section A.2 and finds even more relations such as *Excited* = *Anticipating* + *Joyful*, *Lonely* = *Sad* + *Afraid*, and *Grateful* = *Trusting* + Joyful.

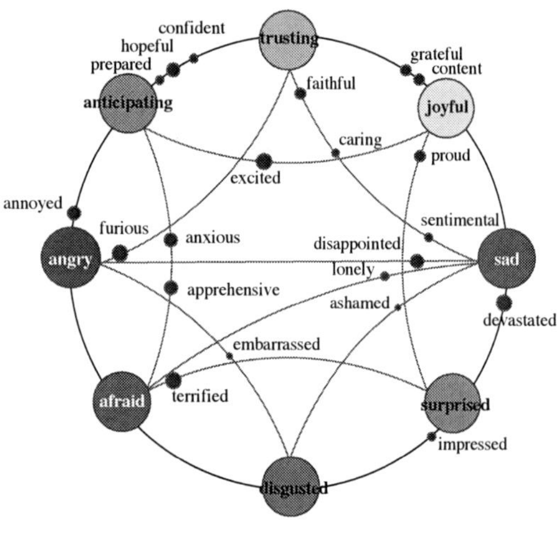

Figure 3: Emotion wheel auto-derived by our approach.

5.3 Augmentation of PAD Model

Russell and Mehrabian (1977) presented the PAD model suggesting that emotions can be denoted by 3 dimensions of pleasure, arousal, and dominance. To verify whether our representations can capture emotional concepts similar to the PAD model, we train a regression model per dimension that takes the emotion embeddings from Eq (1) and learns the corresponding PAD values in Section A.3 manually assessed by Russell and Mehrabian (1977).

[3] 3 complex emotions whose cosine similarity scores are less than 0.1 are omitted in Figure 3: *guilty*, *jealous*, *nostalgic*.

Note that the original PAD model provides the PAD values for only 22 emotions. Given the 3 regression models trained on those 22 emotions, we are able to predict the PAD values for the other 10 emotions missing from the original model.[4] Figure 4 shows the 2D plot of the PA values predicted by our regression models for Pleasure and Arousal, where the 10 emotions, whose PAD values are newly discovered by our models, are indicated with the red labels.[5] It is exciting to see that the newly discovered emotions blend well in this plot (e.g., *anticipating* in between *anxious* and *excited*). Similar emotions are closer in this space (e.g., *sentimental* / *nostalgic*, *trusting* / *faithful* / *confident*), implying the robustness of the predicted values. Notice that the P value of *nostalgic* is predicted as positive, which is understandable because *nostalgic* is related to a memory with happy personal associations; thus, it is found to be positive by distributional semantics.

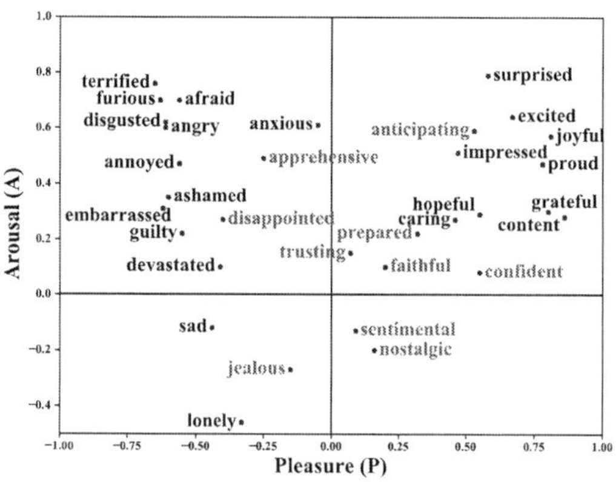

Figure 4: The 2D plot from the PAD values of 32 emotions predicted by our regression models.

6 Conclusion

This paper presents a multi-head probing model to derive emotion embeddings from neural model interpretation. Our model is applied to an emotion detection task and shows a state-of-the-art result. These emotion embeddings can derive an emotion graph, depicting how abstract concepts are learned in neural models, and an emotion wheel and PAD values, verifying their potential of augmenting cognitive models for more diverse groups of emotions that have not been explored by cognitive theories.

[4] Section A.3 provides configurations for all three models.

[5] The 3D plot including the dominance values is in Section A.3.

References

Yossi Adi, Einat Kermany, Yonatan Belinkov, Ofer Lavi, and Yoav Goldberg. 2017. Fine-grained Analysis of Sentence Embeddings Using Auxiliary Prediction Tasks. *5th International Conference on Learning Representations*.

Margaret M. Bradley, Mark K. Greenwald, Margaret C. Petry, and Peter J. Lang. 1992. Remembering pictures: Pleasure and arousal in memory. *Journal of Experimental Psychology: Learning, Memory, and Cognition*, 18(2):379–390.

Sven Buechel and Udo Hahn. 2017. EmoBank: Studying the Impact of Annotation Perspective and Representation Format on Dimensional Emotion Analysis. In *Proceedings of the 15th Conference of the European Chapter of the Association for Computational Linguistics: Volume 2, Short Papers*, pages 578–585, Valencia, Spain. Association for Computational Linguistics.

Giovanna Colombetti. 2009. From affect programs to dynamical discrete emotions. *Philosophical Psychology*, 22(4):407–425.

Jacob Devlin, Ming-Wei Chang, Kenton Lee, and Kristina Toutanova. 2019. BERT: Pre-training of Deep Bidirectional Transformers for Language Understanding. In *Proceedings of the 2019 North American Chapter of the Association for Computational Linguistics: Human Language Technologies*, pages 4171–4186.

Paul Ekman. 1992. An Argument for Basic Emotions. *Cognition & Emotion*, 6(3/4):169–200.

Paul Ekman. 1999. Basic Emotions. *Handbook of Cognition and Emotion*, 98(45-60):16.

Maria Gendron and Lisa Feldman Barrett. 2009. Reconstructing the Past: A Century of Ideas About Emotion in Psychology. *Emotion Review*, 1(4):316–339.

John Hewitt and Christopher D Manning. 2019. A Structural Probe for Finding Syntax in Word Representations. In *Proceedings of the 2019 Conference of the North American Chapter of the Association for Computational Linguistics: Human Language Technologies, Volume 1 (Long and Short Papers)*, pages 4129–4138.

Mandar Joshi, Danqi Chen, Yinhan Liu, Daniel S. Weld, Luke Zettlemoyer, and Omer Levy. 2020. SpanBERT: Improving Pre-training by Representing and Predicting Spans. *Transactions of the Association for Computational Linguistics 2020*.

Richard S Lazarus and Bernice N Lazarus. 1994. *Passion and Reason: Making Sense of Our Emotions*. Oxford University Press, USA.

Yanran Li, Hui Su, Xiaoyu Shen, Wenjie Li, Ziqiang Cao, and Shuzi Niu. 2017. DailyDialog: A Manually Labelled Multi-turn Dialogue Dataset. In *Proceedings of the Eighth International Joint Conference on Natural Language Processing (Volume 1: Long Papers)*, pages 986–995, Taipei, Taiwan. Asian Federation of Natural Language Processing.

Yinhan Liu, Myle Ott, Naman Goyal, Jingfei Du, Mandar Joshi, Danqi Chen, Omer Levy, Mike Lewis, Luke Zettlemoyer, and Veselin Stoyanov. 2019. RoBERTa: A Robustly Optimized BERT Pretraining Approach. *arXiv*, 1907(11692).

Saif M. Mohammad, Parinaz Sobhani, and Svetlana Kiritchenko. 2017. Stance and Sentiment in Tweets. *ACM Transactions on Internet Technology*, 17(3):1–23.

Matthew E. Peters, Mark Neumann, Mohit Iyyer, Matt Gardner, Christopher Clark, Kenton Lee, and Luke Zettlemoyer. 2018. Deep Contextualized Word Representations. In *Proceedings of the 2018 North American Chapter of the Association for Computational Linguistics*, pages 2227–2237.

Robert Plutchik. 1980. A General Psychoevolutionary Theory of Emotion. In *Theories of Emotion*, pages 3–33. Elsevier.

Hannah Rashkin, Eric Michael Smith, Margaret Li, and Y-Lan Boureau. 2019. Towards Empathetic Open-domain Conversation Models: A New Benchmark and Dataset. In *Proceedings of the 57th Annual Meeting of the Association for Computational Linguistics*, pages 5370–5381, Florence, Italy. Association for Computational Linguistics.

James A Russell and Albert Mehrabian. 1977. Evidence for A Three-Factor Theory of Emotions. *Journal of Research in Personality*, 11(3):273–294.

Herbert Spencer. 1895. *The Principles of Psychology*, volume 1. Appleton.

Ian Tenney, Patrick Xia, Berlin Chen, Alex Wang, Adam Poliak, R. Thomas McCoy, Najoung Kim, Benjamin Van Durme, Samuel R. Bowman, Dipanjan Das, and Ellie Pavlick. 2019. What Do You Learn From Context? Probing for Sentence Structure in Contextualized Word Representations. In *9th International Conference on Learning Representations*, pages 55–65.

Ashish Vaswani, Noam Shazeer, Niki Parmar, Jakob Uszkoreit, Llion Jones, Aidan N. Gomez, Lukasz Kaiser, and Illia Polosukhin. 2017. Attention is All you Need. In *31st Conference on Neural Information Processing Systems*.

David Watson and Auke Tellegen. 1985. Toward a Consensual Structure of Mood. *Psychological Bulletin*, 98(2):219–235.

Zhilin Yang, Zihang Dai, Yiming Yang, Jaime Carbonell, Russ R Salakhutdinov, and Quoc V Le. 2019. XLNet: Generalized Autoregressive Pretraining for Language Understanding. In *Advances in Neural Information Processing Systems 32*, pages 5753–5763.

Sayyed Zahiri and Jinho D. Choi. 2018. Emotion Detection on TV Show Transcripts with Sequence-based Convolutional Neural Networks. In *Proceedings of the AAAI Workshop on Affective Content Analysis*, AFFCON'18, pages 44–51, New Orleans, LA.

A Appendix

A.1 Experimental Settings

The BERT model used in our experiment is *BERT-base*, and Table 3 shows the hyperparameters used to develop the models in Table 2.

Hyperparameter	Value
n: max document length	128
m: number of classes	32
k: number of feature vectors in each layer	8
d_0: dimension of the feature vector e_0	768
batch size	32
learning rate	5e-5

(a) Shared hyperparameters.

	128:64:32	64:32	32
l: # of probing layers	3	2	1
d_1: dimension of e_1	128	64	32
d_2: dimension of e_2	64	32	-
d_3: dimension of e_3	32	-	-

(b) Model-specific hyperparameters.

Table 3: Hyperparameter configurations for all models.

A.2 Plutchik's Emotion Wheel

The emotion wheel described in Section 5.2 is inspired by Plutchik (1980) which proposed the eight basic emotions that can constitute other complex emotions through various combinations shown by the emotion wheel in Figure 5, where emotions displayed on the edges are the compositions of those two basic emotions. As can be seen, our derived emotion wheel has some identical emotion relations as the Plutchik's emotion wheel such as *Hope* = *Anticipation* + *Trust*, *Anxiety* = *Anticipation* + *Fear*, and *Sentimentality* = *Trust* + *Sadness*. It suggests the robustness of the emotion wheel derived by the proposed method in Section 5.2.

A.3 Russell and Mehrabian's PAD Model

All regression models in Section 5.3 are based on 2-layer multilayer perceptron using the mean square error (MSE) loss, including a hidden layer with the `ReLU` activation and an output layer with the `Tanh` activation. The hidden layer dimension is 128, and the dropout rate is 0.3, and early stopping is applied to avoid overfitting. The MSE losses of the three regression models to predict the Pleasure (P), Arousal (A), and Dominance (D) values are 0.028, 0.019, and 0.016, respectively. Table 4 describes the original PAD values of the 22 emotions from Russell and Mehrabian (1977), and Figure 6 shows the 2D plot from the PAD values of those 22 emotions. Table 5 describes the PAD values predicted

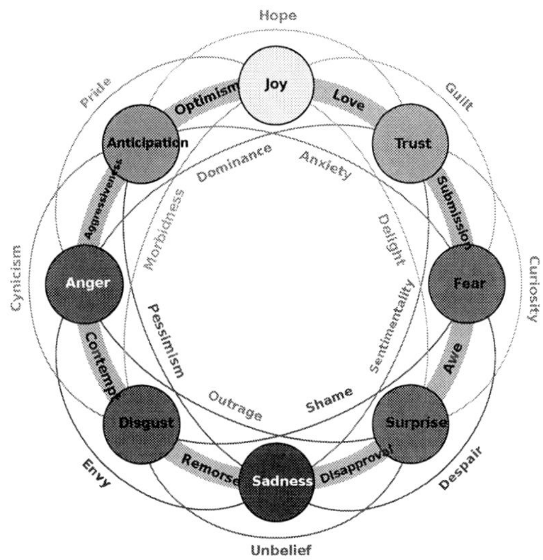

Figure 5: Emotion wheel proposed by Plutchik (1980).

by our regressions models, which are plotted in Figure 4. Finally, Figure 7 plots those predicted PAD values in the 3D space to depict the dominance values with respect to the other two PA dimensions. By comparing the PAD values of 22 emotions in Table 4 and Table 5, most of the predicted values are close to their gold values. Also, we can observe that the predicted values of some newly discovered emotions are consistent with our perception of emotions. For example, *Anticipating* is very close to *Hope* in terms of pleasure but with higher intensity.

Emotion	Pleasure	Arousal	Dominance
afraid	-0.64	0.6	-0.43
angry	-0.51	0.59	0.25
annoyed	-0.28	0.17	0.04
anxious	0.01	0.59	-0.15
ashamed	-0.57	0.01	-0.34
caring	0.64	0.35	0.24
content	0.86	0.2	0.62
devastated	0.14	0.45	-0.24
disgusted	-0.6	0.35	0.11
embarrassed	-0.46	0.54	-0.24
excited	0.62	0.75	0.38
furious	-0.44	0.72	0.32
grateful	0.64	0.16	-0.21
guilty	-0.57	0.28	-0.34
hopeful	0.51	0.23	0.14
impressed	0.41	0.3	-0.32
joyful	0.76	0.48	0.35
lonely	-0.66	-0.43	-0.32
proud	0.77	0.38	0.65
sad	-0.64	-0.27	-0.33
surprised	0.4	0.67	-0.13
terrified	-0.62	0.82	-0.43

Table 4: The original PAD values of 22 emotions provided by Russell and Mehrabian (1977).

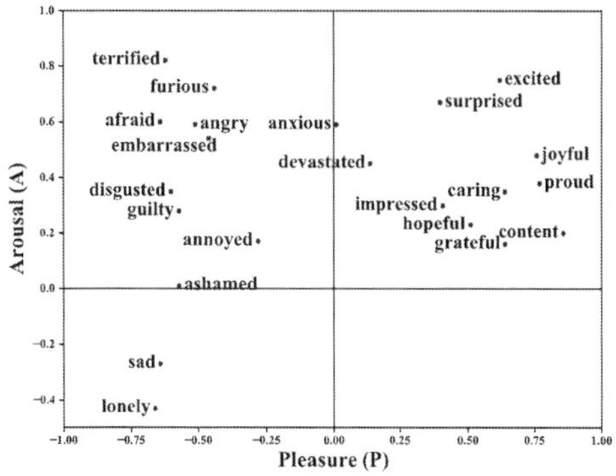

Figure 6: The 2D plot from the PAD values in Table 4.

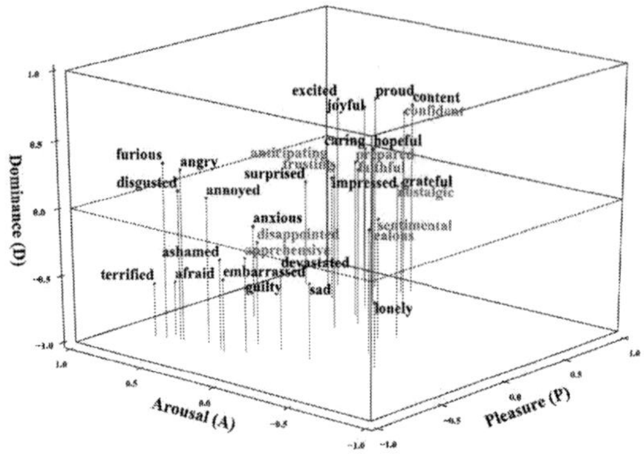

Figure 7: The 3D plot from the PAD values in Table 5.

Emotion	Pleasure	Arousal	Dominance
afraid	-0.56	0.7	-0.6
angry	-0.61	0.6	0.28
annoyed	-0.56	0.47	0.09
anticipating	**0.53**	**0.59**	**0.03**
anxious	-0.05	0.61	-0.31
apprehensive	**-0.25**	**0.49**	**-0.46**
ashamed	-0.6	0.35	-0.33
caring	0.46	0.27	0.22
confident	**0.55**	**0.08**	**0.51**
content	0.86	0.28	0.44
devastated	-0.41	0.1	-0.4
disappointed	**-0.4**	**0.27**	**-0.24**
disgusted	-0.61	0.62	0.12
embarrassed	-0.62	0.31	-0.46
excited	0.67	0.64	0.45
faithful	**0.2**	**0.1**	**0.18**
furious	-0.63	0.7	0.31
grateful	0.8	0.3	-0.14
guilty	-0.55	0.22	-0.52
hopeful	0.55	0.29	0.19
impressed	0.47	0.51	-0.06
jealous	**-0.15**	**-0.27**	**-0.08**
joyful	0.81	0.57	0.37
lonely	-0.33	-0.46	-0.51
nostalgic	**0.16**	**-0.2**	**0.14**
prepared	**0.32**	**0.22**	**0.17**
proud	0.78	0.47	0.46
sad	-0.44	-0.12	-0.43
sentimental	**0.09**	**-0.13**	**-0.11**
surprised	0.58	0.79	-0.19
terrified	-0.65	0.76	-0.6
trusting	**0.07**	**0.15**	**0.23**

Table 5: The PAD values of 32 emotions predicted by our regression models. The 10 emotions that are missing from the original work in Table 4 are indicated with bold font.

A.4 Combinatory Emotions Details

In Section 5.2, we propose a framework to find the combinatory basic emotion pairs for each complex emotion by calculating a weighted sum vector of two basic emotion embeddings. Table 6 lists the basis emotion pairs, weights, and cosine similarity for 24 complex emotions derived by our framework. The weight indicates how much each basic emotion in the pair contributes to the complex emotion and can be interpreted in a proportional manner. For example, *Annoyed* can be composed of 90% *Angry* and 10% *Anticipating*.

c	b_i	b_j	w	cos
annoyed	angry	anticipating	0.9	0.80
anxious	anticipating	afraid	0.5	0.79
apprehensive	anticipating	afraid	0.3	0.76
ashamed	sad	disgusted	0.6	0.17
caring	trusting	sad	0.5	0.28
confident	anticipating	trusting	0.5	0.31
content	joyful	trusting	0.9	0.63
devastated	surprised	sad	0.1	0.93
disappointed	sad	angry	0.7	0.64
embarrassed	disgusted	angry	0.5	0.13
excited	anticipating	joyful	0.5	0.95
faithful	trusting	sad	0.9	0.59
furious	angry	trusting	0.9	0.98
grateful	joyful	trusting	0.8	0.56
guilty	trusting	sad	0.1	0.07
hopeful	anticipating	trusting	0.8	0.67
impressed	surprised	disgusted	0.9	0.40
jealous	disgusted	angry	0.3	0.02
lonely	afraid	sad	0.2	0.33
nostalgic	anticipating	joyful	0.1	0.04
prepared	anticipating	trusting	0.9	0.31
proud	joyful	surprised	0.9	0.45
sentimental	trusting	sad	0.1	0.33
terrified	afraid	surprised	0.9	0.98

Table 6: The combinatory basic emotion pairs for each complex emotion.

Production vs Perception: The Role of Individuality in Usage-Based Grammar Induction

Jonathan Dunn
Department of Linguistics
University of Canterbury
jonathan.dunn@canterbury.ac.nz

Andrea Nini
Linguistics and English Language
University of Manchester
andrea.nini@manchester.ac.uk

Abstract

This paper asks whether a distinction between production-based and perception-based grammar induction influences either (i) the growth curve of grammars and lexicons or (ii) the similarity between representations learned from independent sub-sets of a corpus. A *production-based* model is trained on the usage of a single individual, thus simulating the grammatical knowledge of a single speaker. A *perception-based* model is trained on an aggregation of many individuals, thus simulating grammatical generalizations learned from exposure to many different speakers. To ensure robustness, the experiments are replicated across two registers of written English, with four additional registers reserved as a control. A set of three computational experiments shows that production-based grammars are significantly different from perception-based grammars across all conditions, with a steeper growth curve that can be explained by substantial inter-individual grammatical differences.

1 The Role of Individuals in Usage-Based Grammar Induction

This paper experiments with the interaction between the amount of exposure (the size of a training corpus) and the number of representations learned (the size of the grammar and lexicon) under perception-based vs production-based grammar induction. The basic idea behind these experiments is to test the degree to which computational construction grammar (Alishahi and Stevenson, 2008; Wible and Tsao, 2010; Forsberg et al., 2014; Dunn, 2017; Barak and Goldberg, 2017; Barak et al., 2017) satisfies the expectations of the usage-based paradigm (Goldberg, 2006, 2011, 2016). The input for language learning, *exposure*, is essential from a usage-based perspective. Does usage-based grammar induction maintain a distinction between different types of exposure?

A first preliminary question is whether the grammar grows at the same rate as the lexicon when exposed to increasing amounts of data. While the growth curve of the lexicon is well-documented (Zipf, 1935; Heaps, 1978; Gelbukh and Sidorov, 2001; Baayen, 2001), less is known about changes in construction grammars when exposed to increasing amounts of training data. Construction Grammar argues that both words and constructions are *symbols*. However, because these two types of representations operate at different levels of complexity, it is possible that they grow at different rates. We thus experiment with the growth of a computational construction grammar (Dunn, 2018b, 2019a) across data drawn from six different registers: news articles, Wikipedia articles, web pages, tweets, academic papers, and published books. These experiments are needed to establish a baseline relationship between the grammar and the lexicon for the experiments to follow.

The second question is whether a difference between perception and production influences the growth curves of the grammar and the lexicon. Most corpora used for experiments in grammar induction are aggregations of many unknown individuals. From the perspective of language learning or acquisition, these corpora represent a *perception-based* approach: the model is exposed to snippets of language use from many different sources in the same way that an individual is exposed to many different speakers. Language perception is the process of hearing, reading, and seeing language use (being exposed to someone else's production). These models simulate perception-based grammar induction in the sense that the input is a selection of many different individuals, each with their own grammar.

This is contrasted with a *production-based* approach in which each training corpus represents a single individual: the model is exposed only to the language production observed from that one individual. Language production is the process of

Proceedings of the Workshop on Cognitive Modeling and Computational Linguistics, pages 149–159
Online Event, June 10, 2021. ©2021 Association for Computational Linguistics

speaking, writing, and signing (creating new language use). From the perspective of language acquisition, a purely production-based situation does not exist: an individual needs to learn a grammar before that grammar is able to produce any output. But, within the current context of grammar induction, the question is whether a corpus from just a single individual produces a different type of grammar than a corpus from many different individuals. This is important because most computational models of language learning operate on a corpus drawn from many unknown individuals (perception-based, in these terms) without evaluating whether this distinction influences the grammar learning process.

We conduct experiments across two registers that simulate either production-based grammar induction (one single individual) or perception-based grammar induction (many different individuals). The question is whether the mode of observation influences the resulting grammar's growth curve. These conditions are paired across two registers and contrasted with the background registers in order to avoid interpreting other sources of variation to be a result of these different exposure conditions.

The third question is whether individuality is an important factor to take into account in induction. On the one hand, perception-based models will be exposed to language use by many different individuals, potentially causing individual models to *converge* onto a shared grammar. On the other hand, production-based models will be exposed to the language use of only one individual, potentially causing individual models to *diverge* in a manner that highlights individual differences. We test this by learning grammars from 20 distinct corpora for each condition for each register. We then compute the pairwise similarities between representations, creating a population of perception-based vs production-based models. Do the models exposed to individuals differ from models exposed to aggregations of individuals?

The primary contribution of this paper is to establish the influence that individual production has on usage-based grammar induction. The role of individual-specific usage is of special importance to construction grammar: How much does a person's grammar actually depend on observed usage? The computational experiments in this paper establish that production-based models show more individual differences than comparable perception-based models. This is indicated by both (i) a significantly increased growth curve and (ii) greater pairwise distances between learned grammars.

2 Methods: Computational CxG

The grammar induction experiments in this paper draw on computational construction grammar (Dunn, 2017, 2018a,b). In the Construction Grammar paradigm, a grammar is modelled as an inventory of symbols of varying complexity: from parts of words (morphemes) to lexical items (words) up to abstract patterns (NP -> DET N). Construction Grammar thus rejects the notion that the lexicon and grammatical rules are two separate entities, instead suggesting that both are similar symbols with different levels of abstraction. In the same way as other symbols, the units of grammar in this paradigm consist of a *form* combined with a *meaning*. This is most evident in the case of lexical items, but also applies to grammatical constructions. For example, the abstract structure NP VP NP NP, with the right constraints, conveys a meaning of transfer (e.g. *Kim gave Alex the book*).

In order to extract a grammar of this kind computationally, an algorithm must focus on the form of the constructions. For example, computational construction grammars are different from other types of grammar because they allow lexical and semantic representations in addition to syntactic representations. On the one hand, this leads to constructions capturing item-specific slot-constraints that are an important part of usage-based grammar. On the other hand, this means that the hypothesis space of potential grammars is much larger. Representing the *meaning* of these constructional forms is a separate problem from finding the forms themselves.

(a) NP-Simple -> DET ADJ N
(b) NP-Construction -> DET ADJ [SEM=335]
(c) "the developing countries"
(d) "a vertical organization"
(e) "this total world"

For example, a simple phrase structure grammar might define just one version of a noun phrase as in (a), using syntactic representations. But a construction grammar could also define the distinct NP-construction in (b), further constraining the semantic domain. Thus, the utterances in (c) through (e) are noun phrases that belong to this more constrained NP-based construction (where the semantic constraint is represented as SEM=335).

The grammar induction algorithm used here employs an association-based beam search to identify the best sequences of slot-constraints (Dunn, 2019a). While a grammar formalism like dependency grammar (Nivre and McDonald, 2008; Zhang and Nivre, 2012) must identify the head and attachment type for each word, a construction grammar must identify the representation type for each slot-constraint. This leads to a larger number of potential representations and the beam search has been used to explore this space efficiently. Previous work has used the Minimum Description Length (MDL) paradigm (Goldsmith, 2001, 2006) to describe the fit between a grammar and a corpus as an optimization function during training.

With the exception of the use of semantic representations for slot-constraints, the meaning of constructions is not taken into account here. This is a necessary simplification. Nonetheless, it is important to remember that – to the extent that these patterns are strong manifestations of association across slots – it is likely that they each possess a distinct meaning as well as a distinct form.

The experiments in this paper are centered on sub-sets of corpora containing 100k words. This is significantly less data than previous work (Dunn, 2018b). The idea is to measure the degree to which the grammar itself changes when the induction algorithm is exposed to a more realistic amount of linguistic usage. Because the impact of training size is not clear on the MDL metric, the grammars in this paper are based on the beam search together with an MDL-based metric for choosing the optimum threshold for the ΔP association measure (Dunn, 2018c) used in the beam search. But a final MDL-based selection stage is not employed.

Previous work represented semantic domains using word embeddings clustered into discrete categories. To provide better representations for less common vocabulary items, the embeddings here are derived from fastText (Grave et al., 2019), using k-means (the number of clusters is set to 1 per 1,000 words). Thus, the assumption is that each lexical item belongs to a single domain. Drawing on the universal part-of-speech tag-set (Petrov et al., 2012; Nguyen et al., 2016), semantic domains are only applied to open-class lexical items, on the assumption that more functional words do not carry domain-specific information. The codebase for grammar induction is open source.[1]

[1] https://github.com/jonathandunn/c2xg

ID	Data Source	Condition
AC-IND	Academic Articles	Production
PG-IND	Published Books	Production
AC-AGG	Academic Papers	Perception
PG-AGG	Published Books	Perception
TW-AGG	Tweets	Background
CC-AGG	Web Crawled	Background
WI-AGG	Wikipedia Articles	Background
NW-AGG	News Articles	Background

Table 1: Sources of Language Data

3 Data and Experimental Design

The basic experimental framework in this paper is to apply grammar induction to independent subsets of corpora drawn from different registers. We find the *growth curve* of grammars and lexicons by measuring the increase in representations as these individual subsets are combined. In this case, we examine the representations learned from between 100k and 2 million words in increments of 100k, for a total of 20 observations per condition. Further, we measure the *convergence* of grammars by quantifying pairwise similarities within each condition. In this framework, a *condition* is defined by the data used for learning representations. For example, we examine the convergence of grammars learned from news articles by measuring pairwise similarity across 200 randomly selected combinations of unique sub-sets of the corpus of news articles.

Because of variation in registers, or varieties associated with the context of production (Biber and Conrad, 2009), some grammatical constructions are incredibly rare in one type of corpus but quite common in another type (Fodor and Crowther, 2002; Sampson, 2002). Along these same lines, some registers have more technical terms and thus a larger lexicon with more rare words. Both of these factors mean that the relationship between grammar and the lexicon could be an artifact of one particular register. To control for this possibility, the experiments in this paper are replicated across six registers, as shown in Table 1.

First, corpora representing unique individuals are taken from academic articles and from Project Gutenberg. In this condition, each additional increment of data represents a new speaker (e.g. Dickens, followed by Austen, followed by James). Second, corpora representing aggregations of individuals are taken from the same registers; the difference here is that each additional increment of data does not represent a unique new speaker, only an increased amount of language use. Third, background corpora representing other aggregations of individuals are taken from tweets, web pages, Wikipedia articles, and news articles. These background corpora provide a baseline against which we compare variation in production-based vs perception-based models. Does any observed difference between the *production* and *perception* conditions fall within the expected range observed within this baseline?

In the first condition, *production*, each increment of data (100k words) represents the production of a single individual. In other words, a model trained on this sub-set of the corpus is a representation of only that one individual's production. A corpus of academic articles is drawn from the field of history (Daltrey, 2020). This corpus represents the AC-IND condition, meaning the *Academic* register representing *Individuals*. A corpus of books from Project Gutenberg is drawn from 20th century authors. This corpus represents the PG-IND condition, meaning the *Project Gutenberg* data organized by *Individuals*. Each grammar and lexicon in this condition is trained on the production of a single speaker.

In the second condition, *perception*, these production-based corpora are contrasted with data from the same registers in which each increment of 100k words represents many unknown individuals aggregated together. In other words, a model trained on this sub-set of the corpus reflects the perception of a single individual exposed to many other speakers. The academic register is represented by the British Academic Written English Corpus (Alsop and Nesi, 2009), drawn from proficient student writing. This provides the AC-AGG condition, representing the *Academic* register but with each increment an *Aggregation* of many unknown individuals. The register of books is drawn from the same Project Gutenberg corpus, this time with at most 500 words in each increment representing a single author. This ensures that there is little individual-specific information present in the corpus. This variant provides the PG-AGG condition, representing *Project Gutenberg* data as an *Aggregation* of many individuals.

To provide a baseline, these paired corpora are contrasted with four further sources which represent an aggregation of many unknown individuals: social media data from tweets (TW-AGG), web data from the Common Crawl (CC-AGG), Wikipedia articles (WI-AGG), and news articles, with no more than 10 articles from the same publication per increment (NW-AGG). This range of sources ensures that the experiments do not depend on the idiosyncratic properties of a single register.

Each *ID* in Table 1 represents 2 million words, divided into increments of 100k words. Representations are learned independently on each increment in isolation. In other words, the grammar induction algorithm is applied to each increment of 100k words, with no influence from the other sections of the overall corpus. Thus, each grammar simulates the representations learned from exposure to a fixed amount of language data. The *amount* of exposure is held constant (at 100k words per grammar), allowing us to measure the influence of individuals (production) vs. aggregations of individuals (perception).

The growth of grammars and lexicons is simulated by creating the union of these independent sub-sets: for example, the grammar from Dickens plus the grammar from Austen plus the grammar from James. This means that, after observing 2 million words, the production-based condition has observed the union of 20 different individuals. This design is required to represent the production-based condition because of the difficulty of finding 2 million words for many different individuals. This means that the perception-based condition at 2 million words samples from potentially tens of thousands of speakers while the production-based condition samples from just 20 speakers.

Thus, the growth curves potentially depend on the order in which different samples are observed. In other words, there is a chance that differences between growth curves are artifacts of particular orders of observation and not actual differences between corpora. To test this possibility, we simulate growth curves from 100 random samples for each condition. For each sample, we calculate the coefficient of the regression between the amount of the data and the number of representations, a measure of the growth curve. This provides a population of growth curves for each condition. We then use a t-test to determine whether this sample of growth curves represents a single population. In every case, there is no difference. This gives us confidence that the order of observations has no influence on the final results; the curves reported here are averaged across these 100 samples.

4 Measuring Growth Curves and Grammatical Overlap

The growth of the lexicon is expected to take a power law distribution in which the number of lexical items is proportional to the total number of words in the corpus, as shown in (1). The challenge in understanding the rate of growth, then, is to estimate the parameter α. The simplest method is to undertake a least-squares regression using the log of the size of the corpus and number of representations, as show in (2). On some data sets, this method is potentially problematic because fluctuations in the most infrequent representations can lead to a poor fit at certain portions of the curve (Clauset et al., 2009). We validated the experiments in this paper by conducting comparisons between estimated α parameters and synthesized data following Heap's law. These comparisons confirm that the traditional least-squares regression method provides an accurate measure of the growth curve.

$$p(x) \propto x^{-\alpha} \tag{1}$$

$$\log p(x) = \alpha \log x + c \tag{2}$$

The first question is the degree to which there is variation in the α parameter across representation type (grammar vs lexicon) or condition (production vs perception). For each case, such as perception-based grammar induction from news articles, we calculate the growth curve as described above using least-squares regression on the mean growth curve. We then report both the estimated α and the confidence interval for determining whether differences in the parameter values are significant.

$$d_J(A, B) = 1 - \frac{|A \cap B|}{|A \cup B|} \tag{3}$$

The second question is the degree to which the representations from individual sub-sets of a corpus agree with one another. To measure this, we use the Jaccard distance between grammars, shown in (3). To calculate the Jaccard distance, we first form the union of the two grammars being compared and, second, create a vector for each with binary values indicating whether a particular item is present or not present. The Jaccard distance then measures the difference between these binary vectors, with higher values indicating that there is more distance between grammars and lower values indicating that the grammars are more similar.

5 Experiment 1. Growth Curves Across Grammar and the Lexicon

We begin by measuring the difference between growth curves for the lexicon and for grammars. Here we compare each of the six perception-based conditions, to see the range of behaviours across registers. This is shown in Figure 1, with the x axis showing the increasing amount of data (from 100k words to 2 million words) and the y axis showing the increasing number of representations (to a max of 80k lexical items). The red line represents the grammar and the blue line represents the lexicon. Each of the perception-based conditions (i.e., each register) is represented by a separate plot.

This figure shows that the lexicon grows much more quickly than the grammar. This is somewhat expected because, even though both of them are symbols in the Construction Grammar paradigm, they are symbols of different complexity and may have different behaviors. The other important observation is that lexical items can only be terminal units in the slots of grammatical constructions, which again suggests that the number of different terminal units should be larger than the number of grammatical constructions.

The growth of both lexicon and grammar is visualized by the slope of the lines, with a steeper curve showing quicker growth. Further, the grammar generally levels off, with the rate of growth slowing more quickly as the amount of data increases. In other words, as we observe new data, we are less likely to continuously encounter new constructions as we are to encounter new lexical items. There is general agreement across registers, except that the corpus of news articles shows a grammar that grows much more quickly, reaching a total of 37k constructions. This is a significantly larger grammar than any of the other registers. We also see variation in the lexicon, with the vocabulary on Wikipedia growing at the quickest rate.

Which of these differences are significant? We examine this in Table 2 by looking at the coefficient of a least-squares linear regression to estimate the α parameter, as discussed above. Each α is also shown with its confidence interval, outside of which the difference is taken to be significant. These regression results formalize what is visually clear from the figure: the difference between grammar and lexicon is quite significant. Because the r^2 values of the regression are so high (Clauset et al., 2009), it is also the case that there is a significant

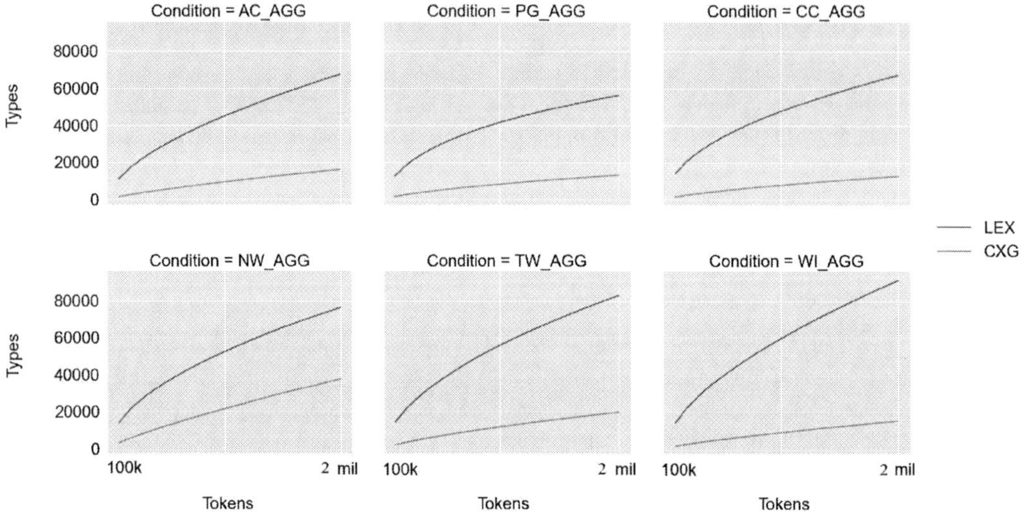

Figure 1: Growth Curve of the Lexicon Contrasted with the Grammar

Lexicon					**Grammar**				
Condition	α	**[0.025**	**0.975]**	**Max** N	*Condition*	α	**[0.025**	**0.975]**	**Max** N
AC-AGG	0.776	[0.772	0.782]	67.4k	AC-AGG	0.660	[0.657	0.664]	16.2k
PG-AGG	0.771	[0.764	0.780]	56.3k	PG-AGG	0.652	[0.652	0.654]	13.3k
CC-AGG	0.782	[0.775	0.790]	67.2k	CC-AGG	0.649	[0.648	0.651]	12.7k
NW-AGG	0.788	[0.782	0.795]	76.2k	NW-AGG	**0.721**	**[0.718**	**0.724]**	**37.7k**
TW-AGG	0.793	[0.787	0.799]	82.9k	TW-AGG	0.678	[0.676	0.680]	19.8k
WI-AGG	0.797	[0.793	0.803]	91.1k	WI-AGG	0.657	[0.654	0.660]	15.2k

Table 2: α Parameters and Confidence Intervals for Growth Curve Estimation by Register

but less meaningful difference across registers in both types of representation. The clearest of these register-specific outliers are Wikipedia (for the lexicon) and news articles (for the grammar); only the second of these is significantly different from all other registers.

6 Experiment 2. Perception vs Production in Growth Curves

Our next experiment takes a closer look at the difference in the growth curves under our two conditions, production (structured around individuals) and perception (structured around aggregations of individuals). The results are shown in Figure 2, again with the growth in number of representations (types) on the y axis and the amount of data observed (tokens) on the x axis. The top row presents the lexicon and the bottom row the grammar. Finally, the blue line represents the perception condition while the red line represents the production or individual condition.

The growth of the lexicon does not show any striking differences. In the academic register (AC), the perception condition shows a faster growth rate; but in the book register (PG) the reverse is true. But the growth of the grammar shows a marked difference: the production-based grammar (in red) grows more quickly in both conditions.

This is formalized in Table 3, showing the estimated α parameters together with their confidence intervals for testing significance. The lexical differences, confirming what we see visually, are not significantly different in either register (i.e., the confidence intervals overlap, or very nearly do). So the difference between production and perception has no influence on the growth of the lexicon.

And yet the growth of the grammar across these two conditions is significantly different in both registers, with an especially large difference in the register of published books (PG). This significance

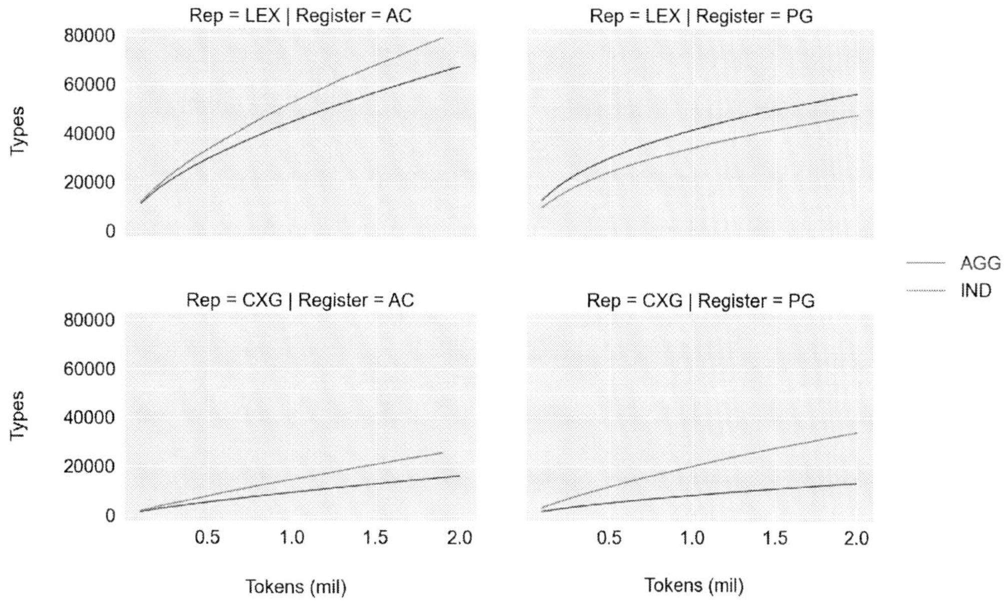

Figure 2: Growth Curves for the Production and Perception Conditions

Lexicon					**Grammar**				
Condition	α	**[0.025**	**0.975]**	**Max** N	*Condition*	α	**[0.025**	**0.975]**	**Max** N
AC-AGG	0.776	[0.772	0.782]	67.4k	AC-AGG	0.660	[0.657	0.664]	16.2k
AC-IND	0.788	[0.784	0.792]	79.1k	AC-IND	**0.691**	[0.686	0.697]	**25.7k**
PG-AGG	0.771	[0.764	0.780]	56.3k	PG-AGG	0.652	[0.652	0.654]	13.3k
PG-IND	0.757	[0.751	0.764]	47.5k	PG-IND	**0.716**	[0.714	0.719]	**34.0k**

Table 3: α Parameters and Confidence Intervals for Growth Curve Estimation by Condition

is shown by the confidence intervals on the estimation of the α parameter; but it is also shown in the final size of the grammars: 16.2 and 13.3k (AGG) vs 25.7k and 34.0k (IND). In other words, given access to data from just one individual, the grammar contains more constructions than an equal amount of data from an aggregation of individuals.

It is important to remember that the grammar induction algorithm is applied independently to each sub-set of the data. What this result shows, then, is that there are considerable individual differences or idiosyncrasies in the grammar but not in the lexicon. In both registers, grammar induction based on the production of individuals acquires more constructions given the same amount of exposure. This is important because most computational approaches to language learning assume that speakers generalize toward a single shared grammar. This implies, incorrectly, that the presence of many speakers in the training corpora is irrelevant, perhaps with the further constraint that each training corpus should represent a single community and register (like written British English).

7 Experiment 3. Perception vs Production in Grammar Similarity

The previous experiments have focused on the *size* and growth of the grammars without focusing on the presence of individual representations (i.e., constructions). To what degree do the grammars from each sub-set of a corpus overlap? Is there a significant difference between the overlap of perception-based and production-based representations? The basic idea in this experiment is to take a closer look at the higher growth curve in production-based grammars identified in the previous experiment: it is possible that a few of the grammars are unique, thus contributing to a higher growth curve, without

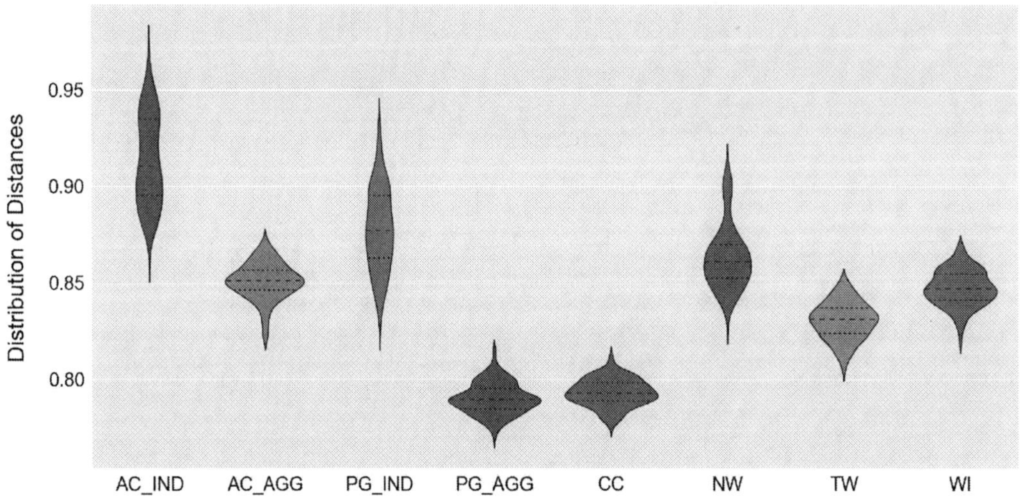

Figure 3: Distribution of Grammar Differences using Jaccard Distance

a pervasive uniqueness distributed across all of the production-based grammars.

This experiment consists in creating pairs of grammars under the two conditions. First, we sample 200 pairs drawn from each condition/register: for example, a pair from different sub-sets of the corpus of news articles. Second, we use Jaccard distance to measure the similarity of each pair. Each comparison is made within a single register, thus controlling for the possibility of register variation. This provides a broader population of pairwise similarities, allowing us to measure the uniqueness of individual grammars in each condition.

We visualize the distribution of grammar similarities using a violin plot in Figure 3. The distance measure ranges from 1 (no overlap) to 0 (complete overlap). The violin plot here shows the distributions, with width representing the density for a particular value and height representing the range of values. This shows, for example, that the AC-IND condition is not normally distributed. Rather, it has a large range of values with two slight peaks. The AC-AGG condition, however, is normally distributed, with a large peak at its mean (shown here by the dotted line in the center).

The values for the Jaccard distances show that, independently of condition, these pairs of grammars are relatively dissimilar. There are many reasons why this is the case, ranging from the amount of data used to train each grammar to the possibility that constructional representations overlap with slightly different slot-constraints. Putting aside the baseline similarity that is observed using this particular measure, the larger point is that there is a clear distinction between production-based and perception-based grammars.

This figure shows a clear distinction between the production-based (IND) and perception-based (AGG) conditions. The grammars learned from individuals vary widely among themselves: some pairs have a high overlap but others a low overlap. Furthermore, the most similar pairs in the individual conditions are as similar or less similar than the average pair for the aggregated condition. This indicates that there are individual differences in these grammars, the same phenomenon that resulted in the higher growth curves identified in the second experiment above.

The perception-based grammars, however, have a low degree of variation: the similarity measures are centered densely around the mean because most grammars have the same degree of similarity. This means that the aggregated or perception-based condition is forcing the induction algorithm to converge onto more stable representations by exposing it to many individuals. The inverse of this generalization is that individuals have unique or idiosyncratic constructions which are only revealed when the training corpus is centered around that individual. This finding fits well with studies in variation (Dunn, 2019b), Dunn2019a which reveal the high degree of syntactic differences across speech com-

Condition	Mean	Variance
AC-IND	91.35	0.053
PG-IND	87.79	0.045
AC-AGG	85.08	0.009
PG-AGG	79.01	0.006
CC-AGG	79.33	0.005
TW-AGG	83.06	0.009
WI-AGG	84.76	0.008
NW-AGG	86.33	0.026

Table 4: Estimated Mean and Variation at Bayesian Confidence Interval of 99% (Each *100 for readability)

munities.

We also notice in Figure 3 that the news register, although part of the perception-based condition, is not as densely centered as the other background registers. This shows the importance of including many registers in a study like this. The likely reason is that different publications enforce their own stylistic conventions. This data set is balanced to ensure that no single publication venue accounts for more than 10 of the articles in any sub-set of the corpus. It remains the case, however, that the presence of a publication-specific style may simulate a different distribution of grammar overlap.

We formalize this violin plot in Table 4 using Bayesian estimates of the mean and variance for each condition at a 99% confidence interval. Because the Jaccard distance is between 0 and 1, we multiply each value by 100 to make the values easier to read. First, the mean distance in the production-based condition is significantly higher in each case; further, the production-based conditions have a higher mean than any of the background conditions. Second and more importantly, the variance for the production-based conditions is greater by an order of magnitude than all other conditions. Only the news register is close; and this is still more similar to the other background data sets than to the individual data sets. The variance is important because it represents the range of overlap caused by individual differences in the grammars.

These Bayesian estimates reinforce the visualization and show that there is more variance and thus more individual differences within grammars that are trained from the production of a single individual. This experiment thus confirms what is suggested by the increased growth curves seen in the second experiment: production-based grammars diverge into more individual-specific representations.

8 Discussion and Conclusions

The three computational experiments in this paper have shown that there is a significant difference between perception-based and production-based grammar induction, even when these conditions are contrasted across many registers. Grammars based on individuals (i) have a significantly steeper growth curve and (ii) a significantly more long-tailed distribution of pairwise similarity. We have also seen that the growth curve of the grammar in general does not have the same α parameter as the lexicon, but does still conform to the generalizations provided by Heap's Law. This supports the idea of a continuum between grammar and the lexicon, with the symbolic representations in the grammar more complex and more abstract, thus showing a slower growth curve.

The results obtained by the three experiments overall reveal that, given a certain number of word tokens, the number of constructions extracted is higher if the sample is taken from one unique individual as opposed to a set of unknown individuals. For example, 100k words of data from academic prose written by the same individual contain 1845 construction types, while the same amount of data from a combination of individuals contains about 1512 construction types, a difference of 333. This is not a trivial result: as a counter-factual, it would also be plausible to expect that the aggregated data would contain a wider variety of constructions because it represents a wider variety of individuals. These results therefore suggest that the constructions that are normally observed in traditional (aggregated) corpora are just the tip of the iceberg: there are many individual-specific constructions that are never observed in aggregated production. In other words, the *uniqueness* of individual construction grammars is disguised when observing the aggregated usage of many individuals.

These findings are consistent with the usage-based proposal that the general grammatical representation of a language emerges as a complex-adaptive system (Beckner et al., 2009). The grammars learned in the perception-based condition contain fewer construction types and are relatively similar to each other. However, these seemingly homogeneous grammars are in fact formed from the shared usage across a number of different individuals. And, as shown in the production-based condition, these aggregated individuals on their own are likely to use very different grammars.

References

A. Alishahi and S. Stevenson. 2008. A computational model of early argument structure acquisition. *Cognitive Science*, 32(5):789–834.

S. Alsop and H. Nesi. 2009. Issues in the development of the British Academic Written English (BAWE) corpus. *Corpora*, 4(1):71–83.

R. H. Baayen. 2001. *Word Frequency Distributions*. Springer Netherlands, Dordrecht.

L. Barak and A Goldberg. 2017. Modeling the Partial Productivity of Constructions. In *Proceedings of AAAI 2017 Spring Symposium on Computational Construction Grammar and Natural Language Understanding*, pages 131–138. Association for the Advancement of Artificial Intelligence.

L. Barak, A. Goldberg, and S. Stevenson. 2017. Comparing Computational Cognitive Models of Generalization in a Language Acquisition Task. In *Proceedings of the Conference on Empirical Methods in NLP*, pages 96–106. Association for Computational Linguistics.

C. Beckner, N. Ellis, R. Blythe, J. Holland, J. Bybee, J. Ke, M. Christiansen, D. Larsen-Freeman, W. Croft, and T. Schoenemann. 2009. Language Is a Complex Adaptive System: Position Paper. *Language Learning*, 59:1–26.

D. Biber and S. Conrad. 2009. *Register, Genre, and Style*. Cambridge University Press, Cambridge; New York.

A. Clauset, C. Shalizi, and M. Newman. 2009. Power-law distributions in empirical data. *SIAM Review*, 51(4):661–703.

A. Daltrey. 2020. *Idiolects and Lexical Bundles*. Unpublished master's dissertation, University of Manchester.

J Dunn. 2017. Computational Learning of Construction Grammars. *Language & Cognition*, 9(2):254–292.

J Dunn. 2018a. Finding Variants for Construction-Based Dialectometry: A Corpus-Based Approach to Regional CxGs. *Cognitive Linguistics*, 29(2):275–311.

J Dunn. 2018b. Modeling the Complexity and Descriptive Adequacy of Construction Grammars. *In Proceedings of the Society for Computation in Linguistics*, pages 81–90.

J. Dunn. 2018c. Multi-unit association measures: Moving beyond pairs of words. *International Journal of Corpus Linguistics*, 23:183–215.

J. Dunn. 2019a. Frequency vs. Association for Constraint Selection in Usage-Based Construction Grammar. In *Proceedings of the Workshop on Cognitive Modeling and Computational Linguistics*. Association for Computational Linguistics.

J. Dunn. 2019b. Global Syntactic Variation in Seven Languages: Towards a Computational Dialectology. *Frontiers in Artificial Intelligence*, frai.2019.

J Fodor and C Crowther. 2002. Understanding stimulus poverty arguments. *The Linguistic Review*, 19(1-2):105–145.

M. Forsberg, R. Johansson, L. Bckstrm, L. Borin, B. Lyngfelt, J. Olofsson, and J. Prentice. 2014. From Construction Candidates to Constructicon Entries: An experiment using semi-automatic methods for identifying constructions in corpora. *Constructions and Frames*, 6(1):114–135.

A. Gelbukh and G. Sidorov. 2001. Zipf and heaps laws' Coefficients depend on language. In *Proceedings of Conference on Intelligent Text Processing and Computational Linguistics.*, volume 2004, pages 332–335. Springer.

A. Goldberg. 2006. *Constructions at work: The nature of generalization in language*. Oxford University Press, Oxford.

A. Goldberg. 2011. Corpus evidence of the viability of statistical preemption. *Cognitive Linguistics*, 22(1):131–154.

A. Goldberg. 2016. Partial Productivity of Linguistic Constructions: Dynamic categorization and Statistical preemption. *Language & Cognition*, 8(3):369–390.

J. Goldsmith. 2001. Unsupervised Learning of the Morphology of a Natural Language. *Computational Linguistics*, 27(2):153–198.

J. Goldsmith. 2006. An Algorithm for the Unsupervised Learning of Morphology. *Natural Language Engineering*, 12(4):353–371.

E. Grave, P. Bojanowski, P. Gupta, A. Joulin, and T. Mikolov. 2019. Learning word vectors for 157 languages. *LREC 2018 - 11th International Conference on Language Resources and Evaluation*, pages 3483–3487.

H Heaps. 1978. *Information Retrieval: Computational and Theoretical Aspects*. Academic Press.

Dat Quoca Dai Quocb Nguyen, Dat Quoca Dai Quocb Nguyen, Dang Ducc Pham, and Son Baod Pham. 2016. A robust transformation-based learning approach using ripple down rules for part-of-speech tagging. *AI Communications*, 29(3):409–422.

J Nivre and R McDonald. 2008. Integrating Graph-Based and Transition-Based Dependency Parser. In *Proceedings of the Annual Meeting of the Association for Computational Linguistics*, pages 950–958. Association for Computational Linguistics.

S. Petrov, D. Das, and R. McDonald. 2012. A universal part-of-speech tagset. In *Proceedings of the Eighth Conference on Language Resources and Evaluation*, pages 2089–2096. European Language Resources Association.

G Sampson. 2002. Exploring the richness of the stimulus. *The Linguistic Review*, 19(1-2):73–104.

D Wible and N Tsao. 2010. StringNet as a Computational Resource for Discovering and Investigating Linguistic Constructions. In *Proceedings of the Workshop on Extracting and Using Constructions in Computational Linguistics*, pages 25–31. Association for Computational Linguistics.

Y Zhang and J Nivre. 2012. Analyzing the Effect of Global Learning and Beam-search on Transition-based Dependency Parsing. In *Proceedings of the International Conference on Computational Linguistics*, pages 1391–1400.

G. Zipf. 1935. *The Psychobiology of Language*. Houghton-Mifflin.

Clause Final Verb Prediction in Hindi: Evidence for Noisy Channel Model of Communication

Kartik Sharma[†*], **Niyati Bafna**[‡*] **and Samar Husain**[†]
[†]Indian Institute of Technology Delhi, [‡]Charles University, Faculty of Mathematics and Physics
kartik.sharma.cs117@cse.iitd.ac.in, 64780815@o365.cuni.cz,
samar@iitd.ac.in

Abstract

Verbal prediction has been shown to be critical during online comprehension of Subject-Object-Verb (SOV) languages. In this work we present three computational models to predict clause final verbs in Hindi given its prior arguments. The models differ in their use of prior context during the prediction process – the context is either noisy or noise-free. Model predictions are compared with the sentence completion data obtained from Hindi native speakers. Results show that models that assume noisy context outperform the noise-free model. In particular, a lossy context model that assumes prior context to be affected by predictability and recency captures the distribution of the predicted verb class and error sources best. The success of the predictability-recency lossy context model is consistent with the *noisy channel hypothesis* for sentence comprehension and supports the idea that the reconstruction of the context during prediction is driven by prior linguistic exposure. These results also shed light on the nature of the noise that affects the reconstruction process. Overall the results pose a challenge to the *adaptability hypothesis* that assumes use of noise-free preverbal context for robust verbal prediction.

1 Introduction

Research on sentence comprehension has conclusively established the widespread role of prediction during online processing (e.g., Marslen-Wilson, 1973; Altmann and Kamide, 1999; Staub and Clifton, 2006; Kutas and Hillyard, 1984). It is known that comprehenders actively anticipate the upcoming linguistic material prior to receiving that information during listening or reading (Luke and Christianson, 2016; Staub, 2015). The role of active prediction during comprehension has particularly been emphasized for processing of SOV languages (e.g., Konieczny, 2000; Yamashita, 1997; Friederici and Frisch, 2000). In particular, it has been argued that preverbal nominal features such as case-markers are effectively used to make precise prediction regarding the clause final verb. Indeed, the ADAPTABILITY HYPOTHESIS states that owing to the typological properties, the prediction system in SOV languages is particularly *adapted* to make effective use of preverbal linguistic material to make robust clause final verbal prediction (Vasishth et al., 2010; Levy and Keller, 2013). Evidence for the *adaptability hypothesis* come from various behavioral experiments that show effective use of case-markers to make clause final verbal prediction (e.g., Husain et al., 2014), facilitation at the verb when the distance between the verb and its prior dependent increase (e.g., Konieczny, 2000), and lack of structural forgetting in the face of complex linguistic environment (e.g., Vasishth et al., 2010). On the other hand, the NOISY CHANNEL HYPOTHESIS assumes that prediction during comprehension is required to accommodate uncertainty in the input (Gibson et al., 2013; Kurumada and Jaeger, 2015). In other words, the hypothesis posits that comprehenders have the knowledge that speakers make mistakes during production, hence, comprehenders need to reconstruct the received input (Ferreira and Patson, 2007).

The two hypotheses stated above make distinct assumptions regarding the utilization of pre-verbal context towards making clause final verbal predictions in SOV languages. One way to operationalize the predictions of the *adaptability hypothesis* is to assume that the preverbal linguistic material will be faithfully used to make verbal prediction, the *noisy channel hypothesis* on the other hand, assumes that the preverbal context is noisy and therefore subject to reconstruction. One consequence of this would be that the *adaptability hypothesis* would predict that verbal prediction should be robust while the *noisy channel hypothesis* would predict that verbal prediction should be susceptible to errors. In

*Equal contribution by KS and NB.

Proceedings of the Workshop on Cognitive Modeling and Computational Linguistics, pages 160–170
Online Event, June 10, 2021.

addition, the two hypotheses would make distinct prediction regarding the nature of errors that might occur during clause final verbal prediction.

In order to probe the two hypotheses stated earlier, in this work, we investigate various incremental models that use local linguistic features to predict clause final verbal prediction in Hindi (an SOV language). The distribution of these model predictions is compared with human data. In particular, we investigate to what extent the models are able to capture the nature of both grammatical as well as ungrammatical verbal predictions when compared to data collected from native speakers of Hindi. Further, in order to probe the assumptions of the *noisy channel hypothesis* more closely, we probe multiple noise functions to investigate the nature of preverbal context reconstruction during prediction.

The paper is arranged as follow, in Section 2 we briefly describe the experimental results that we model. Section 3 provide the necessary details regarding methodology (data/tools, model evaluation, etc.). In Sections 4 and 5 we respectively discuss the n-gram surprisal and the lossy-surprisal models. Section 6 presents the results. Section 7 discusses the current findings and its implications. We conclude the paper in Section 8.

2 Background

In spite of the proposed central role of verb prediction during online processing of Hindi (e.g., Vasishth and Lewis, 2006; Agrawal et al., 2017; Husain et al., 2014), there is a surprising lack of any modeling attempt to understand the processes that subserve verbal predictions in the language. While there are computational metrics that model reading time data (e.g., Hale, 2001; Shain et al., 2016; Futrell et al., 2020), a computational model that makes precise verbal prediction in SOV languages has not been investigated thoroughly (but see, Grissom II et al., 2016, for an initial attempt). Understanding the mechanisms that subserve verbal prediction in SOV languages is critical to understanding how these languages are processed (cf. Konieczny, 2000; Vasishth et al., 2010; Husain et al., 2014; Levy and Keller, 2013; Kuperberg and Jaeger, 2016). Our work fills this gap in the literature. In this section we summarize the key results of a recent study by Apurva and Husain (2020) who investigated the nature of verbal prediction in Hindi using a series sentence completion studies (Staub et al., 2015). Later, in sections 4, 5 we present three computational models to account for these results.

2.1 Completion Study Results

Apurva and Husain (2020) used the sentence completion paradigm (Taylor, 1953) to probe the nature of clause final verbal prediction when differing the number of preverbal nouns that precede the to-be-completed target verb. The number of nouns ranged from 1 to 3 and appeared in different case-marker order. All preverbal nouns were proper nouns. Example 1 shows some of the conditions where 3 preverbal nouns preceded the target verb. In the example, *ne* is the Ergative case-marker, *ko* is the Accusative case-marker and *se* is the Ablative case-marker. In all, there were 6 conditions in this experiment (ne-ko-se, ne-se-ko, ko-ne-se, ko-se-ne, se-ko-ne, se-ne-ko). 36 native speakers participated in the 3-NP condition experiments. Similar to the 3-NP conditions, the 1-NP and 2-NP items had proper nouns and the nouns occurred in various case-marker order. 25 native speakers participated in the 1-NP and 2-NP condition experiments.

(1) a. ne-ko-se
pooja-**ne** urmila-**ko** suneet-**se** ...
Pooja-ERG Urmila-ACC Suneet-ABL ...

b. ne-se-ko
pooja-**ne** urmila-**se** suneet-**ko** ...
Pooja-ERG Urmila-ABL Suneet-ACC ...

The key result from these completion studies was that the number of ungrammatical verbal completions increased as the number of preverbal nominals increased. For the 1-NP conditions the percentage ungrammatical completions was 4%, for the 2-NP conditions this was 8%, while for the 3-NP conditions the ungrammatical completions increased to 15%.

In addition, the completion data was also analyzed for the nature of grammatical and ungrammatical verbal completions. Completions were analyzed based on the verb classes rather than lexical identity (cf. Luke and Christianson, 2016). The data contains a distribution over a total of 18 verbs classes for the 2-NP and 3-NP conditions. In majority of the grammatical completions, Hindi native speakers posit simple syntactic structures (in terms of the number of clausal embeddings and the number of core argument structure). For the 2-NP conditions, the topmost verb classes were *T* (Transitive verb), *IN* (Intransitive verb), and *DT* (Ditransitive verb). For the 3-NP conditions, *CAUS* (Causative verb) and *T DT* (Transitive non-finite verb followed by a ditransitive matrix verb) were consistently the most frequent, covering at least 50% of completions between them for all conditions. Some of the other classes observed were *DT*, *N T DT*, and *DT DT*. Interestingly, while the 3-NP conditions can be grammatically completed using a double embedded structure (e.g., IN DT DT), such cases were not found in the completion data.

Among the ungrammatical verb completions across various conditions, *N DT*, *IN DT* and *CAUS* were consistently the most frequent verb classes predicted. Similar to the trend in the grammatical completions discussed above, the parser posits simple structures even when making mistakes. Additionally, a closer analysis of the ungrammatical completions showed the formation of *locally coherent* parses (Tabor et al., 2004) for the various 3-NP conditions where the first noun was ignored and only the 2nd and the 3rd nouns were used to make the prediction (we call these N2-N3 errors). Other errors were made when either N2 or N3 were ignored to make the prediction (we call these N1-N3, N1-N2 errors respectively). The errors also show a subject primacy effect (Häussler and Bader, 2015; Knoedler et al., 1999) where the presence of an Ergative case marker on N1 is not forgotten. This leads to lack of passive predictions in such cases.[2]

To sum up, the key results of the completion studies were, (a) verb prediction was good in 1-NP and 2-NP conditions, (b) predictions deteriorated in 3-NP conditions, (c) grammatical verbal completions are syntactically simple rather than complex (e.g., clausal embeddings are avoided), (d) error types for the 3-NP conditions show use of two preverbal NPs to make predictions, as well as being sensitive to subject primacy.

Table 1 provides the details on the number of grammatical and ungrammatical completions over all conditions. Also see Table 3 for verb class numbers for the 2-NP conditions. Table 2 shows examples of various error types in the 3-NP conditions.

3 Methodology

3.1 Data and Tools

We use the monolingual Hindi corpus developed by IIT Bombay (Kunchukuttan et al., 2017). It is a collection of raw sentences of Hindi taken from various sources (HindMonoCorp (Bojar et al., 2014), BBC, Wikipedia etc.). For training our models, we use the first 5 million sentences of this data. For the sentence simplification step (described in the Section 3.2), we use the ISC dependency parser for Hindi.[3] Moreover, as the sentence completion experiment included only animate nouns in various items (see Section 2), we use an additional animacy annotation (Jena et al., 2013) to label the nouns accordingly.

3.2 Sentence Simplification

A key aim of the behavioral experiments discussed in Section 2 was to investigate the role of preverbal arguments on clause final verbal prediction. Consequently, our models had to be trained on sentences with various features (e.g., case-marker, animacy) of the preverbal arguments . Since the raw data may contain other intervening material (nominal modifiers, verbal adjuncts, etc.),[4] the task necessitated removal of such material from the training corpus to render it more tractable to the appropriate computational model. Thus, we simplify each sentence in the training data by removing these intervening materials while ensuring that the grammaticality of the sentence remains intact.[5] This, of course, implies that the model only uses the local argument structure to make the necessary verbal prediction.

The sentence simplification process preserves verbal and nominal arguments, such as direct/oblique objects, case-markers, and auxiliaries, but removes adjective phrases, relative clauses, and adjuncts. It treats conjunct structures as separate components. It identifies intra-sentential noun ellipsis and truncates a sequence that displays such a structure, while processing its other verbs. For example:

police-**ne** giraftari warrant
Police-ERG arrest warrant
milne-ke baad somwar raat-ko
get-INF-ACC-GEN after Monday night
Ratan-ke vakeel-**se**
Ratan-GEN-ACC lawyer-ABL

[2]See Sections 1 and 2 of the supplementary material for additional details regarding the word order in Hindi, experimental conditions, predicted verb classes predicted and examples of various errors during the completion study.

[3]`https://bitbucket.org/account/user/iscnlp/projects/ISCNLP`. It is an implementation of the incremental transition-based arc-eager parsing algorithm (Nivre, 2008). The parser is trained on the Hyderabad Dependency Treebank (Bhatt et al., 2009) and is reported to have a UAS of 93.52% and an LAS of 87.77% (Bhat, 2017)

[4]Refer to Section 3 of the supplementary material for statistics on the same.

[5]Additional details regarding procedure and testing have been provided in Section 4 of the supplementary material.

Verb Class	Grammatical completions	Ungrammatical completions
T+DT	170	6
CAUS	140	9
N+DT+DT	51	1
DT+DT	24	0
T+T	21	0
N+CAUS	19	0
N+T+DT	17	5
DT	10	1
CAUS+T	5	0
CAUS+DT	4	0
IN+DT	2	8
T	2	5
N+DT	2	15
N+T	1	2
DT+IN	0	1
DT+T	0	1
IN	0	1
IN+DT	0	2
Other	7	4

Table 1: Grammatical and ungrammatical completions across all 2-NP and 3-NP conditions. *v1+v2* signifies an embedded structure with *v1* as the embedded non-finite verb and *v2* as the matrix verb. In the case of *n+v1+v2*, *n* is part of the *v1* non-finite clause and *v2* is the matrix verb. IN: Intransitive, CAUS: Causative, T: Transitive, DT: Ditransitive, N: Noun.

Error type	Example
N1 N2	N1-ne N2-ko N3-se peeta tha 'hit PAST'
N1 N3	N1-ne N2-ko N3-se kuchaa mangaa 'something asked'
N2 N3	N1-se N2-ne N3-ko introduce kiya 'introduce do'

Table 2: Sample completions for various error types in some 3-NP conditions. Completions are underlined. Note: the completions are grammatical if we ignore the striked-out phrase; else they are ungrammatical. ne=Ergative case-marker, ko=Accusative case-marker, se=Ablative case-marker.

sampark-kiya-tha
communicate-P.Perf

↓

police-**ne** vakeel-**se** sampark-kiya-tha
Police-ERG lawyer-ABL communicate-P.Perf

We also flatten all the nouns in the data to "noun tokens" by merging the noun and its corresponding case-marker. Since we are interested in capturing the variations of the completions for different order of case-markers in the prompt, we can abstract away from the lexicality of the nouns. Thus, we replace the nominal lexical item with its corresponding label depending on whether it is animate (**A**) or not (**N**). Such an abstraction is well motivated considering that humans are known to be sensitive to both syntactic part-of-speech tags as well as lexical semantics during sentence processing (e.g., Demberg and Keller, 2008; Trueswell et al., 1994).

3.3 Experiment Design

Given the abstract nominals and their case-marker, a model's task is to complete the input string with an appropriate verb phrase. For example, if the model is given 3 noun tokens (each with a unique case-marker) with the lexical item replaced with a label **A** denoting *animate*, the task is to predict a verb phrase from this context. End of prediction is signalled as a punctuation.

We note that, given a context, the model makes the prediction in an incremental fashion, rather than producing a one-shot phrase. This means that once a word is predicted, the model considers it as part of the context for the prediction of the next word. For example, given "**A**-ne **A**-ko **A**-se", the model completes the sentence with $w_1w_2w_3$ in the following manner:

A-ne **A**-ko **A**-se $\Rightarrow w_1$

A-ne **A**-ko **A**-se $w_1 \Rightarrow w_2$

A-ne **A**-ko **A**-se $w_1\ w_2 \Rightarrow w_3$

All implemented models discussed in Section 4 and Section 5, use the 1/2/3 preverbal arguments as context. The rationale for use of local context is driven by the goal to model the role of argument structure in verbal prediction (see Section 2). Interestingly, the automatically parsed Hindi corpus (Bojar et al., 2014) shows that arguments (when compared to adjuncts) tend to be closer to the verb[6] suggesting that the critical information needed to

[6]Arguments are at an average distance of 3.8 from the verb while adjuncts have mean dependency distance of 4.5.

Cond	M_Vc	Total	VC count	Cond	M_Vc	Total	VC count	Cond	M_Vc	Total	VC count
n1c1n2c1	COP	1	3	n1c2n2c4	DT	8	23	n1c3n2c4	T	71	84
n1c1n2c1	T	2	3	n1c2n2c4	T	14	23	n1c4n2c1	IN	10	23
n1c1n2c3	DT	3	22	n1c3n2c1	DT	3	22	n1c4n2c1	T	13	23
n1c1n2c3	T	19	22	n1c3n2c1	T	19	22	n1c4n2c2	CAUS	8	82
n1c1n2c4	COP	4	23	n1c3n2c2	DT	30	89	n1c4n2c2	DT	32	82
n1c1n2c4	EXP	2	23	n1c3n2c2	T	59	89	n1c4n2c2	IN	2	82
n1c1n2c4	IN	3	23	n1c3n2c3	DT	2	6	n1c4n2c2	T	40	82
n1c1n2c4	T	14	23	n1c3n2c3	T	4	6	n1c4n2c3	CAUS	2	77
n1c2n2c1	DT	4	21	n1c3n2c4	CAUS	1	84	n1c4n2c3	DT	5	77
n1c2n2c1	T	17	21	n1c3n2c4	COP	1	84	n1c4n2c3	T	70	77
n1c2n2c3	DT	6	24	n1c3n2c4	DT	1	84	n1c4n2c4	T	1	1
n1c2n2c3	T	18	24	n1c3n2c4	EXP	5	84				
n1c2n2c4	CAUS	1	23	n1c3n2c4	IN	5	84				

Table 3: 2-NP Predictions: c1=Nom, c2=Erg, c3=Acc, c4=Abl; IN: Intransitive, CAUS: Causative, T: Transitive, DT: Ditransitive, N: Noun. 'Total' refers to the number of instances of the condition, 'VC count' refers to the number of instances of the corresponding verb class.

predict the verb should be accessible locally. In addition, we place an upper limit on the no. of predicted words – 2 words for 2-NP conditions and 3 for 3-NP.[7] Given the cognitive validity of limited beam-size (e.g., Boston et al., 2011), we only pick the top 50 predictions for further analyses.

Both human and model completions are manually annotated with verb classes based on the valency of the predicted verb. In addition, any nominal argument prediction was also annotated. Verb classes were labeled as *IN* (intransitive), *T* (transitive), *DT* (ditransitive), *CAUS* (causative), or combinations of the above in case a combination of non-finite and matrix verbs is predicted.

For example, the following phrase contains a transitive verb preceded by its object noun:

(2) khaana khaaya ⟶ N T
food eat-PT

Verb classes are used for comparing model output with human data as predictions are known to be graded rather than all-or-nothing lexical prediction (Luke and Christianson, 2016; Staub, 2015). Additionally, we don't predict the verb classes directly to keep the model output consistent with the human data. These completions are then labelled for grammaticality automatically; given the prompt condition and the verb class of the completion, we can infer the grammaticality of the sentence.[8]

[7]No significant change in the set of predictions was observed on increasing these numbers any further.

[8]We use information from our human-annotated completion data as well as native speaker knowledge to construct an exhaustive list of valid completions per condition for this purpose.

3.4 Model Evaluation

All the models are evaluated by comparing the model output with the sentence completion data obtained from the native speakers; specifically, model output is evaluated in terms of the nature of the predicted verb class. We let $\mathbb{VC}$ denote the set of all verb-classes, $h(x)$ denotes the probability distribution of verb-class predictions made by humans, and $m(x)$ denotes the corresponding distribution of the model. We measure KL-divergence between these two distributions, replacing zero probabilities with a fixed value[9] ($= 10^{-5}$); this is shown in (1)

$$KLp(h||m) = KL(h||m') \tag{1}$$

where KL denotes the KL-divergence and m' is a distribution such that $m'(x) = \max(m(x), 10^{-5})$ for each $x \in \mathbb{VC}$.

Apart from this primary measure, we use two other metrics F and D to quantify the span and quality of model predictions with respect to the predicted verb classes, respectively, in order to better understand these characteristics of each model (see Section 6.1).

Further, to ascertain a qualitative understanding of the model performance, we also evaluate each model on the basis of the following characteristics that are displayed in the completion data discussed in Section 2:

- Deterioration in the number of grammatical completions on the 3-NP conditions compared to the 2-NP conditions

[9]It is equal to the minimum probability that we allowed in our model predictions

- Within the grammatical completions, a preference for simpler structures as opposed to complex or embedded constructions
- Exhibition of similar types of errors as humans; for example, in 3-NP conditions, N1-N2 errors, as well as a sensitivity to subject primacy with the Ergative case.

For the 3-NP conditions, we classify errors into types based on their compatibility with a 2-NP sub-context (N1-N2, N1-N3, N2-N3). For example, an error type of N1-N2 would mean that the corresponding ungrammatical prediction is compatible only with first two NPs and not the full 3-NP context. This scheme follows the error types found in the completion data discussed in Section 2. Additionally, see Section 2 of the supplementary material for examples of various errors.

4 N-gram Based Surprisal Model

In order to evaluate the *adaptability hypothesis* where the prediction of upcoming verb is driven by local nominal arguments, we implement an n-gram language model using the data discussed in Section 3.2. Such models are typically used to compute the surprisal metric (Hale, 2001; Levy, 2008) given local context (e.g., Levy et al., 2012). Recall that we have at most 3 NPs as the preverbal context, and therefore, we use a 4-gram model so that the model has access to the complete context in a given condition to make a verbal prediction. Unlike the models discussed in Section 5, the preverbal context in this model is free of noise.

5 Lossy-context Surprisal Models

In this section, we discuss two models to test the *noisy channel hypothesis*. As stated in Section 1, the underlying assumption is that human communication is noisy (Gibson et al., 2013; Kurumada and Jaeger, 2015) and the comprehender has to reinterpret the input to make prediction about upcoming linguistic material. In order to evaluate this hypothesis, we implement different versions of the *lossy-context surprisal* metric (Futrell et al., 2020). Lossy-context surprisal holds that processing difficulty at a word in a context is proportional to the surprisal of a word given a *lossy memory representation* of the context. The two models discussed in sections 5.1 and 5.2 differ in their noise functions that affect the interpretation of the preverbal context.

For the current investigation, lossy-context surprisal is extended to model the sentence-completion task. The word with the highest probability in a given context is assumed to be most likely to complete the sentence (cf. Staub et al., 2015; Levy, 2008; Smith and Levy, 2013).

As noted by Futrell et al. (2020), the lossy surprisal model is not representation-agnostic. Its predictions are dependent on a noise distribution (M). One can then obtain:

$$p(w|r) \propto \sum_{c} p_M(r|c)p(c)p_L(w|c), \qquad (2)$$

where w is the predicted word and r is the result of adding noise to the context c. Here, we consider L to be a 4-gram model, same as the one discussed in Section 4. Moreover, for $c = w_1 w_2 \cdots w_n$ we calculate $p(c)$ also using L

$$p(c) = \prod_{i=1}^{n} p_L(w_i|w_{i-3}w_{i-2}w_{i-1})$$

In addition, if $|c| = n \leq 2$, we don't add any noise to the context and simply use the n-gram model L for prediction. In other words, if $c = w_1 w_2$ or $c = w_1$, then we consider $p(w|r) = p_L(w|c)$. Since we only consider erasure-based noise distributions, this is done to ensure that the whole context is not lost during prediction. In order to get an average behavior of the model, we run the model 10 times and then take the top 50 predictions based on the total probability of each prediction. In other words, suppose a phrase s is predicted to follow a given preverbal arguments in a condition. Then, the total probability of s to be predicted in the given condition by the average model is equal to $\frac{1}{10}\sum_{i=1}^{10} p_i(s)$, where $p_i(s)$ denotes the probability of prediction s in the ith run. Note that if s is not predicted in the ith run, then $p_i(s) = 0$. In the next subsections, we present two models with different noise distribution.

5.1 Predictability Bias Noise (LC-Surp Pred-Bias)

We first consider a noise distribution such that the context is reconstructed based on the predictability of a sub-context. This is driven by the idea that reconstruction of context given a noisy input will be influenced by prior linguistic exposure (Futrell et al., 2020). When the input is less frequent, its reconstruction will be influenced by frequent linguistic patterns in the language. Note, however, that a single word is obviously more frequent than two. Hence, we needed to control for the reduction in the size of the context that may arise due to this predictability bias. We do this by selecting sub-contexts based on their size with a preference to a larger size. Starting from the complete context, we thus iteratively reduce the size by 1 with a high probability ($d = 0.8$).[10] Thus, a sub-context of size m is considered with a probability d^{n-m} where m is the size of the corresponding context. Hence,

$$p_M(r|c) \propto d^{n-m} p_L(r) \tag{3}$$

5.2 Predictability Recency Noise (LC-Surp Pred-Rec)

We next consider a noise distribution which exploits both predictability bias as well as recency. It is well attested that recent input is easier to retrieve from memory compared to non-recent input (e.g., Lewis and Vasishth, 2005). The function therefore is motivated by the fact that while previous linguistic exposure should influence context reconstruction (Futrell et al., 2020), this reconstruction should bias recent linguistic material. In a way, this model combines the properties of the Predictability bias noise model and the n-gram surprisal model.

The conditional probability $p(r|c)$, here, thus can be seen as the multiplication of two parts - (a) predictability of r, $p_L(r)$; and (b) decaying erasure factor, $p_{rec}(r|c)$. Let $c = w_1 w_2 \cdots w_n$, $r = w_{i_1} w_{i_2} \cdots w_{i_k}$ for some n, k, then

$$p_M(r|c) \propto \prod_{j=1}^{n-k} f^{n-i_j} p_L(r), \tag{4}$$

where f is a constant fixed at 0.8.[11]

Thus, a context which is both predictable and can be formed from a recent subcontext is favored. The further a word is from the last uttered word, the lesser its likelihood of being a part of the reduced context r.

6 Results

Table 4 compares the verb class results for the three models discussed above. The key finding is that the values of KLp for the LC-Surp Pred-Rec model is lower than the other models for most of the conditions. This suggests that the model performs better in capturing the verb class distribution found in the human data.

[10]We also evaluated the model with $d = 0.9$ but the model with $d = 0.8$ gave better results.

[11]Following the value fixed for d in Section 5.1.

Condition	4-gram	LC-Surp Pred-Bias	LC-Surp Pred-Rec
ne-ko-se	6.05	5.97	**3.93**
ne-se-ko	7.00	9.14	**5.32**
ko-ne-se	9.40	**9.39**	9.40
ko-se-ne	8.25	8.53	**8.24**
se-ko-ne	5.38	7.87	**5.35**
se-ne-ko	8.57	8.52	**8.37**
Average	7.44	8.24	**6.77**

Table 4: Comparison of the considered models for each condition based on the KLp metric (Equation 1) rounded to 2 places. Smaller (bold) means better.

In order to test if the improvement seen in the LC-Surp Pred-Rec model is indeed significant, we also performed the chi-square test to see if the categories of verb class predicted in the LC-Surp Pred-Rec model were significantly different from other models. Results showed that this was indeed true – categories of verb classes in the LC-Surp Pred-Rec model were significantly different ($p < 0.05$) from both 4-gram model and the LC-Surp Pred-bias model.[12]

KLp provides a measure to quantify the divergence between the human and model prediction distributions. However, the nature of this divergence is still unclear. In order to understand the output of the models better, we evaluate them on some additional metrics. Finally, we report a qualitative analysis of the model output.

6.1 Span and Quality of the Models

In this section we assess the span and quality of the predictions made by the models when compared to the human data.

The `span` of verb prediction made by the model can be computed by the proportion of human distribution that the model misses on. Formally,

$$F(h||m) \propto \sum_{\substack{x \in \mathbb{VC} \\ m(x)=0}} h(x) \tag{5}$$

Since the model will not be able to predict all verb classes that humans produce, we formulate a metric to evaluate the `quality` of the predictions that the model makes. For this, we restrict the verb classes to only those that are predicted by the model and find the KL-divergence (Kullback and Leibler,

[12]See Section 5 of the Supplementary material for details.

Condition	4-gram		LC-Surp Pred-Bias		LC-Surp Pred-Rec	
	F	D	F	D	F	D
ne-ko-se	0.58	2.42	0.58	2.30	**0.31**	**2.15**
ne-se-ko	0.68	2.12	0.94	**0.50**	**0.31**	4.06
ko-ne-se	0.96	0.33	0.96	0.35	0.96	**0.25**
ko-se-ne	**0.87**	0.32	0.90	0.37	**0.87**	**0.23**
se-ko-ne	0.51	2.05	0.83	**0.96**	**0.43**	2.87
se-ne-ko	0.90	0.23	0.90	0.35	**0.88**	**0.15**
Average	0.75	1.99	0.85	**1.63**	**0.63**	2.91

Table 5: Comparison of the considered models for each condition based on the metrics F, D as defined in Equations 5, 6. Smaller means better (bold represents the best in that row for each metric).

1951) on those verb classes between the model and the human; this is shown in (6)

$$D(h||m) = \sum_{\substack{x \in \mathbb{VC} \\ m(x) \neq 0}} h'(x) \log \frac{h'(x)}{m(x)} \tag{6}$$

where $h'(x)$ is normalized from $h(x)$ after removing x where $m(x) = 0$.

Note that higher the F, lower is the model's span; and similarly, higher the D, lower is its quality of predictions (as compared to humans). Table 5 shows that for both F and D, the LC-Surp Pred-Rec model consistently outperforms the LC-Surp Pred-Bias and the 4-gram surprisal model. This suggests that when compared to the human data, the LC-Surp Pred-Rec is better in predicting the valid verb class both in terms of span and the quality of the predictions.

6.2 Qualitative Analysis

In order to interpret the metrics mentioned in Table 5, we did a detailed analysis of the model output in terms of the nature of verb class and the type of prediction errors. This is summarized in Table 6. One can note that

- Grammaticality in all models drops in 3-NP conditions as compared to 2-NP conditions, in line with the human data (cf. Section 2) [13].
- The models prefer simple outcomes, and largely predict DT, $CAUS$ (grammatical) and T, $N\ DT$ (ungrammatical).

Investigating the reason for the better span of the Pred-Rec model, we find that it is primarily due to the important *T DT* verb class. This embedded structure is often used by humans, and neither of the 4-gram or the Pred-Bias model managed to predict it; thus, we can link the better span numbers of the Pred-Rec model to an observable improvement in the nature of verbal predictions.

We also study the error types made by the models and compare them to human errors. The 4-gram model by its nature is only capable of making the locally coherent N2-N3 errors, whereas both the Pred-Bias and Pred-Rec models produce N1-N3 and N1-N2 errors as well. However, while the human data was sensitive to the subject primacy effect – presence of Ergative case-marker never lead to passive verb completion; none of the models is able to fully replicate this pattern. However, the 4-gram model produces the least percentage of passives, followed by the Pred-Rec model. See Section 6 of the supplementary material for more details about error types.

7 Discussion

Results show that the Lossy context surprisal model with Predictability Recency Bias noise performs best in terms of the distribution of predicted verbs and the error types vis-à-vis the completion data. This provides support for the *noisy channel hypothesis* and poses a challenge to the *adaptability hypothesis*. In addition, the comparison of the two lossy surprisal models sheds light on the nature of the noise during the reconstruction process.

Results show that qualitatively all the models capture the completion data to a certain extent (see, Section 6.2). At the same time, overall the noisy context models performed better than the n-gram model in two clear ways. First, the models were able to capture the differential nature of case-marker combination in a limited context. This leads to better coverage of error sources (both in terms of errors made and not made). Second, the models were therefore also better at making better verb predictions compared to the n-gram model. In particular, the overall success of the Pred-Rec model showed that reconstruction of the noisy context in influenced by both past exposure of preverbal sub-context and the recency of the context (cf. Futrell et al., 2020). Put differently, the reconstruction of the context is driven by sub-strings that are more frequent (e.g., ne-ko) and that are closer to the verb. Critically, this shows that the reconstruction process is not random.[14]

[13]See Section 5 of the supplement for actual percentages.

[14]In addition to the two noise functions reported in Sec-

Characteristic	4-gram	LC-Surp Pred Bias	LC-Surp Pred-Rec
Gm% (2-NP) > Gm% (3-NP)	**Yes**	**Yes**	**Yes**
Grammatical classes	*DT, CAUS*	*DT, CAUS*	***DT, CAUS, T DT***
Embeddings predicted	No	No	**Yes**
% of passives	**2.5%**	4.2%	3.1%
Errors made	Only N2 N3 errors	**All error types**	**All error types**

Table 6: Qualitative analysis of the models' predictions. The best/desired outcomes appear in bold font. Gm% denotes the proportion of grammatical completions predicted. High % of passives signifies insensitivity to subject primacy.

While the performance of the predictability recency model is good, it suffers from three issues (a) it overestimates the number of errors made by humans, (b) its overall coverage for various verb class is low, and (c) it is insensitive to subject primacy. The model is able to successfully predict verb phrase involving no clausal embedding, and to a limited extent, those with embeddings. While certain complex structures such as *N DT DT*, predicted rarely by humans, are dropped entirely by the model, its prediction for the *T DT* structure which is frequent in the completion data is not that high. An investigation into the data also shows a scarcity of training examples that exhibit an animate 3-NP context followed by such *T DT* continuations.[15] One reason for this could be the size of the training data, currently 5 million sentences; future work can train on a larger data set. Another possibility is that certain patterns in the human data are not captured in the written corpus used for training and requires a dialogue corpus. Unfortunately, such a corpus currently does not exist for Hindi and attempts to modeling using such a data will have to wait its availability. Relatedly, Staub et al. (2015) argue that prediction based on corpus frequency of syntactic information may not be able to fully capture the notion of preactivation during the completion task. Hence, future work will need to incorporate other sources of information. Finally, the results show that the 4-gram model is more sensitive to subject primacy. This is because, the 4-gram model (unlike noisy context models) has access to the N1 features when making predictions. It can thus correctly use the N1 case feature to avoid predicting passive verbs. This suggests that a noise function relying only on local information will be limited in accounting for the current data.

tion 5, we also investigated a purely random noise function. Due to space constraint, details of this model have been mentioned as supplementary material (Section 7).

[15] See Section 3 of the supplementary material for more details on training data.

The current work provided the first set of detailed results towards modeling clause final verb prediction in an SOV language. The work demonstrated the effectiveness of lossy surprisal models and probed the nature of the noise function during the reconstruction process. In addition to the quantitative analyses demonstrating the success of the Predictability Recency lossy surprisal model, a key contribution of the work was that it highlighted the nature of model's closeness to the human data, both in terms of verb class prediction and the error type. Overall, the results support the proposals that highlight the detrimental effect of increased complexity of the preverbal linguistic material in SOV languages (e.g., Gibson et al., 2013; Ueno and Polinsky, 2009; Ros et al., 2015; Yadav et al., 2020). Future models need to explore other noise functions to investigate the interaction of context predictability with recency as well as primacy of non-local information (e.g., subject). Further, these models need to be tested to investigate the effect of distance (e.g., Vasishth and Lewis, 2006) and structural complexity (Vasishth et al., 2010) on verbal prediction in SOV languages.

8 Conclusion

We implemented three models to predict clause final verbs in Hindi. Model outputs were compared with verb predictions of native speakers of Hindi using quantitative measures as well as qualitatively. Results show that the model that uses limited preverbal context with a predictability recency bias noise function captures the distribution of human data best. The success of this model is consistent with the idea that the reconstruction of the noisy context during prediction is influenced by prior linguistic exposure and that this process interacts with recency of input. These results support the *noisy channel hypothesis* to language comprehension.

References

Arpit Agrawal, Sumeet Agarwal, and Samar Husain. 2017. Role of expectation and working memory constraints in hindi comprehension: An eyetracking corpus analysis. *Journal of Eye Movement Research*, 10(2):1–15.

G. T. Altmann and Y. Kamide. 1999. Incremental interpretation at verbs: Restricting the domain of subsequent reference. *Cognition*, 73:247–256.

Apurva and Samar Husain. 2020. Parsing errors in hindi: Investigating limits to verbal prediction in an sov language. *In submission*.

Riyaz Bhat. 2017. *Exploiting Linguistic Knowledge to Address Representation and Sparsity Issues in Dependency Parsing of Indian Languages*. Ph.D. thesis, IIIT Hyderabad India.

Rajesh Bhatt, Bhuvana Narasimhan, Martha Palmer, Owen Rambow, Dipti Misra Sharma, and Fei Xia. 2009. A multi-representational and multi-layered treebank for hindi/urdu. In *Proceedings of the Third Linguistic Annotation Workshop (LAW III)*, pages 186–189.

Ondřej Bojar, Vojtěch Diatka, Pavel Rychlý, Pavel Straňák, Vít Suchomel, Aleš Tamchyna, and Daniel Zeman. 2014. HindEnCorp - Hindi-English and Hindi-only Corpus for Machine Translation. In *Proceedings of the Ninth International Conference on Language Resources and Evaluation (LREC'14)*, Reykjavik, Iceland. European Language Resources Association (ELRA).

Marisa Ferrara Boston, John T Hale, Shravan Vasishth, and Reinhold Kliegl. 2011. Parallel processing and sentence comprehension difficulty. *Language and Cognitive Processes*, 26(3):301–349.

Vera Demberg and Frank Keller. 2008. Data from eyetracking corpora as evidence for theories of syntactic processing complexity. *Cognition*, 109(2):193–210.

F. Ferreira and N. D. Patson. 2007. The 'good enough' approach to language comprehension. *Language and Linguistics Compass*, 1:71–83.

Angela D Friederici and Stefan Frisch. 2000. Verb argument structure processing: The role of verb- specific and argument-specific information. *Journal of Memory and Language*, 43(3):476–507.

Richard Futrell, Edward Gibson, and Roger P Levy. 2020. Lossy-context surprisal: An information-theoretic model of memory effects in sentence processing. *Cognitive science*, 44(3):e12814.

Edward Gibson, Steven T. Piantadosi, Kimberly Brink, Leon Bergen, Eunice Lim, and Rebecca Saxe. 2013. A noisy-channel account of crosslinguistic word-order variation. *Psychological Science*, 24(7):1079–1088.

Alvin Grissom II, Naho Orita, and Jordan Boyd-Graber. 2016. Incremental prediction of sentence-final verbs: Humans versus machines. In *Proceedings of The 20th SIGNLL Conference on Computational Natural Language Learning*, pages 95–104, Berlin, Germany. Association for Computational Linguistics.

John Hale. 2001. A probabilistic earley parser as a psycholinguistic model. In *Proceedings of the second meeting of the North American Chapter of the Association for Computational Linguistics on Language technologies*, pages 1–8. Association for Computational Linguistics.

Samar Husain, Shravan Vasishth, and Narayanan Srinivasan. 2014. Strong Expectations Cancel Locality Effects: Evidence From Hindi. *PloS one*, 9(7):e100986.

Jana Häussler and Markus Bader. 2015. An interference account of the missing-vp effect. *Frontiers in Psychology*, 6:766.

Itisree Jena, Riyaz Ahmad Bhat, Sambhav Jain, and Dipti Misra Sharma. 2013. Animacy annotation in the Hindi treebank. In *Proceedings of the 7th Linguistic Annotation Workshop and Interoperability with Discourse*, pages 159–167, Sofia, Bulgaria. Association for Computational Linguistics.

A. J. Knoedler, K. A. Hellwig, and I. Neath. 1999. The shift from recency to primacy with increasing delay. *Journal of Experimental Psychology: Learning, Memory, and Cognition*, 25(2):474–487.

Lars Konieczny. 2000. Locality and parsing complexity. *Journal of Psycholinguistic Research*, 29(6):627–645.

Solomon Kullback and Richard A Leibler. 1951. On information and sufficiency. *The annals of mathematical statistics*, 22(1):79–86.

Anoop Kunchukuttan, Pratik Mehta, and Pushpak Bhattacharyya. 2017. The iit bombay english-hindi parallel corpus. *arXiv preprint arXiv:1710.02855*.

Gina R. Kuperberg and T. Florian Jaeger. 2016. What do we mean by prediction in language comprehension? *Language, Cognition and Neuroscience*, 31(1):32–59.

Chigusa Kurumada and T. Florian Jaeger. 2015. Communicative efficiency in language production: Optional case-marking in japanese. *Journal of Memory and Language*, 83:152 – 178.

M. Kutas and S.A. Hillyard. 1984. Brain potentials during reading reflect word expectancy and semantic association. *Nature*, 307:161 - 163.

Roger Levy. 2008. Expectation-based syntactic comprehension. *Cognition*, 106(3):1126–1177.

Roger Levy, Evelina Fedorenko, Mara Breen, and Edward Gibson. 2012. The processing of extraposed structures in english. *Cognition*, 122(1):12–36.

Roger Levy and Frank Keller. 2013. Expectation and locality effects in german verb-final structures. *Journal of memory and language*, 68(2):199–222.

Richard L Lewis and Shravan Vasishth. 2005. An activation-based model of sentence processing as skilled memory retrieval. *Cognitive science*, 29(3):375–419.

Steven G. Luke and Kiel Christianson. 2016. Limits on lexical prediction during reading. *Cognitive Psychology*, 88:22 – 60.

W. Marslen-Wilson. 1973. Linguistic structure and speech shadowing at very short latencies. *Nature*, 244:522–523.

Joakim Nivre. 2008. Algorithms for deterministic incremental dependency parsing. *Computational Linguistics*, 34(4):513–553.

Idoia Ros, Mikel Santesteban, Kumiko Fukumura, and Itziar Laka. 2015. Aiming at shorter dependencies: the role of agreement morphology. *Language, Cognition and Neuroscience*, 30(9):1156–1174.

Cory Shain, Marten van Schijndel, Richard Futrell, Edward Gibson, and William Schuler. 2016. Memory access during incremental sentence processing causes reading time latency. In *Proceedings of the Workshop on Computational Linguistics for Linguistic Complexity (CL4LC)*, pages 49–58, Osaka, Japan. The COLING 2016 Organizing Committee.

N. J. Smith and R. Levy. 2013. The effect of word predictability on reading time is logarithmic. *Cognition*, 128(3):302–319.

A. Staub. 2015. The effect of lexical predictability on eye movements in reading: Critical review and theoretical interpretation. *Language and Linguistics Compass*, 9:311–327.

A. Staub and Jr. Clifton, C. 2006. Syntactic prediction in language comprehension: Evidence from either ... or. *Journal of Experimental Psychology: Learning, Memory, and Cognition*, 32:425–436.

A. Staub, M. Grant, L. Astheimer, and A. Cohen. 2015. The influence of cloze probability and item constraint on cloze task response time. *Journal of Memory and Language*, 82:1–17.

Whitney Tabor, Bruno Galantucci, and Daniel Richardson. 2004. Effects of merely local syntactic coherence on sentence processing. *Journal of Memory and Language*, 50(4):355 – 370.

W. Taylor. 1953. 'cloze' procedure: A new tool for measuring readability. *Journalism Quarterly*, 30:415–433.

J. Trueswell, M. K. Tanenhaus, and S. M. Garnsey. 1994. Semantic influences on parsing: Use of thematic role information in syntactic ambiguity resolution. *Journal of Memory and Language*, 33:285–318.

Miekko Ueno and Maria Polinsky. 2009. Does headedness affect processing? a new look at the vo–ov contrast. *Journal of Linguistics*, 45(3):675–710.

Shravan Vasishth and Richard L Lewis. 2006. Argument-head distance and processing complexity: Explaining both locality and antilocality effects. *Language*, pages 767–794.

Shravan Vasishth, Katja Suckow, Richard L. Lewis, and Sabine Kern. 2010. Short-term forgetting in sentence comprehension: Crosslinguistic evidence from verb-final structures. *Language and Cognitive Processes*, 25(4):533–567.

Himanshu Yadav, Ashwini Vaidya, Vishakha Shukla, and Samar Husain. 2020. Word order typology interacts with linguistic complexity: a cross-linguistic corpus study. *Cognitive Science*, 44(4).

Hiroko Yamashita. 1997. The effects of word-order and case marking information on the processing of japanese. *Journal of Psycholinguistic Research*, 26(2):163–188.

Dependency Locality and Neural Surprisal as Predictors of Processing Difficulty: Evidence from Reading Times

Neil Rathi
Palo Alto High School
neilrathi@gmail.com

Abstract

This paper compares two influential theories of processing difficulty: Gibson (2000)'s Dependency Locality Theory (DLT) and Hale (2001)'s Surprisal Theory. While prior work has aimed to compare DLT and Surprisal Theory (see Demberg and Keller, 2008), they have not yet been compared using more modern and powerful methods for estimating surprisal and DLT integration cost. I compare estimated surprisal values from two models, an RNN and a Transformer neural network, as well as DLT integration cost from a hand-parsed treebank, to reading times from the Dundee Corpus. The results for integration cost corroborate those of Demberg and Keller (2008), finding that it is a negative predictor of reading times overall and a strong positive predictor for nouns, but contrast with their observations for surprisal, finding strong evidence for lexicalized surprisal as a predictor of reading times. Ultimately, I conclude that a broad-coverage model must integrate both theories in order to most accurately predict processing difficulty.

1 Introduction

Computational theories of language processing difficulty typically argue for either a memory or expectation-based approach (Boston et al., 2011). Memory based models (eg. Gibson, 1998, 2000; Lewis and Vasishth, 2005) focus on the idea that resources are allocated for integrating, storing, and retrieving linguistic input. On the other hand, expectation-based models (eg. Hale, 2001; Jurafsky, 1996) propose that resources are proportionally devoted to maintaining different potential representations, leading to an expectation-based view. (Levy, 2008, 2013; Smith and Levy, 2013).

Here, I focus on one representative theory from each group. The first is the **Dependency Locality Theory**, or DLT, which was initially proposed by Gibson (2000). The DLT quantifies the processing difficulty, or *integration cost* (IC) of discourse referents (i.e. nouns and finite verbs), as the number of intervening nouns and verbs between a word and its preceding head or dependent, plus an additional cost of 1. Thus, the IC is always incurred at the second word in the dependency relation in linear order. This is shown in Figure 1. Note that IC only assigns a non-zero cost to discourse referents.

Meanwhile, Hale (2001) and Levy (2008)'s **Surprisal Theory** formulates the processing difficulty of a word w_n in context $C = w_1 \dots w_{n-1}$ to be its information-theoretic surprisal, given by

$$\text{difficulty}(w_n) \propto -\log_2 P(w_n \mid C) \quad (1)$$

so that words that are more likely in context will then be assigned lower processing difficulties.

Some work has attempted to compare DLT and surprisal as competing predictors of processing difficulty. Most notably, Demberg and Keller (2008) compared processing difficulties from DLT and surprisal to the Dundee Corpus (Kennedy et al., 2003), a large corpus of eye-tracking data. Specifically, they examined lexicalized surprisal (where the model assigned probabilities to the words themselves), unlexicalized surprisal (where the model only had access to parts of speech), and integration cost. They found that unlexicalized surprisal was a strong predictor of reading times, while IC and lexicalized surprisal were weak predictors. They also observed that IC was a strong positive predictor of reading times for nouns, and found little correlation between IC and surprisal.

Notably, however, Demberg and Keller's study relied on older methods of calculating surprisal, using a probabilistic context free grammar (PCFG). Other similar work (eg. Smith and Levy, 2013) has used n-gram models, which do not account for structural probabilities. Computational language models (LMs) such as n-grams and PCFGs are suboptimal for estimating the probabilities of words in context compared to humans.

Proceedings of the Workshop on Cognitive Modeling and Computational Linguistics, pages 171–176
Online Event, June 10, 2021.

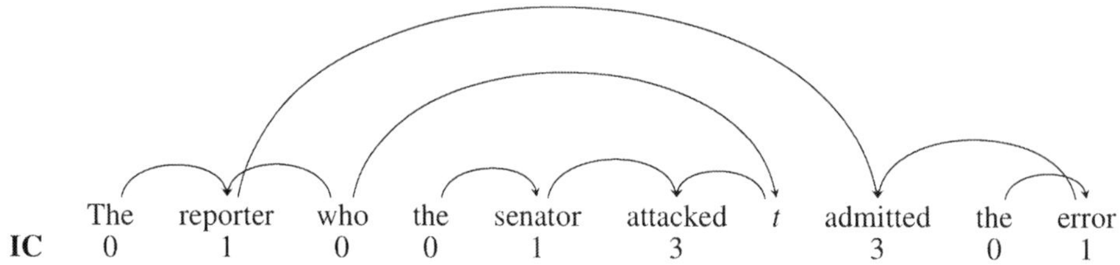

Figure 1: Dependency Locality Theory integration costs

However, recent work in neural network language modeling has shown that recurrent neural networks (RNNs) and Transformers are capable not only of learning word sequences, but also underlying syntactic structure (Futrell et al., 2019; Gulordava et al., 2018; Hewitt and Manning, 2019; Manning et al., 2020). This makes them suited for more accurate estimations of surprisal.

In this paper, I examine the correlation between reading times, DLT integration cost, and surprisal. Specifically, I compare results from a manually parsed treebank for IC and two neural LMs for surprisal, to eye-tracking times sourced from the Dundee Corpus. I additionally examine the correlation between IC and surprisal.

2 Methods

The method in this study is similar to that of prior work on empirically testing theories of sentence processing (eg. Demberg and Keller, 2008; Smith and Levy, 2013; Wilcox et al., 2020), using reading time data in order to estimate processing difficulty.

2.1 Corpus

Specifically, I used a large corpus of eye-tracking data, the **Dundee Corpus** (Kennedy et al., 2003). The corpus consists of a large set of English data taken from the Independent newspaper. Ten English speaking participants read selections from this data, comprised of 20 unique texts, and their reading times were recorded. The final corpus contained 515,020 data points.

As with other work done on reading times (see Demberg and Keller, 2008; Smith and Levy, 2013), I excluded data from the analysis if it was one of the first or last in a sentence, contained non-alphabetical characters (including punctuation), was a proper noun, was at the beginning or end of a line, or was skipped during reading. I also excluded the next three words that followed any excluded words to account for spillover in the regression. This left me with 383,791 data points. For the RNN, I additionally removed any data (and the three following words) that was not part of the Wikipedia vocabulary.

As a second analysis, I restricted the data solely to nouns, as well as to nouns and verbs (see Demberg and Keller, 2008), given that DLT only makes its predictions for discourse referents.

2.2 Integration Cost

For calculating IC, I used the Dundee Treebank (Barrett et al., 2015), a hand-parsed Universal Dependencies style treebank of texts from the Dundee Corpus. This hand-parsed dataset is more accurate than the automatic parser used by Demberg and Keller (2008). To account for syntactic traces, which are not explicitly marked in the annotation, I added traces based on the dependency relations in the parsed sentence. Traces contributed a cost of one as intervening referents, and were added after the following UD relations: acl:relcl, ccomp, dobj, nsubj:pass, and nmod, as in Howcroft and Demberg (2017).

2.3 Surprisal Models

I used two language models (LMs) to calculate Surprisal. While earlier work has relied on PCFGs and n-grams to estimate surprisal, some recent work suggests that these neural models are capable of learning and generating syntactic representations to the same degree as grammar-based LMs (van Schijndel and Linzen, 2018). Thus, I used neural LMs in order to generate probability distributions without explicitly encoding symbolic syntax.

The first model was a recurrent neural network (RNN) model from Gulordava et al. (2018) trained on 90 million words of English Wikipedia.[1] The

[1]The RNN consisted of two LSTM layers with 650 units each, with a batch size of 128 and a dropout rate of 0.2.

	All Data				Nouns			
	RNN		GPT-2		RNN		GPT-2	
	Coeff.	p	Coeff.	p	Coeff.	p	Coeff.	p
Intercept	164.1	***	170.0	***	144.0	***	154.6	***
s_0	1.847	***	1.606	***	1.752	***	1.561	***
s_1	1.738	***	0.853	***	2.042	***	0.864	***
IC	–0.823	***	–0.767	**	1.374	*	1.593	*
IC_1	–0.566		–0.1332		0.154		–0.957	

Table 1: Combined Surprisal and IC regression. *** $p < 0.001$, ** $p < 0.01$, * $p < 0.05$.

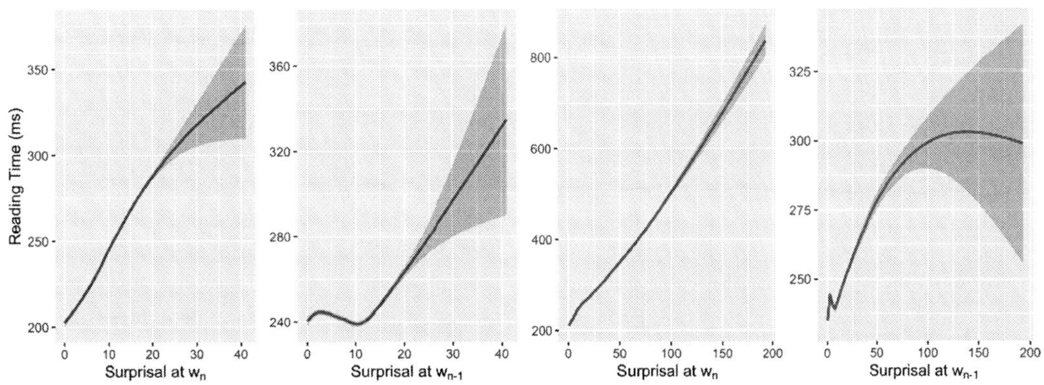

Figure 2: GAM plots from RNN (blue) and GPT-2 (red) surprisals at words n through $n-3$. Shaded region indicates a 95% confidence interval.

second model was the GPT-2 Transformer model from Radford et al. (2019). This study used the 1.5 billion parameter version of GPT-2 trained on the English WebText corpus.

2.4 Analysis

The reading times used for the analyses were first pass gaze durations. As in previous work (Boston et al., 2008; Demberg and Keller, 2008; Monsalve et al., 2012), IC and estimated surprisal values were entered into a mixed-effects model in order to account for other predictor and random effects. I used `lme4` to construct linear models, and obtained approximate p-values via Satterthwaite's degrees of freedom with the `lmerTest` package (Bates et al., 2015; Kuznetsova et al., 2017).

To account for spillover effects, where the processing difficulty of prior word impacts the reading time of the current word (Rayner, 1998), as in previous work (see Smith and Levy, 2013; Wilcox et al., 2020) I used the previous word in the model:

$$\text{rt} \sim s_0 + s_1 + l * f + l_1 * f_1 + p + (1 \mid \text{subj}) \quad (2)$$

Here, s refers to the surprisal or IC, s_1 indicates the surprisal/IC of the previous word, l is word length, f is frequency, $l * f$ indicates that there is a relationship between l and f, and p is the word position. Additionally, I performed GAM regressions on the raw surprisals. I also examined the correlation between the surprisal estimates and IC.

3 Results

Table 2 shows the coefficients of the regression for the RNN and GPT-2 surprisal estimates. The RNN and GPT-2 surprisal regressions resulted in significant positive coefficients, with spillover effects contributing strongly to reading times. The GAM regressions are shown by Figure 2. Surprisal of w_n had a strong linear effect in both models, as well as a slightly weaker effect for w_{n-1}.

Table 3 shows the coefficients for the IC regression on the Dundee Corpus. There was significant negative coefficient for integration cost across the full dataset, with insignificant spillover effects ($p = 0.49$). Restricting data solely to nouns yields a strong positive coefficient. A model fit on both

	RNN		GPT-2	
	Coeff.	p	Coeff.	p
Intercept	163.9	***	169.8	***
s_0	1.826	***	1.609	***
s_1	1.733	***	0.854	***

Table 2: Surprisal regression results from RNN and GPT-2. *** $p < 0.001$, ** $p < 0.01$, * $p < 0.05$.

	All Data		Nouns	
	Coeff.	p	Coeff.	p
Intercept	166.8	***	153.6	***
IC	−1.298	***	1.134	*
IC_1	−0.201		0.127	

Table 3: IC regression results for all data and nouns. *** $p < 0.001$, ** $p < 0.01$, * $p < 0.05$.

nouns and verbs missed significance by a wide margin. For the RNN and GPT-2, regressions on solely nouns were similar to those on all data, with coefficients of 1.75 and 1.560 for s_0.

There was minimal correlation between surprisal and IC across both models, and moderately high correlation between GPT-2 and RNN surprisal values (Table 4). The results from the regression containing both IC and Surprisal are shown in Table 1. Surprisal continued to be a significant positive predictor, whereas IC was a significant negative predictor, albeit weaker than on it's own. On nouns, IC was again a much stronger positive predictor. Again, spillover effects for IC were insignificant.

4 Discussion and Conclusion

This study examined the strength of two different theories of processing difficulty as predictors of eye-tracking data. Overall, neural surprisal has a significant positive relationship with reading times, indicating that it is a strong candidate for a broad-coverage model of sentence processing difficulty. Contrary to the predictions of DLT, there was a significant negative relationship between reading times and integration cost, as in Demberg and Keller (2008).

	All Data	
	IC	GPT-2
GPT-2	0.128	
RNN	0.267	0.684
	Nouns Only	
	IC	**GPT-2**
GPT-2	−0.0163	
RNN	−0.0188	0.562

Table 4: Correlations (Pearson's r) between surprisal and IC for all data and nouns only, $p < 0.001$ for all.

This negative coefficient is likely due to the fact that DLT only makes its reading time predictions for discourse referents, assigning non-referents a processing difficulty of zero. When comparing IC solely to noun reading times, there was a strong positive coefficient, as expected. Additionally, dependency locality has a well-documented cross-linguistic impact on word order (Futrell et al., 2015; Liu et al., 2017; Temperley and Gildea, 2018), suggesting that a modified form of IC which predicts non-discourse referent processing difficulties may be a stronger and more accurate model.

Our results for surprisal are promising evidence that Surprisal Theory can accurately measure sentence processing difficulty. As hypothesised by Surprisal Theory, there was a positive linear effect for both GPT-2 and the RNN. This differs from Demberg and Keller (2008), who found that lexicalized surprisal had an insignificant correlation with reading times from a grammar-based LM. As the corpus used in this study was identical to that in Demberg and Keller (2008), these findings support work which indicates that neural LMs are capable of simulating human language processing better than grammar-based LMs (Monsalve et al., 2012; van Schijndel and Linzen, 2018). I also found a moderately high correlation between RNN and GPT-2 surprisal values, implying that neither model significantly differs from the other.

Similarly to Demberg and Keller (2008), IC and neural surprisal were minimally correlated. When both were added as factors in a mixed effects model, the results remained similar, with IC being negative for all data, and strongly positive for nouns. Given our results as a whole, this suggests that as IC is a strong predictor for nouns, a true broad-coverage model must integrate ideas from both DLT and Surprisal Theory. While I did not note any major gaps in predictions of surprisal, other work has found that it cannot fully account for reading time differences in ambiguities (van Schijndel and Linzen,

2018). Our positive results are in part due to the fact that the Dundee Corpus consists mostly of common syntactic constructions, and therefore does not provide a perfect generalized picture of sentence processing. Thus, this work is consistent with the hypothesis that while appealing, a broad-coverage measure of processing difficulty cannot simply use one model of processing. Potential future work could aim to combine expectation-based models with memory-based theories, such that processing involves both discarding potential representations and integration into the prior structure.

5 Acknowledgements

I would like to thank Richard Futrell and Michael Hahn for their helpful comments, as well as the anonymous reviewers for their feedback.

References

Maria Barrett, Željko Agić, and Anders Søgaard. 2015. The Dundee treebank. In *The 14th International Workshop on Treebanks and Linguistic Theories (TLT 14)*, pages 242–248.

Douglas M. Bates, Martin Mächler, Ben Bolker, and Steve Walker. 2015. Fitting linear mixed-effects models using lme4. *Journal of Statistical Software*, 67(1):1–48.

Marisa Ferrara Boston, John T. Hale, Reinhold Kliegl, Umesh Patil, and Shravan Vasishth. 2008. Parsing costs as predictors of reading difficulty: An evaluation using the Potsdam Sentence Corpus. *Journal of Eye Movement Research*, 2(1).

Marisa Ferrara Boston, John T. Hale, Shravan Vasishth, and Reinhold Kliegl. 2011. Parallel processing and sentence comprehension difficulty. *Language and Cognitive Processes*, 26(3):301–349.

Vera Demberg and Frank Keller. 2008. Data from eye-tracking corpora as evidence for theories of syntactic processing complexity. *Cognition*, 109(2):193–210.

Richard Futrell, Kyle Mahowald, and Edward Gibson. 2015. Large-scale evidence of dependency length minimization in 37 languages. *Proceedings of the National Academy of Sciences*, 112(33):10336–10341.

Richard Futrell, Ethan Wilcox, Takashi Morita, Peng Qian, Miguel Ballesteros, and Roger Levy. 2019. Neural language models as psycholinguistic subjects: Representations of syntactic state. In *Proceedings of the 2019 Conference of the North American Chapter of the Association for Computational Linguistics: Human Language Technologies, Volume 1 (Long and Short Papers)*, pages 32–42, Minneapolis, Minnesota. Association for Computational Linguistics.

Edward Gibson. 1998. Linguistic complexity: Locality of syntactic dependencies. *Cognition*, 68(1):1–76.

Edward Gibson. 2000. The dependency locality theory: A distance-based theory of linguistic complexity. In *Image, Language, Brain: Papers from the First Mind Articulation Project Symposium*, pages 95–126, Cambridge, MA. MIT Press.

Kristina Gulordava, Piotr Bojanowski, Edouard Grave, Tal Linzen, and Marco Baroni. 2018. Colorless green recurrent networks dream hierarchically. In *Proceedings of NAACL*.

John T. Hale. 2001. A probabilistic Earley parser as a psycholinguistic model. In *Proceedings of the Second Meeting of the North American Chapter of the Association for Computational Linguistics and Language Technologies*, pages 1–8.

John Hewitt and Christopher D. Manning. 2019. A structural probe for finding syntax in word representations. In *Proceedings of the 2019 Conference of the North American Chapter of the Association for Computational Linguistics: Human Language Technologies, Volume 1 (Long and Short Papers)*, pages 4129–4138, Minneapolis, Minnesota. Association for Computational Linguistics.

David M. Howcroft and Vera Demberg. 2017. Psycholinguistic models of sentence processing improve sentence readability ranking. In *Proceedings of the 15th Conference of the European Chapter of the Association for Computational Linguistics: Volume 1, Long Papers*, pages 958–968, Valencia, Spain. Association for Computational Linguistics.

Daniel Jurafsky. 1996. A probabilistic model of lexical and syntactic access and disambiguation. *Cognitive Science*, 20(2):137–194.

Alan Kennedy, Robin Hill, and Joël Pynte. 2003. The Dundee corpus. Poster presented at the 12th European Conference on Eye Movement.

Alexandra Kuznetsova, Per B. Brockhoff, and Rune H. B. Christensen. 2017. lmerTest package: Tests in linear mixed effects models. *Journal of Statistical Software*, 82(13):1–26.

Roger Levy. 2008. Expectation-based syntactic comprehension. *Cognition*, 106(3):1126–1177.

Roger Levy. 2013. Memory and surprisal in human sentence comprehension. In Roger P. G. van Gompel, editor, *Sentence Processing*, page 78–114. Hove: Psychology Press.

Richard L. Lewis and Shravan Vasishth. 2005. An activation-based model of sentence processing as skilled memory retrieval. *Cognitive Science*, 29(3):375–419.

Haitao Liu, Chunshan Xu, and Junying Liang. 2017. Dependency distance: A new perspective on syntactic patterns in natural languages. *Physics of Life Reviews*, 21:171–193.

Christopher D. Manning, Kevin Clark, John Hewitt, Urvashi Khandelwal, and Omer Levy. 2020. Emergent linguistic structure in artificial neural networks trained by self-supervision. *Proceedings of the National Academy of Sciences*, 117(48):30046–30054.

Irene Fernandez Monsalve, Stefan L. Frank, and Gabriella Vigliocco. 2012. Lexical surprisal as a general predictor of reading time. In *Proceedings of the 13th Conference of the European Chapter of the Association for Computational Linguistics*, pages 398–408, Avignon, France. Association for Computational Linguistics.

A. Radford, Jeffrey Wu, R. Child, David Luan, Dario Amodei, and Ilya Sutskever. 2019. Language models are unsupervised multitask learners.

Keith Rayner. 1998. Eye movements in reading and information processing: 20 years of research. *Psychological Bulletin*, 124:372–422.

Nathaniel J. Smith and Roger Levy. 2013. The effect of word predictability on reading time is logarithmic. *Cognition*, 128(3):302–319.

David Temperley and Daniel Gildea. 2018. Minimizing syntactic dependency lengths: Typological/cognitive universal? *Annual Review of Linguistics*, 4:1–15.

Marten van Schijndel and Tal Linzen. 2018. Modeling garden path effects without explicit hierarchical syntax. In *Proceedings of the 40th Annual Meeting of the Cognitive Science Society*.

Ethan Gotlieb Wilcox, Jon Gauthier, Jennifer Hu, Peng Qian, and Roger Levy. 2020. On the predictive power of neural language models for human real-time comprehension behavior. *arXiv preprint arXiv:2006.01912*.

Modeling Sentence Comprehension Deficits in Aphasia: A Computational Evaluation of the Direct-Access Model of Retrieval

**Paula Lissón, Dorothea Pregla, Dario Paape,
Frank Burchert, Nicole Stadie, Shravan Vasishth**

University of Potsdam
{lissonhe, pregla, paape, nstadie, burchert, vasishth}@uni-potsdam.de

Abstract

Several researchers have argued that sentence comprehension is mediated via a content-addressable retrieval mechanism that allows fast and direct access to memory items. Initially failed retrievals can result in backtracking, which leads to correct retrieval. We present an augmented version of the direct-access model that allows backtracking to fail. Based on self-paced listening data from individuals with aphasia, we compare the augmented model to the base model without backtracking failures. The augmented model shows quantitatively similar performance to the base model, but only the augmented model can account for slow incorrect responses. We argue that the modified direct-access model is theoretically better suited to fit data from impaired populations.

1 Introduction

Comprehending a sentence involves building linguistic dependencies between words. In the sentence processing literature, several researchers have argued that linguistic dependency resolution is carried out via a cue-based retrieval mechanism (Van Dyke and McElree, 2006; Lewis and Vasishth, 2005). Cue-based retrieval theory assumes that word representations are retrieved from working memory via their syntactic and semantic features. Consider the following sentences:

(1) a. The boy who tickled the girl greeted the teacher.
    b. The boy who the girl tickled greeted the teacher.

In (1a), the noun *boy* would be encoded in memory with features such as [+animate, +subj]. When the reader reaches the verb *tickled*, a retrieval is triggered with retrieval cues that match the features of *boy*. At this point in time, *boy* is the only element that matches the retrieval cues of the verb. By contrast, in (1b), another noun intervenes between *tickled* and *boy* that partially matches the cues set at the retrieval: *girl* [+animate, -subj]. The partial feature overlap causes similarity-based interference between the two items, making the dependency more difficult to resolve in (1b) compared to (1a).

Interference effects have been attested in multiple studies, see for example Jäger et al. (2020); Gordon et al. (2006); Jäger et al. (2017); Van Dyke (2007). One model of cue-based retrieval that predicts these interference effects is the direct-access model developed by McElree and colleagues (McElree, 2000; McElree et al., 2003; Martin and McElree, 2008). The direct-access model (DA) assumes that retrieval cues allow parallel access to candidate items in memory, as opposed to a serial search mechanism. Due to the parallelism assumption, the speed of retrieval is predicted to be constant across items (aside from individual differences and stochastic noise in the retrieval process).

Factors such as increased distance between the target and the retrieval point and the presence of distractor items can lower the probability of retrieving the correct dependent (also known as *availability*). Low availability of the target dependent can lead to failures in parsing or to misretrievals of competitor items. When such errors occur, a backtracking process can be initiated, which by assumption leads to the correct retrieval of the target (McElree, 1993). The backtracking process requires additional time that is independent of the retrieval time. According to the direct-access model, (1a) should have shorter processing times than (1b) on average, because in (1b) some trials require costly backtracking due to lower availability of the target item *boy*.

The direct-access model can be adapted to explain impaired sentence comprehension in individuals with aphasia (IWA; Lissón et al., 2021). However, there is one crucial aspect of the direct-access model that is at odds with the aphasia literature, specifically with the finding that IWA have

Proceedings of the Workshop on Cognitive Modeling and Computational Linguistics, pages 177–185
Online Event, June 10, 2021.

longer processing times for incorrect than for correct responses (e.g., Hanne et al., 2015; Pregla et al., 2021). The direct-access model assumes that some percentage of correct interpretations are only obtained after costly backtracking, and thus predicts that the average processing time for incorrect responses should be *faster* than for correct responses. To address this issue, we implement a modified version of the direct-access model that is specifically relevant for sentence processing in IWA. In this model, backtracking can lead to correct retrieval of the target, as in the base model, but can also result in misretrieval and parsing failure.

1.1 Sentence Comprehension in Aphasia

Aphasia is an acquired neurological disorder that causes language production and comprehension impairments. In the aphasia literature, there are several theories that aim to explain the source of these impairments in language comprehension. One possibility is that IWA carry out syntactic operations at a slower-than-normal pace, which could cause failures in parsing. This is the *slow syntax* theory (Burkhardt et al., 2008). By contrast, Ferrill et al. (2012) claim that the underlying cause of slowed sentence processing in IWA is *delayed lexical access*, which cannot keep up with structure building. Another theory, *resource reduction*, assumes that IWA experience a reduction in the resources used for parsing (Caplan, 2012), such as working memory. Finally, Caplan et al. (2013) claim that IWA suffer from *intermittent deficiencies* in their parsing system that lead to parsing failures. Previous computational modeling work has shown that these theories may be complementary (Patil et al., 2016; Lissón et al., 2021), and that IWA may experience a combination of all of these deficits (Mätzig et al., 2018).

Assuming that a direct-access mechanism of retrieval subserves sentence comprehension, this mechanism could interact with one or more of the proposed processing deficits in IWA. One way to assess whether these deficits are plausible under a direct-access model is the computational modeling of experimental data. Lissón et al. (2021) tested the direct-access model against self-paced listening data from individuals with aphasia, finding the model to be in line with multiple theories of processing deficits in aphasia. Despite this encouraging result, the model could not fit slow incorrect responses, due to its assumptions about backtracking and its consequences.

In what follows, we present our implementation of the original direct-access model and the modified version with backtracking failures. We fit the two models to data from individuals with aphasia and compare their quantitative performances. In order to assess the role of the different proposed deficits of IWA in sentence comprehension, we also map the models' parameters onto theories of processing deficits in aphasia.

2 Data

The data that we model come from a self-paced listening task in German (Pregla et al., 2021). 50 control participants and 21 IWA completed the experiment. Sentences were presented auditorily, word by word. Participants paced the presentation themselves, choosing to hear the next word by pressing a computer key. The time between key presses (here called listening time) was recorded. At the end of the sentence, two images (target and foil) were presented, and participants had to select which image matched the meaning of the sentence they had just heard. Accuracies for the picture-selection task were also recorded. To assess test-retest reliability, each subject completed the task twice, with a break of two months in between. Our modeling is based on the pooled data of both sessions.

2.1 Items

We investigate interference effects in a linguistic construction that is understudied in IWA: Control constructions. In control constructions, the subject of an infinitival clause is not overly specified, but understood to be coreferential with one of the overt noun phrases in the matrix clause of the same sentence (e.g, *Brian promises Martha to take out the trash* $\rightarrow$ Brian takes out the trash). In linguistic theory, it is assumed that a a phonologically empty element (PRO) occupies the subject position of *take out* (Chomsky, 1981). PRO is co-indexed with a noun phrase in the matrix clause that acts as its antecedent. The verb in the matrix clause specifies, according to its semantic and syntactic properties, which noun phrase in the matrix clause triggers the interpretation of PRO in the subclause.

In sentence (2a) below, the verb *verspricht* (promises) is lexically specified as a **subject-control** verb, and the subject noun phrase of the main clause, *Peter*, is chosen as the antecedent of PRO. By contrast, in (2b), the **object-control** verb *erlaubt* (allows) specifies that the object noun phrase of the main clause, *Lisa*, is the antecedent of PRO.

(2) a. **Subject control**
Peter$_i$ verspricht nun Lisa$_j$, PRO$_i$ das kleine Lamm zu streicheln und zu kraulen.
'Peter now promises Lisa to pet and to ruffle the little lamb'

b. **Object control**
Peter$_i$ erlaubt nun Lisa$_j$, PRO$_j$ das kleine Lamm zu streicheln und zu kraulen.
'Peter now allows Lisa to pet and to ruffle the little lamb'

Cue-based retrieval theory assumes that control clauses require completion of the PRO dependency through memory access to the correct noun phrase. The direct-access model would predict (2b) to be easier to process than (2a), because the target (*Lisa*) is linearly closer to the retrieval site at PRO, and thus more available. Therefore, at PRO, the probability of retrieval of the target should be higher in (2b) relative to (2a). In line with this prediction, unimpaired subjects show a processing advantage for object control over subject control (Kwon and Sturt, 2016). Similarly, IWA exhibit more difficulties understanding subject control conditions in acting-out tasks (Caplan and Hildebrandt, 1988; Caplan et al., 1996). However, the object control advantage in IWA has not been previously tested using online methods.

Our experimental items were 20 sentences (10 per condition) similar to (2a) and (2b). The corresponding pictures for the picture-selection task are shown in Figure (1). The top picture is the target picture for (2a), whereas the bottom picture is the target for (2b). We assume that trials where the foil picture has been selected (i.e., the picture that shows the distractor noun as the agent of the action) correspond to a misretrieval.

2.2 Dependent Variables

The dependent variables used for modeling were the listening times (henceforth, LT) at the retrieval site (PRO) and the accuracy of the picture-selection task. Given that PRO is phonologically empty, we assumed that the retrieval process takes place at some point between the second and the third noun phrase (*Lisa* and *das kleine Lamm* in (2a)). We

Figure 1: Example pictures used in the picture-selection task.

therefore summed the listening times of these regions within each trial. In order to evaluate the slowed lexical access hypothesis (Ferrill et al., 2012), we also used data from an auditory lexical decision task that participants performed in addition to the experiment. This task was based on LEMO 2.0 (Stadie et al., 2013). Participants had to decide whether an auditorily presented item was a word or a neologism, and the response times were recorded. For each participant, we computed the mean response times for correct responses. These were then centered and scaled within groups and used as continuous predictors in the models. We will refer to the scaled lexical decision task reaction times as the *LDT* predictor.

3 Direct-Access Model

Our implementation of the direct-access model follows Nicenboim and Vasishth (2018). The model assumes that listening times for correct responses come from a mixture distribution, given that there are trials with backtracking, where an additional processing cost δ is added, and trials without backtracking, where no such cost is added. By contrast, incorrect responses never involve backtracking, and the average listening time should be the same as for correct responses without backtracking. A graphical representation of the model is displayed in Figure (2). The three possible cases are as follows:

(a) Retrieval of the target succeeds at first attempt, with probability θ:
$LT \sim lognormal(\mu, \sigma)$

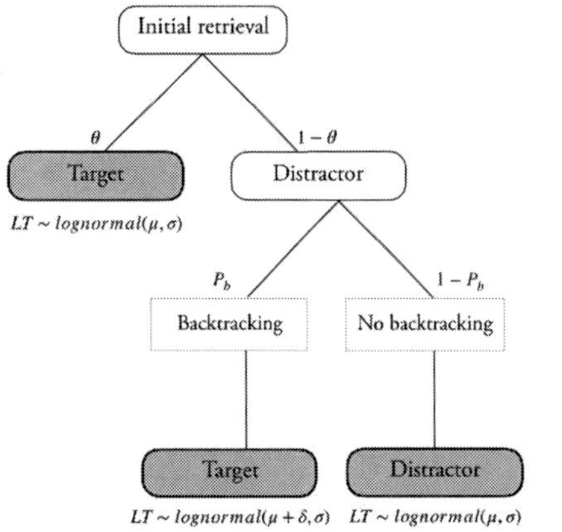

Figure 2: Graphical representation of the direct-access model.

(b) Retrieval fails at first attempt, backtracking is initiated, with probability
$(1-\theta)\cdot P_b$: $LT \sim lognormal(\mu+\delta,\sigma)$

(c) Retrieval fails, no backtracking, and a misretrieval occurs, with probability
$(1-\theta)\cdot(1-P_b)$: $LT \sim lognormal(\mu,\sigma)$

The model includes both fixed and random effects in order to account for sentence complexity, group differences, and individual variability. The hierarchical structure is shown in Equation (1). All parameters have an adjustment by group (IWA versus control), because we expect IWA to have different parameter estimates from control participants. Since DA assumes that retrieval times are not affected by sentence complexity, the average listening times (μ) do not have an adjustment for condition. By contrast, the probability of retrieval of the target, θ, includes a condition adjustment. This parameter can be thought of as indexing memory availability. The probability of backtracking P_b, the cost of backtracking δ, and σ do not depend on sentence complexity, but may vary between IWA and controls. The hierarchical structure is embedded within the parameters when possible (we report the maximal hierarchical structure that could be fit). In Equation (1), the terms u and w are the by-participant and by-item adjustments to the fixed effects, respectively. These are assumed to come from two multivariate normal distributions. All parameters had regularizing priors, listed in Appendix B.

$$\begin{aligned}
\mu &= \mu_0 + u_{\mu 0} + w_{\mu 0} + \beta_1 \cdot group \\
\theta &= \alpha + u_\alpha + w_\alpha + \beta_2 \cdot LDT + \\
&\beta_3 \cdot LDT \cdot group + \\
&(\beta_4 + w_{\beta_4}) \cdot group \\
&(\beta_5 + u_{\beta_5}) \cdot condition + \\
&\beta_6 \cdot group \cdot condition \\
P_b &= \gamma + u_\gamma + \beta_7 \cdot group \\
\delta &= \delta_0 + \beta_8 \cdot group \\
\sigma &= \sigma_0 + \beta_9 \cdot group
\end{aligned} \tag{1}$$

The model was implemented in the probabilistic programming language Stan (Stan Development Team, 2020), and fit via the rstan package (Carpenter et al., 2017) in R (R Core Team, 2020). The model was fit with 3 chains and 8,000 iterations, half of which were used as warm-up.

3.1 Predictions

Based on the theories of processing deficits in aphasia discussed in Section (1.1), and on the findings in Lissón et al. (2021), we make the following predictions:

1. IWA's μ and δ values should be higher than controls'. This would be in line with slow syntax, assuming that both the initial retrieval and the backtracked retrieval are accompanied by appropriate structure-building processes.

2. The probability of initial retrieval of the target θ should be lower for IWA relative to controls, across conditions.

3. Object control conditions should have a larger θ, relative to subject control. In addition, IWA should have a bigger interference effect, i.e., the difference in θ between the two conditions should be larger in IWA than in controls. This pattern would be expected under the resource reduction theory, which states that IWA should have greater difficulties in more complex sentences.

4. Slower lexical decision (LDT) should be associated with a decrease in θ across groups. Strong support for delayed lexical access would come from an interaction between LDT and group, such that an increase in LDT predicts a greater decrease in θ for IWA than for controls: Slow lexical access could cause

parsing problems for controls, but if delayed lexical access is the main cause of difficulty in IWAs, parsing failures should occur more often in this group for individuals whose lexical access is particularly slow.

5. The probability of backtracking should be lower for IWA, which would be in line with resource reduction.

6. Finally, the dispersion parameter σ of the listening-time distribution should be larger for IWA, which would indicate that IWA have more noise in their parsing system. This would be in line with intermittent deficiencies, since more noise could be due to more breakdowns in parsing.

These predictions build on the previous work by Lissón et al. (2021), but other options for the mapping between parameters and theories of comprehension deficits in aphasia are possible, see Mätzig et al. (2018); Patil et al. (2016).

3.2 Results

We begin by assessing the posterior distribution of the probability of retrieval of the target, θ, shown in Figure (3).

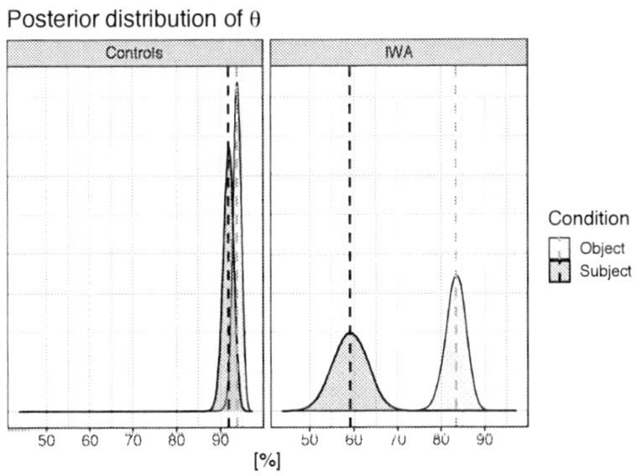

Figure 3: Posterior distribution of θ across conditions and groups.

Controls are estimated to retrieve the target at the first retrieval attempt in both conditions in more than 90% of trials. The mean of the subject-control condition is slightly lower than the mean for the object-control condition. By contrast, IWA display a greater effect of interference: In object-control sentences, where the antecedent is close to PRO, IWA are estimated to correctly retrieve the target at the first attempt 85% of the time, compared to 60% for subject-control. An increase in LDT leads to a decrease in θ of -6% CrI: $[-11\%, -2\%]$, but there was no interaction with group $\times$ LDT (-2% CrI: $[-6\%, 2\%]$). The credible intervals for the remaining parameters are shown in Table (1).

Par.	Control participants	IWA
μ	[1668 ms, 1901 ms]	[2508 ms, 3073 ms]
δ	[1084 ms, 1385 ms]	[2897 ms, 6836 ms]
P_b	[63%, 78%]	[3%, 10%]
σ	[0.15, 0.16]	[0.27, 0.3]

Table 1: Parameter credible intervals, DA model.

As expected under the slow syntax theory, IWA's mean listening times (μ) and the time needed for backtracking (δ) are higher than controls'. Similarly, σ is also higher for IWA, as predicted by intermittent deficiencies. Finally, the probability of backtracking is much lower for IWA than for controls. Assuming that backtracking uses general parsing resources, this estimate is in line with resource reduction.

3.3 Posterior Predictive Checks

One way to assess the behavior of the model is to check the posterior distribution of data generated by the model against the empirical data. If the mean of the empirical data falls within the range of predicted values of the model, the model could have generated the empirical data. By contrast, if the empirical data are outside of the range of the generated values, this indicates a suboptimal fit. Figure (4) shows the posterior predictive distributions of the direct-access model across groups and conditions. Overall, correct responses are modeled reasonably well, except in the object-control condition for IWA. The model also underestimates the listening times for incorrect responses, except for IWA in the subject-control condition. In all other design cells, incorrect responses are slower than correct responses, contrary to the model's assumption that slow backtracking responses are always correct.

4 Modified Direct-Access Model

Based on the original DA model's suboptimal fit, we propose a modified version (MDA). In this version, the distribution of listening times for both correct and incorrect responses is a mixture of directly accessed and backtracked retrievals. The MDA model assumes that backtracking can fail.

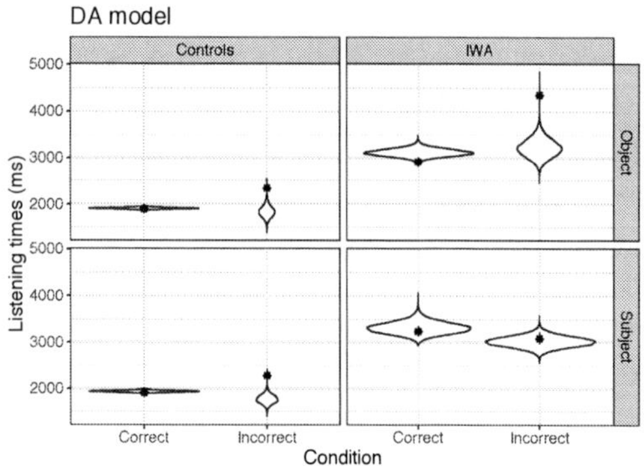

Figure 4: Posterior predictive checks of the direct-access model split by accuracy, group, and condition. The violin plots indicate the distribution of listening times generated by the model. The black stars stand for the mean of the empirical data.

In terms of implementation, the main difference between the models is a newly-introduced parameter θ_b, which is the probability of correct retrieval after backtracking. Figure (5) displays a graphical representation of this new model: After backtracking, the target is retrieved with probability θ_b, and a misretrieval occurs with probability $1 - \theta_b$. The hierarchical structure is the same as in the DA original model, except for θ_b, whose adjustments are shown in Equation (2).

$$\theta_b = \alpha_b + u_{\alpha_b} + \beta \cdot group \tag{2}$$

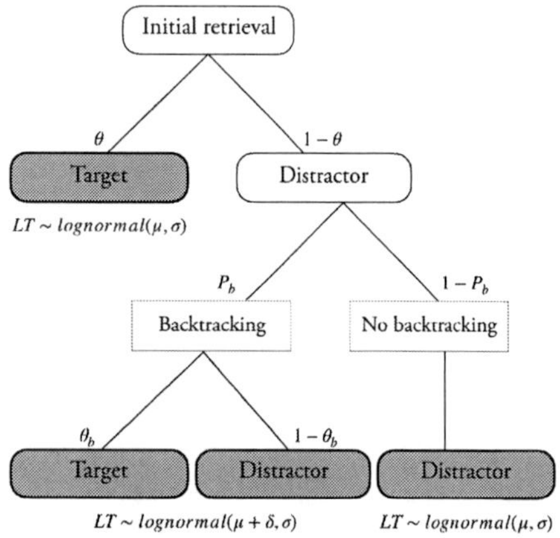

Figure 5: Graphical representation of the modified direct-access model.

The model was run with 10,000 iterations, half of which were used as warm-up.

4.1 Predictions

All predictions are carried over from the base DA model. In addition, the probability of retrieval of the target after backtracking θ_b should be lower for IWA than for controls. This would indicate that IWA are more likely to experience parsing failure or misretrieval even after backtracking.

4.2 Results

We begin by assessing the probability of first correct retrieval, θ. The posterior distribution across groups and conditions is shown in Figure (6). The estimates are quite similar to the ones in the original DA model: Controls have a very high probability of initial correct retrieval across conditions, and IWA display a greater interference effect.

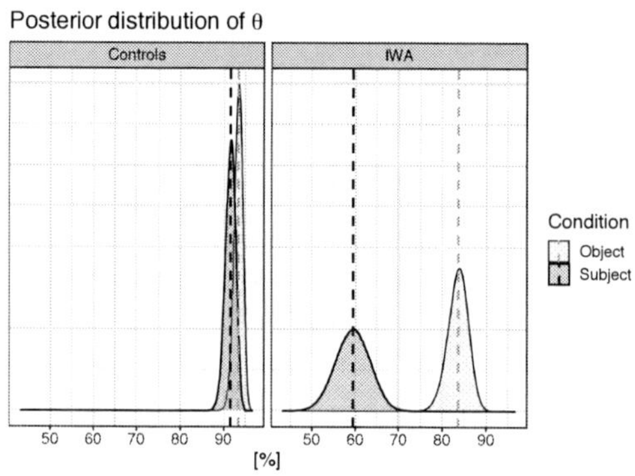

Figure 6: Posterior distribution of θ across conditions and groups.

As in the base model, IWA have a low probability of backtracking in this model (7% CrI: [4%, 12%]) relative to controls (80%, CrI: [72%, 86%]). The probability of correct retrieval after backtracking, θ_b, determines the amount of slow incorrect responses. The posterior distribution of θ_b is shown in Figure (7). After backtracking, controls are estimated to retrieve the target 90% of the time, compared to around 70% for IWA.

The rest of estimates are also similar to the ones in the original DA model: IWA's μ is higher than controls' (2751 ms, CrI: [2477, 3046] versus 1770 ms, CrI: [1654 ms, 1890 ms]). The cost of backtracking, δ, is very high for IWA (6394 ms CrI: [4235, 9468]) relative to controls (1238 ms, CrI: [1103 ms, 1387 ms]). Finally, σ is also higher for IWA (0.27 CrI: [0.25, 0.28]) than for controls (0.15 CrI: [0.14, 0.15]).

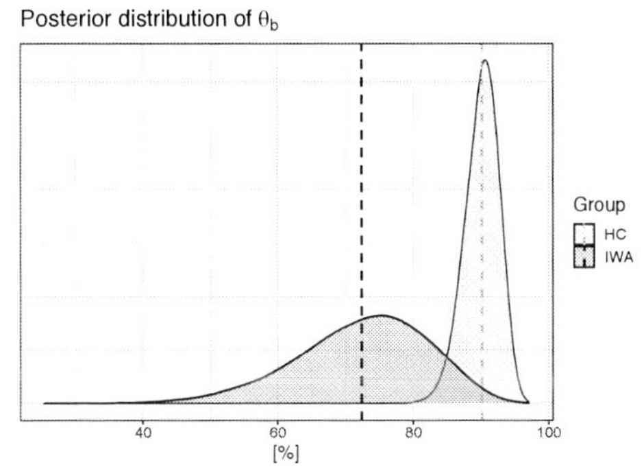

Figure 7: Posterior distribution of θ_b across conditions and groups.

4.3 Posterior Predictive Checks

The posterior predictive checks for the modified direct-access model are shown in Figure (8).

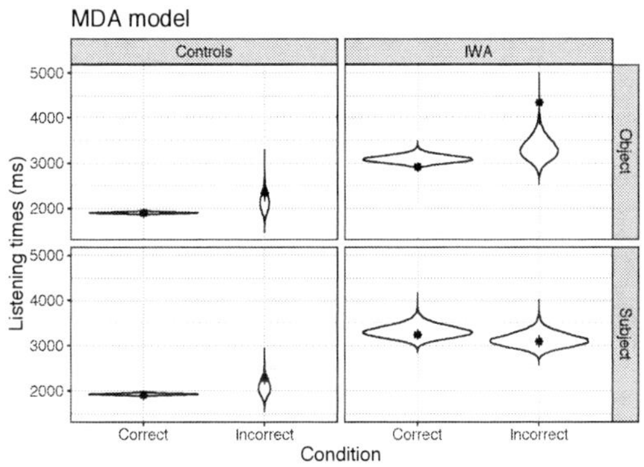

Figure 8: Posterior predictive checks of the modified direct-access model split by accuracy, group, and condition. The violin plots indicate the distribution of listening times generated by the model. The black stars stand for the mean of the empirical data.

Like the base model, the MDA mostly correctly estimates listening times for correct responses across the board. The fits for incorrect responses seem to have improved, except for object-control in IWA, where the predicted listening times are still faster than the observed listening times.

5 Model Comparison

In order to quantitatively compare the performance of the models, we computed Bayes factors. We chose Bayes factors over other alternatives (e.g. cross-validation), because the two models seem to predict similar distributions, and Bayes factors are especially suited for nested models, or models that make very similar predictions. The hypothesis being tested is whether there is a non-zero parameter θ_b that indexes the probability of successful backtracking, assumed by the MDA model, or whether backtracking is always successful, as assumed by the base DA model.

In order to perform the comparison, the models were run for 40,000 iterations, of which 3,000 were used for warm-up. Bayes factors were computed using the *bridgesampling* package (Gronau et al., 2020) in R. The Bayes factor of DA over MDA was estimated to be 2. This result is inconclusive, and indicates that the models provide similar quantitative fit to the data.

6 Discussion and Conclusion

In the present paper, we implemented and tested two versions of the direct-access model of cue-based retrieval and evaluated their predictive performance on data from individuals with aphasia and control participants. Specifically, we modeled interference in an under-studied linguistic construction, namely control structures.

Both the base model and the modified model are in line with a combination of processing deficits in IWA: slow syntax, resource reduction, and intermittent deficiencies. Neither of the two models showed support for delayed lexical access as a source of retrieval difficulty specifically for IWA. Although a delay in LDT was connected to a decrease in the probability of correct retrieval, the effect of LDT was similar for IWA and control participants. In general, our results are consistent with other studies showing that a combination of processing deficits may be the source of impairments in sentence comprehension in IWA (Caplan et al., 2015; Mätzig et al., 2018; Lissón et al., 2021).

Unlike the base direct-access model, our modified DA model (MDA) assumes that backtracking can fail, resulting in slow, incorrect retrievals. However, this added assumption does not result in a decisive advantage in fit for the MDA model, as shown by the posterior predictive checks and the Bayes factor analysis. This result is unexpected, and leads us to think that the MDA model may be overparametrized. In MDA, all of the main parameters include a group adjustment. As a consequence, for instance, the mean listening times, μ, are estimated to be higher for IWA than for controls. The cost of backtracking, which is only added to μ if backtracking is performed, accounts for slower responses. However, because IWA's μ is estimated to be higher than controls' μ, the model may not need to rely on backtracking in order to account for slow responses in IWA. This could be the reason why the probability of backtracking for IWA is very low (7%) relative to controls (80%). In addition, IWA's θ_b has to be estimated from the 7% of trials that include backtracking. Given the size of the IWA group (21 participants), and the small amount of trials that include backtracking, perhaps the model cannot correctly estimate the θ_b parameter. This could be investigated in several ways. One possibility would be to remove the group adjustments from μ, P_b, δ, and θ_b one at the time, and see which of these models shows a better quantitative fit for the data (see Lissón et al., 2021). Another possibility would be to evaluate how these parameters interact with and without group adjustments (e.g., do P_b and/or δ for IWA increase if there is no group adjustment in μ?). We will address these questions in future work.

The present paper contributes to the aphasia literature by proposing a modification of the direct-access model that can account for incorrect slow responses. Despite our inconclusive results, we believe that the modified direct-access model offers a more appropriate set of assumptions for individuals with aphasia than the direct-access model. The modified-direct access model can account for slow incorrect responses, which are frequently found in studies on sentence processing in IWA (e.g., Hanne et al., 2015; Lissón et al., 2021; Pregla et al., 2021). It remains to be seen, by testing the new modified direct-access model against more data from individuals with aphasia, whether there is a difference in predictive performance between the two models.

References

Petra Burkhardt, Sergey Avrutin, Maria M. Piñango, and Esther Ruigendijk. 2008. Slower-than-normal syntactic processing in agrammatic broca's aphasia: Evidence from Dutch. *Journal of Neurolinguistics*, 21(2):120–137.

David Caplan. 2012. Resource reduction accounts of syntactically based comprehension disorders. In C. K. Thompson and R. Bastiaanse, editors, *Perspectives on Agrammatism*, pages 34–48. Psychology Press, London, New York.

David Caplan and Nancy Hildebrandt. 1988. *Disorders of syntactic comprehension*. MIT Press, Cambridge.

David Caplan, Nancy Hildebrandt, and Nikos Makris. 1996. Location of lesions in stroke patients with deficits in syntactic processing in sentence comprehension. *Brain*, 119(3):933–949.

David Caplan, Jennifer Michaud, and Rebecca Hufford. 2013. Dissociations and associations of performance in syntactic comprehension in aphasia and their implications for the nature of aphasic deficits. *Brain and Language*, 127(1):21–33.

David Caplan, Jennifer Michaud, and Rebecca Hufford. 2015. Mechanisms underlying syntactic comprehension deficits in vascular aphasia: new evidence from self-paced listening. *Cognitive Neuropsychology*, 32(5):283–313.

Bob Carpenter, Andrew Gelman, Matthew D. Hoffman, Daniel Lee, Ben Goodrich, Michael Betancourt, Marcus Brubaker, Jiqiang Guo, Peter Li, and Allen Riddell. 2017. Stan: A probabilistic programming language. *Journal of Statistical Software*, 76(1):1–32.

Noam Chomsky. 1981. *Lectures on government and binding*. Foris, Dordrecht.

Michelle Ferrill, Tracy Love, Matthew Walenski, and Lewis P. Shapiro. 2012. The time-course of lexical activation during sentence comprehension in people with aphasia. *American Journal of Speech-Language Pathology*, 21(2):S179.

Peter C Gordon, Randall Hendrick, Marcus Johnson, and Yoonhyoung Lee. 2006. Similarity-based interference during language comprehension: Evidence from eye tracking during reading. *Journal of experimental Psychology: Learning, Memory, and Cognition*, 32(6):1304–1321.

Quentin F. Gronau, Henrik Singmann, and Eric-Jan Wagenmakers. 2020. Bridgesampling: An R package for estimating normalizing constants. *Journal of Statistical Software*, 92(10):1–29.

Sandra Hanne, Frank Burchert, Ria De Bleser, and Shravan Vasishth. 2015. Sentence comprehension and morphological cues in aphasia: What eye-tracking reveals about integration and prediction. *Journal of Neurolinguistics*, 34:83–111.

Lena A Jäger, Daniela Mertzen, Julie A Van Dyke, and Shravan Vasishth. 2020. Interference patterns in subject-verb agreement and reflexives revisited: A large-sample study. *Journal of Memory and Language*, 111:104063.

Lena A. Jäger, Felix Engelmann, and Shravan Vasishth. 2017. Similarity-based interference in sentence comprehension: Literature review and Bayesian meta-analysis. *Journal of Memory and Language*, 94:316–339.

Nayoung Kwon and Patrick Sturt. 2016. Processing control information in a nominal control construction: an eye-tracking study. *Journal of Psycholinguistic Research*, 45(4):779–793.

Daniel Lewandowski, Dorota Kurowicka, and Harry Joe. 2009. Generating random correlation matrices based on vines and extended onion method. *Journal of Multivariate Analysis*, 100(9):1989–2001.

Richard L. Lewis and Shravan Vasishth. 2005. An activation-based model of sentence processing as skilled memory retrieval. *Cognitive Science*, 29(3):375–419.

Paula Lissón, Dorothea Pregla, Bruno Nicenboim, Dario Paape, Mick L van het Nederend, Frank Burchert, Nicole Stadie, David Caplan, and Shravan Vasishth. 2021. A computational evaluation of two models of retrieval processes in sentence processing in aphasia. *Cognitive Science*, 45(4):e12956.

Andrea E Martin and Brian McElree. 2008. A content-addressable pointer mechanism underlies comprehension of verb-phrase ellipsis. *Journal of Memory and Language*, 58(3):879–906.

Brian McElree. 1993. The locus of lexical preference effects in sentence comprehension: A time-course analysis. *Journal of Memory and Language*, 32(4):536–571.

Brian McElree. 2000. Sentence comprehension is mediated by content-addressable memory structures. *Journal of Psycholinguistic Research*, 29(2):111–123.

Brian McElree, Stephani Foraker, and Lisbeth Dyer. 2003. Memory structures that subserve sentence comprehension. *Journal of Memory and Language*, 48(1):67–91.

Paul Mätzig, Shravan Vasishth, Felix Engelmann, David Caplan, and Frank Burchert. 2018. A computational investigation of sources of variability in sentence comprehension difficulty in aphasia. *Topics in Cognitive Science*, 10(1):161–174.

Bruno Nicenboim and Shravan Vasishth. 2018. Models of retrieval in sentence comprehension: A computational evaluation using Bayesian hierarchical modeling. *Journal of Memory and Language*, 99:1–34.

Umesh Patil, Sandra Hanne, Frank Burchert, Ria De Bleser, and Shravan Vasishth. 2016. A computational evaluation of sentence processing deficits in aphasia. 40(1):5–50.

Dorothea Pregla, Paula Lissón, Shravan Vasishth, Frank Burchert, and Nicole Stadie. 2021. Variability in sentence comprehension in aphasia in German. PsyArXiv:7hfpx.

R Core Team. 2020. R: A language and environment for statistical computing. Version 4.0.2.

Daniel J Schad, Michael Betancourt, and Shravan Vasishth. 2020. Toward a principled Bayesian workflow in cognitive science. *Psychological Methods*, 26(1):103–126.

Nicole Stadie, Jürgen Cholewa, and Ria De Bleser. 2013. *LEMO 2.0: Lexikon modellorientiert: Diagnostik für Aphasie, Dyslexie und Dysgraphie*. NAT-Verlag, Hofheim.

Stan Development Team. 2020. RStan: the R interface to Stan. R package version 2.21.2.

Julie A Van Dyke. 2007. Interference effects from grammatically unavailable constituents during sentence processing. *Journal of Experimental Psychology: Learning, Memory, and Cognition*, 33(2):407.

Julie A. Van Dyke and Brian McElree. 2006. Retrieval interference in sentence comprehension. *Journal of Memory and Language*, 55(2):157–166.

Acknowledgements

This work was funded by the Deutsche Forschungsgemeinschaft (DFG, German Research Foundation) – Projektnummer 317633480 – SFB 1287, Project B02. PIs: Frank Burchert, Nicole Stadie, Shravan Vasishth.

A Data and Code

Data and code are available at `https://bit.ly/30VVOYb`.

B Priors

Equation (3) shows the priors used. These are regularizing priors (Schad et al., 2020) and allow for a broad range of parameter values. We used the same priors as Lissón et al. (2021), so that the model results could be comparable. In Lissón et al. (2021), the priors were selected by plotting the predictive prior distribution for each parameter. Plots of the prior predictive distributions can be found in the supplementary materials at `https://osf.io/wkdrz`.

The priors for α and γ are in logit space, the rest of priors are in log space. In the modified direct-access model, α_b has the same priors as α.

$$\begin{aligned} \alpha &\sim normal(1, 0.5) \\ \beta_{1,\ldots,12} &\sim normal(0, 0.5) \\ \mu_0 &\sim normal(7.5, 0.6) \\ \gamma &\sim normal(-1, 0.5) \\ \delta_0 &\sim normal(0, 1) \\ \sigma_0 &\sim normal(0, 0.5) \end{aligned} \tag{3}$$

A LKJ(2) (Lewandowski et al., 2009) prior was used for the correlation matrix of the variance-covariance matrix of the random effects.

Sentence Complexity in Context

Benedetta Iavarone[*◇], **Dominique Brunato**[◇], **Felice Dell'Orletta**[◇]
[*]Scuola Normale Superiore, [◇]Istituto di Linguistica Computazionale "Antonio Zampolli", Pisa
ItaliaNLP Lab – *www.italianlp.it*
benedetta.iavarone@sns.it
{dominique.brunato, felice.dellorletta}@ilc.cnr.it

Abstract

We study the influence of context on how humans evaluate the complexity of a sentence in English. We collect a new dataset of sentences, where each sentence is rated for perceived complexity within different contextual windows. We carry out an in-depth analysis to detect which linguistic features correlate more with complexity judgments and with the degree of agreement among annotators. We train several regression models, using either explicit linguistic features or contextualized word embeddings, to predict the mean complexity values assigned to sentences in the different contextual windows, as well as their standard deviation. Results show that models leveraging explicit features capturing morphosyntactic and syntactic phenomena perform always better, especially when they have access to features extracted from all contextual sentences.

1 Introduction

From a human-based perspective, sentence complexity is assessed by measures of processing effort or performance in behavioral tasks. In this respect, a large part of studies has focused on reading single sentences and correlating syntactic and lexical properties with observed difficulty, being it captured by cognitive signals, such as eye-tracking metrics (Rayner, 1998; King and Just, 1991), or by explicit judgments of complexity given by readers (Brunato et al., 2018). However, models of language comprehension underline the importance of contextual cues, such as the presence of explicit cohesive devices, in building a coherent representation of a text (Kintsch et al., 1975; McNamara, 2001). This implies that a sentence can be perceived as more or less difficult according to the context in which it is presented.

The effect of context on how humans evaluate a sentence has been investigated concerning its acceptability and grammaticality, two properties different from complexity, yet somehow related. In Bernardy et al. (2018) speakers were asked to evaluate the degree of acceptability of sentences from Wikipedia, both in their original form and with some grammatical alterations artificially introduced by a process of round-trip machine translation. Results showed that ill-formed sentences are evaluated as more acceptable when presented within context (i.e. along with their preceding or following sentence) rather than in isolation. More closely related to our study is the one by Schumacher et al. (2016) on readability assessment. In that work, authors gathered pairwise evaluations of reading difficulty on sentences presented with and without a larger context, training a logistic regression model to predict binary complexity labels assigned by humans. They observed that the context slightly modifies the perception of the readability of a sentence, although their predictive models perform better on sentences rated in isolation.

Our study aims to understand how the context surrounding a sentence influences its 'perceived' complexity by humans. As we consider linguistic complexity from the individual's perspective, following Brunato et al. 2018, we use the term complexity as a synonym of difficulty. Also, we assume that sentence complexity is a gradient rather than a binary concept and we operationalize perceived complexity as a score on an ordinal scale. These scores were collected for a new dataset of sentences, where each sentence has been evaluated in three contextual windows, which change according to the position the sentence occupies within them. This enables us to deeply inspect the role of context, allowing us to determine if the perceived complexity of a sentence changes when the context is introduced, and also which contextual window may impact more. To do so, we consider the average complexity score assigned to each sentence as well as the degree of agreement among annotators, calculated in terms of standard deviation. We think

Proceedings of the Workshop on Cognitive Modeling and Computational Linguistics, pages 186–199
Online Event, June 10, 2021.

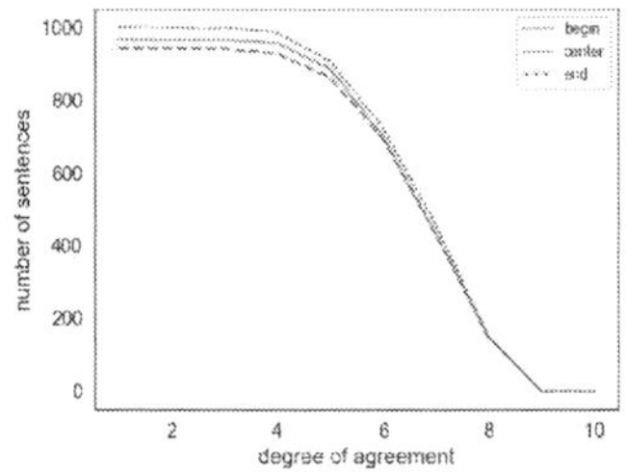

Figure 1: Number of sentences for each degree of agreement.

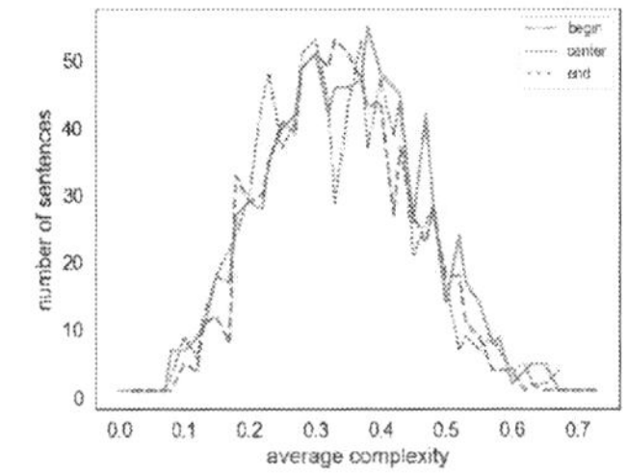

Figure 2: Number of sentences at different average complexity ratings.

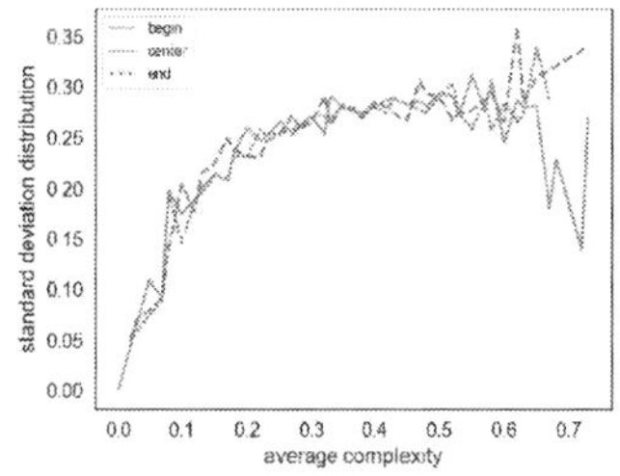

Figure 3: Mean standard deviation at different average complexity ratings.

that this measure is also relevant to comprehend perceived sentence complexity since this is a highly subjective task that cannot be tackled by following specific annotation guidelines. Moreover, knowing that sentence length is a prominent predictor of sentence complexity, we study how complexity scores and annotators' agreement vary for sentences of the same length. Finally, we run experiments to evaluate the accuracy of different regression models in predicting the mean complexity label and standard deviation assigned to a sentence. In particular, we compare models leveraging explicit linguistic features related to a wide set of morphosyntactic and syntactic properties of a sentence, to models exploiting the predictions of a state-of-the-art bidirectional transformer encoder, i.e. BERT (Devlin et al., 2019). To the best of our knowledge, the assessment of sentence complexity in context has never been tackled as a downstream task for evaluating the effectiveness of neural representations in modeling aspects of sentence complexity. Despite the remarkable performance that neural language models have achieved so far in a variety of NLP tasks (Rogers et al., 2020) – also close to ours such as the prediction of perceived sentence acceptability in context (Lau et al., 2020) – our results show that this is not the case as regards to the prediction of sentence complexity: models using explicit linguistic features perform better in all contextual windows, suggesting that information embedded in neural representations could be less effective in modeling the examined task, particularly when few labeled data will be made available.

Contributions. *i)* We release a new dataset of ∼2,900 English sentences rated with human judgments of complexity elicited by presenting sentences in their contexts; *ii)* we model a wide set of morphosyntactic and syntactic phenomena, extracted from the single sentence and contextual ones, and we study which of them are more correlated with sentence complexity judgments in different contextual windows; *iii)* we show that models relying explicitly on these features achieve higher performance in predicting complexity judgments than state–of–the art neural language models, proving the effectiveness of these features to address this task in particularly in a low resource scenario.

All the data discussed here will be made available at: `www.italianlp.it/resources/`.

2 Approach

We first collected an appropriate corpus to evaluate the effect of context on the perception of sentence complexity. We started from the crowdsourced dataset by Brunato et al. (2018), which contains $1,200$ sentences annotated for perceived complexity on a 7-point Likert scale. We similarly built a crowdsourcing task, asking native English speakers to read each sentence and rate its complexity on the same scale. However, while in Brunato et al. all sentences were rated in isolation, in our task sentences were presented in three contextual windows, as illustrated in Section 2.1.

To study which linguistic phenomena may affect annotators' ratings, we represented sentences (the rated one and the contextual ones) with ∼100 linguistic features, based on those described in Brunato et al. (2020). These features model a wide range of sentence properties, which can be viewed as proxies of sentence complexity at different levels of linguistic annotation. The features were first used to study the influence of context-level and sentence-level phenomena on perceived complexity. We did this by analyzing the correlations between the features and the complexity ratings, and the correlations between the features and the standard deviation of complexity. Then, we assessed the automatic prediction of sentence complexity and of the standard deviation of complexity judgments, evaluating if adding information from the context helps in the prediction. We tested two predicting approaches: one based on a linear SVM regression model which leverages the linguistic features discussed so far, and one that employs BERT, one of the most prominent pre-trained neural language model. We compared the accuracy of the models across various scenarios, considering their predictions both for sentences rated in different contextual windows and for sentences distinguished into same-length bins.

2.1 Data Collection

As already mentioned, our dataset was built starting from the sentences collected by Brunato et al. (2018). These sentences were extracted from the Wall Street Journal section of the Penn Treebank and grouped in 6 bins, according to their length in terms of tokens (i.e. 10, 15, 20, 25, 30, 35), as it is well-known that sentence length correlates with complexity. By analyzing sentences with the same length we would understand whether other linguistic features still play an influence on complexity or if their effect is nullified by controlling length. We then proceeded to add context to all sentences, defining context as the sentences that precede and/or follow a given one. For each sentence we created 3 different contextual windows, according to the position occupied by the sentence in relation to the one occupied by the context. In the *begin window*, the sentence appears first and is followed by two contextual sentences; in the *center window*, the sentence is in the middle and is preceded by a contextual sentence and followed by another contextual sentence; in the *end window*, the sentence appears as the last one and is preceded by two contextual sentences. The resulting dataset is composed of 2,913 windows of context: 1,002 for the begin window, 968 for the center window and 943 for the end window.

We carried out a crowdsourcing task to collect complexity ratings through the platform Prolific[1]. For each contextual window, the sentence to be evaluated was highlighted in bold, while the contextual sentences were left in plain style. The windows were randomly ordered and presented on different pages, containing ten windows each. Due to the high number of windows to be evaluated, we split the dataset into smaller sections, containing at most 200 windows each, ending up creating 15 evaluation tasks. For each task, we recruited 10 native English speakers. We then asked participants to read the full paragraph (the whole window of context) and to rate the complexity of the sentence in bold on a 7-point Likert scale, where 1 stands for "very easy" and 7 stands for "very difficult". As complexity perception is very subjective, we then aggregated the ratings to account for the individual bias of annotators, as there could be the case in which a participant always gave low scores, while another one always gave very high scores. Thus, ratings were re-scaled between 0 and 1 and normalized by the range of ratings given by each annotator.

	begin		**center**		**end**	
	judg	*std*	*judg*	*std*	*judg*	*std*
Length 10	.28	.23	.28	.28	.28	.28
Length 15	.27	.23	.32	.28	.30	.28
Length 20	.27	.22	.35	.27	.33	.26
Length 25	.26	.21	.36	.26	.35	.26
Length 30	.26	.22	.38	.26	.36	.25
Length 35	.25	.21	.39	.26	.38	.26
All sents	.26	.22	.35	.27	.33	.27

Table 1: Mean complexity judgment and mean standard deviation on complexity, for all sentences and at different lengths.

2.2 Data Analysis

Firstly, we looked at the *degree of agreement*[2] (DAE) between annotators. Figure 1 reports the number of sentences for every DAE, considering the different sentence positions within the context windows. We found a strong DAE, as most sentences have up to 5 annotators that assigned a complexity judgment within the same range. As the DAE increases, the number of sentences decreases consistently. The highest DAE is found at 8 annotators, but on a small amount of sentences (< 200), while there are no sentences on which 9 or 10 annotators agree. Also, this first examination showed that the sentence position has little to no influence on the DAE, as the numbers for the context windows mostly follow the same trend. To confirm this view, we looked at the distribution of complexity values among the three windows. For each window, we computed the number of sentences that were assigned the same average complexity value. Figure 2 shows that average complexity follows a Gaussian distribution for all the windows of context, as most sentences received an average complexity between 0.2 and 0.4.

[1] www.prolific.co

[2] The degree of agreement is intended as the number of annotators who gave a complexity score within the same range. The range is defined as the standard deviation from the mean of the judgments given to each sentence.

	Zero Variance	BCE	Highest Variance	B	C	E
Length 10	Tokyo's Nikkei index fell 84.15 points to 35442.40.	.38	Nashua announced the Reiss request after the market closed.	.22	.42	.63
Length 15	Elsewhere in Europe, share prices closed higher in Stockholm, Brussels and Milan.	.23	Last year, the prisons' sales to the Pentagon totaled $336 million.	.62	.32	.20
Length 20	Dow Jones industrials 2645.08, up 41.60; transportation 1205.01, up 13.15; utilities 219.19, up 2.45.	.50	The cash dividend paid on the common stock also will apply to the new shares, the company said.	.12	.12	.55
Length 25	In the nine months, Milton Roy earned $6.6 million, or $1.18 a share, on sales of $94.3 million.	.38	Yesterday, Compaq plunged further, closing at $100 a share, off $8.625 a share, on volume of 2,633,700 shares.	.25	.67	.42
Length 30	SsangYong, which has only about 3% of the domestic market, will sell about 18,000 of its models this year, twice as many as last year.	.32	Though not reflected in the table, an investor should know that the cost of the option insurance can be partially offset by any dividends that the stock pays.	.23	.50	.57
Length 35	In the nine months, net rose 35% to $120.1 million, or $1.64 a share, from $89.20 million, or $1.22 a share, a year earlier.	.48	William Kaiser, president of the Kaiser Financial Group in Chicago, said the decline was almost certainly influenced by the early sell-off in the stock market, which partly reflected a weakening economy.	.45	.23	.58
All sents	Dow Jones industrials 2645.08, up 41.60; transportation 1205.01, up 13.15; utilities 219.19, up 2.45.	.50	The cash dividend paid on the common stock also will apply to the new shares, the company said.	.12	.12	.55

Table 2: Sentences that vary the least or the most within context windows. B, C, and E respectively indicate the begin, center and end windows.

Furthermore, we computed the standard deviation of the complexity judgments that were assigned to each sentence. In Figure 3, we plot the standard deviation of each sentence[3] against the average complexity assigned to that same sentence, for the three windows of context. The standard deviation tends to increase with the average complexity score assigned to sentences. This means that annotators agree more on rating a sentence as simple, suggesting that the perception of a sentence as more complex may be less homogeneous. This trend is quite similar for all contextual windows, though we observe a more uniform behaviour in rating a sentence as more complex when it is surrounded by both contextual sentences (i.e. the center window).

Besides sentence positioning, also sentence length may affect the perception of complexity. Thus, we calculated the average of complexity judgments assigned to sentences of the same length, for all the three context windows, along with the mean standard deviation. As shown in Table 1, for the center and the end window average complexity values tend to increase with the length of the sentences, as expected. On the contrary, standard deviation follows the opposite trend, showing that subjects agree more on the complexity of long sentences (e.g. length 30 and 35), while their perception about shorter sentences is more diversified. It also emerges that when the sentence is at the beginning of the paragraph, it is overall perceived as simpler. This may indicate that the following contextual sentences help annotators in the processing and understanding of the first sentence.

Table 2 shows examples of sentences whose complexity scores vary the least or the most within the different windows of context. In the case of *Zero Variance*, the sentence received the same average complexity, regardless of the relative position in the contextual window (begin, center, end). Instead, sentences with the highest variance received very different average values, according to the position the sentence occupies in the contextual windows. This table also reports the actual average complexity values that the sentences got for each position.

Linguistic Features
Raw Text Properties
Sentence Length
Word Length
Vocabulary Richness
Type/Token Ratio for words and lemmas
Morphosyntactic information
Distribution of UD and language-specific POS
Lexical dens
Inflectional morphology
Inflectional morphology of lexical verbs and auxiliaries
Verbal Predicate Structure
Distribution of verbal heads and verbal roots
Verb arity and distribution of verbs by arity
Global and Local Parsed Tree Structures
Depth of the whole syntactic tree
Average length of dependency links and of the longest link
Average length of prepositional chain and distribution by depth
Clause length
Relative order of elements
Order of subject and object
Syntactic Relations
Distribution of dependency relations
Use of Subordination
Distribution of subordinate and principal clauses
Average length of subordination chain and distribution by depth
Relative order of subordinate clauses

Table 3: Linguistic features.

[3]If more than one sentence was assigned the same average complexity value, we plot the average standard deviation of all the sentences.

3 Correlation between Linguistic Features and Complexity

To detect which linguistic phenomena are more involved in the assessment of sentence complexity, and to verify whether these phenomena capture information about the sentence itself or about the context, we performed a correlation analysis between the complexity score assigned to each sentence and a wide set of linguistic features extracted from the sentence. For each sentence, we computed the Spearman's rank correlation coefficient between the average complexity score and the value of each linguistic feature extracted from *i*) the rated sentence, *ii*) its preceding one and *iii*) its following one, according to the contextual window. We performed the correlation analysis on the sentences altogether and then dividing them into bins according to their length. The same process was repeated correlating the standard deviation of complexity scores with the linguistic features of each sentence. As stated in Section 2, we focused on features that model a wide range of sentence properties extracted from different levels of linguistic annotation, from raw text features (i.e. sentence and word length) to morphosyntactic information (e.g. distribution of verbs according to morphological features such as tense, mood, person), to more complex aspects of the syntactic structure capturing global and local information (e.g. parse tree depth, length of dependency link, use of subordination). Table 3 reports the list of features used for our analysis.

In what follows, we discuss the correlation results for the subset of sentences presented in the *center window*, since this is the only one in which the rated sentence was always surrounded by both a left and a right sentence, allowing us to compare the effect of the two context positions[4].

Considering first the average complexity score, we found statistically significant correlations (p-value< 0.05) with $\rho \geq \pm 0.20$ for 103 features out of the whole set. Among them, 44% belongs to the rated sentence (i.e. 45 features) and 56% to the contextual ones (i.e. 23 and 35 features to the left and the right sentence, respectively). Although we could expect that many features extracted from the rated sentence were correlated to complexity judgments, these results also suggest that humans have paid attention to the whole context when rating the middle sentence, and especially to the following

Features	L10	L15	L20	L25	L30	L35	All
B_dep_aux:pass	-	-	-	−1	-	-	-
B_dep_compound	-	-	5	-	-	-	-
B_dep_compound:prt	−4	-	-	-	-	-	-
B_dep_flat	-	-	-	−5	-	-	-
B_dep_nmod	-	-	-	5	-	-	-
B_dep_nsubj	-	−5	-	-	-	-	-
B_dep_nsubj:pass	-	-	-	−2	-	-	-
B_dep_nummod	-	-	3	-	-	-	-
B _princ_prop	-	-	−4	-	-	-	-
B_verb_root_perc	-	-	−3	-	-	-	-
C_aux_Fin	-	-	−1	-	−4	-	-
C_aux_num_pers_+	−5	-	−5	-	-	-	-
C_aux_Pres	-	-	-	-	−5	-	-
C_avg_max_depth	-	5	-	-	-	-	4
C_avg_max_link	-	-	-	-	-	-	8
C_avg_sub_chain	-	-	-	-	-	−1	-
C_avg_tok_clause	-	-	4	-	-	-	-
C_char_tok	-	-	-	-	-	−5	-
C_dep_aux	-	-	-	-	−2	-	-
C_dep_det	-	−3	-	-	-	-	-
C_dep_nmod	5	-	-	-	-	-	-
C_dep_nummod	-	4	2	-	2	2	5
C_dep_root	-	−1	-	-	-	-	−1
C_dep_xcomp	-	-	-	−3	-	-	-
C_max_link	-	-	-	-	-	-	7
C_n_prep_chain	-	-	-	-	-	-	6
C_n_tok	3	2	-	-	-	-	2
C_tok_sent	4	3	-	-	-	-	3
C_upos_ADJ	-	−4	-	-	-	-	-
C_upos_AUX	-	-	−2	-	−3	−2	−2
C_upos_DET	-	−2	-	-	-	-	-
C_upos_NUM	1	1	1	-	1	1	1
C_upos_PRON	-	-	-	-	-	−3	-
C_upos_SYM	2	-	-	-	-	3	-
C_verb_edge_1	-	-	-	-	−1	-	-
C_verb_Fin	-	-	-	-	3	-	-
C_verb_Ind	-	-	-	-	5	-	-
E_aux_Pres	−3	-	-	-	-	-	-
E_avg_link	−2	-	-	-	-	-	-
E_avg_max_depth	-	-	-	2	-	-	-
E_dep_ccomp	-	-	-	-	-	−4	-
E_dep_nummod	-	-	-	4	-	5	-
E_lexical_dens	-	-	-	−4	-	-	-
E_upos_NUM	-	-	-	1	-	4	-
E_upos_SYM	-	-	-	3	-	-	-
E_verb_edge_4	−1	-	-	-	-	-	-
E_verb_Fin	-	-	-	-	4	-	-

Table 4: Ranking of correlations between the top 10 linguistic features and the average complexity score for all sentences and for all length bins. The number indicates the position the feature occupies in the ranking: the higher the number(positive or negative), the higher the correlation. B_*, C_*,E_* mean that the features characterize the beginning, the central and the ending sentence, respectively.

sentence. The influence of context is suggested as well by the fact that we observe much lower coefficients for all correlating features belonging to the rated sentence, unlike those reported by Brunato et al. (2018) for the same sentences evaluated in isolation. Tables 4 shows the top ten features ranked by the correlation score with average complexity, for all sentences and for groups of sentences of the same length. A positive number indicates that the feature is linked to a higher perceived complexity, meaning that linguistic phenomenon makes the sentence more complex in the eyes of annotators. Conversely, a negative number is linked to lower complexity, meaning the linguistic phenomenon helps annotators in the evaluation of the sentence complexity.

When all sentences are considered, we observe

[4] We report in the Appendix the whole tables of correlation results for all contextual windows.

Features	L10	L15	L20	L25	L30	L35	All
B_aux_Inf	2	-	-	-	-	-	-
B_dep_compound:prt	−5	-	-	-	-	-	-
B_subj_pre	-	-	-	−5	-	-	-
B_upos_SYM	-	-	-	−3	-	-	-
B_verb_edge_1	-	−2	-	-	-	-	-
B_verb_Past	-	−1	-	-	-	-	-
C_avg_sub_chain	-	-	-	-	-	-	−1
C_char_tok	-	-	-	-	-	-	−5
C_dep_aux	-	-	-	-	−1	-	-
C_dep_nummod	-	-	-	-	-	-	2
C_dep_punct	-	-	-	−4	-	-	-
C_princ_prop	-	-	-	-	-	−2	-
C_sub_prop	-	-	-	-	-	3	-
C_upos_AUX	-	-	-	-	-	-	−2
C_upos_NUM	-	-	-	-	-	-	1
C_upos_PRON	-	-	-	-	-	-	−3
C_upos_PUNCT	-	-	-	−2	-	-	-
C_upos_SYM	-	-	-	-	-	-	3
C_verb_edge_1	-	-	-	-	-	2	-
C_verb_root_perc	-	-	-	-	-	−1	-
E_avg_link	−4	-	-	-	-	-	-
E_avg_max_link	−2	-	-	-	-	-	-
E_dep_aux	−6	-	-	-	-	-	-
E_dep_ccomp	-	-	-	-	-	-	−4
E_dep_nummod	-	-	-	-	-	-	5
E_dep_parataxis	−7	-	-	-	-	-	-
E_dep_root	1	-	-	-	-	-	-
E_max_link	−3	-	-	-	-	-	-
E_upos_ADV	-	-	1	-	-	-	-
E_upos_NUM	-	-	-	-	-	-	4
E_verb_edge_3	-	-	-	−1	-	1	-
E_verb_Past	3	-	-	-	-	-	-
E_verb_Pres	−1	-	-	-	-	-	-

Table 5: Ranking of correlations between the top 10 linguistic features and complexity standard deviation for all sentences and for all length bins. Feature labels and ranking numbers are used as in 4.

that the first ten ones all belong to the middle sentence and refer to features modeling linguistic phenomena of different nature, although we can distinguish two main groups, positively correlated with the perception of sentence complexity. The first group is related to the presence of numerical information (i.e. literal numbers in the sentence), as conveyed by both POS and syntactic features (*C_upos_NUM, C_dep_nummod*). The second one, as more expected, concerns sentence length (*C_tok_sent, C_dep_root*) and features still related to length but capturing aspects of structural complexity, e.g. the depth of the whole parse tree and specific sub-trees, i.e. nominal chain headed by a preposition (*C_avg_max_depth, C_n_prep_chain*). Notably, the effect of sentence length is observed only for the middle sentence, while the length of contextual sentences is never correlated with judgments. Again, the correlation is much lower with respect to the one obtained by sentences judged in isolation (i.e. 0.31 vs 0.84 reported in the previous study). Within bins of same-length sentences, we notice a more prominent role of features from the context, as suggested by the presence of features characterizing both the sentence preceding and following the rated one in the first ten position of the ranking. Interestingly, for all bins numerical information turned out to be the feature most correlated with complexity score, being it extracted from the rated or from contextual sentences (specifically, the right sentence, for the bin composed by sentences with 25 tokens).

For standard deviation, we found 29 statistically significant ($p < 0.05$) features with correlation $\rho \geq 0.20$. These include 24% of features belonging to the rated sentence (i.e. 7 features), while the remaining features belong to the contextual sentences (i.e. 6 features for the left sentence, 15 for the right one). In this case we found far less correlations, with most features being significant for the length bins but not when considering the sentences altogether. These results confirm that humans have paid attention to the whole context when evaluating the sentence, but also that standard deviation, and thus annotators' agreement, is a phenomenon harder to describe and subjective to factors that linguistic features cannot fully detect. Similarly to what done for average complexity, in Table 5 we report the first ten features mostly correlated with standard deviation, for all rated sentences and for sentences of the same length. As we can see, the ranking is mostly different from the one resulting from correlating feature values and average complexity scores.

4 Predicting Sentence Complexity

The results of the correlation analysis have shown that linguistic information of the context affects the perception of sentence complexity and the extent to which this perception is shared by annotators. We thus proceed to assess the contribution of the context from a modeling standpoint. We built two regression tasks, one to predict the average complexity value assigned to each sentence, and one to predict the standard deviation of complexity for each sentence. In both scenarios, we employed two different models: the first is a linear SVM regression model with standard parameters that leverages the explicit linguistic features presented in Table 3, the second is obtained by fine-tuning the BERT base model (i.e. bert-base-uncased) on our dataset using the FARM[5] regression implementation. Both models were evaluated with a 5-fold cross validation for each of the three windows of context.

For every window, we carried out different runs of the models, varying the amount of contextual features to be considered. For the *begin window*

[5] github.com/deepset-ai/FARM

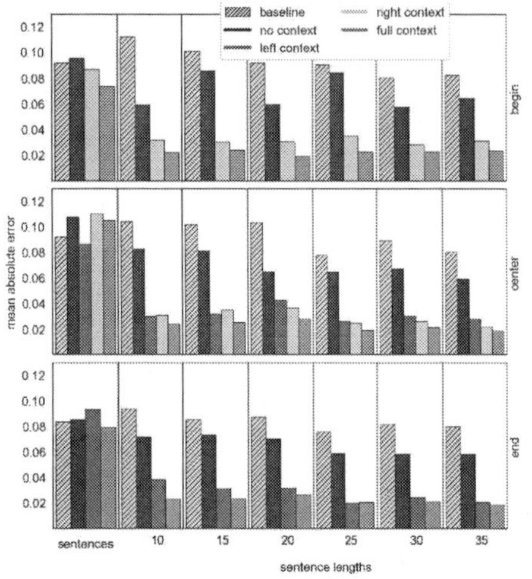

(a) SVM models

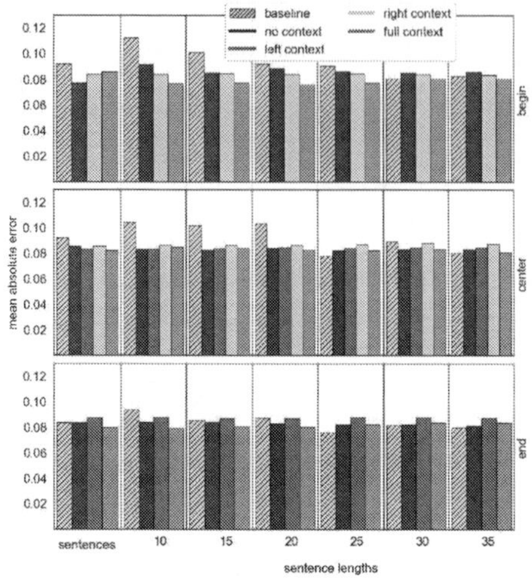

(b) BERT models

Figure 4: Performance (MAE) of SVM regression model on avg complexity ratings prediction. In different windows of context and with different context spans, for all sentences and at different sentence lengths.

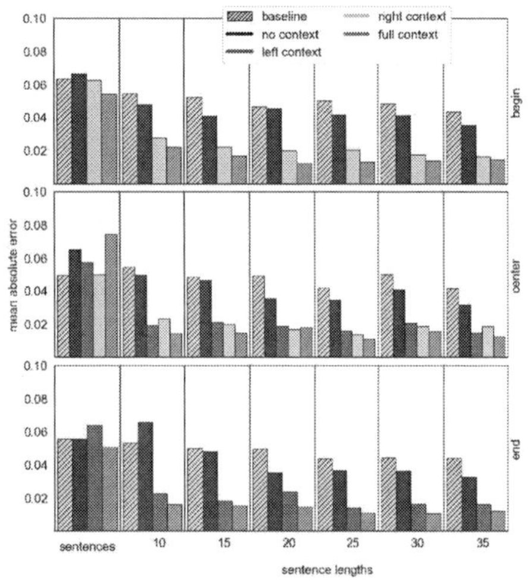

(a) SVM models

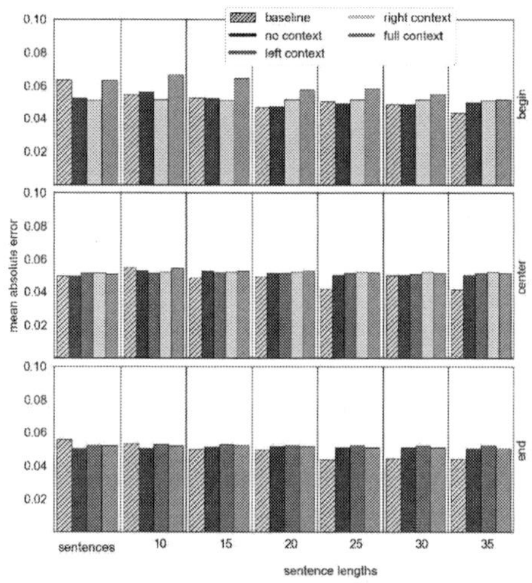

(b) BERT models

Figure 5: Performance (MAE) of SVM regression models and BERT models in the prediction of complexity standard deviation. In different windows of context and with different context spans, for all sentences and at different sentence lengths.

and the *end window* we ran the models with *i*) the features of the single sentence (no context), *ii*) the features of the sentence + the features of the next sentence (right context) for the *begin window*, or + the features of the previous sentence (left context) for the *end window*, *iii*) the features of all the three sentences (full context, i.e. the whole window of context); for the *center window*, we trained the models with *i*) no context features, *ii*) left or right context features, *iii*) full context features. We measured the performance of the models in terms of *mean absolute error* (MAE), evaluating their accuracy in predicting the same average judgment of complexity assigned by humans and the standard deviation of the complexity judgments. We then repeated the same experiments grouping the sentences according to their length. The baseline for the models evaluation was calculated (i) in the case of all sentences, by giving in input to the linear regression model only the length of the sentence as feature for the prediction, (ii) in the case of different lengths (binned sentences), by having the model always assigning the average complexity value (calculated on the whole set of sentences) to each sentence.

Figure 4 reports the results for the prediction of the average complexity, showing the average MAE obtained after the 5-fold validation, both for SVM models and BERT models. The SVM models with linguistic features outperform BERT models overall. BERT models remain close to the baseline in all cases, despite the amount of context considered and the length of the sentences. Instead, the SVM models show significant differences as appropriate. In the case of all sentences, the performances of the model are close to the baseline. Adding contextual features slightly helps in the case of the begin and the end window, while performances worsen in the case of the center window. When considering sentences of the same length, the performance of the model is always helped by the presence of contextual features and best results are achieved when the full context is taken into account, for all the windows of context. This behavior confirms on one side that linguistic characteristics of the context are indeed very influential on complexity, on the other side that the length of the sentence plays an important role on the perception of complexity, as it is only by binning the sentences that we can exploit the effect of context in predicting complexity.

Figure 5 shows the results for the prediction of the standard deviation of complexity, for SVM models and BERT models. As in the previous case, BERT models obtain results that are in line with the baseline and that are not influenced by different amounts of context. When looking at the results obtained with the explicit linguistic features, the outcome is quite different. For the all sentences case, the SVM model cannot predict the standard deviation of complexity, although the error gets lower for the begin window and the end window when the full context is used. Conversely, the model shows large improvement when working on sentences of the same length. In all windows and for all lengths, using the features of the whole context significantly decreases the error in the prediction of standard deviation. When running the model with the features of the single sentence (i.e. no context), the performances of the model are in general close to the ones of the baseline. This suggests that the context is particularly relevant in predicting how people will agree on their perception of complexity.

Overall, our results show that information about the complexity of a sentence is better encoded in its explicit linguistic features, thus its syntactic and morphosyntactic structures. On the other hand, although BERT has been proven to embed a wide range of linguistic properties, including syntactic ones (Tenney et al., 2019; Miaschi et al., 2020), our findings seem to suggest that this model does not exploit these kind of features to solve a downstream task like ours, for which few data are available. Indeed, it has been shown that BERT performs better on datasets larger than ours (Kumar et al., 2020). Thus, it is fair to assume that more data may be needed for BERT to detect phenomenon about perceived complexity.

Moreover, our results show that the presence of context plays an important role on complexity. As the SVM models are always helped by the contextual features, it is fair to assume that annotators have taken into account the whole context when expressing their judgment upon complexity, and that the presence of the context has strongly influenced their perception. Also, contextual linguistic phenomena are the ones that impact more on the variation of complexity perception between annotators as they are the ones that help more in the prediction of this variation.

5 Conclusion

We studied how the context surrounding a sentence influences the perception of its complexity by humans. Starting from a newly collected dataset, we investigated which linguistic phenomena, among a wide set of lexical, morphosyntactic, and syntactic ones, are more correlated with complexity judgments and the degree of agreement between annotators. From a modeling standpoint, we observe that models using explicit linguistic features achieve higher accuracy than state-of-the-art neural language models in predicting the average complexity score assigned to a sentence, as well as the variation among scores. This is especially true when they use explicit linguistic features from all contextual sentences in addition to the linguistic features of the sole rated sentence.

As many NLP applications are concerned with the analysis of linguistic complexity, particularly for text readability and text simplification purposes, we think that our results emphasize the importance of considering contextual information both in the creation of gold benchmarks, which are typically based only on data paired at sentence level and in the development of cognitively inspired evaluation systems driven by how people perceive complexity.

References

Jean-Philippe Bernardy, Shalom Lappin, and Jey Han Lau. 2018. The influence of context on sentence acceptability judgements. In *Proceedings of the 56th Annual Meeting of the Association for Computational Linguistics (Volume 2: Short Papers)*, pages 456–461, Melbourne, Australia. Association for Computational Linguistics.

Dominique Brunato, Andrea Cimino, Felice Dell'Orletta, Giulia Venturi, and Simonetta Montemagni. 2020. Profiling-ud: a tool for linguistic profiling of texts. In *Proceedings of The 12th Language Resources and Evaluation Conference*, pages 7147–7153, Marseille, France. European Language Resources Association.

Dominique Brunato, Lorenzo De Mattei, Felice Dell'Orletta, Benedetta Iavarone, and Giulia Venturi. 2018. Is this sentence difficult? do you agree? In *Proceedings of the 2018 Conference on Empirical Methods in Natural Language Processing*, pages 2690–2699.

Jacob Devlin, Ming-Wei Chang, Kenton Lee, and Kristina Toutanova. 2019. Bert: Pre-training of deep bidirectional transformers for language understanding. In *Proceedings of the 2019 Conference of the North American Chapter of the Association for Computational Linguistics: Human Language Technologies, Volume 1 (Long and Short Papers)*, pages 4171–4186.

Jonathan King and Marcel Adam Just. 1991. Individual differences in syntactic processing: The role of working memory. *Journal of Memory and Language*, 30(5):580 – 602.

W. Kintsch, E. Kozminsky, W.J. Streby, G. McKoon, and J.M. Keenan. 1975. Comprehension and recall of text as a function of content variables. *Journal of Verbal Learning and Verbal Behavior, 14(2).*

Varun Kumar, Ashutosh Choudhary, and Eunah Cho. 2020. Data augmentation using pre-trained transformer models. In *Proceedings of the 2nd Workshop on Life-long Learning for Spoken Language Systems*, pages 18–26.

Jey Han Lau, Carlos S Armendariz, Shalom Lappin, Matthew Purver, and Chang Shu. 2020. How furiously can colourless green ideas sleep? sentence acceptability in context. *arXiv preprint arXiv:2004.00881.*

Danielle S. McNamara. 2001. Reading both high-coherence and low-coherence texts: Effects of text sequence and prior knowledge. *Canadian Journal of Experimental Psychology*, 55(1):51–62.

Alessio Miaschi, Dominique Brunato, Felice Dell'Orletta, and Giulia Venturi. 2020. Linguistic profiling of a neural language model. *arXiv preprint arXiv:2010.01869.*

Keith Rayner. 1998. Eye movements in reading and information processing: 20 years of research. *Psychological bulletin*, 124 3:372–422.

Anna Rogers, O. Kovaleva, and Anna Rumshisky. 2020. A primer in bertology: What we know about how bert works. *ArXiv*, abs/2002.12327.

Elliot Schumacher, Maxine Eskenazi, Gwen Frishkoff, and Kevyn Collins-Thompson. 2016. Predicting the relative difficulty of single sentences with and without surrounding context. In *Conference on Empirical Methods in Natural Language Processing, pages 1871–1881.*

Ian Tenney, Dipanjan Das, and Ellie Pavlick. 2019. BERT rediscovers the classical NLP pipeline. In *Proceedings of the 57th Annual Meeting of the Association for Computational Linguistics*, pages 4593–4601, Florence, Italy. Association for Computational Linguistics.

A Appendix. Results of Correlations between Linguistic Features and Complexity Average Scores (*judg*) and between Linguistic Features and Complexity Standard Deviation (*std*).

Features	Length 10		Length 15		Length 20		Length 25		Length 30		Length 35		All sents	
	judg	*std*	*judg*	*std*	*judg*	*std*	*judg*	*std*	*judg*	*std*	*judg*	*std*	*judg*	*std*
B_aux_+	−0.20	-	-	-	-	-	-	-	-	-	-	-	-	-
B_aux_Fin	−0.29	-	-	-	−0.25	-	-	0.22	-	-	-	-	-	-
B_aux_Ind	−0.27	-	-	-	-	-	-	-	-	-	-	-	-	-
B_avg_link	0.31	-	-	-	-	-	-	-	-	-	-	-	0.21	-
B_avg_max_depth	0.25	-	0.23	-	-	-	-	-	-	-	-	-	0.29	-
B_avg_max_link	0.36	-	-	-	-	-	-	-	-	-	-	-	0.26	-
B_avg_prep_chain	-	-	-	-	-	-	-	-	-	0.20	-	-	-	-
B_avg_sub_chain	-	-	-	-	-	-	−0.23	-	-	-	-	-	-	-
B_avg_tok_clause	−0.20	-	0.25	-	-	-	-	-	-	-	-	-	-	-
B_char_tok	-	-	−0.24	-	-	-	-	-	-	-	-	-	-	-
B_dep_advmod	-	-	-	-	0.20	-	-	-	-	-	-	-	-	-
B_dep_amod	−0.25	-	-	-	-	-	-	-	-	-	-	-	-	-
B_dep_appos	0.54	-	-	-	-	-	-	-	-	-	-	-	-	-
B_dep_compound	0.27	-	-	-	-	−0.22	-	-	0.20	-	0.21	-	0.22	-
B_dep_cop	−0.25	-	-	-	-	-	-	-	-	-	-	-	-	-
B_dep_det	−0.33	-	-	-	-	-	-	-	-	-	-	-	−0.21	-
B_dep_nsubj	−0.43	-	-	-	-	-	-	-	-	-	-	-	−0.22	-
B_dep_nummod	0.39	-	0.20	-	0.30	-	0.23	-	0.33	-	0.35	-	0.33	-
B_dep_obl:tmod	-	-	-	-	-	-	-	-	-	−0.26	-	-	-	-
B_dep_punct	-	-	-	-	0.20	-	-	-	-	-	-	-	-	-
B_dep_root	−0.34	-	−0.33	-	-	-	-	-	-	-	-	-	−0.32	-
B_dep_xcomp	-	-	-	-	-	-	−0.25	-	-	-	-	-	-	-
B_lexical_dens	-	-	-	-	−0.22	-	−0.21	-	-	-	-	-	-	-
B_max_link	0.36	-	-	-	-	-	-	-	-	-	-	-	0.26	-
B_n_prep_chain	-	-	-	-	-	-	0.20	-	-	-	-	-	0.24	-
B_n_tok	0.34	-	0.33	-	-	-	-	-	-	-	-	-	0.32	-
B_obj_post	-	-	0.22	-	-	-	-	-	-	-	-	-	-	-
B_princ_prop	−0.27	-	-	-	-	-	-	-	-	-	-	-	-	-
B_sub_1	−0.24	-	-	-	-	-	-	-	-	-	-	-	-	-
B_sub_prop	-	-	-	-	-	-	−0.22	-	-	-	-	-	-	-
B_subj_pre	−0.42	-	-	-	-	-	-	-	-	-	-	-	-	-
B_tok_sent	0.34	-	0.33	-	-	-	-	-	-	-	-	-	0.32	-
B_ttr	−0.20	-	-	-	-	-	-	-	-	-	-	-	-	-
B_ttr_lemma	−0.21	-	-	-	-	-	-	−0.20	-	-	-	-	-	-
B_upos_ADJ	−0.26	-	-	-	−0.24	-	-	-	-	-	-	-	-	-
B_upos_ADP	−0.20	-	-	-	-	-	-	-	-	-	-	-	-	-
B_upos_AUX	−0.29	-	-	-	-	-	-	0.23	-	-	-	-	-	-
B_upos_DET	−0.33	-	-	-	-	-	-	-	-	-	-	-	−0.21	-
B_upos_NUM	0.40	-	0.30	-	0.33	-	0.30	-	0.34	-	0.30	-	0.34	-
B_upos_PART	-	-	-	-	-	-	-	-	-	-	−0.20	-	-	-
B_upos_PRON	−0.25	-	−0.24	-	-	-	-	-	-	-	-	-	-	-
B_upos_PUNCT	-	-	-	-	0.20	-	-	-	-	-	-	-	-	-
B_upos_SYM	0.30	-	0.22	-	-	-	0.27	-	0.29	-	0.31	-	0.28	-
B_upos_VERB	−0.30	-	-	-	-	-	-	-	-	-	-	-	-	-
B_verb_edge_0	-	-	−0.25	-	-	-	-	-	-	-	-	-	-	-
B_verb_head_sent	−0.42	-	-	-	-	-	−0.21	-	-	-	-	-	-	-
B_verb_root_perc	−0.43	−0.22	-	-	-	-	-	-	-	-	-	-	-	-
C_aux_+	-	-	-	-	-	−0.21	-	-	-	-	-	-	-	-
C_aux_Fin	−0.31	-	-	-	−0.21	-	-	-	-	-	-	-	-	-
C_aux_Ind	−0.32	-	-	-	-	-	-	-	-	-	-	-	-	-
C_aux_Pres	−0.23	-	-	-	-	-	-	-	-	-	-	-	-	-
C_aux_Sing+3	−0.29	-	-	-	-	-	-	-	-	-	-	-	-	-
C_avg_link	−0.23	-	-	-	-	-	-	-	-	-	-	-	-	-
C_avg_sub_chain	−0.24	-	-	-	-	-	-	-	-	-	-	-	-	-
C_avg_tok_clause	−0.33	-	-	-	-	-	-	-	-	-	-	-	-	-
C_avg_verb_edge	−0.30	-	-	-	−0.21	-	-	-	-	-	-	-	-	-
C_char_tok	0.28	-	-	-	-	-	-	-	-	-	-	-	-	-
C_dep_aux	-	-	-	-	−0.21	-	-	-	-	-	-	-	-	-
C_dep_aux:pass	-	-	-	-	-	-	-	-	-	0.23	-	-	-	-
C_dep_cc	−0.23	-	-	-	−0.20	-	-	-	-	-	-	-	-	-
C_dep_ccomp	−0.23	-	-	-	-	-	-	-	-	-	-	-	-	-
C_dep_compound	0.21	-	-	-	0.24	-	-	-	-	-	-	-	-	-
C_dep_nmod:poss	−0.24	-	-	-	-	-	-	-	-	-	-	-	-	-
C_dep_nsubj	-	-	-	-	−0.31	-	-	-	-	-	-	-	-	-
C_dep_nsubj:pass	-	-	-	-	-	-	-	-	-	0.23	-	-	-	-
C_dep_nummod	-	-	-	-	0.28	-	0.27	-	0.22	-	0.26	-	0.23	-
C_dep_obj	−0.21	-	-	-	-	-	-	-	-	-	-	-	-	-
C_dep_obl	−0.25	-	-	-	-	-	-	-	-	-	-	-	-	-
C_dep_root	0.30	-	-	-	-	-	-	-	-	-	-	-	-	-
C_n_tok	−0.30	-	-	-	-	-	-	-	-	-	-	-	-	-
C_obj_post	−0.24	-	-	-	−0.21	-	-	-	-	-	-	-	-	-
C_prep_3	0.37	-	-	-	-	-	-	-	-	-	0.22	-	-	-
C_princ_prop	−0.27	-	-	-	-	-	-	-	-	-	-	-	-	-
C_sub_1	−0.30	-	-	-	-	-	-	-	-	-	-	-	-	-
C_sub_post	−0.28	-	-	-	-	-	-	-	-	-	-	-	-	-
C_sub_pre	-	-	-	-	−0.24	-	-	-	-	-	-	-	-	-

continued on next page

continued from previous page

Features	Length 10		Length 15		Length 20		Length 25		Length 30		Length 35		All sents	
	judg	*std*	*judg*	*std*	*judg*	*std*	*judg*	*std*	*judg*	*std*	*judg*	*std*	*judg*	*std*
C_sub_prop	−0.22	-	-	-	-	-	-	-	-	-	-	-	-	-
C_subj_pre	−0.39	-	-	-	-	-	-	-	-	-	-	-	-	-
C_tok_sent	−0.30	-	-	-	-	-	-	-	-	-	-	-	-	-
C_upos_AUX	−0.22	-	-	-	−0.23	-	-	-	-	-	-	-	-	-
C_upos_CCONJ	−0.21	-	-	-	-	-	-	-	-	-	-	-	-	-
C_upos_DET	−0.23	-	-	-	-	-	-	-	-	-	-	-	-	-
C_upos_NUM	-	-	-	-	0.24	-	0.35	-	0.23	-	0.26	-	0.24	-
C_upos_PART	−0.25	-	-	-	-	-	-	-	-	-	-	-	-	-
C_upos_PRON	−0.27	-	−0.23	-	-	-	-	-	-	-	-	-	-	-
C_upos_VERB	−0.29	-	-	-	−0.27	-	-	-	-	-	-	-	-	-
C_verb_edge_5	−0.31	-	-	-	-	-	-	-	-	-	-	-	-	-
C_verb_head_sent	−0.38	-	-	-	−0.28	-	-	-	-	-	-	-	-	-
C_verb_Ind	−0.23	-	-	-	-	-	-	-	-	-	-	-	-	-
C_verb_Inf	−0.21	-	-	-	-	−0.20	-	-	-	-	-	-	-	-
C_verb_Part	−0.24	-	-	-	-	-	-	-	-	-	-	-	-	-
C_verb_Past	−0.29	-	-	-	-	-	-	-	-	-	-	-	-	-
C_verb_Pres	-	-	-	-	−0.26	-	-	-	-	-	-	-	-	-
C_verb_root_perc	−0.44	-	-	-	−0.29	-	-	-	-	-	-	-	-	-
C_verb_Sing+3	-	-	-	-	−0.25	-	-	-	-	-	-	-	-	-
E_aux_Fin	−0.29	-	-	-	−0.21	-	-	-	-	-	-	-	-	-
E_aux_Ind	−0.22	-	-	-	−0.22	-	-	-	-	0.22	-	-	-	-
E_aux_Pres	-	-	-	-	−0.24	-	−0.21	-	-	-	-	-	-	-
E_avg_link	0.32	-	-	-	0.31	-	-	-	-	-	-	-	-	-
E_avg_max_link	-	-	-	-	0.29	-	-	-	-	-	-	-	-	-
E_avg_prep_chain	0.26	-	-	-	-	-	-	-	-	-	0.23	-	-	-
E_avg_verb_edge	−0.23	-	-	-	-	-	-	-	-	-	-	-	-	-
E_dep_advmod	-	-	−0.25	−0.24	-	-	-	-	-	-	-	-	-	-
E_dep_appos	0.37	-	-	-	0.21	-	0.23	-	-	-	-	-	-	-
E_dep_det	−0.25	-	-	-	-	-	-	-	-	-	-	-	-	-
E_dep_list	-	-	-	-	0.22	-	-	-	-	-	-	-	-	-
E_dep_nmod	0.35	-	-	-	-	-	-	-	-	-	0.25	-	-	-
E_dep_nsubj	−0.29	-	-	-	−0.25	-	-	-	-	-	-	-	-	-
E_dep_nummod	0.40	-	-	-	-	-	-	-	-	-	-	-	0.21	-
E_dep_obj	−0.31	-	-	-	-	-	-	-	-	-	-	-	-	-
E_lexical_dens	−0.30	-	-	-	-	-	-	-	-	-	-	-	-	-
E_max_link	-	-	-	-	0.29	-	-	-	-	-	-	-	-	-
E_n_prep_chain	0.32	-	-	-	0.22	-	-	-	-	-	0.20	-	-	-
E_obj_post	−0.28	-	-	-	-	-	-	-	-	-	-	-	-	-
E_prep_1	0.29	-	-	-	-	-	-	-	-	-	-	-	-	-
E_princ_prop	−0.23	-	-	-	-	-	-	-	-	-	-	-	-	-
E_sub_pre	-	−0.21	-	-	-	-	-	-	-	-	-	-	-	-
E_subj_pre	−0.45	-	-	-	-	-	-	-	-	-	-	-	-	-
E_ttr	−0.31	-	-	-	−0.29	-	-	-	-	-	-	-	-	-
E_ttr_lemma	−0.30	-	-	-	−0.29	-	-	-	-	-	-	-	-	-
E_upos_ADP	0.22	-	-	-	-	-	-	-	-	-	-	-	-	-
E_upos_AUX	−0.24	-	-	-	−0.27	-	-	-	-	-	-	-	-	-
E_upos_DET	−0.27	-	-	-	-	-	-	-	-	-	-	-	-	-
E_upos_NUM	0.39	-	-	-	0.23	-	-	-	-	-	0.21	-	0.23	-
E_upos_PRON	−0.34	-	-	-	-	-	-	-	-	-	-	-	-	-
E_upos_VERB	−0.38	-	-	-	-	-	-	-	-	-	−0.24	-	-	-
E_verb_edge_1	−0.29	-	-	-	-	-	-	-	-	-	-	-	-	-
E_verb_edge_3	−0.23	-	-	-	-	-	-	-	-	-	-	-	-	-
E_verb_Ger	-	-	-	-	0.20	-	-	-	-	-	-	-	-	-
E_verb_head_sent	−0.30	-	-	-	-	-	-	-	-	-	-	-	-	-
E_verb_root_perc	−0.41	-	-	-	−0.21	-	-	-	-	-	-	-	-	-

Table 6: Values of correlation for statistically significant (p-value<0.05) linguistic features with $\rho \geq 0.20$ that correlate with either the average judgment of complexity or the complexity standard deviation. For the *begin context window*, for all sentences and for sentences divided according to their length.

Features	Length 10		Length 15		Length 20		Length 25		Length 30		Length 35		All sents	
	judg	*std*	*judg*	*std*	*judg*	*std*	*judg*	*std*	*judg*	*std*	*judg*	*std*	*judg*	*std*
B_aux_+	−0.21	-	-	-	-	-	-	-	-	-	-	-	-	-
B_aux_form_Ger	-	-	0.21	-	-	-	-	-	-	-	-	-	-	-
B_aux_form_Inf	-	0.20	-	-	-	-	-	-	-	-	-	-	-	-
B_aux_Pres	-	-	-	-	-	-	-	-	−0.21	-	-	-	-	-
B_avg_prep_chain	-	-	-	-	-	-	0.23	-	-	-	-	-	-	-
B_avg_sub_chain	−0.24	-	-	-	-	-	-	-	-	-	-	-	-	-
B_dep_aux	-	-	-	-	-	-	-	-	-	-	−0.28	-	-	-
B_dep_aux:pass	-	-	-	-	-	-	−0.32	-	-	-	-	-	-	-
B_dep_compound	-	-	0.20	-	0.21	-	-	-	-	-	0.22	-	0.21	-
B_dep_flat	-	-	-	-	-	-	−0.22	-	-	-	-	-	-	-
B_dep_nmod	-	-	-	-	-	-	0.25	-	-	-	-	-	-	-
B_dep_nsubj	-	-	−0.24	-	-	-	-	-	-	-	−0.21	-	-	-
B_dep_nsubj:pass	-	-	-	-	-	-	−0.29	-	-	-	-	-	-	-
B_dep_nummod	-	-	0.27	-	0.23	-	-	-	-	-	0.26	-	-	-
B_n_prep_chain	-	-	-	-	-	-	0.23	-	-	-	-	-	-	-

continued on next page

continued from previous page

Features	Length 10		Length 15		Length 20		Length 25		Length 30		Length 35		All sents	
	judg	*std*	*judg*	*std*	*judg*	*std*	*judg*	*std*	*judg*	*std*	*judg*	*std*	*judg*	*std*
B_princ_prop	-	-	-	-	−0.24	-	-	-	-	-	-	-	-	-
B_sub_post	−0.22	-	-	-	-	-	-	-	-	-	-	-	-	-
B_subj_pre	-	-	-	-	-	-	-	−0.20	-	-	-	-	-	-
B_upos_NUM	-	-	0.22	-	-	-	-	-	-	-	0.29	-	-	-
B_upos_PRON	-	-	-	-	-	-	-	-	−0.22	-	-	-	-	-
B_upos_PROPN	-	-	0.21	-	-	-	-	-	-	-	-	-	-	-
B_upos_SYM	-	-	-	-	-	-	-	−0.21	-	-	0.21	-	-	-
B_upos_VERB	-	-	−0.21	-	−0.22	-	-	-	-	-	-	-	-	-
B_verb_edge_1	-	-	-	−0.20	-	-	-	-	-	-	-	-	-	-
B_verb_Past	-	-	-	−0.21	-	-	-	-	-	-	-	-	-	-
B_verb_root_perc	-	-	-	-	−0.25	-	-	-	-	-	-	-	-	-
C_aux_+	−0.24	-	-	-	−0.24	-	-	-	-	-	−0.20	-	-	-
C_aux_form_Fin	−0.21	-	-	-	−0.28	-	-	-	−0.22	-	-	-	-	-
C_aux_Ind	-	-	-	-	−0.23	-	-	-	-	-	-	-	-	-
C_aux_Past	-	-	-	-	−0.21	-	-	-	-	-	-	-	-	-
C_aux_Pres	−0.21	-	-	-	-	-	-	-	−0.22	-	−0.24	-	-	-
C_avg_max_depth	0.21	-	0.31	-	-	-	-	-	-	-	-	-	0.29	-
C_avg_max_link	-	-	-	-	-	-	-	-	-	-	-	-	0.25	-
C_avg_sub_chain	-	-	-	-	-	-	-	-	−0.20	-	−0.38	-	-	-
C_avg_tok_clause	-	-	-	-	0.22	-	-	-	-	-	0.26	-	-	-
C_char_tok	-	-	-	-	-	-	-	-	-	-	−0.30	-	-	-
C_dep_amod	-	-	-	-	−0.24	-	-	-	-	-	-	-	-	-
C_dep_aux	-	-	−0.22	-	−0.21	-	-	-	−0.28	−0.25	−0.29	-	-	-
C_dep_case	-	-	-	-	-	-	-	-	-	-	0.22	-	-	-
C_dep_ccomp	-	-	-	-	-	-	-	-	-	-	−0.27	-	-	-
C_dep_det	-	-	−0.28	-	−0.22	-	-	-	-	-	-	-	-	-
C_dep_mark	-	-	-	-	-	-	-	-	-	-	−0.23	-	-	-
C_dep_nmod	0.23	-	-	-	-	-	-	-	-	-	-	-	-	-
C_dep_nsubj	−0.22	-	-	-	-	-	-	-	-	-	-	-	-	-
C_dep_nummod	0.21	-	0.32	-	0.25	-	-	-	0.26	-	0.35	-	0.29	-
C_dep_punct	-	-	-	-	-	-	-	−0.21	-	-	-	-	-	-
C_dep_root	−0.24	-	−0.33	-	-	-	-	-	-	-	-	-	−0.31	-
C_dep_xcomp	-	-	-	-	-	-	−0.26	-	-	-	−0.28	-	-	-
C_lexical_dens	-	-	−0.23	-	−0.21	-	-	-	-	-	−0.27	-	-	-
C_max_link	-	-	-	-	-	-	-	-	-	-	-	-	0.25	-
C_n_prep_chain	0.23	-	-	-	-	-	-	-	-	-	-	-	0.25	-
C_n_tok	0.24	-	0.33	-	-	-	-	-	-	-	-	-	0.31	-
C_princ_prop	-	-	-	-	-	-	-	-	-	-	0.23	−0.21	-	-
C_sub_2	-	-	-	-	-	-	-	-	-	-	−0.20	-	-	-
C_sub_4	-	-	-	-	-	-	-	-	-	-	−0.24	-	-	-
C_sub_post	-	-	-	-	-	-	-	-	-	-	−0.28	-	-	-
C_sub_prop	-	-	-	-	-	-	-	-	-	-	−0.29	0.20	-	-
C_tok_sent	0.24	-	0.33	-	-	-	-	-	-	-	-	-	0.31	-
C_upos_ADJ	−0.21	-	−0.25	-	−0.22	-	-	-	-	-	−0.26	-	-	-
C_upos_AUX	−0.24	-	-	-	−0.27	-	-	-	−0.23	-	−0.32	-	−0.23	-
C_upos_DET	-	-	−0.28	-	−0.21	-	-	-	-	-	-	-	-	-
C_upos_NUM	0.30	-	0.41	-	0.31	-	-	-	0.28	-	0.39	-	0.33	-
C_upos_PRON	−0.21	-	-	-	−0.21	-	-	-	-	-	−0.31	-	-	-
C_upos_PUNCT	-	-	-	-	-	-	-	−0.21	-	-	-	-	-	-
C_upos_SYM	0.26	-	0.30	-	-	-	-	-	-	-	0.34	-	0.24	-
C_upos_VERB	-	-	-	-	-	-	-	-	-	-	−0.24	-	-	-
C_verb_+	-	-	-	-	-	-	0.22	-	-	-	-	-	-	-
C_verb_edge_1	-	-	-	-	-	-	-	-	−0.28	-	-	0.20	-	-
C_verb_edge_2	-	-	-	-	-	-	-	-	-	-	−0.26	-	-	-
C_verb_form_Fin	-	-	-	-	-	-	-	-	0.24	-	-	-	-	-
C_verb_form_Inf	-	-	-	-	-	-	-	-	-	-	−0.27	-	-	-
C_verb_head_sent	-	-	-	-	−0.23	-	-	-	-	-	−0.28	-	-	-
C_verb_Ind	-	-	-	-	-	-	-	-	0.21	-	-	-	-	-
C_verb_root_perc	-	-	-	-	-	-	-	-	-	-	-	−0.22	-	-
E_aux_Pres	−0.27	-	−0.21	-	-	-	-	-	-	-	-	-	-	-
E_avg_link	−0.29	−0.23	-	-	-	-	-	-	-	-	-	-	-	-
E_avg_max_depth	-	-	-	-	-	-	0.30	-	-	-	-	-	-	-
E_avg_max_link	−0.23	−0.25	-	-	-	-	-	-	-	-	-	-	-	-
E_avg_sub_chain	−0.21	-	-	-	-	-	-	-	-	-	−0.26	-	-	-
E_avg_tok_clause	-	-	-	-	-	-	-	-	-	-	0.25	-	-	-
E_avg_verb_edge	−0.21	-	-	-	-	-	-	-	-	-	-	-	-	-
E_dep_advmod	−0.24	-	−0.20	-	-	-	-	-	-	-	-	-	-	-
E_dep_aux	-	−0.22	-	-	-	-	-	-	-	-	-	-	-	-
E_dep_case	-	-	-	-	-	-	0.20	-	-	-	-	-	-	-
E_dep_ccomp	-	-	-	-	-	-	-	-	-	-	−0.31	-	-	-
E_dep_nummod	-	-	-	-	-	-	0.28	-	-	-	0.33	-	0.22	-
E_dep_parataxis	-	−0.22	-	-	-	-	-	-	-	-	-	-	-	-
E_dep_root	0.21	0.21	-	-	-	-	-	-	-	-	-	-	-	-
E_dep_xcomp	-	−0.21	−0.23	-	-	-	-	-	-	-	-	-	-	-
E_lexical_dens	-	-	-	-	-	-	−0.25	-	-	-	−0.22	-	-	-
E_max_link	−0.23	−0.25	-	-	-	-	-	-	-	-	-	-	-	-
E_n_tok	−0.21	−0.21	-	-	-	-	-	-	-	-	-	-	-	-
E_prep_1	-	-	-	-	−0.22	-	-	-	-	-	-	-	-	-
E_prep_2	-	−0.20	-	-	-	-	0.20	-	-	-	-	-	-	-
E_sub_post	-	-	-	-	-	-	-	-	-	-	−0.22	-	-	-
E_sub_pre	-	-	−0.22	-	-	-	-	-	-	-	-	-	-	-
E_sub_prop	−0.23	-	-	-	-	-	-	-	-	-	-	-	-	-

continued on next page

continued from previous page

Features	Length 10		Length 15		Length 20		Length 25		Length 30		Length 35		All sents	
	judg	*std*	*judg*	*std*	*judg*	*std*	*judg*	*std*	*judg*	*std*	*judg*	*std*	*judg*	*std*
E_tok_sent	−0.21	−0.21	-	-	-	-	-	-	-	-	-	-	-	-
E_upos_ADV	-	-	−0.23	-	-	0.22	-	-	-	-	-	-	-	-
E_upos_NUM	-	-	-	-	-	-	0.33	-	-	-	0.34	-	0.22	-
E_upos_PART	-	-	-	-	-	-	-	-	-	-	−0.23	-	-	-
E_upos_PRON	−0.22	-	-	-	-	-	-	-	-	-	-	-	-	-
E_upos_SYM	-	-	-	-	-	-	0.28	-	-	-	0.30	-	-	-
E_upos_VERB	-	-	-	-	-	-	-	-	-	-	−0.21	-	-	-
E_verb_edge_3	-	-	-	-	-	-	-	−0.22	-	-	-	0.21	-	-
E_verb_edge_4	−0.30	-	-	-	-	-	-	-	-	-	-	-	-	-
E_verb_form_Fin	-	-	-	-	-	-	-	-	0.21	-	-	-	-	-
E_verb_form_Inf	-	-	-	-	-	-	-	-	-	-	−0.22	-	-	-
E_verb_head_sent	−0.24	-	-	-	-	-	-	-	-	-	-	-	-	-
E_verb_Past	-	0.20	-	-	-	-	0.23	-	-	-	-	-	-	-
E_verb_Pres	−0.20	−0.30	-	-	-	-	-	-	-	-	-	-	-	-
E_verb_Sing+3	−0.20	−0.21	-	-	-	-	-	-	-	-	-	-	-	-

Table 7: Values of correlation for statistically significant (p-value<0.05) linguistic features with $\rho \geq 0.20$ that correlate with either the average judgment of complexity or the complexity standard deviation. For the *center context window*, for all sentences and for sentences divided according to their length.

Features	Length 10		Length 15		Length 20		Length 25		Length 30		Length 35		All sents	
	judg	*std*	*judg*	*std*	*judg*	*std*	*judg*	*std*	*judg*	*std*	*judg*	*std*	*judg*	*std*
B_aux_Fin	-	-	-	-	−0.23	-	-	-	-	-	-	-	-	-
B_aux_Ind	-	-	-	-	−0.21	-	-	-	-	-	-	-	-	-
B_avg_link	-	-	-	-	−0.25	-	-	-	-	-	-	-	-	-
B_avg_max_link	-	-	-	-	−0.24	-	-	-	-	-	-	-	-	-
B_dep_acl	-	-	-	-	-	−0.23	-	-	-	-	-	-	-	-
B_dep_advcl	-	-	-	-	-	-	-	-	−0.20	-	-	-	-	-
B_dep_case	-	-	-	-	−0.21	-	-	-	-	-	-	-	-	-
B_dep_ccomp	-	-	-	-	-	-	-	-	-	-	−0.21	-	-	-
B_dep_nmod:poss	-	-	-	-	-	-	-	−0.22	-	-	-	-	-	-
B_dep_obj	-	-	−0.25	-	-	-	-	-	-	-	-	-	-	-
B_dep_obl	-	-	-	-	−0.26	-	-	-	-	-	-	-	-	-
B_dep_xcomp	-	-	−0.21	-	-	-	-	-	-	-	-	-	-	-
B_max_link	-	-	-	-	−0.24	-	-	-	-	-	-	-	-	-
B_prep_3	-	-	-	-	-	-	-	−0.20	-	-	-	-	-	-
B_sub_1	-	-	-	-	−0.23	-	-	−0.25	-	-	-	-	-	-
B_subj_pre	-	-	-	-	−0.21	-	-	-	-	-	-	-	-	-
B_ttr	-	-	-	-	−0.25	-	−0.20	-	-	-	-	-	-	-
B_ttr_lemma	-	-	-	-	−0.22	-	−0.22	-	-	-	-	-	-	-
B_upos_ADP	-	-	-	-	−0.23	-	-	-	-	-	-	-	-	-
B_upos_AUX	-	-	-	-	−0.26	-	-	-	-	-	-	-	-	-
B_upos_NOUN	-	-	-	-	-	-	-	-	-	-	0.22	-	-	-
B_upos_SYM	0.23	-	-	-	-	-	-	-	-	-	-	-	-	-
B_upos_VERB	-	-	-	-	−0.23	-	-	-	−0.24	-	-	-	-	-
B_verb_head_sent	-	-	-	-	−0.21	-	-	-	-	-	-	-	-	-
B_verb_Part	-	-	-	-	−0.26	-	-	-	-	-	-	-	-	-
B_verb_root_perc	-	-	-	-	-	-	-	-	-	-	-	−0.20	-	-
C_aux_Fin	−0.21	-	−0.21	-	−0.26	-	-	-	-	-	-	-	-	-
C_char_tok	-	-	-	-	-	-	-	-	-	-	−0.20	-	-	-
C_dep_appos	-	-	-	-	0.26	-	-	-	-	-	-	-	-	-
C_dep_aux	-	-	−0.27	-	-	-	-	-	-	-	-	-	-	-
C_dep_case	0.22	-	-	-	-	-	-	-	-	-	-	-	-	-
C_dep_compound	-	-	0.22	-	0.22	-	-	-	-	-	-	-	-	-
C_dep_det	−0.21	-	-	-	-	-	-	-	-	-	-	-	-	-
C_dep_fixed	-	-	-	-	-	−0.21	-	-	-	-	-	-	-	-
C_dep_nmod	0.22	-	-	-	-	-	-	-	-	-	-	-	-	-
C_dep_nsubj	-	-	-	-	−0.20	-	-	-	-	-	-	-	-	-
C_dep_nummod	-	-	-	-	0.26	-	-	-	0.20	-	-	-	-	-
C_dep_obl	-	0.20	-	-	-	-	-	-	-	-	-	-	-	-
C_dep_obl:tmod	-	−0.25	-	-	-	-	-	-	-	-	-	-	-	-
C_dep_punct	-	-	-	-	0.23	-	-	-	-	-	-	-	-	-
C_sub_2	-	0.22	-	-	-	-	-	-	-	-	-	-	-	-
C_sub_post	-	0.27	-	-	-	-	-	-	-	-	-	-	-	-
C_sub_pre	−0.22	−0.23	-	-	-	-	-	-	-	-	-	-	-	-
C_sub_prop	-	0.22	-	-	-	-	-	-	-	-	-	-	-	-
C_subj_pre	-	-	-	-	−0.27	-	-	-	-	-	-	-	-	-
C_ttr	-	-	-	-	−0.24	-	-	-	-	-	-	0.23	-	-
C_ttr_lemma	-	-	0.22	-	−0.27	-	-	-	-	-	-	0.22	-	-
C_upos_AUX	−0.25	-	−0.21	-	−0.21	-	-	-	-	-	-	-	-	-
C_upos_DET	−0.23	-	-	-	-	-	-	-	−0.22	-	-	-	-	-
C_upos_NUM	-	-	-	-	0.26	-	-	-	0.21	-	-	-	-	-
C_upos_PRON	-	-	−0.21	-	-	-	-	-	-	-	-	-	-	-
C_upos_PROPN	-	-	0.25	-	-	-	-	-	-	-	-	-	-	-
C_upos_PUNCT	-	-	-	-	0.23	-	-	-	-	-	-	-	-	-
C_upos_SYM	-	-	-	-	-	-	-	-	-	-	0.26	-	-	-
C_verb_Past	-	-	0.28	-	-	-	-	-	-	-	0.23	-	-	-

continued on next page

continued from previous page

Features	Length 10		Length 15		Length 20		Length 25		Length 30		Length 35		All sents	
	judg	*std*	*judg*	*std*	*judg*	*std*	*judg*	*std*	*judg*	*std*	*judg*	*std*	*judg*	*std*
C_verb_Pres	-	-	−0.20	-	-	-	-	-	-	-	-	-	-	-
C_verb_root_perc	-	-	-	-	−0.28	-	-	-	-	-	-	-	-	-
E_aux_Fin	-	-	-	-	−0.23	-	-	-	-	-	-	-	-	-
E_aux_Inf	-	-	-	-	-	-	-	-	-	-	−0.25	-	-	-
E_aux_Pres	−0.20	-	-	-	-	-	-	-	−0.21	-	-	-	-	-
E_avg_link	-	-	-	-	-	-	-	-	-	-	-	-	0.24	-
E_avg_max_depth	0.21	-	0.22	-	-	-	-	-	-	-	-	-	0.27	-
E_avg_max_link	-	-	-	-	-	-	-	-	-	-	-	-	0.28	-
E_avg_sub_chain	-	-	-	-	-	-	-	-	-	-	−0.28	-	-	-
E_avg_tok_clause	-	-	-	-	-	-	-	-	0.20	-	-	-	-	-
E_avg_verb_edge	−0.28	−0.21	-	-	-	-	-	-	-	-	-	-	-	-
E_char_tok	-	-	-	-	-	-	−0.22	-	-	-	-	-	-	-
E_dep_acl:relcl	-	-	-	-	-	-	0.21	-	-	-	-	-	-	-
E_dep_advcl	-	-	-	-	-	-	-	-	−0.20	-	-	-	-	-
E_dep_advmod	-	-	−0.23	-	-	-	-	-	-	-	-	-	-	-
E_dep_amod	-	-	−0.23	-	-	-	-	-	-	-	-	-	-	-
E_dep_appos	0.28	-	-	-	-	-	-	-	-	0.23	-	-	-	-
E_dep_aux	-	-	-	-	-	-	-	-	-	-	−0.32	-	-	-
E_dep_compound	0.20	-	0.27	-	-	-	-	-	0.22	-	-	-	0.21	-
E_dep_det	-	-	−0.30	-	−0.33	-	-	-	-	-	-	-	-	-
E_dep_mark	-	-	-	-	-	-	-	-	-	-	−0.29	-	-	-
E_dep_nmod	0.20	-	-	-	-	-	-	-	-	-	-	-	-	-
E_dep_nsubj	-	-	-	-	-	-	-	-	-	-	-	-	−0.21	-
E_dep_nummod	-	-	-	-	0.27	-	0.23	-	0.21	-	0.25	-	0.22	-
E_dep_obj	-	−0.22	-	-	-	-	-	-	-	-	-	-	-	-
E_dep_obl	-	-	-	-	-	-	-	-	-	-	−0.27	-	-	-
E_dep_parataxis	-	-	-	-	-	-	0.22	-	-	-	-	-	-	-
E_dep_punct	-	-	-	-	0.22	-	-	-	-	-	-	-	-	-
E_dep_root	-	-	−0.33	-	-	-	-	-	-	-	-	-	−0.33	-
E_lexical_dens	-	-	-	-	-	-	−0.29	-	-	-	-	-	-	-
E_max_link	-	-	-	-	-	-	-	-	-	-	-	-	0.28	-
E_n_tok	-	-	0.33	-	-	-	-	-	-	-	-	-	0.33	-
E_obj_post	-	−0.23	-	-	-	-	-	-	-	-	-	-	-	-
E_sub_2	-	-	-	-	-	-	−0.21	-	-	-	−0.23	-	-	-
E_sub_post	-	-	-	-	-	-	-	-	-	-	−0.25	-	-	-
E_subj_pre	−0.32	−0.23	-	-	-	-	-	-	-	-	-	-	-	-
E_tok_sent	-	-	0.33	-	-	-	-	-	-	-	-	-	0.33	-
E_ttr	-	-	-	-	−0.22	-	−0.21	-	-	-	−0.23	-	−0.20	-
E_ttr_lemma	-	-	-	-	−0.22	-	-	-	-	-	−0.20	-	-	-
E_upos_ADV	−0.21	-	-	-	-	-	-	-	-	-	-	-	-	-
E_upos_AUX	-	-	-	-	−0.24	-	-	-	-	-	-	-	-	-
E_upos_DET	-	-	−0.30	-	−0.33	-	-	-	-	-	-	-	-	-
E_upos_NOUN	-	-	-	-	−0.25	-	-	-	-	-	-	-	-	-
E_upos_NUM	-	-	0.21	-	0.28	-	0.27	-	-	-	0.28	-	0.25	-
E_upos_PART	-	-	-	-	-	-	-	-	-	-	−0.23	-	-	-
E_upos_PRON	−0.22	-	-	-	-	-	-	-	−0.21	-	−0.24	-	-	-
E_upos_PROPN	-	-	-	-	-	-	-	-	-	0.24	-	-	-	-
E_upos_PUNCT	-	-	-	-	0.22	-	-	-	-	-	-	-	-	-
E_upos_SYM	-	−0.23	-	-	-	-	0.23	-	-	-	0.27	-	0.21	-
E_upos_VERB	-	-	-	-	-	-	-	-	−0.24	-	−0.25	-	-	-
E_verb_edge_2	-	-	-	-	-	-	-	-	-	-	−0.24	-	-	-
E_verb_edge_3	−0.24	-	-	-	-	-	-	-	-	-	-	-	-	-
E_verb_edge_6	-	-	-	-	-	−0.21	-	-	-	-	-	-	-	-
E_verb_Fin	-	-	-	-	0.22	-	-	-	-	-	-	-	-	-
E_verb_Ger	-	-	-	-	-	-	-	-	−0.25	-	-	-	-	-
E_verb_head_sent	-	-	-	-	−0.20	-	-	-	−0.20	-	-	-	-	-
E_verb_Inf	-	-	-	-	−0.23	-	-	-	-	-	−0.22	-	-	-
E_verb_Pres	−0.22	-	-	-	-	-	-	-	-	-	-	-	-	-
E_verb_root_perc	−0.20	-	-	-	-	-	-	-	-	-	-	-	-	-
E_verb_Sing+3	-	-	-	-	0.23	-	-	-	-	-	-	-	-	-

Table 8: Values of correlation for statistically significant (p-value$<$ 0.05) linguistic features with $\rho \geq 0.20$ that correlate with either the average judgment of complexity or the complexity standard deviation. For the *end context window*, for all sentences and for sentences divided according to their length.

Evaluating the Acquisition of Semantic Knowledge from Cross-situational Learning in Artificial Neural Networks

Mitja Nikolaus[1,2]
mitja.nikolaus@univ-amu.fr

Abdellah Fourtassi[1]
abdellah.fourtassi@gmail.com

[1]Aix Marseille Univ, Université de Toulon, CNRS, LIS, Marseille, France
[2]Aix-Marseille Univ, CNRS, LPL, Aix-en-Provence, France

Abstract

When learning their native language, children acquire the meanings of words and sentences from highly ambiguous input without much explicit supervision. One possible learning mechanism is cross-situational learning, which has been successfully tested in laboratory experiments with children. Here we use Artificial Neural Networks to test if this mechanism scales up to more natural language and visual scenes using a large dataset of crowd-sourced images with corresponding descriptions. We evaluate learning using a series of tasks inspired by methods commonly used in laboratory studies of language acquisition. We show that the model acquires rich semantic knowledge both at the word- and sentence-level, mirroring the patterns and trajectory of learning in early childhood. Our work highlights the usefulness of low-level co-occurrence statistics across modalities in facilitating the early acquisition of higher-level semantic knowledge.

1 Introduction

In order to acquire their native language, children learn both how to associate individual words with their meanings (e.g., the word "ball" refers to the object ball and the word "kick" refers to that act of kicking) and how to map the relationship between words in a sentence onto specific event configurations in the world, e.g., that the sequence of words "Jenny kicks the ball" maps on to the event where the referent of the first noun (i.e., Jenny) is performing the act of kicking on the second (i.e., the ball). This is a difficult task because it requires that children learn these associations and rules in a largely unsupervised fashion from an input that can be highly ambiguous (Quine, 1960). It is still unclear how children overcome this challenge.

Previous experimental studies on child language acquisition have focused on *evaluating* children's learning using controlled tasks that typically take the form of a two-alternative forced-choice paradigm. For example, in order to test the learning of an individual word meaning, we can utter this word to the child (e.g., "ball") and present her with two pictures representing correct (i.e., a ball) and incorrect referents (e.g. a cup), and we test if the child reliably prefers the correct one (Bergelson and Swingley, 2012). Similarly, in order to evaluate children's understanding of sentence-level semantics such as a the agent-patient relationship, we can utter a sentence such as "Jenny is tickling Mike" and present the child with two pictures where either Jenny or Mike are doing the tickling, and we test if the child reliably prefers the correct picture (e.g. Noble et al., 2011; Gertner and Fisher, 2012).

While we have been able to evaluate children's knowledge using such controlled tests, research has been less compelling regarding the *mechanism of learning* from the natural, ambiguous input. One promising proposal is that of cross-situational learning (hereafter, XSL). This proposal suggests that, even if one naming situation is highly ambiguous, being exposed to many situations allows the learner to narrow down, over time, the set of possible word-world associations (e.g. Pinker, 1989).

While in-lab work has shown that XSL is cognitively plausible using toy situations (Yu and Smith, 2007), effort is still ongoing to test if this mechanism scales up to more natural learning contexts using machine learning tools (e.g. Chrupała et al., 2015; Vong and Lake, 2020). This previous work, however, has focused mainly on testing the learning of individual words' meanings, while here we are interested in testing and comparing both word-level and sentence-level semantics.

1.1 The Current Study

The current study uses tools from Natural Language Processing (NLP) and computer vision as

Proceedings of the Workshop on Cognitive Modeling and Computational Linguistics, pages 200–210
Online Event, June 10, 2021. ©2021 Association for Computational Linguistics

research methods to advance our understanding of how unsupervised XSL could give rise to semantic knowledge. We aim at going beyond the limitations of in-lab XSL experiments with children (which have relied on too simplified learning input) while at the same time integrating the strength and precision of in-lab learning evaluation methods.

More precisely, we first design a model that learns in an XSL fashion from images and text based on a large-scale dataset of clipart images representing some real-life activities with corresponding – crowdsourced – descriptions. Second, we evaluate the model's learning on a subset of the data that we used to carefully design a series of controlled tasks inspired from methods used in laboratory testing with children. Crucially, we test the extent to which the model acquires various aspects of semantics both at the word level (e.g., the meanings of nouns, adjectives, and verbs) and at the sentence level (e.g. the semantic roles of the nouns).

Further, in order for an XSL-based model to provide a plausible language learning mechanism in early childhood, it should not only be able to succeed in the evaluation tasks, but also mirror children's learning trajectory (e.g., a bias to learn nouns before predicates). Thus, we record and analyze the model's learning trajectory by evaluating the learned semantics at multiple timesteps during the training phase.

1.2 Related Work and Novelty

While supervised learning from images and text has received much attention in the NLP and computer vision communities, for example in the form of classification problems (e.g. Yatskar et al., 2016) or question-answering (e.g. Antol et al., 2015; Hudson and Manning, 2019), here we focus on *cross-situational learning* of visually grounded semantics, which corresponds more to our understanding of how children learn language

There is a large body of work on cross-situational word learning (Frank et al., 2007; Yu and Ballard, 2007; Fazly et al., 2010), some of them with more plausible, naturalistic input in the form of images as we consider in our work (Kádár et al., 2015; Lazaridou et al., 2016; Vong and Lake, 2020). However, these previous studies only evaluate the semantics of single words in isolation (and sometimes only nouns). In contrast, our paper aims at a more comprehensive approach, testing and comparing the acquisition of both word-level meanings (including adjectives and verbs) and sentence-level semantics.

There has been some effort to test sentence-level semantics in a XLS settings. For example, Chrupała et al. (2015) also introduces a model that learns from a large-scale dataset of naturalistic images with corresponding texts. To evaluate sentence-level semantics, the model's performance was tested in a cross-modal retrieval task, as commonly used to evaluate image-sentence ranking models (Hodosh et al., 2013). They show that sentence to image retrieval accuracy decreases when using scrambled sentences, indicating that the model is sensitive to word order. In a subsequent study, Kádár et al. (2017) introduces *omission scores* to evaluate the models' selectivity to certain syntactic functions and lexical categories. Another evaluation method for sentence-level semantics is to compare learned sentence similarities to human similarity judgments (e.g. Merkx and Frank, 2019).

Nevertheless, these previous studies only explored broad relationships between sentences and pictures, they did not test the models' sensitivity to finer-grained phenomena such as dependencies between predicates (e.g., adjectives and verbs) and arguments (e.g., nouns) or semantic/ roles in detail.

2 Methods

2.1 Data

We used the Abstract Scenes dataset 1.1 (Zitnick and Parikh, 2013; Zitnick et al., 2013), which contains 10K crowd-sourced images each with 6 corresponding short descriptive captions in English. Annotators were asked to "create an illustration for a children's story book by creating a realistic scene" given a set of clip art objects (Zitnick and Parikh, 2013). The images contain one or two children engaged in different actions involving interactions with a set of objects and animals. Further, the children can have various emotional states depicted through a variety of facial expressions. The corresponding sentences were collected by asking annotators to write "simple sentences describing different parts of the scene"[1] (Zitnick et al., 2013).

While some studies have used larger datasets with more naturalistic images (e.g. Lin et al., 2014;

[1]The annotators were asked to refer to the children by the names "Jenny" and "Mike".

Plummer et al., 2015), here we used the Abstract Scenes dataset since it contains many similar scenes and sentences, allowing us to create balanced test sets (as described in the following section). In other words, the choice of the dataset was a trade-off between the naturalness of the images on the one hand and their partial systematicity, on the other hand, which we needed to design minimally different pairs of images to evaluate the model.

For the following experiments, we split the images and their corresponding descriptions into training (80%), validation (10%) and test set (10%).

2.2 Model

We use a modeling framework that instantiates XSL from images and texts in the dataset. To learn the alignment of visual and language representations, we employ an approach commonly used for the task of image-sentence ranking (Hodosh et al., 2013) and other multimodal XSL experiments (Chrupała et al., 2017; Vong et al., 2021).

The objective is to learn a joint multimodal embedding for the sentences and images, and to rank the images and sentences based on similarity in this space. State-of-the-art models extract image features from Convoluatinal Neural Networks (CNNs) and use LSTMs to generate sentence representations, both of which are projected into a joint embedding space using a linear transformation (Karpathy and Fei-Fei, 2015; Faghri et al., 2018).

As commonly applied in other multimodal XSL work (Chrupała et al., 2015; Khorrami and Räsänen, 2021), we assume that the visual system of the learner has already been developed to some degree and thus use a CNN pre-trained on ImageNet (Russakovsky et al., 2015) (but discard the final classification layer) to encode the images. Specifically, we use a ResNet 50[2] (He et al., 2016) to encode the images and train a linear embedding layer that maps the output of the pre-final layer of the CNN into the joint embedding space.

The words of a sentence are passed through a linear word embedding layer and then encoded using a one-layer LSTM (Hochreiter and Schmidhuber, 1997). Using a linear embedding layer, the hidden activations of the last timestep are then transformed into the joint embedding space.

The model is trained using a max-margin loss[3] which encourages aligned image-sentence pairs to have a higher similarity score than misaligned pairs, by a margin α:

$$\mathcal{L}(\theta) = \sum_a [\sum_b max(0, \gamma(i_a, s_b) - \gamma(i_a, s_a) + \alpha) + \sum_b max(0, \gamma(i_b, s_a) - \gamma(i_a, s_a) + \alpha)] \quad (1)$$

$\gamma(i_a, s_b)$ indicates the cosine similarity between an image i and a sentence s, (i_a, s_a) denotes a corresponding image-sentence pair. The loss is calculated for each mini-batch, negative examples are all examples in a mini-batch for which the sentence does not correspond to the image.

We train the model on the training set until the loss converges on the validation set. Details about hyperparameters can be found in the appendix.

2.3 Evaluation Method

In order to evaluate the model's acquisition of visually-grounded semantics, we used a two-alternative forced choice design, similar to what is typically done to evaluate children's knowledge in laboratory experiments (Bergelson and Swingley, 2012; Noble et al., 2011; Gertner and Fisher, 2012). Each test trial consists of an image, a target sentence and a distractor sentence: (i, s_t, s_d). We measure the model's accuracy at choosing the correct sentence given the image.

Crucially, we design the test tasks in a way that allows us to control for linguistic biases. Consider the example trial on the left in Figure 1. The model could posit that, say, Jenny (and not Mike) is the agent of an action even without considering the image, and only because Jenny may happen to be the agent in most sentences in the training data. To avoid such linguistic biases, we paired each test trial with a counter-balanced trial where the target and distractor sentence were flipped (cf. Figure 1, right side), in such a way that a language model without any visual grounding can only perform at chance level (50%).

[2]We also tried the more recent ResNet 152, but found results to be inferior. Also, we did not attempt to fine-tune the parameters of the CNN for the task, which could improve performance further.

[3]In preliminary experiments we also applied a max-margin loss with emphasis on hard negatives (Faghri et al., 2018), but observed a performance decrease. This could be due to the fact that our dataset contains many repeating sentences and semantically equivalent scenes, and consequently we could find "hard negatives" that should actually be positive learning examples (because they are semantically equivalent) in many situations.

Figure 1: Counter-balanced evaluation of visually-grounded learning of semantics: Each test trial has a corresponding counter-example, where target and distractor sentence are flipped.

More precisely, we made the tasks as follows. First we searched in the heldout test set for image-sentence pairs $[(i_x, s_x), (i_y, s_y)]$ with *minimal differences* in the sentences given the phenomenon under study. For example, to study the acquisition of noun meanings, we look for pairs of sentences where the difference is only one noun such as $s_x =$ "jenny is wearing a crown" and $s_y =$ "mike is wearing a crown" (the corresponding images i_x and i_y depict the corresponding scenes, as shown in Figure 1). Second, based on such a minimal pair, we construct two counter-balanced triads: (i_x, s_x, s_y) and (i_y, s_y, s_x). The target sentence in one triad is the distractor in the other triad (and vice-versa). Using such a pair of counter-balanced triads, we test whether a model can both successfully choose the sentence mentioning "Jenny" when presented with the picture of Jenny *and* choose the sentence mentioning "Mike" when presented with the picture of Mike.

In the following we describe in more detail the phenomena of semantics we investigated using this testing setup. We provide an example for each category of task in Figure 2.

3 Tasks

3.1 Word-level Semantics

To study the acquisition of word meanings, we collect minimal pairs for the most commonly occurring nouns, adjectives and verbs. An example can be seen in Figure 1. Across all word-level categories, we make sure that there is only one referent present in the scene (this could be a child, an animal, or inanimate object, depending on the noun category under study). This ensures that we only evaluate word learning, and not more complex sentence-level semantics.[4]

Nouns We group the nouns into *persons*, *animals* and *objects*. Regarding persons, we consider the two children talked about in the dataset, i.e., *Jenny* and *Mike*. Regarding animals, we consider all 6 animals present in the dataset.[5] Regarding objects, we consider the 12 most frequently occurring words that are describing physical objects.[6]

Verbs The category of verbs is a bit tricky to evaluate because verbs are usually followed with an object that is tightly connected to them (e.g. *kicking* is usually connected to a ball whereas *eating* is connected to some food), resulting in a very limited availability of minimally different sentences with respect to verbs in the dataset. To be able to create a reasonable number of test trials, we trimmed the sentences[7] after the target verb and only consider verbs that can be used intransitively, e.g., "Mike is eating an apple" becomes "Mike is eating".

Further, we ensure, that the trials do not contain pairs of target and distractor sentences where the corresponding actions can be performed at the same time. For example, we do not include trials where the target sentence involves *sitting* and the distractor sentence *eating*, because the corresponding picture could be ambiguous: If the child in the picture is *sitting* and *eating* at the same, both the target and distractor sentences could be semantically correct. The resulting set of possible verb pairings is: ("sitting", "standing"), ("sitting", "running"), ("eating", "playing"), ("eating", "kicking"), ("throwing", "eating"), ("throwing", "kicking"), ("sitting", "kicking"), ("jumping", "sitting").

Adjectives The most common adjectives in the dataset are related to mood (e.g., happy and sad) and are displayed in the pictures using varied facial expressions (happy face vs sad face). Due to the lack of other kinds of adjectives[8], we only

[4] For example, if *Mike* (without a crown) was present in the picture to the left in Figure 1, the model would not only need to understand the difference between *Jenny* and *Mike*, but also understand what it means to *wear a crown* in order to correctly judge which sentence is the correct one, that is, which of Mike and Jenny is the one with the crown.

[5] ("dog", "cat", "snake", "bear", "duck", "owl")

[6] ("ball", "hat", "tree", "table", "sandbox", "slide", "sunglasses", "pie", "pizza", "hamburger", "balloons", "frisbee")

[7] The trimming was only done for the test trails and not in the training set.

[8] In the dataset, most of the properties for objects are fixed (e.g. colors and shapes) and are thus very rarely referred to in the descriptions. Consequently, we did not find minimal pairs

Figure 2: Examples for the evaluation of word and sentence-level semantics. Each test trial consists of an image, a target and a distractor sentence.

focused on mood-related adjectives. In addition, as there is no clear one-to-one mapping between each adjective and a facial expression, we only test the broad opposition between rather positive mood (smiling or laughing face) and rather negative mood (all other facial expressions). The resulting set of pairings was: ("happy", "sad"), ("happy", "angry"), ("happy", "upset"), ("happy", "scared"), ("happy", "mad"), ("happy", "afraid"), ("happy", "surprised").

Similar to what we did in the case of verbs, we trimmed the sentences after the target adjective in order to obtain more minimal pairs in our test set.

3.2 Sentence-level Semantics

In addition to evaluating the learning of word-level semantics, here we evaluate some (rudimentary) aspects of sentence-level semantics, that is, semantic phenomena where the model needs to leverage *relationships* between words in the sentence to be able to arrive at the correct solution. We focused on the following three cases for which a reasonable number of minimal pairs could be found.

Adjective - Noun Dependency In this task, we test if the model is capable of recognizing not only a given adjective (e.g., sad), but also the person experiencing this emotion (i.e. Jenny or Mike). The procedure used here is similar to the one we used to test individual adjectives, except that here the picture contains not only the person experiencing the target emotion but also the other person who is experiencing a different emotion (cf. examples on bottom left in Figure 2).

Take the following example: "mike is happy" and its minimally different distractor sentence "mike is sad" associated with a picture where Mike is happy and Jenny is sad (see Figure 2). In order to choose the target sentence over the distractor, the model needs to associate happiness with Mike but not with Jenny. In fact, since both persons appear in the picture and the word Mike appears in both sentences, the model cannot succeed by relying only on the individual name "mike" (in which case performance would be at chance). Similarly, it cannot succeed only by relying on the contrast "happy" vs. "sad" since Mike is happy but Jenny is sad (in which case performance would also be at chance).

Moreover, it cannot succeed even if it combines information in the words "mike" and "happiness" without taking into account their dependency in the sentence (say, if it only relied on a bag-of-

for adjectives describing simple properties like color.

	Evaluation task	Accuracy	p (best)	p (worst)	Size
Word-level Semantics	Nouns: Persons	0.78 ± 0.05	< 0.001	< 0.01	50
	Nouns: Animals	0.93 ± 0.02	< 0.001	< 0.001	360
	Nouns: Objects	0.86 ± 0.01	< 0.001	< 0.001	372
	Verbs	0.83 ± 0.05	< 0.001	< 0.001	77
	Adjectives	0.64 ± 0.06	< 0.01	0.25	56
Sentence-level Semantics	Adjective-noun dependencies	0.57 ± 0.01	< 0.05	< 0.05	192
	Verb-noun dependencies	0.72 ± 0.04	< 0.001	< 0.001	400
	Semantic roles	0.75 ± 0.06	< 0.001	< 0.05	50

Table 1: Accuracy, p-values (for the best and for the worst performing model) and evaluation set size (in number of trials) for all semantic evaluation tasks. The high variance in terms of number of trials is caused by the limited availability of appropriate examples in the dataset for some tasks (cf. Footnote 10).

words representation) because both the sentence and distractor would be technically correct in that case. More precisely, the bag of words of the target sentence {"mike", "happy"} and of the distractor {"mike", "sad"} both describe the scene accurately since the latter contains Mike, Happy, and Sad. The model can only succeed if it correctly learns that happiness is associated with Mike in the picture, suggesting that the model learns "happy" as modifier/predicate for "mike" in the sentence.

To construct test trials for this case, we used the same adjectives as for the word-level adjective learning, but we searched for minimal pair sentences with a second child in the scene with the opposite mood compared the target child.

Verb - Noun Dependencies Similar to adjective-noun dependencies, we aim to evaluate learning of verbs as predicate for the nouns they occur with in the sentence. We use the same verbs as in the word-learning setup as well as trim the sentences after the verb. We look for images with a target and distractor child engaged in different actions and construct our test dataset based on these scenes (see example in Figure 2, bottom right).

Semantic Roles In this evaluation, we test the model's learning of semantic roles in an action that involves two participants. We test the model's learning of the mapping of nouns to their semantic roles (e.g., agent vs. patient/recipient).

We look for scenes where both children are present and engaged in an action. In this action, one of the children is the agent and the other one is the patient/recipient. For example, in the sentence "jenny is waving to mike" the agent is Jenny and the recipient is Mike (see Figure 2, top right). The distractor sentence is constructed by flipping the subject and object in the sentence, i.e., "mike is waving to jenny". To succeed in the task, the model should be able to recognize that Jenny, not Mike, is the one doing the waving. This task is a more challenging version of the verb-noun dependency we described above because, here, Jenny and Mike are not only both present in the picture, they are also both mentioned in the sentences. To succeed, the model has to differentiate between agent and recipient in the sentence. Here again, a null hypothesis that assumes a bag-of-word representation of the sentence would not succeed: We need to take into account how each noun *relates* to the verb.

As with all other evaluation tasks, for each test trial we have a corresponding counter-balanced trial where the semantic roles are flipped.

4 Results

To evaluate the learned semantic knowledge, we measure, for each task, the model's accuracy at rating the similarity of the image and the target sentence $\gamma(i, s_t)$ higher than the similarity to the distractor sentence $\gamma(i, s_d)$. We report both final accuracy scores after the model has converged as well as intermediate scores before convergence, which we take as a proxy for the learning trajectory.

To ensure reproducibility, we make the semantic evaluation sets as well as the source code for all experiments publicly available.[9]

4.1 Acquisition Scores

We ran the model 5 times with different random initializations and evaluate each converged model

[9] https://github.com/mitjanikolaus/cross-situational-learning-abstract-scenes

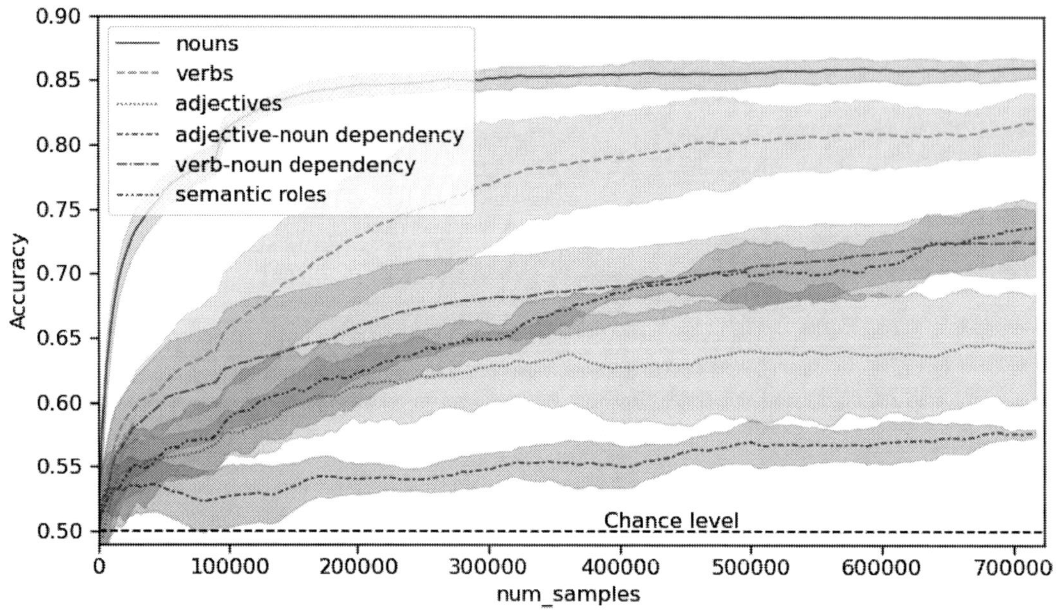

Figure 3: Learning trajectory of the models (mean over 5 runs, shaded areas show standard deviation). Accuracies for all noun categories were averaged. We calculated a rolling average over 30 data points to smooth the curve. The training set contains ~$50K$ examples, which means that the graph displays development over 15 epochs.

using the proposed tasks. Mean and standard deviation of the resulting accuracy scores can be found in Table 1. As some of the evaluation sets are rather small[10], we also performed binomial tests to evaluate whether the accuracy in the binary test is significantly above chance level (50%). We report the p-values' significance levels for the best and for the worst performing model[11] for each evaluation task.

The results show that the model has learned the semantics for most nouns very well. The score for verbs is also relatively high. As for adjectives, performance is only slightly above chance level and not always statistically significant, depending on the random initialization (e.g. the worst model is not significantly better than chance).

Regarding sentence-level semantics, the results suggest that the model has learned verb-noun dependencies and semantic roles relatively well. In contrast, Adjective-noun dependencies are not learned very well, which is not surprising given the poor adjective word-learning performance.

4.2 Acquisition Trajectories

In addition to the final evaluation scores, we are also interested in the *learning trajectory* of the model. We calculated the accuracy scores of the model every 100 batches. Figure 3 shows how the performance on the semantic evaluation tasks develops during the training of the model.

The model converged after having seen around 700K training examples (around 14 epochs). The trajectories show that the model first learns to discriminate nouns and only slightly later the verbs and then more complex sentence-level semantics.

5 Discussion

This paper dealt with the question of how children learn the word-world mapping in their native language. As a possible learning mechanism, we investigated XSL, that has received much attention in the literature. While laboratory studies on XSL have typically used very simplified learning situations to test if children are cognitively equipped to learn a toy language in an XSL fashion. The question remains as whether such a mechanism scales up to the learning of real languages where the learning situations can be highly ambiguous.

[10]Some evaluation sets are smaller than others due to the fact that all image-sentence pairs are taken directly from the test set and no new artificial images or sentences were created. This was done to ensure that the tests are performed using data that comes from the same distribution as the training set, i.e. data that the model has been exposed to.

[11]Each model corresponds to a different random initialization.

The novelty of our work is that we were interested not only in the scalability of XSL to learn from more naturalistic input, but also its scalability to the learning of various aspects of semantic knowledge. These include both the meanings of individual words (belonging to various categories such as nouns, adjectives, and verbs) and the meanings of higher level semantics such as the ability to map how words relate to each other in the sentence (e.g., subject vs. object) to the semantic roles of their respective referent in the world (e.g., agent vs. patient/recipient). We were able to perform these evaluations using a simple method inspired from the field of experimental child development and which has usually been used to test the same learning phenomena in children, i.e., the two-alternative forced choice task.

Using this evaluation method, we found that an XSL-based model trained on a large set of pictures and their descriptions was able to learn word-level meanings for nouns and verbs relatively well, but struggles with adjectives. Further, the model seems to learn some sentence-level semantics, especially verb-noun dependencies and semantic roles. Finally, concerning the learning trajectory, the model initially learns the semantics of nouns and only later the semantics of verbs and more complex sentence-level semantics.

Concerning word-level semantics, the fact that the model learns nouns better than (and before) the predicates (adjectives and verbs) resonates with findings in child development about the "noun bias" (Gentner, 1982; Bates et al., 1994; Frank et al., 2021). The model also learns verbs better than adjectives. However, we suspect this finding is caused by the limited availability of adjectives in the dataset.[12] In fact, the verb-related actions (e.g. "sitting" vs. "standing") were arguably more salient and easier to detect visually than adjective-related words ("happy" vs. "sad") which require a fine-grained detection of the facial expressions.

Concerning sentence-level semantics, the model performed surprisingly well on verb-noun dependency task where the model assigned a semantic role to one participant and on the similar but (arguably) more challenging task of assigning semantic roles to two participants. Further, the fact that the model shows a rather late onset of understanding of semantic roles, only after a set of nouns and verbs have been acquired (cf. Figure 3) mirrors children's developmental timeline. Indeed, children become able to assign semantic roles to nouns in a sentence correctly when they are around 2 years and 3 months old (Noble et al., 2011), at an age when they have already acquired a substantial vocabulary including many lexical categories such as nouns and verbs (Frank et al., 2021)

In this paper, we used artificial neural networks to study how properties the input can (ideally) inform the learning of semantics. Our modeling did not purport to account for the details of the cognitive processes that operate in children's minds nor did it take into account limitations in children's information-processing abilities. Thus, this work is best situated at the computational level of analysis (Marr, 1982), which is only a first step towards a deeper understanding of the precise algorithmic implementation. That said, we can speculate about the internal mechanisms used by the model to succeed in the tasks and about their potential insights into children's own learning. For example, it is very likely that the model leverages simple heuristics to recognize the agent in a sentence, e.g., it may have learned to associate the first appearing noun in the sentence to the agent of the action. Research on child language suggest that children also use such heuristics (e.g. Gertner and Fisher, 2012). This suggests that the model, like children, might use partial representations of sentence structure (i.e., rudimentary syntax) to guide semantic interpretation.

Exploiting structural properties of the input (e.g., order of words in a sentence) may be insightful when it mirrors genuine learning heuristics in children. However, a neural network model may also capitalize on idiosyncratic biases in the dataset (that do not reflect the natural distribution in the world) to achieve misleadingly high performance.[13] For example, a misleading bias in the linguistic input is if a certain noun (e.g., Jenny) occurs more frequently in the dataset as agent, leading the model to, say, systematically map "Jenny" to agent. Similarly, an example of a misleading bias in visual data is if the agent is always depicted on the left or right side of the image, leading the model to capitalize on this artificial shortcut.

In the current work, we controlled for linguistic biases by counter-balancing all testing trials. As for the visual bias, we ruled out some artificial bi-

[12]The data contained mostly mood-related adjectives.

[13]For example, Goyal et al. (2017) finds that grounded language models trained on a visual question answering task are exploiting linguistic biases of the training set.

ases such as the agent spatial order in the images. Indeed, investigation of our semantic roles test set shows that the agent occurs roughly equally on the right (52%) and left sides, which means that a model exploiting such a bias could only perform around chance level. There could be other biases we are not aware of and which require performing further controls. That said, this is an open question for all research using neural networks as models of human learning. More generally, our understanding of language acquisition would greatly benefit from further research on the interpretation of neural network learning, revealing the content of these black box models. This would allow us to tease apart genuine insights about realistic heuristics that could be used by children and artificial shortcuts that only reflect biases in the learning datasets.

In future work, we plan to study visual datasets with even more naturalistic scenes such as COCO (Lin et al., 2014). In this regard, maybe closer to our work is the study by Shekhar et al. (2017a,b) who used COCO to create a set of distractor captions to analyze whether vision and language models are sensitive to (maximally difficult) single-word replacements. Our goal is to go beyond these analysis to test specific semantic phenomena as we did here with the Abstract Scenes dataset. Another step towards more naturalistic input is the use speech input instead of text (Chrupała et al., 2017; Khorrami and Räsänen, 2021).

Finally, this work focused on testing how XSL scales up to natural language learning across many semantic tasks. Nevertheless, children's language learning involves more than the mere tracking of co-occurrence statistics: They are also social beings, they actively interact with more knowledgeable people around them and are able to learn from such interactions (Tomasello, 2010). Future modeling work should seek to integrate both statistical and social learning skills for a better understanding of early language learning.

Acknowledgements

We thank Mostafa Abdou, Jasper Bischofberger, Bissera Ivanova, Chiara Mazzocconi and the reviewers for their feedback and comments.

This work, carried out within the Labex BLRI (ANR-11-LABX-0036) and the Institut Convergence ILCB (ANR-16-CONV-0002), has benefited from support from the French government, managed by the French National Agency for Research (ANR) and the Excellence Initiative of Aix-Marseille University (A*MIDEX)

A Appendix

A.1 Model Details

The hyperparameters of the model were chosen on general best-practices and not any further tuned.

Minimum word frequency for vocab	5
Word Embeddings Size	100
Joint Embeddings Size	512
LSTM Hidden Layer Size	512
Optimizer	Adam
Initial Learning Rate	0.0001
Batch size	32
α (margin for loss term)	0.2

References

Stanislaw Antol, Aishwarya Agrawal, Jiasen Lu, Margaret Mitchell, Dhruv Batra, C Lawrence Zitnick, and Devi Parikh. 2015. Vqa: Visual question answering. In *Proceedings of the IEEE international conference on computer vision*, pages 2425–2433.

Elizabeth Bates, Virginia Marchman, Donna Thal, Larry Fenson, Philip Dale, J Steven Reznick, Judy Reilly, and Jeff Hartung. 1994. Developmental and stylistic variation in the composition of early vocabulary. *Journal of child language*, 21(1):85–123.

Elika Bergelson and Daniel Swingley. 2012. At 6–9 months, human infants know the meanings of many common nouns. *Proceedings of the National Academy of Sciences*, 109(9):3253–3258.

Grzegorz Chrupała, Lieke Gelderloos, and Afra Alishahi. 2017. Representations of language in a model of visually grounded speech signal. In *Proceedings of the 55th Annual Meeting of the Association for Computational Linguistics (Volume 1: Long Papers)*, pages 613–622.

Grzegorz Chrupała, Ákos Kádár, and Afra Alishahi. 2015. Learning language through pictures. In *Proceedings of the 53rd Annual Meeting of the Association for Computational Linguistics and the 7th International Joint Conference on Natural Language Processing (Volume 2: Short Papers)*, pages 112–118, Beijing, China. Association for Computational Linguistics.

Fartash Faghri, David J. Fleet, Jamie Ryan Kiros, and Sanja Fidler. 2018. VSE++: improving visual-semantic embeddings with hard negatives. In *British Machine Vision Conference 2018, BMVC 2018, Newcastle, UK, September 3-6, 2018*, page 12. BMVA Press.

Afsaneh Fazly, Afra Alishahi, and Suzanne Stevenson. 2010. A probabilistic computational model of cross-situational word learning. *Cognitive Science*, 34(6):1017–1063.

Michael C Frank, Mika Braginsky, Daniel Yurovsky, and Virginia A Marchman. 2021. *Variability and consistency in early language learning: The Wordbank project*. MIT Press.

Michael C Frank, Noah D Goodman, and Joshua B Tenebaum. 2007. A bayesian framework for cross-situational word-learning.

Dedre Gentner. 1982. Why nouns are learned before verbs: Linguistic relativity versus natural partitioning. *Center for the Study of Reading Technical Report; no. 257*.

Yael Gertner and Cynthia Fisher. 2012. Predicted errors in children's early sentence comprehension. *Cognition*, 124(1):85–94.

Yash Goyal, Tejas Khot, Douglas Summers-Stay, Dhruv Batra, and Devi Parikh. 2017. Making the v in vqa matter: Elevating the role of image understanding in visual question answering. In *Proceedings of the IEEE Conference on Computer Vision and Pattern Recognition*, pages 6904–6913.

Kaiming He, Xiangyu Zhang, Shaoqing Ren, and Jian Sun. 2016. Deep residual learning for image recognition. In *Proceedings of the IEEE conference on computer vision and pattern recognition*, pages 770–778.

Sepp Hochreiter and Jürgen Schmidhuber. 1997. Long short-term memory. *Neural computation*, 9(8):1735–1780.

Micah Hodosh, Peter Young, and Julia Hockenmaier. 2013. Framing image description as a ranking task: Data, models and evaluation metrics. *Journal of Artificial Intelligence Research*, 47:853–899.

Drew A Hudson and Christopher D Manning. 2019. Gqa: A new dataset for real-world visual reasoning and compositional question answering. In *Proceedings of the IEEE/CVF Conference on Computer Vision and Pattern Recognition*, pages 6700–6709.

Ákos Kádár, Afra Alishahi, and Grzegorz Chrupała. 2015. Learning word meanings from images of natural scenes. *Traitement Automatique des Langues*, 55(3).

Akos Kádár, Grzegorz Chrupała, and Afra Alishahi. 2017. Representation of linguistic form and function in recurrent neural networks. *Computational Linguistics*, 43(4):761–780.

Andrej Karpathy and Li Fei-Fei. 2015. Deep visual-semantic alignments for generating image descriptions. In *Proceedings of the IEEE conference on computer vision and pattern recognition*, pages 3128–3137.

Khazar Khorrami and Okko Räsänen. 2021. Can phones, syllables, and words emerge as side-products of cross-situational audiovisual learning? - a computational investigation.

Angeliki Lazaridou, Grzegorz Chrupała, Raquel Fernández, and Marco Baroni. 2016. Multimodal semantic learning from child-directed input. In *Knight K, Nenkova A, Rambow O, editors. Proceedings of the 2016 Conference of the North American Chapter of the Association for Computational Linguistics: Human Language Technologies; 2016 Jun 12-17; San Diegio, California. Stroudsburg (PA): Association for Computational Linguistics; 2016. p. 387–92*. ACL (Association for Computational Linguistics).

Tsung-Yi Lin, Michael Maire, Serge Belongie, James Hays, Pietro Perona, Deva Ramanan, Piotr Dollár, and C Lawrence Zitnick. 2014. Microsoft coco: Common objects in context. In *European conference on computer vision*, pages 740–755. Springer.

David Marr. 1982. Vision: A computational investigation into the human representation and processing of visual information.

Danny Merkx and Stefan L Frank. 2019. Learning semantic sentence representations from visually grounded language without lexical knowledge. *Natural Language Engineering*, 25(4):451–466.

Claire H Noble, Caroline F Rowland, and Julian M Pine. 2011. Comprehension of argument structure and semantic roles: Evidence from english-learning children and the forced-choice pointing paradigm. *Cognitive science*, 35(5):963–982.

Steven Pinker. 1989. *Learnability and Cognition: The Acquisition of Argument Structure*. MIT press.

Bryan A Plummer, Liwei Wang, Chris M Cervantes, Juan C Caicedo, Julia Hockenmaier, and Svetlana Lazebnik. 2015. Flickr30k entities: Collecting region-to-phrase correspondences for richer image-to-sentence models. In *Proceedings of the IEEE international conference on computer vision*, pages 2641–2649.

Willard Van Orman Quine. 1960. *Word and object*. MIT Press.

Olga Russakovsky, Jia Deng, Hao Su, Jonathan Krause, Sanjeev Satheesh, Sean Ma, Zhiheng Huang, Andrej Karpathy, Aditya Khosla, Michael Bernstein, et al. 2015. Imagenet large scale visual recognition challenge. *International journal of computer vision*, 115(3):211–252.

Ravi Shekhar, Sandro Pezzelle, Aurélie Herbelot, Moin Nabi, Enver Sangineto, and Raffaella Bernardi. 2017a. Vision and language integration: Moving beyond objects. In *IWCS 2017—12th International Conference on Computational Semantics—Short papers*.

Ravi Shekhar, Sandro Pezzelle, Yauhen Klimovich, Aurélie Herbelot, Moin Nabi, Enver Sangineto, and Raffaella Bernardi. 2017b. Foil it! find one mismatch between image and language caption. In *Proceedings of the 55th Annual Meeting of the Association for Computational Linguistics (Volume 1: Long Papers)*, pages 255–265.

Michael Tomasello. 2010. *Origins of human communication*. MIT press.

Wai Keen Vong and Brenden M. Lake. 2020. Learning word-referent mappings and concepts from raw inputs. In *Proceedings of the 42th Annual Meeting of the Cognitive Science Society - Developing a Mind: Learning in Humans, Animals, and Machines, CogSci 2020, virtual, July 29 - August 1, 2020*. cognitivesciencesociety.org.

Wai Keen Vong, Emin Orhan, and Brenden Lake. 2021. Cross-situational word learning from naturalistic headcam data. In *34th CUNY Conference on Human Sentence Processing*.

Mark Yatskar, Luke Zettlemoyer, and Ali Farhadi. 2016. Situation recognition: Visual semantic role labeling for image understanding. In *Proceedings of the IEEE conference on computer vision and pattern recognition*, pages 5534–5542.

Chen Yu and Dana H Ballard. 2007. A unified model of early word learning: Integrating statistical and social cues. *Neurocomputing*, 70(13-15):2149–2165.

Chen Yu and Linda B Smith. 2007. Rapid word learning under uncertainty via cross-situational statistics. *Psychological science*, 18(5):414–420.

C Lawrence Zitnick and Devi Parikh. 2013. Bringing semantics into focus using visual abstraction. In *Proceedings of the IEEE Conference on Computer Vision and Pattern Recognition*, pages 3009–3016.

C Lawrence Zitnick, Devi Parikh, and Lucy Vanderwende. 2013. Learning the visual interpretation of sentences. In *Proceedings of the IEEE International Conference on Computer Vision*, pages 1681–1688.

Representation and Pre-Activation of Lexical-Semantic Knowledge in Neural Language Models

Steven Derby, Paul Miller, Barry Devereux
Institute of Electronics, Communication and Information Technology ECIT
Queen's University Belfast, United Kingdom
{sderby02, p.miller, b.devereux}@qub.ac.uk

Abstract

Neural network language models have the ability to capture the contextualised meanings of words in a sentence by dynamically evolving a representation of the linguistic input in a manner evocative of human language comprehension. While researchers have been able to analyse whether key linguistic regularities are adequately characterised by these evolving representations, determining whether they activate lexico-semantic knowledge similarly to humans remains challenging. In this paper, we perform a systematic analysis of how closely the intermediate layers from LSTM and transformer language models correspond to human semantic knowledge. Furthermore, in order to make more meaningful comparisons with theories of human language comprehension in psycholinguistics, we focus on two key stages where the meaning of a particular target word may arise: immediately before the word's presentation to the model (comparable to *forward inferencing*), and immediately after the word token has been input into the network. Our results indicate that the transformer models are better at capturing semantic knowledge relating to lexical concepts, both during word prediction and when retention is required.

1 Introduction

A wide variety of Natural Language Processing (NLP) tasks have been improved dramatically by the introduction of LSTM (Hochreiter and Schmidhuber, 1997) and transformer-based (Vaswani et al., 2017) neural language models, which can encode the meanings of sentences in such a way that facilitates a range of language tasks (Bengio et al., 2003; Peters et al., 2018; Radford et al., 2018; Dai et al., 2019). Furthermore, both recurrent and transformer networks have been shown to capture a broad range of semantic phenomena and syntactic structure (Dyer et al., 2016; Linzen et al., 2016; Bernardy and Lappin, 2017; Gulordava et al., 2018; Marvin and Linzen, 2018; Lin et al., 2019; Liu et al., 2019; Hewitt and Manning, 2019; Tenney et al., 2019a). Although such models clearly learn aspects of lexical semantics, it remains unclear whether and how these networks capture semantic features associated with conceptual meaning. Some work has demonstrated that word embeddings do reflect conceptual knowledge captured by property norming studies (Rubinstein et al., 2015; Collell and Moens, 2016; Lucy and Gauthier, 2017; Derby et al., 2018), in which human participants produce verbalisable properties for concepts, such as *is green* or *is an amphibian* for concepts such as FROG (McRae et al., 2005; Devereux et al., 2014). Such features correspond to *stereotypic tacit assumptions* (Prince, 1978); common-sense knowledge we have about the real world. There is some evidence that language models implicitly encode such knowledge (Da and Kusai, 2019; Weir et al., 2020); however, coverage of different types of knowledge may be inconsistent, with evidence to suggest that these models fail to capture some types of semantic knowledge such as visual perceptual information (Sommerauer and Fokkens, 2018; Sommerauer, 2020), as well as questions about the completeness of such empirical studies (Fagarasan et al., 2015; Bulat et al., 2016; Silberer, 2017; Derby et al., 2019). In general, there has been only limited work that attempts to investigate whether these neural language models activate lexico-semantic knowledge similarly to humans, further restricted by the fact that such knowledge probing is only performed on latent representations that have received the target concept, ignoring theories of language comprehension and acquisition that emphasise the importance of prediction (Graesser et al., 1994; Dell and Chang, 2014; Kuperberg and Jaeger, 2016).

In this paper, we contribute to the analysis of neural language models by evaluating latent semantic knowledge present in the activation patterns extracted from their intermediate layers. By performing a layer-by-layer analysis, we can uncover

Proceedings of the Workshop on Cognitive Modeling and Computational Linguistics, pages 211–221
Online Event, June 10, 2021.

how the network composes such meaning as the information propagates through the network, eventually emerging as a rich representation of semantic features that facilitates conditional next word prediction, which is directly dependent on the past knowledge. We perform our layer probing analysis at two temporal modalities. That is, we investigate the hidden layer activations of the NNLMs both **before** the concept word occurs (which facilitates next word prediction), and **after** the concept word has been explicitly given to the model. In this way, we determine how richly these latent representations capture real-world perceptual and encyclopaedic knowledge commonly associated with human conceptual meaning.

2 Related Work

The recent popularity of interpretability in NLP has resulted in strong progress on understanding both recurrent (Alishahi et al., 2019) and transformer-based networks (Rogers et al., 2020). A number of these studies rely on probing techniques, where supervised models are trained to predict specific linguistic phenomena from model activations (Adi et al., 2016; Wallace et al., 2019; Tenney et al., 2019b; Hewitt and Liang, 2019).

There exists some work that analyses semantic knowledge in such networks, though to date this has been more limited than investigations of syntax. Koppula et al. (2018) focused on the recurrent layers of LSTM and GRU networks and attempted to interpret their semantic content by using a set of decoders to predict the previous network inputs. Ettinger (2020) devised a set of psycholinguistic diagnostic tasks to evaluate language understanding in BERT, demonstrating that some phenomena such as semantic role labelling and event knowledge are well-inferred, though others such as negation are less so. Similar to our work, Ethayarajh (2019) mined sentences with words in context to demonstrate that context representations are highly anisotropic, while Bommasani et al. (2020) built static word embeddings from contextual representations using pooling methods, analysing their performance on semantic similarity benchmarks.

Language models have also been successfully employed for predicting activation patterns in the brain during human language comprehension (Jain and Huth, 2018; Toneva and Wehbe, 2019). Such work is particularly relevant from the perspective of predictive coding theories of human language comprehension (Kuperberg and Jaeger, 2016), which posits that high-level representations of an unfolding utterance facilitate active prediction of subsequent lexical content in the sentence. Neurolinguistic studies provide evidence that such predictions can be of wordform identity (DeLong et al., 2005), or of the semantic features that are expected for the upcoming word (for example, whether the upcoming word is animate or not; Wang et al., 2020).

3 Neural Language Models

Due to the compatibility issues, we limit our investigation to left-to-right language models that are trained to perform conditional next word prediction, as other SOTA models such as **Bert** (Devlin et al., 2018) fail to capture the desired criterion that facilities similar mechanisms in language comprehension. For the LSTM-based network, we make use of a very large-scale and influential neural language model developed by Jozefowicz et al. (Jozefowicz et al., 2016), which we refer to as **JLM**[1]. The model's architecture consists of character-level embeddings with CNNs, followed by a two-layer LSTM with projection layers to reduce dimensionality and a final linear layer with softmax activation. The vocabulary of the output layer consists of 800000 words, and the model is trained using the One Billion Word corpus (Chelba et al., 2013). For the transformer-based model, we make use of the **GPT-2** (345M) model (Radford et al., 2019), which consists of 24 multi-head attention layers.

3.1 De-Contextualising Representations

There are several problems that emerge when looking to compare concrete conceptual representations of meaning with these neural layer activations. The first is that representations from these latent layers are highly contextualised, which may make it difficult to recover semantic information about a particular concept. The second problem is that recovering a pre-target representation is challenging since it requires contextual information to be supplied to the network before the target word occurs. For our work, we follow a similar approach to Bommasani et al. (2020), and mine a number of sentences from a corpus of text where each target word occurs and then extract representations from each layer of the network **before** and **after** the words are presented. For this, we choose a

[1] `https://github.com/tensorflow/models/tree/archive/research/lm_1b`

predefined set of target words which are based on the overlap of words in the **JLM** vocabulary and several intrinsic evaluation benchmarks which are employed in the analyses below. We then sample the training corpus for up to 500 sentences for each target, selecting sentences in which the target word occurred in any position except the start of the sentence. By analysing how the representations perform on the semantic benchmarks, we can infer how these language models compose meaning over the layers of the network.

3.2 Feature Pooling

To construct these decontextualized representations, we first compute a hidden state from each of our sentences, and then aggregate them into a single static vector, both at the position of the target word and immediately before. More formally, for each word $w \in W$, where W is our lexicon, we retrieve a set of K sentences $\{S_1, S_2, \ldots S_k\}$ from the corpus with corresponding timepoints $T = \{t_1, t_2 \ldots t_k\}$ denoting the position of the word w in the sentences, such that $S_i[t_i] = w$ for $1 \leq i \leq K$. Let f_L be the function that maps each sentence fragment to a contextual representation from the model f for each layer L in the network. We construct our word-level representation *before* and *after* the word w occurs at layer L as follows:

$$\text{before}[w]_L = \frac{1}{K} \sum_{i=1}^{K} f_L(S)[t_{i-1}]$$

$$\text{after}[w]_L = \frac{1}{K} \sum_{i=1}^{K} f_L(S)[t_i]$$

This gives us two sets of word embedding vectors for each layer in each network, one set built from activations immediately before the target words and one built from activations immediately after the target words. Since the context differs depending on the sentence, the aggregation performed in the calculations above should preserve only the information associated with the target word. As the model is tasked with predicting the word w, the vectors from the **before** timestep should contain some semantic information relevant to the target word, even if the word has not been explicitly given to the network.

In the case of GPT-2, input tokens are determined using byte pair encodings, and a given word will correspond to several input units in this encoding. For target words that consist of a number of smaller units that combine into the word, we average the representation over all these positions for the **after** representations. For the **before** representations, we take the token immediately before the target word. In the results that follow, we refer to the two sets of embedding vectors for language model M and layer L using the naming convention ***M*[*L*]-before** and ***M*[*L*]-after**. For example, for GPT-2, the word vectors for the fifth multi-head attention layer just before the target word is presented to the network would be **GPT2[5]-before**.

Note that while LSTMs accumulate a representation of the unfolding utterance at each timestep, this is not entirely true for transformers, which directly combine information from all previous words in the sequence at every layer of the network, guided by attention. In our work, we only care about how the semantic information of the network evolves when it must predict the target word and immediately after.

4 Evaluation Tasks

For our empirical analysis, we first analyse these layers on classic intrinsic benchmarks that determine their ability to explain human semantic judgments scores on word association, to first determine how well these networks capture the semantic content of the word. We then probe these layers to determine whether they capture a rich set of semantic features related to upcoming concepts and whether such representations are retained by the network for functional use on the prediction task.

4.1 Semantic Similarity Benchmarks

Semantic similarity benchmarks, where a set of word pairs are scored by human annotators based on how similar they are, can be used to determine how correlated word pair distances from a set of embedding vectors are with human judgements of similarity for the same words. For the embedding vectors (from each network and network layer), cosine similarity can be used to determine how similar the word vectors are, and these cosine similarities can then be compared with the human judgements using Spearman correlation. Of course, the notion of similarity that informs human judgements is highly dependent on a number of factors such as context, the stimulus set of word pairs, and the instructions given to the human raters (Batchkarov et al., 2016). For this reason, we make use of a number of benchmarks which can be partitioned into two types of relationships, known as *semantic similarity* and *semantic relatedness*. For semantic relatedness, we use **WordSim353-rel** (Agirre et al., 2009) and **MEN** (Bruni et al., 2012), where a high score between word pairs indicates a greater chance of occurring in the same sentence with some syntactic relation (for example "coffee" and "cup"). For semantic similarity, we use **WordSim353-sim** (Agirre et al., 2009) and **SimLex999** (Hill et al., 2015), where a high score between word pairs indicates a high overlap in semantic attributes or replaceability in a sentence (for example "coffee" and "tea"). Though it does not clearly fall into either the similarity or relatedness categories, we also include the original version of the WordSim judgements, **WordSim353** (Finkelstein et al., 2001). Evaluations were performed using the Vecto-ai python package (Rogers et al., 2018).

4.2 Neural Activation Similarity

As an extension to these results, we also evaluate how reliable the vector representations from each layer of the networks are in terms of their ability to predict brain imaging data gathered from participants viewing a set of concept words. In this analysis, we use BrainBench (Xu et al., 2016)[2], a semantic evaluation platform that includes fMRI and MEG neuroimaging data from humans for 60 concept words. This benchmark evaluates how well the semantic models can make predictions about the patterns of neural activations observed in the human participants. For a set of words V, we calculate two pairwise word correlation matrices $M_D, M_B \in R^{|V|\times|V|}$ for a distributional semantic model (D) and the brain imaging data (B). We then perform a 2 vs. 2 test between M_D and M_B, where, for all pairs of words $w_1, w_2 \in V$, we count how often the similarity structure observed for D agrees with B, i.e. how often

$$r(M_D(w_1), M_B(w_1)) + r(M_D(w_2), M_B(w_2)) \\ > r(M_D(w_1), M_B(w_2)) + r(M_D(w_2), M_B(w_1))$$

where r is Pearson's correlation and $M(w_1)$ and $M(w_2)$ denote the rows of values corresponding to the concepts w_1 and w_2, omitting the columns that correspond to the correlation between w_1 and w_2. The final score is the proportion of positive cases across all word pairs, with 0.5 indicating chance. Intuitively, this is a measure of how well the similarity profile of the semantic model matches the similarity profile of the brain data.

4.3 Human Property Knowledge

Next, we determine how well the embedding vectors for each network and layer capture commonsense aspects of meaning reflected in conceptual models from cognitive psychology. We achieve this by using probes to determine whether explicit lexico-semantic knowledge from human-derived property norms can be reliably decoded from these embeddings. For example, for the concept APPLE, can we predict from the embedding vector whether human-elicited properties of that concept such as *is-round* or *grows-on-trees* are true? For this analysis, we make use of a dataset of human-elicited property knowledge (the CSLB norms; Devereux et al., 2014)[3], which lists semantic properties for 638 concept words. These semantic properties are partitioned into five distinct categories, which characterise the different types of information they represent: **visual** (e.g. *is-green*; *is-round*), **functional** (e.g. *is-eaten*; *used-for-cutting*), **taxonomic** (e.g. *is-a-fruit*; *is-a-tool*), **encyclopedic** (e.g. *has-vitamins*; *uses-fuel*), and **other-perceptual** (e.g. *is-tasty*; *is-loud*). While property norming studies provide an insight into the types of information characterised by human conceptual representations, supported by human agreement on feature attributes, it should be noted that they are not a literal description of human lexical-semantic representation (Barsalou, 2003).

4.3.1 Probing methodology

For the probing analysis, we fit a number of $L2$-regularised logistic regression models, in order to predict whether or not a semantic feature is decodable from our embedding vectors, largely following previous work (Collell and Moens, 2016; Lucy and Gauthier, 2017; Derby et al., 2018). Due to the small sample size, each model uses class weight balancing and decodability is scored using the F1 score over 5 cross-validation folds. More specifically, we preprocess the CSLB dataset to exclude features occurring for fewer than five words. For each feature, we then partition the concepts into five folds using stratified sampling and perform 5-fold cross-validation on each feature.

Due to the high likelihood of overfitting, we also regularise each logistic regression by adding λ

[2] http://www.langlearnlab.cs.uvic.ca/brainbench/

[3] https://cslb.psychol.cam.ac.uk/propnorms

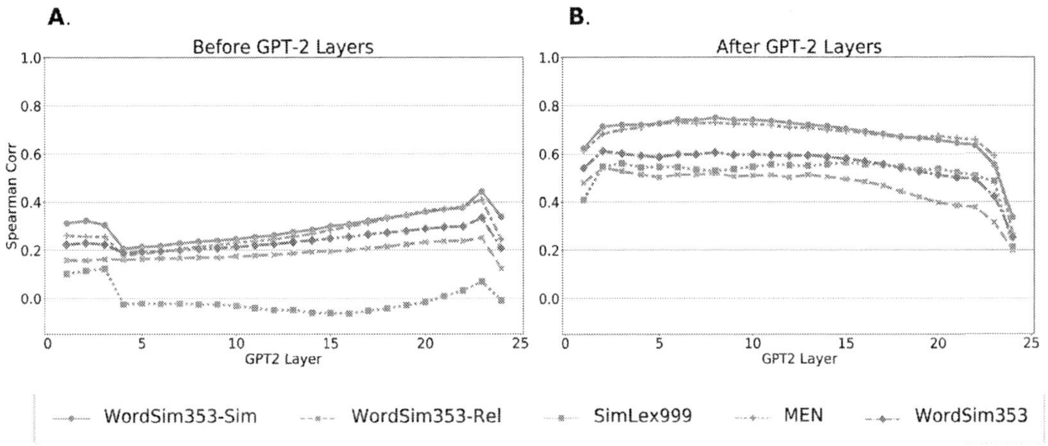

Figure 1: Results (Spearman correlations) for the **before** (on the left) and **after** word embedding vectors across all 24 **GPT-2** layers.

Model	WS353-Rel	WS353-Sim	WS353	SimLex999	MEN	fMRI	MEG
LSTM-based Representations							
JLM[1]-before	0.198	0.496	0.338	0.151	0.353	0.636	0.625
JLM[2]-before	0.314	0.549	0.428	0.115	0.423	0.650	0.638
JLM[1]-after	0.444	0.709	0.557	0.409	0.644	**0.681**	**0.701**
JLM[2]-after	0.280	0.580	0.414	0.423	0.544	0.669	0.692
Transformer-based Representations							
GPT2[Best]-before	0.251 [23]	0.439 [23]	0.334 [23]	0.124 [3]	0.409 [23]	0.627 [23]	0.648 [23]
GPT2[Best]-after	**0.544 [2]**	**0.749 [8]**	**0.612 [2]**	**0.561 [3]**	**0.730 [6]**	0.673 [14]	0.696 [16]

Table 1: Results (Spearman correlations) for each embedding model on the word similarity benchmarks, along with BrainBench results (accuracy) for the fMRI and MEG data. For GPT-2, we include the best performance across all 24 layers from the **before** and **after** representations (best layer number given in [brackets]).

times the $L2$ norm of the coefficient weights to the loss, where λ is a scaling parameter. Since we want to predict each individual property, we determine what value of λ to use by first performing 5-fold cross-validation for each property over a range of potential values, and choosing the best for each feature.

To calculate a decodability score for each feature, we run 5-fold cross-validation using the best λ value for each feature, for which we obtain the final F1 score on the predictions from the test folds. Furthermore, we repeat this cross-validation process three times and take the average score over each run. We note that just because a linear model does not predict the presence of a property does not mean that it is not encoded in the representation (Collell and Moens, 2016). Nevertheless, linear read-out from model activation patterns (and brain activation patterns) remains a useful tool for determining the presence of high-level information such as linguistic structure in those representations (Hewitt and Liang, 2019).

5 Results

5.1 Semantic Similarity Benchmarks

The similarity benchmark results are displayed in Table 1 and Figure 1. For both JLM and GPT-2, the word vector representations computed **after** the target word has been presented as an input token to the model perform better in comparison to when the network must predict the target word (the **before** representations). This result is not surprising, since in the **after** scenario the models have access to the target word itself. Nevertheless, we still see high correlations for the **before** representations for most models and layers, indicating that the representational state of the language models immediately before the target word reflect semantic content of the to-be-predicted word. GPT-2 produces the strongest correlations with human similarity judge-

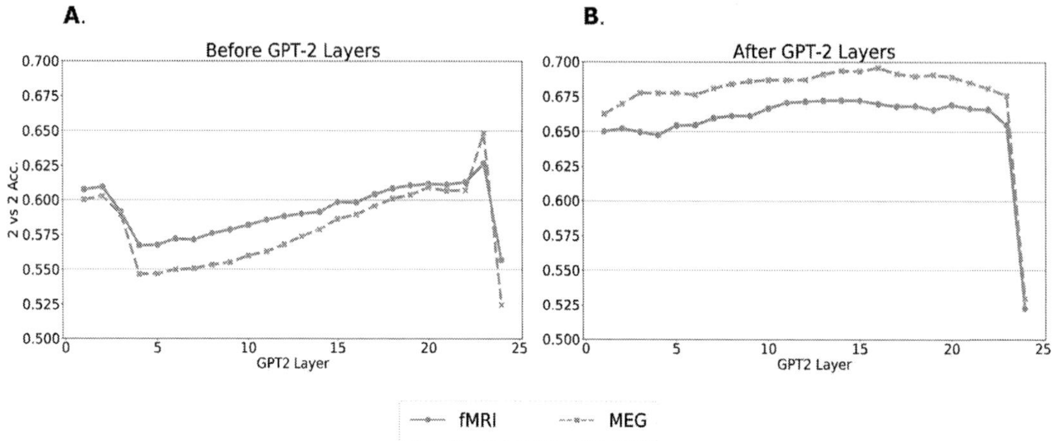

Figure 2: Results (accuracy %) on BrainBench for the MEG and fMRI data for each **before** (on the left) and **after** (on the right) word embedding models for each of the 24 layer of **GPT-2**. Scores are measured using accuracy from a $2vs.\ 2$ test, with a score of 0.5 indicating random chance (see text).

ments overall (particularly in earlier layers of the **after** representations; Fig. 1B). Interestingly, JLM outperforms GPT-2 in how accurately it predicts the brain data, perhaps due to a more cognitively plausible neural architecture that incrementally integrates information over the course of a sentence.

Focusing on the **before** representations, we see that the **JLM-before** semantic representations tend to perform better than the **GPT2-before** representations. This is likely because the LSTM is directly trained on the sampled sentences, which produces a lower perplexity measure than the transformer network, and thus it yields more accurate predictions about the target word. Comparing the **before** representations from different layers in each model, we see that JLM better represents semantic information in the second of its two layers, while for GPT-2 the results are more complex, though later layers are generally better, with the second last layer (23) being best for most evaluations. For both models, then, the upper layers tend to have the best overall semantic representations of the upcoming target word, which follows from the fact that the upper layers directly feed into predictions about the upcoming word in the language modelling task, with the models reflecting the predicted semantic content of that word.

When the target word is available to the model (the **after** representations), we would expect the network to represent meaningful information about the concept, which is why this approach is the most common method for building contextual representations. Our results support this notion, since the **after** representations consistently outperform the **before** representations, on both the word similarity and brain imaging data (see Fig. 2 for the GPT-2 BrainBench results). Notably, **JLM[1]-after** outperforms **JLM[2]-after**, since the activation patterns from the second layer should aim to predict the next word in the sequence (i.e. the word following the target word). Similarly, the **GPT2-after** representations retain semantic information of the word quite well for all but the final layer, with early layers performing well in the semantic similarity evaluations (Fig. 1B and Fig. 2B). **GPT2[24]-after** experiences a dramatic loss in performance, similar to what is observed for the **JLM[2]-after** representations.

Overall, this pattern or results supports the hypothesis that later layers of the language models best reflect semantic information about the to-be-predicted word, whilst earlier layers best reflect semantic information about the just-presented word, though all layers in both models reflect this information to some extent. In the next section, we investigate in more detail the specific kinds of semantic knowledge that is available in different layers of the models.

5.2 Semantic Feature Decoding

The results on the property decoding task are presented in Table 2 and Figure 3. Overall, we see that the GPT-2 layers encode more information about common sense property knowledge than the JLM layers, particularly in the **after** representations.

Focusing on the **before** representations we see

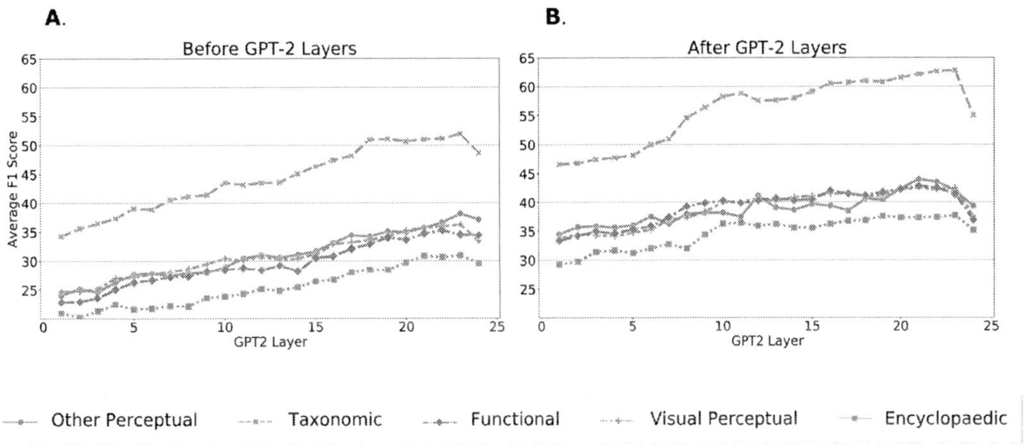

Figure 3: Graph which displays the average cross-validation F1 scores $\times 100$ for each **before** (on the left) and **after** (on the right) transformer-based representations from each layer of **GPT-2**.

Model	Encyclo.	Functional	Taxonomic	Visual	Other Perceptual	Overall
LSTM-based Representations						
JLM[1]-before	21.74	24.92	42.31	29.48	28.91	28.56
JLM[2]-before	26.41	30.22	47.75	32.66	33.39	32.85
JLM[1]-after	33.21	38.29	60.71	38.44	36.83	40.01
JLM[2]-after	33.86	39.06	**62.82**	39.32	40.01	41.14
Transformer-based Representations						
GPT2[Best]-before	30.94 [23]	35.25 [23]	51.95 [23]	36.25 [23]	38.12 [23]	38.35 [23]
GPT2[Best]-after	**37.69 [23]**	**42.74 [21]**	62.79 [23]	**42.47 [23]**	**43.98 [23]**	**45.72 [21]**

Table 2: Average cross-validation F1 scores $\times 100$ for each model and for each of the five property classes. For GPT-2, we include the best performance for each property type across all layers.

that GPT-2 tends to capture more knowledge about conceptual properties than JLM. Most notably, compared to JLM, the GPT-2 model does better at encoding knowledge related to attributive properties (i.e. non-taxonomic properties), which tend to be much more difficult to capture (Rubinstein et al., 2015). Both models show better property decoding performance in the later **before** layers. As these properties are related to conceptual knowledge plausibly associated with the upcoming word, it makes sense that the embedding vectors converge on some particular space related to the semantic restrictions on the upcoming word, which is particularly reflected in the case of taxonomic properties.

Turning to the **after** representations, we see that property knowledge seems to be best reflected in the upper layers of both language models. This is a particularly interesting result, as previous work has demonstrated that the lower layers contain more explicit information relating to the target word such as part-of-speech (Peters et al., 2018) and word association (see Section 5.1). Furthermore, while the **JLM-after** and **GPT2-after** representations perform similarly when predicting taxonomic features, GPT-2 does much better at capturing perceptual, functional, and encyclopedic knowledge. The results indicate that the GPT-2 representation appear to narrow the gap between taxonomic and attributive properties, which distributional models have historically struggled to accomplish. Finally, the network seems to retain and improve performance as we move through the layers.

6 Discussion

6.1 Last Layer Performance

First, we wish to discuss why there is a consistent loss in performance from the representations constructed from the final layer of the network, which is notable given the widespread use of the final layer for transfer learning. To better understand the results for the **GPT2-before** embedding vectors on our evaluation tasks, consider the work of Ethayarajh (2019), who demonstrated that the layers of GPT-2 become more context-specific as we move through the network, more so than LSTM-based networks such as *Elmo*. In particular, Ethayarajh (2019) investigated *intra-sentence similarity*, which measures the average cosine distance between the individual word representations and the sentence representation. In their work, sentence representations were constructed by averaging over the hidden states from all time steps in the sentence, which is similar to the **before** representations (averaging the vectors across sentences given the target word's position). They showed that, when adjusted for anisotropy, the intra-sentence similarity of GPT-2 tends to decrease until layer 4, before uniformly increasing again through the rest of layers. Hence, word representations from different time steps tend to be highly dissimilar from one another by the nature of the network, which demonstrates one limitation of feature pooling. While a limitation, we also note that this approach works well in general for building static word embeddings, supported by previous work (Bommasani et al., 2020)

6.2 Semantic Knowledge

From our initial results on the human judgement benchmarks, we can infer at what layers of the network semantic information about the concept is most representative. When the network must perform next word prediction on the concept, we see that the final layer is most representative, whilst after the word has been given to the network, we see that the semantic information about the concept decreases through as we move through the network. Such a result is not surprising as the network must gradually accumulate information that may be related to the next possible word, focusing less on the previous concept. Generally, the transformer outperforms the LSTM model after the network has received the concept in the lower layers, though the LSTM contained more representative information about the concept during next word prediction.

When probing for human conceptual knowledge, we see that the transformers perform better than the LSTMs, with the transformers performing quite well at predicting attributive features in comparison to taxonomic properties, for which there has historically been a large gap in performance (Rubinstein et al., 2015). These results may indicate that context, for which transformers produce highly contextualised representations (Ethayarajh, 2019), plays an important role in representing conceptual knowledge such as that reflected in semantic property norms. The most interesting result from our investigation is that the semantic knowledge is not forgotten in the later layers of both LSTM and transformer-based networks after receiving the concept, unlike the previous results. These findings may indicate that these networks gradually accumulate such knowledge as the sentence is processed in order to facilitate anticipation of the future. Such ideas have recently been proposed by Ferreira and Chantavarin (2018) who suggested that, in order to reconcile the differences between earlier models of integration (building associations between new concepts and previous information (Kintsch and Van Dijk, 1978; Gernsbacher, 1991)) with more recent theories of prediction, we should replace the notion of *Prediction* with *Preparedness*. Instead of considering direct prediction of future lexical items, which is usually rare (Luke and Christianson, 2016), the authors suggest that given some new information which is processed along with the past information with appropriate background knowledge, a new rich semantic representation is produced containing informative semantic features that facilitate anticipation. Our results indicate that these language models may similarly build and retain rich semantic representations that aid the network in its learning objective (conditional next word prediction).

7 Conclusion

In this paper, we present a novel approach to gaining a better understanding of the kinds of semantic information encoded within the layers of large-scale language models. Our analysis allows us to peer inside the hidden state representations of neural language models, and examine how semantically relevant information is encoded in each layer of the networks. We examine the language models on their ability to capture semantic meaning from two perspectives, when the network is predicting the target word, and when the target word is the most recent input. The results demonstrate that the transformer model is much better at capturing attributive features than the LSTM model, whilst both models are able to retain rich semantic representations of the concept after the concept has been given to the network.

References

Yossi Adi, Einat Kermany, Yonatan Belinkov, Ofer Lavi, and Yoav Goldberg. 2016. Fine-grained analysis of sentence embeddings using auxiliary prediction tasks. *arXiv preprint arXiv:1608.04207*.

Eneko Agirre, Enrique Alfonseca, Keith Hall, Jana Kravalova, Marius Paşca, and Aitor Soroa. 2009. A study on similarity and relatedness using distributional and wordnet-based approaches. In *Proceedings of Human Language Technologies: The 2009 Annual Conference of the North American Chapter of the Association for Computational Linguistics*, pages 19–27. Association for Computational Linguistics.

Afra Alishahi, Grzegorz Chrupała, and Tal Linzen. 2019. Analyzing and interpreting neural networks for NLP: A report on the first BlackboxNLP workshop. *Natural Language Engineering*, 25(4):543–557. ZSCC: 0000012 Publisher: Cambridge University Press.

Lawrence W Barsalou. 2003. Abstraction in perceptual symbol systems. *Philosophical Transactions of the Royal Society of London. Series B: Biological Sciences*, 358(1435):1177–1187.

Miroslav Batchkarov, Thomas Kober, Jeremy Reffin, Julie Weeds, and David Weir. 2016. A critique of word similarity as a method for evaluating distributional semantic models. In *Proceedings of the 1st Workshop on Evaluating Vector-Space Representations for NLP*, pages 7–12. Association for Computational Linguistics.

Yoshua Bengio, Réjean Ducharme, Pascal Vincent, and Christian Jauvin. 2003. A neural probabilistic language model. *Journal of machine learning research*, 3(Feb):1137–1155.

Jean-Philippe Bernardy and Shalom Lappin. 2017. Using deep neural networks to learn syntactic agreement. *LiLT (Linguistic Issues in Language Technology)*, 15.

Rishi Bommasani, Kelly Davis, and Claire Cardie. 2020. Interpreting pretrained contextualized representations via reductions to static embeddings. In *Proceedings of the 58th Annual Meeting of the Association for Computational Linguistics*, pages 4758–4781.

Elia Bruni, Gemma Boleda, Marco Baroni, and Nam-Khanh Tran. 2012. Distributional semantics in technicolor. In *Proceedings of the 50th Annual Meeting of the Association for Computational Linguistics: Long Papers-Volume 1*, pages 136–145. Association for Computational Linguistics.

Luana Bulat, Douwe Kiela, and Stephen Clark. 2016. Vision and feature norms: Improving automatic feature norm learning through cross-modal maps. In *Proceedings of the 2016 Conference of the North American Chapter of the Association for Computational Linguistics: Human Language Technologies*, pages 579–588.

Ciprian Chelba, Tomas Mikolov, Mike Schuster, Qi Ge, Thorsten Brants, Phillipp Koehn, and Tony Robinson. 2013. One billion word benchmark for measuring progress in statistical language modeling. *arXiv preprint arXiv:1312.3005*.

Guillem Collell and Marie-Francine Moens. 2016. Is an image worth more than a thousand words? on the fine-grain semantic differences between visual and linguistic representations. In *Proceedings of COLING 2016, the 26th International Conference on Computational Linguistics: Technical Papers*, pages 2807–2817. The COLING 2016 Organizing Committee.

Jeff Da and Jungo Kusai. 2019. Cracking the contextual commonsense code: Understanding commonsense reasoning aptitude of deep contextual representations. *arXiv preprint arXiv:1910.01157*.

Zihang Dai, Zhilin Yang, Yiming Yang, Jaime Carbonell, Quoc V Le, and Ruslan Salakhutdinov. 2019. Transformer-xl: Attentive language models beyond a fixed-length context. *arXiv preprint arXiv:1901.02860*.

Gary S Dell and Franklin Chang. 2014. The p-chain: Relating sentence production and its disorders to comprehension and acquisition. *Philosophical Transactions of the Royal Society B: Biological Sciences*, 369(1634):20120394.

Katherine A. DeLong, Thomas P. Urbach, and Marta Kutas. 2005. Probabilistic word pre-activation during language comprehension inferred from electrical brain activity. *Nature Neuroscience*, 8(8):1117–1121. 00359.

Steven Derby, Paul Miller, and Barry Devereux. 2019. Feature2vec: Distributional semantic modelling of human property knowledge. *arXiv preprint arXiv:1908.11439*.

Steven Derby, Paul Miller, Brian Murphy, and Barry Devereux. 2018. Using sparse semantic embeddings learned from multimodal text and image data to model human conceptual knowledge. In *Unpublished Manuscript*.

Barry J Devereux, Lorraine K Tyler, Jeroen Geertzen, and Billi Randall. 2014. The centre for speech, language and the brain (cslb) concept property norms. *Behavior research methods*, 46(4):1119–1127.

Jacob Devlin, Ming-Wei Chang, Kenton Lee, and Kristina Toutanova. 2018. Bert: Pre-training of deep bidirectional transformers for language understanding. *arXiv preprint arXiv:1810.04805*.

Chris Dyer, Adhiguna Kuncoro, Miguel Ballesteros, and Noah A Smith. 2016. Recurrent neural network grammars. *arXiv preprint arXiv:1602.07776*.

Kawin Ethayarajh. 2019. How contextual are contextualized word representations? comparing the geometry of bert, elmo, and gpt-2 embeddings. *arXiv preprint arXiv:1909.00512*.

Allyson Ettinger. 2020. What bert is not: Lessons from a new suite of psycholinguistic diagnostics for language models. *Transactions of the Association for Computational Linguistics*, 8:34–48.

Luana Fagarasan, Eva Maria Vecchi, and Stephen Clark. 2015. From distributional semantics to feature norms: grounding semantic models in human perceptual data. In *Proceedings of the 11th International Conference on Computational Semantics*, pages 52–57.

Fernanda Ferreira and Suphasiree Chantavarin. 2018. Integration and Prediction in Language Processing: A Synthesis of Old and New. *Current Directions in Psychological Science*, 27(6):443–448. ZSCC: 0000022 Publisher: SAGE Publications Inc.

Lev Finkelstein, Evgeniy Gabrilovich, Yossi Matias, Ehud Rivlin, Zach Solan, Gadi Wolfman, and Eytan Ruppin. 2001. Placing search in context: The concept revisited. In *Proceedings of the 10th international conference on World Wide Web*, pages 406–414. ACM.

Morton Ann Gernsbacher. 1991. Cognitive processes and mechanisms in language comprehension: The structure building framework. In *Psychology of Learning and Motivation*, volume 27, pages 217–263. Elsevier.

Arthur C Graesser, Murray Singer, and Tom Trabasso. 1994. Constructing inferences during narrative text comprehension. *Psychological review*, 101(3):371.

Kristina Gulordava, Piotr Bojanowski, Edouard Grave, Tal Linzen, and Marco Baroni. 2018. Colorless green recurrent networks dream hierarchically. In *Proceedings of the 2018 Conference of the North American Chapter of the Association for Computational Linguistics: Human Language Technologies, Volume 1 (Long Papers)*, pages 1195–1205. Association for Computational Linguistics.

John Hewitt and Percy Liang. 2019. Designing and interpreting probes with control tasks. *arXiv preprint arXiv:1909.03368*.

John Hewitt and Christopher D Manning. 2019. A structural probe for finding syntax in word representations. In *Proceedings of the 2019 Conference of the North American Chapter of the Association for Computational Linguistics: Human Language Technologies, Volume 1 (Long and Short Papers)*, pages 4129–4138.

Felix Hill, Roi Reichart, and Anna Korhonen. 2015. Simlex-999: Evaluating semantic models with (genuine) similarity estimation. *Computational Linguistics*, 41(4):665–695.

Sepp Hochreiter and Jürgen Schmidhuber. 1997. Long short-term memory. *Neural computation*, 9(8):1735–1780.

Shailee Jain and Alexander Huth. 2018. Incorporating context into language encoding models for fmri. In *Advances in Neural Information Processing Systems*, pages 6628–6637.

Rafal Jozefowicz, Oriol Vinyals, Mike Schuster, Noam Shazeer, and Yonghui Wu. 2016. Exploring the limits of language modeling. *arXiv preprint arXiv:1602.02410*.

Walter Kintsch and Teun A Van Dijk. 1978. Toward a model of text comprehension and production. *Psychological review*, 85(5):363.

Skanda Koppula, Khe Chai Sim, and Kean Chin. 2018. Understanding recurrent neural state using memory signatures. *arXiv preprint arXiv:1802.03816*.

Gina R. Kuperberg and T. Florian Jaeger. 2016. What do we mean by prediction in language comprehension? *Language, Cognition and Neuroscience*, 31(1):32–59. ZSCC: 0000414 Publisher: Routledge _eprint: https://doi.org/10.1080/23273798.2015.1102299.

Yongjie Lin, Yi Chern Tan, and Robert Frank. 2019. Open sesame: Getting inside bert's linguistic knowledge. *arXiv preprint arXiv:1906.01698*.

Tal Linzen, Emmanuel Dupoux, and Yoav Goldberg. 2016. Assessing the ability of lstms to learn syntax-sensitive dependencies. *arXiv preprint arXiv:1611.01368*.

Nelson F Liu, Matt Gardner, Yonatan Belinkov, Matthew E Peters, and Noah A Smith. 2019. Linguistic knowledge and transferability of contextual representations. *arXiv preprint arXiv:1903.08855*.

Li Lucy and Jon Gauthier. 2017. Are distributional representations ready for the real world? evaluating word vectors for grounded perceptual meaning. *arXiv preprint arXiv:1705.11168*.

Steven G Luke and Kiel Christianson. 2016. Limits on lexical prediction during reading. *Cognitive Psychology*, 88:22–60.

Rebecca Marvin and Tal Linzen. 2018. Targeted syntactic evaluation of language models. *arXiv preprint arXiv:1808.09031*.

Ken McRae, George S Cree, Mark S Seidenberg, and Chris McNorgan. 2005. Semantic feature production norms for a large set of living and nonliving things. *Behavior Research Methods*, 37(4):547–559.

Matthew E Peters, Mark Neumann, Mohit Iyyer, Matt Gardner, Christopher Clark, Kenton Lee, and Luke Zettlemoyer. 2018. Deep contextualized word representations. *arXiv preprint arXiv:1802.05365*.

Ellen F Prince. 1978. On the function of existential presupposition in discourse. In *Papers from the... Regional Meeting. Chicago Ling. Soc. Chicago, Ill*, volume 14, pages 362–376.

Alec Radford, Karthik Narasimhan, Tim Salimans, and Ilya Sutskever. 2018. Improving language understanding by generative pre-training. *URL https://s3-us-west-2. amazonaws. com/openai-assets/research-covers/languageunsupervised/language understanding paper. pdf*.

Alec Radford, Jeffrey Wu, Rewon Child, David Luan, Dario Amodei, and Ilya Sutskever. 2019. Language models are unsupervised multitask learners. *OpenAI Blog*, 1(8):9.

Anna Rogers, Shashwath Hosur Ananthakrishna, and Anna Rumshisky. 2018. What's in your embedding, and how it predicts task performance. In *Proceedings of the 27th International Conference on Computational Linguistics*, pages 2690–2703.

Anna Rogers, Olga Kovaleva, and Anna Rumshisky. 2020. A primer in bertology: What we know about how bert works. *arXiv preprint arXiv:2002.12327*.

Dana Rubinstein, Effi Levi, Roy Schwartz, and Ari Rappoport. 2015. How well do distributional models capture different types of semantic knowledge? In *Proceedings of the 53rd Annual Meeting of the Association for Computational Linguistics and the 7th International Joint Conference on Natural Language Processing (Volume 2: Short Papers)*, pages 726–730.

Carina Silberer. 2017. Grounding the meaning of words with visual attributes. In *Visual Attributes*, pages 331–362. Springer.

Pia Sommerauer. 2020. Why is penguin more similar to polar bear than to sea gull? analyzing conceptual knowledge in distributional models. In *Proceedings of the 58th Annual Meeting of the Association for Computational Linguistics: Student Research Workshop*, pages 134–142.

Pia Sommerauer and Antske Fokkens. 2018. Firearms and tigers are dangerous, kitchen knives and zebras are not: Testing whether word embeddings can tell. *arXiv preprint arXiv:1809.01375*.

Ian Tenney, Dipanjan Das, and Ellie Pavlick. 2019a. Bert rediscovers the classical nlp pipeline. *arXiv preprint arXiv:1905.05950*.

Ian Tenney, Patrick Xia, Berlin Chen, Alex Wang, Adam Poliak, R Thomas McCoy, Najoung Kim, Benjamin Van Durme, Samuel R Bowman, Dipanjan Das, et al. 2019b. What do you learn from context? probing for sentence structure in contextualized word representations. *arXiv preprint arXiv:1905.06316*.

Mariya Toneva and Leila Wehbe. 2019. Interpreting and improving natural-language processing (in machines) with natural language-processing (in the brain). *arXiv preprint arXiv:1905.11833*.

Ashish Vaswani, Noam Shazeer, Niki Parmar, Jakob Uszkoreit, Llion Jones, Aidan N. Gomez, Lukasz Kaiser, and Illia Polosukhin. 2017. Attention Is All You Need. *arXiv:1706.03762 [cs]*. ZSCC: 0008106 arXiv: 1706.03762.

Eric Wallace, Yizhong Wang, Sujian Li, Sameer Singh, and Matt Gardner. 2019. Do nlp models know numbers? probing numeracy in embeddings. *arXiv preprint arXiv:1909.07940*.

Lin Wang, Edward Wlotko, Edward Alexander, Lotte Schoot, Minjae Kim, Lena Warnke, and Gina R. Kuperberg. 2020. Neural Evidence for the Prediction of Animacy Features during Language Comprehension: Evidence from MEG and EEG Representational Similarity Analysis. *Journal of Neuroscience*, 40(16):3278–3291. ZSCC: NoCitationData[s1] Publisher: Society for Neuroscience Section: Research Articles.

Nathaniel Weir, Adam Poliak, and Benjamin Van Durme. 2020. On the existence of tacit assumptions in contextualized language models. *arXiv preprint arXiv:2004.04877*.

Haoyan Xu, Brian Murphy, and Alona Fyshe. 2016. Brainbench: A brain-image test suite for distributional semantic models. In *Proceedings of the 2016 Conference on Empirical Methods in Natural Language Processing*, pages 2017–2021.

Relation Classification with Cognitive Attention Supervision

Erik S. McGuire
DePaul University
Chicago, IL
emcguir8@depaul.edu

Noriko Tomuro
DePaul University
Chicago, IL
tomuro@cs.depaul.edu

Abstract

Many current language models such as BERT utilize attention mechanisms to transform sequence representations. We ask whether we can influence BERT's attention with human reading patterns by using eye-tracking and brain imaging data. We fine-tune BERT for relation extraction with auxiliary attention supervision in which BERT's attention weights are supervised by cognitive data. Through a variety of metrics we find that this attention supervision can be used to increase similarity between model attention distributions over sequences and the cognitive data without significantly affecting classification performance while making unique errors from the baseline. In particular, models with cognitive attention supervision more often correctly classified samples misclassified by the baseline.

1 Introduction

For humans, the task of determining semantic relationships may entail complicated inference based on concepts' contexts (Yee and Thompson-Schill, 2016; Zhang et al., 2020) and commonsense knowledge (e.g., causal relations; Chiang et al., 2021), and for labeling relations between entities in texts the task may depend on the genre of the text (e.g. biomedical, biographical) and constraints indicated by annotator instructions (Mohammad, 2016). The advent of crowdsourcing for machine learning approaches to Natural Language Processing (NLP) creates challenges in collecting high quality annotations (Ramírez et al., 2020). A platform such as Amazon Mechanical Turk (MTurk) allows accessible, sophisticated task design (Stewart et al., 2017) but defaults to simple templates for NLP tasks, and is susceptible to self-selection bias (raters may not represent the population) and social desirability bias or demand effects, where judges seek to confirm the inferred hypotheses of experimenters (Antin and Shaw, 2012; Mummolo and Peterson, 2019; Aguinis et al., 2020).

Cognitive research has shown that self-reports are frequently inaccurate (Vraga et al., 2016), and that subjects are unable to effectively introspect about or recall their eye movements during reading (Võ et al., 2016; Clarke et al., 2017; Kok et al., 2017). This encourages the use of precise, objective recordings of non-conscious language processing behavior to use as model training data, rather than relying solely on reader annotations. As emphasized by Hollenstein et al. (2019), when reading humans produce reliable patterns that can be recorded, such as tracking gaze trajectories or measuring brain activity. These signals can associate linguistic features with cognitive processing and subsequently be applied to NLP tasks. The recording of eye movements during reading can be traced to psychology and physiology in the late 1800s (Wade, 2010), but the use of eye-tracking data in NLP is a relatively new phenomenon (Mishra and Bhattacharyya, 2018). Brain data has a longstanding relationship with language processing and in recent years has been investigated with NLP models (Schwartz et al., 2019), leveraged notably by Mitchell et al. (2008) to predict fMRI activity from novel nouns.

The working intuition in using cognitive data in recent NLP studies is that signals produced by humans during naturalistic reading can be leveraged by artificial neural networks to induce human-like biases and potentially improve natural language task performance. For example, recognizing and relating entities while reading sentences might elicit patterns of activation or particular gaze behaviors in human readers which can be transferred to and recovered by models given the same text sequences as inputs. Models might then generalize learned biases to similar text inputs. One route for augmenting neural networks with cognitive data is to regularize attention, such as with eye-tracking (Barrett et al., 2018) and/or electroencephalography (EEG) data (Muttenthaler et al., 2020). Eye-

Proceedings of the Workshop on Cognitive Modeling and Computational Linguistics, pages 222–232
Online Event, June 10, 2021. ©2021 Association for Computational Linguistics

Phrase	Relation
<e> ford </e> became an engineer with the <e> edison illuminating company </e>	Employer
<e> ford </e> became an <e> engineer </e>	Job Title
<e> ford </e> was born on a prosperous farm in <e> springwells township </e>	Birthplace
<e> mary litogot </e> (c1839-1876) , immigrants from <e> county cork </e>	Visited

Table 1: Some example phrases for sentences 3 and 5.

tracking (ET) is an indirect estimate of processes such as attentional focus and cognitive strategies (Eckstein et al., 2017) by associating eye movements with performance; EEG is a direct measurement of brain activity, by recording the electric potentials along the scalp generated by the firing of populations of neurons. We focus in this work on deep learning-based approaches to NLP and seek to induce human-like biases in the self-attention distributions produced by BERT[1] (Devlin et al., 2019) by fine-tuning the base language model for relation classification (RC) with a multi-task learning (MTL) approach, supervising attention with ET and EEG data taken from the Zurich Cognitive Language Processing Corpus (ZuCo[2]; Hollenstein et al. 2018) as the auxiliary task.

2 Related Work

Mathias et al. (2020) describe the key terms used in gaze behavior studies; eye-tracking appears to be the more robust and proven measurement modality for augmenting machine learning models. In particular, **fixations** are the eyes' focused pauses on Areas of Interest (AOIs); **saccades** are rapid movements from one point to another. These movements can be progressive or regressive, moving to later or earlier AOIs (e.g., the words in a sentence), and occur on the order of milliseconds. Hollenstein et al. (2019) combine the indirect signals of ET with EEG data, moving beyond inferences based on eye-screen positioning (e.g., that content words are more likely to be fixated upon, and unfamiliar words have longer fixation durations). In general, EEG provides a high temporal resolution but due to interference from the scalp exhibits a poorer spatial resolution than other brain imaging methods such as magnetoencephalography (MEG; Hollenstein et al., 2020). To understand cognitive processes involved in, e.g., longer fixation durations, EEG can complement ET, where larger amplitudes for event-related potentials (ERPs) such as N400 correspond to less frequent or less predictable words and semantic processing (Frank et al., 2015).

A number of studies have applied cognitive data to NLP tasks, among them: sentiment analysis (Mishra et al., 2016), part-of-speech (POS) tagging (Barrett et al., 2016), and named entity recognition (NER) (Hollenstein and Zhang, 2019). Hollenstein et al. (2019) apply both gaze and brain data to a suite of NLP tasks (Hollenstein et al., 2019), including relation classification. For sentiment analysis, Mishra et al. (2018) use MTL for a bidirectional Long Short-Term Memory (biLSTM) network, learning gaze behavior as the auxiliary task. Malmaud et al. (2020) predict ET data with a variant of BERT as an auxiliary to question answering. Bautista and Naval (2020) predict gaze features with an LSTM to evaluate on sentiment classification and NER tasks. Barrett et al. (2018) supervise model attentions with ET data by adding attention loss to the main classification loss so the model jointly learns a sentence classification task and the auxiliary task of attending more to tokens on which humans typically focus. Muttenthaler et al. (2020) follow this paradigm using EEG data.

A number of studies impose schemata or mechanisms to encourage BERT to learn more structured RC representations: Soares et al. (2019) fine-tune BERT for RC, experimenting with the use of additional special entity tokens from BERT's final hidden states to represent relations, rather than the last layer's classification token, [CLS]: the [CLS] token is conventionally used as the sentence representation for tasks such as classification (Devlin et al., 2019), as well as attention analysis (Clark et al., 2019). For joint entity and relation extraction Xue et al. (2019) fine-tune BERT using focused attention to mask what the [CLS] token attends to, so that it attends only to entities. Su and Vijay-Shanker (2020) fine-tune BERT for RC by summarizing the other tokens' final hidden states with either LSTM or attention, concatenating the result to the [CLS] representation.

[1] https://huggingface.co/bert-base-uncased

[2] https://osf.io/2urht/

Relation	Train	Train %	Test	Test %	Total
Awarded	9	1.77%	1	1.75%	10
Birthplace	68	13.36%	8	14.04%	76
Deathplace	17	3.34%	2	3.51%	19
Education	36	7.07%	4	7.02%	40
Employer	31	6.09%	3	5.26%	34
Founder	13	2.55%	1	1.75%	14
Job Title	136	26.72%	15	26.32%	151
Nationality	38	7.47%	4	7.02%	42
Political Affiliation	13	2.55%	2	3.51%	15
Visited	129	25.34%	15	26.32%	144
Wife	19	3.73%	2	3.51%	21
Totals	509	100%	57	100%	566

Table 2: Statistics for the static, stratified train and test splits on 566 phrase samples derived from 300 ZuCo sentences, as a given sentence may contain multiple binary relations among entities.

3 Data

Hollenstein et al. (2018) created ZuCo, a corpus of ET and EEG recordings in which 12 adult subjects (fluent English speakers) read full sentences at their own speed, with brain recordings synchronized to eye fixations. The sentences used by the corpus were written English: 400 review excerpts from Stanford Sentiment Treebank (Socher et al., 2013) and 707 biographical sentences from a Wikipedia relation extraction dataset (Culotta et al., 2006). In this work we use a subset of 300 relation sentences (7,737 tokens) divided into 566 phrases[3] by Hollenstein et al. (2019) to encompass the multiple binary relation statements, and annotated with markers around entity mentions. The dataset uses 11 relation types, as seen in Table 2.

For ET we had access to five features for each word, including first fixation duration (FFD), gaze duration (sum of fixations), and total reading time (TRT: the sum of the word's fixations including regressions to it). The features for EEG we use are the 105 electrode values mapped to first-pass fixation onsets to create fixation-related potentials (FRPs), so that each word has 105 values. We average ET and EEG values over all subjects, which has been shown to reduce variability of results (Hollenstein et al., 2020) and overfitting (Bingel et al., 2016). To obtain a single ET value for each token, Barrett et al. (2018) used the mean fixation duration (MFD), by dividing TRT by number of fixations. There is no best practice to our knowledge, and in this study we use TRT as a proxy for overall attention to a word. For EEG electrode values, we obtain a scalar for each word by taking the mean (Hollenstein et al., 2019), rather than the maximum (Muttenthaler et al., 2020).

4 Method

We split the English-language ZuCo samples into 90% training and 10% test sets. We perform 9-fold cross-validation on the training data for 6 epochs with batch size 16 and otherwise default hyperparameters, averaging validation results over folds. We fine-tune the final models on the full training data, choosing 4 epochs based on cross-validation accuracy, reserving the test data for later comparison. For the main RC task, categorical cross-entropy loss $\mathcal{L}_{RC}$ is calculated for each sequence j in batches of size M with sequence-level predictions for the C classes, $\hat{y} \in \mathbb{R}^{M \times C}$, and a vector of target class indices $t \in \mathbb{Z}^M$ where $0 \leq t_j < C$:

$$\mathcal{L}_{RC}(\hat{y}, t) = -\frac{1}{M} \sum_{j}^{M} \ln\, a_{t_j} \tag{1}$$

where a_{t_j} is the t_j-th value of the softmax of sample j's C prediction scores $\varphi(\hat{y}_j)$:

$$a = \varphi(\hat{y}_j) \qquad a_{t_j} = \frac{e^{\hat{y}_{jt_j}}}{\sum_{k}^{C} e^{\hat{y}_{jk}}}$$

We additionally compute auxiliary attention losses. BERT takes an input of sequence hidden states $\in \mathbb{R}^{N \times d}$ (N tokens, $d = 768$ features) and uses 12 attention heads at each layer to create 12 token-token attention weight matrices $\in \mathbb{R}^{N \times N}$.

[3] `https://github.com/DS3Lab/zuco-nlp/tree/master/relation-classification/data`

Model	Loss	Accuracy	Precision	Recall	Weighted F1
Baseline	0.61	**0.88**	**0.83**	**0.80**	**0.88**
ET	**0.60**	0.87	0.82	**0.80**	0.87
EEG	0.62	0.86	0.80	*0.77*	0.87
ET+EEG	0.63	0.86	0.82	**0.80**	*0.85*
Random ET	*0.64*	*0.85*	*0.78*	0.78	0.86
Random EEG	0.62	0.86	0.82	0.79	0.86
Random ET+EEG	0.62	0.87	**0.83**	**0.80**	0.86

Table 3: Metrics at 4 epochs, averaged over 4 runs. Bold are best values, italics worst. Weighted macro-F1 is intended to account for class imbalances.

Specifically, in these matrices, there is a row for every token in the sequence–a distribution of N attention weights, where each scalar weight corresponds to a token's similarity to a token in the sequence. The resulting matrices are multiplied with the input to transform the tokens' features and produce a context matrix $\in \mathbb{R}^{N \times d}$. Each token context vector c contains a blend of features from the sequence's tokens: each feature for c is a weighted sum dominated by that feature's values from tokens most attended by c. For instance, the features in the context vector for [CLS] will reflect the features of those tokens given highest attention by [CLS], with the features of lower weighted tokens scaled down and contributing minimally.

These operations are founded on the conception of attention emerging from relationships between tokens in sequence contexts, or the notion of each token attending to the others, and computations occur in the subspaces of heads' attention weights: this is incompatible with the concept of a single abstracted human reading a displayed word sequence. Therefore, to intervene on the production of contextualized model representations using the ZuCo data as proxies for attention, we seek a single distribution of weights from the multiple token-token attention matrices for a given sequence, analogous to the competitive attention given by a human reader. Due to its use as the sequence representation used for classification, we take from each matrix the row of weights accorded by [CLS], resulting in 12 vectors, treating [CLS] as our model reader. We average these vectors along the head axis to obtain a [CLS]-token vector $\alpha \in \mathbb{R}^{1 \times N}$ of attention weights. This aggregate is supervised during training: in this way, each independent representation subspace (head) is informed by the human values, influencing the features of the sequence representation used for the RC task.

We then obtain human scores for the sequence tokens. Previous studies used "type-aggregated" (Barrett et al., 2016; Hollenstein et al., 2019) cognitive data, where values are averaged over corpus word occurrences to obtain an aggregated value for that word type. This method exchanges specific sample contexts for the ability to synthesize distributions for samples not in the original data through type lexicon queries, using 0 for unknown word types. For relation extraction, previously Hollenstein et al. (2019) discretized and binned ZuCo features which were used in an auxiliary task. To preserve context, we extract from ZuCo the raw ET and EEG values for each sample without type-aggregating, so that ZuCo coverage of tokens in the samples is complete: every token has a ZuCo value, excluding special model tokens, which are assigned zeros.

Because BERT uses subword tokenization, to allow matching entries to be found in the ZuCo word-level data we split the ZuCo words into BERT tokens, evenly dividing values between each subword piece (e.g., "delicacy" $\rightarrow$ "del", "##ica", "##cy", each piece allotted a third of the ZuCo value), a technique used by Malmaud et al. (2020). We preserve entity markers "<e>" and "</e>" in each sample by adding them as special tokens to the BERT tokenizer so their embeddings are learned with other tokens during fine-tuning. Human ET and EEG token values z_{ET} and z_{EEG} are passed through softmax to obtain two distributions over sequences, vectors α''_{ET} and α'_{EEG}. ET features such as TRT are much larger, measured in milliseconds, than the small EEG microvoltages (μV), so the raw ET values' softmax output α'_{ET} would be much peakier than α'_{EEG}, providing an extremely low entropy signal where weights are forced onto one or two tokens. To combat this, we reduce each ET token value by dividing by the maximum value

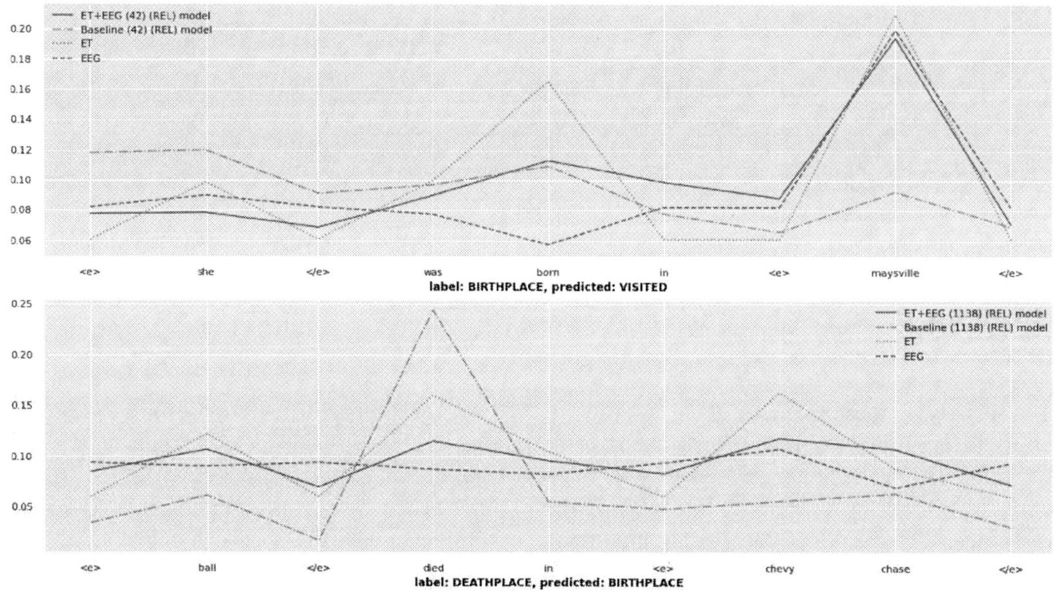

Figure 1: Plots of baseline and attention-supervised model attentions against ZuCo ET and EEG values where the baseline is correct and attention-supervised model is incorrect. Note that piece attentions are combined (e.g., "may": 0.1004 + "##sville" 0.0939 → "maysville": 0.1943). The ET+EEG model in the top plot was influenced to emphasize the location "maysville" alongside "born in" and predicts "Visited" rather than the correct "Birthplace", whereas the baseline places relatively more emphasis on "she was" and "born". At bottom, the baseline attends strongly to "died" whereas the ET+EEG model has learned a more uniform attention distribution.

for its sequence (Eq. 3), returning softmax output α''_{ET}. Each sequence thereby has a context-specific distribution, reflecting the averaged responses of the human subjects. Following other studies that implemented attention supervision (Qiuxia et al., 2020; Sharan et al., 2019; Sood et al., 2020; Zhang et al., 2019), we compute attention losses based on the Kullback-Leibler divergence (D_{KL}[4]) from the aggregate model attention weights α to the human weights α''_{ET} and α'_{EEG}. We do so for each sequence j in batches of size M for each modality, obtaining eye-tracking loss $\mathcal{L}_{ET}$ and EEG loss $\mathcal{L}_{EEG}$. By toggling binary coefficients λ, one or both losses are added to RC categorical cross-entropy loss to give us the overall multi-task fine-tuning loss, $\mathcal{L}_{MTL}$.

$$\mathcal{L}_{ET} = \frac{1}{M} \sum_{j}^{M} D_{KL}(\alpha_j''^{ET} || \alpha_j) \quad (2a)$$

$$\mathcal{L}_{EEG} = \frac{1}{M} \sum_{j}^{M} D_{KL}(\alpha_j'^{EEG} || \alpha_j) \quad (2b)$$

[4]For this computation, zeros are set to 1e-12.

$$\mathcal{L}_{MTL} = \mathcal{L}_{RC} + \lambda_{ET}\mathcal{L}_{ET} + \lambda_{EEG}\mathcal{L}_{EEG} \quad (2c)$$

where $\alpha_j''^{ET}$ is the softmax of the max-normalized vector of ET token values for sequence j:

$$\frac{z_j^{ET}}{\max(z_j^{ET})} \quad (3)$$

5 Experimental Results

5.1 Ablations

We perform ablations comparing base BERT fine-tuned for four runs with arbitrary random seeds and varying combinations of the cognitive data. The baseline used in ablations is the result of fine-tuning on the ZuCo data without attention supervision. For the ET model, we add only the loss computed from the ET data. For the EEG model we do likewise with the EEG loss, and for the combined ET+EEG model we compute and add both auxiliary losses to the main classification loss. We similarly create random ET, EEG, and ET+EEG

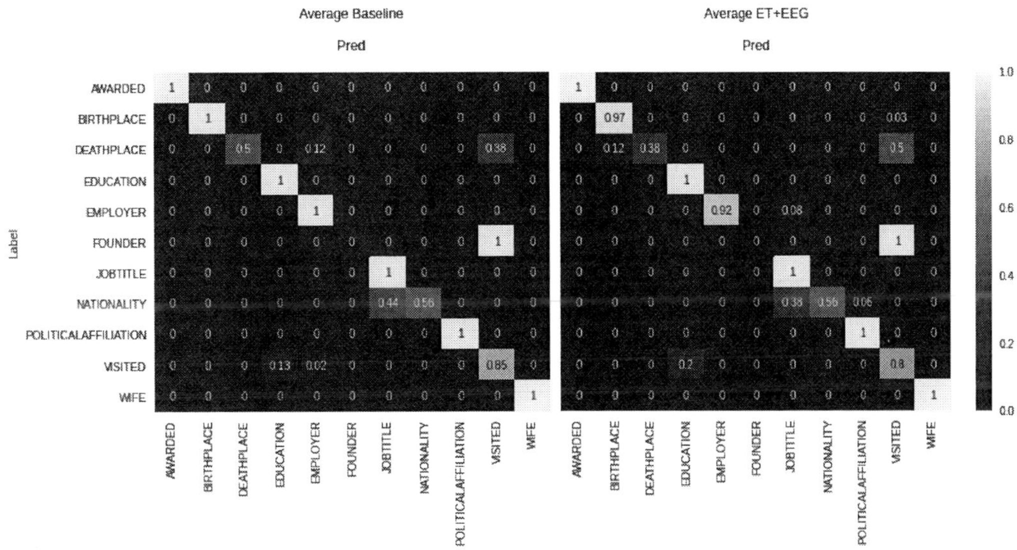

Figure 2: Confusion matrices of accuracies averaged over four runs for baseline and ET+EEG models. Models often misclassified "Deathplace" (which comprises roughly 3.5% of the splits' samples) as "Visited" (25%) or "Nationality" (7%) as "Job title" (26%), and "Visited" was occasionally misclassified as "Education" (7%).

models. For random models, we replace the modality's ZuCo values with values uniformly sampled from the fixed minimum and maximum range of the modality's ZuCo values. This should allow us to distinguish the effects of learning regularities in ZuCo token attention values versus the effects of constraining the range of magnitudes given by the ZuCo values.

After training, we evaluated the final models on the held-out test data of 57 samples. Table 3 shows evaluation results. Two-sided Pitman's permutation tests (Dror et al., 2018) were performed on final accuracies to assess statistical significance, comparing each of the six models against the baseline. Averaging over four runs, there are no statistically significant differences ($p > 0.05$) between baseline vs. ET, EEG, ET+EEG, and random versions thereof, respectively. Figure 2 displays confusion matrices for the models, showing similar per-class results, with some cases where classes with few samples such as "Deathplace" (19 samples) were classified as more dominant categories such as "Visited" (144 samples).

5.2 Attention Similarity

Sen et al. (2020) define a *behavioral similarity* metric to quantify the extent to which model attentions focus on the same words as the human attention; in their work, human attention maps are binary vectors used as the ground truth against which the continuous model attention maps are compared using Area Under the Curve (AUC), a binary classification metric. In a similar vein, in order to assess whether models learn a generalizable bias in attention we create a measurement to assess the amount of token overlap between continuous human and model attention vectors for phrases in the test set. Results of this measurement as well as relative entropies are shown in Table 4.

We compare a fixed top-k tokens for sequences using a variety of k values, for tokens scored by model attentions after fine-tuning and the scores given by human data. We run the models on all splits, using the methods described in §4 to obtain model attentions α, and compute the attention similarity for the test set by pairwise comparison of each model's attentions with the human data. Specifically, as Equation 4 describes, for each model we obtain sets of all samples' token indices and values for the top k attention weights from both ZuCo values α' and α, and divide the cardinality of the sets' intersection by k to obtain an overlap ratio. To factor the k weights' salience into the similarity, we divide their total weight given by the model by their total ZuCo weight and multiply this percentage–capped at 1.0–with the overlap ratio. For example, if both the baseline and an attention-supervised model have the same tokens in the top k

Model	k=1		k=2		k=3		k=4		D_{KL}	
	EEG	ET	EEG	ET	EEG	ET	EEG	ET	EEG	ET
Baseline	*4.26*	3.50	*8.23*	*7.70*	*12.90*	*13.69*	*20.10*	*17.37*	*0.36*	*0.44*
ET	12.11	**26.09**	**27.53**	**36.28**	32.57	**45.59**	36.35	**48.58**	0.05	**0.04**
EEG	9.48	*3.29*	16.38	9.09	21.58	16.06	25.49	20.33	**0.02**	0.07
ET+EEG	**14.21**	18.48	25.64	26.62	**33.21**	35.57	**36.61**	41.39	0.03	0.05
Random ET	11.92	6.82	20.61	16.99	29.80	29.28	33.88	33.79	0.04	0.05
Random EEG	13.11	9.29	17.50	18.27	27.77	30.38	34.68	36.69	0.06	0.07
Random ET+EEG	12.98	8.09	20.11	16.88	29.35	30.26	34.67	36.87	0.05	0.06

Table 4: Overlapping top-k and batch Kullback-Leibler divergence for model vs. sample-specific human attentions on the test set. Averaged over 4 runs, bold cells are best, italics worst.

attention, the model that weighs these tokens similarly to the ZuCo data should have a greater score. We take the average over each sample j in dataset D:

$$\text{sim}(\alpha_j, \alpha'_j) = \frac{1}{D}\sum_{j}^{D}\left[\frac{|o_j^k|}{k} \times \min\left(1, \frac{\sum_i^{o_j^k} \alpha_{ji}}{\sum_i^{o_j^k} \alpha'_{ji}}\right)\right] \quad (4)$$

where o_j^k is the set of intersecting indices of the top k attention values for sequence j and α' corresponds separately to α''^{ET} (Eq. 3) or α'^{EEG}:

$$o_j^k = \alpha_j^k \cap \alpha_j'^k \quad (5)$$

As Table 4 shows, baseline and random models have less overlap than the ET model for all sets. Curiously, after the baseline, EEG overlap was weakest for the model supervised with EEG, including for the random models. This might indicate a diffusion of attention that makes top-k overlap difficult to differentiate, as EEG overlap values reach parity with non-EEG models with $k > 10$. Figure 1 visualizes the respective final [CLS] attention weights averaged over attention heads for baseline vs. attention-supervised models against the ET and EEG ZuCO data values used to supervise the latter models.

5.3 Unique Errors

While task performance is not significantly different, we can see that model attentions are affected. To detect the possible effects of these attentional differences, where alternative features may be emphasized or diminished in the sequence representations used for RC, we analyze errors made by

Model	MM	Fixes	Breaks	AvB
Baseline	0.00	0.00	0.00	0.00
ET	20.59	0.07	*0.02*	*0.16*
EEG	24.16	**0.11**	*0.02*	*0.16*
ET+EEG	**28.90**	**0.11**	**0.04**	**0.22**
Random ET	*20.24*	*0.03*	0.03	0.18
Random EEG	20.83	*0.03*	0.03	0.18
Random ET+EEG	25.55	**0.11**	0.03	0.18

Table 5: *MM* (*mismatches*): The percentage of unique errors between model errors and baseline errors out of all errors for both models. *Fixes* refers to the percentage of all $\mathcal{M}_b$'s errors that $\mathcal{M}_a$ correctly predicted. *Breaks* refers to the percentage of all $\mathcal{M}_b$'s correct answers that $\mathcal{M}_a$ incorrectly predicted. *AvB* refers to the percentage of all $\mathcal{M}_a$'s errors that $\mathcal{M}_b$ correctly predicted. Bold cells are the highest, italicized lowest.

the baseline models against those of the attention-supervised models on a sample by sample basis. For each model $\mathcal{M}_a$ paired with baseline model $\mathcal{M}_b$ (fine-tuned without attention supervision), we examine the proportion of the pair's mismatched errors out of all errors on the test set (Equation 6); that is, the size of the symmetric difference ($\triangle$) between $\mathcal{M}_a$'s errors $\mathcal{M}_a^{\text{inc}}$ and $\mathcal{M}_b$'s errors $\mathcal{M}_b^{\text{inc}}$ divided by the size of the union of errors made by each model:

$$\text{mismatches}(\mathcal{M}_a, \mathcal{M}_b) = \frac{|\mathcal{M}_a^{\text{inc}} \triangle \mathcal{M}_b^{\text{inc}}|}{|\mathcal{M}_a^{\text{inc}} \cup \mathcal{M}_b^{\text{inc}}|} \quad (6)$$

As seen in Table 5, we note that models with non-random ZuCo attention supervision have more unique errors compared with the baseline than those with random supervision. In this case, the EEG-based attention loss seems to be the source of the small differences, as ET and Random ET models have similar mismatches. Lin et al. (2020)

examine *fixes*: instances where the baseline is in error, but the modified baseline is correct. We analyze the percentages of *fixes* and also *breaks*, which we define to occur when the baseline is correct, but the model with supervised attention is incorrect. These are also shown in Table 5. Compared to random models, the ZuCo models seem to more frequently predict correctly samples that the baseline labeled incorrectly.

6 Conclusions and Future Work

Overall, BERT models with multiple modes of human attention supervision converged to accuracy for the relation classification task that does not differ significantly from the fine-tuned base BERT model, despite possessing attention distributions that were shifted toward the cognitive data. Measured by overlap, attention supervision with eye-tracking data was most influential on the final layer's [CLS]-assigned attention weights. In addition, we have shown that the behavior of these models differs from the baseline consistently by misclassifying different samples, exposing pathologies which may be of interest for research in neural network-based human language processing.

Barrett and Hollenstein (2020) have pointed to distinct reading patterns evident in eye-tracking studies for unfamiliar proper nouns which may be more readily apparent in the ET values. On the other hand, it may be that the EEG data were too noisy and that dimensionality reduction to find the most predictive electrode values, such as performed by Muttenthaler et al. (2020), is needed to provide a consistent signal. Additionally, Hollenstein et al. (2019) and Muttenthaler et al. (2020) incorporated EEG frequency bands into their ZuCo-based studies; the α frequency band has been associated with attention (Feldmann-Wüstefeld and Awh, 2020) and supervision with this band might yield different results. The cognitive data used in this study were not specifically produced from an entity-related reading task, but Brédart (2017) has noted the increased difficulty of processing proper names which is reflected in behavioral studies, with a double dissociation between common nouns and proper names where production of one type of noun is impaired but the other is intact. A more careful use of neuroimaging data may be needed to leverage signals reflecting the differing brain mechanisms involved in human lexical access.

Typically, researchers implicitly seek to induce a human-like bias in classifiers so they correlate more highly with human judgments by using self-reported annotations to supervise learning. This supervision is limited insofar as self-reports can not specify responses inaccessible to annotator introspection, such as the brain's electrical activity or detailed gaze behavior. Models additionally biased by non-conscious physiological responses may learn to more robustly reflect human language processing, incorporating both subjective and objective signals. Human annotations are conventionally taken as ground truth. Yet cognitive data may offer valid judgments, as well. For example, in sentiment analysis, a false negative according to a self-report could be a true negative according to physiological affective responses. Cognitive data may reveal inconsistencies and gradations obscured by labels. In the case of relation extraction, cognitive data might uncover patterns more reflective of different, potentially novel categories of semantic relation, or different dynamics, due to linguistic ambiguity and/or changing contexts and readerships. In terms of limitations, we did not investigate the breadth or depth of influence of our method of [CLS]-based aggregate attention supervision on the model attentions across layers and heads, nor the supervision of specific layers or heads as done by Strubell et al. (2018). We did not explore trade-off coefficients on the multiple losses, such as the convex combination used by Malmaud et al. (2020). We used a relatively small English dataset, which limited generalizability and robustness.

Hollenstein et al. (2020) describe some ethical concerns in the recording and use of cognitive data, including voluntary data procured but not recorded by NLP researchers. This includes loss of privacy with the identification of subjects, an overrepresentation and normalization of particular demographics, and the perpetuation of fossilized human prejudices. Sen et al. (2020) have described the potential for human attention supervision to address the validity of attention as a faithful, human-like explanation for model decisions while Pruthi et al. (2019) have discussed the potential for deception by manipulating attention to make models appear less biased. Future work could scrutinize whether human attention supervision can provide a basis for exploring cognitive biases learned by models, or align attention-based explanations to model outcomes: enabling performant models to adhere faithfully to auditor expectations.

References

Herman Aguinis, Isabel Villamor, and Ravi S Ramani. 2020. MTurk research: Review and recommendations.

Judd Antin and Aaron Shaw. 2012. Social desirability bias and self-reports of motivation: A study of Amazon Mechanical Turk in the US and India. In *Proceedings of the SIGCHI Conference on Human Factors in Computing Systems*, pages 2925–2934.

Maria Barrett, Joachim Bingel, Nora Hollenstein, Marek Rei, and Anders Søgaard. 2018. Sequence classification with human attention. In *Proceedings of the 22nd Conference on Computational Natural Language Learning*, pages 302–312.

Maria Barrett, Joachim Bingel, Frank Keller, and Anders Søgaard. 2016. Weakly supervised part-of-speech tagging using eye-tracking data. In *Proceedings of the 54th Annual Meeting of the Association for Computational Linguistics (Volume 2: Short Papers)*, pages 579–584, Berlin, Germany. Association for Computational Linguistics.

Maria Barrett and Nora Hollenstein. 2020. Sequence labelling and sequence classification with gaze: Novel uses of eye-tracking data for Natural Language Processing. *Language and Linguistics Compass*, 14(11):1–16.

Louise Gillian Bautista and Prospero Naval. 2020. Towards learning to read like humans. In *International Conference on Computational Collective Intelligence*, pages 779–791. Springer.

Joachim Bingel, Maria Barrett, and Anders Søgaard. 2016. Extracting token-level signals of syntactic processing from fMRI-with an application to PoS induction. In *Proceedings of the 54th Annual Meeting of the Association for Computational Linguistics (Volume 1: Long Papers)*, pages 747–755.

Serge Brédart. 2017. The cognitive psychology and neuroscience of naming people. *Neuroscience & Biobehavioral Reviews*, 83:145–154.

Jeffrey N Chiang, Yujia Peng, Hongjing Lu, Keith J Holyoak, and Martin M Monti. 2021. Distributed code for semantic relations predicts neural similarity during analogical reasoning. *Journal of Cognitive Neuroscience*, 33(3):377–389.

Kevin Clark, Urvashi Khandelwal, Omer Levy, and Christopher D. Manning. 2019. What Does BERT Look at? An Analysis of BERT's Attention. In *Proceedings of the 2019 ACL Workshop BlackboxNLP: Analyzing and Interpreting Neural Networks for NLP*, pages 276–286, Stroudsburg, PA, USA. Association for Computational Linguistics.

Alasdair DF Clarke, Aoife Mahon, Alex Irvine, and Amelia R Hunt. 2017. People are unable to recognize or report on their own eye movements. *The Quarterly Journal of Experimental Psychology*, 70(11):2251–2270.

Aron Culotta, Andrew McCallum, and Jonathan Betz. 2006. Integrating probabilistic extraction models and data mining to discover relations and patterns in text. In *Proceedings of the Human Language Technology Conference of the NAACL, Main Conference*, pages 296–303, New York City, USA. Association for Computational Linguistics.

Jacob Devlin, Ming-Wei Chang, Kenton Lee, and Kristina Toutanova. 2019. BERT: Pre-training of deep bidirectional transformers for language understanding. In *Proceedings of the 2019 Conference of the North American Chapter of the Association for Computational Linguistics: Human Language Technologies, Volume 1 (Long and Short Papers)*, pages 4171–4186, Minneapolis, Minnesota. Association for Computational Linguistics.

Rotem Dror, Gili Baumer, Segev Shlomov, and Roi Reichart. 2018. The hitchhiker's guide to testing statistical significance in natural language processing. In *Proceedings of the 56th Annual Meeting of the Association for Computational Linguistics (Volume 1: Long Papers)*, pages 1383–1392, Melbourne, Australia. Association for Computational Linguistics.

Maria K Eckstein, Belén Guerra-Carrillo, Alison T Miller Singley, and Silvia A Bunge. 2017. Beyond eye gaze: What else can eyetracking reveal about cognition and cognitive development? *Developmental cognitive neuroscience*, 25:69–91.

Tobias Feldmann-Wüstefeld and Edward Awh. 2020. Alpha-band activity tracks the zoom lens of attention. *Journal of cognitive neuroscience*, 32(2):272–282.

Stefan L Frank, Leun J Otten, Giulia Galli, and Gabriella Vigliocco. 2015. The ERP response to the amount of information conveyed by words in sentences. *Brain and language*, 140:1–11.

Nora Hollenstein, Maria Barrett, and Lisa Beinborn. 2020. Towards best practices for leveraging human language processing signals for natural language processing. In *Proceedings of the Second Workshop on Linguistic and Neurocognitive Resources*, pages 15–27, Marseille, France. European Language Resources Association.

Nora Hollenstein, Maria Barrett, Marius Troendle, Francesco Bigiolli, Nicolas Langer, and Ce Zhang. 2019. Advancing NLP with cognitive language processing signals. *arXiv preprint arXiv:1904.02682*.

Nora Hollenstein, Jonathan Rotsztejn, Marius Troendle, Andreas Pedroni, Ce Zhang, and Nicolas Langer. 2018. ZuCo, a simultaneous EEG and eye-tracking resource for natural sentence reading. *Scientific data*, 5(1):1–13.

Nora Hollenstein and Ce Zhang. 2019. Entity recognition at first sight: Improving NER with eye movement information. In *Proceedings of the 2019 Conference of the North American Chapter of the Association for Computational Linguistics: Human Lan-*

guage Technologies, Volume 1 (Long and Short Papers), pages 1–10, Minneapolis, Minnesota. Association for Computational Linguistics.

Ellen M Kok, Avi M Aizenman, Melissa L-H Võ, and Jeremy M Wolfe. 2017. Even if i showed you where you looked, remembering where you just looked is hard. *Journal of Vision*, 17(12):2–2.

Chen Lin, Steven Bethard, Dmitriy Dligach, Farig Sadeque, Guergana Savova, and Timothy A Miller. 2020. Does BERT need domain adaptation for clinical negation detection? *Journal of the American Medical Informatics Association*, 27(4):584–591.

Jonathan Malmaud, Roger Levy, and Yevgeni Berzak. 2020. Bridging information-seeking human gaze and machine reading comprehension. In *Proceedings of the 24th Conference on Computational Natural Language Learning*, pages 142–152, Online. Association for Computational Linguistics.

Sandeep Mathias, Diptesh Kanojia, Abhijit Mishra, and Pushpak Bhattacharya. 2020. A survey on using gaze behaviour for natural language processing. In *Proceedings of the Twenty-Ninth International Joint Conference on Artificial Intelligence, IJCAI-20*, pages 4907–4913. International Joint Conferences on Artificial Intelligence Organization. Survey track.

Abhijit Mishra and Pushpak Bhattacharyya. 2018. *Cognitively Inspired Natural Language Processing: An Investigation Based on Eye-tracking*. Springer.

Abhijit Mishra, Diptesh Kanojia, Seema Nagar, Kuntal Dey, and Pushpak Bhattacharyya. 2016. Leveraging cognitive features for sentiment analysis. In *Proceedings of The 20th SIGNLL Conference on Computational Natural Language Learning*, pages 156–166, Berlin, Germany. Association for Computational Linguistics.

Abhijit Mishra, Srikanth Tamilselvam, Riddhiman Dasgupta, Seema Nagar, and Kuntal Dey. 2018. Cognition-cognizant sentiment analysis with multitask subjectivity summarization based on annotators' gaze behavior. In *Thirty-Second AAAI Conference on Artificial Intelligence*.

Tom M Mitchell, Svetlana V Shinkareva, Andrew Carlson, Kai-Min Chang, Vicente L Malave, Robert A Mason, and Marcel Adam Just. 2008. Predicting human brain activity associated with the meanings of nouns. *science*, 320(5880):1191–1195.

Saif Mohammad. 2016. A practical guide to sentiment annotation: Challenges and solutions. In *Proceedings of the 7th Workshop on Computational Approaches to Subjectivity, Sentiment and Social Media Analysis*, pages 174–179, San Diego, California. Association for Computational Linguistics.

Jonathan Mummolo and Erik Peterson. 2019. Demand effects in survey experiments: An empirical assessment. *American Political Science Review*, 113(2):517–529.

Lukas Muttenthaler, Nora Hollenstein, and Maria Barrett. 2020. Human brain activity for machine attention. *arXiv preprint arXiv:2006.05113*.

Danish Pruthi, Mansi Gupta, Bhuwan Dhingra, Graham Neubig, and Zachary C Lipton. 2019. Learning to deceive with attention-based explanations. *arXiv preprint arXiv:1909.07913*.

LAI Qiuxia, Salman Khan, Yongwei Nie, Sun Hanqiu, Jianbing Shen, and Ling Shao. 2020. Understanding more about human and machine attention in deep neural networks. *IEEE Transactions on Multimedia*.

Jorge Ramírez, Marcos Baez, Fabio Casati, Luca Cernuzzi, and Boualem Benatallah. 2020. Challenges and strategies for running controlled crowdsourcing experiments. *arXiv preprint arXiv:2011.02804*.

Dan Schwartz, Mariya Toneva, and Leila Wehbe. 2019. Inducing brain-relevant bias in natural language processing models.

Cansu Sen, Thomas Hartvigsen, Biao Yin, Xiangnan Kong, and Elke Rundensteiner. 2020. Human attention maps for text classification: Do humans and neural networks focus on the same words? In *Proceedings of the 58th Annual Meeting of the Association for Computational Linguistics*, pages 4596–4608, Online. Association for Computational Linguistics.

Komal Sharan, Ashwinkumar Ganesan, and Tim Oates. 2019. Improving visual reasoning with attention alignment. In *International Symposium on Visual Computing*, pages 219–230. Springer.

Livio Baldini Soares, Nicholas FitzGerald, Jeffrey Ling, and Tom Kwiatkowski. 2019. Matching the blanks: Distributional similarity for relation learning. In *Proceedings of the 57th Annual Meeting of the Association for Computational Linguistics*, pages 2895–2905, Florence, Italy. Association for Computational Linguistics.

Richard Socher, Alex Perelygin, Jean Wu, Jason Chuang, Christopher D Manning, Andrew Y Ng, and Christopher Potts. 2013. Recursive deep models for semantic compositionality over a sentiment treebank. In *Proceedings of the 2013 conference on empirical methods in natural language processing*, pages 1631–1642.

Ekta Sood, Simon Tannert, Diego Frassinelli, Andreas Bulling, and Ngoc Thang Vu. 2020. Interpreting attention models with human visual attention in machine reading comprehension. In *Proceedings of the 24th Conference on Computational Natural Language Learning*, pages 12–25, Online. Association for Computational Linguistics.

Neil Stewart, Jesse Chandler, and Gabriele Paolacci. 2017. Crowdsourcing samples in cognitive science. *Trends in cognitive sciences*, 21(10):736–748.

Emma Strubell, Patrick Verga, Daniel Andor, David Weiss, and Andrew McCallum. 2018. Linguistically-informed self-attention for semantic role labeling. pages 5027–5038.

Peng Su and K. Vijay-Shanker. 2020. Investigation of BERT model on biomedical relation extraction based on revised fine-tuning mechanism.

Melissa L-H Võ, Avigael M Aizenman, and Jeremy M Wolfe. 2016. You think you know where you looked? you better look again. *Journal of Experimental Psychology: Human Perception and Performance*, 42(10):1477.

Emily Vraga, Leticia Bode, and Sonya Troller-Renfree. 2016. Beyond self-reports: Using eye tracking to measure topic and style differences in attention to social media content. *Communication Methods and Measures*, 10(2-3):149–164.

Nicholas J Wade. 2010. Pioneers of eye movement research. *i-Perception*, 1(2):33–68.

K. Xue, Y. Zhou, Z. Ma, T. Ruan, H. Zhang, and P. He. 2019. Fine-tuning BERT for joint entity and relation extraction in chinese medical text. In *2019 IEEE International Conference on Bioinformatics and Biomedicine (BIBM)*, pages 892–897.

Eiling Yee and Sharon L Thompson-Schill. 2016. Putting concepts into context. *Psychonomic Bulletin & Review*, 23(4):1015–1027.

Yizhen Zhang, Kuan Han, Robert Worth, and Zhongming Liu. 2020. Connecting concepts in the brain by mapping cortical representations of semantic relations. *Nature Communications*, 11(1):1–13.

Yundong Zhang, Juan Carlos Niebles, and Alvaro Soto. 2019. Interpretable visual question answering by visual grounding from attention supervision mining. In *2019 IEEE Winter Conference on Applications of Computer Vision (WACV)*, pages 349–357. IEEE.

Graph-theoretic Properties of the Class of Phonological Neighbourhood Networks

Rory Turnbull
Newcastle University
rory.turnbull@newcastle.ac.uk

Abstract

This paper concerns the structure of phonological neighbourhood networks, which are a graph-theoretic representation of the phonological lexicon. These networks represent each word as a node and links are placed between words which are phonological neighbours, usually defined as a string edit distance of one. Phonological neighbourhood networks have been used to study many aspects of the mental lexicon and psycholinguistic theories of speech production and perception. This paper offers preliminary graph-theoretic observations about phonological neighbourhood networks considered as a class. To aid this exploration, this paper introduces the concept of the *hyperlexicon*, the network consisting of all possible words for a given symbol set and their neighbourhood relations. The construction of the hyperlexicon is discussed, and basic properties are derived. This work is among the first to directly address the nature of phonological neighbourhood networks from an analytic perspective.

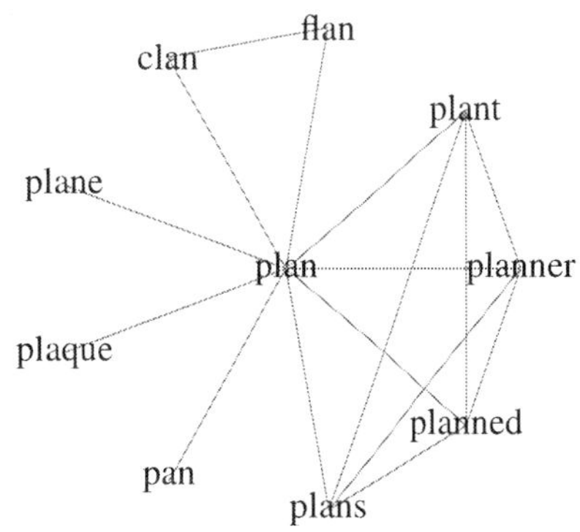

Figure 1: Example phonological neighbourhood network centred around the English word *plan*. Note that some neighbours of a word are neighbours of each other. Adapted from Turnbull and Peperkamp (2017).

1 Motivation

Recent work in phonological psycholinguistics has investigated the structure of the lexicon through the use of phonological neighbourhood networks (Chan and Vitevitch, 2010; Turnbull and Peperkamp, 2017; Siew, 2013; Siew and Vitevitch, 2020; Shoemark et al., 2016). A phonological neighbourhood network is a representation of the lexicon where each word is treated as a node and a link is placed between nodes if and only if those two nodes are phonological neighbours. Two words are neighbours if their string edit distance, in terms of phonological representation, is one. In other words, the neighbours of a word w are all the words that can be formed by the addition, deletion, or substitution of a single phoneme from w. The neighbourhood relation is symmetric (if w is a neighbour of w', then w' is necessarily a neighbour of w), intransitive (if w is a neighbour of w', and w' is a neighbour of w'', it is not necessarily the case that w is a neighbour of w''), and anti-reflexive (w cannot be a neighbour of itself).

Figure 1 shows an abbreviated phonological neighbourhood network for some words of English. One advantage of this representation is that it permits analysis with the methods of network science and graph theory, and work so far has shown a good deal of promise in modeling psycholinguistic properties of the lexicon with these methods (Chan and Vitevitch, 2010; Vitevitch, 2008). A common analysis technique within network science is to compare a given network with a randomly generated one that has the same number of nodes and links. Notable features of the target network relative to the random network are likely due to intrinsic properties of the target network, rather than chance. From this structure one can then infer details about the organising principles that generated the network originally.

For phonological neighbourhood networks, however, this method is often inappropriate, as many

Proceedings of the Workshop on Cognitive Modeling and Computational Linguistics, pages 233–240
Online Event, June 10, 2021. ©2021 Association for Computational Linguistics

logically possible network structures are not possible phonological neighbourhood networks. This fact is because the links between nodes—the neighbourhood relations—are intrinsic to the definitions of the nodes themselves. Changing a link between nodes necessarily means changing the content of a node, which then could entail other changes to other links. This problem was highlighted by Turnbull and Peperkamp (2017),[1] who instead chose to randomly generate *lexicons* and derive networks from those lexicons. However, randomly generated lexicons do not guarantee the same number of links will be present in the resulting network, making it difficult to compare like with like. For this reason, studying phonological neighbourhood networks as a class, and discovering their defining characteristics, is an important methodological goal for psycholinguists.

This research therefore seeks to answer the following broad questions: What are the distinctive characteristics of phonological neighbourhood networks, including their definitions in terms of edge sets and vertex sets, their extremal properties, and characterization of forbidden subgraphs? Is there an effective and efficient method by which phonological neighbourhood graphs can be distinguished from other graphs? The present paper lays the mathematical foundations for future investigations of both of these questions.

2 Preliminaries

This section briefly defines the basic mathematical definitions and operations used in the remainder of the paper. The reader is referred to standard textbooks in graph theory, such as Trudeau (1993) or Diestel (2005), for more details. As mathematical terminology and notation can vary between subfields, alternative names and characterizations of some objects are mentioned in the ensuing sections, but they are not strictly necessary to understand the arguments of this paper.

Networks can be modeled as mathematical objects known as *graphs*, which consist of vertices (nodes) and edges (links). Let G be an undirected graph with no self-loops with vertex set $V(G)$ and edge set $E(G)$. Let K_n denote the complete graph with n vertices and all possible edges.

A graph H is said to be a *subgraph* of a graph G if $V(H) \subseteq V(G)$ and $E(H) \subseteq V(G)$, that is, if the the edges and vertices of H are subsets of those of G. A subgraph H is an *induced subgraph* of G if every edge in $E(G)$ whose endpoints are both in $V(H)$ is present in $E(H)$. In other words, an induced subgraph can be obtained by the process of removing vertices (and any incident edges) from a graph, but not removing edges on their own. Figure 2 provides illustrative examples.

The *diamond* is K_4 with one edge removed. A *circle* C_k has the set of nodes $\{1, 2, ..., k\}$ and edge set $\{\{1, 2\}, \{2, 3\}, ..., \{(k-1), k\}, \{k, 1\}\}$. (Circle graphs that are induced subgraphs of a larger graph are also known as *k-holes*.) Figure 3 depicts the diamond and C_5.

A *star* S_k is a graph with one central vertex which is connected to k other unique vertices. No other vertices or edges exist. Figure 4 depicts the stars S_3 (also known as a *claw*), S_4, and S_6.

The *Cartesian product* $A \times B$ of two sets A and B is defined as

$$A \times B = \{(a, b) | a \in A, b \in B\}, \tag{1}$$

that is, the Cartesian product of A and B is the set of all ordered pairs where the first element is a member of A and the second element is a member of B. For example, the Cartesian product of $\{a, b, c\}$ and $\{x, y\}$ is $\{(a, x), (a, y), (b, x), (b, y), (c, x), (c, y)\}$.

The Cartesian product $G \square H$ of two graphs G and H has the vertex set

$$V(G \square H) = V(G) \times V(H). \tag{2}$$

A given vertex (a, x) is linked with another vertex (b, y) if $a = b$ (the first elements are identical) and $\{x, y\} \in E(H)$ (the second elements are linked in H), or if $x = y$ (the second elements are identical) and $\{a, b\} \in E(G)$ (the first elements are linked in G). To aid understanding, Figure 5 depicts an example of the Cartesian product of two graphs, G and H. Graph G has $V(G) = \{a, b, c\}$ and $E(G) = \{\{a, b\}, \{b, c\}\}$. Graph H has $V(H) = \{x, y\}$ and $E(H) = \{\{x, y\}\}$. Observe how G and H can be seen in $G \square H$ as two orthogonal dimensions. Note also that the total number of vertices in $G \square H$ is equal to the product of the number of vertices in G and H.

We further denote the *Cartesian exponent* of a graph G as

$$G^{\square n} = \underbrace{G \square G \square G \dots G}_{n}, \tag{3}$$

[1] See also Gruenenfelder and Pisoni (2009) for related concerns.

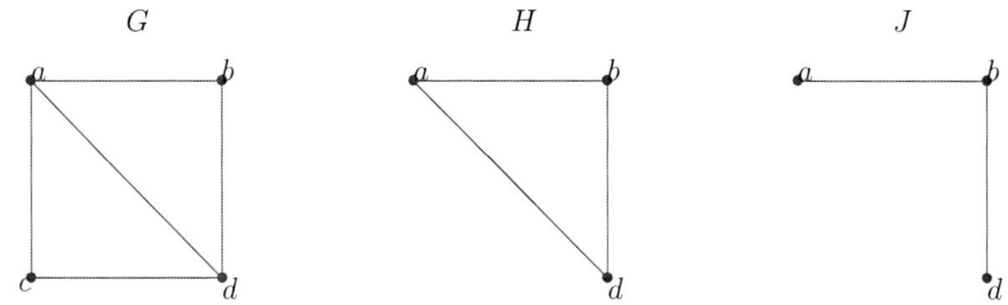

Figure 2: Three graphs. H is an induced subgraph of G formed through the removal of vertex c and its incident edges. J is also a subgraph of G, but it is not an induced subgraph due to the fact that the edge between vertices a and d is missing.

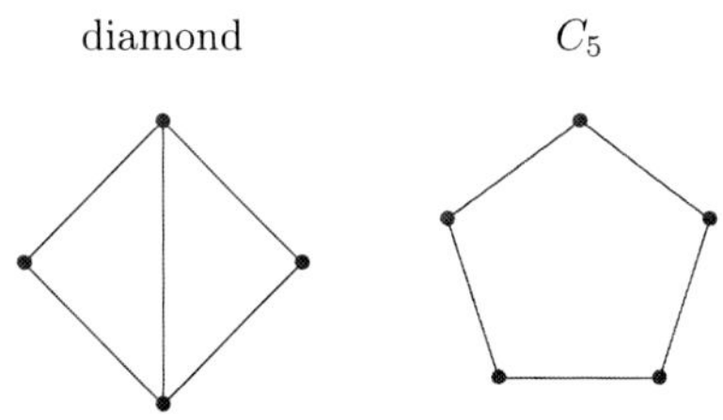

Figure 3: The diamond graph and C_5.

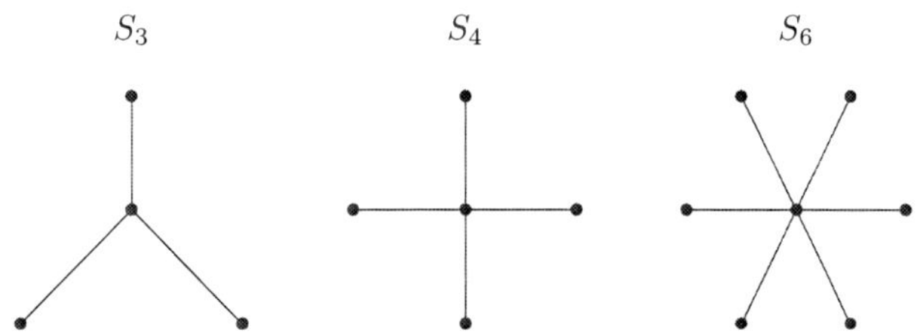

Figure 4: Star graphs S_3, S_4, and S_6.

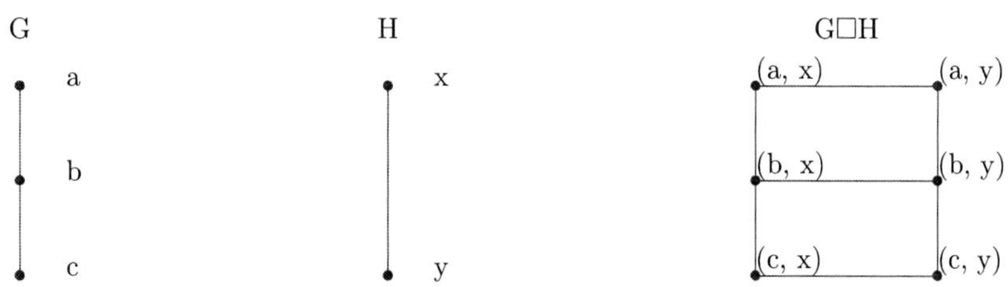

Figure 5: Graphs G and H and the Cartesian product $G \square H$.

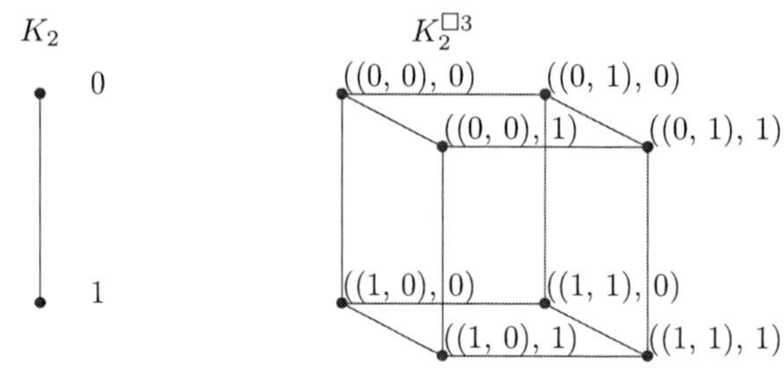

Figure 6: The complete graph K_2 and Cartesian exponent $K_2^{\square 3}$, i.e. $K_2 \square K_2 \square K_2$.

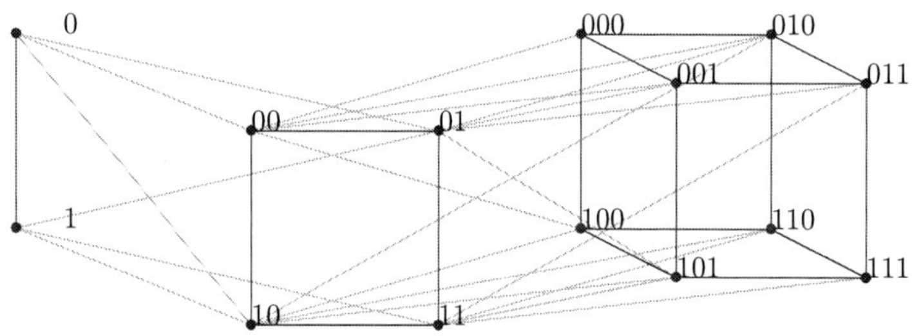

Figure 7: The hyperlexicon $\mathcal{H}(2, \{1, 2, 3\})$. Here the alphabet is defined as $\{0, 1\}$ but any set of two symbols is possible. Edges between layers (i.e. phoneme additions/deletions) are drawn in grey; edges within layers (i.e. phoneme substitutions) are drawn in black.

that is, the Cartesian product of G with itself $n-1$ times. Figure 6 depicts the graphs K_2 and $K_2^{\square 3}$.

It can be seen that $K_2^{\square 2}$ is a square, $K_2^{\square 3}$ is a cube, and $K_2^{\square n}$ is an n-dimensional hypercube.[2] Likewise, the vertex labels of $K_m^{\square n}$ are equivalent to all strings of length n drawn from an alphabet of m symbols. The edges of $K_m^{\square n}$ are equivalent to the neighbourhood relations of such strings. These facts establish the basis upon which we can use these tools to model phonological neighbourhood networks.

3 The Hyperlexicon

In this paper we introduce the concept of the *hyperlexicon*. A hyperlexicon $\mathcal{H}(\phi, L)$ is defined as the phonological neighbourhood network generated from all possible string sequences of lengths $\{\ell_1, \ldots \ell_n\}$ for $\ell \in L$ over an alphabet of length ϕ.

Figure 7 depicts the hyperlexicon of all 'words' of length 1, 2, and 3, over the alphabet of `0` and `1`. Stella and Brede (2015) observed that the set of all possible phoneme sequences (i.e. the hyperlexicon) is composed of multiple 'layers', each corresponding to a distinct member of L. This layered structure can be clearly seen in Figure 7. Edges within a layer correspond to neighbours by substitution, while edges between layers correspond to neighbours by deletion or insertion. Note further that each layer is isomorphic to $K_\phi^{\square \ell}$, the ℓth Cartesian exponent of the complete graph with ϕ vertices.[3]

Imagine now a hypothetical lexicon consisting of the words `1`, `00`, `10`, and `110`. The phonological neighbourhood network of this lexicon is depicted in Figure 8, overlaid on the hyperlexicon from Figure 7. It can be seen that this lexicon's network is an induced subgraph of the hyperlexicon.

Indeed, phonological neighbourhood networks are necessarily induced subgraphs of the hyperlexicon. For example, the English lexicon consists of strings of varying lengths, with the set of English phonemes as its 'alphabet'. There are some strings of English phonemes which are not part of the English lexicon—i.e. nonwords such as *blick* and *pmisgkr*. The set of words in the English lexicon, then, is a subset of the set of all logically possible strings of English phonemes. A hyperlexicon corresponds to the neighbourhood network derived from a set of all logically possible strings

[2]More generally, $K_m^{\square n}$ is an $m \times m$ Rook's graph in n dimensions.

[3]Each layer can also be characterized as an expansion of the hypercube graph Q_ℓ, or as a Hamming graph $\text{Ham}(\ell, \phi)$.

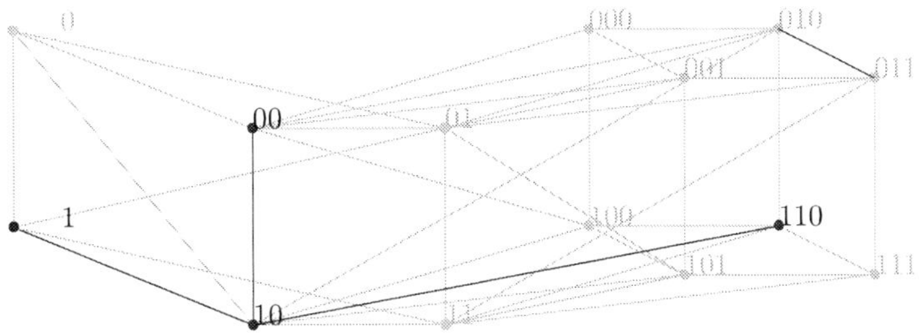

Figure 8: The phonological neighbourhood network (in black) of the lexicon 1, 00, 10, and 110, depicted as a subgraph of the hyperlexicon $\mathcal{H}(2, \{1, 2, 3\})$ (in grey).

of length L, given some set of phonemes of length ϕ. Any subset of this set of strings will correspond to an induced subgraph of the hyperlexicon. Any phonological neighbourhood network, then, with words of lengths in L constituted from ϕ distinct phonemes, is necessarily an induced subgraph of the hyperlexicon $\mathcal{H}(\phi, L)$. Studying properties of the hyperlexicon therefore gives us insight into the possible structures of phonological neighbourhood networks.

The vertex set of the hyperlexicon is given by

$$V(\mathcal{H}(\phi, L)) = \bigcup_{\ell \in L} V(K_\phi^{\Box\ell}), \tag{4}$$

that is, the set union of each layer's vertices. The number of vertices of $\mathcal{H}(\phi, L)$ is the sum of the size of each layer, which is

$$\sum^{L} \phi^{\ell}. \tag{5}$$

If L is contiguous, $\mathcal{H}(\phi, L)$ is necessarily connected (i.e. there is exactly one connected component); if L is not contiguous,[4] then $\mathcal{H}(\phi, L)$ has multiple connected components.

4 The Edges between the Layers of the Hyperlexicon

Defining the edge set of $\mathcal{H}(\phi, L)$ is less straightforward than the vertex set and is not fully solved. Within each layer, the edges are the same as in the graph $K_\phi^{\Box\ell}$. Between the layers the situation is considerably more complex. To begin, we first determine the number of possible unique neighbours for any word. For a word of length ℓ in a language with ϕ distinct phonemes, neighbours are generated through the addition, deletion, or substitution of a single phoneme. The number of possible neighbours can be shown to depend upon word length ℓ, alphabet size ϕ, and the number of pairs of adjacent identical phonemes, described below.

4.1 Substitutions

It is straightforward to demonstrate that there are

$$\phi\ell - \ell \tag{6}$$

possible substitutions. This statement follows from the fact that neighbourhood is an anti-reflexive relation, so vacuously substituting a phoneme for itself will not generate a neighbour.

4.2 Additions

The number of additions can be derived from the fact that each of ϕ symbols can be added to $\ell + 1$ positions, which gives $\phi(\ell + 1)$. However, for each insertion position, one of these ϕ phonemes will result in a string which is identical to an insertion of the same phoneme at a different location. For example, prefixing a onto the beginning of ab is equivalent to inserting a into the middle of ab: they both result in aab. The number of additions is therefore

$$\phi(\ell + 1) - \ell \tag{7}$$

which simplifies to Equation (6) plus ϕ:

$$\phi\ell - \ell + \phi. \tag{8}$$

4.3 Deletions

The number of deletions is not constant and depends upon the structure of the word. For example, although there are three distinct deletion positions in a possible word aaa, all three of them lead to the same unique word aa; so practically speaking

[4] Such a scenario is plausible for languages with strict phonotactics requiring an obligatory onset and forbidding codas, i.e. all syllables must be CV. For such languages, $L = \{2, 4, 6, 8, \dots\}$. Hua (Blevins, 1995) and Senufo (Kientz, 1979) have been reported to have this kind of syllable structure.

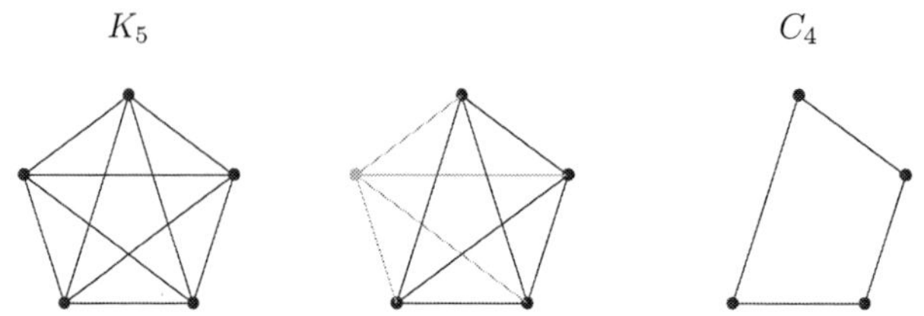

Figure 9: In attempting to generate C_4 (right) from K_5 (left), a single vertex must be removed. However, as shown by the middle graph, removal of a single vertex (in grey) results in a graph with too many edges. This is true no matter which vertex we choose to remove. C_4 is therefore not an induced subgraph of K_5; we can call C_4 a *forbidden subgraph* of K_5.

there is only one possible deletion. On the other hand, all three possible deletions on abc result in three unique strings (namely, bc, ac, ab), so it has three deletions.

The actual number of possible deletions depends on the number of pairs of identical adjacent symbols.[5] Pairs of identical adjacent symbols act as a single symbol for the purposes of counting possible deletion sites. The number of deletions is therefore

$$\ell - a, \tag{9}$$

where a is the number of pairs of adjacent identical symbols in the word. For example abba has only 3 possible deletions, despite being of length 4. (For this word, a deletion at position 2 is equivalent to a deletion at position 3; the sequence bb can be essentially treated as a single symbol for the purposes of counting deletion sites.)

All words allow at least 1 deletion, and some words allow as many as ℓ deletions.

4.4 Vertex Degree

From the sections above, it follows that each vertex in $\mathcal{H}(\phi, L)$ has $\phi\ell - \ell$ edges to other nodes in the same layer as it. If there is a higher layer, then each node also has $\phi\ell - \ell + \phi$ edges leading to nodes in that layer. If there is a lower layer, then each node has between 1 and ℓ edges leading to that layer.

5 Forbidden Subgraphs

Finally, we begin to attempt to characterize the class of hyperlexicons in terms of forbidden subgraphs. A forbidden subgraph of G is any graph which is not isomorphic to any induced subgraph of G. For example, there is no induced subgraph of K_5 which is isomorphic to C_4. This fact is illustrated in Figure 9. C_4 is therefore a *forbidden subgraph* of K_5. Graph structures which are impossible within a hyperlexicon are also impossible within real phonological networks, because real phonological networks are induced subgraphs of a hyperlexicon. Understanding the forbidden subgraphs of a hyperlexicon therefore allows us to understand possible natural language networks.

5.1 Forbidden Subgraphs of individual layers

A hyperlexicon is composed of layers. Each layer is $K_\phi^{\square\ell}$, the ℓth cartesian exponent of K_ϕ. For the special case of $\ell = 2$ (i.e. words of length two), these graphs have been studied in the mathematical literature under the names of *Rooks' graphs*, *grid-line graphs*, *adjacency graphs*, and *graphs of* $(0, 1)$ *matrices*. Peterson (2003) studied these graphs in cases where $\ell > 2$, and established that the diamond and C_5 are among the forbidden subgraphs of $K_\phi^{\square\ell}$.

The 3-star S_3 has been shown to be a forbidden subgraph of $K_\phi^{\square 2}$ (Hedetniemi, 1971). More generally, no layer at length ℓ has $S_{\ell+1}$ as an induced subgraph. This observation follows from the pigeonhole principle: the first ℓ vertices of $S_{\ell+1}$ can be found in the ℓ dimensions of the graph. The final vertex must be in one of the dimensions already considered, and therefore must be adjacent to an existing vertex. This leads to a triangle, meaning the induced subgraph is no longer a star.

These structures, forbidden from each individual layer of the hyperlexicon, are not forbidden from the hyperlexicon as a whole. Within the hyperlexicon $\mathcal{H}(3, \{1, 2, 3\})$ we observe both the diamond and C_5; see Figures 10 and 11.[6] Similarly, for a hy-

[5] Using the terminology of combinatorics on words, a "pair of identical adjacent symbols" can be understood as a square of length 2.

[6] We have been unable to find any induced C_5 in cases where $\phi < 3$. While this conjecture might be of mathematical interest, it is not relevant to our main use-case of phonological

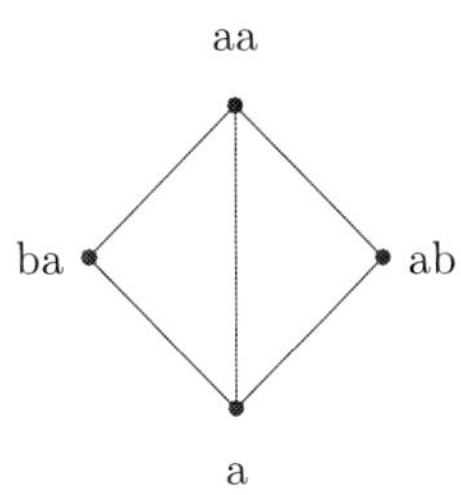

Figure 10: The diamond graph as an induced subgraph of a hyperlexicon.

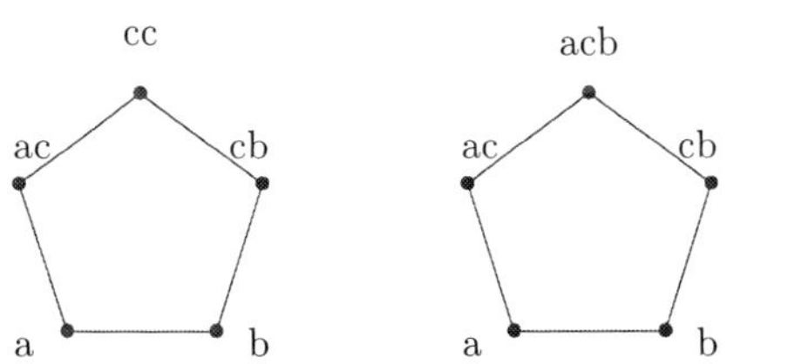

Figure 11: C_5 as two induced subgraphs of a hyperlexicon.

perlexicon with $\max(L) = 4$, the star S_5 is present as an induced subgraph, as shown in Figure 12.

Since these structures cannot occur within each layer, it follows that their existence within a hyperlexicon must necessarily span more than one layer. Indeed, we hypothesize that in the case of $S_{\ell+1}$ where $\ell = \max(L)$, this structure must necessarily span three layers.

5.2 Forbidden Subgraphs of the Entire Hyperlexicon

No hyperlexicon has $K_{\phi+2}$ as an induced subgraph. K_ϕ exists, as this constitutes the 'dimensions' of each layer. From K_ϕ it is possible to induce $K_{\phi+1}$ by adding a vertex from one layer down. For example, the string `a` is adjacent to `aa`, `ab`, `ac`, and so on. However there is no other vertex in the lower layer which is adjacent to all of `a`'s neighbours and to `a` itself. $K_{\phi+2}$ is therefore not an induced subgraph of the hyperlexicon.

6 Conclusion

This paper has reviewed the basic structure of hyperlexicon graphs. Induced subgraphs of hyperlexicon graphs typify the class of phonological neighbourhood networks. It is hoped that the preliminary results presented here will spur further work on the

networks, as all known natural languages possess considerably more than 3 phonemes.

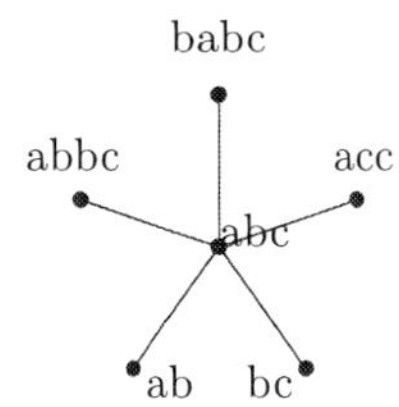

Figure 12: S_5 as an induced subgraph of a hyperlexicon with $\max(L) = 4$.

nature of phonological neighbourhood networks as formal objects. This work in turn has methodological implications for evaluating and measuring phonological neighbourhood networks derived from natural languages.

Acknowledgements

I am grateful to Paul Tupper and several anonymous reviewers for their comments on an earlier draft. All errors and omissions are my own.

References

Juliette Blevins. 1995. The syllable in phonological theory. In John Goldsmith, editor, *Handbook of phonological theory*, pages 206–244. Blackwell.

K Y Chan and M S Vitevitch. 2010. Network structure influences speech production. *Cognitive Science*, 34(4):685–697.

Reinhard Diestel. 2005. *Graph Theory*, 3rd edition. Springer, New York, NY.

Thomas M Gruenenfelder and David B Pisoni. 2009. The lexical restructuring hypothesis and graph theoretic analyses of networks based on random lexicons. *Journal of Speech, Language, and Hearing Research*, 52(2):596–609.

Stephen T Hedetniemi. 1971. Graphs of (0,1)-matrices. In M Capobianco, J B Frechen, and M Krolik, editors, *Recent Trends in Graph Theory*, pages 157–171. Springer, Berlin.

Albert Kientz. 1979. *Dieu et les génies: Récits étiologiques senoufo (Côte-d'Ivoire)*. Centre national de la recherche scientifique, Paris.

Dale Peterson. 2003. Gridline graphs: a review in two dimensions and an extension to higher dimensions. *Discrete Applied Mathematics*, 126:223–239.

Philippa Shoemark, Sharon Goldwater, James Kirby, and Rik Sarkar. 2016. Towards robust cross-linguistic comparisons of phonological networks. In *Proceedings of the 14th ACL SIGMORPHON Workshop on Computational Research in Phonetics, Phonology, and Morphology*, pages 110–120.

Cynthia S Q Siew. 2013. Community structure in the phonological network. *Frontiers in Psychology*, 4:553.

Cynthia S Q Siew and Michael S Vitevitch. 2020. Investigating the influence of inverse preferential attachment on network development. *Entropy*, 22(9):1029.

Massimo Stella and Markus Brede. 2015. Patterns in the English language: Phonological networks, percolation and assembly models. *Journal of Statistical Mechanics: Theory and Experiment*, 5:P05006.

Richard J Trudeau. 1993. *Introduction to Graph Theory*. Dover, New York, NY.

Rory Turnbull and Sharon Peperkamp. 2017. What governs a language's lexicon? determining the organizing principles of phonological neighbourhood networks. In Hocine Cherifi, Sabrina Gaito, Walter Quattrociocchi, and Alessandra Sala, editors, *Complex Networks & Their Applications V*, volume 693 of *Studies in Computational Intelligence*, pages 83–94. Springer, Cham, Switzerland.

Michael S Vitevitch. 2008. What can graph theory tell us about word learning and lexical retrieval? *Journal of Speech, Language, and Hearing Research*, 51:408–422.

Contributions of Propositional Content and Syntactic Category Information in Sentence Processing

Byung-Doh Oh
Department of Linguistics
The Ohio State University
oh.531@osu.edu

William Schuler
Department of Linguistics
The Ohio State University
schuler@ling.osu.edu

Abstract

Expectation-based theories of sentence processing posit that processing difficulty is determined by predictability in context. While predictability quantified via surprisal has gained empirical support, this representation-agnostic measure leaves open the question of how to best approximate the human comprehender's latent probability model. This work presents an incremental left-corner parser that incorporates information about both propositional content and syntactic categories into a single probability model. This parser can be trained to make parsing decisions conditioning on only one source of information, thus allowing a clean ablation of the relative contribution of propositional content and syntactic category information. Regression analyses show that surprisal estimates calculated from the full parser make a significant contribution to predicting self-paced reading times over those from the parser without syntactic category information, as well as a significant contribution to predicting eye-gaze durations over those from the parser without propositional content information. Taken together, these results suggest a role for propositional content and syntactic category information in incremental sentence processing.

1 Introduction

Much work in sentence processing has been dedicated to studying differential patterns of processing difficulty in order to shed light on the latent mechanism behind online processing. As it is now well-established that processing difficulty can be observed in behavioral responses (e.g. reading times, eye movements, and event-related potentials), recent psycholinguistic work has tried to account for these variables by regressing various predictors of interest. Most notably, in support of expectation-based theories of sentence processing (Hale, 2001; Levy, 2008), predictability in context has been quantified through the information-theoretical measure of surprisal (Shannon, 1948). Although there has been empirical support for n-gram, PCFG, and LSTM surprisal in the literature (Goodkind and Bicknell, 2018; Hale, 2001; Levy, 2008; Shain, 2019; Smith and Levy, 2013), as surprisal makes minimal assumptions about linguistic representations that are built during processing, this leaves open the question of how to best estimate the human language comprehender's latent probability model.

One factor related to memory usage that has received less attention in psycholinguistic modeling is the influence of *propositional content*, or meaning that is conveyed by the sentence. Early psycholinguistic experiments have demonstrated that the propositional content of utterances tends to be retained in memory, whereas the exact surface form and syntactic structure are forgotten (Bransford and Franks, 1971; Jarvella, 1971). This suggests that memory costs related to incrementally constructing a representation of propositional content might manifest themselves in behavioral responses during online sentence processing. In addition, there is evidence suggesting that parsing decisions are informed by the ongoing interpretation of the sentence (Brown-Schmidt et al., 2002; Tanenhaus et al., 1995).

Based on this insight, prior cognitive modeling research has sought to incorporate propositional content information into various complexity metrics. A prominent approach in this line of research has been to quantify complexity based on the compatibility between a predicate and its arguments (i.e. *thematic fit*, Baroni and Lenci 2010, Chersoni et al. 2016, Padó et al. 2009). However, these complexity metrics can only be evaluated at a coarse per-sentence level or at critical regions of constructed stimuli where predicates and arguments are revealed, making them less suitable for studying online processing. A more distribu-

Proceedings of the Workshop on Cognitive Modeling and Computational Linguistics, pages 241–250
Online Event, June 10, 2021.

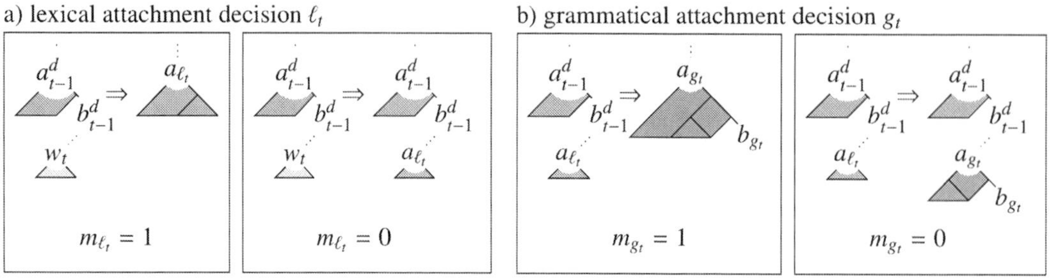

Figure 1: Left-corner parser operations: a) lexical match (m_{ℓ_t}=1) and no-match (m_{ℓ_t}=0) operations, creating new apex a_{ℓ_t}, and b) grammatical match (m_{g_t}=1) and no-match (m_{g_t}=0) operations, creating new apex a_{g_t} and base b_{g_t}.

tional approach has also been explored that relies on word co-occurrence to calculate the *semantic coherence* between each word and its preceding context (Mitchell et al., 2010; Sayeed et al., 2015). Although these models allow more fine-grained per-word metrics to be calculated, their dependence on an aggregate context vector makes it difficult to distinguish 'gist' or topic information from propositional content.

Unlike these models, our approach seeks to incorporate propositional content by augmenting a generative and incremental parser to build an ongoing representation of *predicate context vectors*, which is based on a categorial grammar formalism that captures both local and non-local predicate-argument structure. This processing model can be used to estimate per-word surprisal predictors that capture the influence of propositional content differentially with that of syntactic categories, which are devoid of propositional content.[1] Our experiments demonstrate that the incorporation of both propositional content and syntactic category information into the processing model significantly improves fit to self-paced reading times and eye-gaze durations over corresponding ablated models, suggesting their role in online sentence processing. In addition, we present exploratory work showing how our processing model can be utilized to examine differential effects of propositional content in memory-intensive filler-gap constructions.

[1]Note that this distinction of propositional content as retained information about the meaning of a sentence and syntactic categories as unretained information about the form of a sentence may differ somewhat from notions of semantics and syntax that are familiar to computational linguists – in particular, predicates corresponding to lemmatized words fall on the content side of this division here because they are retained after processing, even though it may be common in NLP applications to use them in syntactic parsing.

2 Background

The experiments presented in this paper use surprisal predictors calculated by an incremental processing model based on a probabilistic left-corner parser (Johnson-Laird, 1983; van Schijndel et al., 2013). This incremental processing model provides a probabilistic account of sentence processing by making a single lexical attachment decision and a single grammatical attachment decision for each input word.[2]

Surprisal can be defined as the negative log of a conditional probability of a word w_t and a state q_t at some time step t given a sequence of preceding words $w_{1..t-1}$, marginalized over these states:

$$\mathsf{S}(w_t) \stackrel{\text{def}}{=} -\log \sum_{q_t} \mathsf{P}(w_t\ q_t \mid w_{1..t-1}) \qquad (1)$$

These conditional probabilities can in turn be defined recursively using a transition model:

$$\mathsf{P}(w_t\ q_t \mid w_{1..t-1}) \stackrel{\text{def}}{=} \sum_{q_{t-1}} \mathsf{P}(w_t\ q_t \mid q_{t-1}) \cdot \mathsf{P}(w_{t-1}\ q_{t-1} \mid w_{1..t-2}) \qquad (2)$$

A probabilistic left-corner parser defines its transition model over possible working memory store states $q_t = a_t^1/b_t^1, \ldots, a_t^D/b_t^D$, each of which consists of a bounded number D of nested derivation fragments a_t^d/b_t^d. Each derivation fragment spans a part of a derivation tree below some apex node a_t^d, lacking a base node b_t^d yet to come.

At each time step, the parser generates a lexical attachment decision ℓ_t, a word w_t, a grammatical at-

[2]Johnson-Laird (1983) refers to lexical and grammatical attachment decisions as 'shift' and 'predict' respectively.

$$\begin{aligned}&\text{many }(\lambda_{x_1}\text{ some }(\lambda_{e_1}\text{ person }e_1\ x_1)\\&\qquad\qquad(\lambda_{e_1}\text{ true}))\\&\quad(\lambda_{x_1}\text{ some }(\lambda_{x_3}\text{ some }\ (\lambda_{e_3}\text{ pasta }e_3\ x_3)\\&\qquad\qquad\qquad\qquad(\lambda_{e_3}\text{ true}))\\&\qquad\qquad(\lambda_{x_3}\text{ some }\ (\lambda_{e_2}\text{ eat }e_2\ x_1\ x_3)\\&\qquad\qquad\qquad\qquad(\lambda_{e_2}\text{ true})))\end{aligned}$$

Figure 2: Lambda calculus expression for the propositional content of the sentence *Many people eat pasta,* using generalized quantifiers over discourse entities and eventualities.

tachment decision g_t, and a resulting store state q_t:

$$\begin{aligned}\mathsf{P}(w_t\ q_t \mid q_{t-1}) = \sum_{\ell_t, g_t} &\mathsf{P}(\ell_t \mid q_{t-1}) \cdot \\ &\mathsf{P}(w_t \mid q_{t-1}\ \ell_t) \cdot \\ &\mathsf{P}(g_t \mid q_{t-1}\ \ell_t\ w_t) \cdot \\ &\mathsf{P}(q_t \mid q_{t-1}\ \ell_t\ w_t\ g_t) \qquad (3)\end{aligned}$$

As shown in Figure 1, the lexical attachment decision ℓ_t generates a new complete node a_{ℓ_t} based on (m_{ℓ_t}) whether the word matches the base of the most recent derivation fragment; and the grammatical attachment decision g_t generates a new derivation fragment a_{g_t}/b_{g_t} based on (m_{g_t}) whether the parent of a grammar rule with this new complete node as a left child matches the base of the most recent remaining derivation fragment.

The semantic processing model described in this paper extends the above left-corner parser to incorporate propositional content by conditioning lexical and grammatical decisions on sparse vectors of predicate contexts $\mathbf{h}_{a_t^d}$ and $\mathbf{h}_{b_t^d}$ in addition to category labels $c_{a_t^d}$ and $c_{b_t^d}$ in apex and base nodes a_t^d and b_t^d. These predicate context vectors for nodes in a derivation tree of a sentence can be defined in terms of argument positions of variables signified by these nodes in predicates of a logical form translation of that sentence. For example, in Figure 2, the variable e_2 (signified by the word *eat*) would have the predicate context EAT_0 because it is the zeroth (initial) participant of the predication (eat $e_2\ x_1\ x_3$).[3] Similarly, the variable x_3 would have both the predicate context PASTA_1, because it is the first participant (counting from zero) of the predication (pasta $e_3\ x_3$), and the predicate context EAT_2, because it is the second participant (counting from

[3]Participants of predications are numbered starting with zero so as to align loosely with syntactic arguments in canonical form.

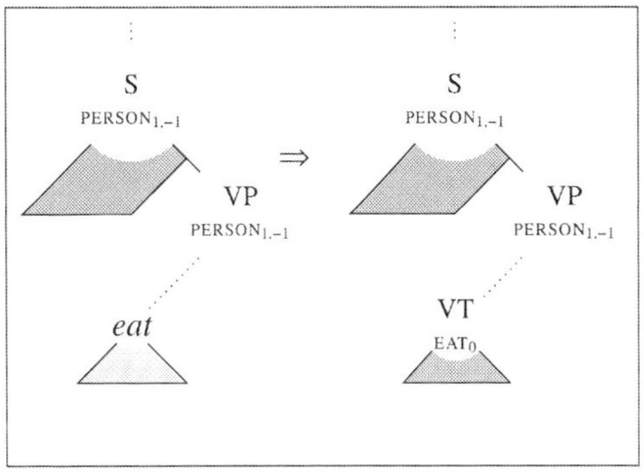

Figure 3: Derivation fragments resulting from example lexical decisions made at the word *eat* in the sentence *People eat pasta.* Note that the *predicate contexts* instead of *predicate context vectors* are displayed here for clarity. The predicate context $\text{PERSON}_{1,-1}$ represents an eventuality that takes the first argument of a PERSON predicate as its first argument.

zero) of the predication (eat $e_2\ x_1\ x_3$). These predicate contexts are obtained by reannotating the training corpus using a generalized categorial grammar of English (Nguyen et al., 2012), which is sensitive to syntactic valence and non-local dependencies.

Lexical attachment probabilities. The probability of each lexical decision ℓ_t in this parser is therefore decomposed into one term for generating a match decision m_{ℓ_t} and a predicate context vector $\mathbf{h}_{\ell_t}$, and another term for generating a syntactic category label c_{ℓ_t} for the new complete node a_{ℓ_t}:

$$\begin{aligned}&\mathsf{P}(\ell_t \mid q_{t-1}) = \\ &\qquad \mathsf{P}(m_{\ell_t}\ \mathbf{h}_{\ell_t} \mid q_{t-1}) \cdot \mathsf{P}(c_{\ell_t} \mid q_{t-1}\ m_{\ell_t}\ \mathbf{h}_{\ell_t}) \quad (4)\end{aligned}$$

The probability of generating the match decision and the predicate context vector depends on the base node b_{t-1}^d of the previous derivation fragment:

$$\begin{aligned}&\mathsf{P}(m_{\ell_t}\ \mathbf{h}_{\ell_t} \mid q_{t-1}) = \\ &\qquad \underset{m_{\ell_t}, \mathbf{h}_{\ell_t}}{\text{SOFTMAX}}(\text{FF}_{\theta_\text{L}}[\delta_d{}^\top, [\delta_{c_{b_{t-1}^d}}^\top, \mathbf{h}_{b_{t-1}^d}^\top]\,\mathbf{E}_\text{L}]) \quad (5)\end{aligned}$$

where FF is a feedforward neural network, δ_i is a Kronecker delta vector consisting of a one at element i and zeros elsewhere, depth d = $\text{argmax}_{d'}\{a_{t-1}^{d'} \neq \bot\}$ is the number of non-null derivation fragments at the previous time step, and $\mathbf{E}_\text{L}$ is a matrix of jointly trained dense embeddings for each syntactic category and predicate context. The probabilities of category labels are calculated using relative frequency estimation on training data based on the base node of the previous derivation fragment. The new complete node a_{ℓ_t} then depends on the match decision m_{ℓ_t} (see Figure 3):

$$a_{\ell_t} \stackrel{\text{def}}{=} \begin{cases} a^d_{t-1} & \text{if } m_{\ell_t} = 1 \\ c_{\ell_t}, \mathbf{h}_{\ell_t} & \text{if } m_{\ell_t} = 0 \end{cases} \quad (6)$$

Word probabilities. Probabilities for generating words are estimated as the probability of generating their character sequence using a recurrent neural network implementation of a character model.

Grammatical attachment probabilities. The probability of each grammatical decision g_t in this parser is similarly decomposed into a term for generating a match decision m_{g_t} and a composition operator for a grammar rule o_{g_t},[4] and terms for category labels c_{g_t} and c'_{g_t} at the apex and base nodes of the new derivation fragment:

$$\begin{aligned} \mathsf{P}(g_t \mid q_{t-1}\, \ell_t\, w_t) = \mathsf{P}(&m_{g_t}\, o_{g_t} \mid q_{t-1}\, \ell_t\, w_t) \cdot \\ &\mathsf{P}(c_{g_t} \mid q_{t-1}\, \ell_t\, w_t\, m_{g_t}\, o_{g_t}) \cdot \\ &\mathsf{P}(c'_{g_t} \mid q_{t-1}\, \ell_t\, w_t\, m_{g_t}\, o_{g_t}\, c_{g_t}) \end{aligned} \quad (7)$$

The probability of generating the match decision and the composition operator depends on the base node of the previous derivation fragment and the new complete node a_{ℓ_t}:

$$\mathsf{P}(m_{g_t}\, o_{g_t} \mid q_{t-1}\, \ell_t\, w_t) = \underset{m_{g_t} o_{g_t}}{\text{SoftMax}}\big(\text{FF}_{\theta_{\text{G}}}[\delta_d{}^{\top}, [\delta^{\top}_{c_{b^{d-m_{\ell_t}}_{t-1}}}, \mathbf{h}^{\top}_{b^{d-m_{\ell_t}}_{t-1}}, \delta^{\top}_{c_{a_{\ell_t}}}, \mathbf{h}^{\top}_{a_{\ell_t}}]\,\mathbf{E}_{\text{G}}]\big) \quad (8)$$

where $\mathbf{E}_{\text{G}}$ is a matrix of jointly trained dense embeddings for each syntactic category and predicate context. The probabilities of category labels c_{g_t} and c'_{g_t} in Equation 7 are calculated using relative frequency estimation on training data based on the base node of the previous derivation fragment. The composition operator o_{g_t} in Equations 7 and 8 is associated with sparse composition matrices $\mathbf{A}_{o_{g_t}}$, which can be used to compose predicate context vectors associated with the apex node a_{g_t} of the new derivation fragment,

$$a_{g_t} \stackrel{\text{def}}{=} \begin{cases} a^{d-m_{g_t}}_{t-1} & \text{if } m_{g_t} = 1 \\ c_{g_t}, \mathbf{A}_{o_{g_t}} \mathbf{h}_{a_{\ell_t}} & \text{if } m_{g_t} = 0 \end{cases} \quad (9)$$

and sparse composition matrices $\mathbf{B}_{o_{g_t}}$, which can be used to compose predicate context vectors associated with the base node b_{g_t} of the new derivation fragment (see Figure 4):

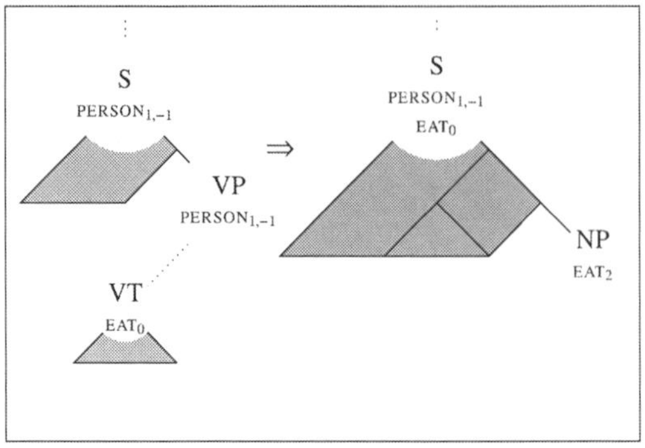

Figure 4: Derivation fragments resulting from example grammatical decisions made at the word *eat* in the sentence *People eat pasta.*

$$b_{g_t} \stackrel{\text{def}}{=} \begin{cases} c'_{g_t}, \mathbf{B}_{o_{g_t}}[\mathbf{h}_{b^{d-m_{\ell_t}}_{t-1}}{}^{\top}, \mathbf{h}_{a_{\ell_t}}{}^{\top}]^{\top} & \text{if } m_{g_t}{=}1 \\ c'_{g_t}, \mathbf{B}_{o_{g_t}}[\mathbf{0}^{\top}, \mathbf{h}_{a_{\ell_t}}{}^{\top}]^{\top} & \text{if } m_{g_t}{=}0 \end{cases} \quad (10)$$

These composition matrices allow predicate contexts to propagate appropriately through the tree to allow parsing decisions to depend on predicates that may be several words away.

Resulting store state probabilities. In order to update the store state based on the lexical and grammatical decisions, derivation fragments above the most recent nonterminal node are carried forward, and derivation fragments below it are set to null ($\perp$),

$$\mathsf{P}(q_t \mid \ldots) \stackrel{\text{def}}{=} \prod_{d=1}^{D} \begin{cases} [\![a^d_t, b^d_t = a^d_{t-1}, b^d_{t-1}]\!] & \text{if } d < d' \\ [\![a^d_t, b^d_t = a_{g_t}, b_{g_t}]\!] & \text{if } d = d' \\ [\![a^d_t, b^d_t = \perp, \perp]\!] & \text{if } d > d' \end{cases} \quad (11)$$

where the indicator function $[\![\varphi]\!] = 1$ if φ is true and 0 otherwise, and $d' = \text{argmax}_d\{a^d_{t-1} {\neq} \perp\} + 1 - m_{\ell_t} - m_{g_t}$. Together, these probabilistic decisions generate the n unary branches and $n-1$ binary branches of a parse tree in Chomsky normal form for an n-word sentence.

3 Isolating Content and Category Contributions

In order to examine the contribution of propositional content on the content-sensitive processing model, the model is modified to allow it to be trained to make lexical and grammatical decisions without conditioning on the predicate context vec-

[4] Examples of composition operators include using the predicate context of the left child as a modifier or an argument, as well as introducing or discharging filler-gap dependencies.

tors,

$$\mathsf{P}(m_{\ell_t}\, \mathbf{h}_{\ell_t} \mid q_{t-1}) = \underset{m_{\ell_t} \mathbf{h}_{\ell_t}}{\textsc{SoftMax}}(\, \mathrm{FF}_{\theta_\mathrm{L}}[\delta_d{}^\top, [\delta^\top_{c_{b^d_{t-1}}}, \mathbf{0}^\top]\, \mathbf{E}_\mathrm{L}]\,) \quad (12)$$

$$\mathsf{P}(m_{g_t}\, o_{g_t} \mid q_{t-1}\, \ell_t\, w_t) = \underset{m_{g_t} o_{g_t}}{\textsc{SoftMax}}(\, \mathrm{FF}_{\theta_\mathrm{G}}[\delta_d{}^\top, [\delta^\top_{c_{b^d_{t-1}}}, \mathbf{0}^\top, \delta^\top_{c_{p_t}}, \mathbf{0}^\top]\, \mathbf{E}_\mathrm{G}]\,) \quad (13)$$

where $\mathbf{0}$ is a vector of 0s.

Likewise, to examine the contribution of syntactic category information on the content-sensitive processing model, the model is modified to allow it to be trained to make decisions without conditioning on the syntactic category labels:

$$\mathsf{P}(m_{\ell_t}\, \mathbf{h}_{\ell_t} \mid q_{t-1}) = \underset{m_{\ell_t} \mathbf{h}_{\ell_t}}{\textsc{SoftMax}}(\, \mathrm{FF}_{\theta_\mathrm{L}}[\delta_d{}^\top, [\mathbf{0}^\top, \mathbf{h}^\top_{b^d_{t-1}}]\, \mathbf{E}_\mathrm{L}]\,) \quad (14)$$

$$\mathsf{P}(m_{g_t}\, o_{g_t} \mid q_{t-1}\, \ell_t\, w_t) = \underset{m_{g_t} o_{g_t}}{\textsc{SoftMax}}(\, \mathrm{FF}_{\theta_\mathrm{G}}[\delta_d{}^\top, [\mathbf{0}^\top, \mathbf{h}^\top_{b^d_{t-1}}, \mathbf{0}^\top, \mathbf{h}^\top_{p_t}]\, \mathbf{E}_\mathrm{G}]\,) \quad (15)$$

These two ablated models will respectively be referred to as the *content-* and *category-ablated* models in the following experiments.

4 Experiment 1: Linguistic Accuracy

4.1 In-domain Linguistic Accuracy

In order to assess the parsing performance of the content-sensitive processing model outlined in Section 2, a linguistic accuracy evaluation was conducted on the development set and test set (i.e. sections 22 and 23 respectively) of the Wall Street Journal (WSJ) corpus of the English Penn Treebank (Marcus et al., 1993). The performance of the content-sensitive processing model is compared to the incremental left-corner parser of van Schijndel et al. (2013), which is based on a PCFG with subcategorized syntactic categories from the Berkeley latent variable inducer (Petrov et al., 2006).

The content-sensitive processing model was trained on a generalized categorial grammar (Nguyen et al., 2012) reannotation of sections 02 to 21 of the WSJ corpus. Choices regarding hyperparameters were made based on the parsing performance on the development set of the WSJ corpus. In order to account for sensitivity to initial parameters, the average performance of the content-sensitive processing model trained using three different random seeds is reported. Likewise, the left-corner parser of van Schijndel et al. (2013) was trained on the same generalized categorial grammar reannotation of sections 02 to 21 of the WSJ corpus, using four iterations of the split-merge-smooth algorithm (Petrov et al., 2006). Both parsers used beam search decoding with a beam width of 5,000 to return the most likely sequence of parsing decisions.

Parsing model	WSJ22	WSJ23	NS
vS et al. (2013)	85.20	84.08	69.60
Full model (avg.)	84.60	82.45	71.64
Con-ablated (avg.)	81.64	79.86	69.88
Cat-ablated (avg.)	75.63	74.45	64.19

Table 1: Bracketing F1 scores on sentences with 40 or fewer words for the incremental parsing models. WSJ: Wall Street Journal, NS: Natural Stories.

The unlabeled WSJ bracketing F1 scores from both parsers are presented in the WSJ22 and WSJ23 columns of the vS et al. and Full model rows of Table 1.[5] The results show that the two parsers achieve comparable performance on WSJ22 and WSJ23, indicating that the current processing model is a reasonable model of syntactic parsing.

4.2 Cross-Domain Linguistic Accuracy

The two parsers were also evaluated on the Natural Stories Corpus (Futrell et al., 2018). This corpus consists of 10 naturalistic stories (10,245 tokens) adapted from existing texts such as fairy tales and short stories. As can be seen in the NS column of the vS et al. and Full model rows of Table 1, parsing accuracy on this corpus is substantially lower. This is likely due to the "deceptively naturalistic" nature of the Natural Stories Corpus; this corpus was designed to over-represent rare words and syntactic constructions, therefore representing a different "syntactic domain" from the WSJ corpus. Interestingly, the content-sensitive processing model seems to generalize better to the Natural Stories domain than the model based on the Berkeley latent

[5]It should be noted that the performance of the van Schijndel et al. (2013) parser here is lower than their reported performance because they trained their parser on data with PTB-style annotation, which has substantially fewer syntactic categories than the GCG annotation scheme.

variable inducer. This could be the result of the latent-variable subcategorized syntactic categories overfitting to the WSJ domain.

4.3 Linguistic Accuracy of Ablated Models

To determine the differential effect of propositional content and syntactic categories, models with each of the propositional content and syntactic category components ablated (i.e. the content- and category-ablated models) were evaluated against the full processing model.[6] As with the full model, the ablated models were trained using three different random seeds to account for sensitivity to initial parameters. The results in the Con-ablated and Cat-ablated rows of Table 1 show substantial contributions of both components to parsing accuracy in all domains. On Natural Stories, bootstrap significance tests revealed that seven out of nine (3 × 3) pairwise comparisons between the full model and the content-ablated model, and all nine pairwise comparisons between the full model and the category-ablated model were statistically significant at the $p < 0.05$ level, which are both highly significant overall by a binomial test.

5 Experiment 2: Self-paced Reading

In order to evaluate the contribution of propositional content and syntactic categories to predicting behavioral responses, surprisal predictors were calculated from the content-sensitive processing model and its two ablated versions, which are outlined in Section 3. Subsequently, linear mixed-effects models containing common baseline predictors and one or more surprisal predictors were fitted to self-paced reading times. Finally, a series of likelihood ratio tests (LRTs) were conducted in order to evaluate the contribution of the surprisal predictor from the full processing model to regression model fit.

5.1 Response Data

Experiments described in this paper used the Natural Stories Corpus (Futrell et al., 2018), which contains self-paced reading times from 181 subjects that read 10 naturalistic stories consisting of 10,245 tokens. The data were filtered to exclude observations corresponding to sentence-initial and sentence-final words, observations from subjects who answered fewer than four comprehension questions correctly, and observations with durations shorter than 100 ms or longer than 3000 ms. This resulted in a total of 768,584 observations, which were subsequently partitioned into an exploratory set of 383,906 observations and a held-out set of 384,678 observations. The partitioning allows model selection to be conducted on the exploratory set and a single hypothesis test to be conducted on the held-out set, thus eliminating the need for multiple trials correction. All observations were log-transformed prior to model fitting.

5.2 Predictors

The baseline predictors commonly included in all regression models are word length measured in characters, index of word position within each sentence, and 5-gram surprisal. The 5-gram surprisal predictor is calculated from a 5-gram language model estimated using the KenLM toolkit (Heafield et al., 2013) trained on the Gigaword 4 corpus (Parker et al., 2009).[7]

In addition to the baseline predictors, surprisal predictors were calculated from the full content-sensitive processing model, the content-ablated model, and the category-ablated model trained as part of Experiment 1 (*FullSurp*, *NoConSurp*, and *NoCatSurp*). To account for the time the brain takes to process and respond to linguistic input, it is standard practice in psycholinguistic modeling to include 'spillover' variants of predictors from preceding words (Rayner et al., 1983; Vasishth, 2006). However, as including multiple spillover variants of predictors leads to identifiability issues in mixed-effects modeling (Shain and Schuler, 2019), the *FullSurp*, *NoConSurp*, and *NoCatSurp* predictors were all spilled over by one position. Moreover, preliminary analysis showed that the surprisal predictors are highly collinear, which may result in identifiability issues for the regression model if included together as predictors. In order to mitigate this problem, the difference between the surprisal predictors from the ablated model and those from the full model (Δ*ConSurp*, Δ*CatSurp*) were also calculated as predictors that represent the contribution of the full model over an ablated model. All

[6] Source code is available at `https://github.com/modelblocks/modelblocks-release`.

[7] Although word frequency is also often included as a baseline predictor in the form of unigram surprisal, it was excluded in the current study in light of results showing no significant effect of unigram surprisal over and above 5-gram surprisal when predicting reading times from the Natural Stories Corpus (Shain, 2019).

predictors were centered and scaled prior to model fitting.

5.3 Likelihood Ratio Testing

Two sets of nested linear mixed-effects models were fitted to reading times in the held-out set using using `lme4` (Bates et al., 2015). The first set manipulated the contribution of propositional content by including *ΔConSurp* in the full regression model over the base model that contains the baseline predictors and *NoConSurp*. Similarly, the second set manipulated the contribution of syntactic categories by including *ΔCatSurp* in the full regression model over a base model that contains the baseline predictors and *NoCatSurp*. All regression models included by-subject random slopes for all fixed effects and random intercepts for each word and subject-sentence interaction. Subsequently, a series of LRTs were conducted between nested regression models in order to assess the contribution of surprisal predictors from the full processing model to regression model fit. As there were three variants of each surprisal predictor, a total of nine (3 × 3) LRTs were performed for each ablated surprisal predictor.[8]

5.4 Results

The results show that the *ΔCatSurp* predictor made a statistically significant contribution to model fit over *NoCatSurp* in eight out of nine LRTs,[9] which is highly significant according to a binomial test ($p < 0.001$). In contrast, no significant contribution of *ΔConSurp* over *NoConSurp* was observed, with none of the nine LRTs indicating significantly improved model fit.[10] This demonstrates that the full processing model captures the influence of propositional content and syntactic category information differentially, the latter of which contributed to predicting self-paced reading times.

6 Experiment 3: Eye-tracking Data

In order to examine whether the results observed in Experiment 2 generalize to other latency-based measures, linear-mixed effects models were fitted on the Dundee eye-tracking corpus (Kennedy et al., 2003). Following similar procedures to Experiment 2, a series of LRTs were conducted to test the contribution of propositional content and syntactic category information.

6.1 Procedures

The set of go-past durations from the Dundee Corpus (Kennedy et al., 2003) provided the response variable for the regression models. The Dundee Corpus contains gaze durations from 10 subjects that read 20 newspaper editorials consisting of 51,502 tokens. The data were filtered to exclude unfixated words, words following saccades longer than four words, and words at starts and ends of sentences, screens, documents, and lines. This resulted in the full set with a total of 195,296 observations, which were subsequently partitioned into an exploratory set of 97,391 observations and a held-out set of 97,905 observations. In the base regression models, word length in characters, index of word position in each sentence, and saccade length were included. Additionally, either *NoConSurp* or *NoCatSurp* spilled over by one position was included as a baseline predictor. Similarly to Experiment 2, the first set of LRTs examined the contribution of propositional content by including *ΔConSurp*, and the second set of LRTs examined the contribution of syntactic category information by including *ΔCatSurp* in the full regression models.

6.2 Results

The results show that the *ΔConSurp* predictor made a statistically significant contribution to model fit over *NoConSurp* in all nine LRTs.[11] A significant contribution of *ΔCatSurp* over *NoCatSurp* was observed as well, with three of the nine LRTs indicating significantly improved model fit ($p = .008$ according to a binomial test).[12] Interestingly, contrary to Experiment 2 that showed only a robust contribution of syntactic category information to

[8]Despite the risk of convergence issues, the LRTs were also replicated with full regression models that include raw *FullSurp* in addition to the baseline predictors and either *NoCatSurp* or *NoCatSurp*.

[9]Any LRT in which either the base or full regression model failed to converge was considered as a null result. Regression models in one LRT failed to converge. In the replication using raw *FullSurp*, regression models in five LRTs failed to converge. However, the remaining four LRTs were statistically significant, which is highly significant according to a binomial test ($p < 0.001$).

[10]Regression models in one LRT failed to converge. In the replication using raw *FullSurp*, regression models in five LRTs failed to converge, with the remaining four LRTs indicating non-significance. Additionally, removing 5-gram surprisal from the baseline did not change the pattern of significance.

[11]In the replication using raw *FullSurp*, regression models in five LRTs failed to converge. However, the remaining four LRTs were statistically significant, which is highly significant according to a binomial test ($p < 0.001$).

[12]Regression models in all LRTs converged. In the replication using raw *FullSurp*, regression models in five LRTs failed to converge, with two out of four remaining LRTs indicating statistical significance ($p = .071$ according to a binomial test).

predicting self-paced reading times, a strong influence of propositional content in predicting eye-gaze durations is observed. This corroborates the finding that the full processing model captures the distinct influence of propositional content and syntactic category information, the ablation of which results in qualitatively different predictions. In addition, this differential contribution of Δ*ConSurp* across self-paced reading and eye-tracking data suggests that these self-paced reading times and eye-gaze durations may capture different aspects of online processing difficulty.

7 Experiment 4: Filler-gap Constructions

Observing that surprisal from the full processing model did not contribute significantly to predicting broad-coverage self-paced reading times on top of its content-ablated counterpart in Experiment 2, we focus on filler-gap constructions,[13] in which information about the extracted object is thought to strongly influence the processing of the verb. In order to explore the extent to which integration costs associated with filler-gap constructions could be explained by the influence of propositional content, a series of LRTs were conducted to assess the contribution of surprisal from the full processing model to predicting reading times of object-extracted verbs.

7.1 Procedures

The subset of self-paced reading times from the Natural Stories Corpus corresponding to object-extracted verbs provided the response variable for the regression models. The object-extracted verbs were identified using a version of the Natural Stories Corpus that had been reannotated using a deep syntactic annotation scheme (Shain et al., 2018). Applying the same data exclusion criteria as Experiment 2 resulted in an exploratory set of 1,537 observations and a held-out set of 1,523 observations. As the number of data points for regression model fitting was substantially smaller in comparison to the full set used in Experiment 2, the regression models had to be simplified for reliable convergence. First, the 5-gram surprisal predictor was excluded as its effect estimate was not stable on the exploratory set. In addition, the random effects structure was simplified to include only the by-subject random intercept.

In the base regression models, word length in characters, index of word position within each sentence, and *NoConSurp* were fitted to the log-transformed reading times in the held-out set. The contribution of propositional content was incorporated by including *FullSurp* in the full regression models. *NoConSurp* and *FullSurp* were spilled over by one position, and all predictors were centered and scaled. The same three variants of each surprisal predictor were used, which resulted in a total of nine LRTs testing the contribution of *FullSurp*.

7.2 Results

The results showed that the *FullSurp* predictor made a statistically significant contribution to model fit over *NoConSurp* in all nine LRTs. The inclusion of *FullSurp* consistently improved model fit, indicating that integration costs associated with object-extracted filler-gap constructions can be partially explained by the influence of propositional content.

8 Conclusion

This paper presents a generative and incremental content-sensitive processing model which factors the contribution of propositional content and syntactic category information. This model can be cleanly ablated to calculate surprisal predictors that differentially isolate the influence of the two components. Subsequent experiments demonstrate the utility of both components in predicting human behavioral responses; the inclusion of propositional content resulted in significantly better fits to broad-coverage eye-gaze durations and self-paced reading times of object-extracted verbs. Additionally, the inclusion of syntactic category information significantly improved fits to both broad-coverage self-paced reading times and eye-gaze durations. Taken together, these results suggest a role for propositional content and syntactic category information in incremental sentence processing.

Acknowledgments

The authors would like to thank the anonymous reviewers for their helpful comments. This work was supported by the National Science Foundation grant #1816891. All views expressed are those of

[13]For example, in the sentence *It was a match that the girl rubbed _ on the wall*, the extracted object *a match* has to be retrieved from memory and integrated to the transitive verb *rubbed*.

the authors and do not necessarily reflect the views of the National Science Foundation.

References

Marco Baroni and Alessandro Lenci. 2010. Distributional memory: A general framework for corpus-based semantics. *Computational Linguistics*, 36(4):673–721.

Douglas Bates, Martin Mächler, Ben Bolker, and Steve Walker. 2015. Fitting linear mixed-effects models using lme4. *Journal of Statistical Software*, 67(1):1–48.

J. D. Bransford and J. J. Franks. 1971. The abstraction of linguistic ideas. *Cognitive Psychology*, 2:331–350.

Sarah Brown-Schmidt, Ellen Campana, and Michael K. Tanenhaus. 2002. Reference resolution in the wild: Online circumscription of referential domains in a natural interactive problem-solving task. In *Proceedings of the 24th Annual Meeting of the Cognitive Science Society*, pages 148–153.

Emmanuele Chersoni, Philippe Blache, and Alessandro Lenci. 2016. Towards a distributional model of semantic complexity. In *Proceedings of the Workshop on Computational Linguistics for Linguistic Complexity (CL4LC)*, pages 12–22.

Richard Futrell, Edward Gibson, Harry J. Tily, Idan Blank, Anastasia Vishnevetsky, Steven Piantadosi, and Evelina Fedorenko. 2018. The Natural Stories Corpus. In *Proceedings of the Eleventh International Conference on Language Resources and Evaluation*, pages 76–82.

Adam Goodkind and Klinton Bicknell. 2018. Predictive power of word surprisal for reading times is a linear function of language model quality. In *Proceedings of the 8th Workshop on Cognitive Modeling and Computational Linguistics*, pages 10–18.

John Hale. 2001. A probabilistic Earley parser as a psycholinguistic model. In *Proceedings of the Second Meeting of the North American Chapter of the Association for Computational Linguistics on Language Technologies*, pages 1–8.

Kenneth Heafield, Ivan Pouzyrevsky, Jonathan H. Clark, and Philipp Koehn. 2013. Scalable modified Kneser-Ney language model estimation. In *Proceedings of the 51st Annual Meeting of the Association for Computational Linguistics*, pages 690–696.

Robert J. Jarvella. 1971. Syntactic processing of connected speech. *Journal of Verbal Learning and Verbal Behavior*, 10:409–416.

Philip N. Johnson-Laird. 1983. *Mental models: Towards a cognitive science of language, inference, and consciousness*. Harvard University Press, Cambridge, MA.

Alan Kennedy, James Pynte, and Robin Hill. 2003. The Dundee corpus. In *Proceedings of the 12th European conference on eye movement*.

Roger Levy. 2008. Expectation-based syntactic comprehension. *Cognition*, 106(3):1126–1177.

Mitchell P. Marcus, Beatrice Santorini, and Mary Ann Marcinkiewicz. 1993. Building a large annotated corpus of English: The Penn Treebank. *Computational Linguistics*, 19(2):313–330.

Jeff Mitchell, Mirella Lapata, Vera Demberg, and Frank Keller. 2010. Syntactic and semantic factors in processing difficulty: An integrated measure. In *Proceedings of the 48th Annual Meeting of the Association for Computational Linguistics*, pages 196–206.

Luan Nguyen, Marten van Schijndel, and William Schuler. 2012. Accurate unbounded dependency recovery using generalized categorial grammars. In *Proceedings of the 24th International Conference on Computational Linguistics*, pages 2125–2140.

Ulrike Padó, Matthew W. Crocker, and Frank Keller. 2009. A probabilistic model of semantic plausibility in sentence processing. *Cognitive Science*, 33(5):794–838.

Robert Parker, David Graff, Junbo Kong, Ke Chen, and Kazuaki Maeda. 2009. English Gigaword LDC2009T13.

Slav Petrov, Leon Barrett, Romain Thibaux, and Dan Klein. 2006. Learning accurate, compact, and interpretable tree annotation. In *Proceedings of the 21st International Conference on Computational Linguistics and 44th Annual Meeting of the Association for Computational Linguistics*, pages 433–440.

Keith Rayner, Marcia Carlson, and Lyn Frazier. 1983. The interaction of syntax and semantics during sentence processing: Eye movements in the analysis of semantically biased sentences. *Journal of verbal learning and verbal behavior*, 22(3):358–374.

Asad Sayeed, Stefan Fischer, and Vera Demberg. 2015. Vector-space calculation of semantic surprisal for predicting word pronunciation duration. In *Proceedings of the 53rd Annual Meeting of the Association for Computational Linguistics and the 7th International Joint Conference on Natural Language Processing*, pages 763–773.

Marten van Schijndel, Andy Exley, and William Schuler. 2013. A model of language processing as hierarchic sequential prediction. *Topics in Cognitive Science*, 5(3):522–540.

Cory Shain. 2019. A large-scale study of the effects of word frequency and predictability in naturalistic reading. In *Proceedings of the Annual Conference of the North American Chapter of the Association for Computational Linguistics: Human Language Technologies*.

Cory Shain, Marten van Schijndel, and William Schuler. 2018. Deep syntactic annotations for broad-coverage psycholinguistic modeling. In *Workshop on Linguistic and Neuro-Cognitive Resources (LREC 2018)*.

Cory Shain and William Schuler. 2019. Continuous-Time Deconvolutional Regression for Psycholinguistic Modeling. *PsyArXiv*.

Claude Elwood Shannon. 1948. A mathematical theory of communication. *Bell System Technical Journal*, 27:379–423.

Nathaniel J. Smith and Roger Levy. 2013. The effect of word predictability on reading time is logarithmic. *Cognition*, 128:302–319.

Michael K. Tanenhaus, Michael J. Spivey-Knowlton, Kathleen M. Eberhard, and Julie C. E. Sedivy. 1995. Integration of visual and linguistic information in spoken language comprehension. *Science*, 268:1632–1634.

Shravan Vasishth. 2006. On the proper treatment of spillover in real-time reading studies: Consequences for psycholinguistic theories. In *Proceedings of the International Conference on Linguistic Evidence*, pages 96–100.

Author Index

Association for Computational Linguistics
209 N. Eighth Street
Stroudsburg, Pennsylvania 18360

ISBN 978-1-7138-3020-7

CURRAN ASSOCIATES INC.
proceedings.com